Constructing Lebanon

Florida A&M University, Tallahassee
Florida Atlantic University, Boca Raton
Florida Gulf Coast University, Ft. Myers
Florida International University, Miami
Florida State University, Tallahassee
University of Central Florida, Orlando
University of Florida, Gainesville
University of North Florida, Jacksonville
University of South Florida, Tampa
University of West Florida, Pensacola

Constructing Lebanon

A Century of Literary Narratives

Elise Salem

University Press of Florida

Gainesville · Tallahassee · Tampa · Boca Raton

Pensacola · Orlando · Miami · Jacksonville · Ft. Myers

Library of Congress Cataloging-in-Publication Data
Salem, Elise, 1955–
Constructing Lebanon: a century of literary narratives / Elise Salem.
p. cm.
Includes bibliographical references and index.
ISBN 0-8130-2596-6 (cloth: alk. paper)
1. Nationalism and literature—Lebanon—History. 2. Arabic literature—
Lebanon—History and criticism. 3. Arabic literature—20th century—
History and criticism. 4. Literature and society—Lebanon. 5. Lebanon—
Intellectual life—History—20th century. I. title.
PJ8072 .S25 2003
892.7'09325692—dc21 2002028984

The University Press of Florida is the scholarly publishing agency
for the State University System of Florida, comprising Florida A&M
University, Florida Atlantic University, Florida Gulf Coast University,
Florida International University, Florida State University, University
of Central Florida, University of Florida, University of North Florida,
University of South Florida, and University of West Florida.

University Press of Florida
15 Northwest 15th Street
Gainesville, FL 32611–2079
http://www.upf.com

In loving memory of my mother,

Phyllis Sell Salem, 1930–2001

Contents

Preface

In this book I examine the evolving and problematic Lebanese nation through the lens of literary narratives. I range over a century of Lebanon's political and cultural development, offering both descriptive and prescriptive models of how nations can be "read" through literary productions. While I am concerned with the fate of the nation, this is neither a political nor a historical study, and although I use literature as an example of cultural production, this book is not a cultural studies monograph. Indeed, I intentionally mix discourses and disciplines and extend its arguments beyond the boundaries of traditionally specialized fields. Also, this project does not present definitive answers on the relationship between nation and culture but rather suggestive theories on how a nation is interpreted through its narratives. Stated differently, this book does something new and useful by systematically analyzing those literary narratives in order to apprehend better their relationship to the political entity of Lebanon. I hope to illustrate that, in the Lebanese context, politics and literature are inseparable.

One of the impulses for this book was personal. I was born, raised, and educated in Lebanon. I lived through the "good" times and then experienced much of the war. I came to the United States for my higher education, earned a Ph.D. in English literature, and became a professor in an American institution, but I felt increasingly drawn to Lebanon during its long war and its messy reconstruction. I studied Lebanon's contemporary literature and was struck both by how revelatory much of it was and by how relatively neglected it was. In part, my project sought to retrieve Lebanon's literature and to read its many narratives in order to understand the nation better.

Another impulse for this book was to counter a disturbing trend of studying "other" literatures in quick surveys or eclectically collected anthologies in a multicultural climate that often disregards the historically contextual components of cultural productions. If anything, this book attempts to complicate readings by illustrating that these literary narratives should not simply be studied under headings current in academia (like gender, class, the diasporic, the postcolonial). Instead, the texts are set against a broad historical, political, and socioeconomic Lebanese backdrop that forces the reader to consider the multiple assignations configuring the intricate relationship between culture and nation.

While I primarily select and study literary texts in order to better describe and prescribe Lebanon, I do not imply that those texts are worthy only insofar as they document the nation. As Milan Kundera asserts, "The novelist is neither historian nor prophet: he is an explorer of existence" (44). Some of the texts transcend the national narrative and the cultural moment, extending toward a universal paradigm of human existence. I hope the selection offered here will encourage readers also to pursue their own interests. Indeed, the word *selection* is key here, as this book in no way pretends to offer a comprehensive study of Lebanon's literary production in the past century. The works chosen for selection advance the various arguments of this project. The many endnotes and extensive bibliography direct the reader to a broader range of primary and secondary materials.

Indeed, there are different ways to read this book. For the uninitiated, it offers a basic outline of Lebanon's political and cultural development in the past century. More specifically, it serves as a guide to Lebanon's published and established literary texts along with samples from performed popular productions, especially in theater. In addition, the book can be read as an example of how a nation's narratives not only are descriptive but can serve a potentially useful or prescriptive function. The book thus intends both to deepen and to enrich thinking on Lebanon by drawing from a body of knowledge generally ignored by those outside literary studies. The work is intended for several complementary but different audiences: for Lebanese as well as for non-Lebanese. As there are only a handful of people "specializing" in Lebanese literature, I am not writing only for them, nor am I writing exclusively for literary critics or cultural historians. This treatment of a century of Lebanon's literature is proposed for a mixed audience either familiar with Lebanon but not with the import of literary criticism or familiar with the latter but not with the richness of the Lebanese case. By bringing the general and the specific together, I hope to shed new light on both. Finally, and perhaps most important, it is directed at those in the process of constructing Lebanon today.

Without leaves and grants from Fairleigh Dickinson University, this book would have taken even longer to complete. I would like to thank Peter Falley, Martin Green, Barbara Salmore, Mary Cross, Geoff Weinman, and my colleagues for their ongoing support. I am also obliged to my students, who helped me test many of the textual and cultural theories put forth in these chapters. I am indebted to comments on this project from scholars both in the United States and in Lebanon, including Mona Amyuni, Miriam Cooke, Sabah Ghandour, Michelle Hartman, Mohja Kahf, Marc Manganaro, Nadim Naimy, Elie Salem, Paul Salem, Stephen Sheehi, and Nadim Shehadeh. Many of the authors discussed here were generous with their time and ideas. I would like to thank Etel Adnan, Rachid al-Daʿif, Hasan Daoud, Elias Khoury, Ghada Samman, and Hanan al-Shaykh. Special thanks to Suzan Masʿad and Fares Abi Saab and the rest of the staff at the Lebanese Center for Policy Studies, where I spent many productive weeks.

My parents, Elie and Phyllis, have always been my greatest teachers and sources of inspiration. I am forever grateful for their undying love, sense of humor, and guidance. I also thank my sister Nina and my brothers Adib and Paul, as well as my extended Salem and Sell families for being a part of me both in Lebanon and in the United States. To my good friends from Washington, D.C., up to Vermont and then west to Seattle, thank you. And finally, this book would never have seen the light of day without the persistent interruptions of Anthony, Thomas, and Rania, my miraculous trio.

Note on Transliteration

I have used a simplified system of transliteration based upon that of the *International Journal of Middle East Studies*. The prefix "al-" is used the first time a transliterated Arabic name appears in the text but omitted later (for example, al-Shaykh, Shaykh). Contemporary names and places are usually spelled out as they are found in standard Western publications (for example, Elias Khoury rather than Ilyas Khuri). In quoted materials, I have preserved existing spellings, even when they differ from the transliteration system used here.

Nation and Culture

An Introduction

In his 1882 essay "What Is a Nation?" Ernest Renan wrote, "Forgetting, I would even go so far as to say historical error, is a crucial factor in the creation of a nation, which is why progress in historical studies often constitutes a danger for [the principle of] nationality" (11).

To talk about Lebanon at all before the 1920s is, in itself, an act of "forgetting" and "historical error." Although the term *Lebanon* had been used by some for centuries to describe the mountainous region between the Mediterranean and the Damascene plains, that region was not a nation-state until 1920, and even then it was under the League of Nations Mandate to France until its official independence in 1943. Yet Lebanon's very emergence as a modern nation-state, contingent upon the vicissitudes of European politics during two world wars, was reflected in local narratives of identity and belonging, fictions derived from realities and myths that sought to link the territory with a people.

In the decades following independence, Lebanon gradually coalesced as a political entity, but divided loyalties, reinforced by cultural and political ideologies in the region, are evident in the many narratives that have been published. With the outbreak of civil war in 1975, Lebanon's landscape was drastically changed. The government collapsed as countless militias and armies took over the country during sixteen years of warfare, but Lebanon did not break up into separate cantons. The political entity survived, shaky and changed, as Lebanon sought to reconstruct itself after 1990. The rich body of literature produced during and after the war is testimony to how complicated the process of narrating the ever-changing nation is and how necessary these narratives are in imagining a new Lebanon.

Much of the scholarship on nation and nationhood has fed directly into this project. The nation, despite its elusive and problematic definitions, is taken seriously because of its concrete influence in shaping political and individual identity in the twentieth century. Although cosmopolitan and globalist models have validly challenged the national paradigm,[1] this only complicates rather than negates the fact that the nation is still the "cornerstone of geopolitical organization," that "access to power has become virtually conditional upon nation status," and that "our world is structured around the general category of nation" (Penrose 30–32).

The "nation-state" is also acknowledged as an important site for ideological formation. Simon During writes, "The nation-state is, for better or worse, the political institution which has most efficacy and legitimacy in the world as it is. Modernity reproduces itself in nation-states; there are few signs of it happening otherwise. To reject nationalism absolutely or to refuse to discriminate between nationalisms is to accede to a way of thought by which intellectuals—especially postcolonial intellectuals—cut themselves off from effective political action" (During 139). The decision to adopt Lebanon—as nation, state, and nation-state—for my site of inquiry is hence neither arbitrary nor merely convenient. As this study will reveal, the idea of the nation is integral to an understanding of literary production in Lebanon.

The terms *nation* and *state* are often used interchangeably, but whereas the state is, according to Walker Connor, the "major political subdivision of the globe," the nation is a very ambiguous and intangible entity. One definition of *nation* is essence, a "psychological bond that joins a people and differentiates it, in the subconscious conviction of its members, from all other people in a most vital way" (Connor 36). Too often this abstract essence of nation is used in place of the tangible state. Indeed, the coining of *nation-state* illustrates (by the hyphen) the actual distinction in academic circles between the words.

In the Arab world, *nation* [al-watan or al-umma] is also a complicated and confused term both conceptually and linguistically. To many it is difficult to distinguish between the Arab *world* [al-ʿalam al-ʿArabi], the regional *nation-state* [al-dawla al-qutriyya], and the Arab *nation* [al-umma al-ʿArabiyya]. These terms are highly inflected in Arabic with multiple definitions. Nation has been defined as "watan," "umma," "qawm," or "shaʿab"; country as "balad" or "dawla"; state as "wilaya," "dawla," or "hukuma." Other related terms include "wilaya" as province and "hukuma" as government. Much can also be made of the roots of these Arabic words and the nuances of their uses.

Though some may argue that as ideology, Arab nationalism died with Gamal 'Abd al-Nasir over three decades ago, others would counter with cultural, political, and economic evidence of its survival. At the same time, certain forces in the Arab world have been calling for a unified Muslim state [dawla Islamiyya] in direct opposition to the implied secularism of the nationalist movement. With Arab and Islamic nationalisms as undeniable trends within the Middle East, any retrieval of Lebanese "nation," as in this project, must be carefully negotiated. Muhammad al-Jabiri, a respected Arab intellectual, peruses the Arab world and notes that since the majority are Muslims, Islam is a true component of Arab identity and hence Arab nationalism. He also admits, however, that for "bilad al-Sham"—the region comprising Syria, Lebanon, Jordan, and Palestine—Islam can be a divisive binary, since minority non-Islamic groups exist in this region (104). In making his case for Arab nationalism, Jabiri plays down this binary, since for him it is only a local and not a universal Arab issue. For Lebanon, however, where a very large minority is indeed Christian, this binary is crucial and formative.

This is not the place to catalog the development of theories on nation or Arab nationalism.[2] Rather, it is to clarify how my study fits into the scholarship on these issues. In the introduction to *Rethinking Nationalism in the Arab Middle East* (1997), editors James Jankowski and Israel Gershoni summarize the history of nation and nationalism, pointing out the need to distinguish between "the political trajectory of nationalism on the one hand and its cultural articulation on the other" (xiii). Writers like Benedict Anderson and Ernest Gellner have helped formulate how nationalism is indeed related to "nonpolitical changes of the modern epoch" such as "printing, literacy, urbanization, changing social roles, and even new ways of comprehending space and time" (xiii). My project on literary narratives, printed and potentially part of social discourse, is a prime example of the "nonpolitical," increasingly regarded as significant in the "cultural articulations" of nationalism. Indeed, one of the shortcomings of *Rethinking Nationalism*, as the editors themselves admit, is that despite essays that draw on "relatively neglected sources such as visual materials . . . and newer forms of communication such as audiocassettes," other sources that "have much to say about nationalist imaginings" are left untapped. These include "literature, music, and contemporary popular art forms such as film, radio, and television" (xxv). Although my book does not deal with all of these cultural forms of expression in detail, it does focus on literature and musical theater and hence redresses the lack of scholarship on the symbiotic relation between nation and culture, especially in Arab studies. Reading a century of literary narratives in order to sharpen our understanding of the evolving and problematic Lebanese nation is hence a fresh approach, though certainly not the last word on the subject. I hope this study will encourage others to pursue the roles of film, contemporary television and radio productions, cartoons, websites, popular music, and the visual/plastic arts in learning about Lebanese identity and nation-formation.

Important work has been done on Arab historiography, including some studies that have problematized Lebanon's narrative histories.[3] Kamal Salibi, in his 1988 A *House of Many Mansions: The History of Lebanon Reconsidered*, for example, acknowledges the subjective nature of history and the specific issues of Lebanon's multiple, usually religious-based, histories. In her 1994 book, *An Occasion for War: Civil Conflict in Lebanon and Damascus in 1860*, Leila Fawaz specifically foregrounds textual narratives in her assessment of a historical event. Enlightening work by other non-Arab scholars (concerning France, India, and Iran, for example) has demonstrated how narratives of historical events have shaped national discourse and political culture.[4] It is my hope that this book on literary narratives will promote other studies on how, specifically, historical narratives have played their part in constructing modern Lebanon.

While assuming the nation to be foundational, this study pays heed to constructionist perspectives: Nations are largely products of myths, subjective social and cultural constructs that have evolved as contingent institutions in specific times. To varying degrees, writers like Ernest Renan and, later, Ernest Gellner, Eric Hobsbawm, and Benedict Anderson have provided important theories on the nation and its formulation, generally positing a vital correlation between the political apparatus and the cultural one. Indeed, Anderson bases his entire theory of nation on that correlation, as cultural narratives that imagine and embody the nation emerged because of political, economic, and social conditions.[5]

Antonio Gramsci's particular approach to nation and culture proved to be most paradigmatic for this project. In his extensive discussion of Italy in the *Prison Notebooks*, Gramsci theorizes on the inner workings of the Italian nation and offers insightful analyses on the role of culture in relationship to the political. His concrete approach, as Stuart Hall has argued, is most useful because it is not purely theoretical.[6] One can read Gramsci on nineteenth-century Italy and then apply or use his findings to think elsewhere. Gramsci helped put into focus for me the underlying inquiries of this study on Lebanon. As this project proceeds chronologically to read literary narratives, it is consciously setting those narratives against the evolving political entity of Lebanon from its early inception through its development to its demise and its current reconstruction. More to the point, this project attempts to understand Lebanon better through its cultural, specifically literary, narrative productions. As such, it subscribes to the Gramscian symbiotic formula between culture and nation.[7]

One of Gramsci's key assertions is that culture does not merely function, in strictly Marxist terms, as a reflection of the economic base, but that it performs a crucial social and political role. Much of Gramsci's writing demonstrates this dynamic nature of culture by examining Italy, especially during the historically formative period of the Risorgimento. Gramsci attributed Italy's failure as a nation to the lack of a strong popular culture and a true cultural revolution, to the recognition that the Italian language was not a "national fact," and to the overdominance of external and cosmopolitan cultural forces. Gramsci further delineated the role of education and of intellectuals, the significance of folklore, the hegemony of a civil society through popular consent, and the commitment to social transformation as relevant components of the Italian nation. Many of these issues helped clarify my own interpretation of Lebanon and suggested the themes around which my inquiry would revolve.

The question of language, for example, is critical to Lebanon's establishment of its own culture, specifically a popular culture. The role of education, at all levels, will be seen to be important in establishing cultural identification and national aspiration. External influences, both ideologically and culturally, would threaten national unity. As I seek to demonstrate the relationship between culture and nation, many other relevant themes, some drawn from Gramsci, are woven in: the function of myths in forming national identity; the role of the intellectual/artist in promoting change; the relation between elite and popular culture; narrative challenges to national discourse; and the difficult issue of Lebanese identity in conjunction with Palestinian, Syrian, or Arab identity.

Although the nation is assumed to be a cultural construct and a myth, its impact on daily lives is real. By studying multiple literary narratives over many decades, I hope to demonstrate that the imagined and fictional renditions of the nation were powerful and formative reflectors of the nation. Romantic myths of an early idealized Lebanon, for example, became fixed national symbols and remain integral validating principles in the wake of a devastated nation. The positive image of pluralistic Lebanon was revealed to be simplistic in light of actual disintegration of the state, yet pluralism remains one of the most distinguishing features of Lebanon. The survival myth of a resilient Lebanon rebuilding itself after war was undermined by the questionable priorities of a guiltless leadership and citizenry, but the myth persists in the national imagination. So while the nation is perceived through texts that are contingent, its constructedness does not reduce its concreteness.

Like *nation*, the word *culture* is a highly ambiguous and powerfully reso-nant term in today's scholarship. This is not the place to take issue with that term, except to acknowledge its central function in the decision to focus on a nation.[8] As the discussion on Gramsci and others reveals, cul-ture is an active component of nation. The decision to look more specifi-cally at narrative suggests that the cultural artifacts chosen almost all have narrative elements to them. Narratives give structure and meaning to expe-rience. We live, according to Brian Wicker, in a "story-shaped world." The narratives that people construct map the world, both descriptively and pre-scriptively. Peter Brooks writes, "We live immersed in narrative, recount-ing and reassessing the meaning of our past actions, anticipating the out-come of our future projects, situating ourselves at the intersection of several stories not yet completed" (3). Indeed, even when some of the cultural artifacts are not, strictly speaking, narratives (for example, some poems or songs), they take on symbolic meaning and function in a national context when they have been narrated, storified, told and retold, recorded.[9]

Many of the cultural materials discussed in this book are novels. Benedict Anderson reserves special importance to the role of novels in providing the "technical means for 're-presenting' the *kind* of imagined community that is the nation" (25).[10] Richard Rorty also discusses the useful social function of the novelist in his *Contingency, Irony, and Solidarity*. He argues, for example, that the utopia of human solidarity will be achieved not by in-quiry but by imagination, by "the imaginative ability to see strange people as fellow sufferers." The novel is especially geared to eliciting that kind of empathy. It, along with the movie and the TV program, has virtually "re-placed the sermon and the treatise as the principal vehicles of moral change and progress" (xvi). Culture needs to be imagined and narrated rather than "rationalized or scientized" (53). The many plots, characters, contexts, and vocabularies within narratives trigger the imagination and allow us to redescribe and thus reconstitute our selves and our world. For Rorty, positive political development is possible.

As cultural critics our function becomes, Homi Bhabha writes, to "establish the cultural boundaries of the nation so that they may be acknowledged as 'containing' thresholds of meaning that must be crossed, erased, and translated in the process of cultural production" (4). An examination of a century of Lebanon's literary narratives will reveal that those national boundaries are forever fluctuating, that increasingly cultural production seems to challenge national discourse. This is not to say that those narratives become irrelevant to the nation but rather that they are questioning national rhetoric. For this reason, the narratives presented in the latter sections of this book offer new ways (prescriptive models) for assessing the nation.

A nation's literature is rarely consulted by those who govern. This is regrettable, because the narratives put forth here often help explicate and occasionally anticipate the nation's trajectory. Artists and intellectuals, often historically in a dubious relationship with the state, not only continue to imagine and hence extend the discourse of the nation but, in more palpable ways, participate in remembering, recording, and transforming it.

The book is divided into three parts, comprising seven chapters. The first part studies Lebanon from before independence until the beginning of the 1975 civil war; the second focuses on the war itself (1975–90); and the last looks at the postwar era (1990–98). Against a brief historical context, the chapters generally proceed chronologically by reading examples of published Lebanese literary narratives. Other cultural modes of expression — theater, music, folklore, journalism, and popular media — are also occasionally consulted. Some of the narratives are already in the Lebanese public domain (published, reprinted, reviewed, anthologized, taught, memorized), but others are not. This book does not set out primarily to "discover" unknown writers and texts, however. Instead, by looking at relatively accessible literary narratives, this project examines the possibility of cross-fertilization between cultural artifacts and constructions of Lebanon.

Although not structurally apparent, the book is also divided into two large segments. The first (corresponding to part I) covers a longer historical period but presents less literary exegesis. The objective here is to demonstrate that cultural narratives can and have been indicative, or descriptive, of the newly constructed nation. The second segment (corresponding to parts II and III) covers a briefer historical period but proceeds more slowly. An analysis of Lebanese novels produced during and after the war is presented here, not just as descriptive models for Lebanon but as prescriptive models in these periods of collapse and reconstruction.

Part I, "Constituting Lebanon," contains three chapters. The first, "Nation Formation," looks at early notions of Lebanon, especially as envisioned by Michel Chiha, leading up to the birth of modern Lebanon in 1920 and the constitution of 1926 and concluding before independence in 1943. Christians in the Mount Lebanon region advocated an independent, French-sponsored state, while Muslims (primarily along the coast) preferred a linkage to a larger Syrian nation. The literature of Khalil Gibran (1883–1931) provides a lens through which the process of nation-building comes into sharp focus. Rereading Gibran with the idea of nation in mind is revealing. He lived and wrote during an era when the very idea of Lebanon was emerging, so it is critical to locate where formative ideas of Lebanese identity might reside. He actively participated in transforming the Arabic language in ways that would help distinguish a Lebanese identity. He isolated certain features of the "homeland" that would come to be essential to any discussion of the Lebanese nation. Many of the ideals that Gibran associated with Lebanon, however, were also romantic myths that would help explain the fault lines upon which that Lebanon was built.

Chapters 2 and 3 examine the seemingly prosperous Lebanon of Michel Chiha's earlier vision. Lebanon was supposedly pluralistic and democratic, known as the Paris of the Middle East, yet in a few decades it was entangled in the conflicting ideologies dominant in the region. The rise of Arab and Syrian nationalisms, Marxist and Ba'thist agendas, and pro-Palestinian sentiment all provided alternative loyalties for the Lebanese, exacerbating an already segmented nation.

Instead of focusing on a single author, this two-chapter section examines a multiplicity of narratives that demonstrate the different perspectives on Lebanon. Some texts, including the popular Rahbani/Fayruz musicals, idealize village life and promote nostalgia for a simple vision of Lebanon. Others disregard Lebanon altogether and foreground a broad Arab context or develop a modernist aesthetic in their narratives. Tewfiq Awwad's 1972 *Death in Beirut* effectively captures the complicated recipe of Lebanese identity in the aftermath of the 1967 Israeli victory and the increasing political activity within Lebanon.

Part II, "Unraveling Lebanon," covers the civil and regional war that collapsed the Lebanese nation-state. The multiple militias, shifting alliances, regional proxies, and urban guerrillas all become fixtures of the seemingly dissolving Lebanon. Rather than assuming total breakdown, this part also examines how national and cultural assignations, like language, survive but are transformed.

Chapter 4, "Disintegration," covers the first seven years of the war beginning in 1975 and leading up to Israel's invasion of 1982. Chapter 5, "Living with War," examines the literary narratives produced in the second half of the war from 1982 to the end of hostilities in 1990. This intense period of Lebanon's history featured literature from new and unexpected sources. Previously unheard voices took advantage of the extensive social collapse to construct new modes of expression. An impressive list of women published novels and stories that confronted the Lebanese war and explored the psychology of the Lebanese. Hanan al-Shaykh, Emily Nasrallah, Hoda Barakat, and others identified new Lebanons in their texts and introduced important feminist/womanist perspectives on the nation.

Another relatively new group of authors emerged from the south of Lebanon, where continued occupation by Israel (especially after the 1982 invasion), resulted in a poetic movement of resistance. Known as Shuʿara al-Junub [Poets of the South], this primarily male and Shiʿite group exploded on Beirut's literary and publishing scene in the 1980s. Most significantly, many authors of fiction, like Elias Khoury, Yusuf Habshi al-Ashqar, Hassan Daoud, and Rachid al-Daʿif, would use the war to construct important new notions of self, of language, and of nation. The popular plays of Ziad al-Rahbani, while debunking the folkloric representations of an earlier idealized Lebanon, also served to validate certain aspects of Lebanese identity.

Part III, "Reconstructing Lebanon," looks at eight years following the implementation of the Taef Agreement in 1990 and the new constitution.[11] Here it is stipulated that Lebanon is a "final" homeland [watan nihaʾi] and that it has an Arab identity [hawiyya ʿArabiyya]. All militias were to be disarmed and foreign armies supposedly evacuated. With the internal wars virtually ended, Lebanon could now embark on a program of massive reconstruction that included rebuilding downtown Beirut, providing basic infrastructure for the country, revising the educational system, instituting reforms in media, labor, and elections. While all seemingly necessary projects, the priorities of Lebanon's reconstruction efforts seem, to many, misguided. While the great bulk of money and energy is steered toward concrete, only a trickle is reserved for human development. With Hizballah still resisting Israel in the South, and with both Israeli and Syrian armies still in Lebanon, the implementation of Taef is hardly complete.

This part divides thematically rather than chronologically. Chapter 6, "Reworking the Past," focuses on postwar novels set in a prewar past or deliberately highlighting Palestinian concerns. Chapter 7, "The Elusive Present," examines narratives explicitly set during the war or in the diffi-cult-to-conceptualize present (up until 1998). Although Beirut has regained much of its status as the cultural and publishing center of the Arab Middle East, much of the current Lebanese literature, though accessible, is little known. Authors Hanan al-Shaykh and Elias Khoury, for example, both write fictions that do not sentimentalize Lebanon or reduce the war. As such, their novels disturb rather than entertain. Many Lebanese are perhaps un-comfortable confronting the difficult questions of their identity and na-tionhood or pondering the significance of the sixteen years of war. Instead, nostalgic and sentimental fictions continue to sell and continue to be in-cluded in even the revised educational programs. With satellite broadcast-ing and innovative Lebanese TV shows, much of the cultural output has shifted from elite literary texts to popular media. The singer Fayruz contin-ues to cast her spell in Lebanon and to enthusiastic expatriates abroad, suggesting that national symbols are still very much in demand.

The afterword to this book reflects upon the role of culture in Lebanon and asserts that literary narratives still have an important role to play in effecting positive change. Not only does culture matter; it especially mat-ters now as Lebanon is at an opportune juncture in its history. Since the end of most fighting in 1990, Lebanon has been involved in a program of rebuilding and rejuvenation, yet the nation has not seriously taken account of its recent tragic history. Although much of the public discourse already revolves around how best to construct Lebanon, little attention is being paid to the difficult, yet necessary, issues raised in the recent narratives from Lebanon. Now is the time to assess that program and offer a healthy critique that might truly assist Lebanon in its reconstruction efforts.

Part I

Constituting Lebanon

If I remind my people of our Phoenician ancestors,
It is because we were at the beginning of history,
Before becoming Muslims or Christians,
But one people united in the same glory.

Charles Corm, *La Montagne Inspirée*, 53

In itself, Arab nationalism for us Ba'thists is a self-evident reality not in need of special investigation or affirmation, but the meaning and content of this nationalism are in dire need of clarification, elaboration, and struggle. . . . In other words, it is not our business to debate whether we are or are not Arabs—for it is evident that we are—but rather to discern and delineate the content of our Arabness at this historical juncture of our Arab nation.

Michel Aflaq, *Fi sabil al-Ba'th* [For the renaissance], 102

1

Nation Formation

You have your Lebanon and I have mine. You have your Lebanon with its
problems, and I have my Lebanon with its beauty. You have your Lebanon with
all its prejudices and struggles, and I have my Lebanon with all its dreams and
securities.

Khalil Gibran, "You Have Your Lebanon and I Have Mine"

In this chapter I trace the early formation of the Lebanese nation by focusing primarily on the texts of Khalil Gibran. Of course, no single literary
oeuvre can fully measure the sociopolitical trends of a region, but sufficient and significant insights can be gained by this analysis of one of the
most formative figures in Lebanon. The main objective here, as in the
next two chapters, is to present narratives that would prove descriptive of
the evolving nation. To begin, however, it is necessary to provide something of a brief historical review. When Gibran's fictional and imagined
narratives are hence contextualized, a more complex and revealing picture emerges of Lebanon before its independence.

In reading various histories of Lebanon, one immediately notices the
variations in nomenclature. Philip Hitti, the doyen of Lebanese history,
refers to the regions now part of the modern nation as Lebanon, even when
they were part of the Ottoman Empire and belonged to distinctly different
wilayat, some now part of Syria or Palestine/Israel. Ilya Harik, however,
points out that the country did not even have a single name, Mount Lebanon, until the late eighteenth century; and then, only the Maronites referred to it as Mount Lebanon. The Druzes called their part Jabal al Shuf
or Jabal al Druze (13). Under the Ottomans, the Mount Lebanon region
was actually referred to by its coastal towns—Jbeil, Batroun, Sidon, Tripoli—and not by the mountain. Kamal Salibi is careful in using the "Lebanon" attribution, clarifying what denomination used what term for what
ends. To the Christians, and especially the Maronites, a historical Leba-

non would serve their political aspirations as modern Lebanon came into being after World War I. To non-Christians, a separate Lebanon made little sense apart from Syria or a larger Arab homeland; consequently, few references to a historical Lebanon are found in those narratives. Walid Phares, on the other hand, insists in his ideologically heavy history of Lebanese Christian nationalism that Lebanon is an ancient Christian nation that existed prior to the Ottoman takeover.

During most of the Ottoman period from the sixteenth century until World War I, what is today Lebanon was part of various sanjaks and wilayat initially under the jurisdiction of Istanbul, but increasingly shifting to local governance. In the nineteenth century, Mount Lebanon was divided into two administrative units, kaymakamats, one for the Maronites and one for the Druzes. This dramatic institutional change in Ottoman policy, however, led to increased tensions and open internal conflict leaving thousands dead.

France, which for centuries had seen itself as a protector of the Maronites, organized a conference of European powers to consider another reorganization of Mount Lebanon. In 1861, the shift was made from a kaymakamat to a mutasarrifah, "or privileged sanjak (administrative region) of the Ottoman Empire, internationally guaranteed, under an Ottoman Christian governor called a mutesarrif who was appointed and sent from Istanbul with the approval of the guaranteeing European powers" (Salibi 16). Until 1915, this special regime for Mount Lebanon remained operative.

With the onset of World War I and the shifting power struggles in the Middle East, dramatic political and geographical transformations began that would lead to the creation of the modern Arab states. For Lebanon, that transformation began in 1915, when Istanbul ended the privileged regime of Mount Lebanon and appointed Jamal Pasha as the commander in chief of Damascus. Jamal Pasha occupied Mount Lebanon, abolished its autonomy, and so began a reign of terror marked by military courts, persecution, and famine. Anyone sympathetic to nationalist causes could be sent to prison or the gallows. On May 6, 1916, fourteen Muslims and Christians in Beirut were killed, and their sacrifice would be commemorated on "Martyrs' Day"—later an important symbol of the Lebanese nation.[1]

In 1916 Husayn, the sharif of Mecca of the Hashimite family, led an Arab revolt against the Turkish regime with support from Britain and promise of independence. Arab nationalism was now a viable force and would

continue to resonate in the region for the rest of the century. The Sykes-
Picot Agreement, however, between Britain and France, while accepting
the principle of Arab independence, actually divided the eastern Arab area
into zones of permanent influence. In addition, in 1917, the Balfour Declaration approved the establishment of a Jewish national home in Palestine. After World War I, the Treaty of Versailles stipulated that the Arab
countries formerly under Ottoman rule could be provisionally independent but under the supervision of either a British or a French mandate.
Thus Britain was mandated over the regions of Iraq and Palestine and
France over Syria and Mount Lebanon. In 1920, under pressure from the
Lebanese Maronites, and partly for France's own reasons, the French annexed parts of the former Ottoman provinces of Beirut and Damascus to
the territory of the old Lebanese mutasarrifah.

In Beirut on September 1, 1920, General Henri Gouraud, the French
commander in chief of the armed forces in Syria and Lebanon, proclaimed
the creation of Greater Lebanon. Philip Hitti provides a quotation of
Gouraud: "At the foot of these majestic mountains which have been the
strength of your country and remain the impregnable stronghold of its faith
and freedom, on the shore of this sea of many legends that has seen the
triremes of Phoenicia, Greece and Rome and now, by a happy fate, brings
you the confirmation of a great and ancient friendship and the blessings of
French peace. . . . I solemnly salute Greater Lebanon in its glory and prosperity in the name of the government of the French Republic" (489).

This proclamation is noteworthy in its omission of any Arab or Islamic
dimension to Lebanon. The country's heritage is Phoenician and European, and the modern state has the blessings of its friend, France. The
national flag became the French tricolor with the cedar, in green, against
the middle white strip.

Not surprisingly, most non-Christians in Lebanon opposed the formation of the new Lebanese state sponsored by France. In fact, a Muslim
delegation from the areas annexed to Lebanon presented a memorandum
to the French High Commission on December 1925. Part of the text reads:
"Confident in France, motherland of liberty, greatest defender of the rights
of man, we are sure that our rights regarding our proper destiny will not be
refused, and, despite a plebiscite, we will never be annexed, against our
wishes, to any land" (Zamir 1995, 292).[2] As the Muslims pleaded their
case against annexation, Lebanese Christians were working toward a localized independence that would ensure Christian dominance and European

protection within a newly constructed state. In 1920 as Greater Lebanon was formed, many Muslims opposed it, rejected the designation "Lebanese" in their identity papers, and refused to enter the civil service (Hanf 65). It is not surprising then, as Salibi wrote, that since the emergence of Lebanon as a state in 1920, "the Christian and Muslim Lebanese have been in fundamental disagreement over the historicity of their country: the Christians by and large affirming it, and the Muslims denying it" (3).[3]

In 1926, Lebanon's constitution was drafted under the leadership of Michel Chiha, a man who promoted a pluralist and nonsectarian view of the new state. One of the creators of Lebanese nationalism, Chiha sought to define Lebanon as distinctly linked to both Europe and the Arab world. It was a Mediterranean civilization, and the Lebanese were conceived as cosmopolitan friends of the world. The drafted constitution then institutionalized a system of administration and representation on the basis of confessionalism, or religious community. Modeled after the Third French Republic, the Lebanese Republic emerged as a parliamentary democracy with wide powers for the president. However, though an electoral system was established for Parliament (as early as 1922), the seats were to be distributed in proportion to the numerical strength of the religious communities. This was the only way that government could supposedly reflect Lebanon's mixed groups.

This prioritization of the communities (actually confessional or sectarian groups) would, of course, have lasting repercussions in Lebanon. By 1936 Pierre Gemayel would form the paramilitary Kata'ib Party with the motto "God, Fatherland, Family." He declared that the party was pro-Lebanon and all enemies were hence antinationalists. At around the same time, another Lebanese Christian, Antun Saadeh, formed the Syrian Social Nationalist Party. Arab nationalist sentiments continued to grow among the Sunni za'ims or leaders like the Karamis of Tripoli or the Salams of Beirut.

At the outset of World War II, relations deteriorated between France and Lebanon, as the former was reluctant to grant full independence to the latter. In 1943, however, after French decline and the rise of British and American power, the French mandate was terminated and the country became independent and a founding member of the League of Arab States and the United Nations shortly thereafter. The divisions among the Lebanese, over whether they were of Phoenician or Arab descent, for example, would have to be reconciled somehow. This reconciliation was politically achieved with the compromise document of the National Pact (to be discussed in the next chapter), which sought to alleviate both Christian and Muslim fears over the future and governance of the new state.

This quick overview of pre-independence Lebanon is provided as context to a discussion of literary texts produced during this period. By looking primarily at the works of Gibran, one can perceive how the seeds of many of the issues prominent at the formation of the Lebanese nation were already imbedded in cultural productions.

At the outset, though, one must acknowledge the strong influence on Gibran of an older Lebanese immigrant writer, Amin Rihani (1876–1940). The critic Nadeem Naimy considers Rihani to be the "forerunner" of Gibran. Rihani arrived in New York in 1888 and helped set the scene for Gibran by publishing works, both in Arabic and English, that exposed the religious and clerical autocracy of his country.[4] His rather doctrinaire style provided numerous depictions of the goodness of Christ in juxtaposition to the corruption of the priesthood—often amid long descriptive passages on the "virgin mystic beauty of nature in Lebanon" (Naimy 21). These themes are evident in Gibran's works.[5]

Another influential Lebanese immigrant writer of the same period was Mikhail Naimy. Born in Mount Lebanon in 1889, Naimy spent years studying in Palestine and then the Ukraine before moving to Washington State and eventually to New York. His publications, both in English and Arabic, also abound in the deification of the Lebanese terrain and reinforce themes that Gibran would make popular.[6]

Gibran Khalil Gibran was born in 1883 and raised in Bsherri, North Lebanon, home of the Maronite Christians. Growing up poor with very little education, Gibran emigrated to Boston, like many Christians from the region, with his mother and siblings in 1895. He returned to Beirut in 1898 for four years to continue his education, and then went back to the United States to live the rest of his life in Boston and New York, where he established himself as a painter and writer and formed, in 1920, the Pen Society [al-Rabita al-Qalamiyya]. Initially writing in Arabic (roughly from 1905 to 1920), he then shifted primarily to English until his death in 1931. His works achieved popularity back in Lebanon, and he soon became a national symbol, even though he was an immigrant, or Mahjar, writer. Much of his writings angered the clerics, however, and he was excommunicated from the Maronite Church. In his will he insisted on being buried back in Bsherri, and he was.

This account of Gibran's life is intentionally minimalist. Many others narrated extensive accounts of his life, as will be demonstrated below. Detailed studies of Gibran's many works can also be consulted elsewhere, as the bibliography indicates. The objective here is to isolate certain features of Gibran's writings and persona in order to demonstrate how they would prove descriptive of Lebanon. These features include Gibran's Phoenician themes, his association of the land with sacredness and natural beauty, his depictions of rebelliousness, his political and national assignations, and his creation of a language that would eventually become, as Gramsci put it, a "national fact." Moreover, the cult of Gibran that he himself helped foster is itself an indicative phenomenon in Lebanon's cultural history.

Gibran's identification with Lebanon even before Lebanon became an independent nation-state is of importance. Not only did he see himself as Lebanese (although he occasionally also referred to himself as a Syrian), but he was and continues to be perceived as a Lebanese author. How that association emerged, how it was reinforced, and what it signifies in the construction of Lebanese identity are all relevant points.

In his proclamation of Greater Lebanon, General Gouraud referred to the Phoenician heritage of the country; this reference would have resonated strongly with many Christians in Lebanon, especially since the vogue of Phoenicianism had been growing for decades. Salibi argues that in 1864 Ernest Renan published his *Mission en Phénicie* after a French archeological team uncovered ancient Phoenician remains in coastal Lebanon (172). These discoveries triggered a deep interest in the connectedness between modern Lebanon and ancient Phoenicia and bolstered theories, advocated primarily by Christians, that Lebanon was Phoenicia resurrected.

Gibran, whose early literary works in Arabic were becoming increasingly popular back in the Ottoman provinces of Lebanon and Syria, makes frequent use of the Phoenician dimension in his stories.[7] Often, the Phoenician is juxtaposed to other ancient civilizations or religions, constructing an image of Lebanon that is rich in cultural heritage. In his 1912 novel *Al-ajniha al-mutakassira*, translated as *The Broken Wings*, the main character, Selma, is compared to the Phoenician goddess Ishtar. In the chapter entitled "Between Christ and Ishtar," the desperate lovers enter an abandoned temple, "a haven for worshippers and a shrine for lonely lovers." Inside, an old Phoenician picture of Ishtar, goddess of love and beauty, hangs beside a Byzantine picture of Christ. "There, the lovers would imagine the ghosts of Phoenician men and women who lived and loved and worshipped beauty in the person of Ishtar" (1:264). Gibran hence links the terrain (and love) to a Phoenician past.

Much of the scholarship that developed around Gibran exaggerates the extent of the Phoenician and other ancient influences and reinforces a narrative of Lebanon that would prove enduring. In a study of Gibran's parables, Annie Salem Otto writes that the author came from a country "rich in legend and Biblical inference. It is the traditional birthplace of Tammuz and Ishtar, the home of the ancient Phoenicians, the setting of the *Song of Songs,* and the seat of the Judeo-Christian tradition" (15). In his translation of Gibran's *Mirrors of the Soul,* Joseph Sheban discusses the poet's deep interest in the Phoenician gods Ishtar, Baal, and Tammuz and in his incorporation of Christian, Muslim, Buddhist, and other theologies in his writings (54).

History textbooks and tourist brochures, for example, perpetuated the narrative that Lebanon was not a recent construction but one with thousands of years of national heritage emphasizing, in particular, the Phoenician element. In his undated *L'art phénicien: petit repertoire,* Charles Corm, the ideologue of Phoenicianism, continued to reinforce the image of Lebanon as the heir to Phoenicia.

Gibran infused that Phoenicianism with spiritual significance, as his Phoenician references were often linked to gods and temples located within a Lebanese landscape. Occasionally that spirituality was clearly associated with Christian symbols. Renan's work was well known to Gibran. He had long been influenced by Renan's *Life of Jesus* and hoped to do justice both in painting and writing to Jesus the artist, the poet, the man. Many of his dreams and visions about Jesus are recorded by his close friend Mary Haskell, and he makes it very clear that "it was [in] Lebanon, as it always is that I see him [Jesus]" (Jean Gibran 385). In one dream he meets Jesus at a Phoenician tomb outside Bsherri; they sit in the sun and converse in simple and ordinary words. As Jesus lies on the ground with his staff, the Gibran character asks: "Is your staff of fig?" "No," Jesus replies. "It's shahbi," a hard wood common in Mount Lebanon (385).

This link between the pagan and the Christian was a key feature of Gibran's writing, labeled by many as romantic, mystic, universalist, etc. But it is also extremely resonant in an emerging nationalist context, as it instills sacred substance into the secular idea of the nation. The Lebanon that was forming and would be declared a republic in 1920 and an independent nation-state in 1943 would fall back time and again on the narratives being constructed (and still taught today) at the beginning of the century.

In fact, part of Gibran's success in propagating the idea of a sacred Lebanon was through his self-fashioning (as will be discussed more fully ahead). Both as narrator of his tales and as literary persona, Gibran constructed himself as the prophet from Lebanon, intent on distilling the spiritual natural essence of Lebanon and expressing that essence in his artistic works. Not surprisingly, most writings on Gibran also promoted him as the "immortal prophet of Lebanon and the savant of his age"; he grew up in "the famous town of Bsharri, which prides itself on being the guardian of the forest of the Holy cedars from whose lumber King Solomon built his temple in Jerusalem" (Ferris, preface). Gibran came from Lebanon and the East from whose soil "the great prophets and seers of old had sprung" (B. Young 31). And like those prophets, Gibran understood the Aramaic parables and used the parabolical method so evident in Jesus' own teachings (Otto 49).

The traditional sacredness of Gibran's image is reproduced in many of the fictional texts themselves, where the unnamed narrator, a clear Gibran persona, is a Jesus prototype. In "Martha," a 1906 story from 'Arais al-muruj [Nymphs of the valley], the female protagonist, once a simple rural girl, is now a prostitute in Beirut, the victim of male deceit and tyranny. As she lies dying, she confesses her life to the narrator, who listens lovingly and bestows forgiveness. She is no leper, he assures her, but oppressed by the rich and powerful; she should be consoled by the thought that "it were better that a person should be the oppressed than that he should be the oppressor" (1:115). She dies taking comfort in that thought. A whole cast of Gibran male protagonists, from Yuhanna the Mad to Khalil the Infidel, embody a supposedly pure spirituality, always in opposition to a corrupt clergy and clearly identified as Christ-like. They preach and lead the simple life, often as shepherds close to the peasants, unjustly victimized by the powerful. The setting is always in Mount Lebanon, usually in a clearly identifiable Bsherri-like environment where actual monasteries, like Deir Quzhayya, have dominated the landscape for centuries. By conjoining the lead characters with his own persona, Gibran consolidates the idea of a sacred Lebanon. With his reputation growing, Gibran took on great authority back home. He is from Lebanon, he locates his fictions there, and he chooses to infuse the characters and the landscape with a sacred quality.

That sacredness is further reinforced by Gibran's lavish descriptions of the terrain's natural beauty. Repeatedly, Gibran locates that terrain in Mount Lebanon, empowering it with a spirituality that predates and precludes any institutionalized religion. The strong sentimentality of these natural descriptions, reminiscent of the Western Romantic movement that was undoubtedly an influence on Gibran,[8] would prove to be powerful in shaping Lebanese consciousness and identity. The natural images of Gibran show up repeatedly in popular song, in poetry, and in letters from immigrants, and they have turned Gibran into one of the most potent symbols of Lebanon itself. Below is a typical example of Gibran's descriptions, one that many Lebanese would already recognize. In a letter to Ameen Ghuraieb, editor of the New York magazine *Al-Mahjar*, who was visiting Lebanon, Gibran writes:

> When you are in a beautiful spot or among learned people, or by the side of old ruins, or on the top of a high mountain, whisper my name so that my soul will go to Lebanon and hover around you and share with you the pleasure of life and all life's meanings and secrets. Remember me when you see the sun rising from behind Mount Sunnin or Fam el Mizab. Think of me when you see the sun coming down towards its setting, spreading its red garment upon the mountains and the valleys as if shedding blood instead of tears as it bids Lebanon farewell. Recall my name when you see the shepherds sitting in the shadow of the trees and blowing their reeds and filling the silent fields with soothing music as did Apollo when he was exiled to this world. Think of me when you see the damsels carrying their earthenware jars filled with water upon their shoulders. Remember me when you see the Lebanese villager plowing the earth before the face of the sun, with beads of sweat adorning his forehead while his back is bent under the heavy duty of labor. . . . Remember me when you hear the songs and hymns that Nature has woven from the sinews of moonlight, mingled with the aromatic scent of the valleys, mixed with the frolicsome breeze of the Holy Cedars, and poured into the hearts of the Lebanese. (Ferris 33)

The spirit of longing for the beautiful homeland in this epistle resonates still with the generations who left the Lebanese region. Some of the most popular songs about Lebanon capture the same sense of idealized village and natural beauty that seem to make what would become Lebanon unique in the Middle East. The tone in all these texts is almost always nostalgic and reverent. The terrain is sacred, demanding love and loyalty. The terrain is also, in Gibran's case, clearly set in monastery-dotted Christian regions (Mount Lebanon), thereby excluding large portions of Lebanon's citizens.

Still, Gibran's early writings in Arabic were formative in Lebanese consciousness, especially as his works were taught in the educational curriculum, published in textbooks and anthologies, and quoted in cultural productions and touristic brochures. In *Broken Wings* he describes springtime in Lebanon (a topic reserved for every Arabic composition class in Lebanese elementary schools): "Spring is beautiful everywhere, but it is most beautiful in Lebanon. It is a spirit that roams round the earth but hovers over Lebanon, conversing with kings and prophets, singing with the rivers the songs of Solomon, and repeating with the Holy Cedars of Lebanon the memory of ancient glory" (24).

Gibran's description of the rising moon in *Broken Wings* is yet another resonant image in Lebanon's folkloric modern tradition: "The moon came out from behind Mount Sunnin and shone over the coast, hills, and mountains; and we could see the villages fringing the valley like apparitions which have suddenly been conjured from nothing. We could see the beauty of all Lebanon under the silver rays of the moon. . . . That night I saw Lebanon dream-like with the eyes of a poet" (50–51).

Although Gibran's later English writings are much more epigrammatic and less conducive to long natural descriptions, whenever a natural setting is offered, it is usually reminiscent of North Lebanon, with references to Bsherri, the Qadisha Valley, rugged mountains, majestic cedars, etc. So while Gibran spent virtually his entire adult life in Boston and New York, he obviously located his textual art in the landscape of his childhood. This transfer explains the nostalgia of the presentation; its innocence, purity, and beauty can be attributed to longing.

Occasionally Gibran situated his narratives in Beirut or chose to describe the city, and yet it is difficult to detect an urban setting. In *Broken Wings*, for example, he writes: "Beirut, free from the mud of winter and the dust of summer, is like a bride in the spring, or like a mermaid sitting by the side of a brook drying her smooth skin in the rays of the sun" (24).

Beirut is often depicted in fictional narratives, poetry, and song as the victimized bride, mermaid, or fallen beauty. As Lebanon entered a conscious period of folklorization, the popular depiction of Beirut remained relatively untainted or was bypassed for more focused depictions of the idealized rural villages. The image of Beirut would obviously change, especially as guerrilla warfare characterized it later during the war years. Interestingly enough, Beirut's pristine and virginal qualities would be resurrected even during war.

Gibran's infusion of the Lebanese landscape with Phoenician elements, mythic and ancient religious symbols, along with Christian imagery, clearly painted a locale that was special. It was recognizable to the Lebanese of the North and the mountains, even to those in Beirut who could spot the peaks at a distance. The unique geographic features of Mount Lebanon helped distinguish it intellectually and emotionally. Gibran's oft-quoted and printed descriptions occurred at a time when Lebanon was trying to imagine itself. The fact that those descriptions still endure signifies their formative value.[9]

Another feature of Gibran's Lebanon was the theme of liberation. Many of his key Lebanese fictional characters rebel openly against political tyrants and religious despots, offering a rejuvenative narrative. Gibran's spiritual advocacy was in clear opposition to the institutionalized Christianity exemplified by the wealthy monasteries and the corrupt clergy. This is not to say that his vision was not Christian, for despite his attack on the religion, he openly espoused the example and teachings of Jesus.[10] Generally, however, Gibran's writings tended to advocate a universalist spirituality that might encompass all religions. He emphasized typically abstract and pervasive multiconfessional qualities like forgiveness, justice, purity, etc. And yet those qualities were significantly linked to characters who loved and rebelled in the mountains of Lebanon. As Gibran continued to produce stories about resistance to oppression, a Lebanese political agenda emerges as well.

In the four stories that form the 1908 *Al-arwah al-mutamarrida*, translated as *Spirits Rebellious*, all the main characters from Wardat al-Hani to Khalil al-Kafir [the Infidel] are examples of rebellious spirits. Khalil, an orphan brought up in a monastery, is thrown out on a snowy night to fend for himself after he questions the immoral ways of the monks. A widow and her daughter nurse him back to health. He falls in love with the daughter, but is condemned and imprisoned by the authorities. As he defends himself in a court of law, Khalil becomes the mouthpiece for many of Gibran's political concerns. Primarily, his is a call for liberation from governmental and religious oppression. In his climactic speech at the end of "Khalil the Infidel," he calls on Freedom to save them—the besieged, the downtrodden, the dispossessed. The oppressors have turned the Druze against the Arab, the Shiʿa against the Sunni, the Kurd against the Bedouin, the Muslim against the Christian. When, Khalil asks, will these battles end between brothers and neighbors? He then praises Freedom, the daughter of Athena, the sister of Roma, the friend of Moses, the lover of Muhammad, and the bride of Jesus (1:205).

The story concludes with Khalil, now "Khaliluna" [our Khalil], successful in mobilizing the masses of victimized peasants against the forces of oppression. The village, happy in its liberation, now "sits like a bride on the shoulder of the valley" (1:208). The fact that Gibran was excommunicated by the Maronite Church as a result of these early writings is testimony to their impact. He was able to feed the frustrations of a people under domination while raising to the status of national symbol certain features of the Lebanese villager. *Spirits Rebellious* remains one of Gibran's most popular writings in Arabic in Lebanon, and its stories are still taught in today's Lebanese curriculum. The images of incorrupt peasants, pure lovers, and poor villagers victimized by larger forces dominates much of the Lebanese folklore and songs, popularized later on by the popular singer Fayruz, the Rahbani brothers, and others.

At the beginning of the twentieth century, when Gibran wrote many of the narratives that would prove so resonant, he could not have foreseen how historical events would unfold culminating in the establishment of a Greater Lebanon under French mandate supported by the Christians. In fact, his political agenda, if it can be called that, remained vague and abstract, never calling specifically for an independent Lebanese, Syrian, or even Arab nation. His incentive was liberation from oppression, ostensibly from the tyranny of the Ottoman Empire but also from the local warlords and religious leaders who served as Turkish proxies in Mount Lebanon.[11] But it is precisely this abstracted, even idealized, vision of liberation that would prove so enduring in the complicated Lebanese political formula. As the nation strove to imagine itself, it incorporated unproblematic idealized narratives to help justify it. The narratives provided by Gibran reflected the dynamics of the emerging nation.

One of his most famous essays in Arabic is the 1920 "You Have Your Lebanon and I Have Mine," written in reaction to the prolonged French mandate. This often quoted essay provides many of the idealistic symbols that would counter the messy Lebanese political formula outlined in the 1926 constitution and the 1943 National Pact. The essay works by juxtaposing two versions of Lebanon. "Your Lebanon" is a political knot, a national dilemma, a place of conflict and trickery. "My Lebanon," on the other hand, is a place of beauty and dreams, of magical valleys and glorious mountains. "Your Lebanon" is inhabited by employees, officers, politicians, committees, and factions. "My Lebanon" is for peasants, shepherds, young boys and girls, parents and poets. "Your Lebanon" is empty and fleeting, whereas "My Lebanon" will endure forever (1:598–602).

Gibran's Lebanon, already described in the letters and stories, is a terrain with geographical features, specific individuals, and pressing needs. It is an imagined community with a climate and a distinct culture, and yet Lebanon did not exist as a nation-state when the above works were written, although they clearly take place in the Mount Lebanon of Gibran's childhood. What is significant about the essay "You Have Your Lebanon and I Have Mine" is the repeated insistence on naming his homeland Lebanon and his clear realization of the different versions of Lebanon already in existence.[12]

Using "Lebanon" as an attribution before the 1943 independence, even after the 1920 declaration of Greater Lebanon opposed by most Muslims, was highly subjective. Although most Maronites were referring to a Lebanon for decades and even centuries, most non-Christians in what would become Lebanon opposed such an attribution. The political fluidity of the region from the end of the Ottoman Empire to the French mandate reflected the uncertainty of the emerging nation-states. Even after independence, many then-Lebanese citizens abroad referred to themselves as Syrian. Prior to that, it was common for people from the region that was to become Lebanon to refer to themselves as Syrian. Gibran was no exception.

In 1912, Gibran allegedly told Mary Haskell that he believed Turkey's hold on Lebanon and Syria could be broken only by an "Allied attack." Jean Gibran continues: "His commitment to war as a means of gaining his country's freedom caused him to guard closely his Arabic ties at just the time when he was forming commitments within the [pacifist] American literary community" (287). But what does "his country" signify in 1912? The biographers have already distinguished between a Lebanon and a Syria even though neither was a nation-state. In a letter to Haskell that same year Gibran writes: "I am not patriotic, Mary; I am too much of an Absolutist, and Absolutism has no country—but my heart burns for Syria" (Jean Gibran 289).

While Gibran most often identified himself as Lebanese, he and his protagonists were also occasionally labeled as Syrian. In a 1913 letter, "To the Muslims from a Christian Poet," published in New York's magazine *al-Funoon,* he wrote:

> I am Lebanese and I'm proud of that,
> And I'm not an Ottoman and I'm also proud of that.
> I have a beautiful homeland of which I'm proud,
> And I have a nation with a past—
> But there is no state which protects me. No matter how many
>   days I stay away . . .
> I shall remain an Easterner—Eastern in my manners,
> Syrian in my desires, Lebanese in my feelings—
> No matter how much I admire Western progress. (4:208)

The political designations—Lebanese, Syrian, Eastern—abound. In 1913 these were obviously not mutually exclusive. Gibran speaks of a "beautiful homeland" and a distinct "nation with a past," but the homeland/nation is never defined. Mount Lebanon, Greater Lebanon, or Syria could have been substituted terms. Even in his later "You Have Your Lebanon and I Have Mine," Gibran reveals the ambiguity of the Lebanon/Syria division: "Your Lebanon alternately separates and rejoins Syria . . . but my Lebanon neither separates nor rejoins, neither expands nor is reduced" (1:600). In 1916, during the famine in Mount Lebanon,[13] Gibran wrote to Haskell soliciting funds for charity: "My people, the people of Mount Lebanon, are perishing through a famine which has been planned by the Turkish government. 80,000 already died. Thousands are dying every day. The same things that happened in Armenia are happening in Syria. Mount Lebanon, being a Christian country, is suffering the most" (Jean Gibran 292). The constant slippage between the two national attributions (Lebanese and Syrian), even while referring to a "Christian country," is disconcerting but would not have been unusual at the time.[14] After the 1916 Arab revolution, Gibran and most of the writers of the region (especially the Lebanese Christians) exhibited an Arab current in their works that did not appear in conflict with any budding Lebanese nationalism. Khalil Mutran, Shibli Mallat, Wadiʿ ʿAql, Bishara al-Khuri, Marun ʿAbbud, Ilyas Farhat, Iliyya Abu Madi, Adib Farhat, al-Akhtal al-Saghir, al-Shaʿir al-Qurawi, Omar Hamad, Muhammad Ali Humani, and Mustapha al-Ghalayini all wrote about past Arab glory, critiqued the Turks, and were inspired by the revolution (Khazen 211–60).

Gibran is important to study for what he wrote and did not write about the political developments of his time. While Lebanon was emerging as a complex political entity characterized by extreme balance and delicate negotiations between its various groups, it was also besieged by larger regional forces that shaped its identity. Gibran's narratives, for the most part, simplified the political reality by repeatedly exposing basic injustices and calling for reformist and liberation agendas. At the same time, though, he understandably conflates national designations, eerily projecting into a future where Lebanon would still be a relatively confused national entity.

Gibran's narratives of place and politics, though clearly formative, would probably never have had the impact they had were it not for the language they were expressed in. Until 1920, Gibran wrote primarily in Arabic. It is these earlier works that had the largest impact on the Lebanese. *The Prophet* was published in English in 1923, and its early influence was most clearly in the West.[15]

Gibran's language would become increasingly identified as Lebanon's and would help consolidate the young nation's perception of itself. A common language, as a criterion in the development of a homogeneous culture, facilitates communication within a nation that has realized its political aspirations. In the scholarship on the rise of nationalisms across the Arab world, the issue of language is central. While there is debate over how instrumental the Lebanese Christians were in theorizing and popularizing the ideology of Arab nationalism in the nineteenth century, there is no doubt that the ideology of nationalism coincided with a revival of the Arabic language during the "Nahda" (literary renaissance).[16] Language is one of the most salient features of the nation if only as the conduit of its narratives. Benedict Anderson writes: "Much the most important thing about language is its capacity for generating imagined communities, building in effect *particular solidarities*" (133). Vernacularizing the language, as happened with Latin and to a certain extent with Arabic, and disseminating it through mass printing hence broaden the base of its users (its imaginers, its narrators). In Europe, this vernacularization and dissemination coincided with the secularization of the language. The modernization of Arabic also had the effect of dislocating Arabic from its most important religious source, the Islamic Quranic text. As the literal language of revelation, Arabic was inherently linked to Islam, which explains why Islamic nationalists adopted language as one of the surest proofs of their cultural unity.

The Arabic language, however, was undergoing a transformation in the nineteenth century that would lead to its increasing adoption in non-Islamic ideologies. For one thing, two important initiatives to translate the Bible into modern Arabic had a profound effect on the Christian authors of the time, including Gibran.[17] Even before they founded the Syrian Prot-estant College (later AUB) in 1866, the American Mission moved its print-ing press from Malta to Beirut, where its first major project was the transla-tion of the Bible by Eli Smith and Cornelius Van Dyke, along with Butros al-Bustani, Nasif al-Yaziji, and Yusuf al-Asir (Hitti 456, 461). This Protes-tant Bible as well as a new Catholic translation sponsored by the St. Joseph University created a biblical style for Arabic that could now coexist along-side a Quranic style. According to Nadeem Naimy, the biblical style was simple; unlike the formalized style of the Quran, the new language was chiseled to fit the meaning. The aesthetics was transferred inward and re-sided now in the meanings rather than in the language itself. This is the style that Gibran helped perpetuate (Naimy interview).

The foregrounding of language at this juncture is critical to discussion of nation-formation. Most of the leading Arab and Western theorists on nation have included key segments on the role of language. Hisham Sharabi succinctly states the importance of this correlation: "The Arab literary re-vival provided the logical base for the political revival. . . . Language, and the cultural heritage in which it was embedded, constituted the basis of national identity" (1970, 115). Gibran, as one of the most important trans-formers of the Arabic language during Lebanon's emergence, also discussed this correlation between nation and language.

In an Arabic essay, "Al-umam wa thawatiha" [Nations and their essences], collected in the 1920 Al-'Awasif [The tempests], Gibran searches for defi-nitions of al-umma [the nation]. He wonders what it is that unites a people, and considers categories like religion, language, ethnicity, and material comforts. Yet while each of these is relevant, Gibran recognizes that nei-ther category in itself can justify the nation. For example, there are many nations that use the same language and single nations that speak many languages. Gibran argues that every people has its general essence, which is similar to the individual's essence. Even though this general essence de-rives its being from the individuals in the same way that the tree is nour-ished from water, dirt, light, and heat, it is independent from the people and has its own life and will (1:505).

These essences, Gibran continues, might fade or transform, but they will never totally disappear. They will find true expression and life in nations such as the Egyptian, Persian, Greek, Roman, or Arab nations—some ancient and some modern. It is only the nation that contains and unites both the general and the individual essences (1:506).

Gibran's typically abstract definition is nonetheless revealing. First, he never isolates a Lebanese or Syrian nation but refers to a larger Arab nation (while also admitting an Egyptian nation). This conflation, confusion, and omission of national labels in Gibran's work has already been discussed. Second, he isolates an unpalpable quality to be the determinant of the nation. This point seems to cohere with his romanticized and idealized notion of the homeland already referred to in his writings. Finally, the categories, like language, that he does consider are ones that continue to be discussed by scholars on nation.

During Gibran's career, Lebanon's "language" was not an indisputable fact. The Lebanon that was to emerge was first under Ottoman rule, which meant that Turkish was often the official language of transaction, although Arabic, of course, was the language of the people. By 1920, French (which already had a hold on the Christians) came to dominate political business while an entire educational infrastructure based on the French baccalaureate system was instated. Arabic was also promoted to official status and remained the language of the people. The presence of a Western language (and culture and political apparatus) in the Lebanon region (and throughout the Arab world) would generate an important intellectual debate that remains central today in Arab thought. The issue was how to consolidate Arab culture in the face of powerful Westernization, how to resist the influence from the West. Arabic language as the vehicle for the transmission of Arab culture was often the locus for this debate, and Arabic language, as already pointed out, was most often singled out as the main criterion of a nationalism to resist the West.[18]

In "The Future of the Arabic Language," collected in the 1923 *Al-Badai' wa al-tara 'if* [Best things and masterpieces], Gibran agonizes over the subordinate role of Arabic. Western dominance is killing Arab creativity; we need to distinguish between what is useful and what is harmful. He writes that, in "our country Syria," we are now infiltrated by different Western nationalisms in the forms of various schools: the student who attends American schools graduates with an American perspective; he who goes to a

French school becomes an ambassador of France; and the student who learns in a Russian school has allegiances to Russia (1:629). Gibran emphasizes the need to concentrate on the Arabic language, to ensure that it is taught throughout the school years to help unite "our political thought" and to help develop "our nationalism" [al-qawmiyya]. Otherwise, as Gramsci had also shown with Italy, Gibran believes "we will never belong to one nation" [watan wahid] (1:630).

This clear link between nation and language takes on concrete significance in the poetry of Gibran, a poetry that not only was innovative in its meanings and styles but would come to be identified very powerfully with Lebanon and only Lebanon, not Syria, not the Arab world. The imagery, idioms, and meanings in his most famous and substantial 1919 poem, "al-Mawakib" [The procession], have become part of Lebanese folklore, and it is worth taking a close look at it. Parts of the poem were immortalized by Fayruz, who sang "A'tini al-Nay" [Give me the flute] composed by Najib Hankash. The poem continues to be taught in the school systems and reified in the collective national memory.

The poem (1:417–26) is structured as a dialogue between two positions similar, in some ways, to those stated in his essay "You Have Your Lebanon and I Have Mine." The first voice is of a world inhabited by ordinary people: fallen, corrupt, pained. But it is also a world of potential inner beauty. The response is lyrical, spiritual, pastoral, and akin to the romanticized natural settings of the stories. Here, in the forest, the refrain "Give me the flute and sing" produces, like the music of the flute, a song that will not die. In contrast to the first world, this spiritual place has no interior or exterior; it is an unfragmented whole. The first ten pages of the poem proceed as dialogue between these two voices on broad subjects like good, evil, life, religion, justice, truth, love, happiness, sadness, and death. The first voice expresses one of those subjects while the second responds that this subject does not exist in the forest. In the last two pages of the poem, the spiritual voice takes over in a long lyrical segment that virtually paints the palpable world of the spirit, the forest. This is the segment that Fayruz sings and children memorize.

It is difficult to translate these last lines into English,[19] as their essence (this term is used deliberately) eludes translation. Essence (in Arabic "that") was one of Gibran's favorite words, and the impact of his writing on even contemporary Lebanese may lie in his ability to have isolated something of what Lebanese consider to be the essence of their culture and nation. (A good English translation by G. Kheirallah, himself a poet, captures something of the rhythm and rhyme of the poem.)[20] There are those who believe that that which is untranslatable is that which distinguishes one culture from the next.[21] In Gibran's poem, many of the images are deeply rooted in a landscape and a culture that has come to signify Lebanon. Those images resonated back when they were written precisely because they were in context; they continue to resonate for a Lebanese readership because Gibran's poem has become a canonical text from which images and values are derived.

The essence of the poem for many Lebanese comes with the lines that begin, "Have you . . . ?" (1:425). The second voice lectures the first, but since these lines are often removed from the larger poem, they read as if the poet/speaker is addressing the reader. The meaning of these questions hence takes on a personal immediacy: Have you, like me . . . taken the forest as a home, bathed in dew and dried in sunlight, drunk the dawn like wine, slept in the grass blanketed by the night, and so on. Stylistically, the power of these lines is also in the choice of words (a combination of colloquial and classical), the internal rhythm and final rhyme, and a syntax that favors an innovative verb. For example, in the line "Have you slept in the grass at night blanketed by the sky," the first verb, *farasha*, does not just mean "to sleep" but to "spread out" and is used in Lebanese dialect to connote spreading out a bed, often on the ground. This "spreading" acts upon the object, *al-'ishb*, the grass, without clarifying whether the bedding is on top of the grass or whether the grass itself is the mattress (or possibly the blanket). The omission of function words (*in, on, with*, etc.) jams verbs with nouns in a startling new way. The second half of the line continues the question "Have you . . ." by adding "been blanketed by the sky?" This second verb, *lahafa*, means to cover or wrap, but in Lebanese dialect it is also used as a noun, *lhaf* or comforter, but not just any comforter. In the north Lebanese villages, the lhaf is a blanket sewn between two sheets; it is both heavy enough for winter cold and refreshing enough for summer nights . . . outside. Indeed, what Gibran has captured here is the feeling of sleeping outdoors on a summer night, a popular practice even now in the Lebanese villages of the mountains. Like the first part of the line, the object, *al-fada*, the sky, is simply juxtaposed to the verb. Is the sky (or space) the actual blanket, or is one sleeping, already covered, beneath it?

Alliteration and assonance further tighten these lines, making them relatively easy to memorize and put into song. The refrain "Give me the flute and sing" (in the Kheirallah translation, "Give to me the reed and sing thou") makes a final appearance, but the meaning is ominous, for Gibran adds, "People are merely lines, written, yet in water." His own poetry, he then admits, is useless in the face of this sad mutability. The poem concludes with three ponderous lines that are rarely reproduced in the popular versions of the poem.

At the end of his essay "Future of the Arabic Language," Gibran writes, "The only way to revive the language is in the heart of the poet and on his lips and between his fingers, for the poet is the link between creativity and proclamation, the conduit that transfers from the world of self to the world of study, from the world of thought to the world of memory and recording. The poet is both the father and the mother of language" (1:631). The poet, Gibran continues, is anyone intent on innovation, creativity, exploration, invention in the face of imitative traditionalism. Certainly one of the most important legacies of Gibran is his innovation of the Arabic language that he spearheaded while writing in the United States.

In 1920, Gibran and a group of other Syrian/Lebanese writers founded the Pen Society in New York. This group discussed, as Mikhail Naimy put it, how to "lift Arabic literature from the quagmire of stagnation and imitation, and to infuse a new life into its veins so as to make of it an active force in the building up of the Arab nations" (qtd. in Jean Gibran 338). As 1920 also marks the beginning of the mandate period in Lebanon and Syria, Naimy's statement on the building of Arab nations has particular significance. Members included Amin Rihani, Mikhail Naimy, and Iliyya Abu Madi—all authors taught still in the Lebanese curriculum. Another Pen Society member, William Catzeflis, wrote about the goals of the group. Gibran, who was undoubtedly the leader, reportedly said: "If the meaning or beauty of a thought requires the breaking of a rule, break it. . . . If there is no known word to express your idea, borrow or invent one. . . . If syntax stands in the way of a needed or useful expression, away with syntax." Catzeflis continues, "Gibran was never a purist, although he took extreme care in furbishing and refurbishing his phrases. His Arabic was never orthodox and he broke the rules right and left" (qtd. in Jean Gibran 339).

Gibran's innovations and liberties with the Arabic language are generally undisputed. There are some disagreements over the extent and impact of his modernized Arabic, but there is little doubt that he coined new words, created fresh expressions and images, liberated the syntax, and generally valorized the colloquial. The critic Salma Khadra Jayyusi summarizes some of the contributions of Gibran:

> What caused Gibran to tower over his contemporary Arab writers both at home and in the Americas . . . was the unrivalled revolution he engineered in the language and style of poetry. . . . Strongly influenced by the Bible, [the "Gibranian style"] is characterized by a striking use of interrogatives, vocatives and aesthetic repetitions. . . . His vocabulary was inventive, his metaphors selective and new. . . . By penetrating the rigid linguistic facade of Classicism, so deeply entrenched in Arab poetic practice up to his time, he hauled diction into the modern age, accomplishing for poetry what would otherwise have taken several generations to achieve. (foreword)

Gibran's original style was also matched, as seen, by his liberated social vision. His repeated writings against all forms of oppression and his call for a progressive society back in his homeland were consistent with his irreverence for the status quo. Jayyusi believes that his ability to be so free "was the fact that he was writing in America, away from the sages of Arabic literature at home" (foreword).

Gibran's huge influence was also a result of his being an immigrant, away from the homeland yet powerfully drawn to it. From afar, the narratives could take on a certain clarity (both thematically and stylistically) that would prove most effective in the process of nation-building. In the case of Lebanon, immigrants played an important role in narrating the nation. Not only did they contribute to literary discourse,[22] but their large numbers, coupled with their general economic success, resulted in significant financial remittances to the "homeland." In addition, their role in defining and perpetuating Lebanese identity (in all its mythology) through festivals, haflis, and cuisine is an interesting (though separate) study. The larger theoretical issue here involves the very meaning of the nation in light of emigration/immigration patterns. A country is not merely defined by what is contained within its borders. Gibran's resonance within Lebanon is testimony to that.

This chapter has focused on Gibran because, despite having been an emigrant, he proved formative to the Lebanese in defining certain aspects of their national identity. He became a national icon where so few existed

before because he vocalized certain themes in a specific style that resonated with a population that would soon find itself part of an emerging
nation. In clear Lebanese settings he constructed stories of love, oppression, and rebellion. He relied on a refreshingly Lebanese diction despite
writing in the more formalized fusha, and he validated simple, rural imagery as he constructed a seemingly Lebanese aesthetic. But the very points
that would link Gibran to the new Lebanon often revealed the fault lines
upon which that Lebanon was built. The Phoenician and Christian em-
phases, the almost exclusive focus on mountain village life, the conflation
of national designations, and the idealized émigré perspective all remain
problematic features of the Lebanese nation. Also, the fact that he lived in
the West and wrote most of his later work in English rather than Arabic
suggests internal schisms, even division of loyalties, features that remain
endemic to the Lebanese mentality.

Gibran's themes and language, as seen in the works discussed above,
would prove resonant in the formation of the Lebanese nation. Gibran's
influence, however, would not have been so strong were it not for his own
efforts at self-fashioning and the excessive adulation he generated among
others. In addition, his growing fame in the United States lent an aura of
greatness to the poet who insisted on being buried in and commemorated
from his humble Lebanon. This last section will trace the cult of Gibran,
culminating in his funeral and reception in Lebanon.

For Americans, Gibran *was* the exotic. As early as 1896, the thirteen-
year-old Gibran was elaborately dressed in "traditional garb" and rented
out to be photographed by the avant-garde artists of Boston like Fred Hol-
land Day. Day himself was often dressed in "oriental garb, smoking a water
pipe." In their biography of Gibran, *Kahlil Gibran: His Life and World*,
Jean and Kahlil Gibran comment upon Day's "accessories—waterpipes,
fezzes, pointed slippers, embroidered robes, and incense . . . [that] were to
Kahlil common objects of everyday life." They continue, "The boy delighted
that a well-educated American enthusiastically responded to his country's
symbols. In turn, he was able in many ways to help his patron's Oriental
fancies become more authentic and elaborate" (53).

This uncritical comment is replete with significance. First, the authors
assume that the "accessories" are genuine symbols of Gibran's "country."
Second, they assume that Gibran further authenticated those symbols to
the American. The symbols, in other words, are unproblematized, fixed

artifacts that have arrived in the West from their obvious source in the East. Yet both the fact that Day adopted the accessories as exotic symbols and that young Gibran perpetuated the signification of those symbols is proof of the complicated attributions and perceptions involved here. There is ample evidence from reading the biographies of Gibran that the author played up the symbols that appealed to his American audience. By the time he was publishing his Arabic stories and exhibiting his paintings in Boston, for example, he had already constructed a persona rich with the supposed mysteries of the East.[23] According to the account of friends, Gibran wanted to emphasize his role as the oriental poet and would consciously wear an Arab costume to social events so that his "rich American friends could see him in his native garb" (157).

Gibran's self-fashioning was also self-promotion that helped catapult him into the imagination of his American readers. More important, back home in Lebanon, Gibran's luster seemed to brighten because of his success abroad. As mentioned earlier, most of Gibran's works up until 1920 (coinciding with the establishment of Greater Lebanon) were in Arabic. After that, most of his published work, including *The Prophet*, was in English. Translated into over forty languages with millions of copies sold worldwide, this text ensured Gibran's international reputation as a populist philosopher. His aphoristic musings on love, marriage, children, work, freedom, friendship, beauty, religion, and death struck a chord with many people inside and outside Lebanon, especially in the United States, making for an interesting connection between East and West. For the growing number of Lebanese immigrants and for their families left behind, the idea of Lebanon was beginning to take on a form partly dictated, ironically perhaps, by the West's perceptions of the East.

It is no wonder that Day's gaze and Gibran's pose would coincide in classical orientalist photographs that framed the very nature of East/West relations. Increasingly it becomes difficult to locate the source of the Lebanese image that emerges from these pictures, for both poser and photographer are implicated in the construction. In trying to assess the development of a Lebanese identity at this juncture, it behooves us to consider again the vital role of the immigrant and, consequently, the foreigner. Gibran's specific case in point is further illustrative because of the emergence of a cultlike following in the West that helped distinguish the poet at home. It is as if Gibran's fame abroad helped validate his significance.

Barbara Young, a friend of Gibran who would initiate this adulation, exaggerated and romanticized his influence in her book *This Man from Lebanon:*

> His boldness and daring became evident in his youth. His country, under the yoke of the Turkish Empire, was stricken in spirit, and hopelessness threaded all the fabric of its weaving. Gibran wrote a poem in his native Arabic, calling it *Spirits Rebellious*. It was published, and in an incredibly short time it was burned in the market place in Beirut by priestly zealots who pronounced it "dangerous, revolutionary, and poisonous to youth." The book was the first fist of the modern free youth to be shaken in the face of that powerful Empire, and it was shaken with unmistakable vigor. (18–19)

Resistance to the Ottomans had been ongoing for centuries, and it took many different forms, from the political success of Fakhr al-Din in the seventeenth century to the Arab intellectual renaissance of the nineteenth.[24] Gibran's collection of stories did not even identify the Turks as villains. (It is implied, of course, but it is the local rulers who are truly vilified.) His text was hardly the catalyst for a revolution. Young continues her assessment of Gibran's book:

> But the burning of the book was not the end. Gibran received in Paris information that for the writing of this poem he had been excommunicated from the Church and exiled from his country, for this unspeakable crime, a book calling upon the youth of his land for a realization of their high heritage and for a revival of the courage and the power and the glory of their forefathers, those men of ancient distinction and splendor, their Phoenician-Chaldean ancestors! (19–20)

Significantly, Young's prime source about Gibran's homeland was Gibran himself, who probably highlighted to her the "ancient heritage" of his country, a heritage increasingly useful to many who sought to de-Arabize and de-Islamicize what would become independent Lebanon. Her narratives on Gibran not only exaggerated his political impact but consolidated narrow definitions of his nation. She and others who knew and wrote about Gibran idealized and essentialized him, labeling him a genius and a prophet, but Gibran himself encouraged those images. The adulation of Gibran during his own lifetime has continued. It is indicative to peruse the many books, in Arabic and English, on Gibran. A quick glance, for example, through the card catalog at the American University of Beirut library on Lebanese literature reveals that most author studies are on Gibran. Second, a great bulk of these studies are not too different in tone from the Barbara Young fan club approach. Besides the 1961 Karami and the 1981 Khuweiri books mentioned below, see Fawzi 'Atweh's 1971 study and Suleiman Kattani's 1983 dramatic rendition for television.[25]

The cult of Gibran is in evidence today more than seventy years after his death. Documentaries, like the 1995 *Death of the Prophet*,[26] along with frequent articles about the author in cultural magazines and countless web pages and Gibran links on the Internet often reinforce the well-known myths about Gibran. Attempts to seriously critique Gibran have been few and far between. In 1934 when Mikhail Naimy published the biography of his friend Gibran, many were outraged at his lack of reverence and some, like Amin Rihani, rallied quickly to Gibran's defense (Jean Gibran 417–18). Naimy had disclosed, for example, that Gibran was a heavy drinker and womanizer. The earliest critical and complex study on Gibran is Khalil Hawi's 1963 book.[27] Besides providing insightful readings of Gibran's major texts, Hawi takes on the character of the poet, dismissing his prophetic posturing as immature and naive (280), while admitting to the worth of his early Arabic writing, which showed a "relative awareness of historical situation and a fresh eye for background and scenery" (281). Naimy's 1964 edition of the complete works of Gibran in Arabic also provided an intelligent and somewhat critical introduction of the author. Recent biographies like Robin Waterfield's *Prophet: The Life and Times of Khalil Gibran* have also placed Gibran under severe scholarly scrutiny.[28] Despite many attempts to deconstruct the legend of Gibran, it has persisted stubbornly in the public sphere. Documentaries, plays, schoolbook texts, and an ongoing scholarship continue to propagate the notion of the exceptional man who has come to symbolize, for many, something of an idealized Lebanon.

Indeed, it is the legend of Gibran that has had as much impact on the formation of a Lebanese consciousness as it is the actual writings of Gibran. Renan and other theorists on the nation have written precisely on the importance of legends, of myths, of narratives, even of lies, in constructing and imagining the nation. The combination of Gibran's writings, his life stories, and his following made for a potent mix. As a final example of his import, one has only to look at the narratives of his death.

Gibran, who chose to live in the United States, where he accumulated much of his fame, decided he wanted to be buried back in Lebanon. He supposedly wrote: "If Mary Haskell is living I desire the heart to be taken from my body and given to her, and my body to be sent to Bechary Syria to be buried in Mar [St.] Mema" (Jean Gibran 213). The final will and testament further stipulated what would become a legal nightmare: requesting that his sister take a good percentage of his money "to my hometown of Becharri, Republic of Lebanon, and spend it upon charities" (403).

And so the "return" begins. And to so many Lebanese, Gibran's return home replicates either their own journeys or those of friends/relatives. The raj'in [we are returning] theme, dominant in Lebanese folklore and popular song, reinforces the glorification of Lebanon: the homeland, the happy childhood, the spectacular mountain range visible from the advancing ship or plane. Lebanon becomes the place one aspires to be, even or especially in death. It takes on an inexplicable essential significance.

The accounts of Gibran's funeral are revealing. The biographers Jean and Kahlil Gibran write that an official delegation boarded the ship at the Beirut port, the casket was lowered before a guard of honor, the minister of education placed the Decoration of Fine Arts on Gibran's body, and important dignitaries marched with the casket to the church where the archbishop blessed the body. That evening Charles Debbas, president of the Republic, held a reception in his honor at which many prominent people spoke, including Amin Rihani. The next day, the funeral procession made its way north to Bsherri. People supposedly lined the roads and "twenty times the swelling cortege stopped for local ceremonies" (408).

Barbara Young's melodramatic description of the reception in Lebanon is worth recording:

> And his own country, Lebanon, from the moment that the ship dropped anchor in the beautiful harbor of Saint Georges at Beirut, added a testimony of tribute and pride that has not been known before "in the hoary history of Lebanon." The Arabic press bears witness that never has such homage been paid to any man, living or dead. From far and near the throngs of the grieving came to their capital city, and even from beyond the bounds of Lebanon itself, from the greater Syria. For the bells had tolled the tidings all up and down that land, the tidings of the death of this man from Lebanon who had achieved the height of their most ardent dreams, and on that day of his passing their greatest

sorrow had been born. From ancient Damascus, from Homs and Hama, from Antioch and Sidon and Tripoli they came, and from the Holy Land to the south, to do honour to their dead. (156)

The same spirit of exaltation characterized the many critical works on Gibran. One, by Nabil Karami, for example, also describes the welcoming of the dead poet in effusive language. As the motorcade advanced north, thousands of people in countless villages came out and put on their own receptions with music, speeches, dances, etc. Schoolchildren lined the streets and, Karami notes, there was a feeling of national unity. Along the road were posters depicting a Cedar, Baalbek, and Gibran, promoting the poet as the third wonder of Lebanon. Overwhelmed by this imagined scenario, Karami's language takes off as he describes the body entering the church of St. Youhanna for the first time since he left Bsherri, the "town he grew up in, with its sweet breeze, pure sky, fresh water, fragrant flowers and grandiose nature."[29]

After the burial in Bsherri, a library of his collection was gradually set up. But when Barbara Young visited that collection in 1939, she was supposedly appalled at its condition: "All the effects, paintings, drawings, and Arabic manuscripts were uncatalogued, untended, and unloved. The ever-growing royalties were abused and misused" (Jean Gibran 419). Antoine Khuweiri wrote in 1981 that Young actually wanted to burn Gibran's personal papers (to remove all traces of Mary Haskell, of whom she was jealous), but Haskell secured the poet's personal works and shipped them to Bsherri, where they remained sealed in boxes for a very long time. The municipality rented an apartment to store and exhibit some of the works, but by the early 1970s they saw the need for a more proper Gibran museum. This led to much quarreling and the eventual formation of a National Committee on Gibran. This group finally decided to establish a museum on the site of the old monastery (the St. Sarkis hermitage), partly set in caves that Gibran used to frequent.[30] The museum was almost ready to open when the war broke out in 1975. The opening had to be postponed for another two decades.[31]

Despite the emotional reception of the poet who, according to some, put Lebanon on an international map, there were few consistent or state-directed plans to commemorate Gibran. In 1970, however, under the patronage of President Charles Helou, the first Gibran International Festival was held in Beirut.[32] This was initiated primarily by Lebanese Americans, who succeeded in monumentalizing Gibran. In Boston, for example, a monument to Gibran was established in Copley Square across from the Boston Public Library in 1977. In 1989, a garden on federal land in Washington, D.C., was located to "honor the Lebanese-American poet and artist" (Jean Gibran 429). Symposiums, exhibits, and seminars across the United States celebrated Gibran's centennial in 1983.[33] That year, Lebanon was reeling from the aftereffects of the massive Israeli invasion and was still enmeshed in civil war. The government of Amin Gemayel sponsored a centennial commemoration in 1983, which basically consisted of a series of lectures over two months. In the introduction to the collection of those essays, *Jubran*, the editor writes that all the contributors are professors at the Lebanese University, the university of the nation, Gibran's nation (6).[34] Now in the postwar period, Lebanon has been more attentive to rebuilding or rediscovering national symbols, and Gibran has not been overlooked. In the summer of 1999, for example, the National Committee on Gibran sponsored a monthlong festival in Bsherri on, as the English *Daily Star* put it, "the country's legendary author and philosopher" (Al-Ali 4). The *Star*'s article continues with a quote by the mayor of the town: "Gibran taught us notions like courage, martyrdom, equality and human rights. He introduced us to sentiments of independence, freedom and brotherhood . . . and taught us about national dignity and invited us to support the needy and the poor."

It is also noted that the festival, with its cultural activities, poetry evenings, films, and book exhibitions, could not have taken place "without the support and generosity of Cardinal Nasrallah Butros Sfeir." Ironically, the powerful and sectarian cardinal would probably have been exactly the type of cleric Gibran would have opposed. In Lebanon, the political and religious leaders continue to officially preside and therefore try to shape the national narratives. This is not to say that the public is totally dominated by authoritarian visions.

In April 1996, after Israel's "Grapes of Wrath" offensive in Lebanon, I attended a well-publicized and lavishly produced play on Gibran.[35] Despite innovative stage directions and a reputable cast, the play reinforced the cliché perspective of Gibran as the visionary prophet. More to the point, the audience, shaken by the Israeli offensive, clearly responded to the recitation of Gibran's famous "Nine waylat" [pity the nation] sequence from his *Garden of the Prophet*. Published by Barbara Young in 1933, two years after Gibran's death, *Garden* consists of works, originally in Arabic, which

Gibran then put into English. These lines were especially resonant: "Pity the nation that doesn't raise its voice except when it walks in a funeral, boasts not except among its ruins, and will rebel not except when its neck is laid between the sword and the block" (2:432).

These lines resonated with a Lebanese audience that night. Lebanon's leaders were visible only at the official ceremonies and only after the tragedies had struck. Once again they had perfected the art of lamentation and relegated Lebanon to the victim role. Gibran's insights on Lebanon, declared decades before its independence, are rather wondrous to behold. He continues to resonate in Lebanon, despite or because of his cultlike following, his own self-aggrandizement, and his seerlike stature.

Rereading Gibran with the idea of nation in mind is illustrative on many levels. He lived and wrote during an era when the very idea of Lebanon was emerging, so it is interesting to locate where formative ideas of Lebanese consciousness might reside. He actively participated in transforming the Arabic language in ways that would help distinguish a Lebanese identity. And he isolated certain features of the "homeland" that would become essential to any discussion of nation. In studying a selection of his works, one can detect an insistence on presenting both a concrete landscape and a spiritual dimension to his narratives. His texts abound in natural description alongside a religious (or moral) vision. Not coincidentally, land and religion (along with language) are key components of the perception of the nation, certainly the Lebanese nation. While the 1926 constitution provides the geographic perimeters of the Lebanese nation, today the Lebanese borders remain permeable and overrun by other nation-states. Whereas prior to the 1920 Republic of Greater Lebanon people were classified according to Ottoman-devised states centered usually around large towns or relatively homogeneous mountain ranges, Lebanese today still identify strongly with ancestral village or urban community, differentiating rather than uniting them as citizens. Though Gibran commends a universalist spiritual moral code, it is often derived from and expressed in Christian terms. In fact, something akin to religion permeates Gibran's entire literary output. The very ideological foundation of the Lebanese nation was, arguably, built upon religious grounds. Some fifty years after independence (including sixteen years of internal warfare), most Lebanese still adhere to their confessional loyalties before all else.

Benedict Anderson, among others, has explored how, in Europe for example, the rise in national sentiments coincided with the demise of "religious modes of thought" (11). Eventually the nation, rather than religion, inspires love and sacrifice among the populace. Perhaps Lebanon's transformation into a nation was never fully accompanied, like the European nations, by a secular transformation. Narratives like Gibran's that repeatedly affirm the sacred significance of the "land" suggest that, in the case of Lebanon, the national and the religious (or at least the quasi-spiritual) remained entwined. This feature might have been less problematic if Lebanon did not encompass a diverse range of confessions.

As if already concerned by the religious divisions that would increasingly torture Lebanon, Gibran wrote in his 1913 "To the Muslims from a Christian Poet": "I am a Christian and I'm proud of that, but I reach for the Arab prophet and I enlarge his name. And I love the glory of Islam and fear its extinction. . . . I hate the Ottoman state because I love Islam and its greatness and I want to restore its glory. . . . Take it, O Muslims, a word from a Christian: Jesus lives in one half of me and Muhammad in the other" (4:208–10).

However, his attempts to speak to the Muslims of the region did not result in him becoming a strong national symbol for many non-Christians, nor did his words fully serve to unite the multiconfessional Lebanon. Although Gibran was respected for his innovations, especially in language, he remained ostensibly a spokesman for a Christian idea of Lebanon that was coalescing into existence.

As I've indicated primarily through endnotes, there were many other writers producing from Lebanon during Gibran's lifetime. Many of them, as William al-Khazen has so carefully documented, reflected the broad ideologies of the time. Some wrote occasional verse praising the Ottoman and other authorities, but most found the opportunity to condemn their policies of oppression. Many poets identified with the East against Western control and imperialism (and eventually Zionism). Most writers, though at times referring to Lebanon, also identified themselves as belonging to a broader Arab community.[36] None of these figures, however, would emerge to take on the significance of Gibran, who also, in complicated ways, touched upon all the ideologies just mentioned. Because Gibran became a national figure, his example has been intentionally highlighted. The marginalization of everyone else suggests the selective process of national mythmaking itself at work.

Reading through Gibran reminds us that *Lebanon* and *Syria* were not always mutually exclusive terms, even when he prioritizes one over the other in differing circumstances. With recent treaties on "Cooperation and Brotherhood" being signed in Damascus and Beirut while Lebanon remains for all intents and purposes under Syrian influence, there is further evidence of the endurance of designations and identities articulated at the turn of the century.

Finally, the Arabic language, which to many is the surest proof of nationhood [al-umma al-'arabiyya], is also what has allowed many to link Gibran's Arabic specifically to Lebanon. The history of Arab nationalism versus Islamic or more local nationalisms, the role of Arab Christians in formulating those nationalisms and modernizing the language, and the admission of absolute Muslim/Arab binaries within Lebanon all speak to the core of Gibran himself—a Christian, an Arab, a nationalist, an innovative transformer of the language, and a lost immigrant pining away nostalgically in the big American city. His "Lebanon," idealized and victimized, becomes a construction that sheds light on the very processes of political and cultural development in the region—processes that need attending to as we confront Lebanon today.

Contest of Ideologies

We used to praise nature (and Trad was the best at praising nature), describing her virtues and beauty, blind to her secrets and her relationship to man and her harshness. We used to sing to the loved one (and Trad did that the most beautifully), as if she was not made of flesh and blood, as if she were a god. And we used to look to love (and Trad befriended love) as napping on an arm in the light of the moon, not as a strange secret that connects the sky and the earth and a deep existential joy whose key is pain. This primitive optimism character-ized Lebanese poets even the melancholic romantic Ilyas Abu Chabaka. All of this was the result of our lack of consciousness to human existence and to human problems in this strange world. This consciousness arrived to us late—in the last ten years—and is still in its infancy.

Yusuf al-Khal

The year 1943 marks the end of the French mandate over Lebanon. The Lebanese Parliament amended the constitution, abrogated all articles re-ferring to mandatory status, and declared Lebanon's independence. Al-though Greater Lebanon had already been created in 1920, and a consti-tution was already drafted in 1926, it was not until 1943 that a legitimate and independent nation-state was launched. This chapter will continue to study Lebanon through its literary narratives, allowing them to be con-textualized against briefly presented historical segments. The intention here is primarily to illustrate how cultural artifacts might reflect and hence bet-ter describe a historic moment, but also to raise questions on the symbiotic relationship between culture and nation, especially at this juncture of Leba-non's development.

Perhaps the most important feature of independence was the 1943 un-written National Pact ("al-mithaq al-watani"), which sought to allocate high government positions according to religious sects. The ongoing division between Muslims and Christians over the existence and identity of Leba-non was hence partially addressed through this pact, drawn up primarily by Maronite Christian (Bishara al-Khuri) and Sunni Muslim (Riad al-Sulh) leaders. A "confessional democracy" was spelled out, providing for the religious denominations in various key governmental posts. The Maronites were given the presidency and the Sunnis the premiership. In order to keep the Christians further secure, a Christian/Muslim ratio of 6:5 was maintained in Parliament and throughout national institutions. Also, the Muslims would have to accept Lebanon's sovereignty and independence as well as its unique openness to the West, in exchange for the Maronites' forsaking French protection and affirming Lebanon's "Arab face."

This compromise deal between the religious sects spelled out the political formula for Lebanon's pluralistic culture. On the one hand it enabled Christians and Muslims to politically coexist within the new state; without the pact, Lebanon might not have survived its inception in 1943. It also offered the potential for a secular, pluralist democracy. Unfortunately, the compromise deal also defined the nature of Lebanon's political culture. Political parties, ideological movements, electoral laws all took on a confessional identity which, arguably, weakened national development. Moreover, every citizen was required by law to belong to a religious sect, clearly marked on the Lebanese identity card. Not surprisingly, this religious insistence promoted or, at the very least, encouraged mixed loyalties among the Lebanese, whose identities were then determined not only by nationality but by confession. In addition, the Lebanese legal system intentionally bypassed personal status issues like marriage, divorce, and inheritance, leaving them to the religious courts.[1] This foregrounding of religious identity at the institutional, political, and legal levels would serve both to distinguish the Lebanese nation and to undermine it.

Lebanese national loyalties were also further challenged by regional ideologies that swept across the Arab world in the 1940s and 1950s. Many Lebanese were more concerned about the possibility of an Arab nation, the migration of Jews to Palestine and the subsequent establishment of Israel, and the pull to a Syrian nationalism, rather than invested in the new Lebanese nation. To the generation growing up in the 1940s, "Lebanon" was hardly an achievement.

It is not surprising that without a strong state structure the new nation was unable to build a strong national allegiance. This problem was exacerbated by an educational system that strongly followed Lebanon's confessional divisions, not a national program. Except for the prerequisite government baccalaureate degree needed for university admission and some employment, schools were free to administer their own curricula. This freedom of education is specified in article 10 of the constitution. Indeed, one of Lebanon's claims to excellence was this educational freedom, as it enabled different communities to invest heavily in their own chosen or perceived cultural heritage.

Many schools not only took on confessional names but were linked to foreign missions. The French had already established a powerful network of schools across Lebanon, and the Lebanese baccalaureate system was modeled closely after the French one. American Protestant and British Evangelical schools had sprouted, as well as orthodox Christian and Islamic schools. These distinct schools (as Gibran had already noted decades earlier) reinforced the heterogeneous cultures within Lebanon and did little to build a unified national Lebanese culture.

In terms of higher education, the universities were mainly products of foreign missionary or cultural activity and continued to divide rather than unite the groups of students they graduated. St. Joseph University was founded by the Jesuits in 1881; it taught in French and tended to serve the Catholic and Maronite communities. Its influential law school would supply most of the top personnel of the political system and national bureaucracy. The American University of Beirut (known earlier as the Syrian Protestant College) founded in 1866 and the Beirut College for Women (now the Lebanese American University) founded in 1926 both served a more heterogeneous population. Their language of instruction was English, and their philosophy was modeled after the liberal, humanist American tradition.

From the outset, the nation appeared fractured. In order to survive, it adopted a compromise policy between the confessions that led to protectionism within the sects. With little drive toward national identity, political culture emerged as individual candidates (linked usually to families representing the various seventeen official confessions) served only their constituents. The central government remained weak as parliamentary blocs, controlled by the traditional leaders or za'ims, determined the national agenda. Successful political leadership was measured by how the za'im could serve his followers, find jobs for them, and service their villages. In fact, "the poorer the people in a community and the stronger their confessional loyalty, the stronger the position of the za'im" (Elie Salem 62). Leaders often opposed the spread of education in their regions for fear of losing the blind support of their constituencies.

Many of the traditional leaders, according to Salibi, thus opposed social and economic development because, without it, they could then blame the central government and be perceived as "the protectors of the people" (190). This unscrupulous mind-set became inscribed within the Lebanese political formula, minimizing healthy development. Instead, national development or, more precisely, development within the new nation-state was fueled by private capitalist initiatives and regional ideological movements. The result was a period of relative peace and seeming economic prosperity within Lebanon.

In a useful assessment of the term of Bishara al-Khuri, Lebanon's first president, Harris notes: "Certainly his presidency, from 1943 to 1952, took independent Lebanon through its teething stage. On the other hand, al-Khuri's enthusiasm for unfettered liberal capitalism and his abuses of presidential power confirmed unattractive features of Greater Lebanon already visible under the Mandate, features incompatible with multisectarian equilibrium" (138). Among his abuses of power was his involvement in widespread fraud in the 1947 parliamentary elections, which led to a pro-Khuri majority. It is this Parliament which then voted to amend the constitution in 1949, authorizing the president to seek a second term. Increasing dissent against Khuri gradually led to his resignation in 1952. This first attempt to extend the term of office has, unfortunately, become a rather common feature of the Lebanese presidency.[2]

Khuri's economic liberalism seemed to validate the philosophy of his brother-in-law, Michel Chiha, the most influential thinker on Lebanese nationhood and the main drafter of Lebanon's constitution. One of Chiha's central ideas was that modern Lebanon had evolved from an ancient culture of traders and seafarers, Phoenicia. It was once the commercial and cultural center of the Mediterranean, it had a distinct climate and geography, and it was the most powerful unifying factor of modern Lebanon. Chiha wrote, "Lebanon is basically a beautiful and noble experiment in peaceful cohabitation of religions, of traditions, of races. It is a natural experiment, which history offers as a still more decisive demonstration than that of Switzerland in the heart of Europe" (1966, 250). Although many would reject these definitions of Lebanon, they remained powerful ones during and after Lebanon's independence.

After all, it was hard to argue with the facts on the ground: Because of Lebanon's freedoms, Arab writers and intellectuals chose to reside and publish there. Because of its economic prosperity, businesses, employment figures, and wage earnings were on the rise. Because of its development, the population was comparatively healthy, life expectancy and per capita calorie intake were relatively high, starvation was virtually nonexistent, and major diseases were under control.

This was a Lebanon that boasted of its cosmopolitanism, of its emigrants, of its Western ties and unique features within a broader Arab-Islamic region. Its moderate climate, snow-capped mountains, Mediterranean coastline, swanky hotels, casinos, and restaurants drew tourists in record numbers who reported back on this "Switzerland of the Middle East"— playground, financial center, cultural and intellectual haven. Here was a country where French and Arabic, and increasingly English, were spoken and taught. Dress codes, architectural structures, public advertisement and media presentations, cultural centers and educational curricula were widely varied, creating a colorful mosaic.

In his 1949 *Liban d'aujourd'hui*, Chiha presented a Lebanon that was fragile but "marvelous," a special nation that required special forms of governance that included compromise, tolerance, and the provisions for ample liberties for its citizens. Although currently situated in the Arab-Islamic world, Lebanon was the product of many conquests and a mix of multiple cultures and civilizations, like the Phoenician. It was, and had always been, multilingual, multicultural, and able to thrive only with an open economic system, confessional pluralism, and democracy.[3]

Some of the ideas spelled out by Chiha were attractive to Lebanon's writers. By 1946, Chiha's ideas inspired the formation of an intellectual group, Cénacle Libanais, and a group of writers, including Charles Corm and Sa'id 'Aql, would express Chiha's brand of nationalism in their verse and prose writing. 'Aql, for example, made a literary career out of fabricating an extensive Phoenician mythology for Lebanon. He also went out of his way, both thematically and stylistically, to dissociate Lebanon from its Arab heritage. Many of his poems, although ostensibly apolitical, take on serious political overtones in 'Aql's decision to publish them in a defiant new Latin alphabet of his own construction. His program to de-Arabize Lebanese culture is hence most powerfully revealed in his own "Lebanese language." Below is a brief example from a poem entitled "Henni? Bxebbun" [Them? I love them]) in *Yara* (some minor adjustments had to be made out of typographical necessity):

Henni? Bxebbun, bass qenti,
Qetr ma tjammay bi yinayqi xala,
Men qabl ma b ha l qawn qenti,
Qent salliliq sala.

[Them? I love them, but you / So much beauty gathered in your eyes /
Before, when you weren't in this world / I used to say a prayer for
you.]

'Aql provides a thorough index of the consonants and short and long vow-
els and a transliteration table that translates the Arabic alphabet into a Latin
one. Achieving something like an ideological following, 'Aql mobilized
groups of mainly young Maronite Lebanese who would, in different con-
figurations, fall into rightist political parties and militias. Obviously inspired
by increasing fears of regional Arabism and sweeping Islamicism that, some
felt, could destabilize Lebanon and the unique position of the Christians
within the state, these groups solidified, through cultural production and
political rhetoric, their distinct narratives of the new nation.

Chapter 1 illustrated how the then "imagined community" of what
would become the nation-state of Lebanon featured strong symbols of
the Phoenician past, the idyllic rural terrain, and the sacred dimension
of Lebanon's history. The texts of Gibran, which served more than any
other literary or cultural texts to shape the narrative of nation, abound in
these references. In the 1930s and 1940s other authors, many influenced
by Gibran and the Mahjar poets, broke away from the neo-classical traditions of Arabic poetry and formed a loose coalition of "Lebanese Romantic Literature" that further reinforced certain narratives of the nation. In
her 1979 book, *Al-Dalala al-ijtima'iyya li-harakat al-adab: al-romantiqiyya
fi Lubnan* [Social conditions for literary movement: Romanticism in Leba-
non], Yumna al-Eid explains how this literary movement came about as
a product of specific socioeconomic factors and cites the authors most
influential in the movement like Omar Fakhoury, Iliyya Abu Madi, al-
Akhtal al-Saghir, Ilyas Farhat, Khalil and Amin Takyeddine, and especially Ilyas Abu Shabaka (1903–47).

Abu Shabaka's poetry is one of the most consistently taught in Lebanese
schools. The politically unthreatening ideas of romantic individualism,
creative imagination, and passionate feeling are expressed in his love poetry. Though written and published in the decades surrounding indepen-

dence, his poetry had no overt political overtones and was easily anthologized and put to memory by generations of students. A typical line from "I Love You" is translated as "You are the perfumed cloud from heaven sent / To rain upon me your enchanted dew" (from Salma Jayyusi's anthology, *Modern Arabic Poetry*, 53).

Significantly, the most important idea or conflict that dominates Abu Shabaka's poetry is what Mounah Khoury calls the "problem of a denatured world." The city, the state, progress, and corruption are all displacing what is truly good and ideal: the pastoral life of Mount Lebanon, site of the poet's sweetest memories:

> Our minds were at peace in those old,
> treasured days. Our conscience was at rest,
> and truly there was peace and life reaping
> its harvest. O time, bring back to us
> what Lebanon has lost! (qtd. in M. Khoury 94)

Lebanon, that imagined pre-independence community, was where, as Gibran narrated, nature resided. Here was the essence of goodness, where shepherds and peasants lived simply and proudly. These "romantic" notions of society proved powerful in continuing to inform the identity of Lebanon.

As Lebanon emerged into a state, some aspects of these romantic symbols persevered and even intensified. In his *Lubnan in haka*, 'Aql creates a document that attempts to validate the Lebanese nation he imagines. His emphasis is on locating references to "Lebanon" from classical and Western, not Arab, sources. He then fabricates a tale—with dialogue, detailed description, and powerful imagery—to bring that location or moment to life. Without providing any references or scholarly notes, 'Aql's text reads like an authoritative document that has taken on the function of national mythmaking. Below are some examples of his stories.

The first tale, "Qasadtuhu Qabl An Akun" [I intended him before I became], is set in Sidon during the Greek Empire. The parents of the great mathematician Pythagoras had spent their honeymoon in Sidon, the most beautiful, civilized, city in the world—magnificent with its Phoenician temples and Greek theaters. And there the genius was born and baptized in the holy water of Afqa in Mount Lebanon. Although Pythagoras would return to Greece for his early education, he pursued his higher learning in Lebanon, a place honored and praised by the immortal Homer. This quick summary illustrates the attempt to glorify Lebanon, which is constantly named as an existent, concrete entity. Further, the associations of glory come from distinctly Phoenician and Greek links. This pattern continues in most of the thirty-eight stories collected here.

For those who might not know, Antony and Cleopatra met in Zahle, Lebanon. Shakespeare's "best heroine," Marina from *Pericles, Prince of Tyre*, was "Lebanese." The "Panegyrics" of Romanos came from "Lebanon." In "Yawm zara yasuʿ Lubnan" [The day Jesus visited Lebanon], we learn of the miracle he performed in Sidon and Tyre when he cured a sick child. Another story, "Al-thurri al-awwal" [The first atomist], introduces the first atomic theorist—a Lebanese, of course. Here ʿAql reports on a Swedish scholar who in 1948 was a visiting member of a UNESCO conference in Lebanon. On a trip to Sidon, he encounters an educated young man and informs him that his city is the birthplace of Mokhos, the first atomist in history. The young man is surprised, since in his schooling he was taught that the Greeks Loseeb and Democritus were the first. The Swede, however, informs him that his education was not thorough. The first atomist was Mokhos, and this is a fact that Lebanon should celebrate (175). The last story, "Ila akhir al-ard" [To the end of the earth], depicts an Austrian teacher well versed in Lebanon's "stupendous" history. Again, it is through a foreign spokesperson that we learn that the Lebanese (i.e., the Phoenicians) discovered the New World 3,000 years before Columbus (297).

Lebanon is hence an important source for great genius, learning, scholarship, art. It is also, as some tales reveal, a haven for justice and freedom—words used repeatedly in the text. Beirut is presented as the ancient city with the greatest Roman law school in the world. Tyre, threatened by Nebuchadnezzar, remains defiant, as one of its watchmen calls out: "Since its inception, Fate has only seen Tyre free!"

Another indicative feature of these tales is that they are located across present-day Lebanon. The myths are centered in Damour, Zahle, Saida (Sidon), Sour (Tyre), Jbeil (Byblos), Tripoli, Beirut, Baalbek, and villages in Akkar and the Bekaa. These are locations that, at different times in the region's history, fell under separate jurisdictions and yet are claimed here as historically and unproblematically Lebanese. There are no references to the Arab and Islamic conquests that altered the Middle East, to the Ottoman Empire and the various states or wilayats under its sway. The artificial construction of 1920 Greater Lebanon is conceived here as ancient, unified, and fixed. Lebanon, with its current borders, has its roots in

Phoenician, Greek, and Roman cultures—all undeniably recognized, especially by the West, as great civilizations. In fact, these are primarily Western cultures themselves. Lebanon is not Arab, nor from the East.

'Aql reconciles the fact that Lebanese speak Arabic by refusing to assign "Arabic" as the label for the language. Throughout *Lubnan in haka* [Should Lebanon speak], the references are not to Arabic but to the "language of Lebanon" (e.g., 294). 'Aql's attempts, of course, to Latinize Arabic illustrate his insistence on redefining, as Ataturk did, by force, one of the most essential criteria of nation, the linguistic one.

Some of the powerful sentiments of 'Aql's narrative on Lebanon could be matched in other local political movements, especially the militant Kata'ib [Phalange] Party of Pierre Gemayel founded in 1937. Although it was a confessional, rather than a secular national, movement, the Kata'ib always prioritized Christian Lebanon as its mission. Feeling increasingly besieged and outnumbered by their Muslim compatriots who had broader allegiances in the Arab world, Lebanese Maronites rallied behind a party that seemed to guarantee Lebanon's survival.

In his *Lebanese Christian Nationalism*, Walid Phares voices (in English and in writing) this survivalist mentality so dominant among the Maronites. In no uncertain terms he outlines how the National Pact initiated the "disastrous" decline of Christian domination in Lebanon. According to Phares: "The country had shifted from a bold pro-Western character, illustrated by centuries of relations between Mount Lebanon and Europe, to that of a satellite of the Arab bloc. From this angle, political Arabization of Lebanon was underway" (89). Severing ties with the West proceeded with the elimination of French as an official language and the declaration of Arabic as the only national language. The victorious independence coalition, Phares laments, further called for the immediate withdrawal of French troops.

As the 1940s drew to a close, the most cataclysmic event in the region, the nakba, took place with the 1948 establishment of the state of Israel and the displacement of thousands of Palestinians. The repercussions of these events will be discussed more thoroughly below, but first it is interesting to see how 'Aql referred to 1948.

Like many Maronites, 'Aql was concerned with how a large influx of primarily Muslim Palestinian refugees would destabilize Lebanon. Rather than focusing attention on the plight of the Palestinians in Lebanon, he worried about the fate of Lebanon. It is indicative to witness his use of the landmark year 1948 in one of the tales mentioned above ("The First Atomist"). The year is marked not for the loss of Palestine but for the UNESCO conference that provided the occasion for yet another creation of a Lebanese national mythology. The new fragile Lebanon, galvanized like its Arab neighbors by Israel's sudden statehood, was exhibiting loyalties and allegiances that seemed irrelevant to the nation itself. One way to read 'Aql is that he strove to make the Lebanese nation relevant. Phares, not a noted historian but a useful spokesperson for a dominant Maronite ideology, explicates the tragic implications of the establishment of Israel in 1948: "The Lebanese government could not refuse to play host to hundreds of thousands of Palestinian refugees who brought considerable political and demographic change to the already precarious balance of power within the small state" (97).

Despite the potentially turbulent political climate in Lebanon, other writers, like the poet Michel Trad (1912–98), steered away from ostensible political engagement, and like 'Aql, consolidated aspects of the young Lebanese nation. Trad did so by composing poetry that used Lebanese colloquialisms and incorporated folksy images and themes set mostly in a village locale. Difficult to translate because of the specific regional dialect, Trad's work has remained the property of the Lebanese and like certain songs, zajal, foods, and practices is often classified under Lebanese folklore.[4] In the epigraph to this chapter, Trad is the poet who, according to Yusuf al-Khal, was best at "praising nature" and at singing beautifully to the "loved one." He represented a "primitive optimism" that, although challenged by al-Khal and others, served its purpose in essentializing the nation, like Gibran before him, through its language.

Another group of writers during this era achieved in prose a new kind of realism that sought to describe their positive perception of Lebanon. A quick look at another group of Christian writers, selected primarily because of their popularity then and their continued visibility in school textbooks now, will provide another dimension to the literary narratives emerging shortly after Lebanon's independence.

Marun 'Abbud (1886–1962) and Anis Freiha (1903–92) published short stories almost exclusively set in the villages of Christian Mount Lebanon. In that respect they come out of a Gibran tradition that gave concrete form to a lifestyle and system of values that would become associated with one of Lebanon's important cultures. Although these stories vary widely in theme, stylistics, and intentions, they do share some significant points. For one, they tend to present a lifestyle that, in its rural simplicity, becomes quaint and idealistic. The tales, which revive village customs and modes of interchange, are set against realistic portraits of traditional homes, schools, churches, and orchards. Some are sentimental, some are funny, and most are nostalgic.

'Abbud's stories are regular features in both elementary and secondary Arabic textbooks throughout Lebanese schools. Born in 'Ayn Kfa' (near Jbeil/Byblos), he was very prolific, publishing many collections, including *Ahadith al-qariya* [Village tales]. The "Lebanese" 'Abbud writes about are Christian villagers who live deep within rugged Maronite terrain. The inhabitants are very religious and have total faith in the powers of St. Maroun. The stories revolve around village characters and their beliefs, generational differences, shocking Western innovations, etc. They are not, however, as innocuous as they might seem. In "Bi munasabat al-dastur wa al-istiqlal" [On the occasion of the constitution and independence], the villagers complain about the lack of government responsiveness to their needs: They still have no road, water, electricity, hospital, or school. "The Constitution is useful to the educated; what have Independence and the Constitution done for us? The villager is poor and weak; he will have no luck from the government unless he is strong" (206). The politicians, it seems, only care when it comes time for reelection. The only difference independence has made is that now they pay more taxes and receive fewer benefits! The bitterness, however, is undermined by a caricature of villagers and their antics. They stubbornly insist on their old ways, refusing advice and counsel, and wallowing in the "happy past" (208). The story concludes with a mother screaming uncontrollably because her son is choking on an apricot pit. While some of the relatives run off to nearby villages to get help or stand by helplessly, a few others race to give offerings and prayers at the church. To the villagers, it is this last group which brings salvation. The story ends happily with a "miracle" as the boy spits out the pit. 'Abbud is obviously depicting something of the poverty and ignorance of these mountain folk, whose daily lives are so consumed by their faith. He is also affectionately capturing a mentality and a generation that would soon begin to change in the 1950s as development and modernization programs would trickle into the villages across Lebanon. He renders something of the Maronite spirit of fierce mountain independence and distance (geographically, psychologically, and culturally) from the sophisticated urban compromising political class. Their lives are, in every way, disconnected from the political process.

Anis Freiha's popular collection *Isma'ya Rida* [Listen, O Rida) addressed to his son, Rida, is ostensibly about his memories from village life.[5] In his preface he admits that these tales have no depth and no political significance. They are written for kids trapped in the city, who want to be liberated by what the village can offer. In a passage reminiscent of Gibran's "You Have Your Lebanon and I Have Mine," Freiha writes: "This book is not for those who want to make of Lebanon a center for learning, or an experiment for multiconfessionalism, or a free market, or a tax-free zone for trade, or a repository for oil pipelines, or a country for play and pleasure. If they read this book they'd say it embodies primitivism, sanctifies ignorance, glorifies backwardness. Their Lebanon is blown out of proportion. Our Lebanon is still the Lebanon of the village, Lebanon of the mountain" (4). As a way perhaps to sidestep criticism, Freiha says that outsiders, city dwellers, and critics would not understand this book. He does not mind, though, because the book is not intended for them; it is specifically for Rida. Each of the stories begins with "Listen, O Rida," and proceeds to relate some heartfelt village custom, scene, incident. Many provide intricate details of children's games, classroom experiences, Christian holidays, kinds of foods, etc. At the end of the story, the son Rida is always asleep, wearied by his father's long reminiscences.

The overall spirit of these stories is one of nostalgia, always associated with a supposedly simple, rural lifestyle of the previous generation. This nostalgia, in fact, remains one of the most dominant features of the spotty national culture that would emerge in the decades after independence. Easily traceable to some of the qualities of Gibran's writing, this kind of cultural text could, and would, be reinforced by inclusion within school curricula and, on a more popular note, by the young entertainment industry.

A quick glance through typical textbooks used in teaching Arabic reveals a whole host of Lebanese writers whose stories or poems foreground a romantic pastoral vision. Examples include the works or excerpts from Gibran, Amin Rihani, Mikhail Naimy, Marun 'Abbud, Michel Trad, Karam Milhem Karam, Khalil Takieddine, Amin Nakhli, Emily Nasrallah, Gibran Mas'ud, Rose Ghreib, Iliyya Abu Madi, Ilyas Abu Shabaka, Sa'id 'Aql, Mansur Rahbani, and Fawzi al-Ma'luf. Most are Christian males and some are from the immigrant Mahjar group discussed in chapter 1. Also, what most of the anthologized examples have in common is a closedness that discourages critical engagement with the text. In other words, the selections are presented as fixed truths about a clearly distinct era or location in Lebanon. It is almost impossible to detect conflict within the narratives and therefore difficult to tease out the potential ironies inherent within them. If there is a political agenda at work, then this might be it. For generations, the Lebanese educational program (sanctioned within the official baccalaureate) has promoted a view of Lebanon that adheres to the ideals imagined by many of the above writers. In a climate of political turbulence that resulted in the nonconfrontational formula of the National Pact, it is perhaps understandable why conflict, at all costs, would not be encouraged within the national education curriculum.

This nostalgic and often sentimental portrait of Lebanon was not just reserved for schoolbooks. Increasingly, a national image linked powerfully to song, dance, and drama would capture the popular imagination of the Lebanese. Significantly, this image would be reinforced as much outside of Lebanon, by the growing number of emigrants, as within it. In the decades leading up to 1975, a whole host of contributions to popular culture would consciously bypass the sensitive difficulties facing the fragile new nation and focus instead on the trials and tribulations of simple village life, the antics of misfits, the romance in the face of societal opposition, etc. Alongside these plotlines developed an effective song-and-dance routine with elaborate costumes that would become the traditional Lebanese dress. A period of intense folklorization of Lebanon was now under way.[6] The poems, songs, and musical dramas of the famous Rahbani brothers (discussed in the next chapter) joined with the unforgettable voice of Fayruz and her dancing dabke troupes to create one of the most powerful and certainly exportable of Lebanese cultural products. The sheer excellence of the product would guarantee its immortality alone, but its dominance within the Lebanese psyche could also be explained by the simple vision of loveliness and nostalgia that it offered. To a society confused over national identity and unsatisfying political formulas, the popular cultural alternative could fill in some gaps. If Lebanon's history was unspoken (and it remains amazingly blotted out even now, more than fifty years after independence), then literary and artistic narratives, intentionally defanged of political implication, could be reinforced—and they were.

As Lebanon entered the 1950s under the presidency of Camille Chamoun, the country was seemingly thriving. Literary narratives of a non-problematic, apolitical past reinforced the climate of luxury, tourism, and laissez-faire economy. Indeed, when social and political realities contradicted (as they often did) that idealized image, they did not necessarily weaken or alter it. The "beautiful" Lebanon was adhered to precisely in the face of "ugliness," and maybe even because of it. The Lebanons of Gibran, of Chiha, of Freiha, and eventually of the Rahbani brothers,[7] different as they were from each other, were all hopeful. They held the promise of a Lebanon that could work, that would be unique, that was beautiful. Perhaps they willed Lebanon to be! Ernest Renan defined the nation as the product of groups which *will* themselves to persist as communities. He defined the nation as a "historical result brought about by a series of convergent facts" (11–12). A nation, however, is also a soul, "a spiritual principle" constituted by two things: "the possession in common of a rich legacy of memories," and "present-day consent, the desire to live together, the will to perpetuate the value of the heritage that one has received in an undivided form" (19). In Lebanon, of course, this will or regard was only within certain groups. For the Maronites and many other Christians and eventually for the Sunni political class, the idea of Lebanon made sense. To those disenfranchised and outside of political representation, the new nation held little meaning.

Already apparent within Lebanon were the widely disparate views of the very notion of Lebanon. There were those, like the authors discussed above, who believed in the very essence of Lebanon. Georges Corm discusses the three most important trends within this "essentialist" camp.[8] For some, Lebanon is essentially a Christian nation that evolved from Mount Lebanon, historically a refuge for Christians within the Islamic world (1996, 32). To others, Lebanon is essentially a secular, democratic, independent nation. Religion and the confessional system, as Gibran advocated, should not be part of the political process (34). The third essentialist view of Lebanon saw the nation as fundamentally unique and therefore requiring a National Pact that would institute confessionalism as a way to ensure representation and sufficient checks and balances (35).

Three powerful nonessentialist views of Lebanon were also at work, according to Corm, to undermine the very existence of the nation. Each viewed Lebanon in terms of a larger regional entity. Some perceived Lebanon as part of the Islamic nation, others as part of the Arab nation, and another group saw Lebanon as part of the Syrian nation (1996, 39–44). Although Corm's classification might, ultimately, be a bit too tidy for our purposes, it certainly serves as a useful transition to a more thorough discussion of the age of ideologies that would contribute so strongly to the shaping of and maybe even dissolution of Lebanon.

An examination of a popular novel written by one of Lebanon's most prominent writers and publishers, Suheil Idriss, gives form to some of these nonessentialist views of Lebanon in circulation during this period. *Al-Khandaq al-ghamiq* (the title is a district in Beirut—The Deep Trench), published in 1958, takes place during World War I. It deals primarily with the coming of age of Sami and his siblings, who confront and rebel against a strict, conservative Muslim father. Much to his father's pleasure, young Sami vows to become a Sheikh and attend religious school. The school is stifling, and most of the students are superficial and more interested in the headdress than the teachings, more intent on recitation than on understanding. Sami quits the school and takes up journalism, travels to France, and pursues a life of enlightenment (including supporting the rights of his sister, Hoda).

Of relevance here is the stark difference between this text and the numerous examples discussed above. For one, there is virtually no mention of Lebanon. The word appears once on page 42 within a line of poetry. There are only a few topical references to a town, a specific location in Beirut, a summer resort. There is absolutely no foregrounding of Lebanon as land, as mountain range, as haven, as Mediterranean coast, as beautiful climate. That entire perspective is irrelevant to the story. The Sunni Muslims of now-Lebanon had for centuries lived within the coastal cities of Tripoli, Beirut, and Sidon—all previously part of Ottoman wilayat connected to Damascus or Palestine, not Lebanon. Not surprisingly, the world which Idris's characters inhabit is the much broader Arab nation. The father has business in Aleppo, Syria; the girlfriend, Sumayya, moves to Egypt; Hoda plans to continue her education in Cairo. The narrative assumes an Arab cultural unity that includes or subsumes Lebanon.

In fact, the main sociopolitical tension within the story has absolutely nothing to do with Lebanon—even though the nation is in its most formative stage. Instead, the battle lines are drawn between the Islamicists and the secularists, again suggesting concerns that dominated the entire Arab world, not just Lebanon.

This quick example reveals some of the rather obvious differences between certain Christian and Muslim writers in Lebanon. Politically, as well as socially and culturally, they often espoused different values and outlined different identities for themselves. Whereas the Christian authors discussed previously insisted upon a palpable rural idealistic Lebanese setting for their texts, Idriss's example suggests a lack of psychological investment in Lebanon; as an idea it does not capture the imagination; it does not have "essence."

Another Lebanese novel appeared in 1958 that complicated the essentialist notion of folkloric Lebanon. Layla Baalbaki's *Ana ahya* [I live] takes place specifically in Lebanon, but because its perspective is almost totally that of its heroine and only main character, Lina Fayad, the novel presents a newly disparaging narrative. Lina systematically opposes most aspects of Lebanese society. She wants to live life fully as an independent woman, not restricted by domestic and cultural roles. She disapproves of her father's capitalism, of her country's labor laws, and of the inequality in marriage relationships. She is animated by many issues like those of class, gender, politics, labor, and religion, but her opinions are not taken seriously by her male counterparts. Even women, she believes, are responsible for keeping females in restricted and demeaning roles. By the end of the novel she feels disconnected from her family, her friends, and her colleagues.[9] This defiant novel written by a Muslim woman about a woman created an uproar when it was published, and Baalbaki was attacked for her outspokenness. In a 1959 lecture entitled "Nahnu bila aqni'ah" [We without masks], Baalbaki assailed traditional Arab society for its restrictive views of women and its sexual segregation. Unfortunately, when her next novel, *Al-Aliha al-mamsukha* [The deformed goddess], was published in 1960, Baalbaki, according to Bouthaina Shaaban, seems to have reduced her intensity and written a less outrageous novel. According to Shaaban, *Ana ahya* remains closer to the heart of the author and a novel "thirty years ahead of its time" (101). Its thematics and its first-person presentation forged a new construction of the nation.

Whether existing as an idea or not, the Lebanese nation began to be associated with the Lebanese state. Ernest Gellner explains nationalism as a consequence of a "new form of social organization, based on deeply internalized, education-dependent high cultures, each protected by its own state" (Nations 48). In the second half of the twentieth century, it is the state that usually presides over a national culture. Indeed, the nation/culture becomes, according to Gellner, "the natural social unit, and cannot normally survive without its own political shell, the state" (143). In Lebanon, however, as the state emerges with the directive to preside over the

nation, it is a nation still undefined and not unified and without a dominant national culture.

One can hypothesize about the function of the state under these circumstances by offering some scenarios. A strong state could impose, under tyranny, a single national culture; or it could promote multiple cultures since, in its security, it felt unthreatened by a plurality of differences.
A weak state could encourage the political divisions and potential breakup
of the nation; by its incapacity to control the factions, it could also allow
them their share of distinctiveness, creating a plural identity.

Lebanon's state apparatus was never strong, but it did begin to make
an impact in the 1950s, providing services and reforms to a wider percentage of its citizens. Yet it never instated a truly progressive program
that would alter Lebanon's postfeudalistic system and offer the chance
for a new national culture. Instead, the state opted for minimal interference in economic affairs, which resulted in a severe class division to go
along with the already dangerous confessional divisions within the nation. During a period of seeming economic prosperity, then, many came
to identify Lebanon in terms of that success. Wealth and the freedoms it
bought hence became features of the Lebanese nation even though they
did not apply to many Lebanese. In those cases, national loyalties became even more mixed.[10]

The 1950s offer useful specifics on how Lebanon, both as nation and
state, would evolve and interrelate. The liberal economic policies under
President Khuri continued with the presidency of Chamoun (1952–58),
although now there was more state money spent on public services. Labaki
writes, "The state began to reap the benefits of its public services, including water, electricity, railroads, tramways, and others. Institutions were established with the goal of assisting economic growth" (Labaki 99).

Although the Lebanese state was beginning to actualize, the internal
political divisions remained strong as ever, especially as Lebanon became
entangled in the affairs of other states. Israel's existence, the plight of the
Palestinians, the toppling of regimes in Egypt, Syria, and Iraq—all deeply
affected the climate in Lebanon. The loss of Palestine mobilized Arab forces
around what was perceived to be an imperialist Western and Israeli Western enemy. Eric Hobsbawm writes that the most effective way to bond "disparate sections of restless people" is to unite them against outsiders (91).
The ideology that best embodied Arab opposition and Arab progress was
Arab nationalism.[11] For Lebanon, Arab nationalism would prove divisive.

In 1955 President Chamoun seemed to come out in favor of the so-called Baghdad Pact, which linked Iraq to the pro-Western and non-Arab "northern tier" of the Middle East. He also seemed to endorse the Eisenhower doctrine recommending U.S. support against the Communist threat in the Middle East, and he refused to expel the British and French ambassadors after the 1956 Suez invasion. All of these foreign policy positions angered Lebanese Muslims, who increasingly identified with the aspirations for a new and politically exciting Arab nation. In 1958, Syria and Egypt united as the United Arab Republic, and radical Arab nationalism under the leadership of Gamal 'Abd al-Nasir nearly toppled the regime in Lebanon. The assassination of a journalist quickly triggered civil strife in Lebanon as various militias representing the Nasirites, Ba'thists, and Communists fought against the National Front, which brought together the unlikely Lebanonist Kata'ib and the proponents of greater Syria, the Syrian Social Nationalist Party (SSNP). Chamoun tried but failed to bring in American troops to "defend" Lebanon under the Eisenhower doctrine, but the 1958 coup in Iraq changed everything. With the sudden dissolution of the Baghdad Pact and the loss of Iraq as an ally in the region, the United States was quick to respond to Chamoun's renewed request for troops. The Marines landed in Lebanon the day after the Iraqi coup, and prolonged negotiations led to another compromise solution. General Fuad Shihab, who successfully kept the army out of the conflict, was deemed acceptable to both sides and was elected president by Parliament to succeed Chamoun.[12]

In retrospect, it seems that Chamoun's pro-West foreign policy along with his active opposition of Nasirism disrupted the internal balance within Lebanon. There was no deeply rooted unified national culture through which to negotiate the competing ideologies within Lebanon. Instead, those ideologies replaced or dramatically transformed the weak and fragmented local cultures within Lebanon. Alongside the essentialist notions of Lebanon, partially expressed in some of the romantic and nostalgic pastoral literature above, there developed a literature that reflected the climate of crisis within Lebanon and the Arab world. At times more ostensibly political, this was a literature that was actively engaged in the intellectual debates of the time. Characterized by experimentalism and a search for meaning, Kamal Abu-Deeb elaborates on this literature: "It is this state of flux and free search which underlies the feeling of angst gripping people in the Arab world today. It is this condition which makes people declare that we live in a state of crisis: crisis in activity, crisis in poetry, crisis in thought, crisis in criticism" (Sharabi, 1988, 180). By the 1950s, Lebanon, and specifically Beirut, had become a leading cultural, intellectual, and publishing center for the entire Arab world. The radical political upheavals across the region reverberated within Lebanon as scholars, journalists, and writers engaged the political process in their classes, editorials, and literature. At times the result was propagandistic and simplistically monologic, but other texts, as will be seen, reveal a more rigorous dialogic commensurate with the challenging political philosophies now on the horizon.

Lebanon was also caught up in its move toward development and liberal economy. The incredible wealth generated from the oil-producing Gulf states poured into Lebanon as well, encouraging a mentality of consumption and political cynicism. This rapid embourgeoisement tended to dilute or isolate the progressive ideologies so that there was never a fully successful partnership between the popular masses and the intelligentsia in a serious drive toward political and social reform. Instead, as Samih Farsoun outlines, the middle classes tended toward rampant consumerism and disenchantment with politics, while the poor searched for salvation in religious revival and "utopian idealism" (Sharabi, 1988, 231).

Under these social conditions, the task of the intellectual is daunting indeed. Some of the literary figures in Lebanon, especially the group of poets linked with *Shi'r* (discussed below), consciously saw themselves as intellectuals, taught at the universities, wrote for the leading journals, gave public lectures, and published texts in engagement with current sociopolitical issues. Although much of their poetry was considered obscure, these writers effectively captured popular sentiments of anxiety and disenfranchisement. Like many Lebanese who were subscribing to the regional ideologies, these poets also were swept by the tide of political discourse sweeping over the nation, especially after the loss of Palestine.

Arab nationalist sentiments became much more radicalized after 1948. Led by middle-class groups, this new Arab nationalism called for immediate pan-Arab unity and advocated for social revolution. In Egypt, Nasir and the Free Officers seized power in 1952, while Ba'th regimes took gradual hold of Syria in 1955 and Iraq in 1963. Rebel Arab nationalist movements nearly toppled the regimes of Lebanon and Jordan in 1958. Other traditional governments fell in Libya, Sudan, and Yemen.

The intellectual most responsible for the founding of modern Arab nationalism was Sati' al-Husri (1882–1968), who was influenced by the Germans Fichte and Herder. Because the Arabs shared a common language and history, they were a united nation. Religion, geography, and race were secondary to language and history. Like Renan, who believed that "forgetting" and "historical error" are necessary in the creation of a nation, Husri maintained that what people remember (rather than the actual facts) shapes the psychology of a nation. He appealed to the mythmakers who "could construct from the debris of the past a grand and glittering edifice to serve as a source of confidence and inspiration for the entire [Arab] nation" (P. Salem 53).

In Egypt, the banner of Arab nationalism would be carried by Nasir, who through the 1950s and 1960s came to be the undisputed leader and mouthpiece of the movement. He was heavily influenced by revolutionary and nationalist ideology of Palestinians and Syrians. His socialist reforms, nationalization of the Suez Canal, and defiance against the West established his reputation as the Arab world's most charismatic figure. His speeches would be broadcast throughout the Arab world as he advocated for political, social, and cultural unity, recalling past narratives of Arab civilization and inciting enthusiasm with talk of collective opposition against the intruder, Israel. Arab nationalism became the avowed ideology of Nasir's regime, and he was the first leader to translate the theory of this movement into statist policies. His influence and popularity were so strong, of course, that Nasirist groups formed in Lebanon, where they seriously threatened the regime in 1958. The Lebanese nation was not perceived to be an essential entity by the advocates of Arab nationalism. They backed the Syrian-Iraqi unity plan of 1954, the Syrian-Egyptian merger of 1958, and the Hashemite Federation of the same year. The objective was consolidation and expansion as ways to create a powerful and glorious Umma 'Arabiyya.

Michel Aflaq, a Greek Orthodox from Damascus, was the leading thinker of the more radical Ba'th Party. Unlike Husri, Aflaq (1910–89) recognized language and then history as the two most important factors in nationhood. His nationalist ideology "was couched primarily in the philosophic concept of national cultural 'inbi'ath,' or 'Ba'th,' i.e., renaissance, or flowering. Aflaq considered the heart of his message to be a call for a general Arab renaissance that would transform Arab civilization in all its aspects—political, economic, intellectual, and moral—and which would provide a unique and historic contribution to humanity and world civilization" (P. Salem 62). Much of the appeal of Aflaq's philosophy lay in the style in which he expressed his ideas. His Arabic language was poetic, resonant, and memorable, and he used it effectively, like Nasir, to mobilize his listeners.

Another political leader instrumental in defining notions of nation and in attracting a generation of Lebanese writers was Antun Saadeh (1904–49). From a Greek Orthodox Lebanese family, Saadeh spent formative years in Brazil, where he developed his ideas of Syrian independence and political secularism. As seen in the previous chapter on Gibran, Lebanese and Syrian identities were especially interchangeable by those who lived abroad. Whereas theories of Lebanese and Arab identity had already been brewing in the Middle East, Saadeh's advocacy was for a Syrian identity that would be housed in a Greater Syria encompassing Syria, Lebanon, Palestine, and Jordan.

Saadeh was especially influenced by European fascism and its ability to mobilize the masses and create a powerful state. He studied German and taught it at the American University of Beirut when he arrived in Lebanon in 1929. In 1934 he founded the SSNP, and it quickly attracted students and intellectuals across Lebanon, especially from the Greek Orthodox community, which was less than enthusiastic about Maronite versions of Lebanon. From its inception, the SSNP opposed the mandate authorities, and after Lebanon's independence in 1943 it opposed the new state. A failed coup in 1949 would lead to Saadeh's execution.

The SSNP moved temporarily to Damascus but came in open conflict with the Ba'thist regime there primarily over the central issue of Arab nationalism. Saadeh and his followers were against the idea of an Arab nation. In his 1938 *Nushu' al-umam* [The origin of nations], Saadeh had written that nations are based on a "shared life over generations within a territorial boundary" (qtd. in P. Salem 248). He prioritized physical and natural surroundings over language or culture. To him there existed a Syrian nation, predating both Christianity and Islam, whose people shared a common history in a specific locale.

The SSNP's ideological differences with the Ba'th led to its relocation to Lebanon and its temporary support of President Chamoun against his Arab nationalist opponents in 1958. But the SSNP was fundamentally opposed to the Lebanese state, which it tried again to overthrow in 1961. One of its most consistent reasons for opposition was its advocacy for total secularism and abolishment of the confessional system within Lebanon. These ideas appealed widely to an intelligentsia eager to reduce the influence of religion within the political system. Saadeh's zeal and charisma were also unforgettable, creating something like a cult following even now, almost fifty years after his death.

The issues and debates surrounding Husri, Aflaq, and Saadeh's versions of nationhood would galvanize many Lebanese. The rigor of their inquiries appealed to many writers and intellectuals who were unsatisfied with the essentialist notions of the new Lebanon. The optimistic and glorifying versions of an ideal pastoral Lebanon were, to them, simplistic myths attempting to validate an erroneous nation-state. A group of authors sought to problematize the very notion of identity and meaning by debating these issues in essays and creating a language, through poetry, that was experimental, creative, and utterly new. Best represented in the groundbreaking journal *Shi'r* [Poetry], these writers narrated an important cultural movement within Lebanon.

In 1957, the Lebanese poet Yusuf al-Khal (1917–87) founded *Shi'r* with the conscious objective of inaugurating a new era in critical and creative discourse. Emulating a famous modernist journal in the United States, *Shi'r* sought to revolutionize Arabic poetry. One of its missions was to translate and hence introduce Arabic readers to Western poetry. The early editions contain samples of Pound's *Cantos*, selections from Emily Dickinson, Walt Whitman, Galway Kinnell, Philip Larkin, W. S. Merwin, e. e. cummings, Edith Sitwell, William Butler Yeats, Paul Valéry, and others. Some of the poems are presented in the original language. At the end of each volume is a "News and Issues" section that includes the latest on publications, lectures, and debates within the Western modernist movement and also across the Arab world. Features on T. S. Eliot appear regularly, as do items on Khal and his changing board of editors and advisors. The Arabic poems, in the first issues, identified the poets by city, with Beirut, Damascus, Cairo, and Baghdad being the most frequent. Soon after, however, the city designations are dropped, and only a date follows the poet's name. In addition to poetry, the journal also featured essays and reviews that expressed the opinions of the editorial staff.

Although Yusuf al-Khal remained chief editor of *Shi'r* for its duration (intermittently from 1957 to 1969), other poets then became members of an editorial board. They included Adonis (Ali Ahmed Sa'id), Shawqi Abi Shaqra, Unsi al-Haj, and Fuad Rifqa—all of whom were located in Lebanon, although Adonis and Rifqa were of Syrian origin. The Lebanese poets Khalil Hawi, Talal Haydar, Issam Mahfuz, Nadia Tueni, Etel Adnan, and Laure Goraieb were also often included. Other poets from the Arab world included Nazik al-Malaika from Iraq, Nizar Qabbani from Syria, Jabra Ibrahim Jabra, Salma Khadra Jayyusi, Fadwa Tuqan, and Samih al-Qasim from Palestine. The poetry and the critiques intend to set a new course for the intellectual output of the Arab world. Essays incite writers to steer away from the traditional, the classical, and the status quo and to forge a new language of inquiry to confront the decrepit cultural/political scene. The call was for a revolution in cultural discourse to match the calls for political revolution espoused by the current nationalist parties.

Some of those involved with *Shi'r* were well versed in Arab nationalism and Ba'thist ideology, and they had all been members of Saadeh's SSNP. This fact irritated those critics who were strongly committed either to an essentialist Lebanese nationalism or to an Arab (rather than a Syrian) nationalism. Jihad Fadil, for example, in his 1996 *Al-Adab al hadith fi Lubnan: Nathra mughayyara* [Modern literature in Lebanon: A different perspective] attacks *Shi'r* for being insufficiently concerned about the larger Arab/Israeli conflict, since its proponents were too interested in larger Syria and "modernism." Fadil says that because Khal and others claimed Arabic language was dead and could only be revived if replaced by spoken language, their agenda was culturally destructive. Fadil also criticized Adonis's journal *Mawaqif* because it is too influenced by the West and is itself critical of Arab culture (57–58).

Although many of the leading contributors to *Shi'r* were Christian Lebanese, they did not foreground Lebanon as an essentialist entity, and they did not promote the popular idealized nostalgic version of Lebanon visible in so many of the cultural artifacts. Instead, their concern was for how the poet was to capture the spirit of the "modern" age. Fraught with political turmoil, rapid technological advancement, and personal isolation, this era demanded a different discourse, one that was experimental, avant-garde, and boldly new. The poetry of Khalil Hawi perhaps best embodied the new angst of the Lebanese Arab poet.[13]

An interesting review (an excerpt of which appears as the epigraph to this chapter) in the fall 1957 issue of *Shi'r* expresses some of the main critiques of the editors. Written by Khal in response to Michel Trad's latest poetry collection, *Dulab* [Wheel], the review systematically attacks traditional poetry for being too conventional, too descriptive, and too romantic. Trad's poetry ignored human and universal conflicts and was therefore isolationist, unconnected to the actual historic moment and its myths. Finally the poetry is too optimistic and unproblematic. Khal presents what we *used* to praise (nature and love), but now "we" are plagued by a modern consciousness. Subsequently, the language has to change. Khal continues to reprimand poets who have frozen themselves in time, who refuse to move beyond the French symbolist poets. Even Sa'id 'Aql, Khal says, admits that he has no idea what has happened since Valéry (111).

In the summer 1959 issue, Adonis's "An Attempt at Defining Modern Poetry" lays out some of the key objectives of his and others' new poetry. First, it is visionary and "should arouse and save us from numbness—from collective narrow thought" (vol. 3.10, 79). Poetry, he argues, should always be a site of conflict, should free itself from localized events, and should release words from their antiquated meanings (80–81). Indeed, the greatest aspect of this new poetry, represented in *Shi'r*, is that it has a "consecrated" mission. This poetic movement is "the wholehearted attempt to nourish, free and complete our current, fallen life" (90).

In the next decades Adonis would become one of the leading advocates for cultural change in the Arab world. His many critical publications, his consistently high-caliber poetry, his editorship of the journal *Mawaqif* (founded in 1968) all have established him as the Arab intellectual most intent on liberating the Arab mind from what he defines as a static, overly traditional, and religious mentality. One of the reasons for a lack of progress in the Arab world is the political system. Mounah Khoury summarizes Adonis's philosophy: "The Arab world must overcome these problems and establish a new culture based on freedom, creativity, and change. In order for this to happen, the Arab intellectual elite must reflect the prevailing culture. Reconciliation and acquiescence on their part perpetuate the old culture with its pattern of suppressing change and innovation. They must stress diversity and individuality, and above all freedom. In fact, it is freedom in all spheres that Adonis sees as the most essential element of the new Arab culture" (Mounah Khoury 23–24). For Adonis, like for Gramsci, culture is formative and plays a crucial sociopolitical role. Adonis relies on the highly educated and elite intellectual to pave the way for social transformation, whereas for Gramsci change must be motivated by the populace. Gramsci further outlined how excessive reliance on foreign ideologies (hardly available to the masses) was not conducive to authentic social transformation.

As one observes some of the leading intellectual voices emerging from Lebanon in the 1950s, it becomes quickly apparent that despite their often progressive tenor they remained strictly in elite spheres doing little to alter the populist agendas necessary for social transformation. Adonis, who after critiquing the Syrian political regime was imprisoned and then exiled, re-located in Beirut in 1956 and soon after became a naturalized Lebanese citizen. He was active with Khal in launching in 1957 both a publishing house, Dar Majallat Shi'r, and the journal. The journal's run was rocky due in part to "the political views and activities of its two editors, al-Khal and Adunis." Jayyusi provides a rather simplistic explanation of the prob-lem: "When, for example, the Civil War broke out in 1958 in Lebanon between the right-wing forces of the president of the republic, Camille Chamoun (viewed by most Arabs in Lebanon and the rest of the Arab world to be at the center of most of the harm, injustice, and disunity that befell Lebanon at the time) and the oppressed people of Lebanon, the two poet editors sided with Chamoun. This stigmatized the magazine while still in its early years" (*Modern Arabic Poetry* 19). This reductionist binary drawn by Jayyusi does not apply to the complicated political divisions within Leba-non. To characterize Chamoun as easily oppressive ignores the reforms he instituted (including female suffrage) and the confidence he had instilled in many Muslims for his defense of "Arab perspectives during his terms in the late 1940s as Lebanese ambassador to Britain and the United Nations" (Harris 140). Moreover, Chamoun did not come from the traditional upper-class za'im elite, but from the middle class, and he did not simply promote the interests of the once-feudalistic ruling families. The complex situation in 1958, as has already been outlined, was greatly determined by the rise of Nasirism and the coup in Iraq, not just by internal class divisions, and pit-ted a host of interests against each other. SSNP supporters (which would have included both Khal and Adonis) sided with Chamoun because they disapproved of the broad Arab nationalism being touted by Nasir's sup-porters. The "oppressed people of Lebanon," in fact, would have included many of those groups friendly to Chamoun and not some monolithic op-positional entity. Jayyusi's implication that the editors of *Shi'r* were politi-cally reactionary does not ring true considering the almost relentless revo-lutionary tenor of their agenda.

What is more significant about the political assessment of those intel-lectuals associated with *Shi'r* is the above observation that they were per-haps too Westernized to be truly responsive to the cultural climate they hoped to change. More pointedly, their Western literary and cultural agenda was not convincingly welded to a Lebanese or Arab social and political program. The forces that led to the modernist movement in the Western world do not easily translate into a modernist perspective in the Arab world a couple of decades later. Fredric Jameson makes the association between three fundamental moments in capitalism and their corresponding cultural forms in *Postmodernism, or the Cultural Logic of Late Capitalism*. Briefly, market capitalism leads to realism; monopoly or the imperialism stage leads to modernism; and multinational capitalism leads to postmodernism.[14] Modernism's appearance in the West can be arguably understood in large economic and political terms. The tenets of modernism forwarded in the 1950s and especially in Lebanon are out of sync with the actual socioeconomic base that best describes Lebanon at this stage in its national development. Barely untangled from a feudalistic economy and recently independent from a mandate force and centuries of Ottoman rule, Lebanon was hardly itself in a stage of high capitalism or monopoly. And the political forces that shaped Lebanon and the region were historically distinct, not reducible to pure economic terms. In fact, as one peruses the many editorials and articles within *Shi'r* during its first ten years (up through the spring of 1967), one is struck by the deliberate attempt to relegate poetry, specifically modern poetry, to a new prominence. The sociopolitical realm is hardly of concern. The focus is on discovering a new poetic aesthetic, defining it, promoting it. The ultimate allegiance is to poetry, for it alone is true, it alone endures. It is a luxurious inquiry, afforded to those relatively untraumatized by current political or economic issues. The rigor of this inquiry, however, would be drastically redirected after the Arab-Israeli 1967 war, setting in relief its discrepancy in the first place.

Certainly one of the recurring laments by contemporary Arab intellectuals has been a condemnation of excessive imitation of Western models by Arab thinkers. Even Khalil Gibran, in one of his nine laments in *The Garden and the Prophet*, recites: "Pity the nation that wears a cloth it does not weave, eats a bread it does not harvest, and drinks a wine that flows not from its own wine-press." Both Hisham Sharabi in *Arab Intellectuals and the West* (1970) and Issa Boullata in *Trends and Issues in Contemporary Arab Thought* (1990) are useful sources on this subject. From Adonis to al-Jabiri to Laroui to Khatibi, there is a call for Arabs to break the cycle of conformism to either their own conservative Islamic culture or to modern Western culture. In short, they have been too imitative and therefore not sufficiently useful. Instead, the Arabs should construct a unique agenda commensurate with their own specific history, drawing from their own particular culture, and attentive to the new demands of their own future.

What the above advice foregrounds, of course, is that this is the agenda for Arabs, irrespective of their nations. This is precisely the discourse that engaged so many of the poets/intellectuals who published their views from within the Arab nation with the most liberal political and economic system in the region. For better or for worse, the already distinct system in Lebanon was largely undermined in order to prioritize non-Lebanese nationalisms. The result is cultural production that is highly erudite, very Western, and almost exclusively atopical. With hardly any concrete references to Lebanon, whether in myth or in reality, there is a steady, almost unspoken chipping away at the political structure that, granted, flimsily sustained Shi'r and its offshoots.

Equally telling, the poetry of Shi'r never achieved the level of national discourse. The sophisticated imagery, oblique meanings, and convoluted syntax (reminiscent of Western modernist poetry) did not appeal to many outside academic circles. The political disagreements that increasingly divided the editors at Shi'r also resulted in a fragmented and isolated production. Their inclusion in this chapter reinforces the ideologically divided Lebanon, unable to coalesce as a nation yet conscious of its complexity.

The first chapter might seem to present a rather unified identity for the new Lebanon, but that is partly attributable to the focus on a single author, Gibran. If Gibran had not so dominated Lebanese consciousness, his narratives would have been studied along with a whole host of others. But Gibran did dominate, and his narratives did describe and shape the Lebanon to come. In the paired chapters 2 and 3, on the other hand, Lebanon appears to be more divided. Not only does the history confirm this fragmentation but the multiple narratives increasingly in the public domain reflect the many forces tugging at the young nation. The fact that Beirut would become the center of publishing in the Arab world meant that diverse texts were being read and assimilated within Lebanon. If no unified national/popular culture is on the horizon in Lebanon, at the very least one can detect a growing culture in the exchange of ideas. Lebanon was not simply fragmented but distinctive in the region as the site for multiple points of view.

3

Development and Dissent

In my grandfather's time there was a quarry in Deir Mutill where the use of gunpowder was forbidden because there was sulphur in its soil. The labourers of the village used to use great caution, handling the rocks with their working tools, with pick and shovel and crowbar. . . . Until one day my grandfather fell ill. Some good-for-nothing among the workers seized the chance of the boss's absence to set an explosive charge of gunpowder under a rock in the quarry while his workmates weren't paying attention. The quarry blew up like a volcano and many were killed and maimed. The village has never forgotten the tragedy.

The quarry of Lebanon is like that, my friends. Beware of gunpowder!

Tewfiq Yusuf Awwad, *Death in Beirut*

As Lebanon adjusted to its independence during the 1940s and 1950s, cultural expressions traditionally limited to village festivals and religious rites became more formalized. Many dramatic troupes, orchestras, and singers performed on stages and in restaurants, especially in Beirut, the new capital city. Here, Egyptian idiom and music heavily dominated dramatic and musical presentations. Occasionally songs were performed to a Badawi accent. Lebanese actors and singers usually spoke in Egyptian dialect,[1] but gradually a more distinctively Lebanese language began to take over. The Lebanese dialects had always been maintained, of course, in the Shi'a 'Ashoura presentations reenacting the suffering of Hassan and Hussein, for example. They also were reinforced through village plays, storytelling, zajal, and poetry recitations often performed during weddings and festivals. Not until the late 1950s and early 1960s, however, did something like national cultural productions begin to occur. These took off when the popular singer Fayruz, her husband, 'Asi Rahbani, and his brother, Mansur, created music that came to define Lebanese culture and folklore.

The Baalbek Festival began in 1956 but was focused at first only on

Western productions. In 1959, however, in a conscious attempt to finally include a Lebanese folk example, the festival committee asked the Rahbanis and Fayruz to perform. For the next two decades, their songs and musicals would project a distinctive and persistent image of Lebanon. A quick look at some of the early plays will help establish what that image was.

Between 1960 and 1965, the Rahbanis produced six popular musicals.[2] All are deeply rooted in a village, carefully prescribed with customs, locations, and characters. The world where the action takes place is complete with the bakery, olive press, village spring, and square. The flora and fauna of Mount Lebanon are there along with village events like the wedding and the central religious feast (eid). The wise mayor (mukhtar), the peddler, farmer, watchman, hunter, thief, old gossip, young beauty, and boastful hero (batal) are all portrayed. It is a fully imagined community, where the characters don traditional costumes and partake in customs, exhibit values, and use expressions that revive a nostalgic sense of rural and past Lebanon. Here, the moon speaks volumes, the evening walks to the spring ('ayn) are full of romantic promise, and hunting is a worthy pastime to swagger about. In this carefully narratized world, the only conflicts involve silly village squabbles juxtaposed against idealized and innocent love relations. In fact, all problems are eventually solved by turning to love.[3]

In this village setting, the mayor is usually the ultimate resource and judge; he is almost always the only representative of the government. Indeed, these musicals make hardly any reference to any political system larger than the village municipality. There are no confessional tensions or any serious or specific references to political underrepresentation. The language is colloquial and wonderfully accessible, not only in humorous and realistic dialogues but in the songs constructed for Fayruz's special delivery. She usually plays the part of the beautiful and wise young woman (sabiyya) who happily restores justice to the village by the end of the play. She is the pacifist, symbol of love and forgiveness, and defender of the downtrodden. Abu Murad notes that she plays the role of the prophet, the angel, the miracle worker. She is always convincing, and her word always goes. She speaks or sings the play's most forceful populist lines against oppression and for the replacement of injustice with love (235).

The Fayruz/Rahbani team constructed a vision of Lebanon that tapped into a yearning for a comforting image of the country. It was an image already propagated in the previous decades by primarily Christian artists, as already seen, who had sought to imagine Lebanon in terms of simple and positive mountain village principles. The Rahbanis succeeded like no one else in "turning on" the nation, as they seasoned their Lebanese image with memorable song, witty dialogue, colorful costumes, and rousing dabke dance. By the 1960s, their performances were also broadcast on television and radio, providing for a major segment of the nation's entertainment. Although they were certainly not the only artists to appear during this era, they led this important trend of "folklorization," which consciously shifted popular music and dramatic expression away from the Egyptian and toward the Lebanese. Although Egyptian films and singers like Umm Kulthum continued to be extremely popular, a new Lebanese media industry was under way in the 1960s. TV programs like *Abu Milhem* and *Abu Selim* centered on simple village antics and humorous family and neighborhood squabbles. Singers like Sabah, Wadiʿ al-Safi, and Nasri Shamseddine also participated in musicals (including those of the Rahbanis) and popularized romantic and lyrical tunes, most often set, again, in a Lebanese rural context. The Lebanon that was already so ideologically divided (as seen in the previous chapter) appeared to coalesce somewhat in terms of entertainment.

The climate of competing ideologies within Lebanon would only worsen as the 1960s progressed, especially after the defeat of 1967, which not only redrew the geographical map of the region but also reconfigured the psychological landscape of the Arab world. For Lebanon, one of the concrete changes was that the pressing Palestinian issue would become increasingly entangled with Lebanese affairs. Under the presidencies of Fuad Shihab (1958–64) and Charles Helou (1964–70), Lebanon continued to make some headway into statehood, but the government failed to administer to Lebanon's lower classes or attend seriously to the Palestinian refugee presence within its borders. Admittedly, Shihabism introduced numerous reforms especially in Christian-Muslim representation and economic development. Shihab was able to implement his policies by distancing himself from the traditional politicians and by relying heavily on the military intelligence [al maktab al thani, or the deuxième bureau]. He strengthened the army, established the Central Bank, modernized the ports, and expanded public education. He maintained friendly relations with Nasir and his Arab neighbors and when, in 1961, Syria broke away from its unity with Egypt, the dampened enthusiasm for Arab nationalism seemed to bolster the integrity of the Lebanese state.[4] The government still did not focus sufficiently, however, on the agricultural and industrial sectors, leaving large segments of the population without sufficient employment and large areas of Lebanon undeveloped. The economic growth remained virtually in the private sector, the result of services like transit, trade, and tourism. Lebanon's undeniable prosperity during the 1960s was also the result of external factors like the Arab-Israeli conflict, closure of the Suez Canal, and the nationalization of Arab economies, all of which resulted in enhancing Lebanon's economic profile in the region.[5] The political process remained highly sectarian, despite some equalization efforts. Services were usually rendered because of personal connections, not because of need or merit. As the private sector continued to grow, and Beirut gradually became an important publishing and financial center for the Arab Middle East (only five banks existed in Beirut before 1951 but the number had risen to ninety-three by 1966), the divisions among the classes and across the religions intensified.[6]

Exacerbating Lebanon's problems was the increasingly deplorable condition of Palestinians. Mainly housed in slumlike camps around the urban centers, the refugees were virtually ignored by the government with the excuse that they were entitled to Palestine and only temporarily dwelled in Lebanon. Lebanese law made it very difficult for a Palestinian refugee to find gainful employment or acquire naturalization. Ironically, other affluent Palestinians thrived in Lebanon's liberal economic system, presenting some competition to Lebanese businesses. In 1966, however, the Palestinian-owned Intra Bank in Beirut collapsed, wreaking havoc among Lebanon's financial investors and entrepreneurs.[7] Intra had become the most powerful financial institution in Lebanon, suggesting the already intertwined economies of the Palestinians and the Lebanese. The following year, of course, brought the devastating Arab *naksa* [defeat] that resulted in Israel acquiring all of Jerusalem, the West Bank, Gaza, the Golan Heights, and the Sinai. Thousands of Palestinians flowed into Lebanon, further complicating the fragile political entity.

The 1967 defeat hit Arab intellectuals like a thunderbolt. Articles, editorials, poems, songs, and media events described the war's impact. A striking example is evident in the poetry journal *Shi'r*, where almost the entire summer 1967 issue is devoted to the defeat. The focus of *Shi'r* had been ostensibly nonideological, since the aim was only to propagate excellent poetry. But the summer 1967 issue is altogether different. For one, the issue opens with four poems by the Palestinian Mahmoud Darwish, followed by poems from Yusuf Khal and Issam Mahfouz specifically on the disaster.

Two "conversations" on the war take place between poets Abi Shaqra and Unsi Haj, and then by Nadia Tueni and Haj. An article, "The Arab Voice Is Lost in the Current Crisis," by Abd al-Karim Abu al-Nasr explores the failure of the Arab Left in communicating with the Western Left. The "News and Issues" section is dominated by commentary on the war, including a long excerpt by Haj from the newspaper *Nahar* on how the Arab intellectual must be brave and ask the truly new and difficult questions that might help explain the defeat. Most other literary and cultural journals including Suheil Idriss's *Al-Adab* devoted considerable attention to this catastrophic political event.

Abdallah Laroui and Constantine Zurayq are among Arab thinkers who wrote about how "catastrophe," in fact, becomes a cornerstone of ideology. For Zurayq, the disaster (nakba) that befell the Palestinians in 1948 and then in 1967 cannot be ignored. He insists on the importance of catastrophes in developing historical consciousness. To ignore catastrophes is worse to a people than the catastrophe itself. One must fully study catastrophes— their causes, persons responsible—in order to come up with a course of action that is meaningful and modern, not founded on an archaic or classical vision.[8] Decades earlier Ernest Renan had also written about the importance of shared glories and regrets in establishing a national idea: "Indeed, suffering in common unifies more than joy does. Where national memories are concerned, griefs are of more value than triumphs, for they impose duties, and require a common effort" (19).

One of the many novels to have been written about the 1967 defeat is Layla Osseiran's *'Asafir al-fajr* [Birds of dawn]. First it reveals the shock and horror of the quick defeat, then it presents the repercussions, specifically, the birth of the Palestinian armed resistance. Bouthaina Shaaban notes, however, that the fervent political motives for the novel result in little distinguishing characterization or plot development (144–47).

After the Arab catastrophe in 1967, the refugee camps in Lebanon and Jordan became the sites for military operations against Israel, resulting in harsh Israeli retaliations against the host countries. The late 1960s were marked by frequent Israeli raids on Palestinian camps and Lebanese villages that housed the growing number of Palestinian military organizations falling under the general umbrella of the Palestinian Liberation Organization (PLO). In 1968, for example, the Israelis destroyed thirteen Lebanese Middle East Airlines aircraft after a Palestinian hijacked an El Al plane to Athens. The political climate within Lebanon was now very tense. To many

Christians, especially Maronites, the Palestinian military presence was an unacceptable threat. Palestinian operations across the border weakened Lebanese sovereignty, armed Palestinian commandos challenged the Lebanese army, and the "Palestinian cause" finessed all other internal and foreign affairs objectives. Indeed, reports from within the Palestinian camps revealed that, increasingly, many refugees saw the Lebanese state as their oppressor.[9] Although many of Lebanon's Muslim leaders were not especially encouraging of increased Palestinian radicalism, they were not averse to a weakening of Maronite preeminence and saw the Palestinian card as useful in shifting the internal Lebanese balance. Significantly, many leftist popular movements within Lebanon, especially among less privileged and Islamic groups, enthusiastically embraced the ideology of Palestinian resistance. So groups within Lebanon were increasingly mobilized according to the Palestinian issue.

Even some of the most Lebanese of Lebanese symbols became linked with Palestinian loss and a call for justice. As far back as the mid-1950s, the Rahbanis had composed the popular song "Raji'un" [We are returning], calling on Palestinians to return to their land and lead the battle of liberation from there. In his 1990 study of the Rahbanis, Abu Murad presents how the brothers flew to Cairo (then the undisputed cultural center of the Arab world and host to the influential radio station Sawt al-Arab) to suggest new ways to promote the Palestinian cause. Most past songs, for example, had been sighing, elegiac laments for the loss of Palestine. This new song offered a different spirit (43–44). A series of other pro-Palestinian songs would follow, immortalized by Fayruz. Perhaps the most popular would be "Zahrat al-mada'in" [The flower of all cities], a moving tribute to Jerusalem after its takeover in 1967.

As mentioned, leading Lebanese poets and artists dedicated works to the "cause," while a growing number of Palestinian and other Arab intellectuals and performers flocked to Beirut and reinforced a cultural output centered around the victimization and injustice suffered by Palestinians at the hands of Israel and its Western imperialist allies. To an already divided and weak nation like Lebanon, the indisputability of a "just" Palestinian cause was very attractive. The always subtle, forever compromising, agonizingly pluralistic aspects of Lebanon that never succeeded in establishing a unified and truly democratic nation-state paled in comparison. No national myths (despite Gibran and Fayruz) were strong enough to speak for all Lebanese; no cultural narratives defined or identified the majority of citizens of this country. The state, despite reforms and economic developments, did not tend to the basic needs of its population; and the political system, despite attempts at fair representation and a spirit of dialogue, remained archaic and largely self-serving.

As the 1960s waned, the Arab and other nationalist movements that had their heyday in the 1950s gave way to more radicalized Marxist and pro-Palestinian movements within Lebanon. For example the Arab National Movement (ANM), formed after the loss of Palestine in 1948 by some students of Constantine Zurayq at the American University of Beirut, became disillusioned with Nasirism after the defeat and adopted radical new political ideologies. After 1967, the ANM disintegrated into various extreme leftist movements such as the PFLP (George Habash's Popular Front for the Liberation of Palestine), the PDFLP (Nayef Hawatmah's Popular Democratic Front for the Liberation of Palestine), the PFLP–GC (General Command of Ahmad Jibril), and the Munathamat al-ishtirakiyyin al-Lubnaniyyin (Organization of Lebanese Socialists). Despite their differences, these groups followed a Marxist line of thinking that understood history in terms of class struggle. They were also antithetical to religious ideology and advocated a totally secular political ideology as witnessed in the works of another professor at AUB, the Syrian Sadiq al-ʿAzm.

Because of the relative freedoms within Lebanon and the convergence of cultural and intellectual forces in Beirut, the city became a vibrant site for political activism. Educational and cultural centers proved hotbeds of dissent in the face of Arab disappointment after 1967. It was only a matter of time before political legislation would confirm Lebanon's direction in foreign policy. This happened in 1969. By that year, the various Palestinian groups had allied themselves with Lebanon's populist, leftist movements primarily among the Islamic (though nonreligious) sector. The Baʿthists, Communists, Nasirites, SSNP, and the Palestinians formed a loose coalition in opposition to the Christian forces represented by the Kataʾib Party of Pierre Gemayel and other Maronite leaders including Camille Chamoun and Suleiman Frangiye. President Helou and the army were caught between these groups at first, but the army soon clashed with Palestinian fighters in April 1969. This confrontation resulted in severe opposition both within and outside Lebanon. Under pressure from Nasir and other Arab states, President Helou was forced to sign the Cairo Agreement (Ittifaq al-Qahirah), which guaranteed PLO supremacy within Lebanese refugee camps and legitimized Palestinian offensives against Israel from within

Lebanon's borders. No other Arab country granted such prerogatives to the Palestinians.

Besides the opposition of the Christian groups within Lebanon (the Phalanges, Chamounists, and the National Bloc), more radical right-wing groups also emerged in 1969. Phares discusses the founding of the underground paramilitary Tanzim [the Organization] that year, which promoted a radical Lebanonism. In 1970, another group, inspired by the poet Sa'id 'Aql, fostered the idea of a Christian-Muslim Lebanese nationalism and created the General Union of the Lebanese Nationalist Students in 1970. Claiming that the Palestinians would overrun Lebanon, these groups sought to assert an "ethnic-nationalism for the Christian people of Lebanon and to call for the implementation of their right for self-determination" (105).

In the next few years, the political climate would deteriorate further, beginning with King Hussein's decision to crush the Palestinian apparatus in Jordan ("Black September") in 1970. The result was a large influx of Palestinian civilians and fighters into Lebanon and an even more severe tipping of Lebanon's internal balancing act. That year also saw a series of violent encounters between Lebanese Christian groups and Palestinians. Under the new presidency of Suleiman Frangiye (1970–76), the Palestinians were not curbed, the Christian opposition forces were not curbed, and the climate was so volatile that it only needed a spark to set it all ablaze in the spring of 1975.

The Arab intellectual world, and Beirut as one of its cultural centers, became imbued with a new spirit of angst, anger, and frustration. Adonis began publishing his monumental study of Arab culture, *Al-Thabit wa al-mutahawwil: Bahth fi al-ittiba' wa al-ibda' Al-'Arabi* [Continuity and change: A study of conformity and creativity among the Arabs] in 1974. Here he faulted the Arabs for an overreliance on theology, on heritage, and on a conformist language.[10] After 1967, Arabs had to take stock of their language that broadcast "victory" as sure "defeat" was taking place. The political rhetoric of Nasir and others that mobilized and sustained millions had to be thrown out. Other intellectuals like Abdallah al-'Arawi (Laraoui), Tayyib Tizini, Hasan Hanafi, Muhammad Abd al-Jabiri, Hisham Sharabi, and Sadiq al-'Azm confronted the new Arab condition after 1967. Despite Lebanon's own shaky foundations, Beirut was the only city that could safely publish and distribute the great majority of intellectual and cultural angst from the Arab world.

The already noted poets writing from Lebanon like Adonis, Nizar Qabbani, Khalil Hawi, and others revised their material to better represent the changing climate. Fouad Ajami's study of Hawi foregrounds this poet's disillusion with previously held ideologies of Syrian and/or Arab nationalisms. Some of the optimism of his earlier poems was set in sharp contrast to the bitter sense of disappointment and alienation that now filtered into his works. His earlier popular poem put to song, "The Bridge" (published in the 1957 collection *Nahr al-ramad* [River of ashes]), exposed some of the problems confronting Arabs, but it also offered promise for the future. In the ending, he is comforted by the "children of my comrades." Despite the coming of snow, the poet has "stores enough of embers and wine" (trans. Diana Der Hovanessian and Lena Jayyusi in Salma Jayyusi, ed., *Modern Arabic Poetry*, 258). In an insightful critical edition of his 1965 *Bayadir al-ju'* [The threshing floors of hunger], Adnan Haydar and Michael Beard maintain the singular importance of Hawi's prophetic poetry. "Lazarus 1962," for example, "foreshadows an entire decade of Arab writing, in which the disillusionment which followed the 1967 war produced a rich tradition of waste-land writing" (*Naked in Exile* 9). His poetry seemed to grow increasingly bleaker in the 1970s, and he committed suicide in 1982, ostensibly in response to the Israeli invasion of Lebanon. In the short poem "Lebanon," written before he died, the persona is "Choked by the tragedy, It was painful to talk" (trans. Abdullah al-Udhari in *Modern Poetry of the Arab World*, 119).

The playwright Issam Mahfouz would also capture the new spirit of disillusionment in his plays of this era. Whereas the main impulse in serious theater had been the translation and performance of European plays, the 1967 defeat led to a big shift in Arab and Lebanese drama. In 1968, Mahfouz published his *Al-Zanzalakht* [China tree];[11] in 1969 his *Al-Diktator* [The dictator]; and in 1970 his *'Arrib ma yali* [Conjugate the following]. This last play was a collaboration with Adonis, the Lebanese playwright George Shehadeh, the Syrian Saadallah Wannous, and the Palestinian poet Mahmoud Darwish. Also in 1970, Mahfouz wrote his *Carte Blanche*, a play then directed by Roger Assaf. Abu Murad provides a fuller list of some of the plays of the late 1960s and early 1970s that present a critical or oppositional stance in light of the 1967 defeat (167).

The comforting and optimistic Rahbani musicals set in the village and mentioned earlier would gradually change. Their plays of the late 1960s and early 1970s involved more social criticism and occasional overt politics; in addition, the action is often set in the city. Attempting to capture something of the new spirit of conflict in the Arab world, these musicals often dealt with injustice and state oppression, but they remained unspecific as to the source of political ills. Despite paying lip service to the somber concerns of this era, they were only marginally interested in serious sociopolitical reform. The plays always ended happily, usually with a celebratory wedding or reunion.[12]

In contrast, a text that did not attempt to blot over the problems facing Lebanon and the region was Tewfiq Awwad's 1972 *Tawahin Beirut*. (I will be referring to the English version, *Death in Beirut*.) The novel takes place during the political turmoil in the region following 1967 and the student riots in Lebanon of 1968–69. Although set against the backdrop of broad regional politics, it focuses on what transpired in Lebanon (specifically in Beirut) during this period. Awwad, a journalist and then diplomat in the Ministry of Foreign Affairs, had written some short stories and two novels in the 1930s: *Al-Sabi al-a'raj* [The crippled boy, 1936] and *Al-Raghif* [The loaf, 1939]. Both described the desperate conditions under Ottoman rule during World War I and came to be read as Arab nationalist narratives popular across the Arab world. Awwad's literary output came to a halt for some three decades until the publication of *Tawahin Beirut*, perhaps one of the most prophetic of cultural documents produced in Lebanon before the outbreak of war in 1975.

The novel centers around Tamima Nassour, a young Shi'a woman from South Lebanon who comes to Beirut in search of education and experience. It is through her encounters that the reader gains a vivid sense of the varied and disparate ideologies at work in the capital city. Her brother, Jaber, a supposed student revolutionary leader, is actually a reactionary and corrupt thug out to punish his sister through his henchman and fraudulent Palestinian supporter, Hussein Qamoo'i. Her lover, Ramzi Raad, a noted journalist, incites passionate revolution while remaining cold and aloof himself. Akram Jurdi, a supposed "leftist" politician and lawyer, is an immoral opportunist and lecher out to get Tamima. Abu-Sharshur, a Palestinian laborer, becomes her protector. Jamil Mawali, a wealthy African émigré from her village, proposes to her, but she refuses. And finally, Hani Raai, her Maronite boyfriend and a student leader, is a man she loves but also refuses as they go their separate ways at the novel's close.

Tamima is not only personally linked to ideologically varied characters. She also becomes a member of the Federation of Student Unions and is literally at the center of a group of political players whose points of view she, as secretary, needs to record. The students had been making demands regarding new facilities for the Lebanese University, guaranteed health insurance, and the abolition of confession as a criterion for student acceptance. Increasingly, however, these rather specific demands had been broadened to include larger political questions affecting the region. After the 1968 Israeli attack on Beirut International Airport, the student leaders in Awwad's novel, already in opposition to the government, now "rose in anger over the question of their country's honour" (108). More strikes and demonstrations were planned against Lebanon's refusal to retaliate and in support of the Palestinians. Awwad carefully describes the climate of the next meeting of "The League of Free Students" discussing the upcoming strike:

> The strike was an all-out one with committees and communiques, speeches and broadcasts; slogans were appearing on the walls, and seminars and discussions were being held everywhere. Permeating these activities was a mixture of enthusiasm, desire for revenge, bitterness and the recklessness and naivete of youth. These were given added impetus by the diverse currents flowing from four universities with disparate syllabuses, numerous languages, and a variety of sects and nationalities. Within a few days, however, the movement had lost its first purity. It was polluted by all kinds of dregs that brought their mud with them. Every wind that blew brought vapours from places where fanaticism and extremism were manufactured and the dust of the street mob began to rise. The traditional political bosses and those who dealt in influence had infiltrated the ranks of the students. They now urged them on to do what they wanted them to do, in the interests of their own factional aims and objectives and their personal goals. They plunged themselves into the cauldrons of ideological dyes which ranged in hue from extreme left to extreme right. (109–10)

The politicians gave lip service to the students, condemning the Israeli aggression, promising a new conscription law for the Lebanese army, and fully supporting the Fedayeen in their "resistance" efforts. As the students staged sit-ins and hunger strikes, however, only their relatives paid attention to them. Their actions, in fact, were totally isolated from "the workers and all other elements of the population who . . . just read about them in the newspapers" (110–11).

Even as the students discuss why they are striking, serious divisions emerge. One student begins to present important statistics on the four universities (American University of Beirut, Lebanese University, St. Joseph University, and the Arab University), including percentages of Lebanese vs. "foreigners."[13] Some then object to the word *foreigners* because it encompasses non-Lebanese Arabs who are not really foreigners to be equated with Europeans. The student is further prevented from giving his statistics on the confessional distribution because of cries of "Down with confessionalism!" and "We reject statistics of confessionalism!" (112). Although Hani is very interested in this information, most listeners are already bored and calling for revolution. More sloganistic speeches follow. These are interrupted by opposing cries. One group calls out, "Long live Arab unity!" The other screams, "Long live free, independent, and sovereign Lebanon!" (113–14). The two sides are on the verge of open confrontation when suddenly "the chairman rose, ringing his bell loudly, stretching out his arm to its full extent. A brilliant thought, a stroke of genius, had occurred to him: 'Long live the Fedayeen! Long live the Fedayeen!'" With this new call, both sides are temporarily diverted from their differences and amazingly unified: "Both sides gave this their approval and the dispute between them was resolved" (114).

This is a revealing scene, as it boldly interjects the Palestinian issue as a red herring. The Lebanese situation as expressed through student unrest is complicated, divided, and not easily resolvable. The Arab nationalist pull, along with calls for Greater Syria, continues to divert loyalties away from the problematic Lebanese nation. The internal problems are a headache; no one is in agreement over what the problems are, how they should be addressed, or how to proceed. The students, representing myriad factions of Lebanese communists, socialists, idealists, Ba'thists, and other nationalist interests, are assembled within a frustrating Tower of Babel unable to truly communicate or activate. Tamima's job to lucidly record their points of view turns out to be an impossible task. The Palestinian option, however, appears to Tamima with the clarity of a bolt of lightning. The "cause" is powerful, just, and captivating, especially when presented in personal terms. Tamima hears Abu-Sharshur's story, when "The Jews had killed his heart's delight in Jaffa on that day of terror in 1948" (69). In graphic terms, he describes how his daughter, Adla (who reminds him of Tamima), resisted the three members of the Irgun gang who tried to rape her. They then shot her and he, the father, witnessed "Adla lying on the ground and on top of her was the third soldier getting from her in death what the three of them hadn't been able to get when she was alive" (69). It is no wonder that the father is devastated and that his son will join the Fedayeen. It is also no wonder that Tamima is captivated. The many ideological options before her lack the clarity of the Palestinian cause.

Tamima's identification with that cause, however, comes with a heavy price. She needs to reinvent herself, be silent, in order to take on a new identity. As she witnesses the Israeli assaults on Mahdiyya, her village in South Lebanon, she takes it personally and feels a new kinship and love for Mahdiyya (120). They are both victims, "silent and submissive."[14] At the end of the novel, she will transfer this victimization mentality toward action and become a resistance fighter for the Palestinian cause. The book, however, concludes with her ominous words: "I shall never speak from this day on. From the moment I set off with the man no more will be heard of the name of Tamima Nassour" (185).

Her Lebanese identity is hence erased in order for her to embrace the Palestinian cause. Awwad, in narrating Tamima's final choice, is not necessarily advocating it. He is careful to delineate the intertwined fates of the Palestinians and the Lebanese and in the process to foreground the difficult choices of Lebanese. For one, Palestinian resistance from within Lebanon resulted in heavy casualties for Lebanese at the hands of Israeli retaliatory forces. Government weakness in the face of Israel led to student unrest, to open public division, and to a regional decision to implement the Cairo Agreement. The Lebanese students' call for revolution had already been confused by Palestinian aspirations to defeat Israel. While the students had legitimate complaints against the state (condemnation of the confessional system, lack of social services for the poor, unacceptable working conditions for laborers, inept town planning, etc.), the main character, Hani, is also specifically against a "bloody revolution for Lebanon" (135). That is not the solution. Awwad includes actual excerpts from leading intellectuals and journalists on some of the problems facing Lebanon (137–39). Yusuf Khal of *Shiʿr* takes a rather conciliatory position as he states that the "fault is not in the system, but in the exercise and implementation of it" (qtd. in Awwad 138). Unsi Haj, also a regular contributor to *Shiʿr*, agrees on the need for an uprising, but he questions the inevitability of killing one another "in order to be true revolutionaries." He continues, "Is it the case that the dream of a new Lebanon will never materialize except through the nightmare of slaying?" (qtd. in Awwad 139). It is soon after that we hear Hani telling the group the story of his village and why gunpowder was forbidden in the quarry (quoted at the beginning of this chapter in an epigram). The sulphur in its soil made it too volatile. Hani concludes, "The quarry of Lebanon is like that, my friends. Beware of gunpowder!" (140).

When Tamima's Palestinian friend and protector's son is killed in the South, his funeral in Beirut promises to be exactly the kind of volatile event that could trigger widespread violence. Hani and his friends are worried, and they discourage linking the student uprisings with Palestinian revenge. Tamima is horrified at what she considers their insensitivity to the Palestinian plight. But hers is not the only voice here, and Awwad is not necessarily agreeing with her outrage. In the following pages he presents a debate on the facts of Israeli aggression, a weak national defense, and refugees from the South. The most important news, however, is that some of the Fedayeen are now "clashing with the Lebanese Army and the local civilians. The Army and the civilians complain of the Fedayeen departing from the terms of the agreement. Some are taking up positions in the villages instead of keeping to the positions assigned to them in remote places. Some of them are committing criminal acts" (176). The Palestinian cause might not be so "pure" anymore as we hear: "Originally the Palestinian movement arose —as it was bound to—to demand a right that is the most sacred of rights. But when it breaks the law in the course of its activities, and departs from accepted international principles, for example by hijacking aircraft, does that not constitute a stab at the very heart of its morality, at its right to demand that right?" (177). Awwad thus complicates the Palestinian cause in Lebanon by offering a perspective of its corruption.

In continuing to identify herself with the plight of Palestine, Tamima herself uses the image of a sham virgin to describe her corrupted state (177). She is quick to explain and defend, however: "But—once treachery and collusion had robbed them of their homeland and squandered their rights and their dignity, contrary to all laws, and once international laws, processes and rituals failed to give them back anything of what they had lost— how do you expect them to respect the law and give due weight to political morality and its accepted principles?" (178). This justification for Palestinian action is understandable, but according to Hani, this action is also not acceptable in Lebanon (178). True revolution is "very far from the clichés and empty slogans mouthed by students." True revolution is "the revolt against the self" (127). Indeed, Hani is a thinker and arguably the novel's protagonist, yet the English version labels him in the introduction as a "right-wing idealist," implying that he adhered to the narrow ideologies of the Kata'ib and other Maronite groups. While Hani's call for internal revolution is a potentially new and liberating ideology, Awwad does not expand upon it in this text. In fact, not until the novels of the war and postwar period will we witness truly interior and psychological narratives.

Certainly an important feature of Awwad's novel is that the various ideologies presented are often themselves undermined, so that they are rarely offered as good or proper solutions for the Lebanese "quagmire." Instead, they serve to complicate the narrative by fully contextualizing it and thereby offering a hard look at a nation on the verge of crisis. To read *Tawahin Beirut* is to better comprehend what were the forces brewing in Lebanon in the few years prior to the outbreak of war in 1975. Yet the novel is in no way propagandistic. It does not promote one ideology over another, nor does it offer a "good solution." It presents a plot that meanders through a rocky terrain that is recognizable as Lebanon. Unlike so much of the literature that came out of Lebanon, that terrain is neither rural nor beautiful nor simple. It is urban, violent, and fragmented, and it is fraught with political, social, and sexual tensions. Reading it in retrospect, one is struck by how so much of what Awwad included in the novel would help explain why the nation-state collapsed in the 1970s.

It is a rare example, in fact, of a cultural artifact that contains within it the many oppositional voices of its society. It has been read in many ways because it is a nonhegemonic text. There are sufficient valid interpretations because oppositional voices are not stifled. They are allowed to exist on the page either through a character's point of view or by reference to an actual editorial excerpted in the local newspaper, *Nahar*. It is almost impossible to reduce Lebanon to any of the single ideologies operational during this era. If one is inclined to favor the Palestinian perspective, Awwad is sure to include examples of their corruption and fanaticism. A Communist point of view is undermined by a chilling lack of concern for human emotion. The Lebanese Christian mentality is too self-centered. The traditional Islamic perspective is reactionary. The political players are all opportunistic. The Arab nationalist and supporters of the SSNP are sloganistic and irrelevant. The feminist perspective is hardly existent, a fact which describes, unfortunately, the Lebanon of the late 1960s.[15]

This next segment elaborates on the above notion of a hardly existent Lebanese feminist perspective. Awwad's text is illuminating on this issue, for although feminism in itself is hardly foregrounded, some important contingent aspects of it are. This suggests perhaps a movement toward a conscious feminism, a necessary component in any true social and political transformation.

Tamima, initially caught between a web of competing ideologies and men, is especially vulnerable. She is a strong woman of principle who is not afraid of making choices and determining her own destiny, especially in the face of a broad range of disappointing male characters. On the other hand, she is presented in highly sexist terms. The following quotation is a typical example of how Awwad chooses to describe her: "The whole of youth asserted itself boldly through that fresh and tender-skinned body, forced into the thin grey dress Tamima had chosen for the day. But there was more than beauty in her. There was invitation in those wide, honey-coloured eyes 'to wander in realms which have a beginning, but no end,' as the poet said" (6). It is no wonder that Tamima is pursued. She is coveted, used, abused, and punished. Her final choice to join the Palestinians becomes, therefore, her salvation. Only with a total refashioning of herself can she survive. Evelyne Accad, in a discussion of this novel, faults Awwad for giving Tamima a "fate connected with male violence. . . . Why not have her choose a life/peace alternative instead?" (109). Accad concludes that because Awwad is a liberal and not a feminist, "the solution he imagines is one of *equality* for Tamima (she gets to act like a man), not radical change, transformation" (110). While Awwad certainly could have been more attentive to gender issues, his novel, nevertheless, is outspoken in its presentation of women's rights and in its depiction of male hypocrisies. Tamima's final decision to join the Fedayeen is a radical one. Her choosing to become a revolutionary is not necessarily an antifeminist choice. On the contrary, it is a provocative choice that extends the possibilities for Arab women.

Awwad further bolsters a quasi-feminist agenda by introducing two other female characters who serve as important foils to Tamima. Her friend and role model, Mary, is a single professional woman who offers steady advice. She will save her friend's life by sacrificing her own as she takes the bullet directed at Tamima by her brother. Her tragic death becomes the culmination of a series of tragedies that will result in Tamima's decision to join the Fedayeen. The good-woman-as-victim motif proves a catalyst for action (and potentially for genuine social transformation).

The maid Zennoub also befriends Tamima, whom she admires and wants to emulate. This young girl, treated like chattel by her own father and the other men she confronts, is raped and impregnated by Tamima's brother,

Jaber. When she is unable to find any honorable way out of her dilemma, she commits suicide. Awwad's inclusion of her tragedy is especially relevant because it reveals the consequences of severe class divisions within Lebanon. As a poor woman from Akkar, one of Lebanon's most neglected regions, she is treated as worthless by everyone except Tamima. Her struggles, her tragedies, her death are inconsequential. Only Tamima feels guilt at her neglect and sorrow for her end. Awwad consciously juxtaposes Zennoub's fate against that of the more privileged Tamima in order to highlight the total lack of options for the very poor.

The fact that Tamima is a Muslim will also allow Awwad to broach the sensitive confessional issue that, in many respects, is the central conflict in this novel. Her relationship to the Maronite Hani and his proposal of marriage will place in relief a taboo in Lebanese society, while complicating the gender concerns of the novel. Hani gives a brief history lesson to Tamima: "We've had the period of conflict between Christians and Moslems that carried on even under the shadow of the French mandate. After that we had the spell of peaceful coexistence, the tightrope walk that followed independence. Now the time's come for the two communities to merge. Blood ties—that's the question for Lebanon" (77). His insistence on their engagement seems to be a political statement, a defiance of a Lebanon still bound to confessionalism. He is threatened by Tamima's brother, who sends ominous notes demanding that the two break off their relationship. Jaber will act on his threats, drawing the blood that Hani had referred to above. This uncompromising religious perspective is presented as a destructive element in Lebanese society, while sadly still a vital component and determinant of one's fate. Indeed, Tamima's decision to join the secular Fedayeen is one way to escape that confining aspect of her Lebanese identity.

Awwad certainly makes the case for the limited options for women while at the same time linking the plight of women to class and confessional issues. His attention to the myriad ideologies of his time explains his inclusion, for example, of a 1968 speech by the popular Syrian poet Nizar Qabbani at the American University of Beirut. Known affectionately as the "young ladies' poet," Qabbani had established a reputation as the poet of political and sexual freedoms. He moved to Lebanon in 1966, started his own publishing company, and helped generate a new kind of rebellious poetry after the 1967 Arab defeat. Along with his condemnation of Arab political conservatism, he constantly advocated for human and women's rights. In his electrifying speech at AUB, primarily to women, Qabbani incites his audience to action:

> Rise, woman! I want you to rise in revolt. Rise against this Orient of slave-prisoners, of resting places for pilgrims, of incense. Rise against history and emerge victorious over the great illusion. Be in awe of no one! . . . We want to give woman back her body. Up to now it has been the possession of history, of laws and codes, of the institutions and establishments of this world and the next. . . . The puritans and prudes will say I am inciting women to love. I am inciting you to the most beautiful thing that is within you, and the most noble. I am inciting you to rise to the level of humanity. (80–81)

Like most of the Arab world, Lebanon's record on women's rights was abominable. In the 1950s Lebanese attorney Laure Nasr Moghaizel had inaugurated a series of movements for improving the situation for women in Lebanon and the Arab world by implementing an organization for the rights of the political woman, the association for the rights of women in inheritance law, the association for amending the penal code, and the Lebanese Federation for Women (see the Moghaizel Foundation Home Page). While a small but growing struggle for women's rights improved the situation for some Lebanese women, significant political awareness and promotion of women's issues was hardly discernible for most women, as social and cultural forces seemed to actively dissuade progress in true gender equality.

Although a few women writers broke through the dominant male literary discourse, they hardly constituted an ideology that would be effective in transforming the nation. Their voices, however, are an important early register of national consciousness. Lebanese authors like Layla Baalbaki and Emily Nasrallah offer insights into the changing national entity as they both provide perspectives that necessarily stretch the conceptual boundaries of Lebanon. In her 1958 *Ana ahya* (discussed in chapter 2), Baalbaki adopts a first-person female narrative (supposedly one of the first in Arabic women's fiction).[16] The novel is striking not only in its social defiance but in its persistent use of Lina's singular voice as the window through which her world is perceived. Her 1964 collection of short stories, *Safinat hanan ila al-qamar* [Spaceship of tenderness to the moon] led to charges of sexual obscenity, and Baalbaki was investigated and put on trial by the chief of the Beirut vice squad. She was accused of "harming the public morality" because two sentences in the title story were deemed too sexually graphic (see Fernea, "Account of Her Trial," 280). The fact that she was a woman openly describing sex, without censure, was objectionable. Although she was cleared of all charges, the case remains a landmark in Lebanese state intervention.

Not surprisingly, Baalbaki's bold discourse earned her both support and condemnation. While some writers and intellectuals (including those linked to *Shi'r*) rallied to her cause during the trial, others, including some women, negatively reviewed her books, labeling them a "damned literature" (qtd. in Zeidan 103). Some believed that she was targeted by the Lebanese state because of her affiliations with the Syrian Social Nationalist Party (Accad, 1985, 33). But others faulted her for her gender, her Muslim religion, and/ or her Arab identity. A Muslim Arab woman should not write such material. Her Shi'a Lebanese identity, however, figures marginally in her texts except as a springboard to her general rebelliousness. Her main contribution, of course, is as a powerful new voice that would help launch a broader ideological movement.

A less known female voice is that of Mona Jabbur, who in 1962 published *Fatat tafiha* [A worthless girl]. The heroine, Nada, comparable in many ways to Baalbaki's Lina Fayad, attempts to assert her individuality and independence in her patriarchal society. Bouthaina Shaaban notes that the author was especially ahead of her time in exposing how the Arabic language favors the male gender. Nada wants to alter the language in her desire for women's equality (Shaaban 130).

The early works of Emily Nasrallah, especially her 1962 *Tuyur aylul* [September birds], were immediately embraced by the public and continue to be reprinted and taught within Lebanon.[17] Also adopting a first-person female narrator who rebels against social traditions, this novel achieves much of its resonance not by foregrounding gender issues (although they are present) but by highlighting the stark differences between the Lebanese traditional village and the increasingly dominant capital, Beirut. The book is disappointing, in fact, in terms of its feminist ideology as its female characters are, as Zeidan puts it, "mere puppets in the hands of fate." Zeidan continues: "Nasrallah uses fatalism as a device to avoid having to deal with the motivations of her characters. In doing this she is, in a sense, reflecting the very 'village mentality' she is attacking" (124). The novel revolves around failed romances, arranged marriages, and protests that result in eventual submission to traditional ways. The central character, Muna, like Lina of *Ana ahya*, rebels against her village and moves to

Beirut where she becomes isolated and therefore longs for the very village she left behind. Her memories and flashbacks, which result in the story told, are tinged with nostalgia and a romantic tone that undermine her critique of village life. When she returns to the village, she realizes she no longer belongs there, and Nasrallah effectively captures the heroine torn between two worlds.

Nasrallah, who has partially built her reputation around depicting village life, succeeds in driving a wedge between that village and those other possibilities now readily available to Lebanese villagers, i.e., either Beirut or emigration. Her texts very much reveal a growing reality within Lebanon of that division and of the growing prominence of Beirut within the nation. If village life was conservative, quaint, and family-oriented, Beirut was depicted as progressive, cosmopolitan, and suited to the pursuits of the individual. Beirut became the alternative—the place for education, for employment, for adventure. Like the emigration alternative, for over a century a real option especially for Christian Lebanese and Syrians, Beirut in the 1960s could offer what immigration, the Mahjar, once did and more. Unlike emigration, which necessitated a painful severing of place, a move to Beirut could be easily negotiated while maintaining that original place. To a great number of Lebanese, especially among the Christian, the Druze, and the Shi'a, the village represented both the place to escape from and the place to return to and, as such, took on symbolic value.

This narrative of division, which clearly offers two contrasting ideas of Lebanon, becomes entrenched in an evolving Lebanese identity. Significantly, this binaric idea of Lebanon (urban/rural) suggests that the idea of Lebanon is more deeply entrenched in the Lebanese psyche, since it allows for far-reaching movement within its borders without threatening the national entity itself. The village/Beirut binary also tends to reduce those places into fixed modes. The village becomes that which is not Beirut; despite its "backwardness," it is the locale of family and "old-fashioned" values. Beirut, on the other hand, becomes the exciting, beautiful, but ultimately corrupt city. Eventually its mythological identity will come to stand for, and even replace, Lebanon.

Beirut '75, completed just a few months before the outbreak of war in April 1975, further serves this narrative shift to urban Beirut. Authored by the Syrian Ghada Samman, who had taken up residence in Lebanon since the 1960s, this activist and pro-feminist text reveals yet another important dimension of the soon-to-collapse Lebanese nation. Again, although Samman is attentive to women's issues, there are other ideologies relating to nation that are of concern here. Since 1967, Samman had promoted Arab nationalist ideas and fought Zionism and imperialism in her many fictional and nonfictional works.[18] In *Beirut '75*, she focuses on Lebanon and specifically on Beirut as an alternative site not for Lebanese villagers (like in Nasrallah's texts) but for young Syrians escaping the drudgery of Damascus. Like Tewfiq Awwad's *Death in Beirut*, this well-crafted and insightful book partially anticipates the collapse of Lebanon and introduces a perspective that might justify that collapse.

To Farah and Yasmeena, two Syrian passengers in a taxi bound for Lebanon, Beirut is their dream. It is where they hope to be transformed, liberated, made rich. Yasmeena thinks, "Beirut is waiting for me with all her glitter, with all the possibilities of freedom, love, and fame" (7). As they reach the mountain range looking down on the capital, the city is described: "In the abyss of darkness, Beirut glowed and twinkled like the jewels of a sorceress who had gone down to bathe in the sea by night, leaving behind on the shore her precious pearls, multihued, enchanted objects, and chests inlaid with ivory and sandalwood and filled with both disaster and good fortune, magic spells and secrets" (8). Farah is worried, though, and senses that his entry into Beirut will be an entry into hell. Much of the subject of Samman's novel is an illustration why.

Despite its beauty and attractiveness, its wealth and opportunities, Beirut is ominous and dangerous. Its citizens are morally depraved, corrupt, and lecherous. During Israeli raids, they are uncaring. The very rich are the worst offenders, controlling the destinies of the vulnerable (including both Farah and Yasmeena). The fishermen are dominated by monopoly holders, the poor have no opportunites, women are forced to become maids or prostitutes, and men are subjected to tribal "blood vengeance." It is a hellish place described as "poisonous," "rapacious," "calamitous," "cruel." In fact, for those who enter its Dantesque gates, only violence awaits them.

While the text becomes increasingly surreal with a series of gory nightmares anticipating Samman's 1976 text of the early war years, *Kawabis Beirut* [Beirut nightmares], it touches upon real gender, class, and political issues that would help describe Lebanon's demise in 1975. Indeed, class divisions would prove volatile, a tribal mentality would fuel vengeance, the selfish rich would disregard warning signals of the ailing nation, etc. Beirut was also glittery; people had fun in it and were attracted to it. A city, however, is a complex place, and Beirut was never simply the repository of evils that it is portrayed as here.

To Yasmeena and Farah, virtual strangers to each other but bonded because as young Syrians they sought Beirut out and were both destroyed in it, Beirut now seems lovely only from a distance (90). They are linked in "silent misery" as they reflect upon their respective falls within the treacherous city. Beirut is sick, insane, and renamed in the novel's final paragraph and nightmare as the "Hospital for the Mentally Ill" (115). Here Yasmeena is beheaded and Farah is made crazy. All the women, all the restaurants, all the newspapers that Beirut has to offer can no longer satisfy Farah. The city is mad and dangerous like "an infernal wild beast preparing to pounce" (115). One is safe only if one escapes.

This is the Beirut which now symbolizes the Lebanon that would soon seemingly disintegrate. It is a Beirut that too easily fit the image of the glittery whore, the vindictive temptress, the poisonous treat. Beirut, which had been a point of difference within Lebanon, would become synonymous with Lebanon. Its metonymic value needs unpacking, but it is used here (as increasingly elsewhere) as easily transferable with the larger nation-state. When Lebanon collapsed in war, it is noteworthy how many elegies were written to the beautiful and fallen "Beirut" of Samman's text. It is also interesting to note the national identities of those who wrote. (The next chapters will provide examples of the Syrian and Palestinian authors who lamented Beirut's demise.) In Samman's text there is no place for the rather obvious irony of victimized Syrians within Lebanon. At the beginning of the twenty-first century, while Lebanon is under clear Syrian hegemony, it is interesting to read about the innocence of Syrians trapped in the ugly quagmire of Lebanon.[19] Whereas Awwad's text clearly allows for inclusion of the thorny Palestinian question, Samman's text leaves virtually no room for the equally thorny Syrian question. In addition, with a sustained depiction of an evil Beirut, *Beirut '75* seems to validate its warranted destruction. This too, unfortunately, was a motivating ideology in the 1970s.

This chapter concludes with an examination of theatrical narratives that shed more light on prewar Lebanon. Ziad Rahbani, the son of Fayruz and 'Asi Rahbani, would prove to be a powerful cultural force in Lebanon, and he presents an interesting contrast to the generation of his parents. Although arguably flawed, his first play, the 1974 *Nazl al-surur* [Inn of happiness], tapped into a popular mood in the country, especially in West Beirut among students, the Left, and the working class. The play is set in a modest hotel, housing a group of funny but pathetic characters who seem resigned to their fate. One of them, Raouf, pontificates in slogans about the need for revolution: "You are the downtrodden proletariat. . . . Rise against the imperialists." But he is always dismissed by more "sensible" characters. After all, things are mashi al-hal [good enough], an expression that becomes a refrain in one of the most popular songs of the play (and the decade). One learns that "out there" are demonstrations and strikes, but the antics of the hotel guests provide comic relief until two thugs, Abbas and Fahd, storm the hotel and take all the customers hostage: "Either we kill you all and bomb the building, or you agree to a revolution. Do you understand?" they blare.

The "revolution" had already been caricatured in the figure of Raouf and is further undermined here as it is taken up by these bullies. Then Rahbani shifts away from the burlesque, allowing the supposed thugs to narrate their serious stories. Abbas's sisters sell Chiclets on the street; no hospital will treat his very sick, impoverished father. Abbas declares, "Someone needs to start the revolution. Why not me?" (34). Fahd then supports this perspective with his own: His younger brother was run over by a rich man, accountable to no one. Both Abbas and Fahd have been fired from their jobs because they encouraged workers to strike. The situation, in other words, is not mashi al-hal. Something needs to change.

This shift into the serious, even melodramatic, mode is once again undercut as it becomes clear that these guys are not fit to ignite or lead any revolution. Abbas decides to "postpone, not cancel" the revolution so that he can marry the rich Sawsan and secure, at least, his own economic future. Not surprisingly, the robotic Raouf delivers the rhetorical speech advocating marriage as the necessary step in the now-planned revolution. Zakaria, the lethargic ne'er-do-well played by Ziad himself, suddenly comes to life at the end of the play: "What's wrong with you guys? You promised, and now you're reneging on the revolution. . . . Give me one machine gun for my child, so that at least we can have one revolution." As he laments, the stage darkens and an explosion is heard from afar.

The theater audience in 1974 responded enthusiastically to all the pro-revolutionary cues of this play. Even though, at times, Rahbani pokes fun at the rhetoric or methodology of the uprising, he does not seem to question the categorical need for a revolution of the have-nots against the privileged and corrupt sociopolitical class. The fact that the thugs were not willing to go through with the revolution serves to drive home the point that Lebanon's political leaders look out only for their own interests in the end. The rhetoric of revolution that had been broadcast across the Arab world for decades is here exposed for the sham that it really is. The truth is that most people are poor and unable to depend on the political system for relief. The rich can often bulldoze their way through the country untouched by any law, while most Lebanese meekly survive under unacceptable conditions. For Ziad Rahbani, revolution was ripe. For the thousands who attended his plays, listened to them on cassettes, and memorized entire dialogues and songs, his message rang true. But it rang true not primarily because of its content; it rang true because of its style.

What is most revolutionary, in fact, about Rahbani's message is not the theme of political upheaval (many had already voiced that ideology) but the very mode of delivery. The entire play transpires in a refreshingly familiar Lebanese colloquialism that becomes the most engaging and memorable subject of the performance. Dialogue often centers on puns and witticisms, twistings of the dialect to create alternate (and bizarre) meanings. The constant contortions of the language, in fact, indicate Rahbani's extreme confidence in it. So though he might be advocating change in Lebanon's sociopolitical system, in no way does he undermine one of the most essential criteria of the nation, language itself. On the contrary, Rahbani's insistence on utilizing, to the fullest, his own national dialect, toying and playing with it the way he does, reinforces his belief in it. For the Lebanese, Ziad (as he is familiarly referred to) spoke their language.

In one sequence, the musicians Barakat and Kaisar talk sarcastically about "our tradition" (turathna) and proceed to list some hackneyed phrases describing nature—"al-tayr al-shadi" [the warbling bird], "kitf al-wadi" [the shouldered valley], "shalh al-zanbaq" [the disrobed lily]—leading them to an outburst of "hayhat ya abu Zuluf," the traditional refrain for the folkloric symbol/reciter of Lebanese song. They then humorously recall the countless songs that feature romantic rendezvous at the village spring. The spring, they joke, must be positively mobbed by now. In this way, the folklore and the myth so popularized by Ziad's own family is tinkered with and, in some ways, dismissed.

With their 1974 musical *Lulu*, the Rahbani brothers attempted to introduce a spirit of conflict after the events of 1967. More significantly, they experimented with the heroine that Fayruz played. Here, the plot takes on an unusual, for the Rahbanis, sinister tone as the heroine is accused of murder. Although she is found innocent in the end, much of the play revolves around her accusation and the implications of this malevolent world. Abu Murad notes that the Lebanese public was not at all prepared for a categorically different Fayruz. For over a decade, she had been the main Rahbani hero, an innocent village girl, embodying love and virtue. There is reason to believe that the public wasn't willing to alter its perception of Fayruz or the Lebanon she had come to represent. It was dangerous indeed to play with the myth of Fayruz. Not surprisingly, *Lulu* did not enjoy the kind of success the Rahbanis had been accustomed to (Abu Murad 185).

Perhaps in a last-ditch effort to regain their audience, the Rahbanis returned to the village in *Mays al-rim* (1975), after a hiatus of some ten years. Here, the heroine is still an urbanite, but she finds herself unexpectedly in a village after her car breaks down. This allows the action to be, once again, set in a village milieu, where the heroine becomes engulfed in all the village ways and conflicts which she, of course, eventually resolves through her usual prescription of love and marriage. The village is similar to the Rahbani depictions in the early plays, but Fayruz is a city gal and not the character the public had come to expect. This play, produced as Lebanon was just about to embark on war, could easily be read (in retrospect) as a stale and desperate effort to capture something of the Lebanon that was so rapidly changing. Perhaps not coincidentally, this would also be the last musical to feature Fayruz in collaboration with the Rahbanis—a rift was on the way.

Much of the impetus of these two paired chapters (2 and 3) has been to illustrate that, despite the growing influence of the Lebanese state after independence, and despite the continuation and emergence of various Lebanese national symbols, there were many pulls toward regional ideologies, toward new perceptions of urban and rural landscapes, and toward gender differences that complicated the mission of the Lebanese nation. The fact that Fayruz was one of the most visible Lebanese symbols suggests that, like all symbols, it was both too simple and too intricate. As women remained on the periphery of the sociopolitical sphere, a woman could be the most potent cultural presence. Yet as a persona, Fayruz was a desexed goddess, an undeniably virtuous prophet. That image was tinkered with as the image of Lebanon itself was changing. As Lebanon increasingly became associated, in the cultural imagination, with Beirut, and as Beirut increasingly harbored the conflicting regional ideologies, it was only a matter of time before someone (like Fayruz's own son Ziad) would come along to question the myth of simple, innocent Lebanon. Ziad Rahbani's inclusion here also suggests that those many pulls were not strong enough to totally obliterate a sense of a Lebanese shared culture. Indeed, the son who seemingly critiqued his family's version of Lebanon also promoted their most important contribution, an acknowledgment of a Lebanese culture.[20]

The selection and analysis of narratives in these first three chapters hence provide a broad archive of Lebanese cultural material. They run the gamut from being popular artifacts to being occasionally esoteric documents. When read against the "thick description" of the contextual process, every text offers a discourse that both furthers our understanding of the complex notion of Lebanese culture and offers a descriptive model of the evolving nation.

Part II

Unraveling Lebanon

Contrary to the isolationists' allegations, the civil war would have broken out even without the presence of the Palestinians. Lebanon needed no such pretext to become the scene of bloody confrontation in 1958. The Palestinian resistance was only one cause of the latest conflict. If the Lebanese had not been ready for an explosion, there would have been no explosion.

Kamal Joumblatt, *I Speak for Lebanon*, 64

The very forces that *enable* the Lebanese at the micro and communal level and from which they derive much of their social and psychic supports, *disable* them at the macro and national level by eroding their civic consciousness and symbols of national identity.

Samir Khalaf, *Lebanon's Predicament*, ix

4

Disintegration

The war was like a weevil that had found its way into the heart of a huge bag
of white flour and settled there. And I, likewise, was destined not to stay in the
village. I would return to Beirut at the first opportunity, to be overtaken by that
same weevil, back in the midst of the fighting.

Hanan al-Shaykh, *The Story of Zahra*, 1980, 119

The deadly outbursts in 1975 that would lead to a sixteen-year war obviously had their origins in the previous formative decades of Lebanon's existence. Regional nationalist aspirations, class struggles, and a weak Lebanese state would help foster an atmosphere of division and heightened
tension and suspicion. The different accounts of "how the war began" seem
only to confirm that war was inevitable.

One narrative of the beginning of the war describes the Christian Phalange April 13 shooting of a busload of Palestinians. With minor provoca-
tion, the massacre took place because the Palestinians were in unwelcome
Maronite 'Ayn al-Rummaneh. Here a new church was being consecrated,
and the armed Phalange (military wing of the Kata'ib) was standing by.
The unfortunate bus was stopped, and twenty-seven men were killed. By
the time the Palestinians retaliated, groups had already aligned themselves
to one faction or another. Muslims and "leftists," forming the National
Movement headed by Kamal Joumblatt, sided with the Palestinians who
were perceived as being attacked by "rightist" Christian militias.

An almost opposite narrative faults the Palestinians for interfering in
Lebanese internal matters. They were accommodated as refugees in camps
across the nation since Israel's establishment in 1948, but they had begun
to form a "state within the state," destabilizing Lebanon's delicate political
and confessional balance. By this account a Kata'ib supporter was shot in
'Ayn al-Rummaneh by four Palestinians on April 13; a few hours later the

above-mentioned bus, filled with armed PLO fighters, drove through bar-ricades in the area opening fire on the crowds gathered for the dedication of the new church. According to the Phalange, they had no choice but to defend their people, and the killings took place.

A third narrative highlights the class and confessional dimensions of the war. Earlier in the year, poor fishermen in Sidon demonstrated against a new fishing consortium run by a wealthy few. This dispute immediately took on a confessional nature, as the fishermen were primarily Muslim and the owners primarily Christian. The Lebanese army (under predomi-nantly Christian command) fired at the demonstration killing the popular Muslim and leftist leader in Sidon, Ma'ruf Sa'd. The violence that ensued mobilized groups that aligned themselves in broad ideological coalitions. The "left" was supposedly out to defend the poor (perceived as predomi-nantly Muslim) against the wealthy powers of the "right" (perceived as pre-dominantly Christian).

In his *Conflict and Violence in Lebanon: Confrontation in the Middle East*, Walid Khalidi focuses on the first two years of the war and carefully explains the roles of the internal and external players. "The Sarajevo of the Lebanese Civil War" was on April 13, 1975, in 'Ayn al-Rummaneh. Un-known assailants fired at a Sunday church gathering attended by Pierre Gemayel, killing his bodyguard and two others. In retaliation, the Pha-lange ambushed and massacred twenty-eight (mostly Palestinian) men aboard a bus that drove by the area (47). This impassioned confrontation between the Palestinians and the Phalange, however, was only one factor in a complicated scenario that, as Khalidi discusses, involved the Arab-Israeli conflict and inter-Arab tension.

However one chooses to narrate the beginning of the war, there is little disagreement that once begun, there were many reasons for the war to continue. There is also no doubt that 1975 was a categorically different year for all Lebanese. Whereas the previous chapters were also divided according to dates, none of them was as definitive in shaping the culture and nation as 1975. As pointed out earlier, the nation had already been pronounced as Greater Lebanon with the current boundaries in 1920; its constitution already drafted in 1926; and independence in 1943 did not drastically alter the reality on the ground. In fact, the choice of 1943 as a dividing point is as much arbitrarily convenient as it is valid. But 1975 meant that whether one was involved in the fighting or not, existence was differ-ent. Shelling, kidnapping, and sniping had become new realities every Lebanese confronted. In addition, schools and businesses would periodically close, electricity and water would be interrupted, bread would become scarce, and travel at times would be impossible. Lebanon had changed profoundly.

It is not surprising that most attempts to deal with this period focus only on the war. The war, after all, drastically altered existence. Consider the number of articles and books written by foreign journalists, former hostages, political scientists, historians—Lebanese, Arab, and Western—on this war. This was a war that would capture the imagination, that tempted photographers and poets, that baffled and fascinated. There are countless reports on the once beautiful Beirut, the "Paris of the Middle East," now the most dangerous and sinister place on earth. It became the site of film noir, literally, as urban guerrillas stalked the nights across films, like the German *Circle of Fear*. For years the world press covered Lebanon, the victim of skyscraper combat and sniping, relentless shelling of civilian neighborhoods, frequent car bombs, senseless kidnappings. Occasionally a report would focus on the resilience of the Lebanese who, like ants, would scurry out of their homes during brief cease-fires and proceed to rebuild, shop, and even have fun.

While the foreign media looked on in amazement, the Lebanese listened to the inimitable Sharif al-Akhawi, whose daily radio reports explained which roads were "amina wa salika" [safe and passable] and which were treacherous due to sniping or shelling. Nothing else was more relevant. Most information delivered over the radio airways was narrow propaganda from one group or another, including the position of the increasingly dysfunctional Lebanese government. The Lebanese printed press was more centrist, but also tended toward the simplistically ideological. Sharif al-Akhawi did not analyze, philosophize, or pontificate. He, like most, was a noncombatant trapped in war. His pleas for calm and his call for demonstrations against the fighting resulted, for example, in a very large peace march in November 1975, when citizens from both sides rallied to meet as church bells and the call from the mosque resounded. In the end, all these efforts were for naught and Akhawi remained the most haunting voice of the early years of the war.[1]

Although Lebanon was consumed by war, the war did not fully define it. Too many assumed that the war was a monolithic template by which one could read Lebanon. There is no doubt that the war effected major and minor changes, but life in all its complexity and triviality continues during war. To proceed with this study of Lebanon is to acknowledge, first off, that despite the division of these chapters into the war years, this period was determined by multiple factors that would shape the nation and its culture. The shifting economic trends of the region,[2] diffusion of Western media, the increased foreign travel and urbanization, and the advances made by women are some of the factors, irrespective of war, that affected Lebanon of the 1970s and 1980s.

This chapter will examine some of the literary narratives produced during or about the early phases of the war. Although there are many ways to divide and study Lebanon's early war years, this chapter uses a historical and chronological structure and focuses on two subperiods: the first years of the war and the interlude leading up to the Israeli invasion of 1982. As in previous chapters, this political framework serves as a backdrop to the study of national culture through the window of literary artifacts. Unlike the previous three chapters, the narratives here are offered not merely as descriptive but as prescriptive models for the nation. In other words, many of the narratives discussed in the remainder of the book offer new ways of perceiving Lebanon and can hence be useful in constructing Lebanon now.

The first period begins in 1975 toward the end of Suleiman Frangiye's presidency (1970–76). Theodor Hanf describes the growing strength of the Palestinian presence within Lebanon and the fateful alliance between the Palestinians and the sociopolitical movement headed by the Druze leader Kamal Joumblatt. Joumblatt was able to "articulate the disappointment and embitterment with post-Chehabist economic and social policies" (127), and he advocated a nonconfessional Lebanon while rejecting the National Pact upon which the country was based. The Palestinians provided the military training and support for the various leftist groups under Joumblatt, and the Lebanese Kata'ib continued to bolster their military wing as well. When the fuse was lit in 1975, Lebanon was poised for conflagration.

This period covers the initial heavy fighting of 1975–76, including the Battle of the Hotels, Karantina, Damour, Tal al-Za'tar, and the Battle of the Mountains. The government (under Frangiye) and Christian forces feared the fall of the Maronite heartland and asked for Syrian intervention. Elias Sarkis was elected president in 1976, and Syrian/Palestinian fighting escalated, leading to the Riad Summit and the deployment of a 30,000 strong Arab Deterrent Force (overwhelmingly made up of Syrian soldiers).

The early war years generated some fictions that promoted the ideologies discussed in previous chapters. Suheil Idriss's short story "Al-Tal wa al-nawrass" [The hill and the seagull], for example, chronicles the fate of those Palestinians and Lebanese who suffered the defeat of Tal al-Za'tar (the Palestinian refugee camp on the eastern outskirts of Beirut that was besieged and bombarded by rightist forces in 1976). Travelers fleeing the war are on a ship bound for Egypt. In the background the radio reports on the fighting in the Tal. The wounded fighter Sa'id is unhappily among this group, lamenting his fate of not becoming a martyr in the Tal battles. He quickly emerges as a larger-than-life figure who protects the downtrodden on the miserable ship. At the story's close, and after Tal al-Za'tar camp has fallen, Sa'id miraculously disappears. The final explanation is offered by the young boy whom Sa'id had rescued earlier. His hero has gone, saved by a flock of seagulls who placed him on a green rug and took him away. The pathos of this tale leaves no room for multiple perspectives. It is elegiac, paying tribute and homage to what is considered a noble group and cause. As narrative it is in the traditional modern Arabist tradition.

An utterly new kind of fiction would be written in 1977 by Elias Khoury. *Al-Jabal al-saghir*, translated as *Little Mountain*,[3] though political in its coverage of battles and the early years of the war, is ostensibly an aesthetic tour de force. Here the political becomes the aesthetic and vice versa. Khoury's attention to style and to language foregrounds his belief that language must take control of events and of its narrators. In a 1981 novel, *Abwab al-medina*, Khoury would perfect this formula, as events are meaningless without the language to narrate them. A study of Khoury's major novels, most written about or during the war, enables one to pursue central issues—including the intersection of nation, culture, and narrative—relevant to the study of Lebanon.

The poet and intellectual Adonis maintains in his *Al-Nizham wa al-kalam* [Order and the word] that great poetry and periods of creativity stem from opposition and dialectic. In his tirade against Arab mentality, Adonis faults a stagnation in perspective, an overreliance on a stifling, tyrannical religion that has taken on a position of political authority. There is little opportunity for hadatha, for modernity, which he characterizes as the ability to find new relationships between language and things. The Arab mind is fettered by tradition and enslaved by worn-out expressions. The rare poet is the one who can conceive of new meanings, new symbols, new ways of perceiving, reading, understanding, and hence living. In this way, the writer might be able to change the world in some small way (Lecture).

A careful reading of *Al-Jabal al-saghir* reveals that important new modes of expression and narration are now at work. One can speculate on whether war itself generates the oppositionally creative environment Adonis is calling for. Certainly great art can and has been produced during war, but so has much that is mediocre and derivative. On the other hand, tranquil historical periods have occasioned truly new ways of expression. Certainly war involves inherent opposition and conflict, but that rarely translates into the oppositional dialectic that Adonis is talking about. Much of the cultural output during war is disappointingly monologic and sloganistic, extolling political leaders, adhering to the maxims of narrow political parties, inciting the passions of the already converted, etc. War can also have a transformative effect, forcing a reassessment of one's existence, of one's priorities, and of one's understanding of language. To read Khoury's novels is to experience that reassessment.

Khoury's *Al-Jabal al-saghir* has been read as a novel that propagates the "male myth" of war (Cooke, 1988, 92). Here, according to Miriam Cooke, the Christian fighters are presented as the clear bad guys versus the good Palestinians who are engaged in a just revolution. The novel offers a "neat dichotomizing of issues and parties" (90) that reduces Lebanon to a paradigm. Evelyne Accad faults Khoury for seemingly celebrating the destruction of Beirut since he treats the war "in such light and sarcastic terms" (1990, 155). Yet the novel is a complex interweaving of voices and perspectives that constantly undermine any single authority. Although there is a bias toward a leftist ideology, it hardly dominates or controls the fiction that Khoury has constructed.

In Edward Said's foreword to the English translation, *Little Mountain*, in 1989, he highlights the quasi-autobiographical trajectory of the narrator who, like Khoury, was born and raised in Ashrafiye (or the "little mountain") district of Beirut, who became involved in the leftist movements, joined the Palestinian Fedayeen and fought in the first years of the war, and is later seen in exile in Paris. Said praises Khoury's "formless" and disorienting postmodern style, characterized by repetition, comedy, irreverence, and informality. It is specifically original in "its avoidance of the melodramatic and the conventional" (xx). The novel is introduced in its relation to other Arab novels, especially those by the Egyptian Nobel Prize–winning Naguib Mahfouz, and Said concludes by placing Khoury within a camp of writers giving voice to "rooted exiles and trapped refugees"; his is the voice of the minority oppositional Arab artist, "infected by rejection, drift, errance, uncertainty" (xxi).

While there is much to agree with in Said's comments, there are three points that need clarification. First, Said assumes and/or implies that Khoury's novel consists of a single narrative voice. Yet the book was originally conceived as separate vignettes, not a novel (Michael Young, Interview with Khoury, 136). It is true that in parts of the novel, one can perceive that quasi-autobiographical trajectory mentioned above, yet it is never alone. The unnamed first-person narrator who dominates much of chapters 1, 2, 3, and 5 is occasionally shifted to a third-person subject or is merged into another named character like the bespectacled Talal. The narrator of chapter 4 is Kamel Abu Mehdi (although he too at times becomes the third-person subject rather than the first-person speaker), who bears no relation to the dominant narrator/s of the surrounding chapters.

Second, Said welcomes an Arab fiction that is not melodramatic. Indeed, Khoury's text only occasionally falls into that category. There are a few instances when the narrative falls off track to sentimentalize political ideology. In the beginning of the book, for example, Ashrafiye is depicted as the rural haven of the narrator's childhood, until it becomes infiltrated by corrupt merchants and, eventually, the vile Christian militias. In the present, these Phalange burst into his home, threateningly interrogate his mother, search through his belongings looking for "Palestinians and Abd al-Nassir and Communism," crossing themselves in "hate or joy" (11). War has arrived, and now the "bodies of my friends" are hurled into collective graves (21), the narrator laments. The militias surround the poor district of Karantina, wanting to oust the beggars and foreigners who, according to them, rob Lebanon (20). The subsequent fall of Maslakh and Karantina is at the "hands of the fascists" (37). Some heavy Christian symbolism further dots the first two chapters: "No one opened the church door" (24) despite the knocking of the young narrator and his family; and later when he is an adult fighting in the war taking refuge in a church, he notes that "Christ is on the floor" (31); his statue has fallen. These obvious symbols and binaric depictions are overlooked by Said and overly focused on by Cooke. Khoury's later works would relinquish any melodramatic or overtly ideological references. Perhaps this early novel illustrates that despite an innovative style and structure, Khoury occasionally lapsed into the sloganistic when he chose to depict political motivations.

A third problem with Said's depiction of Khoury is his insistence on placing him generically within Arab culture. Admittedly Khoury is an Arab writer and can be studied as such, but he is also an idiosyncratically Lebanese writer, drawing on specifically Lebanese society and adopting a distinct Lebanese dialect. While it might be true that Khoury has features in common with the Palestinian Ghassan Kanafani, they hardly define this author who, despite his pro-Palestinian sentiments, is so wholly rooted in the Lebanese context.

Khoury provides new ways of conceiving of Lebanon, now coincidentally engaged in war, and he does so primarily through structural and stylistic, not thematic, innovations. It is surprising that his novels, quickly translated into French, sell relatively well in France, and the English translations have found a market (though small) in the United States. Khoury's novels are difficult in translation because there are many topical references to specific dates, urban areas, and cultural/political events that would be unfamiliar to foreigners. In translation, the largely thematic and potentially ethnographic sociopolitical issues take on an exaggerated significance. Yet it is the experience of reading these novels in the original Arabic that is so significant. One of the primary features of that Arabic is Khoury's attention to the spoken language in its Lebanese dialect and colloquial syntax. There is a wide gap between the classical written Arabic and the spoken colloquial, challenging authors to capture, in writing, what one thinks or says. This is a thorny issue indeed that only a handful of writers are seriously grappling with. As mentioned earlier, Ziad Rahbani is one of those writers, and much of his success was due to his tapping into a familiar Lebanese dialect.

Like his earlier play *Nazl al-surur*, Rahbani's 1978 *Bilnisbi la bukra shu?* [So, what about tomorrow?] also foregrounds the language itself. Here, an upper-class slang (with its overuse of the word *fahl*) is put down, as well as the overreliance on foreign words and phrases. The play is riddled with an odd assortment of French, English, and Italian expressions spoken by the various foreign customers of the bar. The main character (also Zakaria played by Ziad) disagrees with his wife's insistence on teaching their kids "foreign languages so that they can get ahead." It is soon apparent that "foreign" is, in essence, evil and dangerous. Zakaria's wife is forced to prostitute herself to the foreigners in order to live, and at the end of the play Zakaria gets in a fight with the American Mr. Harold, who turns him in to the police. That which is not Arabic is clearly unwholesome seems to be one of the readings of the play.

The most memorable segments of the play, however, are actually the songs, in colloquial Lebanese dialect, that were quickly committed to memory by most Lebanese irrespective of class, religion, or political incli- nation. The vegetable vendor, Ramez, sings the famous "Tghayyar hawana" [Our times have changed] with the popular line "sarat hayati kulha shi bahdali" [my whole life has become a mess/an insult]. He also sings the satirical and pastoral "'a hadir al-bosta" [to the drone of the bus] and "'ayshi wahda balak" [she's living alone without you]. These songs would become some of the most popular in Lebanon for the next ten years, while Leba- non was still at war with itself. What is noteworthy is not the context from which the songs were pulled—the ideologically heavy play of Ziad Rahbani —but the simple and refreshing diction and music along with everyday situations that most Lebanese could identify with and find amusing. These songs would lose (as they already have) almost everything in translation, but they endure because of the language and hence the culture that Rahbani effectively tapped into. Indeed, Rahbani helped sustain or pro- mote a Lebanese identity, even while the themes of his play were seri- ously undercutting the current Lebanese system.

Examining some of these narratives strongly suggests the significant role of language in both expressing and identifying aspects of the national cul- ture. Though the nation was torn apart politically, socially, and economi- cally, it retained or even developed cultural features that need to be ac- knowledged. The language adopted in certain fictions and other popular forums, especially during these war years, would help define a Lebanon that seemed ostensibly threatened.

Like Rahbani, Khoury's use of Arabic is especially significant, as he sets out in novel after novel to do new things with the language. The effect of reading the opening pages of *Little Mountain*, for example, is to realize that the written has become the spoken. Although Khoury preserves the essential qualities of the classical grammar, he loosens up the syntax and inserts slang words and expressions. Also, by relying on repetition and a simple cadence, the written text quickly becomes an aural one as well. For Khoury, "in Arabic the spoken is the true; the written is lies." One of his functions is to attempt to introduce the spoken into the written; otherwise, one cannot tell stories (1995 interview). When reading the Arabic text, one quickly learns to trust it. This does not necessarily mean believing the stories it chooses to tell, but trusting the language through which the narrations take place. By the time one gets to the third chapter and a prolonged description of a battle on Mount Sannine, one is receptive to the mode and style of its unusual depiction.

The reader is suddenly *in medias res*, on the snowy top of a big mountain in the middle of a military confrontation. The warring sides are not clearly defined, nor are the reasons for this battle, but Khoury is relying totally on historic precedence. In 1976, the Palestinian and leftist coalition of fighters decided in a bold move to close off the Phalange by taking over the Maronite heartland. This strategy could be achieved if the leftists gained the high ground on Mount Sannine and encircled the Christian enclave north of Beirut. In fact, it was this real possibility of a Christian defeat that led to them calling in the Syrians to put a stop to the leftist offensive. This was certainly one of the most critical battles in the beginning of the war. Khoury says virtually nothing about the historic specifics of this battle. He occasionally describes the shooting and confused shelling on the foggy mountaintop, but the bulk of the narration is told in terms of minutiae: a fighter who complains about his wife, the chitchat among the fighters on issues large and small, and the real problem in this battle of cold, wet, swollen feet.

As the narrative continues, the lens zooms in on the village fighter Nazih, pontificating and gesticulating while the reader's gaze is made to focus on the orange he holds in his hand. This then becomes the real locus of the story as the narrator cannot keep his eyes off of it. As one, through the narrator, continues to trace the path of the orange, the reader understands something of the utter deprivation the narrator must feel after days of fighting on a stranded mountain. The craving, intensity, and barbarism of these miserable men are also captured, as they fight desperately over possession of the sole orange. One also grasps the total absurdity and gravity of this situation.

The primary narrator, as mentioned above, periodically melds into other characters. For example, the narrator describes how the orange rolls away from the village fighter's hand and Talal picks it up. They get into an argument, and then the village fighter "jumps up and takes the orange from *my* hand" [my emphasis]. But the orange was clearly in Talal's hand, so Talal and the narrator seem, for now at least, to be one and the same (85–86). A surprise battle resumes, and the corpse of the village fighter known as "The

Tree" is brought in on the back of a white mule: "The mule stopped before me. Talal leaned. The smell of death resembles the smell of orange. Death is an orange tree. When I die I want my smell to be that of an orange tree" (87). Here the reader believes the narrator to be the affected Talal, leaning to look at the body of the freshly killed village fighter. But when one jumps ahead to the last paragraph of this chapter entitled "The Last Option," one learns that the procession walking behind the white mule includes Nazih, the village fighter. It is Talal who lies dead on the mule's back!

The narrator has masterfully linked the orange to death and specifically to the death of his good friend and fellow fighter, Talal, perhaps a man so close to him during their intense existence in battle that their identities are merged. This, of course, is a contradiction. In fact, the narrator is accused of contradicting himself, and he responds: "Life is like that. Contradiction doesn't mean that I contradict myself. Contradiction means contradiction" (89). That is the way it is. Talal is me and I am him.

In chapter 4, "The Steps," the narrator is confused, disturbed, possibly insane as he muses about the woman hanging from the ceiling. One might assume that he is our previous narrator, devastated from the experience of war and the death of Talal. But no, this is Kamel Abu Mehdi, stinking drunk, a petty employee and a painfully ordinary man watching his wife change the bulb on a chandelier. The loose trajectory of this man's life takes the reader from prewar to postwar Lebanon, but the narrative foregrounds the mundane details of a daily, and somewhat unsavory, life. The focal point becomes the car he purchases and worships. Unfortunately, it is hit by a shell. Note the slippage, again, between the narrators:

> I wept. The corpse is before me, the people around the corpse, and the corpse before me alone. Kamel Abu Mehdi stood there in shock. . . .
>
> I said to my wife that the car.
> I said to the woman standing in front of me that the car. But she was pointing to a child running and laughing in the street.
> I said to her that I.
> She said that the shells.
>
> Kamel Abu Mehdi stood there alone. She was before me alone. Shrapnel filled the street. Glass filled the street. Cars filled the street. But she died. He approached her. (120–21)

Kamel's shock is so great that his sentences are aborted; he cannot express his grief. The dueling first- and third-person narrators further confuse this bizarre tale that borders on the ridiculous, especially as Kamel mournfully follows what becomes the funeral procession of his bombed car. In juxtaposition, however, is the truly tragic. These indiscriminate daytime bombs hit playing children, like the girl Kamel's wife focused on above. She is struck and picked up by a man in glasses who takes her away in his orange car. They later learn that she died, paralleling the "death" of the car. Soon after, a poster of the man in glasses, now martyred, is also put up. His name is Talal. The narrator Kamel stares at that poster, and the reader is left wondering what Talal and the orange (here, the color of his car) are doing in this tale.

Khoury's indiscriminate and seemingly incomprehensible tactics parallel the Lebanese war itself. The mode of telling becomes integral to the tale, inseparable from it. The war hence takes on a new level of verity as it is conceived as an aesthetic and not solely as an ideology. This is not to deny the artist specific political views, but it does set in relief how art might be able to transform perception and hence expression.

Khoury's politics are certainly evident in his highlighting of class differences as the main cause for the war. He presents the plight of the poor, workers' strikes, and student demonstrations from the early 1970s. The narrator reminisces about that time and notes that "we didn't realize that the war had already begun" (148). This attention to class would be adopted into the pro-Palestinian or leftist position during the war, but this ideology does not dominate or determine Khoury's fiction. On the other hand, Rahbani's 1978 *Bilnisbi la bukra shu?* indoctrinates. From the very outset, the play foregrounds the dramatic rise in the cost of living in Beirut and the lack of good jobs. Toward the end of the play, the once carefree Zakaria (similar in many ways to the lead character of *Nazl al-surur*) delivers a humorless speech on the terrible economic conditions that have led his family to ruin: "Poverty is really frightening; when we were in it we didn't notice it, but as soon as we came out of it a bit, we saw it. . . . We can never go back" (129). His eyes now open, Zakaria forces his wife to quit her prostituting and walk out on the job, but he is challenged by the American and thrown into prison, where he remains at the play's close. The plot is predictable and the political message simplistic. The humor and nuanced exchanges of the earlier scenes virtually disappear by the end. After all, in 1978 Lebanon had already been at war for three years, and that is not funny.

This Rahbani play makes no mention of the war. The situation is disastrous because of economic inequities that lead to violence and injustice. Perhaps there is no need to bring in the actual war which, to many, was explained primarily in these economic terms. This simplistic binaric political depiction did not seem to reduce the popularity of Ziad's play, however. Khoury's novel, on the other hand, is essentially complicated and perhaps consequently less accessible. Despite the instances where strong political partisanship is visible, Khoury's text is dialogic, frequently undermining any authoritative voice with a multiplicity of perspectives.

In the novel, almost every account of the war is refracted. The fighters differ on their assessment of the battle around the church in chapter 2. One says it was a great fight; another admits he remembers nothing; Talal muses that the battle was like a movie (36). The battle on Mount Sannine is similarly recollected through multiple vignettes culminating in the orange sequence already discussed. In chapter 4, the narrator Kamel decides to become more active in the events (i.e., the war) in his neighborhood. But rather than taking on an ideology, Kamel participates in the rampant looting. The supposed fighters seem more interested in material accumulation than in achieving social justice. At the end of the novel when the narrator ruminates over the Egyptian obelisk in the center of Paris, he becomes the pathetic ancient Egyptian king himself climbing on top of the column to rule his land. This strange scene oscillates between condemnation of imperialism and a call for total destruction (161), but the narrator lacks credibility. While the topsy-turvy world of this novel foils all attempts at pontification or even certainty, the collective production achieves something like truth.

Little Mountain never reduces Lebanon solely to war. Many passages deal with flashbacks or buildups to earlier periods. Storytellers like Abu George, for example, provide a history of Ashrafiye. The narrator reconstructs his childhood memories of that section of Beirut. Most of the content of Kamel's narrative in chapter 4 has nothing to do with the war. Even when war is described, as already pointed out, the focus is often on incidentals.

One cannot make the same claims about Etel Adnan's *Sitt Marie Rose*. Written in French and published in 1978, this novel also covers the period of the early war years. Despite some beautifully lyrical sections, the text is weakened by a dominant preachy voice that seeks to explain and understand this war. The Christian militia men are caricatures: rich, spoiled, misogynistic, and brutal. The Palestinians are downtrodden, haggard, and terrorized. The Christian section of Beirut is "fierce and puritanical, arrogance flies its flag at half mast." In the Muslim quarter "there is less bravado in the eyes and more sorrowful resignation" (20). These binaric depictions lead to a one-sided offensive whereby on April 13, 1975, "Hatred erupts": "A bus full of Palestinians returning to their camp passes a church." The rest really is history.

The novel focuses on the factual murder by Phalangists of Marie Rose Boulos, a Christian Syrian/Lebanese, who supported the Palestinian resistance and taught disadvantaged children. Her tragic death is passionately depicted and serves as an example of the horrors of the Lebanese war. Adnan is especially successful in her inclusion of multiple perspectives on this event: Marie Rose's deaf-mute students, Marie Rose herself, the specific Phalange fighters, a priest, and the dominant narrator. It is this last voice, however, which proves most problematic as it pontificates and dominates. This is the voice that explains who the players in this war are and why they are who they are. These Lebanese citizens are sexually frustrated men; they are insecure and fearful men; they are violent men. In short, they are "Arabs":

> Thus, the Arabs let themselves go in a tearing, killing, annihilating violence, and while other peoples, virulent in their own obsession with cleanliness, invent chemical products, they seek a primitive and absolute genocide. In their fights they don't try to conquer lands, but to eliminate each other. And if after death they persist in mutilating the corpse, it's to diminish the enemy's body still more, and erase if possible the fact that he ever existed, the existence of the enemy being a kind of sacrilege which exacts a purification equally as monstrous. (66)

One gets the strong sense that this novel was written by an outraged outsider. Despite Adnan's involvement in, love for, and knowledge of Lebanon and the Palestinians, her text is essentially a study and an indictment of Arabs as exemplified by a minority offshoot of, ironically, wanna-be Europeans—in other words, Lebanese Christians. It is difficult to reconcile a text replete with condescending and demeaning generalizations like the example above.

This text has served its purpose well in certain Western academic contexts by providing an accessible third world voice, a readable narrative on war and, even more important, a third world female voice on war. Unlike the texts of Elias Khoury or, to be discussed, the texts of Hanan al-Shaykh, Adnan's work is not especially transformative. Because it is written in French and not Arabic, the possibilities for altering the national language are reduced; because it is heavily ideological, it tends to simplify rather than to capture complex Lebanon; and because it is accusative rather than participatory, it is set outside and beyond the Lebanese experience itself. To read *Sitt Marie Rose* is to reinforce the image that dominated the Western press for years: Lebanon was *only* a repository for war.

Ghada Samman's *Kawabis Beirut* (1976), translated as *Beirut Nightmares*, certainly focuses on Lebanon at war, but it is not primarily reductionist. It is a wrenching first-person account, clearly based on Samman's own experiences of what it was like to be trapped for a week in close proximity to the hotel district during the raging battles of the hotels in the fall of 1975. Samman clearly identifies when and what she was composing, culminating in her bold move to save her manuscript at the end of the book. Although her previous novel, *Beirut '75*, seemed to anticipate much of the violence, this next novel, situated in the midst of that violence, is uttered partly in disbelief. Cooke assesses:

> Throughout the *Beirut Nightmares* that hurtle from dream to reality Samman maintains a tight authorial control and vision, never allowing the narration to become an abstraction whose only impact is to convey numbness. The balance between a frightening present and its exaggerated possibilities is struck in such a way that the reader enters a fevered imagination, and does not reject as too much, as too implausible, the recounted horrors. There is no limit to what can be imagined, but there is a very definite limit to what can be tolerated in experience. (45)

The 196 nightmares related in the book vacillate from the surreal to the mundane, but they all communicate what Samman was going through (physically, emotionally, intellectually) during this period, and they also are testimony to her absolute need to write, to record her experiences.

In Nightmare #35, Samman confronts her own dilemma as a writer during war. As she gazes over her extensive library and her own books with the word *revolution* in the titles, she wonders if she herself has participated in creating this war, for she has always called for transformation and for "wiping away the ugliness from this nation and washing it with equality, joy, freedom, and justice" (41). Yet she realizes she wanted a revolution without blood. The narrative now takes on the form of an internal dialogue over the nature of revolution, on whether the pen or the bullet is the more effective weapon, on whether the silent majority is in fact guilty, etc. One voice accuses her of being irrelevant; the artist caught in her library just scuttles off to hide when the bombs fall. This recalls a section in Khoury's *Little Mountain* when the narrator of the last chapter criticizes a group of university professors who preach revolution but who hypocritically refrain from any action (145–46). Another voice in Samman's head counters that poets and artists often make terrible fighters; besides, "to drag an artist into battle would be like forcing Marie Curie from her lab to the kitchen because the country is in need of cooks!" (43).

"A writer should create revolution, not practice it," insists this voice. But why should the artist be so privileged and protected? responds the other voice. Because, comes the answer, the artist is different, constructed in such a way that "he" cannot be a good fighter. Samman's narrator continues: "I cannot kill or torture any human being—I will think that he was once an innocent babe. . . . I will think of his mother, his lover. . . . I will imagine what he looks like while laughing, while praying, while making love" (44).

Despite the dialogue, it is very clear where the "truth" lies. The artist might struggle with what her function is in society, especially when that society is at war, but there is no doubt that in the end Samman sees herself as both an artist and a revolutionary. Her action becomes the attempt to save what she has written. The product, in fact, is worth sacrificing one's life for. After days of entrapment, the narrator is finally rescued by an armored vehicle, but she accidentally leaves her case, containing the manuscript to this text, in the vehicle. She then heroically braves shelling and sniping in order to retrieve the significant text that will become the foundation of the one before us. This not too subtle self-aggrandizement is not too difficult to take, since it is balanced by genuine moments of self-deprecation. The self, so overtly focused on, becomes indistinguishable from the authoritative narrator, who is completely lacking in Khoury and poorly camouflaged in Adnan. One could perhaps argue that the dominant voice is claustrophobic, paralleling the condition of claustrophobia experienced by the author/narrator during her period of entrapment under heavy shelling.

This voice is nonetheless definitive and provides explanations for why this Lebanese nation was doomed. Zeidan interprets two analogies for Lebanon in Samman's text. One is her frequent reference to a pet shop that, from the outside, looks wonderful (paralleling "the deceptive showcase of the Lebanon the tourists see"). To enter into the pet shop is to reveal the miserable condition of the caged animals (who clearly "stand for the Lebanese people"). When the narrator (and heroine) tries to free them, they at first refuse to leave, but then, driven by hunger, they attack and mutilate their owner (203). Obviously, Samman blames stifling socioeconomic conditions for the violent outburst that has resulted in war. A second analogy comes at the very end of the series of nightmares in Dream #1.[4] Here, Lulu (representing Lebanon) searches for her father's identity (i.e., Lebanon's national identity). Was her dad an American sailor of the Sixth Fleet or a soldier during the Crusades? These Western designations conform, Zeidan points out, to the Maronite vision of Lebanon. Lulu's mother, however, insists that Lulu, like her twenty-one other siblings (representing the other Arab nations), is unmistakably Arab. Lulu then falls in love with a poor stranger (i.e., a Palestinian) who, despite his bad fortune, knows very well his Arab heritage. In April 1975 (official beginning of civil war), she is impregnated and, along with her husband, fights the forces of the king (the Lebanese authorities). Her child is not born after the usual nine months and might not appear for another nine years. He is different and will be born many times and in many places (symbolizing, perhaps, the spirit of revolution). This dream, not nightmare, provides a possible optimistic read on the Lebanese war, which seems to lead to a justified revolution.

Without a doubt, Samman does take a political position on the war and, by extension, provides a critique of the nation. In addition, her perspective, like Adnan's, is a gendered one, adding yet another important dimension to a discussion of this period of Lebanon's nationhood. There have been important studies on how cataclysmic events like wars can so totally disrupt a society as to reconfigure gender relations. There are reasons to argue that Lebanon, a traditionally male-oriented society, was shaken up so violently that new opportunities for women began to emerge. There is also evidence to illustrate that societies at war, though transformed, are not necessarily more conducive to women during or after the turbulence. This is not the place to assess whether the war fundamentally altered the situation for Lebanese women, but one can note that a disproportionately large number of women seemed to enter into the literary arena during Lebanon's war years. Many of these women, however, were writing from outside Lebanon; some, though not all, moved away to escape the undeniable dangers of war. It is not difficult to see how war would dominate the imagination and impose itself as a subject, especially when the writer, living abroad, had the time and the compulsion to narrate it.

In *War's Other Voices: Women Writers on the Lebanese Civil War* (1987), Cooke isolated a group of female writers and studied their contribution and their distinction from male writers on the war. She labeled these women the Beirut Decentrists and sought to analyze their texts in gendered terms, highlighting the impact of war on the female imagination. Accad also examined a group of primarily Lebanese authors in *Sexuality and War: Literary Masks of the Middle East* (1990) in terms of sexuality and violence in an attempt to better comprehend the relationship between war and gender. In his 1995 *Arab Women Novelists: The Formative Years and Beyond*, Joseph Zeidan spends part of chapter 4, "The Quest for National Identity," on female authors who wrote about the Lebanese civil war. In Bouthaina Shaaban's 1999 study, in Arabic, of Arab women novelists, she devotes most of her seventh chapter, "Tajalliyat" [Clarifications], to those Lebanese authors, like Shaykh, Hoda Barakat, and Nasrallah, who wrote about the war.[5]

Adnan and Samman figure as authors who helped constitute new narratives on Lebanon from a female perspective. Adnan, as already seen, blames men's sick sexuality for an unhealthy outlook on life that was destined to lead to violence. Samman, by focusing on daily existence during war rather than on the participation in battle, offers the perspective of most women who were trapped, though not necessarily politically uncommitted, during the war years. Emily Nasrallah, on the other hand, wrote mostly children's stories in the early stages of the war, books like *Al-Bahira* (1977) and *Shadi al-saghir* (1977). Cooke writes that Nasrallah felt that "at least one possible solution to the strife that was tearing her country apart was to educate the children differently" (Cooke, 1995, 184). In 1978, Nasrallah published a novel, *Tilka al-thikrayat* [Those memories], which features a dialogue between two women on how their lives have changed because of the war. *Al-Iqla' 'Aks al-zaman* (1981), translated as *Flight against Time* (1987), and many of her short stories describe varying war-related situations like forced emigration and the effects of brutal violence. Many other women (both Lebanese and not Lebanese) wrote poetry, journals, prose texts (in Arabic, English, and French) that dealt with the war but that I have not discussed. They include Nadia Tueni, Nazek Saba Yared, Daisy al-Amir, Umayya Hamdan, Claire Gebeyli, Venus Khoury-Ghata, Evelyne Accad, Liana Badr, Jean Said Makdissi, May Rihani, and Dominique Edde.

The most significant female voice to emerge from the early war years, however, was Hanan al-Shaykh's. A commendable effort to translate her major texts along with a scholarly recognition of her work has meant, primarily, that Shaykh is relatively known to Western academics interested in third world and gender studies. Shaykh herself, however, resists all designations that reduce her to a female writer or a representative of third world women's writing. Moreover, despite positive reviews, she is not widely read in Lebanon and is virtually ignored in the Lebanese educational system. This is not necessarily to say that women writers have no following in Lebanon (after all, Nasrallah still manages to be popular), but it does raise some difficult questions.

Shaykh's 1980 *Hikayat Zahra* (translated in 1986 as *The Story of Zahra*) is an utterly innovative text.[6] The first part of the novel is divided into five chapters, three of which are narrated by Zahra, a young Shiʻa woman who reminisces about her relationships with her mother, her uncle, Hashem, and her future husband, Majed. Forced as a young girl to accompany her mother on her adulterous affairs, Zahra recollects her desperate need for her mother's love and her uncontrollable fear of her father's tyranny. Both her parents cater to her brother, Ahmed, saving the choicest meats for him and allocating education funds to him alone. In stream of consciousness fashion, Zahra recollects moments of incest by a cousin (or grandfather?) and by her uncle, and one also learns of her frequent rapes (or was she a passive consensual partner?) by Malek, a friend of the family. Her acne, made worse by her own incessant scratching, along with her abortions and occasional suicide attempts and nervous breakdowns, reveal a woman much troubled by her existence. A telling image is of her "escaping" by cowering in a locked bathroom. Toward the end of this first part, turned off by men, she lashes out: "I wanted to live for myself. I wanted my body to be mine alone. I wanted the place on which I stood and the air surrounding me to be mine and no one else's" (78). She feels that in all her relations with men she was only a spectator (96). The impulse to blame the men in her life is thwarted by Shaykh's inclusion of two other points of view. Both Hashem and Majed, located in Africa, narrate chapters, allowing the reader a glimpse of insecure but hopeful men, clinging to an image of Lebanon they associate with Zahra. It is also a Lebanon of rhetoric: Hashem was a fanatic member of the PPS, noted for the rhetoric [balagha] of its founder, Antoine Saadeh, whose slogans he lived by; Majed receives letters from his father, who "would address his letters to me as if they were written to God rather than to his son" (62). Zahra, who also keeps a journal, seems free from this rhetoric, which arguably has a stronger hold on Arab men.

The second part of the novel is told only by Zahra, who has left her husband in Africa and moved in with her parents in Beirut. Lebanon is in the early stages of the civil war (1975–76): The reader can tell by references to the radio announcer Sharif al-Akhawi, the death of the comedian Shushu, and named battles like Karantina. Ironically, Zahra comes out of her shell, so to speak. Her face clears, she ventures out of the house, and as the battles rage fiercely outside, she locates a peace within herself: "I felt calm. It meant that my perimeters were fixed by these walls, that nothing which my mother hoped for me could find a place inside them" (107). Her parents leave for the village, her brother joins a militia, and Zahra seeks out the sniper who terrorizes their neighborhood. In an attempt to distract him from killing, she offers herself to him sexually. Every day they meet on the rooftop from whence he kills. For the first time in her life, she experiences true pleasure and depends on the sniper for her happiness. When she becomes pregnant and is too far along for an abortion, the sniper reassures her that he will marry her the next day. As she walks home basking in her good fortune, he guns her down. The novel ends as she continues to narrate her own death.

This powerful text provides an important new narrative on the Lebanese nation. For one, the society that Zahra inhabits prior to war is unwholesome. This is especially revealed in the makeup of the strongest traditional institution of society, the family. Unlike so many of the cultural artifacts from Lebanon that assume the sanctity of the family, Shaykh goes out of her way to create a story where the central figure is tormented on every level by the relationships within her family. In addition, the unhappiness generated within the family is primarily linked to gender and sex issues. This perspective suggests the second reason for Shaykh's unique approach. While much of the book is set against the backdrop of Lebanon's war, the focus is only incidentally political. The manifestation of frustration/violence/war is primarily imparted through sex. Moreover, the mode of expressing this link between violence and sex is also new. By relying mostly on the internal narrative of the troubled Zahra, the text becomes a psychological map and provides the grid through which one now reads Lebanon. In other words, Shaykh does not write about the war; she presents it obliquely through the consciousness of Zahra. This psychological approach permits the war to be woven into the very fabric of Zahra's internal narrative. The war itself is internalized, it stems from within, and it resides within. Shaykh provides a new way of thinking about Lebanon, by intertwining war, family, gender, sex, and narrative into a single text.

By juxtaposing Shaykh's part two (war years) to her part one (prewar years), one is able to perceive parallels that shed light on the troubled nation. Without resorting to any kind of authoritative posing, Shaykh gains trust by simply illustrating. In different ways, Adnan and Samman break through their fictions to expose their own passions and political agendas. This strategy weakens the effectiveness of the texts themselves. *The Story of Zahra* convinces because the aesthetic and the thematic meld, erasing all traces of the author and her idiosyncratic beliefs, for if the power of a literary text is to reside in the declaration of the author's agenda, then she had best spell it out in a nonfictional text. When the charge is creative, like literary fiction, then the burden must lie elsewhere. Shaykh's genius is in her ability to construct art (possibly charged with her own attitudes on politics) without sacrificing her art to her ideology. The product, the narrative itself, then can be judged on its merits, irrespective of the beliefs of the author.

This point is further evidenced by Shaykh's refreshing writing style, which, as the novelist Rachid al-Da'if maintains, is "uneducated" in the most positive sense, since it is "unburdened by traditional Arabic rhetoric" (interview with Da'if, January 31, 1998). Although she does not rely as much on the "spoken word" as Elias Khoury does, this particular text (primarily an internal narrative rather than an actual dialogue) may not warrant that approach. Shaykh succeeds, as Cooke writes, in introducing a "stylistic device that subtly and powerfully illustrates Zahra's integration into the war and into others' psyches" (57).

Because the war arrives in part two, after the personal and troubled accounts of part one, it does not take the reader by surprise. The war seems to evolve rather naturally from an already disintegrated and unhealthy society. Despite this perspective, Zahra's own reflections on the war acknowledge its insanity: The shelling is indiscriminate, innocents are victimized, the political and military players serve their own interests, and the rhetoric of the fighters is hypocritical as they loot and take drugs. Hers is a totally cynical and critical point of view made all the more poignant because of its sanity—this by the woman institutionalized for her "crazy" behavior.[7] Shaykh's obvious play with in/sanity highlights a perspective not only on the war but on the society that produced it. In addition, it foregrounds the issue of the reliable/questionable narrator. Zahra, or any narrator for that matter, is not necessarily to be trusted.

As if to confuse the reader and posit the theory of the unreliable narrator, Shaykh introduces a passage early in the book where Zahra reflects on her brother, Ahmed, who is seven years her senior. "Between us," she continues, "had been a set of twins, girl and boy, who lived but briefly in a porcelain soup dish after my mother aborted them." Although Zahra had obviously not even been born then, she pursues her story: "I remember the neighbors pouring into the bedroom to greet my mother, then peering into the soup dish where the tiny embryos swam" (20).

The above quotations not only undermine Zahra's reliability but they disclose something of Shaykh's unique style in graphically and humorously capturing the physical. One of the women who gathers around the porcelain dish exclaims, "In the name of Allah, the All Merciful. Blessed be the Creator. Look, here is a fully developed creature." Another more outspoken one "spat, swearing and shoving the dish aside: 'I spit on the human being. Is this how we all are created—as minute as a finger nail becoming as huge as mules!'" (20). Shaykh's attention to detail, all detail, is especially noteworthy when she depicts sexual or traditionally taboo subjects (especially for Arab women). In one scene, Zahra recalls the incestuous advances of her uncle, Hashem. She feigns sleep as he approaches her in bed: "Then he came closer and took my hand, which still carried faint menstrual traces on the nails, left there when I had checked in the night to see whether my period had begun. As he started to lick my fingers, he noticed a strange taste, but drew closer, saying how sharply he longed for his family. At that point, even through his trousers and my nightgown, I felt his penis throbbing against my thigh" (28). This is a new kind of writing, and Shaykh has been both criticized and praised for her explicit style. Noted as one of the most "sensual" of Arab writers (Accad, 1990, 45), Shaykh brings a relatively new vitality and honesty to Lebanese writing.

When Zahra is killed by the sniper who impregnated her, one is confronted by the stark paradoxes that shoot through this text and through the nation it narrates. Nothing but a violent end that fuses life with death, love with hate, closure with beginning can express the intensity of Zahra herself, sacrificed in the end, but enabled in the telling of her story. Zeidan writes that Zahra's hopes about her future are "illusory." "Because the war has not brought about true revolution, especially with respect to women and sexuality, Lebanon is doomed to remain an oppressive patriarchal state even after the war" (Zeidan 213). He then quotes Accad, who writes: "Sexuality is much more fundamental in social and political problems than previously thought, and unless a sexual revolution is incorporated into political revolution, there will be no real transformation of social relations" (Accad, 1990, 12). Perhaps one hope is that in exposing the societal ills and presenting a fresh alternative in the form of an aesthetic, a step toward transformation is possible. Shaykh's potentially prescriptive text stands in contrast to Tewfiq Awwad's primarily descriptive novel discussed in the previous chapter.

These women who wrote during Lebanon's war are testimony, perhaps, to the notion that traditional paradigms and authority figures are displaced during social upheaval, making room for new possibilities for imagining one's community, one's nation. Zahra's own life seemed, at first, to be more liberated during war. With her family "elsewhere" (literally and figuratively), Zahra is free to locate her self, yet she is never really free from the fears and paradoxes of her childhood and adolescence that have shaped her. She as much seeks the sniper out to self-destruct as she does to purportedly stop him from shooting. Her personal tale becomes the tale of Lebanon, also self-destructing. Those women who wrote Lebanon's war were also, perhaps, caught in that double helix. By offering a gendered perspective, they contributed to a more pluralistic version of Lebanon; unfortunately, this came at a time when Lebanon's pluralisms were effectively at war with each other.

It is also easy to see how these female fictions could be adopted to serve a pacifist agenda that opposed the war. In fact, all of the women writers discussed or cited above disapproved of the violence. This would not mean that all Lebanese women could be absolved. Women, like men, preserved a mentality and a disposition that would lead to war. Arguably, women raised and nurtured the boys who would become the combatants in 1975, reinforced some of their prejudices, valorized their heroisms, mourned their martyrdoms. In addition, women, like men, struggled with the poverty and lack of representation that explains revolution. For those who sought to interpret the beginning of the war in Lebanon in terms of class issues, then women's support of war might be justified. So it is simplistic to readily link feminist and pacifist agendas, although that has been the dominant pattern. Moreover, the isolation of women writers as a group has tended to falsely pit them against male writers, who were also overwhelmingly cynical of the war.[8]

This examination of the first two years of the war sets in relief some of the salient concerns of this project. Suddenly in 1975 (despite decades of deliberating over what Lebanon's identity was) the very idea of Lebanon emerged just as it was put to the physical test. Almost all of the parties and militias warring in Lebanon assigned nationalist objectives to their agendas. Kamal Joumblatt headed the oppositional Lebanese National Movement, which served as an umbrella organization for over a dozen Lebanese groups and Palestinian factions; he maintained that his primary concern was always the preservation of the country's unity (92). He vehemently opposed the Syrian intervention in 1976, which violated Lebanese sovereignty and interrupted, as he put it, the "social revolution" under way (49). The Kata'ib who prayed for the unique trinity of God, Family, and Lebanon persisted in claiming that they were fighting for the preservation of Lebanon now threatened by the likes of Joumblatt. Sami Fares established the Lebanese Nationalist Front (not to be confused with Joumblatt's movement), calling for Christian self-determination in the face of the Arab-Islamic "new form of imperialism" (qtd. in Fares 131). All parties were in the "resistance" against something. "What is Lebanon" was no longer a hypothetical question but a lived-out, fought-over conundrum.

Georges Corm writes, "Any situation involving violence calls for the forging of mythologies that aim to justify the death of innocent people." Indeed, the leaders of local factions responsible for the senseless deaths of thousands "are turned into heroes of mythological causes" (Corm in *Lebanon: A History of Conflict*, ed. Shehadi and Mills, 258). Lebanon's civil war was gruesome, especially in its attacks on the civilian population. Sniping, car bombs, shifting (flying) roadblocks, shelling of civilian areas, and massacres all took their toll primarily on noncombatants. The political rhetoric, however, remained above the fray, always able to justify a "victory" in terms of ideology and doctrine—nationalism, religion, honor, and justice. Corm openly condemns this "militia order" (272); worse still, its existence was legitimized by subsequent postwar governments.

During this early period of the war, when most were simply wondering where to spend the night and secure the next meal for the family, certain texts, like the ones above, were produced. It is important to discern the creative possibilities within those texts. Most, for example, had already demystified the war. Khoury with his supposed "revolutionary" dreams actually went out of his way in *Little Mountain* to depict the absurd and the horrific. The war seemed to have gone sour. For those who believed that the war initially had a legitimate purpose, then the display of excessive looting, drug addiction, personal vendettas, and senseless violence would perhaps cause one to question. Even Joumblatt, who in the quotation at the opening of the chapter absolves the Palestinians of blame, admits that their behavior (detaining Lebanese officials, holding armed demonstrations and military funerals) in Lebanon was impolitic and made them hated. He then quotes a wonderful line from Marx: "We know the role stupidity has played in history and how it has been exploited by rascals" (55). Joumblatt even admits to the stupid mistakes of his own movement,[9] but in the end, he held fast (at least rhetorically) to the notion of a just revolution.

During these early years of the war, many historians sought to understand it by researching the bloody nineteenth-century sectarian conflict in Mount Lebanon. The sociologist Ahmad Beydoun notes that such historians felt the "need for a 'precedent' — if not an 'origin' — capable of strengthening the interpretation [they] were giving the present war" (66). Although their interpretations differed on whether the past conflict (like this one) was a result of "communal search for autonomy, veiled class struggle, examples of foreign interference," etc., they were all based on a "firm acceptance of Lebanese unity, at once the cause and the victim of recurring conflict" (66). A search for a logical explanation (historical precedence), however, did not mean that those historians approved of the current conflict. Most lamented Lebanon's violent trajectory, even while they sought to comprehend it.

Sa'id 'Aql, discussed earlier, was one of the few writers who seemed receptive to war. In the summer of 1975, Etienne Sacre formed Hurras al-Arz [Guardians of the Cedars]. This paramilitary group was heavily influenced by 'Aql's version of Lebanese nationalism, which insisted on Lebanon's Phoenician, not Arab, heritage. It also lobbied for replacing classical Arabic with a colloquial Lebanese dialect written in Latin script, an alphabet that 'Aql had developed. By 1976, the Guardians had joined the unified command of the Lebanese Forces. While a number of Lebanese authors were members of political parties and some were involved in the fighting of this early period, most became quickly disillusioned by the war or remained highly skeptical of its objectives.

Perhaps all who supported the war believed in some myth. Is it any coincidence that Joumblatt would write: "Bad news is always listened to attentively, and any secret which is leaked soon takes on the dimensions of myth" (53)? Interesting line, but Joumblatt has a specific axe to grind here as he accuses the Maronites of spreading rumors about the threat of an increasingly militant Palestinian presence in Lebanon. Whether this was a myth or reality, Joumblatt would offer revolution as the solution: "the silent struggle of honest people against mercantilism and political opportunism" (89). Perhaps this rhetoric masked another myth as well.

This is not to say that the myths that once and were now circulating about Lebanon were necessarily divorced from a reality of Lebanon. They constituted essential perspectives on how the nation was perceived and narrated.

The next phase of the war (following the intense battles of 1975–76 and ending with the Riad Summit and deployment of the inter-Arab force) was the period leading up to the 1982 Israeli invasion. This was a time of more intermittent warfare, punctuated by major political and military events, such as the March 1977 assassination of Kamal Joumblatt, the March 1978 Israeli invasion of South Lebanon, the summer 1978 Kata'ib attack on the rival Frangiye clan, 1978 Syrian and Kata'ib warfare, the summer 1980 Kata'ib militia victory over the rival Chamoun militia, and the 1979–82 Palestinian/Shi'a confrontation. In the region, not only were the Camp David Agreements signed in 1978, but the Iranian Revolution took place in 1979. Both would have lasting effects on Lebanon.

The Lebanese war that began as a result of an already complex mélange of factors was quickly becoming even more convoluted. The Syrians who entered ostensibly in defense of the Christians were now engaged in battle with them; the Christian forces were entwined in internal warfare with each other; and the Palestinians and Shi'a who fought side by side in the early war years were now engaged in prolonged combat over dominance of Beirut. The victory of Bashir Gemayel's Lebanese Forces over all other rival Christian groups coincided with increased cooperation with the Israelis. The Maronites, primarily restricted to the "Christian enclave" north and east of Beirut, began to talk more of Lebanese partition or cantonization rather than continuing to exist within the compromise system of the confessionally structured National Pact. Beirut was a divided city, and Lebanon was broken up into opposing sectors governed by armed militias. The government of Elias Sarkis was ineffectual, and the Lebanese army was a weak and divided armed group among dozens.

Despite the obvious instability and danger, some thought the war was over. The Lebanese were able to come out of their shelters for long periods at a time. Schools, universities, and businesses reopened, and many attended to the necessary repairs of their homes and workplaces. The displaced, many in and around Beirut, dug their heels deeper into the abandoned buildings or shantytowns illegally put up to meet their dire needs. Many exiles flew back to reassess their lives and consider their futures. Others remained abroad; many wrote from there. Books were also written and published in Beirut, TV and radio shows were produced, and theaters were reopened—but all in a limited capacity. In Elias Khoury's 1981 *Al-Wujuh al-bayda'* [The white faces], one of the narrators naively notes that the posters of martyrs are now being replaced by others: "This was normal because the war had ended, and the walls were full of poster ads for movies and theater" (22). Khoury and others could reflect on this period of shaky calm and appraise its meaning.

Many sought to evaluate the earlier 1975–76 war years, to place them in some context, to historicize and analyze them. In *The White Faces* Khoury contributes to this discourse by offering multiple, often conflicting readings of the war. Now that the war seems to be over, artists, filmmakers, writers, and intellectuals are trying to make sense of it. Khoury undermines this impulse by introducing a team of leftist quasi-intellectuals keen on making a documentary on the war. They seek out Fahd Badr al-Din (one of the six main narrators of this novel), a student and a fida'i pro-Palestinian fighter, to "act" his part. Unable to act, he methodically reads their stilted script:

> I am Muhammad al-Sayyid, fighter in the combined forces of the Palestinian Revolution and the Lebanese National Movement. We fight for the sake of Lebanon's Arabness, independence, and unity, and for the liberation of Palestine, against imperialism, Zionism, fascism, and reactionism. Stop. Look at the crimes of fascism. Stop. War, we do not love war; we fight for peace. Stop. Fascism commits brutal crimes, and we defend women and children. Stop. Many of my friends were martyred. I myself carried them in my arms and with their dying breaths they called out for freedom. Stop. I was shot in the eye; do you know my eye? Stop. (174)

The film director explains that after every "stop," the camera will focus on scenes from Tell al-Za'tar and the shelling of West Beirut. He encourages Fahd to put more feeling into his reading, to "act." But Fahd is resistant to the very idea of attempting to represent the war. His friend Samar argues for the important role of the media (especially film) in the revolution. "Imagine," she says as she lights up a Marlboro, "that we can picture death in a new way." She continues: "We film, for example, a corpse, a corpse thrown in the business souks, around it wild grasses, . . . The camera revolves quietly, then stops at the corpse, then zooms in on a wild flower blossoming alone in the middle of the grass. Isn't that a wonderful scene?" (178). The corpse will be stinking, replies Fahd. She smiles. Fahd muses that she knows nothing about death; she only knows what she sees in movies. "What if I told her about what happened to Samih?" (179). In a flashback, we learn about the death of his comrade Samih, who died in the Battle of the Mountains, a battle Khoury also focuses on in *The Little Mountain*. Like Talal's death there, Samih's death also has had a powerful effect on the narrator, who cannot reduce or explain it in words.

What Fahd does know is that war is ugly and terrible. Samar continues excitedly about the film project that will expose the fascists and their corrupt ways: "their killings, kidnappings, thefts, forced evacuations, destruction of homes." At this point, Fahd interrupts: "But we also . . . I told her that we also make mistakes and kill and . . ." She vehemently disagrees, but he reminds her of Damour, the Christian town that was destroyed in January 1976. She fires back, "Did you forget al-Maslakh, al-Karantina, al-Nabʿa, and Tal al-Zaʿtar?" (These are all areas destroyed by the Christian forces in 1975–76.) Wearily, he responds that what he is telling her is the truth. "No," she answers, "that is not the truth. The truth must serve the revolution!" (184).

This exchange reveals how readily and easily events can be molded to suit one history or another—how differing perspectives result in dramatically opposing narratives that seek to justify or explain or condemn. For Fahd, the war cannot be idealized or glorified. There were mistakes, and they were horrible. Perhaps the spirit of the revolution (if there was one) really is corrupt. If so, the war was all for naught; the deaths of comrades and ordinary citizens were meaningless.

Alongside these flashbacks, analyses, and artistic attempts of the early war years, Khoury's novel primarily takes place in 1980. Joumblatt has been assassinated, the Israelis have invaded, but many act as if, again, the war is finished and life has gone back to normal. The text provides evidence to the contrary. It centers on the mysterious death of Khalil Ahmed Jaber, a petty government employee whose mutilated corpse is found in a garbage heap. The primary narrator/journalist/quasi-autobiographical writer conducts a series of interviews with people associated with Jaber. Their narratives, which only occasionally make reference to Jaber, constitute the bulk of the novel. "These are unbelievable stories," according to Fatma Fakhru, one of the three female narrators whose husband kills their son and is killed himself, "but everything is possible these days; who would have believed that what happened would have happened, but it did" (121). We learn that Jaber changes drastically after his only son, Ahmed, is "martyred" in 1976. His hair turns white, and he becomes increasingly depressed. He spends his time collecting posters of his hero son and plastering them on walls. He buys erasers and proceeds to erase all newspaper references to his son. He no longer goes to work but isolates himself in his room, where he whites out the faces of the family photos, cuts them out, and exchanges faces with bodies. This is his new work. Later, he leaves his house and walks the streets whitewashing the walls of the city. It is this sad man whose death is the subject of this novel.

"This is not a story; it doesn't draw the attention of the reader in any special way, for people are busy these days with other more important issues than reading stories or listening to them; and the people are right. But the story did happen" (9). Khoury begins his novel this way with a focus on one of thousands of seemingly senseless murders. There is a name, but no motives, no solutions, no meaning. This is just one of many stories, not special or worthy, presented with a read-it-if-you-want attitude. Once the story is somehow told, Khoury provides the "Temporary Conclusion." Here he admits that he, the creator, does not know how to tell the story, that maybe he should have chosen a worthier subject instead of pursuing this ordinary corpse of an ordinary citizen (249). In the end, this story doesn't even "deserve the effort to read it," for "Khalil Ahmed Jaber, he's one of millions of original inhabitants of this country, and they're all exposed to death every day" (275). It is the ordinariness of violent death in current Lebanon that is precisely the point. If the war is over, then how do we account for killings that are performed as leisurely as if one were "drinking a Coke" (45). These are skewed times, and society is out of kilter.[10]

As Sweidan has convincingly demonstrated in his long chapter on this novel in *Abhath fi al-nass al-riwa'i al-'Arabi* [Studies in Arabic literary texts, 1986], Khoury's structure here is innovative and impressive. His complex layerings of narrators, each telling multiple stories, serve to ironically affirm, while denying, the significance of the text itself (193). The piecemeal way in which information is revealed about Khalil Jaber is not only unique but perfectly suited to the crime and to the puzzling situation Lebanon now finds itself in. Moreover, the multiple narratives tend themselves to dominate the text as oral narratives. Sweidan notes that the "expression is overcome by the mode of spoken narration" (241). These varied perspectives, together, offer the story.[11]

In Khoury's novel *Abwab al-medina* published in the same year (1981), he adopts a different style that, according to Stefan Meyer, represents perhaps an "extreme point of experimentation, from which he subsequently drew back" (194–95). Translated as *Gates of the City* in 1993, this fablelike novel only obliquely refers to Lebanon or its war, adopting a highly symbolic and abstract narrative style. An unnamed man stands before the walls of an unspecified city, women appear and lead him in various directions, his suitcase is lost and needs to be retrieved, the city is finally engulfed in destructive flames, and the sea floods the city and ends all. This minimalist plot is paralleled by the language, which features short, declarative sentences and repetition. It is both simple and ambiguous. The man, like the language, is deliberate in his every step/word. His absurdist world appears closed and frozen, with few meanings and little communication.

A structuralist aesthetic is partially achieved by Khoury's attention to binaries: man/woman, blindness/vision, clothes/nakedness, lost/found, enter/exit, fire/water, etc. It reads, in some ways, like a symbolist poem or short story. In fact, Meyer notes a parallel to the experimental short fiction of Khalil Gibran, "in its very abstract method of describing situations, its anonymous narrator, and its dreamlike events" (235).[12] Its vision, however, unlike Gibran's, is dark. It indirectly reflects a state of mind during war. It is a bleak reality where truth or fiction hardly make a difference: "The man said that he did not believe the story, but suppose it's true, and I accepted and we went, what changes? We would have sat before the sea and waited, gone to the tomb and waited, had children and waited, then the children die as do we" (104).

In her foreword to the English version of *Gates*, Sabah Ghandour insightfully discusses how Khoury's language changes in order to capture the "disintegration of the state. This formal effect is discerned in discursive change: something is happening to the narrative itself with respect to syntax, word choice, languages employed, narrative coherence, reference, and so on" (xv). Moreover, Khoury, in his war novels, "dismantles the traditional way of writing where cause and effect dominate the narrative structure" (xv). Neither is the plot chronological nor is the subject unified or whole. In *Gates*, the "dream verges on being real, and the real becomes slippery and intangible" (xvii). Like Samman's *Beirut Nightmares*, the surreal quality of war is also captured to a certain extent. The most striking feature of Khoury's text is that the narrative itself is worth nothing outside of its mode of telling. The language *is* the text and embodies all meanings and all possibilities of interpretation. The plot and characterization are worthless outside of the style in which they are presented.

It is clear that Khoury was very concerned with the theoretical issues that his novels raise. In the fall 1981 issue of *al-Mawaqif*, he published "Al-Naqd wa al-nass al-naqdi" [Criticism and the critical text], where he develops an argument for the kind of writing he does. On page 11 he writes: "The text that opens itself up to critique, must itself be a critical text structurally; i.e., it must be a diverse text, able to sustain more than one reading, and it must participate in establishing a critical language." He continues that writing is unable to effect "social transformation" when it is crushed, as it is now, during this era of quick "media consumption" and these times when "political authority has no popular support" whatsoever (14). True criticism, he believes, begins with a "critique of current Arab life—to read it and present different readings of it and to admit of this diversity. Diversity alone is the way to arrive at some sort of social unity. . . . In this way, criticism is created and it is freed from it being simply selective translation" (21).

Khoury's writing is important because it attempts to rethink the language and in the process prescribe new ways of imagining the nation. During the period of Lebanon's early war years (1975–76) and the interlude (1976–82) that followed, Khoury wrote three indicative novels that stretched the limits of previous perceptions of Lebanon. In all of them he foregrounded language itself as the vehicle not only of expression but of perception as well.

Another writer very intent on transforming language is Rachid al-Daʿif. His early publications of poems, aphorisms, short pieces, and fablelike stories are indicative of this concern.[13] In his 1980 *La Shayʾ yafuq al-wasf* [Nothing is beyond description], the language is the text as Daʿif puns, molds, and transforms Arabic to say new things. In the process, he also comments on the social reality of war. One sentence states, "Kul man qal qutil" (14); the repetition of k/q and l sounds cleverly intensifies this phrase so that it becomes a powerful poetic utterance which, when translated, blandly reads, "Whoever speaks is killed." In fact, the project of changing the language is literally under way here. Daʿif writes:

I hereby declare that the *n* is a *d*
Come and announce with me that the *n* is a *d*
I forget
Come and forget with me.
Come, let's do away with the verb and favor the object against the
subject.
Come, let's favor the crowds of the alphabet against the *dh*.
Dh is the heart of [in the middle of] ghadhab [anger].[14]
Come, let's toss the alphabet in the river, then go to the sea and
search for it, and the first letter one of us finds will become his
name, then it is thrown to a fish.
. . . .
Everything is memory except forgetfulness
And the nation is memory. (42–43)

In a section titled "Beirut," the narrator insists that the city is like his brain, "since in my brain cars move and park on sidewalks exactly as they do in Beirut." More ominously, "Places explode in my brain as they do in Beirut. . . . In my brain people's bloody bodies are torn and scattered everywhere. Exactly as in Beirut." The only difference between the two is that "my brain is unable to rest like Beirut. My brain is weaker than Beirut" (72–73). Da'if's whimsical and poignant narrative oscillates from descriptions of an innocent child discovering its belly button in the bath to depictions of inner rage and explosion. Amyuni writes that Da'if's style is "iconoclastic and rebellious, angry and ironic, tender, full of humor and flights of fantasy. . . . Al-Da'if's prose is highly poetic, moving by means of images, repetitions, echoes, and leitmotiv, while his poems come in vignettes, aphorisms, or just a few words that make up one line, lying there between empty spaces on a white page, shimmering with great vulnerability and delicacy of feeling" (1996, 180). In his 1979 *Hin halla al-sayf 'ala al-sayf* [When the sword cut short the summer], Da'if writes, "My country [watani], you've lost your W and T and N" (55). Only the *I* remains, suggesting not only the possessive pronoun, but the "ee" sound of lament. Language is indeed "betrayal," for it opposes change and preserves "forgetfulness" (51). Da'if's project is to mold the language into something new—this he does here and effectively in the many poems and novels that would follow in the 1980s and 1990s.

Because the novel clearly replaces the poem as forceful narrative during this period, there are only brief discussions of poetry here. Of course, many poets (some mentioned in the previous chapters) continued to be productive during the war. Joseph Abi Daher, Shawqi Abi Shaqra, Adonis, Sa'id 'Aql, Unsi al-Haj, Huda al-Naamani, Khalil Hawi, Fuad Rifqa, Nadia Tueni, Henri Zoghaib, and others continued to write.[15] The Syrian poet Nizar Qabbani, who had lived many years in Lebanon and established a publishing company there, wrote a series of poems elegizing Beirut. One poem, "Ya sitt al-dunia ya Beirut" [Beirut, mistress of the world], was put to song and popularized by Majida al-Roumi in the late 1970s.

Qabbani's poem reinforces what had already become a distinguishing mark of Lebanon: Beirut's preeminence. In some of the texts studied in the previous chapters, one saw the gradual shift from imagining Lebanon in terms of its villages to focusing on Beirut as the psychological center of the country. The war, although it spread to most areas of Lebanon, was concentrated in the city as most of the fictions just examined bear out. It was primarily an urban war that took dramatic tolls on the once popularly perceived beautiful city. Qabbani's rendition of Beirut's fall and his call for its resurrection captured the imagination and was quickly committed to memory with these lines, which begin in Arabic: "qumi min taht al mawj al-azraq, ya 'Ishtar":

> Rise from under the blue waves, O Ishtar,
> Rise like a poem of roses,
> Or rise like a poem of fire.
> There is nothing before you . . . after you . . . like you.
> You are the essence of the ages.
> O field of pearls
> O harbor of love.

The poet, continuing to address Beirut, laments that, like all beauties, she has paid a high price for her beauty. The persona then confesses that we all took advantage of the feminized city: We loved and left you, we joined the killers and witnessed your execution, we envied you. Consumed with guilt, the poet pleads:

> We confess before the one God
> That we used to envy you
> And your beauty irritated us.

This long lyrical poem then ends with "I still love you, O Beirut / Why don't we begin now?"[16] Beirut is Ishtar, the Phoenician goddess, as much mystified in her fall as she was in her supposed days of glory (as Gibran and others have demonstrated). Qabbani's poem was collected in *Ila Beirut al-untha . . . ma'hubbi* [To Beirut the woman, with my love]. The introduction (dated 1976) clearly imagines the city in terms of an idealized (and now fallen) womanhood. The poem above and four others constitute a crystallizing and mythologizing tribute to Beirut, now in the midst of violence, providing a powerful and increasingly popular narrative on Lebanon.

Other poetic talents began to emerge as well. In her *Al-Kitaba: Tahawwul fi al-tahawwul: Muqaraba li al-kitaba al-adabiyya fi zaman al-harb al-Lubnaniyya* [Writing: Transformation of the transformation: A study of comparative literature during the Lebanese war years, 1993], Yumna al-Eid devotes a few chapters to poetry. She says that most poets opposed the war and stood by its victims, writing poetry as a way of resistance. She cites poets like Hasan Abdallah, Muhammad Abdallah, Shawqi Bzai', and Muhammad Ali Shamseddine. They were known as "al-Shu'ara al-Shabab" (the young poets), and their collections of the late 1970s focus on martyred sons, weeping mothers, the suffering of the nation, and the hope of resistance, etc. (121–27). A more detailed examination of these poets' works of the 1980s will follow in the next chapter.

In terms of musical theater, the popular Rahbani brothers had failed to produce successful musicals in the period just before the outbreak of war. The safe, idealized village settings no longer rang true in a sociopolitical urban environment increasingly filled with tension. After 1975, the Rahbani spirit, according to Abu Murad, seemed to break. Where were the people and the nation they sang to about stability and tranquility (189)? To make matters worse, Fayruz broke away from the creative Rahbani team and would never again star in their musicals. Her husband 'Asi also suffered serious illness. Abu Murad writes that it was as if the Rabhanis, like Lebanon, were falling apart. Not surprisingly, for the first five years of the war they did not produce any musicals. Their last two plays were the 1980 *Al-Mu'amara mustamirra* [The plot continues] and the 1981 *Al-Rabi' al-sabi'* [The seventh spring]. Both take on the war with scenes of checkpoints, armed figures, and family victims, but they are thematically and stylistically timid, lacking any overt political statements and virtually doing away with the memorable poetic language that captured the Lebanese imagination for decades.

In contrast, the play and musical by Ziad Rahbani, *Film Amirki tawil* [Long American film, 1980], opens with a voice-over stating that the action occurs in September 1980, or maybe 1979, or even 1978. There is really no difference, since the political situation hasn't changed. Taking place in a hospital in the slums of southern Beirut (overrun by the sound of planes coming in to land at the nearby airport), patients, staff, and relatives engage in absurd conversations about the "situation." Some suggest that it is an American conspiracy after all (170). The confusion in the ward parallels the confusion in the political arena, as political parties, confessionalism, partition, and conspiracy theories all circulate.

Rahbani continues his humorous word play. In one scene, for example, two patients scorn the confessional group [ta'ifi] and ply the word until it becomes tayifi [flooded (also in Arabic "tayifi")] (52). In the course of the dialogue, political agendas and ideological positions are whittled down to words, puns, and bizarre expressions. In another scene, the patients Rachid and Nizar discuss the latter's membership in a party. Is it the "social" or the "national" movement? Well, it is the national movement, but it can also be social. Rachid seems disbelieving that the movement can encompass so much: "What . . . Why . . . For what . . . all these movements, boy?" Nizar replies: "These are for the society, to develop society, the struggle, to defeat conspiracies, imperialism, reactionism, all of it!" Rachid finally resigns himself to this sweeping agenda; he obviously likes the sound of the rhetoric and concludes with a frankly untranslatable line: "Ah . . . look . . . I very much, I mean, like to encourage these things" (51) [Ah . . . wallah layk . . . ana shee ktir ya'ni bhibb shajji' hal shi]. The astoundingly familiar colloquial itself validates whatever nonsense Rachid has just uttered.

With his humor still intact, Rahbani has added an element of bitter cynicism to the sociopolitical fabric of his fictional world. Whereas the two plays produced in the 1970s made fun of that system, the need for war or revolution seemed at least partially understandable, even justifiable. After five years of war, however, it became increasingly difficult to locate any redeeming or restorative qualities to it, nor was it clear who the enemies and allies were. As one of Rahbani's characters yells out, "No one understands anything anymore" (178). Some of Khoury's characters had already arrived at the same conclusion. The war had set everything in flux. The commemoratives by Qabbani and the exaltations by Fayruz remained popular but, to many, outdated. Adopting the same formats, the same rhetoric, the same language, when one's reality was so categorically altered seemed hypocritical.

Instead, a willingness emerged to experiment, to reconceive the nation linguistically, and to reconstruct Lebanon psychologically. Without a doubt, the war years yielded important novels, new kinds of narratives that ironically consolidated the nation while it seemed on the verge of collapse. Benedict Anderson discusses how the novel's arrival in Europe coincided with the evolution of the nation; it became the nation's most significant mode of confirmation. In the case of Lebanon, the novel per se does not emerge as a cultural force until the nation is seemingly self-destructing. The next chapter will continue this narrative of war, beginning with perhaps the most significant event of the sixteen-year conflict, Israel's 1982 invasion of Lebanon.

5

Living with War

I went towards the door to open it, as I heard knocking. . . . Six people. I
went towards the door, opened it with my left hand . . . took one step outside,
and said in a loud voice, "Yes?"
    After that I can't remember a thing.
    I was killed at once.

Rachid al-Da'if, *Fusha mustahdafa bayna al-na'usi wa al-nawm*, 1986

The 1982 Israeli invasion was a watershed year for Lebanon. It devastated
entire sections of the country, altered the political and military players,
and revised the discourse on Lebanon significantly. The invasion acted as
a catalyst for various kinds of cultural production. It shook—and in some
ways awakened—the fatigued nation in ways that need to be acknowledged.

On June 3, 1982, the Israeli ambassador was shot in London, providing
the needed excuse for an Israeli offensive against its neighbor to the north.
According to David Gordon, the time was right for Israel to strike, because
the government wanted to destroy Syria's SAM-6s in Lebanon, crush the
PLO, and seize the headwaters of the Litani River (141). The Israelis also
sought to reshape Lebanon, linking their offensive with the political aspirations of the rising militia leader, Bashir Gemayel. With tacit approval by
the United States, the Israeli military, under the leadership of Ariel Sharon,
crossed the border on June 6 with a massive force of over 80,000 soldiers
and 500 tanks, along with complete air and sea control. By June 9, the
Israelis had occupied most of the South, and by June 13, Beirut was totally
surrounded. The siege would last seventy days, during which civilian and
military targets were shelled and basic supplies were cut off. Over 18,000
Lebanese and Palestinians were killed with over 30,000 wounded. The
material damages ran into the billions of dollars.

The literary critic Yumna al-Eid abandoned her usual professional style when writing about this period in her 1993 book, *Al-Kitaba* [Writing]. Although ostensibly a critical book about the literature of the war years, she cannot contain herself as she describes the Israeli atrocities in Saida, her city. "How could they call themselves a Defense force when they killed Lebanese on their own soil?" (27). Indeed, the army was "Israel's Defense Force," and its mission was labeled "Peace for Galilee." It was a milestone event that many (primarily Maronites) hoped would secure for the Christians a prominent political role once again in a Lebanon devoid of Palestinians and Syrians. In fact, some Muslims also greeted the Israelis with flowers and celebratory rice, since they were disillusioned by the strong PLO presence on their land. The opposition by most Arab states was primarily rhetorical, calling on all Lebanese and Palestinians to "resist the Zionist enemy" and persist with the "just revolution against the oppressor." Although the Syrian army and air force offered resistance, they were forced to retreat systematically in the face of superior Israeli strength.

It soon became clear that the Israelis were not simply retaliating for the wounding of the Israeli ambassador, nor were their far-reaching objectives in Lebanon achievable without huge civilian casualties. As the media broadcast the devastation abroad, even the United States seemed appalled and put pressure on General Ariel Sharon to choose a diplomatic rather than a military solution to the problem. By August, Philip Habib, a personal emissary of President Reagan, was shuttling between world capitals trying to work out a way to end the hostilities and to evacuate the PLO from Lebanon. An arrangement was worked out, and by September 1 the Palestinian guerrillas had left Beirut.

More violence, however, was in store for Lebanon. The term of President Elias Sarkis was over, and Bashir Gemayel, bolstered by the Israeli presence, had announced his candidacy. On August 23, he was elected president on the second ballot by fifty-seven votes out of a bare quorum of sixty-two at the Lebanese Military Academy under Israeli surveillance. Although he had been the leader of the Lebanese Forces, there were signs that, as president, he was willing (and eager) to broaden his support and steer Lebanon on a centrist course not necessarily in Israel's camp. On September 14, he was assassinated. Israel moved into West Beirut, allowing the angry members of Gemayel's Lebanese Forces to enter the Palestinian camps of Sabra and Chatila immediately and massacre hundreds of civilians in four days. World outrage at these atrocities reverberated within

Israel itself, where many called for a swift withdrawal and reassessment of Israel's "Vietnam."

On September 21, Bashir's older brother Amin was elected president by a majority of seventy-seven out of eighty parliamentarians present. More political and diplomatic than Bashir, with closer ties to the Arab and Muslim world, Amin hoped to save Lebanon from its invaders and internal morass. With no substantial political or social changes, though, it was unlikely that a resolution for Lebanon's problems was forthcoming. Indeed, until the Taef Agreement of 1989, Lebanon continued to be at war with itself, although intermittently.

The 1980s are primarily characterized by taking stock of the 1982 invasion and its aftermath. Other than Palestine's Jerusalem, never before had an Arab capital been occupied by Israel, never had the Lebanese and Palestinians, already accustomed to seven years of fighting, been exposed to such a level of high-tech military destruction. The tanks were so large that they crushed cars on both sides of the streets as they advanced, and the shelling was so powerful that it brought down tall buildings like pancakes. Nothing was spared. Hospitals, shelters, and schools were hit. Even those who supported the Israelis in the beginning quickly became suspicious of their motives and tactics. Their presence on Lebanese soil rallied the nation in new ways with an outpouring of cultural expression.

Eid talks about how, despite the savage destruction of Beirut, the Israelis were unable to "prevent cultural resistance" to their invasion. In fact, it flourished with the production of songs, posters, poetry, plays, and novels (29). The city, which had already become the synecdoche for Lebanon, now took on more poignant significance. Beirut, the once beautiful queen, seductress, jewel of the Mediterranean, was raped, mutilated, fallen. The invasion, like the 1967 *naksa* or defeat, made for perfect poetic subject. Poets from around the Arab world competed to lament the tragedy of Beirut. From the Palestinian Mahmoud Darwish to the Syrian/Lebanese Adonis, works were composed on Beirut, the new symbol of the Arab tragedy.[1]

In 1985, Adonis's book of sixteen poems on the invasion, *Kitab al-hisar* [Book of the siege], was published. This powerful and moving rendition captures the magnitude of the Israeli action. What follows are stanzas 24 and 25:

The airborne killer
circles the wounded city.
The wound is the fall of the city.

It shivers at the mention of its name —
its name now written in blood.
Everything changes around us.
Houses have no interiors.
Even I am not myself any longer

Bombs are mirrored in books
along with prophecies and ancient wisdom
and hidden places.
Memory is a needle
that stitches a carpet of words like threads
over the face of Beirut.[2]

The locale of destruction resides in the city where, not coincidentally, many of the Arab world's leading writers once lived. The aura of Beirut, already huge before the war, and made more complicated and tragic by the urban guerrilla warfare of 1975–76, now takes on yet another dimension with the Israeli siege. Beirut, more than ever before, became a mythic and symbolic city that warranted extensive commentary and lament.

Although published in 1989, Khoury's *Rihlat Ghandi al-saghir*, translated in 1994 as *The Journey of Little Gandhi*,[3] looks back to the dark days of the siege and particularly to September 15, 1982, when the Israelis entered West Beirut after the assassination of Bashir Gemayel. While Gandhi the shoe shiner and many others are killed on that day, it is Beirut, personified, that is forever transformed. As the planes soar and the bombs fall, Gandhi realizes that "the bullets weren't aimed at him, but rather at the heart of a city that destroyed itself" (194). Beirut seems to weep as "the salt that was spreading through the city melted in the raindrops" (18)—this was the "rain that scorched Beirut the morning of September 15, 1982" (187). Before, Beirut "never cried. Beirut was a city of sparkling nights that trotted across the surface of the sea" (134), but it changed, becoming a "Tower of Babel" (111). Gandhi spends most of his working life in Beirut, not realizing that, as a result, he has "traveled more than all the shoe shiners in the world." For Beirut has itself traveled: "You stay where you are and it travels. Instead of you traveling, the city travels. Look at Beirut, transforming from the Switzerland of the East to Hong Kong, to Saigon, to Calcutta, to Sri Lanka. It's as if we circled the world in ten or twenty years" (5). On that fateful day when Gandhi would die on his shoe shine box, "the Israelis entered Beirut and the city was filled with their black boots, their beards, and their stench" (61). They shot Gandhi, and his friend Alice would cover his body with newspapers:

> The newspapers covering the body of the little man dissolved under the light September rain. The color black oozed from the body, and the body swelled. The light rain poured down silently, and the newspapers got soaked and became transparent, the black words seeped out of them. The color black rolled onto the street to the curb filled with black trash bags.
>
> Everything was black. Soldiers' boots, their rifles, their faces, their screams in the streets, and the hissing of bullets as they tore out buildings and windows.
>
> Bullets, and silence. A dawn of light rain and boots, the city awakened as if it were asleep. (84)

Beirut represents more than its streets, buildings, and inhabitants; it is a living organism that laughs, cries, breathes, speaks, is awakened. The city completes the tragedy of the nation. As Ghandour notes in her introduction to *Gandhi*, Beirut is "the major character in the novel" (xvii). Significantly, the novel reveals how Beirut falls apart, is altogether altered and torn to pieces by the impact of Israel's offensive in Lebanon.

Khoury, who is a prolific journalist as well as novelist, also wrote frequent editorials to the leftist newspaper *Safir* on the aftermath of the invasion. Collected in 1985 as *Zaman al-ihtilal* [Time of occupation], these articles are conceived as a "cycle in our national resistance" (5). Like other Arab intellectuals, Khoury, along with Adonis and others, also participated in forums and joint collections that sought to appraise the implications of 1982. The literary journal *Al-Adab*, for example, devoted a special winter 1983 issue to the invasion. Entitled "Istifta' al-adab al-kabir: al-Muthaqqafun wa al-hazima" [*Al-Adab*'s Big Referendum: The Intellectuals and the Defeat], the issue is a consortium of thirty-six Arab intellectuals from Damascus, Baghdad, Beirut, Kuwait, Morocco, Tunis, Yemen, Paris, and London. The editorial charge laid out at the beginning of this issue reads:

> There is no doubt that the Defeat upon the Arab nation as a result of the Zionist enemy against the Lebanese and Palestinian people warrants Arab intellectuals, and especially writers, to review their ideas and

reassess their role in the Arab struggle against imperialism, Zionism, reactionism, and backwardness.

How do you look at new Arab culture and education and to the role that they should take in leading us out of the Defeat and in saving future Arab generations from despair? (vol. 1, p. 2)

Each of the thirty-six then attempts to address this question in light of the 1982 assault. The collection provides some worthwhile insights to the discussion of Lebanon at this juncture. One might note at the outset the rhetorical and sloganistic flavor of the journal's mission. The editor, Suheil Idriss, is known for his Arab nationalist sentiments; the choice of invitees, not surprisingly, reflects that ideology. For the most part, the Israeli Invasion of Lebanon is presented as an Arab problem. Most of the respondents are non-Lebanese, and very few of those make any specific reference to Lebanon. The overall sentiment of these writers is anger at the passivity of Arab regimes that remained silent at the destruction, even while Israel "slaughtered" children on Arab land. Israel has succeeded not only in a military defeat but in a defeat of the Arab spirit. The year 1982 is now added to the list of other devastating dates (the *nakba* of 1948 and the *naksa* of 1967) that mark Israel's victories over the Arabs. According to these writers, the Arabs are to blame for lacking the courage and the moral rectitude to stand up against this humiliation of an Arab capital subjected to three months of a terrible siege. In other words, the fate of the Arab nation is further compromised by Israel's actions in Lebanon, one of the twenty-two states that compose that umma.

As far as the role intellectuals and culture can play, many blame Arab regimes for discouraging healthy debate. In his response, "Khitab al-fikr wa khitab al-mal" [Speech of thought and speech of money], Adonis questions *Al-Adab*'s assumption that there even is a "new Arab culture and education" and that it could have any "new role," for that presupposes that the Arab climate today is one that encourages freedom and truth. Instead, there is an atmosphere of political and religious surveillance that constantly reduces humanity and human rights. As for Arab thaqafa [culture], it is either, according to Adonis, old, traditional, and inactive or new, media-oriented, superficial, but active (17). Unless and until the whole nature of thaqafa changes, it can have no substantial and positive transformative effect.

The many responses by leading Arab literary figures like Adonis, Jabra

Ibrahim Jabra, and Abdel Rahman Munif, along with the comments by Arab critics and professors, reinforces the idea of Lebanon as consumed under the larger Arab watan or umma. The 1982 invasion is pertinent in its clarification of Arab culture, Arab regimes, Arab defeat. A grouping of Lebanese writers provides a slightly different perspective, as Elias Khoury and three Poets of the South (or Young Poets) write from within Beirut itself.

Khoury's entry, entitled "Liyasqut al-fikr al-irhabi awwalan" [First, may the terrorist thinking fall], refers repeatedly to Beirut, Lebanon, and the Lebanese/Palestinian tragedy, but the Arab context remains absolutely relevant. He berates the Arabs who still claim victory in the face of the most obvious defeats, and then he cynically reconsiders: Perhaps they were victorious in their restraint against the enemy and in their conquest over their own people. A writer composing under these conditions is either a slave or killed. We cannot, Khoury asserts, participate in the program of social transformation unless we save ourselves first. He concludes by wondering if this resistance in Beirut, this Lebanese/Palestinian tragedy, can plant the seeds of a new consciousness. Here we are in a city "occupied by the ghost of occupation and besieged by Arab death" (37). This strong indictment against the Arabs serves to reinforce the tragedy of the Lebanese and Palestinians who are as much defeated by Israel as they are by fellow Arabs.

In "Thaqafat tams al-haqa'iq" [The culture that buries truths], the Lebanese poet Hasan Abdallah also claims his geographical perspective within Lebanon, but he speaks to the larger Arab public:

> I speak from Lebanon, where the ground is still shaking and the thick smoke clouds the horizons. The Israeli tanks are on the hills, and the prospects for this country are still open to the worst options. Lebanon's fate, and the fate of the Palestinian people, and the fate of the Arabs collectively . . . I can only record by truthful testimony and share my personal experiences. Sometimes I wonder if I am able to say everything. . . .
>
> No one can capture what I saw and heard and discovered. Others will want to make excuses and cover up, to make the disaster a festivity. Because it is a culture that eradicates truths. . . . What is required instead is a new culture that is bold and hard, that can transform the broken Arab spirit to a positive struggle for change. (45)

The Iraqi-born writer Daisy al-Amir, who never left Beirut during the war, believes that those who stayed earned the right to speak, whether they were Lebanese or not. After she describes what life was like on a daily basis during this war, she announces that if she had despaired she would have left or committed suicide (perhaps a reference to her friend, the poet Khalil Hawi, whose suicide in 1982 many attributed to the invasion).[4] Instead, she remained, reinforcing her hope in the future: "And I still wait, for I am the Arab that does not despair" (73).

The pan-Arab quality of *Al-Adab*'s referendum reminds one again of the complicated nature of Lebanese identity. When the nation is, by many, defined in terms of a larger nation, then its problems are never solely its own, nor are the Arab regional issues irrelevant to it. This constant interplay between "al-qadiyya al-Lubnaniyya" [the Lebanese problem] and the Arab one became itself yet another reason for the armed conflict. Many experienced the Israeli Invasion as a specifically Lebanese tragedy, so were upset when the Arabs claimed victimization and defeat. Also, the Palestinian qadiyya, which had already so powerfully displaced many of the Lebanese myths of nationhood, was able to capitalize, so to speak, on the invasion. Many Lebanese, for example, were offended when reports of Palestinian casualties were broadcast alongside the tragic scenes of forced evacuation of the PLO.[5] The invasion touched many already raw nerves, as the varied cultural output it generated illustrated. The intellectual and creative spirit that dominated the pages of *Al-Adab* was matched by other journals that devoted special sections to the invasion. In addition, the daily press was filled with editorials, poems, essays, and tributes on the effects and implications of Israel's actions in Lebanon. Songs, plays, novels, like Khoury's 1989 *Rihlat Ghandi*, now had to take account of this significant event.

One of the important effects of the invasion on Lebanon was that it fueled not only a new political ideology but a cultural and literary movement as well. Another qadiyya emerged: the South (al-Junub). Whereas Beirut, as symbol and site, had dominated the cultural psyche for decades, the rural South now took on growing importance in the Lebanese imagination. For decades, of course, the South had its special features and problems. Primarily the site of repeated Israeli attacks and the region of Lebanon's poorest Shi'a sect, most attempted to make a living growing tobacco with little if any government assistance. The area fell behind most regions of the country (especially the Christian-dominated ones) with regards to basic infrastructure (roads, electricity, decent schools and hospitals). Also, since the 1969 Cairo Agreement, which legitimized Palestinian commando activity from parts of South Lebanon into Israel, the South had to share turf with Palestinians engaged in their war against Israel. Consequently, the South suffered the almost constant wrath of Israeli bombardment. The invasion of 1978 and then 1982 sealed the fate of hundreds of thousands of southern Shiʿa, many of whom finally fled their villages to seek shelter and employment in what would become known as the "belt of misery," the southern suburbs [al-Dahia] of Beirut.

In the late 1960s, the Iranian-educated Imam Musa Sadr founded the Movement of the Deprived [Mahrumin], representing the poor Shiʿa within Lebanon. Traditionally, this group had been under the political leadership of wealthy Shiʿa landowners. Sadr's movement foregrounded economic issues dealing with the need for proper infrastructure, cost controls, etc. By 1974, the Amal, an acronym meaning "hope" but standing for "afwaj al-muqawama al-Lubnaniyya" [Brigades of the Lebanese Resistance], was formed as the military wing of the Movement of the Deprived. With the outbreak of war in 1975, Amal fought on the side of the Left (combined forces of the Palestinian resistance and the Lebanese National Movement). In September 1978, the Shiʿa suffered a huge shock when Sadr disappeared while on a visit to Libya. However, in January 1979, the successful revolution in Iran proved to be a boost for the Shiʿa, and they mobilized to become more significant players within Lebanon's political system.

Since the 1976 expulsion of Palestinians from the camps in East Beirut, more Palestinian refugees had moved into already crowded camps and suburbs in the southwest section of Beirut, primarily inhabited by Shiʿa. The PLO was still heavily armed and quickly took control of these areas much to the frustration of the Shiʿa. In addition, the Palestinians had, in many cases, taken over Shiʿa homes, farms, and land in the South to lob their shells into northern Israel, resulting in intense Israeli shelling of Shiʿa villages. From 1979 on, bitter fighting erupted between Amal (now under the leadership of Nabih Berri) and the PLO.

The 1982 Israeli Invasion incurred such heavy losses in the South and displaced so many Shiʿa that it is no wonder a new political party would emerge, breaking off from the relatively moderate Amal leadership. During that invasion, Syria allowed a few hundred Iranian Revolutionary Guards to enter Lebanon, participate in the war against Israel, and establish a branch of Hizballah [Party of God]. Under the leadership of Hussein Moussavi,

this new party broke away from Amal and allied itself with Islamic fundamentalists, calling for an Islamic state within Lebanon. Funded by Iran
and supported by Syria, Hizballah easily established training camps in Lebanon and recruited thousands of young men to wage a constant war, primarily against the Israeli occupiers in the South and the Western peacekeep-
ing troops brought in to monitor the PLO evacuation of 1982. By 1983,
suicide bombers brought down the barracks of the American and French
troops, forcing them to withdraw the following year. Hizballah's bold assaults against Israeli troops within the so-called security zone gained them
increased respect across broad areas of Lebanon. Additionally, Hizballah's
popularity rose as it sought to actively improve the daily lives of poor Shi'a.
They secured water and electricity, built schools and hospitals, and instituted an extensive network of charities throughout the South, the Bekaa
region, and Dahia.

In fact, Hizballah's popularity was undermining the political agenda of
Amal, which found itself not only locked in battle with Palestinians (roughly
from 1979 to 1988) but in clear opposition to the Lebanese government.
Displeased with the policies of Gemayel's regime, Amal clashed with the
Lebanese army in 1983, and in 1984 initiated the division of that army. In
1985, Amal clashed with the Druze militias; in 1987 they fought the com-
bined forces of the Left, which led to yet another Syrian entry into the
Lebanese capital on February 22. Amal's ongoing battles with the PLO
simmered to a stop by 1988 and the beginning of the Palestinian Intifada.
As Hanf puts it, Amal could now turn its attention to a "new adversary":
Hizballah (314).

These two Shi'a groups had very different visions of Lebanon. Amal
called for a "majority democracy" vote, whereby the Shi'a (since they were
the largest sect) would play a leading role; Hizballah wanted an Islamic
Republic modeled after Iran. Heavily financed by Iran, Hizballah managed to gain control of most of the southern suburbs, clashing in fierce
battles with Amal in 1988. Syria once again intervened and put a halt to
the fighting, but the Shi'a groups were already both powerful and destined
to play increasingly important roles in Lebanon.

The Shi'a, once the most underrepresented and downtrodden of Lebanese sects, became pivotal players in the politics of the 1980s. Throughout
this period of Shi'a ascendancy, however, Shi'a villagers continued to be
subjected to Israeli offensives with minimal regard by the official government. Their cause began to be heard increasingly in the popular songs of

Marcel Khalife, Khaled al-Habr, and Julia and in the rhetoric of politicians of the opposition and among journalists and the intelligentsia.

Irrespective of the military posturing of the militias, the plight of the South came to dominate the Lebanese imagination. Politicians began to insert the word *al-Junub* into their rhetorical speeches and essays—almost a sure way to win applause. Typical phrasing is evident in Ali al-Khalil's essay, "The Role of the South in Lebanese Politics."[6] The South "is the key to the Lebanese settlement, aspiring to liberate the national homeland from without and the human individual from within. . . . It is the base of the noble and heroic resistance holding the torch of confrontation before the aggressors" (305). This hortatory style, so typical of politicians using the latest qadiyya, contrasted with a more genuine lament and show of outcry in other cultural outputs, especially in a new school of poetry represented by Shu'ara al-Junub [Poets of the South].

Primarily Shi'a, these poets drew much of their inspiration from the specific tragic fate of the displaced and dispossessed Shi'a of South Lebanon. "Al-Junub" often figures as a metaphor for oppression, alienation, and despair. Even when located in Beirut, most identify with a "village," often in the shrit [occupied zone]. In some ways, the contrast between urban Beirut and rural village is maintained here, paralleling earlier contrasts within the Lebanese literary tradition. Both versions of the village suggest an idealized or nostalgic quality that has been shattered. For the earlier writers, that idealism is threatened by Ottoman oppression, religious dominance, and corrupt urban ways. For the new poets, the village is shattered by clear Israeli aggression. While Beirut remained at the center of Lebanese concerns, a new consideration of the village now takes place. More specifically, a new attention to the villages of the rural South is now evident, signifying yet another changing perception of the nation.

Eid analyzes the poetry of Shawqi Bzai' and notes the intense lyricism filled with sorrow depicted alternately in funerals and weddings, scenes of southerners before the waters of the Litani River, thrown across the tobacco plants, captivated by the memory of Karbala. In his 1984 poem "Al-'Ai'd" [He who returns], Bzai' describes the funeral of a martyr from the South, including phrases of the mourners and the lamentation of his mother:

The Southerners walk behind the bier,
Their Koufiyyas stained by his covered forehead,

A woman follows
She smells his shirt
. . . .
He returns to the earth
Wrapped in a sandbag and a torn flag,
. . . .
Thorn of the age
Lost is the age
. . . .
But oh! . . . if only time could return again!
Or the shots reach
If the baker could heal you
If a live grass could restore you
We'd plant all the grasses of earth on your tomb.

Eid points out that despite the elegiac tone, the poem concludes with a strong, confident voice of the poet who seems to address the martyr:

A road will emerge from your bones
To cut a path with its beautiful spear
And to resist the occupier
And to resist the occupier.[7]

Abbas Beydoun also writes elegiac and funereal poems, especially about the destruction of his town, Sur (Tyre), memorialized in a 1985 poem by that name. Here is an excerpt:

We danced in your souks
Between the rounds of mad bullets,
Walked with eyes fixed on the ground
Searching for bonds lost in the wild.
And so it went—
We ended up with eunuchs' hearts
Faces numb as shoe soles
Fear of going where the night's rats go.
We denied the sound of your thunder and rain
And were condemned to learn each day the language
Of the crabs that rot in the sea.[8]

Eid notes that the poet has gradually disappeared in a world where war is the only active element. Unlike the prophetic voice of the Gibranic poet, the traditional rhetoric of Shawqi, or the lyricism of Qabbani, this new experimental poetry like that of Beydoun disturbs rather than resolves. Poetry is no longer simply oratory or a declaration (Eid 135).

Another example of the import of the wounding of the city is witnessed in Jawdat Fakhr al-Din's short poem, "A Handful of the Southern Wind":

Our migration just doesn't end
And the wheat—before our eyes—its plains are endless
All the alleys and the curving hills are acquainted
        with us
And our tears know only one path
And the sun still waits for "Aitaroun"
To escort it on its journey towards blood
That frightens the tribes
Aflame with tobacco and spikes of wheat
The evening suddenly halted at the villages' gates
While the sea came closer:
Advance ye tireless fighter
And grant the farmers a handful of the southern wind
Then depart into the crimson of dust
Though they besiege our grief, the trees continue to grow
Oh, you beautiful fighter do you see
How beautiful death is at the villages' gates?[9]

Tropes of the land, the vegetation, familiar nature, dominate the landscape of this poetry, broadening the notion of Lebanon as being only represented through Beirut. It is still a poetry presenting war, though now in new terms and with a different set of priorities.

The poems of Muhammad 'Ali Shams al-Din also offer a new and powerful perspective on loss, on lament:

We are finished.
Everyone went to his death
and waited,
but we learned no wisdom from
the lovers
who were finished
before us.
Love is mindless:
Vision is the source

of misery.
I was not blind
but I had bad timing, bad luck,
and bad friends.[10]

Lebanon's tragedy and narrative have now shifted to the South, where political choices and unfortunate fate play themselves out.

Intellectuals and journalists who had previously identified with the city
took on the new cause of the South and published numerous pieces on the
Israeli Invasion and its aftermath. Many of these essays were published in
Beirut in a 1985 book called *Al-Muqawama fi al-ta'bir al-adabi*. Among
more than forty contributors are the Poets of the South along with critics
like Yumna al-Eid and Samah Idriss and writers who usually conceptual-
ized the city like Elias Khoury and Adonis. Perhaps the most striking aspect of Adonis's article, "Junub al-kitaba: 'Ara'iss al-ruh wa 'Ara'iss al-jasad"
[South of the writing: weddings of the spirit and weddings of the body], is
that it was written at all. For someone who usually concerns himself with
broad theoretical issues relating to Arab culture, literature, and society, the
focus on a specific locale, South Lebanon, as a new and worthy site of
inquiry, is significant. He scorns Western labels of "Shi'ite Terrorism" as
he depicts the "slaughtered villages" of the South. The resistance there
gives a whole new meaning to death, he writes (53). He notes that his critics wonder why he is writing about the South, but it is here that the big
questions of humanity are played out. Perhaps what is happening in the
South, he writes, can serve as a wake-up call and help generate new meanings and a new kind of discourse.

As usual, the popular critic and playwright Ziad Rahbani put a cynical
spin on the situation after the invasion and specifically on the new pre-
dominance of the South. His 1983 play *Shi fashil* [What a failure] offered
a biting satire on many aspects of Lebanese politics and culture. The
main character, Nur, is the director of a musical he is in the process of
rehearsing. It is a typically "folkloric" setting complete with villagers,
mayor [mukhtar], and young woman [sabiyyi], all dressed in traditional
garb. The villagers are happy, frequently breaking into song and dance
[dabke], until the disaster occurs: The symbolic village jug is stolen from
the square. This obviously ridiculous crisis is set against 1983 Beirut, where
the actors and stage crew have to deal with Israeli occupation, a divided
city, unsafe roads, shelling, etc. The play continues with its idealistic songs
(complete with simplistic rhymes in the Arabic):

We are all brothers and will remain so
We'll bring back the good days, our village square
        will light up again . . .
In faith and love, we will rebuild Lebanon
We'll create a new Lebanon, full of song and grape
        bunches
O our country.

The chorus sings as the crew tries to lower a cedar onto the stage. The juxtaposition is both comical and painful. With a plot and a dramatic mood reminiscent of his own family's musicals, Ziad Rahbani resurrects the hero mayor and the savior young woman (usually played by Ziad's own mother, Fayruz). A journalist from the French Beirut daily *L'Orient le Jour* praises Nur's play for "le vrai folklore libanais" (163).

As the rehearsals continue, we learn that the jug thief is a "gharib" [stranger]. As the characters wonder if there is a hidden meaning here, a lightbulb goes off. In fact, in a hilarious interview between the unsuspecting Nur and a reporter from the leftist newspaper *Safir*, the latter deduces that the play is a sophisticated political critique and the "outsider" must mean the aggressor Israel (101). The French-speaking journalist above, however, interprets the "outsider" to be the Palestinian [le falastinien] who was invited into Lebanon only to cause a rift among the Lebanese (165). "Whatever," responds Nur—he is too busy putting the final touches on the still messy production.

When the producer Nazih realizes that the play is costing too much money, he curses folklore and then strongly suggests that Nur put in some sex to draw a crowd. Nur persists that this is a simple village play with no place for sex. Nazih suggests a hot affair between the mayor and the sabiyyi, but Nur dissuades him. Perhaps the patriotism and nationalism of the villagers against the "outsider" will excite the public, offers Nazih; besides, "you've certainly put in something on the South, right?" Nur hits himself on the head with an "oops, I totally forgot to" kind of response. He agrees the situation must be remedied. After all, the South is the hottest "qadiyya" [issue] in town these days. There's still time to add a quick line. Nazih is pleased: "Our area [West Beirut] supports this kind of thing. Just insert a short sentence. You can remove it when we perform in East Beirut" (147). So Nur gets to work to compose a rousing sentence on the South that he then teaches to the actor playing the role of the mayor. It keeps changing, but goes something like this: "O South, O South . . . O wound of the little (no, big) nation. O you who stand alone in the middle of the heart" (168). By now the play is in total chaos, and tensions are rising as opening night approaches.

Suddenly Abu Zuluf (traditional symbol of the village) appears onstage, in person, to furiously attack Nur for his stupid play. The italicized words appear in English. "Can't you all leave me alone?" he screams. "I turn on Lebanese *TV* and get a goat. I change the *channel* and don't get a goat but people singing Abu Zuluf. *Shit*, what is this? I turn on the radio and find a sheep; I move the dial and the sheep moves with it and they're all singing Abu Zuluf. *Shit*, what's this?" He continues reprimanding Nur for gathering all these people, dressing them in shirwals [traditional Mount Lebanon pants], and making them sing these old songs: "Hey, who told you I ride on a donkey? What are these rumors you're spreading about me? I have a Kawazaki-900 ZX, with incredible take-off speed, *man*" (196–97). Nur trembles as Abu Zuluf continues his tirade against the village so persistently idealized in Lebanese myth and folklore:

> "Hey, by what right do you make plays and stick us in the valley and the village, while you're off having a good time? Who told you I'm still able to live in the village and the valley? I went up once to the valley and the guys training [for the militias] caught me and almost killed me! You think I still dare to go up to some valley? What valley are you talking about in your plays, *man?*" (197)

Nur meekly replies that he means the valley "full of love." Abu Zuluf responds scornfully: "Love in the valley. Love in the village. Love in the square. Where are you getting all this love from, *man?*" (198). Stop writing these useless plays full of lies. He concludes, "Mr. Nur. There are satellites recording your backwardness from morning until night. In the name of Lebanese tradition I curse you. . . . Lebanon cannot progress with your goats standing in the way" (204). Finally, Nur is made to strip and put on traditional garb and go to one of these villages. He is petrified, as the village named is not of his religious persuasion. Oh, don't worry, Abu Zuluf sarcastically tells him. Just stand in the village square and recite your play (207).

The caustic humor is reinforced throughout by the language. Rahbani typically adopts the colloquialisms of his generation and effectively captures village and mountain dialects as well. In the character of Abu Zuluf, he also brilliantly puts down the clichéd rhymes of traditional self-glorifying Lebanese songs and poetry. "We're in 1983, for God's sake. Why do you still place overused words after 'layali' [nights]? Have you ever thought of using 'mallali' [troop carrier]?" Nur feebly answers that a troop carrier just doesn't fit in the song. "Really, so can the song fit in the troop carrier, then?" (198–99). Rahbani is forcing the issue of confronting our national myths. The safe village, lyrical poems, harmonious brotherhood of people, just do not exist. The war, and especially the Israeli Invasion, so radically transformed the discursive landscape of Lebanon.

As the 1980s wore on, Lebanon negotiated a withdrawal of Israeli forces from Beirut, who then settled in the so-called security zone of South Lebanon. Their presence along with the South Lebanon Army (SLA) ensured that Lebanon remained an arena for Shi'a-sponsored military and political action. In addition, most of the earlier combatants of the war resumed their battles—this time with a different set of enemies. Not only did Amal fight previous allies like the PLO and the entire left wing, but it fought another Shi'a group, Hizballah. In 1986 as Amal and the PLO fought, the Lebanese Forces lent support to the Palestinians (as a way to weaken the Syrian-sponsored Amal). In the following years, the LF would fight each other with Elie Hobeika's pro-Syrian Christian faction taking on Samir Geagea's. Different factions of the Palestinian resistance fought each other on Lebanese soil.[11] Finally, the Lebanese Forces and the Aounists (followers of General Aoun), both Maronites, fought to the bitter end. Whatever reasons for fighting in the first place seemed altogether lost as the battles, like so many forest fires, continued to spurt haphazardly across the horizons.

By the mid to late 1980s the various histories of Lebanon, according to Ahmad Beydoun, began to shift their focus. The earlier explanations of the war assumed a Lebanese unity and advocated pluralism, but the newer histories promoted isolationism. Much research now went into "micro (local or confessional) history" (67). Moreover, cultural production was often housed and financed by the militias themselves as they ran radio and television channels, controlled many newspapers and magazines, and filled "libraries with fanatical literature" (71). The selections of narratives chosen for discussion here were clearly not sponsored by the militias, although their authors might have strong ideological positions, but it is important to remember that cultural propaganda usually thrives during wartime.

By the mid-1980s, more organized mass protests against the war also took place from various constituencies including women, the handicapped, professional groups like lawyers and doctors, and trade unions.[12] Conferences and debates were held in Beirut (and abroad) in order to discuss aspects of life under war.[13] Nazek S. Yared spells out, in fact, that contrary to Western media presentations of war-damaged Lebanon, there was "un autre visage du Liban." Education was hardly ever interrupted, books and journals continued to be published in Beirut, conferences and roundtables persisted, as did dozens of art exhibits, innovative theater, music, and dance shows.

The large exodus of Lebanese to France also generated publications and conferences in Paris. Authors who composed in French—like George Shehadeh, Claire Gebeyli, Etel Adnan, Evelyne Accad, Amin Maalouf, and others—would add their contributions to an increasingly global Lebanese literature.[14] Andrée Chedid, for example, wrote *La maison sans racines* (1985), translated as *The Return to Beirut* in 1989. Like Adnan's depiction of Sitt Marie Rose, Chedid also foregrounds the actions of female pacifists whose lives are devastated by the incomprehensible violence of the war. Emily Nasrallah continued to write short stories that first appeared in the magazine *Fayruz*. Cooke notes that in these stories Nasrallah focuses on women and "celebrates their resistance to the senseless violence and their survival as a testimony to their commitment to their nation" (1995, 186). In 1988 Hanan al-Shaykh published her *Misk al-ghazal* (translated in 1989 as *Women of Sand and Myrrh*), structured around a cast of narrators situated in an unnamed Gulf state. The main character, Suha, is a Lebanese woman who has left her country now at war and whose perspective offers a glimpse of the increasingly significant exiled Lebanese. Shaykh herself had moved to London in the 1970s, but by the 1980s many writers (including Adonis and Qabbani) had relocated to Europe. Lebanon's story could and would be told from abroad. After all, almost a century earlier, Gibran, living in the United States, would offer some of the most enduring narratives on Lebanon.

In Lebanon itself, an important novel by Hassan Daoud captured the outrageous condition of the changing nation. A journalist and novelist, Daoud published the 1983 *Binayat Matilde* [translated in 1999 as *The House of Mathilde*],[15] which is first set in a prewar Beirut apartment building. Here, the rather routine lives of primarily female relatives and neighbors unfold. It is a new kind of narrative that recounts the lives of a diverse mix of tenants: Muslim families from the South now squarely situated in Beirut, Armenian and Russian neighbors, and extended families. Daoud succeeds in providing a detailed social and physical reality, with minimal overt politicking, of previously unfictionalized groups. Then the war starts. Tenants begin to move away, squatters arrive, and life in the building gradually changes. An ominous tension now pervades the lives of the remaining neighbors, but the war is not the only culprit. The relatively quiet Mathilde takes on a renter, who kills and dismembers her. Although a massive bomb also destroys most of the building, Mathilde is already dead. The building hence chronicles the prewar to war era, but offers a complex and disturbing analysis of human beings. Without any commentary or analysis, Daoud's novel suggests that war doesn't just happen; it is not some external unrelated occurrence. It is created by people, even familiar people, who do terrible things. Other novels by Daoud, discussed below, would ensure that his voice would be added to the list of innovative writers from Lebanon.

Another important writer of this period is the prolific Rachid al-Daʿif. His 1983 *Ansi yalhu maʿ Rita* [Ansi plays with Rita] puts an especially interesting spin on the situation.[16] The main character, Ansi (whose name also means "I forget"), narrates how he is born out of forgetfulness. A sequence of tales features him as a child in a warped reality where he, for example, communicates with an elephant on television. In another story he enters the television screen to save a girl from drowning, but his mother, seeing no one in front of the set, turns it off, leaving her son stranded. In another tale Ansi shrinks so he can drive his matchbox car around. These seemingly children's stories reveal Daʿif's ability to extend the language; it is pliable in his hands, molded to describe the incomprehensible and unacceptable new reality of Lebanon.

Another 1983 work, *Al-Mustabidd* [The tyrant], presents perhaps a more realistic backdrop (the Israeli bombing of Beirut) but certainly no less bizarre reality than the one above. As the citizens resort, like rats, to the city's shelters, the main character searches obsessively for a woman he had sex with in a darkened basement. To relive the intensity of that lovemaking, in total fear and anonymity, becomes his life's work, but the outcome is futile. Amyuni writes: "He chases the girl in vain and once again meets all sorts of physical and human obstacles, objective correlatives to his own psyche. The novel comes to its conclusion as he screams, drives his car and goes away. The novel ends on the same absurd note with which it started: with the translation of *The Plague*" (1996, 86).

Daʿif published three more novels between 1986 and 1989. Two will be quickly discussed here and the third later in the chapter. The first novel, *Fusha mustahdafa bayna al-naʿusi wa al-nawm* [Trapped between drowsiness and sleep, 1986], has received much critical acclaim by Lebanese and French critics and has been translated into French.[17] This striking novel begins (as the epigraph to this chapter shows) with the narrator/protagonist recounting his own death. He then provides different accounts of his killing that contradict one another over whether the watchman, for example, was with him when he was shot or actually participated in the shooting. The narrator realizes another inconsistency in his account, for the watchman appears unarmed: "The watchman was with them. . . . They all, even the watchman, shot at me. But the watchman was unarmed. This is a weak point in my statement, I do admit. But I did see him with both my eyes. I saw him, unarmed, shooting at me. His bullets went through me, as did the others' bullets" (7). Although the narrator seems unreliable, the novel reads like an authentic narrative precisely because of the absurd stories of the narrator. The new reality of haphazard violence is absurd and cannot be rationally scripted. Da'if's structural and stylistic innovations reflect something of the reality of war. It is a war that also put a nation on tranquilizers. The final page of the novel, once again narrating the upcoming killing of the protagonist, concludes with the narrator taking a double-dose of sleeping pills and waiting to be knocked out (125).

The novel effectively captures the alienation and resignation of the narrator who has endured (indeed been severely wounded by) the war. The recourse to sedatives, paralleling the extensive use of drugs by militiamen, reinforces the need to numb the senses during war. Without necessarily focusing on the horrors of war, the need to block it out is also powerful. By extension, the drugs distort, so the narratives bend and blend into the surreal. War distorts and is surreal. As Da'if expressed in the text quoted in chapter 4, his brain and Beirut at war are exactly the same.

His next novel, *Ahl al-zhull* [People of the shadow, 1987], was translated into French.[18] To escape the violent city, the protagonist goes back to the village, where he is engaged in building the ephemeral house. Amyuni writes that "the story revolves around that dream of a house, how it was built or is meant to be built, the threat of snakes and scorpions, and is salvaged by lyrical flights of fantasy about honey and herbs, love and tenderness" (188). The French translator, Edgard Weber, was interviewed in the *Nahar al-kutub* newspaper supplement. One of the reasons he was so taken by this novel was because it effectively captured the war. Indeed, its narrative is structured like war. He provides three examples. First, the main character is nameless and incomplete, correlating to war killings of unspecified enemies (not specific individuals). Like war participants, he also does not take responsibility for his action, leading to a feeling of victimization. Second, the place—the house he says he is building—is either true or a fantasy. As in war, the real, according to Weber, becomes the imagined. The third example concerns time. This novel, like other recent ones, defies chronology. War too explodes normal human time, not differentiating between night and day, summer and winter, past or future (Weber 3). The very mode of narration hence captures something real about the Lebanese war without recourse to thematics or any overt politics. Like Khoury, Da'if challenges traditional methods of expression and breaks new ground.

Yusuf Habshi al-Ashqar (1926–92) is less innovative in his style, but he published a lengthy novel in 1989 called *Al-Zhull wa al-sada* [The shadow and the echo],[19] which offered a critical perspective on the war. Written in 1988, the novel powerfully captures the weariness of war. For thirteen years, the narrative offers, Lebanon has been engulfed in a bizarre series of never-ending battles. The cease-fires only prove to be temporary, as the stakes grow higher and new opportunities for power-grabbing arise. The war has been a terrible mistake, and its devastation is as much internal as it is physical. In the introduction, Beirut is depicted as ruined with everything and everyone affected. No one can escape war "because it is war, and it has entered into everyone's hearts." This war has conquered all, and the only way to escape fear is through "whiskey, tobacco, weapons, hashish, heroin. . . . They are all cheaper than water, flour, oil, sun, or air" (7). This cynical and negative perspective is also that of Iskander, who dominates the text, although he is neither the main narrator nor actor.

The novel begins with an old friend visiting Iskander, who in his depression has locked himself up in his palatial home with a decrepit dog. When the war started on April 13, 1975, he read all the newspapers diligently for days, and then he stopped altogether, shut off the radio, no longer consulted a watch, and refused to leave his mansion (375). Now he has no feelings, no hope—he is surrounded by war and can barely muster the energy to live. In fact, he has considered suicide. But he could not kill himself while his parents were alive. The news of his mother's death unleashes an extensive flashback (with multiple narrators) on his origins, his village, and himself.

He comes from the Christian village of Kfarmallat, which like many villages suffered famine and oppression during World War I and which witnessed the extensive emigration of its inhabitants either to Beirut or

abroad. This emigration, however, leads to a specific problem as place de-
termines both freedom and identity. Neither is possible when there is no
place (91). The Christians are confused: "We sit between two chairs—our
hand is in the eastern pocket and our heart is with the Western song. . . .
We must cease being twentieth century's sick man of the Middle East"
(197). The Christians continue to emigrate, as does the young Iskander
when he leaves the village to go to school in Beirut. In the big city, no one
knows or cares who he is. He is totally alone, close only to God (108). His
reason for leaving the village is itself linked to emigration. His boyhood
friend Asmar is a filthy rich and spoiled Lebanese emigrant, whose powerful gang destroys the village school. Asmar's priorities of materialism and
gangsterism violate, at first, the traditional values of the village, but much
to Iskander's disgust, the village soon follows suit. The war, in fact, clarifies
everything. "The war revealed the difference; the war is like a magnifying
glass that exposed people and groups" (145). Asmar's childhood pranks
metamorphose easily into brutality, the villagers prove to be immoral, and
only Iskander retains his decency.

Ironically, Iskander has also become rich as a result of a major inheritance, so Iskander and Asmar are both potentially powerful players once
the war begins. When the villagers come to Iskander asking him to help
fund a militia, buy some M-16s, or contribute in any way, he unequivocally refuses: "He didn't pay one penny toward killing" (127). The villagers
are furious and call him a traitor; after all, it was rumored he had sympa-
thies for Palestinians and the Left. But the issue was not whose side he was
on. Iskander consistently and categorically denounces war: "The Right and
the Left both kill, steal, lie, and get excited. The result is the same: destruction" (190). Asmar, on the other hand, participates in the war with gusto.
Now is his opportunity to use his wealth to achieve political power. He
fully funds a militia to defend his interests and, only by association, the
interests of the village. To the villagers he is a hero and a nationalist (128),
unlike the coward and traitor Iskander. As Asmar rallies the villagers against
Iskander, the latter stops being a misunderstood pariah and instead becomes
an object of intense loathing. At the very end of the novel when Iskander
slips into the village to visit his mother's grave, the militiamen of the village are poised for assault.

The Christian village, the once idealized locale of many Lebanese writers, is here transformed (as it was in Rahbani's *Shi fashil*) into a dangerous
place where militiamen train. Its inhabitants blindly follow the rich and

the strong, propagating the centuries-old political za'im system of the region. Asmar, the new za'im, is presented with no redeeming features whatsoever; even as a boy he was cruel, envious, and greedy. Now as an adult he is vengeful and maniacal, but the villagers treat him with adoration and aspire to be like him.

Only Iskander is different. He is the "pure self" (76), who from the beginning, according to Eid, knew that the war was only "a shadow and an echo" (78). He laments the fate of his generation that had to be the one to "lose faith" (39). Everything has now withered away, all is fake, and a deep depression has set in. The war has exposed all. The conflict brought on by the war is played out, however, not in Iskander but in the son of his friend Khalil. The young man, Yusuf, with plenty of time to ruminate since he has chosen to remain in prison, becomes the primary narrator of this novel. It is he who is most torn by the opposing ideologies embodied in Asmar and Iskander. He grows to despise his weak and poor father, who cannot even see that his wife is in love with another man. Their house is puny and a source of embarrassment to Yusuf. In fact, when people ask him why he fights, this is what he says:

> I responded with a slogan: [I fight] for the nation's honor, the nation's permanence, the nation's roots, the warmth, the security. The nation is the big house and the house is the small nation; I used to respond to the question with another: since I did not find security or warmth or roots, neither in my village house nor the village, neither in my Beirut house nor Beirut; since I never felt the significance of the nation, any place in this world could become my house, my village, my city, my nation; did I fight fanatically? No, no, for the sake of a za'im? Ha, ha, ha. (256)

Yusuf's home never offered much, so his perception of the nation (the larger home) is not comforting. Instead, he covets Iskander's house and all it represents. After his father is killed at a checkpoint, Yusuf becomes a thief and a looter as well as a fighter. Now he is able to finally provide for his widowed mother and sisters who, thanks to him, live "like queens." In a symbolic gesture, he decides to knock down his father's old shack and build a real house for his family. The father is forgotten, and Yusuf realizes he has become like Asmar. He, along with everyone else engaged in battle, has profited from the war and doesn't want it to end: "We are like insects that only thrive on garbage heaps" (512).

Although Yusuf admires Iskander, he is far away (literally and figuratively); his good father has been killed; and kind Marthe (Iskander's partner and Yusuf's love) has left the country. He misses all of them (514) and is left with no options but Asmar's. Not surprisingly, in the final scene he participates in the ambushing of the grieving Iskander. He is a man of two minds, however, for he recognizes, like Iskander, the charade of this war: "It's no harm if innocents are killed for the nation, I mean for the cause. The nation is no longer the slogan; the cause has defeated the nation. What is the cause? At the time I didn't ask, but now I do. The cause has become causes; each of us here and there has started to defend our causes" (463). As Iskander predicted, this would be a terrible war. All those engaged in the war are secretive, and they fight at night like "shadows" (470). Yusuf's voice is like the "echo" to Iskander's (Eid, 1993, 76). Nothing is solid or sacred anymore. With the malaise of a fin de siècle period piece, Ashqar's text wearily completes itself.

It is a text rich with astute political analysis and posturing. The war figures as a clear evil in an already corrupt and corruptible society. In fact, the war clarifies rather than simply destroys. The novel proceeds thematically to challenge clichéd versions of Lebanon and thereby forces one to take a harsh look at the machinations of Lebanon itself, not just fallen because of the war, but already tarnished.

Khoury's novel of the same year (*The Journey of Little Gandhi*, 1989) takes place in the early 1980s but was published later, when the war-weariness visible in Ashqar is paramount. Unlike Ashqar, however, Khoury is less concerned with a thematic analysis of war and more interested in confronting how one can narrate at all. While the war is the ostensible subject of this novel, its absurdities are not necessarily less narratable than other life experiences. Perhaps the war, like Ashqar said, simply served as a "magnifying glass." What was there was always there, though not necessarily seen. In any case, Khoury is intent on foregrounding the slippage, the uncertainties, the constant unreliabilities of discourse. In a complicated sequence of passing-on-the-story, the reader learns that the prostitute Alice is the person most responsible for telling the narrator the stories of Gandhi the shoe shiner (a nickname, by the way, given to him by an American professor). He then decides to write them down, but:

> I discovered that the things Alice told me weren't lies. A woman in love
> doesn't lie. Alice wasn't in love and she didn't lie. That's how she was,

told lies like everyone else, but she told me everything, and all of it was true. . . . He died when death ceased to have any value.

"Death has always been cheap," Alice said when she was telling me his story. But she was lying, because she knew death does have a price — death itself. (2–3)

Any assurance that what we read is truthful is here quickly undermined. In fact, "truth" as a concept is highly suspect throughout Khoury's discourse. He flirts with the idea of pliable knowledges. The narration (and hence conceptualization) of reality is all we have. This outlook, however, is countered by some hard-hitting descriptive accounts of the war, for example, as we saw earlier. The result is a new kind of narration of war, one that is always already incomplete and imprecise: "When I tell it, I don't tell anything. I tell about it and I don't quench my thirst, and I go on my journey to it, and don't find it. I find words that dangle like a rope, I climb the rope and I slip, and when I tumble to the ground, I see the walls collapse and the city migrate" (191). The act of recording is always a process, continual, like life itself. Ghandour promotes this idea of storytelling in her introduction to the English version of the novel: "Although the 'journey' is tragic for most of the characters in this novel, the narrator, like Sheherazade, wards off death by his stories. Writing in this context provides life and continuation to the act of creativity in the midst of war and destruction" (xix). Ironically, this very act of creation is only possible in conjunction with a cycle of death. War and its narration are now indelibly linked, aesthetically and structurally: "If Kamal al-Askary hadn't died, then Alice wouldn't have met up with Gandhi, and if she hadn't met Gandhi, then he wouldn't have told her his story. And if Gandhi hadn't died, Alice wouldn't have told me the story. And if Alice hadn't disappeared, or died, then I wouldn't be writing what I am writing now" (14). Indeed, as Ghandour maintains: "Death allows the narrator to tell everything" (xviii). True, but this "everything" is intentionally perspectival and contestable; its language does not "tell mere facts" (Ghandour xiv). So Khoury offers an important and unique mode of telling that scripts the war in new ways. He constantly tests the possibilities of the Arabic language, forging new perspectives on the Lebanese nation.

As a foil to Khoury, Da'if's novel of the same year also consciously foregrounds language and style in depicting the war. Instead of the frequent questionings of the narrator or the constant undermining of the text, Daʿif tends to concretize reality by close scrutiny of particulars. The choice of subject matter along with the clarity of description also make for a powerful new aesthetic on war.

Daʿif's 1989 novel, *Tiqniyyat al-buʾs* [Techniques of misery] was composed (like Khoury's and Ashqar's novels just discussed) in what would effectively be the last years of the civil war. And like *The Shadow and the Echo*, the novel reveals the weariness of the Lebanese who have lived through these interminable hostilities. Unlike Ashqar's novel, the text offers no political analysis whatsoever. Instead, the novel focuses on Hashem, a schoolteacher who is temporarily out of work because his school has been war damaged. He wakes up, makes coffee, washes, looks out the window, takes the elevator downstairs, talks to neighbors, meets cronies for a smoke, tries to cook lunch while talking on the phone to his fiancée, frequents the bathroom, takes tranquilizers, sleeps. There are hardly any changes in his life. In fact, he always correctly anticipates who is knocking on the door or who is on the phone. This humdrum daily routine is set against a backdrop that scarcely mentions the war. Hashem's major concerns are not profound but unabashedly mundane: how many lentils to put in the pot, how to clean off the toilet seat before he sits, what has become of the gristle stuck in his friend's teeth, how to create an internal water tank for his apartment, how to pay for lunch, which taxi to grab, how to prevent his armpits from stinking. The war simmers in the background, and its most pervasive effects are discovered in these daily performances.[20]

The war, for example, has led to severe water shortages. As a result, much of Hashem's day is spent working to ensure more water for his flat and trying to make do with what little water he does have. In fact, his most jubilant moment in the novel comes not when he reunites after many weeks with his fiancée but when the water comes through the pipes and he successfully fills every possible container in the house and washes the dishes before the water is cut off again. This ordinarily lethargic and passive man is seen racing all over the apartment as he completes this task. When it is over, he smiles:

> The tub is overflowing with water.
> And the three gallons.
> And tens of bottles.
> And the small barrel on the sink.

And the toilet is clean.

And what else?

He carefully scrutinizes every corner to see whether he forgot any container, but no. All is well with the world. "And he smiled again" (111).

Complete satisfaction has been whittled down to this. As if to reinforce the "shitty" situation that has reduced the Lebanese to this level of existence, Da'if pursues the narrative of Hashem's plentiful water in a most scatological way. The war has made his relationship with his girlfriend, Maryam, very difficult. Not only is it almost impossible to meet, but they can only communicate rarely by phone (since the lines break down). More seriously, she is becoming impatient with him as he seems hesitant to commit. ("Get your affairs in order," she keeps warning him.) But he seems increasingly distant from her and her bourgeois concerns: He is out of work and can hardly make ends meet. Besides, he is much more interested in when the next supply of water can be secured. After halfhearted attempts at a meeting, she succeeds in coming to his apartment to spend the night. Tension is high.

Before bed, she goes into the bathroom (where only just recently Hashem has happily saved all that water). She is in there a long time and Hashem starts hearing the pouring of water. One can sense him tensing up, concerned over how much water she is using. We know he is wondering if she is bathing, perhaps in preparation for a night of sex. This thought seems to appease his apprehension over wasted water. Water continues to flow, and finally she leaves the bathroom and plops herself on the bed. Hashem now enters the bathroom, anticipating signs of the bath. The toilet seat is closed. He opens it only to find her bowel movement, which she had unsuccessfully tried to flush down the toilet with the water saved in the tub (122–23). This is a huge disappointment, as he is now faced with no sex and, more seriously, no water.

Da'if captures what war means: no water, no electricity, no phone lines. By 1987, the war also meant the total collapse of the Lebanese lira.[21] As the novel unfolds, Hashem is flabbergasted at the news that one dollar, which used to be worth around 3 lira, is now worth 600 lira. He calculates the unbelievable cost of a simple lunch and decides he must learn to cook with cheap lentils. The extent of the economic collapse is so huge, it is grotesque. It is no wonder that Hashem focuses on the ever-reliable fresh spit in the corner of the elevator or on the dab of hummus that rests on the corner of his friend's mouth.

In an amazing sequence, Hashem describes in detail (27–28) the fate of a tiny bit of meat, stuck in the teeth, and then released to rest against a white napkin. His first telling is brief, followed by a play-by-play report that covers over a page of script. The reader is left both amused and awed by a language that can actually describe these minutiae. In another sequence (50–52), Hashem's bath is described, taking about as much time to read as it would to perform. "Nothing is beyond description" (the title of his earlier book) certainly rings true here. Da'if has created a style that, like the war, is interminable.

Throughout the novel, Hashem occasionally recalls that he has "seven million ideas" he has not been able to formulate. Serious thinking now eludes him, as he is reduced in many ways to an animal sniffing about his den searching for sustenance. He hears the humming of the electric generators, smells the garbage and his own body odor, performs his bodily functions, notes and measures the dimensions of his living space, eats, sleeps. Amyuni writes: "Al-Da'if's originality lies precisely in this stripping of human beings, feelings, and things down to absolute nakedness in the midst of a war that tore apart the artist's nation. He expresses himself in a language stripped to its bare essentials, as well, breaking away from the traditional Arabic mode, in which rhetoric and lyricism dominated" (177). Indeed, the style is so pared down as to read like stage directions for an actor. In the supposedly climactic scene when Hashem and Maryam finally meet on the bed after the embarrassing bathroom incident, what transpires is depicted only clinically. The kissing and groping is precisely and mechanically described: "Hashem brought his lips closer and kissed her on her lips. She didn't part them at first, then she did" (128). The language, as Eid contends, is cold, dry, unemotional—as if it were unrelated to the writer: "The writing is merely a witness" (63).

Perhaps, but the writing is arguably more active, creating the ideas everyone (including Hashem) is struggling to formulate. A tiny example will illustrate this point. Hashem boards the elevator to ride to his sixth-floor apartment: "The trace of the spit—in the right corner under the row of buttons with the numbers of the floors on them—was still clear" (15). Note that the "trace" remains despite a long parenthetical interruption. Thus the structure of the sentence itself parallels the endurance of this spit. Da'if's writing is new because it captures what one saw or felt (or didn't feel) during this new epoch of Lebanon's existence. At no point does one feel numbed by traditional Arabic rhetoric.

The novel winds down with Hashem descending in the elevator at night to deliver a dish of lentils to a neighbor. The electricity is cut off, leaving him stranded. He decides not to respond to neighbors' calls, so the elevator is assumed to be empty. Totally alone in the dark, Hashem passes the night in the elevator. He eats the lentils like an animal and places the dish under his clothes. Then he hears dogs roaming the building, and a wild dog enters the lobby, sniffing at the elevator. Shut off from the world, he swallows a tranquilizer, preparing himself for the calm ahead. The next sentence reads: "Hashem did not observe the reaction of the man who opened the elevator door in the early morning, to find him dead on the floor of the elevator! And he didn't hear his screams!" (141). The shock of Hashem's death, however, is countered by the realization that he has simply appeared dead. He is, in fact, asleep after taking a tranquilizer. The novel concludes with him being escorted to his flat while he fibs about what happened in the elevator. He falls asleep musing about those unrealized "seven million ideas" (142).

In the end, Eid seems to fault Da'if for a text that bypasses big issues like national liberation (63). Again, that is exactly the text's point—that war has so transformed the nation that oblivion is a consequence, a reality to be narrated. "Techniques" of survival replace larger issues that consume the war-weary ordinary citizens of Lebanon. The villains and heroes of some early war fiction have all but disappeared by the end of the war, nor is there any energy for earnest soul-searching and analyses. The war has taken its toll on the nation in this way as well; one needs to take account of it, narrate it, record it.[22]

The war still did not end. In fact, its last years were some of the most vicious, pitting the least likely foes against each other. For all the war-weariness, surprising bursts of energy continued to alter the political landscape and to reconfigure the nation.

In June 1987, Prime Minister Rashid Karami was assassinated, and Selim Hoss replaced him. Since Karami had resigned four weeks before he was killed, questions arose as to whether Hoss was the official or acting prime minister. If "acting," then the president could appoint a new government before his term ended. When President Amin Gemayel's term ended in September 1988 without agreement on a successor candidate, Gemayel tried, but failed, to form a new government. In the last minutes of his presidency, he then dismissed Hoss's caretaker government and appointed an interim government of army officers under the leadership of Michel Aoun, the head of the army. Hoss refused to resign, and Aoun took on his new position. The country had no president but two governments that denied each other's legitimacy.

In the meantime, during the Iran/Iraq war, Syria alone had supported Iran against Iraq. When that war ended in 1988, Iraq was eager to arm Syria's enemies in Lebanon (the Lebanese Forces and the Lebanese army). As Aoun began to consolidate control over the country in 1989, he met with resistance both from the LF in the Christian heartland and from the non-Christian segment of the country under Syrian control. In March 1989, Aoun announced his war of liberation [harb al-tahrir] against Syria, and he succeeded in mesmerizing a certain segment of the population (primarily Christian and young), desperate for a hero. He captured the imagination, as he spoke in unadorned colloquialisms, contrasting drastically with the rhetorical political speeches of Lebanon's traditional leaders: "You are the liberation generation, you are the nation and the national will. . . . Tell the deputies you didn't elect them, so they've got no right to speak for you. . . . Tell the church the reason you're here is to speak the truth. . . . The state is not the people; the people are the state" (qtd. in Hanf 577). Aoun's slogans mobilized a generation disillusioned by the political system and weary of a self-propagating war that did not end. His forces engaged in battles with the Syrians for about six months until Arab diplomacy arranged a cease-fire in September 1989 and called for a meeting of Lebanon's deputies in Taef, Saudi Arabia, to arrive at true "reconciliation and peace." The result was a document, known as the Taef Agreement (or Accord), that both affirmed and revised Lebanon's constitution.

In brief, the document asserted Lebanon's independence *and* its Arab identity (compared with the National Pact, which mentions Lebanon's "Arab face"). While it maintained the principle of confessional representation, it prescribed a new formula of parity between Muslims and Christians, 1:1 rather than the original 6:5 formula of the unwritten National Pact. More deputies were added, the powers of the Maronite presidency were reduced, and both the Sunni prime minister and the Shi'a speaker of the House became stronger. The document also called for the future abolition of confessionalism, and sanctioned the role of Syria for helping resolve the Lebanese crisis, without offering a clear timetable for Syrian withdrawal.[23]

Aoun rejected Taef, although the LF along with most other parties and participants in Lebanon accepted the reconciliation document. Again, the prospect of continued Lebanese-politics-as-usual mobilized huge groups of supporters against Taef, against Syria, and for Aoun. In November 1989, the Parliament elected René Mou'awad as president, but he refused to move militarily against the "renegade" general. Mou'awad was assassinated on Independence Day a few weeks later. Elias Hrawi, under strong Syrian presence, was elected the next day and was ready to oust Aoun by force. The prospect of an attack on Aoun in the presidential palace of Baabda instigated a massive show of support. For weeks, a festival atmosphere dominated the grounds of the palace, as tens of thousands of Lebanese joined the sit-ins and cheered the poets, singers, and musicians who had come to entertain the crowds. Schools in the district regularly arranged for their students to be bused after school to attend the events. However one felt about Aoun, there was no doubt that there was a genuine populist enthusiasm for the phenomenon that he had unleashed. Although the great majority of attendees were Christian, the spirit was not confessional but nationalist. Surveys of demonstrators indicate that most were for a united Lebanon, for direct presidential elections, for a new electoral law, against existing parties, and against Taef.[24]

This Aounist movement insisted on an independent Lebanon, free from foreign forces. It demanded not only an end to the war but also the creation of a new leadership that did not rely on the corrupt machinations of the old system. It called for popular representation, a new language, and a positive secular vision of Lebanon. It was a nationalistic and unabashedly cultural movement that spawned dozens of popular songs by leading singers like Majida al-Roumi and Laure 'Abs. The senior composer, Zaki Nassif, and others composed music and lyrics that spoke for the movement. "Raji' yit 'ammar Lubnan" [Lebanon will be rebuilt] became an anthem, along with many other songs, like "Aounak Raji' min Allah," playing on Aoun's name, which means help or support. Poetry recitals and competitions were regularly held. The poet Père Simon Assaf, for example, composed poems that pitted Aoun against the deputies. The poet Sa'id 'Aql was often seen by Aoun's side at these festivals, promoting the idea of a free, strong, and proud Lebanon. Pro-Aounist magazines like Al-Sahwa al-Lubnaniyya or L'Eveil [The awakening] were also published and widely distributed. The movement even generated its own car horn–blowing rhythm that was honked on roads and in tunnels as a political statement.

As the presidential palace in Baabda, where Aoun was bunkered in, was dubbed "qasr al-sha'b" or "la maison de peuple," it was difficult for President Hrawi to order an assault. The spirit of resistance and defiance only strengthened. In addition, Aoun began to put muscle behind his verbal assaults on the Christian militias. By January 1990, tired of continued refusals by the Lebanese Forces to surrender their ports and weapons, Aoun turned against the LF under the leadership of the increasingly unpopular Samir Geagea. These battles, some of the most brutal of the entire war (in part because of Iraq's previous arming of both groups), confirmed to many the unconfessional spirit of Aoun's agenda. As a Maronite himself, he was fighting Maronites who valorized their militia over what he considered the legitimate Lebanese government and army. The cult of Aoun grew as he persisted not only in representing the "true" state but in advocating himself as the only true leader for that state.

The situation would once again change in the region when in August 1990 Iraq invaded Kuwait and Syria joined the U.S. alliance against Iraq. The Americans, unhappy with Aoun's intransigence, anti-American rhetoric, and support of Iraq, now saw their interests coinciding with that of the Hrawi pro-Syrian government. Within weeks, Hrawi requested Syrian military support, and on October 13, 1990, the Syrian air force bombed Baabda and moved ground troops alongside anti-Aoun Lebanese army brigades. This forced the ouster of Aoun, who would eventually seek political asylum in France. The Taef Agreement had already been adopted by Parliament, and Lebanon could now embark on a new future based on a revised constitution. For many in Lebanon, the coast looked clearer than it had in decades as Aoun, the only serious hindrance to peace, was removed, ensuring the role of a single president and a single government. To others, the Syrian action of October 13 meant the end of the political role of Christians in Lebanon and the end of "their cultural identity" (Phares 179). Almost all agreed that Syria was now calling the shots as Lebanon embarked on its Second Republic.

Two important novels were published in 1990: Hoda Barakat's *Hajar al-duhk*, translated in 1995 as *The Stone of Laughter*, and Hassan Daoud's *Ayyam za'ida* [Extra days]. Barakat's award-winning text extends and complicates the discourse established by women writers on the war.[25] Like Shaykh in *Story of Zahra*, Barakat adopts a psychological and sexual approach to her subject, but she inverts her hero, constructing a male figure, Khalil, whose effeminacy and homosexuality ensure that he is, at first, outside the realm of fighting. As the novel progresses, however, Khalil sheds his true self and becomes an aggressor who can "belong" in the group, the militia. The novel ends with him not only engaged in drug and arm smuggling but also raping a neighbor. He now appears powerful and broad-shouldered as he drives away (out of the text and away from the author's vision), fully transformed into the violent Lebanese male. Barakat laments: "Khalil is gone, he has become a man who laughs. And I remain a woman who writes" (209). Like Adnan in *Sitt Marie Rose,* Barakat seems to offer the thesis that the war is a male enterprise that women are victims of, marginalized by, or narrators of. Unlike Adnan, however, Barakat allows the fiction to unfold and tell its own tale, introducing a sympathetic narrator rather than projecting a judgmental authorial voice.

Like the Da'if novels discussed above, Barakat's novel is also situated in the 1980s. Without too many overt references, we recognize this era of the devaluation of the Lebanese currency, the constant electrical blackouts, the propensity for car bombs, and the relatively new phenomenon of martyrs. For ordinary citizens like Khalil, it is a time of limbo, of waiting: "The real pity is that the body is not yet completely lost because it has not died. . . . It still breathes. . . . If you were to tie a plastic bag up over the body the sides of the bag would steam up as if that flesh were breathing, although it lies still" (43). It is an existence that barely qualifies as human; in fact, to exist during the war is to become dehumanized. In a powerful sequence at a social gathering, the guests laugh at any mention of the horrific life around them. An explosion tears apart a friend, mixes drinking water with sewage, puts live electricity wires into the water. People are robbed in broad daylight. The guests can't stop laughing. The narrator interjects: "This is the place where people laugh more than anywhere else in the world. When the bombing is in full swing, the children laugh and the government employees laugh because it's a holiday. . . . They eat plenty and well. . . . They bring the best videotapes to their parties because they will be staying up late and there is no work or school early next morning" (122). The women, the shopkeeper, the baker, the owners of the restaurant and gas station, the moneychanger, the journalist, the landlord all laugh. Even the poet laughs because someone in his family will be martyred, making him sadder, and thus inspiring him to compose moving lyrics to a receptive crowd. Barakat pokes fun at the tradition of lament and rhetorical outcry exhibited increasingly in this era of martyrs, for the poet is begged by the crowds to "lament and warble in that unique voice of his, made for calamities and the power of words and wisdom will return, in the name of the clan, of the tribe, of kin" (123).

The entire country laughs because "it does not object to the open sew-ers," nor does it "protest against bombing or death or humiliation or the lack of water or electricity or flour, because it wants the warring powers to become more deeply embroiled, wants more scorn and accusation and so stays silent, so it can laugh more" (123–24). As so many other narra-tives of Lebanon, Beirut takes on a metonymic quality, as it replaces the nation. The laughter is like a "tempestuous festival": "A city thrown onto its back waving its arms and legs like a huge cockroach under a massive joke. Laughter that fate does not give a chance to catch its breath, the chance to draw a little oxygen . . . laughter whose blood is blue and turns black from laughter . . . dies of laughter" (125). The personified city is here reduced to a grotesque insect that will choke to death laughing. This is the new image of Beirut. It is the site of violence, of depravity; indeed, it is a "uniquely hideous city." But its inhabitants don't see its ugliness: "To see it in its hideousness would take them back to their own hideousness, its vileness would take them back to their own vileness and so they prefer to fabricate stories about it and to keep the stories going" (200). In this way the Lebanese do not have to confront themselves, and the myths continue.

Samir Khalaf concludes his study of Lebanon with this idea of mystifi-cation. The "Lebanese miracle" was inexplicable, but "now that this myth is being shattered, we turn back and mystify Lebanon's descent into anomie. Hence, much of the tension and violence is attributed to 'mysterious forces,' 'borrowed ideologies,' and 'shadowy organizations'" (290). Khalaf is intent on understanding the real source of Lebanon's collapse (see his epigraph at the beginning of part II), and like Barakat, he refuses to blame others. The ugliness lies within. Lebanon can no longer exclude the excessive and random violence that shaped its destiny. These new narratives pre-scribe, at the very least, a need to look within.

As Khalil walks through the city, he realizes that he never loved it, so he need not lament it: "It gave him nothing and had promised him nothing." Unlike the score of poets from across the Arab world who eulogized the fallen queen, the tainted sorceress, the bejeweled lover, Khalil has not been betrayed by Beirut. It was always like this. He reflects on the idyllic symbol of Lebanon, Fayruz (who "continues to gather together the skies of the nation"),[26] and realizes that this "woman's songs had nothing to do with him." They were nothing but a "mistake." Her words were "empty to the core. Because it was a symbol to the core. A symbol that symbolizes nothing to him" (201). He is full of hatred, reminding us perhaps of Ashqar's Yusuf.

The title of Barakat's novel resonates meaningfully in the last lines of the text, as Khalil, now metamorphosed into a tough man, drives away. The narrator grieves for him: "You've changed so much since I described you in the first pages. You've come to know more than I do. Alchemy. The stone of laughter" (209). War transforms as well as exposes. War is like Ashqar's "magnifying glass," which reveals the hideousness within, while it is also the Kafkaesque cockroach. War is a condition that many of Lebanon's writers attempted to understand through writing, through narrative.

Hassan Daoud's *Ayyam za'ida* was also published in 1990. One of the more remarkable features of this novel is that it doesn't mention the war in any way, although it was composed in 1987–88. As such it offers a fascinating look at Lebanon without having to be distracted by the phenomenon of war. Some texts discussed earlier also did not ostensibly mention the war, but were clearly set in a ravaged society, like Rahbani's *Bilnisbi la bukra shu?* or Khoury's *Gates of the City*. In the next chapter, there will be discussion of other texts (like Nasrallah's *Al-Jamr al-ghafi*) that are specifically set before the war. The omission of the war in Daoud's novel is revelatory because, although the text might be set in a prewar period (when the Lebanese lira had its value, for example), it certainly feels like it is set in the miserable war-torn present.

Daoud's entire text is presented from the point of view of a ninety-four-year-old man who is ailing but still lucid. He reminisces about his relationships with siblings, his move to Beirut to work in a bakery, his visits to the village in the South, his dealings with neighbors, workers, and family. He recalls what he bought with his earnings, how he divvied up his will to his male children, and what he gave away. He lives now in the decrepit village house with his son and his family. His days are passed sitting, sleeping, moving slowly from his bed to the kitchen to the bathroom. He listens to the radio, eats, pees from the balcony, and shouts at his noisy grandchildren. His routinized life is somewhat reminiscent of Da'if's Hashem character.

As the novel progresses, the old man becomes more infirm and restricted in his movements. Increasingly, he and the land and the house are neglected. The trees on the land have dried up, the ceiling sheds dirt, and the old father withers away, ignored like a discarded piece of furniture. The great bulk of his narrative hence focuses, in King Lear fashion, on the ingratitude of his offspring. He gave all to his sons—his land, his house, his money. He had saved a small piece of land for himself for security reasons, but his younger son griped about his share of the inheritance, so the old man turned it over as well. He lives as an unwanted guest in his own house and is forced to listen to his family scolding him constantly. They refuse to fix anything in the house, obviously awaiting his death so they can quickly sell the property. They refuse to summon the doctor when he is ill, they feed him cold leftovers as if he were a dog, and they only grudgingly clean his room. Although they hate his long hair and disheveled beard, they never offer to take him to a barber. One of his daughters-in-law cannot even bear to look at him. They all disapprove of his loud radio playing, complaining that he wakes them up with the Quranic call to prayer each morning. They criticize his screaming at the kids, who seem to be a special nemesis for the old man.

In a powerful scene, one of the grandsons verbally attacks his grandfather, who narrates: "He said to me, after he ran down their steps, that I had lived my life and others' lives as well, and that it was time for me to die. His voice was even louder than mine had been when I had screamed at the kids since noon. He took to raising and lowering his arm while he yelled as if he wanted to capture me. He also said that I needed to give others a rest of me" (83). The old man is dumbstruck as he recalls that this is the boy he used to affectionately give 100 liras to cut his hair, the one he used to cook his favorite dishes for, the one he would put on the donkey and play with (84).

Everyone awaits his death. Early in the novel when the father complains about his pain, the older son, who is tidying up the room, is irritated, and without looking at his father tells him loudly to stop fearing death (12). But the grandfather cannot escape from this fear, and sixty pages later he comes back to it. He fears not just any death "but that which comes to us as we are spread out on our beds. Real death that has killed our people, not that which happens noisily, dripping blood, coming to us while we stand like a stab in the waist" (72). This violent, bloody death (perhaps a reference to the war that Daoud himself was living in) is nothing compared with the kind of death he now fearfully awaits. What he fears has already stricken ahlina [our family, also translated as our people].

In her chapter on Daoud, Eid interprets the grandfather's fear of death to be symbolic. She writes that "this deeper death is the death of life from its own dirt, laziness, negligence, and routine." The novel seems to reflect upon the social condition of the neglected, especially in the South, in Lebanon (1993, 92). The slighted house, in fact, is a symbol of the nation, reminding us of Yusuf's response to why he fights in Ashqar's novel. Eid writes: "The dilapidated house ready to collapse appears to stand for more than the individual or family house. It is the refuge, or the place to which the citizen takes shelter. Perhaps it is the nation itself" (93). Perhaps, but the thrust of the novel suggests that the house is only an extension of those who care (or not) for it. One need not see the house (or the nation, for that matter) as separated entities. The novel is about people, about the family—traditionally the strongest of all Lebanese institutions. In one of his chapters from *Lebanon's Predicament*, Khalaf focuses on kinship, probably "Lebanon's most solid and enduring social bond" (164). The extended family is more supportive than subversive, according to Khalaf, affecting all aspects of one's identity, employment, personal and political behavior. It is "still the major security device in society," although its influence has been gradually eroding (165). As in Shaykh's *Story of Zahra*, Daoud's novel totally demystifies the family. Whereas Shaykh focuses on spousal violence, infidelity, gender preference, and sexuality, Daoud looks at greed, materialism, selfishness as the main motivators for family relations. As a result of his treatment by his family, the story of this old man is tragic. Like during war, his society is ravaged and violent.

In the last chapter of Daoud's novel, one of the old man's granddaughters and her friend, callous girls, come into his room to change his soiled bed and clean him. During the whole procedure, they treat him like a disgusting object, moving him roughly from side to side and finally plopping him on the floor, where they spray him with cold water. They talk about him scornfully in the third person, never exhibiting even the slightest human concern for him. He has been reduced to Kafka's cockroach, dirty, dusty, disgusting, cursorily cleaned up and tossed away to die. Meyer notes that Daoud has, in fact, depicted the grandfather's condition as "existential" (300). Throughout his physical (and even arguably his mental) deterioration, he is fully aware that he is increasingly becoming an object to those around him. In the last paragraphs of the novel, the grandfather notes that "they washed me like they would a corpse, and they returned me, dirty, to my bed" (132). In a taunting voice, one of the girls menacingly approaches him and calls out, "Are you cleaner now than last time?" The last sentence reads: "The other one proceeded to stuff the rose up her nostril so that she could not smell my stench" (133).

Daoud depicts a level of heartlessness, of brutality even, between members of the same family. There are no competing clans, no village conflicts, no civil wars. There is just this one family, in many ways shockingly familiar, systematically torturing its supposedly most revered member. One need not resort to a landscape of actual war to depict destruction, death, and tragedy. It already resides here, within this society, within the hallowed family structure. Daoud's narrative written and published during the last years of the war suggests some of the more disturbing ways of constructing Lebanon. As in his earlier *House of Mathilde*, Daoud exposes something of the depravity of human beings. He forces the Lebanese to consider themselves and, as such, offers an important prescriptive model for the nation.

This two-chapter sequence on the war years introduces the idea that the period 1975–90 could not simply be contained or defined by that war. Certainly most writers presented here deal explicitly with war, and even those like Daoud who at times do not deal with war cannot be read without reference (as has just been done) to that war. Most of these writers also confront a Lebanese lifestyle, a mentality, a dialect or mode of expression that existed or grew irrespective of (though not divorced from) war.

The cultural artifacts produced during the war, and especially the novels, expand the limits of traditional boundaries. They seek in many ways to express thematically, stylistically, and structurally the new fictions that the war revealed or exposed. Because of the uniqueness of the war era, readers then as now approach those texts with preconceived questions and expectations. It is no wonder that one might look for answers (for the war) in these narratives, but one must also be open to the possibilities of meaning (irrespective of the war) that those narratives reveal. Ziad Rahbani's 1983 play *Shi fashil*, for example, can certainly reveal something about the war, but it also brilliantly can inform about the behavior of narcissistic women, obsessed with their diets and the latest fashions. It is also a play that illustrates how mongrelized our language has become, with humorous and familiar English and French intrusions into Arabic dialogue. It pokes fun at the jargon of journalists and intellectuals, trapped within their impressive sounding slogans. Rahbani recognizes the growing influence of Western media and, alongside the critical and ostensibly political conclusion to his play, introduces a character's clear preference for *Dallas* over the traditional Lebanese television fare (204). Like in so many of the novels already discussed, that which is backdropped or assumed can be highly indicative. As a result, a writer's depiction of family and gender relations, of urban life, of media issues, of household chores and daily routines can sometimes tell more about a people and a nation than a catalog of dates and battles.

What is most striking about the literary production of the war years is that it is diverse, exhibiting a healthy pluralism that, in the political arena, was expressing itself in battles. The level of discourse, especially in the newly conceived Lebanese war novel, reached a new height that, ironically, placed Lebanon on the cultural map while the country was at risk of disintegrating. In the introduction, Rorty is mentioned as advocating the imagination and specifically the novel (with its new vocabularies) as a guide to future action. Adonis also called repeatedly for new ways of thinking and writing if the Arabs aspired to progress. The novels of Khoury, al-Shaykh, al-Ashqar, Barakat, Da'if, and Daoud, set here against a historical context, all aspire to break the yoke of traditional rhetoric and to offer new thematics and stylistics for Lebanon. Their narratives presuppose a concrete nation, where its inhabitants and their plots unfold. All speak in a language and on topics that are recognizable and at times strikingly Lebanese. The recorded literature of the war years, as compared with most that came before, is much less derivative, more experimental, and more solidly situated within Lebanon. As such, these narratives probe deeper into the Lebanese psyche, into Lebanese institutions and cultural values, and thereby further our understanding of a nation trapped in war. They trigger a self-consciousness about the nation by prescribing an internal evaluation.

Part III

Reconstructing Lebanon

The Lebanese Republic and the Arab Republic of Syria, motivated by the brotherly and distinctive bonds between them that draw strength from their geographic propinquity and their common history, allegiance, fate, and mutual interests, and confident that realizing the widest cooperation and coordination shall serve their mutual interests, guarantee their progress and development, ensure their national security, secure their prosperity and stability, enable them to confront all regional and international developments, and fulfill the ambitions of the peoples in both countries in line with the Lebanese National Reconciliation Pact approved by [the Lebanese] Parliament on November 5, 1989, have agreed on the following [six articles].[1]

From the Treaty of Brotherhood, Cooperation, and Coordination between Syria and Lebanon, 1991

The dream of a reconnected city, a renewed and active center, and of a capital that can play a major role in the changing and competitive regional economy, is rapidly becoming a reality. It is the dream of a new and optimistic generation and of those now returning to their country to aid the reconstruction: the vision of Beirut reborn.

Beirut Reborn: The Restoration and Development of the Central District

6

Reworking the Past

Literature, in our situation, must put together two elements: seeing and inventing; it must tell the truth and lie; it must combine the real and the fantastic at the same level and at the same moment. This is the line of my research in literature.

Elias Khoury, 1993 *Beirut Review* interview

This final section examines the nation in the post-Taef, postwar period (1990–98). It is divided into two chapters to accommodate the large number of published texts, mainly novels. Breaking with the previous chronological structure of the book, the next two chapters could not be sensibly divided according to separate time frames. The eight-year period treated here is both too brief and void of a major dividing line. The usual historical backdrop for the entire period will be provided in this chapter, the first of the postwar chapters, followed by a treatment of texts that are primarily set in a prewar past or that do not focus on contemporary Lebanon. Chapter 7 then continues the literary analysis by focusing on texts that are set either during the war or afterward.

This phase of Lebanon's history coincided with the declaration of a New World Order, witnessed in the American-led international coalition against Iraq in 1991. The unchallenged position of the United States after the crumbling of the Soviet Union, and the division within the Arab world over supporting or opposing Iraq, propelled an American-Israeli peace process that did not necessarily serve Lebanon's interests. In addition, changing power structures in the region resulted in increasing Syrian hegemony over Lebanon as it entered a new phase of its existence.

Lebanon's so-called Second Republic was created after the constitutional amendments of the Taef Agreement (fall 1989) were approved by Parliament in August 1990 and signed into law by President Hrawi on September 21. A few weeks later, as discussed in the previous chapter, a Syrian offensive approved by Hrawi led to the removal of General Aoun from the presidential palace in Baabda. Under clear Syrian influence, the Second Republic emerged and would gradually consolidate its hold over the war-weary nation.

Soon after Aoun's departure, the Syrian/Lebanese plan for Greater Beirut Security and plans for dissolving the militias, for incorporating militiamen into the state institutions, for collecting small arms were all drawn up. Negotiations for returning displaced peoples began. Mandatory service in the army was instituted. The destruction of hashish fields in the Bekaa Valley by Syrian and Lebanese troops was highly publicized. Millions of dollars were promised by Arab regimes to help in reconstruction. By the end of 1991 all of the Western hostages were released. Many flights resumed to the Beirut International Airport, and citizens, especially among young Lebanese, began to travel to parts of the country they had never seen. For the first time in sixteen years, the nation was virtually free of war.

All was not rosy, however. Hizballah, recognized as fighting a legitimate war against the Israeli occupier, was not dissolved. The South remained a battlefront with almost daily exchanges and casualties. Many militia heads, now ministers in the government, continued to jostle for political supremacy. To increase the size of the new Parliament, around forty deputies were appointed (not elected) by the Council of Ministers (this in accordance with Taef). The hashish fields were publicly destroyed, but only after the earlier opium crop was harvested. Hostages were released in the same period when AUB's main administrative building, College Hall, was blown up (November 1991). The Lebanese lira continued its decline, unemployment was high, and the cost of living skyrocketed. Strikes by labor unionists, trade workers, and teachers reflected the disheartening economic conditions.

The most significant feature of this postwar period is Syrian hegemony, which exhibits itself not only in a visible military presence but in most political, economic, and increasingly cultural transactions. A slew of treaties and pacts, beginning with the 1991 Treaty of Brotherhood, Cooperation, and Coordination, between the two countries, clearly marks the future for Lebanon. The opening to the treaty (quoted at the outset to this section) introduces the six articles agreed upon by Syria and Lebanon. The treaty then stipulates that the "highest levels of cooperation and coordination" shall be sought in all fields, including political, economic, security, educational, scientific, agricultural, industrial, trade, transport, customs, and communications. Article 4 states that both governments "shall decide on the redeployment of Syrian troops" and also on the "size and dura-tion-of-stay of the force that will be redeployed." At no point in the treaty is there mention of a Syrian withdrawal. Article 5 outlines the principles that should govern the foreign policy of both countries, and Article 6 provides any "future confederal structure with a central authority: the Syrian-Lebanese Higher Council" (Tinaoui 101). By 1993, Lebanon had signed multiple agreements with Syria, including the Social and Eco-nomic Cooperation Agreement, where Lebanon is described as a "qutr" [province]. According to Simone G. Tinaoui, "This is a key word in the rhetoric of the Syrian Ba'th, for which Arab states are mere provinces in a united Arab nation" (102).

In terms of Lebanon's internal politics, parliamentary elections long overdue were scheduled in the late summer of 1992, but it soon became obvious that Syria's candidates were being pushed through and many (primarily Christians) boycotted the entire process, making the elections a total "sham" (pun intended). In the fall of 1992, the Lebanese/Saudi bil-lionaire Rafiq Hariri was asked to serve as prime minister and form a gov-ernment, and Nabih Berri was elected as speaker of Parliament. For the next six years, Hrawi, Hariri, and Berri would form the Lebanese ruling troika.

The growing hold of Syria over Lebanon is visible in attempts to censor and regulate previously unmonitored productions, especially in the me-dia. The Taef Agreement stated that "all media should be reorganized to serve the goals of national reconciliation and the termination of the state of war." The post-Taef period had witnessed a proliferation of unautho-rized TV and radio stations, which a series of regulatory draft laws then sought to change, but the limits they proposed for broadcasting and the audiovisual media were so restrictive that they were heavily criticized. The proposals strongly discouraged stations from showing political programs and news with severe penalties in case of transgressions.[2] The year 1993 also saw the rare banning of a text by the journalist and poet 'Abdo Wazen. His *Hadiqat al-hawass* (discussed in the next chapter) caught the attention of the censoring bureau of the Interior Ministry, which labeled it "porno-graphic," promptly banned it, and confiscated all copies. In the same year, several newspapers were shut down or taken to court, including *al-Safir*, *Nida' al-watan*, *al-Liwa'*, and *al-Sharq*.³

Four months before the Wazen ban, Elias Khoury anticipated the sure harm to come from a censorship bureau housed in the Ministry of the Interior: "Any policeman can come and censor Shakespeare."⁴ Khoury was also concerned about the creation of a new Ministry of Culture that could only, in the current political climate, be dominated by the state. One of the unique virtues of Lebanon was that it, alone among the Arab nations, had provided a forum for the free exchange of ideas. Khoury cites the example of a current play, *Al-Ightisab* [The rape] by the Syrian playwright Saʿdallah Wannus, with Palestinian actors and an Iraqi director. No performances were allowed in any Arab capital except Beirut (134). For Khoury, Lebanon must maintain its democratic function; in fact, he continues: "The main role of Lebanon today is to be a place where all the democratic forces in the Arab world can congregate, debate, and plan the future of the Arab world. This is the real meaning of this country, if we want to give it any meaning" (134).

The economic situation continued to worsen despite (or because of) efforts by Hariri, who ushered in a major program of reconstruction focusing on Lebanon's physical infrastructure. While most would argue for the need for such an initiative, many faulted the regime for failing to bolster other ravaged segments of the society. In addition, many noted that Hariri's policies were often wedded to his private business empire. The Solidere group, a private-sector company established in 1994 and responsible for the reconstruction of Beirut's downtown, was largely a Hariri venture, although the original plan for Beirut began even before he became prime minister.

Spurred by petro-dollars and the vision of an Arab Hong Kong, the new Beirut was conceived as a financial center in concrete and glass towers. The 1991 Master Plan of Beirut was commissioned by the Council for Development and Reconstruction (CDR), financed by the Hariri Foundation, and prepared by Dar al-Handasah. The plan provided very little public space in the new downtown, but was dominated by large highways and buildings and hundreds of parking lots. A wall of high rises (glass and iron) would essentially block the view of the sea; new sectors of land created from rubble would greatly profit a select few; little attention to reviving the old souks or preserving the archeological treasures of the area was given.

The idea was a financial center with exclusive shops that in no way renewed the once centralizing function of the "Burj" (Beirut's downtown area). Without attempting to salvage some 300 old buildings, a major demolition took place in the spring of 1992.[5]

Hariri's vision for Lebanon was also evident in the changing media regulations that largely favored the prime minister, who in 1993 owned 49 percent of the shares in Lebanon's state-run TV station, Tele-Liban (the only station with exclusive rights to broadcast via Arabsat), as well as owning another station outright, Future Television. In October 1994, a new law regulating the audiovisual media was passed. The government still owned broadcast frequencies and issued licenses, but censorship was much relaxed. The new law, however, required a large monetary backing for every station, greatly reducing the number of stations able to survive financially. Not coincidentally, those few stations which could then split the lucrative advertising revenues were primarily linked to political figures with high positions in the government. The survivors were as follows: Tele-Liban (official government station), Future Television (owned by Prime Minister Hariri), Murr Television or MTV (owned by the brother of the interior minister, Michel al-Murr), the National Broadcasting Network or NBN (controlled by Speaker of the House Berri), and the Lebanese Broadcasting Company (LBC, originally established by the Christian militia but controlled mainly by Christian oppositional figures critical of the government). Hizballah's "Manar" station was allowed to survive, despite its overt religious and political material, because it was perceived to be a major promoter of the resistance against Israel.

By 1995, new programs began to sprout, especially on LBC, that criticized the regime. TV programs like Jubran Tueni's 1995 *Fakhamat al Ra'is* [His excellency the president] made fun of the entire political process. Tueni's show featured presidential pretenders and hopefuls who were then asked questions on national and international affairs. A 128-member audience (equaling the number of deputies in Parliament) then voted and gave the candidate a grade. Under Syrian pressure, however, presidential elections did not take place, and Hrawi's mandate for the presidency was extended three more years (until the fall of 1998). Article 49 of the Constitution was amended to accommodate the extension.

In 1996, Benjamin Netanyahu became the new prime minister of Israel and in April launched the Grapes of Wrath operation in southern Lebanon, resulting in devastating losses, especially at the UN compound in Qana. This Israeli offensive was the largest since 1982 and represented a huge setback for Lebanon, but it also served to seemingly unify the country. Many Christians and Muslims joined not only in the condemnation but in charity efforts, while an outpouring of elegiac poetry and laments flooded the newspapers. National attempts to mark the Qana tragedy were largely successful, and the state quickly capitalized on the tragedy to transform the Qana site into a national symbol.

In the meantime, Hizballah was gaining legitimacy in Lebanon. Some of its members were elected to Parliament and were noted for their seriousness and dedication. Perceived as fighting a just battle against Israel for the liberation of Lebanese territory, Hizballah also secured the gratitude and respect of constituents by providing much needed social services.

The summer 1996 parliamentary elections were, as expected, marred by fraud in all regions. For the first time, private monitoring groups observed and reported on the polling, engaging citizens in the political process. The massive reconstruction effort in the old city center of Beirut remained controversial, and Elissar, a project for the development of Beirut's southwest suburb, was launched. In May 1997, the pope visited Lebanon, drawing almost a third of the population to greet him. In July, Lebanon hosted the delayed Pan-Arab Games, which featured a memorable semifinals soccer match between Lebanon and Syria. After a Lebanese goal, the Syrian fans broke plastic seats and threw garbage on the field. The Syrians won the game, and rioting followed. This embarrassing incident was kept muted in government reporting. In 1998 the Hikma (Sagesse) Lebanese basketball team won the Arab championship, causing an unprecedented show of support. However, this national victory was primarily celebrated in Christian, not Muslim, areas of Lebanon where Hikma is located.

The long-delayed municipal elections (last held in 1963) finally took place in May and June 1998. Despite some postponements and reports of fraud, the elections mobilized large segments of the population and were conducted in a relatively democratic fashion. Candidates, representing a broad range of the populace, positioned themselves either as pro-government or in the opposition. Besides the already exhibited dominance of pro-Syrian nominees and supporters of Hariri or Berri, the powerful presence of the interior minister, Michel Murr, was evident in many elections. This disturbing trend, however, was countered by a new spirit of participation and engagement by young people, women, pro-environment activists, and oppositionists. The elections in Mount Lebanon, for example, proved that many districts were willing to go against the authorities, and Hizballah's victory over a formidable Hariri/Berri ticket sent a clear message across the nation.

As Lebanon emerged relatively intact as a nation-state after sixteen years of war, the promise of liberal democracy seemed elusive. The leaders seemed intent on rebuilding the country on shaky foundations. Questions and issues that were necessarily postponed or eclipsed during Lebanon's long night of war were now suddenly quite visible. Besides the obvious destructions produced by the war, Lebanon's environment appeared to be devastated, its children troubled, its educational system outdated, its civic sense weak. Large groups of people were either out of work or falling rapidly out of the middle class to below the poverty line. While the government spent huge amounts of (borrowed) money to rebuild the nation, those efforts focused on roads, tunnels, and buildings, with little attention to bolstering the industrial and agricultural sectors that might produce jobs. In addition, a huge infiltration of low-wage foreign workers (estimated close to 1 million) funneled labor wages out of the country.

This quick survey of almost a decade since the official end of the civil war serves primarily to complicate facile perceptions of Lebanon as the "phoenix rising from the ashes," or of Beirut as the amazingly "reborn city." While there is certainly reason to celebrate the end of a war that devastated but did not destroy the country, there is also evidence to warrant great caution. At the end of his massive study of Lebanon, Hanf optimistically concluded that the Lebanese had an independent state, but that they "became a nation only when the state was in mortal danger" (642). A nation, however, is a complicated entity, and though most combatants in the civil war agreed that Lebanon should not be partitioned, this did not imply that the nation was united. Unlike the fragmentation of Yugoslavia after its internal battles, Lebanon seemingly survived, but its cultural narratives continued to critique, offering a significant discourse in the 1990s.

Examining selections from the cultural output during this period helps problematize Lebanon, still very much under construction and, to many, undergoing a misguided reconstruction. Perhaps it is no coincidence that a large number of fictions written during this period choose not to focus on contemporary Lebanon. Many novels, in particular, are either set in an earlier period or focus on a distinct cultural group only partially linked to the Lebanon of the 1990s. The latest novels by Elias Khoury, Rachid al-Da'if, Hasan Daoud, Emily Nasrallah, and Amin Maalouf all fit loosely, despite differences, into this category.

The last three novels by Khoury, though not a trilogy, are intricately bound together by occasional thematics and stylistics. The 1993 *Mamlakat al-ghuraba'* [Kingdom of strangers] and 1998 *Bab al-shams* [Gate of the sun] both revolve around Palestinian lives and stories. In fact, after completing the latter novel, which contains more than 500 pages, one can see how the earlier one was, in some ways, a warm-up text. Between the two is the 1994 *Majma' al-asrar* [Collection of secrets], which, though focusing on the Lebanese, is an obvious pair with *Mamlakat*.

Published only a year apart, *Mamlakat* and *Majma'* both revolve around strangers and secrets. Often set in the past, both continue to foreground the teller/tale and male/female binaries, and both make frequent references to other authors. In the first novel, three women (Maryam, Wadad, and Samia) set in relief the male narrators and their stories, which, in the telling, are perceived to be either fictions or truths. At one point, the character Maryam accuses the narrator scornfully of always searching for the truth in order to write it, and that when he writes it he distorts it into a story. The narrator agrees: "What else can we do? We write means to lie—but I try not to lie" (65). She then realizes that he wants her because he doesn't write about her; he writes about others.

Another woman, Wadad the Circassian once-servant, is loved by her literal owner, Iskander, who bought her in 1920 and then married her. She becomes fluent in Arabic, but in all his years with her, she remains a quiet mystery, a cross between a nun and a nurse. In 1976, an old and sick woman, she reverts back to her native language, escapes from the hospital (perhaps in search of her country), and is found dead along the road. In 1988, the narrator tells this story to the author Salman Rushdie (before the appearance of *Satanic Verses*), who agrees that it is material for a novel, but the narrator is scared to write the story because "we fear that it might swallow and marginalize us" (96). His attempts here to then narrate the story of Palestine is testimony to that fear. No language is totally appropriate for the telling; besides, the narrator's relationship to the language is uncertain.

In reaction to these issues, Rushdie smiles and talks about how he left behind a language (Urdu) when he moved to Britain, how he still dreams in Urdu and English, but how English has definitely come to dominate all his languages. The narrator draws a parallel to the story of Wadad and reflects upon Rushdie's account of an Indian who moves to London and writes stories in English. He wonders what would happen if Rushdie were struck by disease, forgot his English, and reverted to his mother tongue, no longer able to read the stories he had written. Rushdie, however, maintains that he never forgot Urdu, but consciously chose English, a language over which he now has total control. The narrator responds: "Language is like land. . . . We are able to occupy the language of others as we can occupy their land. The problem is who are we?" (97).

The story of Wadad allows Khoury to introduce a subject dealt with expertly by another Arab writer and intellectual, Abdelkebir Khatibi, on the relationship between author and language. In his *Love in Two Languages*, Khatibi demonstrates how the colonized (Arab) can achieve a level of supremacy by adopting and transforming the language of the colonizer (French). Some Lebanese authors have also consciously chosen to write in French and have expressly talked about it.[6] The Palestinian Israeli Anton Shammas wrote his novel *Arabesques* in Hebrew rather than his native Arabic. By insisting on expressing themselves, their cultures, and their nations in French and Hebrew, not Arabic, these authors have achieved a new kind of occupation. For Khoury, enmeshed here in a tale of Palestinian loss to Israeli occupation, the political implications of these remarks are evident. Reclaiming loss through language is, in fact, at the core of Khoury's project. By weaving the Wadad tale (with her losses and adoptions of languages) throughout the narrative of Palestinians, Khoury attempts yet another way of "getting at" the essence of his story—the difficult narration of Palestine.

By the end of his tale, though, the tentative teller can only question what he has produced: "Is this land which we call Palestine just a story that mesmerizes us with its secrets and talismans? Why is it that when we listen to this story we don't sleep . . . but die?" (127).

This is no bedtime story for sleepy children; it is real life tragedy, translated, transmitted, and communicated with difficulty. Indeed, the narrator wonders if oral narratives, or perhaps journalism, would be more reliable (119). Much to his surprise, the narrator discovers that the legend of the

Lebanese monk Jirgi, killed in Jerusalem in 1946, is true. This supposed apocryphal story of the monk was forgotten, but it gradually made its way into legend or folklore to become part of the unconscious and transfer into children's stories. In contrast now, according to the narrator, "We live in an era of registration. This means that when we record an event as it occurs we cancel its legendary possibilities" (118).

In his next novel, *Majmaʿ al-asrar,* Khoury also toys with legends, wondering how to piece together historical fragments and how to construct meaning out of strange and secretive lives. Much of the story takes place in Beirut of the 1940s, with references to the killing of one of the main characters' ancestors in 1860. This old tale is taken up by the Nobel Prize–winning author Gabriel Garcia Marquez in his novel *Chronicle of a Death Foretold,* a portion of which is translated into Arabic in Khoury's novel (44). Khoury's interest in Latin American writers was also revealed in *Mamlakat,* when the narrator offers the contribution of these authors who have resorted to the oral past to reconstruct their contemporary stories (118). In both novels, Khoury is attentive to that past in creating the legends and the stories that reside with the people in the public domain.

The narrator of *Majmaʿ* maintains that in traditional or oral stories like *One Thousand and One Nights,* there was no need for naming. Giving names to characters is a problem of the modern story, for "modernism involves a shift to the individual, and the individual has no presence without a name" (*Majmaʿ* 36). Khoury confronts this in his own writing. On the one hand he yearns for anonymity, for his characters and stories to enter the public imagination by osmosis and to become part of a collective unconscious. On the other hand, he lives in an "era of registration," increasingly competing with forces (like the visual media) that defract and distract. There is a compulsion to name and record lest one forever forget, but recording or naming also limits the possibilities of meaning.

In his *Majmaʿ,* Khoury attributes secrets to all of his main characters and their relationships. As in earlier works, gender presents a foiling mechanism. Here, Norma is in a sexual relationship, secretly, with two old friends, Ibrahim Nassar and Hanna Salman. The first seems gentle while the second is rough. Ibrahim, however, leads a secretive life with his spinster aunt, who dies, by strangling, at the beginning of the novel. We learn later that Ibrahim suffers from occasional impotence with Norma and has the desire to kill her, that he detests his aunt's insistence on her virginity and wants to rape her, that he has recurring sexual dreams about the jockey Abbas. When Ibrahim dies, the reader realizes he is a dangerous man, shrouded in mystery. Hanna, on the other hand, is an overtly violent man who sexually assaults Norma and is accused of raping and killing prostitutes. He is thrown in prison, where he is tortured until he confesses to his crimes, but Hanna is innocent. The real killer, the historically accurate Victor Awwad, is condemned and executed in 1948. Hanna is released as a quieter and gentler man. Most significantly, as he attends Awwad's execution, he realizes and is terrified by the "truth"—that he could have committed these crimes—man can be anything, is capable of anything (169).

Indeed, the novel explores this dialectic between Ibrahim and Hanna, both alternately dangerous and innocent. Norma is trapped between the two, offering a glaring look at the complex and sinister human species. *Majma'* combines fictional with factual accounts from the present and the past to weave a tale that gradually unfolds and becomes, both in the reading and the telling, the experience itself. The strange and the secretive—those prime qualities of human relations—are narrated in increasingly confident tones, so that by the time we reach Khoury's 1998 novel *Bab al-shams*,[7] the tentative experimentation gives way to a bold tour de force. Here the narrator in an obviously unrealistic formula persists in narrating his subject, the glorious subject that Khoury unabashedly puts forth, Palestine.

Unavoidably a Lebanese concern, as earlier chapters have indicated, the intensive focus on Palestine so late in the century, and as Lebanon itself recovers from years of war, is perhaps curious. It is as if to say that despite the tragedies of Lebanon and in spite of Palestinian involvement in Lebanon's internal affairs, the question of Palestine remains legitimate. For Khoury, Palestine's story needs to be told and retold, as it is threatened with extinction, with forgetfulness. Khoury's *Bab al-shams* is an act of chivalry, a grandiose gesture of empathy, an epic love story. In tone, it is very similar to *Mamlakat*, also featuring primarily Palestinian lives and tales. In format, it draws from earlier works, but ostensibly foregrounds an oral tradition, as Khoury consciously constructs a massive text from already existing tales within the popular imagination.

The premise for the narration is knowingly forced: a quasi-doctor, Khalil, watches over the coma-stricken Yunus in the Galilee Hospital within the Chatila Palestinian camp in Beirut. For months he tends to the patient, telling him one story after the next hoping to cure him through talk. As the object (and often subject) of these tales is unresponsive, Khalil is free to make mistakes. "This is freedom," he declares, but he is exhausted from all the telling and "drowning in all these stories" (236). At the end of the long first part, "Galilee Hospital," Khalil's voice is hoarse and he needs respite. He turns on the radio, listening to soothing Fayruz, and then exits Yunus's room and the book . . . for a while.

After two weeks, he returns to tell other stories. These are personal accounts, primarily by others, that capture in important new ways what happened in 1948 as Palestine was torn in war and Israel established; in 1967 when more Arab lands were lost to Israel in the short war; in 1970 when the Palestinian resistance was liquidated in Jordan; in 1982 when the Israelis invaded Lebanon, forcing the relocation of the PLO, and the subsequent massacres in Sabra and Chatila; and in 1985 when the War of the Camps pitted the Shiʿa Amal group against Palestinians in the Lebanese capital. The stories, however, do not simply reinforce the public narrative of Palestinian losses just listed above. They provide the much needed human dimension of that loss, the intricate, often incomprehensible, even humorous qualities of people's lives during the various junctures of history. Khalil, like Khoury himself, is eager to narrate and hence register these stories. He takes great pride in them because they are not just his but public property, so to speak. He is the facilitator, the spokesman, but the tribute (as he insists in his acknowledgments) goes to the many women and men in the Palestinian camps in Lebanon who "opened up the doors of their stories to me, and who took me on a journey to their memories and dreams" (528). He also thanks the many intellectuals, writers, and researchers who helped prepare him for this large project.

The novel begins with the death of the remarkable Umm Hasan in Chatila. Khalil has inherited a videotape of her visit back to Palestine. All want to preserve and consecrate the video, but it hardly captures the essence of what occurred on her visit. This true story (confirmed by Khoury during a 1998 interview) is worth summarizing quickly here. Umm Hasan, now an old woman, had the opportunity to visit Israel and locate the village and house that she was forced to evacuate in 1948. The village has been renamed and is hardly recognizable. Most of the houses were destroyed decades ago, except for a few new houses on the top of a hill, one of which was Umm Hasan's. So her house still stands and she walks slowly to the door, taking in every detail of the surroundings. A fifty-year-old Israeli woman opens the door, speaks to her in Arabic, and invites her in. Umm Hasan is surprised she knows Arabic, but the Israeli responds that she never forgot Arabic but had to learn Hebrew. The house has not changed a bit; even the water jug is where Umm Hasan left it years ago. They introduce themselves, and the Israeli woman offers the jug to the Palestinian as a token gift, but Umm Hasan refuses. The silence is deafening as the old woman continues her tour of the house, but the Israeli continues talking (in Arabic) about the difficulty of life here. As Umm Hasan looks around, all she can mutter is "Palestine is heaven."

Their conversation becomes more specific, and the Israeli wants to know exactly where Umm Hasan lives in Lebanon. When she finds out she lives in Beirut, she screams out: "I too am from Beirut, from Wadi Abu Jamil, the Jewish neighborhood downtown. They brought me here when I was twelve. I left Beirut and came to this godforsaken place. . . . I don't understand. You live in Beirut and you come to cry here. I'm the one who wants to cry. Get up and leave; get up, sister, and leave. Return Beirut to me and take all this barren land" (109).

Later, Umm Hasan would recount how the Israeli told her how badly treated she and her family were in Israel. As Eastern Jews, they were tormented and humiliated constantly. Umm Hasan returned to Lebanon and told everyone that she cried when the Israeli woman occupying her house told her her story. She couldn't help it (112). Nothing is as simple as it at first seems. When it is time for Umm Hasan to leave her former house, the Israeli again offers her the jug, and she takes it without looking at it. She returns to Beirut, to the Chatila camp where she has been a refugee for over forty years and places the jug in the corner of her abode. It is there when she dies in the camp in 1995, as sure as the Israeli woman is still living in her home back in Palestine (111).

In another story regarding houses, Nahila (the wife of the patient Yunus) tells how in 1948 they followed Yunus's blind father not toward Lebanon, as the Israelis wanted, but in the opposite direction, to a village just evacuated. There they chose an empty house at random, a house that belonged to people who fled to Lebanon. Here they remained—in a village that was no longer a village, unable to harvest the fields, so they resorted to stealing fruits at night (393). In that house they lived for decades like strangers. "What must the Jews feel who live in our houses?" she wonders (396).

The unleashing of these and myriad other stories thwarts all attempts to reduce and simplify the Palestinian tragedy. Not only is it complex, but it is alive and mesmerizing. Khoury's retelling is testimony to the fact that these stories are still operative in the camps. They need to be preserved now, especially now, as the inclination toward one-dimensional videos is sadly taking over and as the Arab political climate is moving quickly away from Palestinian concerns.

Khoury chooses to focus his narrative of Palestine not on political issues but on the relationship between Yunus and his wife, Nahila. Khalil has been talking to the comatose and obviously dying Yunus for months. We know that Yunus, who goes by many names, has proved to be a hero and father figure to Khalil. He has been in the resistance for decades, establishing political and military organizations and becoming a leading member of Fateh (391), but we hear surprisingly little about his pro-Palestinian activities. Instead, Khalil focuses on the unlikely love story between a husband and wife. Here, he recalls what Yunus told him: "I lived with her [Nahila] and for her. For Palestine is not a cause. Well, in a way it is, but it isn't. The land is going nowhere. And the problem isn't over who controls the land: controlling land is a delusion. No one can rule over the land as long as he is going to be buried in it. The land controls all and takes all to her. I, my friend, did not fight because of history. I fought because of the woman I loved" (25–26).

Yunus and his wife were separated in 1948, as she remained inside the new state, and he fought that state from the outside. In the first decades after the establishment of Israel, Yunus could move relatively easily across the borders where his wife and growing family resided, but he had to be careful, as he was a wanted man. He and Nahila of the long dark hair would meet in the caves, called *Bab al-shams* [door/gate of the sun], outside the village, where they would talk, eat, make love—year after year. Even when the border crossings became almost impossible in the 1970s and 1980s, he persisted. Now this is a story, according to Khalil, that is worth retelling, but it has not been told before.

We learn that Yunus actually told it to Ghassan Kanafani, the prominent Palestinian writer, who took some notes but never wrote the story because it wasn't symbolic enough; it was just a love story (43). Khalil realizes, however, that the story really didn't have to be told to anyone, since everyone already knew it: "Real stories are not narrated, because the people know them" (43). They have already become legends and part of a collective consciousness.

In a 1998 interview, Khoury related a personal story of when he was a budding author along with his friend, the poet Mahmoud Darwish. Both met and fawned over the very distinguished and prominent Egyptian writer Yusuf Idris. He dismissed their adulation with a remark that went something like this: I am not a great writer and won't be until I become like the writer of the Juha tales.[8] When his young protégés remarked that no one authored the Juha tales, Idris replied, "Exactly. The people think that they wrote them. They are very natural and come out of the culture. That's the kind of writer I aspire to be."

In an insightful review, Samira Issa points out how *Bab* is like *One Thousand and One Nights*, as Khalil, like Scheherazade, tells his and others' stories as a way to overcome his own death. In both texts, the original author has also disappeared, melding into the personalities of his own heroes. The reader forgets the author's existence (Issa 18).

Certainly in *Bab*, Khoury demonstrates the power of an oral tradition that keeps afloat popular narratives on the Palestinian experience. He weaves together those stories alongside a fictional composition that is also dotted with historical facts. The result is orchestral and harmonious. The many different contributions to the text serve a similar function of bringing to light the lived Palestinian ordeal. Although the stories vary from being funny, pragmatic, quirky, and tragic, they are rarely melodramatic, and all serve to challenge reductionist and traditional notions of Palestinian history.

The story of Yunus and Nahila, for example, ends up not simply glorifying the man for his military exploits but highlighting the woman's heroism in dealing with an increasingly impossible situation. Yunus's heroism is exposed only by implication. Nahila's, on the other hand, is consistently foregrounded. It is she who is reported to have stood up to the Israeli authorities during her fourth pregnancy. To protect her husband, she denied that Yunus was the father, insisting that she was a whore (288). When they accuse her of having no shame, she yells out: "Shame! You stole the country and kicked out its people, and you come to give me lessons in morality. Sir, we're free, and no one is entitled to ask me about my sex life" (289). This powerful woman has spent her life waiting, living "on hold." She finally (perhaps in her most heroic act) confronts her husband under the olive tree. She spells out their dilemma in no uncertain terms: She has lived her life in Israel, where her children now work and plan to marry. What will she do in Lebanon? Live in a refugee camp? She also knows that he will be killed if he comes to Israel. They are divided. The real story, she says, "is about people who have become strangers. Do you know who we are, what we have become?" (392). She is afraid for her kids, whom she doesn't understand: "They live as if this is it." She holds Israeli citizenship, she votes, but realizes that they have paid the ultimate price and were defeated. "I want to end the delusion," she concludes (398–99). It is time to lead separate lives.

Khalil is, of course, the transmitter of all this material. His own love and passion for a Fida'i woman, Shams, who is later killed, haunts him. When she died, he says, he feared his own death and became aware of all the parts of him that died as well. Death was creeping up on him, and then Yunus came. Khalil turns to him pleadingly: "I didn't want you to die, so that the last part of me that separates me from death would not die" (506). Khalil's incessant talking can be interpreted as a desperate search for life, for meaning, for love. Yunus becomes for Khoury the ultimate symbol of hope and resurrection. His survival, he thinks, is necessary for his own.

After seven months in a coma, Yunus does die, and Khalil remains behind. He cannot grieve, and he regrets having ended his last session with Yunus talking about Nahila's death. He doesn't want to end the story that way; he wants a different one, so he now resurrects a different ending that has Yunus risking his life to cross the border to see Nahila again some nine months after the "talk" under the olive tree and their decision to separate. He recalls a time when the two of them went to Acca and ate fresh fish as if they were in Palestine. Khalil wants to tell Yunus of his children and grandchildren and the growing numbers of Palestinian offspring—good things.

Khalil, unable to absorb Yunus's death, still talks to him and recounts an incomprehensible experience whereby he stumbles upon a veiled woman who ends up in his house, cooking a dinner of fresh fish, letting down her long dark hair, and making passionate love to him. When he wakes up, she is gone with no trace. This is Khalil's epiphany. He realizes he is in love and breaks down sobbing:

I never cried for Shams, the way I cried for you and her.
I never cried for my father, the way I cried for you and her.

I never cried for my mother, the way I cried for you and her.
I never cried for my grandmother, the way I cried for you and her.
I left my house barefoot and ran to your grave. (527)

The last lines of the novel switch to the present tense with Khalil standing
in the rain before Yunus's grave with the conviction that the stories did not
end this way. He reaches out to the pouring rain and walks. The talking to
Yunus is now over, and Khalil has been released to walk away from the
grave and out of the text.

Coming to the end of this long novel, one has the feeling that, perhaps
like the author, Khalil has made his peace. There is a powerful cathartic
undertow that is finally snapped in the last lines to release the reader as
well. Whereas at the end of *Mamlakat al-ghuraba'* the stories are read not
to sleep but to die, in *Bab* there is the clear assertion that "stories are for
sleep, not for death" (485). Not all is death and loss. There is also love,
loyalty, faith, persistence—qualities represented in Nahila, in Nahila and
Yunus's relationship, and in Khalil's final understanding of Nahila, of Yunus,
and of Palestine. This realization, however, comes at a painful price. Khalil
is able to fully understand the big picture only after he has gone through a
purgatory of guilt. Issa highlights the Oedipal dimension of Khalil's relationship with Yunus (his now dead adopted father) and Nahila (the woman
he makes love to) at the novel's close. It is this realization which finally
leads Khalil to confront his own guilt and to finally break down in tears
standing in the rain. Issa wonders if Khoury is suggesting that the Palestinian must be purified by remorse and self-confrontation prior to overcom-
ing death (Issa 18).

Khoury's latest narrative drew a lot of attention and praise from the Palestinian community.[9] Though ostensibly on Palestine, this novel also re-
lates specifically to Lebanon. As earlier chapters have illustrated, the Palestinian issue has, from its inception, been linked to the fate of Lebanon.
Even before the civil war and certainly during the war years, as Khoury's
and other narratives have indicated, the Palestinian/Lebanese dialectic has
been unavoidable. In both *Mamlakat* and *Bab*, the Palestinian stories have
been told primarily from the Lebanese camps, involving both Lebanese
and Palestinian characters and scenarios. Indeed, there are specific and
powerful moments when the Palestinian and the Lebanese are conjoined.
For example, Khalil recalls meeting the Kata'ib now in Ashrafiyye, but he
is surprised to discover that he no longer regards them as the enemy: "It

was as if I was before a mirror. As if I saw myself reflected there. . . . I want to say that true war begins when your enemy becomes your mirror, and you kill him to kill yourself" (283). This moment of painful recognition suggests shared experiences, so that the multiple narratives ultimately reflect not only on the state of Palestinian nationhood but on the Lebanese state. In fact, one can argue, narrating Palestine from within the Lebanese context (as Khoury is doing as a Lebanese author who writes and publishes in Lebanon) propels the stories to become part of the national consciousness—not just the Palestinian, but specifically the Lebanese consciousness. As such, the narrative offers a prescription for Lebanese reconstruction.

It is in this same spirit of awareness that writers and intellectuals like Khoury reasserted Lebanon's place as a cultural haven in the Arab world with a bold commemoration of Palestine fifty years after the *nakba*. At the Théâtre de Beyrouth (where Khoury had been director for years) from April through June 1998, a series of events on political, cultural, scientific, and artistic subjects were scheduled. Some, like the invitation to a number of Arab Jewish scholars, caused considerable controversy leading to the unfortunate cancellation of their talks. For Khoury, Lebanon must continue the struggle for intellectual freedom in the Arab world. The forum on Palestine (like the narratives on Palestine in Khoury's novels) is inherently also a project for Lebanon's reconstruction.

Khoury's three novels are not war novels per se. The war (as most of Khoury's previous novels attest) has been narrated. In fact, in his 1993 *Kingdom*, the narrator wonders, "How come we didn't tell our stories before this war?" (103). For many reasons the war provided a rich opportunity for telling. In these later novels, although all three make necessary reference to Lebanon at war, there are other stories that now need to be told as well. This postwar era allowed writers to throw their nets further.

The Lebanese Najwa Barakat sets her 1996 *Bas al-Awadim* [Bus of decent folk] in Morocco, although it could really be any Arab locale. Here, a group of men and women are brought together on a bus, like pilgrims on a journey. They are a disparate bunch who are compelled to hear each other's tales and to experience similar fates. One man clutches a plant stolen from his beloved's garden; another carries a bag of sugar for a wife he deserted forty-five years ago in order to follow the Palestinian "cause"; a third journeys to her wedding with her bedroom as a dowry on the bus's roof. The bus stops during a violent storm, and the passengers share tea and food together. They enter a forest of olive trees and rescue a young man who is pursued by an angry mob because he won't play music for their dying trees. The passengers tell stories to pass the time. One of them recalls an old vibrant city with its bustling souks and a rich variety of merchandise and artisans (28) that might suggest a lost Beirut, but the novel is not specific in its geography or its time in history. Like Khoury's *Gates of the City*, it proceeds allegorically with references to walled cities, the North, the South, a sea, a desert.[10]

Other novelists writing in this period chose to relocate their fictions not geographically but temporally by going to Lebanon's past. One of Da'if's novels written after the official end of the civil war also seeks to tell new stories, by focusing its fiction on an era before (though leading up to) the war.

After a 1991 novel, *Ghaflat al-turab* [Negligence of the dirt], and a 1993 collection of short pieces and poems, *Ay thalj yahbut bi-salam* [What snow falls], Da'if published *'Azizi al-Sayyed Kawabata* in 1995 (translated in 1999 by Paul Starkey as *Dear Mr. Kawabata*). Set primarily before the war, this novel is structured as a string of uninterrupted letters by the narrator Rachid (who is like but not identical to the author, he cautions on p. 19) to the Nobel-winning Japanese novelist Yasunari Kawabata. This odd correspondence allows the narrator many privileges. For one thing, Da'if's narrator can be comfortably confessional because he speaks to a total stranger. He can, for example, safely reveal that as kids they used to be plagued by tapeworms. Now if a "Christian told this to a Muslim the latter would say: you Christians are worm-infested! Or the Christian would accuse all Muslims of being worm-infested" (85). Talking to a foreigner, a Japanese no less, is much easier. The narrator can also take advantage of his recipient's ignorance of Arabic and Arabs to explain (usually parenthetically) certain features he is obviously eager to criticize. He uses particular expressions or turns of phrases in Arabic and then points out how hackneyed and rhetorical they are. He also can generalize about Arabs to this foreigner, telling how prone they are to a literature of sorrow, lament, and blame. He promises that, here, he will not be following this tradition (21). Finally, the narrator Rachid is also writing to a fellow novelist, one who understands, as Da'if said,[11] how to express feelings and ideas.

With all these excellent excuses for free narration, Rachid has plenty of

good stories to tell. Like other novelists in the 1990s, Daʿif chooses to situate his drama outside of contemporary Beirut. Much of this tale takes place
decades ago in the mountain village, ending with the protagonist seriously
wounded in Beirut at the outset of the war in 1975. The stories are all
revealing, even and perhaps especially if they are delusions. Rachid writes:
"I know, Mr. Kawabata, that people are in need of delusion or myth or
religion, etc." (26). His own father used to tell a story that could not possibly have happened to him, since a simple calculation (on his son's part)
revealed that the dad was not even there.

Rachid himself admits that he clearly recalls his parents' honeymoon
night and his own birth. He then proceeds to carefully narrate both; this
allows him to broach the subject of sex—a definite taboo topic and source
of great speculation on the part of the village boys. As anecdotes of his
childhood continue, it soon becomes apparent that illiteracy, superstition,
ignorance, and blind faith characterize his parents, who refuse to encourage him in his pursuit of knowledge and questioning of God's vision: "Even
the dumb chicken raises her head when she drinks in thanks to her creator," affirms his mom (116). What is a schoolboy to do? He has just learned
that the earth is round and revolves around itself and the sun. This is knowledge to make one swoon; indeed, the young Rachid is so shocked by this
information that he needs to be revived in class (47). The first part of
Kawabata is replete with endearing and funny stories that bring to life a
village mentality that the author, rather lovingly, records.

In contrast to the village and childhood culture that Rachid inhabits is
Beirut, that faraway, dazzling place of promise and adventure. It is there
that Rachid heads for college, for political activism, and for sex. He describes the student and worker strikes of the late 1960s,[12] his involvement
with the Communist Party, and his vision to bring down the Lebanese system and other Arab regimes, resulting in a war of liberation against Israel
(152). This idealism is matched by an innocence exhibited, for example,
when the young Rachid and his buddies decide to look for a prostitute
(122–27). All of this action takes place in Beirut's downtown in Martyr's
Square, popularly known as the Burj. Here the young men rent a room,
participate in demonstrations, seek out the prostitutes, take cabs, eat, go to
the movies, shop. As he reminisces, Rachid cannot help his enthusiasm:
"Allah, Allah! Dear Mr. Kawabata, don't prevent me now from going on
about Martyrs' Square! You'll see how this will interest you" (156): "Before

the war it was the heart of the capital, with its souks, banks, movie houses, popular theaters, hotels, prostitutes, cab stations, so that one could get to it from all over Lebanon. It was the heart of Lebanon" (157). It was a truly public and popular living space. Today, of course, it no longer exists. The Burj was destroyed in the early 1975–76 battles, and for the duration of the war it remained an isolated no-man's-land with collapsed buildings, over-grown vines, and stray cats. In the postwar period, debate over how to re-construct the downtown raged on, resulting in multiple plans. But debate did not prevent a massive demolition of much of the Burj in 1993. Besides Da'if, other writers—like Nasrallah and Shaykh—focused portions of their texts on Beirut's Burj. All serve a vital purpose of preservation in the face of obliteration.

Da'if's description of this prewar period (both from the village and Beirut), however, is never simply nostalgic. He effectively captures the contradictions that form a past life, while offering something of a retro-spective on troubled Lebanon. As he is writing from the vantage point of the postwar period, Da'if can now look back with a modicum of cyni-cism. The youthful zeal, for example, of the young Rachid's political vi-sion is tempered much later when he recalls how he participated in the fighting of 1975. Then, the leftist political party distributed forged iden-tification cards to all Christian members, listing them with Muslim names. At the time, he writes, "we didn't wonder why it was necessary to be Mus-lims so as not to be kidnapped and killed in the areas that we were defend-ing with our weapons!" (172). The hypocrisy of a party that supposedly was fighting against overt confessionalism is hence exposed retrospectively. By the novel's close, Rachid has been seriously hit and left for dead (204)—no cheery optimism here.

Hassan Daoud's beautifully written 1996 *Sanat al-automatik* [Year of the Automatic] is also set before the war (in the mid-1960s) and never even leads up to that war. In a nonnostalgic style, Daoud brings to life the people and activities surrounding a Ras Beirut family bakery. Narrated by the son of the bakery's owner, we learn about every detail of the changing busi-ness: the employees, the equipment, the materials, the finances, and the distribution. As time goes by, different machines are introduced (often with negative results), culminating in the year when the "automatic" oven is installed. Against this backdrop, which almost reads like a history of Beirut bakeries, the novel proceeds by vignettes (in separate chapters) rather than a traditional plot. These interconnected stories revolve around the narrator's friends and family, offering a glimpse at lives not often told. Here, the adolescent boys flunk out of school, pursue body-building, and spend every waking hour plotting how to get laid. They build a bamboo tent on the apartment building roof so as to improve their chances of spotting naked girls. They speed around in the bakery car or take a ride on a flimsy boat in dangerous waters—all in the hopes of a glimpse. Almost every woman is a candidate for their imaginative exploits.

All the characters are connected, somehow, to the bakery situated on a busy street in Ras Beirut.[13] The boys either work at the bakery or are related to the owner. Others come in to buy bread (like the two pretty sisters) or to use the restroom. The bakery it seems is the only store on the street to have a restroom; as such, it humorously draws in a wide array of owners and employees from the vicinity. Even the American Peter is embarrassed but compelled to use the restroom, and Daoud carefully narrates the polite verbal exchange between the baker and this foreigner during the now-routine awkward visit (178–80). Another restroom frequenter is the Armenian woman who, late in the novel, will be offended by an incident involving the urinating brother of the narrator. She will now boycott the bakery and seek relief elsewhere (172).

The world Daoud reconstructs is stable, lively, funny, and comfortable. Like Da'if and, as we shall see, Nasrallah, he resurrects a Beirut that no longer exists. He also chronicles an era (as exemplified in adolescence) that must, of necessity, sadly end. As in his previous work, he often indicates that youthful era by providing the costs of things in Lebanese piasters and liras, reminding one of the shocking devaluation of the currency that would take place in the 1980s. In his vivid depictions of the daily bustle about the bakery, we see the mixed neighborhood that once thrived with Christians, Muslims, Armenians, and foreigners all sharing urban space side by side. Here are the neighboring bookstore, restaurant, cinema, and sundry shops. The church is nearby as is a university, and a wide assortment of people float in and out of the bakery. We only know in retrospect that this lifestyle will change during the civil war.[14] As for the tattooed adolescent boys, they remain occupied with the bakery, their schoolwork, and their social and family lives. It is difficult to imagine that some of these same boys would, ten years later, pick up guns and take to the streets, but perhaps there are some telltale signs.

When the boisterous Farhat, to some a ruffian, travels to Egypt, he is wept over by family and friends alike. His letter (182–84) to his buddy Ramez is carefully written and surprisingly sweet, expressing his great longing for his friend, while sharing (who knows if truthfully) his sexual exploits with an older woman. A few pages later, however, Farhat is described cruelly beating this Egyptian woman. We soon realize that this scene is imagined (or experienced) by Ramez (190). In either case, the seeds of violence seem present. More to the point, these young men will change as the novel ends. The fun-loving Ramez is sadly altered when we witness his wedding, which he sits through like a man at a funeral. Now when he smiles from afar, the narrator notes that "his teeth had extended in length and size because of smoking that weakened his gums" (212). As his friends dance, he gestures to the narrator, reminding him of the good old days, for he has grown up now, joining the ranks of his adult brothers. He has also, in his newfound wealth, distanced himself from the likes of the poorer Muhammad Harqus, once a real buddy to him. Others will also change. The narrator's brother, the beautiful but reticent body-builder, discovers how offended he is at the competition and decides to stop training. In a matter of six months to a year (as the narrator keeps reminding us), his body will turn to unattractive fat. His prime time is already past.

The novel, however, does not just foreground violence or loss. In his earlier book, *Extra Days* (1990), discussed at the end of the previous chapter, Daoud also wrote about a prewar period, but he highlighted the dark side of family life, suggesting the sinister makeup of the human species that would later find itself at war. The tone of *Sanat al-automatik* is quite different, as family members, friends, and neighbors generally look out for each other; indeed, a whole world consists rather cozily in their interrelationships. The current problems involve two brothers jealously fighting, an offended restroom visitor, another baccalaureate test failed, a mild rise in the cost of living, a decline in the quality of bread, and a natural passing from childhood to adulthood. The father worries that increased automation will result in less qualified laborers and a new generation of dishonest, gambling workers (198). Despite the obvious changes that the novel catalogs, the text's structure is static. Machines may have been introduced, but the characters and their lives seem secure in a routine, in a year when things seem to run "automatically."

Farhat's letter to Ramez, mentioned earlier, is dated January 1966, the year preceding the devastating Arab-Israeli war of 1967 and almost a whole decade before the Lebanese war of 1975 would break out. Politics seem remote from the world Daoud retrieves here. A passing reference to the then Egyptian president Nasir (49) and to the Palestinian "cause" are incidentals to the daily concerns of the adolescents. Daoud's striking omissions are what, in part, draw attention to his novel. His deliberate writing style and attention to detail successfully bring to light a newly imagined Lebanon.

Some Lebanese authors chose to situate their fictions even further back in the past, narrating yet another version of Lebanon. The francophone Amin Maalouf's *Le Rocher de Tanios* focused specifically on Lebanon and earned him the prestigious 1993 Prix Goncourt.[15] That an Arab author, as Khatibi and others had alerted, could so dominate the French language was perhaps itself cause for celebration. For Lebanon it reminds us of the presence of the French legacy and the linguistic choices afforded some of its citizens like Maalouf, enabling him to write both in Arabic (as a journalist) and in French (as a novelist).

Tanios takes place in the first half of the nineteenth century in Mount Lebanon, where Turkish authorities, Egyptian dignitaries, local za'ims, shaykhs, and religious men all control the destinies of the common village folk. Referring loosely to the actual murder of a patriarch by Abou-Kishk Maalouf, the author weaves a complicated tale of the young Tanios, supposed son of the eventual murderer. The story of Tanios suggests his illegitimacy and presents his struggle for identity, his thirst for knowledge, his early love, his relationships with multiple father figures, his life in Cyprus, his role with the rebels, and his sudden disappearance from the rock that would forever bear his name. The enigmatic Tanios, who holds both a unique and precarious relationship within his village, is seen as a player and a pawn in the social and political intrigues of the region.

One is struck by the fact that, although set over a century ago, the world Maalouf constructs is familiar. The innumerable political maneuvering involving not only local but regional and international forces is today's Lebanon. The active role of religious figureheads from different confessions, the powerful za'im mentality, the ubiquitous family, and a system that thrives on honor and revenge are all still features of Lebanon. By digging deep into Lebanon's past, Maalouf succeeds (as Da'if has also done) in broadening one's understanding of contemporary Lebanon. This is a world, as the reviewer Sassine argues, of filial relations. Tanios becomes the example of one "burdened by the weight of the fathers" (141). It is difficult to act at all when one is confronted by so many different authority figures. The result is paralysis only broken by a magical disappearance. In the end, Maalouf has written, according to Sassine, a "profoundly uneasy and disturbing work" (141).

He has also done so distinctively. He masterfully brings together accounts from supposedly authentic but clearly bogus sources that intermittently construct Tanios's tale. With deadpan humor, the narrator cleverly consults the notebooks of a muleteer, the chronicles and journals of monks and missionaries, and relies for further authority on oral accounts. Many of these sources are meticulously (and extensively) quoted as if to validate their authenticity and the subsequent tale's verity. In contrast to Khoury's *Bab al-shams*, which relies genuinely on others' accounts, Maalouf's borrowings are utterly counterfeit. The result is a dazzling tour de force, where intertextuality steals the show. The combination of a Lebanese subject set in a postmodern mold is startling and refreshing. Perhaps because the author roams in a world set safely in the past, he is relatively free to offer yet another way to conceive of Lebanon.

Emily Nasrallah also continued to publish after the war. Many of her short stories appeared in *Fayruz*, a women's magazine, and a collection of her stories, *Mahattat al-rahil* [Stations of departure] came out in 1996. In 1995, she published her first novel in eight years, *al-Jamr al-ghafi* [Sleeping embers], to positive reviews. Unlike the writings of many Lebanese novelists discussed here, her work remains relatively popular. She is one of the only Lebanese female authors whose work is regularly anthologized in textbooks, and because her stories are often first printed in popular magazines, her audience is considerable.

Perhaps the most striking aspect of most of her post-1990 works is that, like some of Daoud's texts, they do not overtly confront the reality of the long war or deal with the predicament of the South (where she is from) or any other social/political cause. Unlike Da'if's or Maalouf's texts, which encourage a juxtaposition between Lebanon's eras, or Khoury's novels, which broaden one's understanding of the Lebanese psyche, Nasrallah's seem comfortably situated in an uncontested political reality.

The novel *Sleeping Embers* (like many written in this postwar period) is set decades before. A first past occurs between the two world wars when emigration from Lebanon to the United States was heavy; the second past occurs some twenty-five years later (pre-1960) as one of the emigrants, Nuzha, returns to the southern village to "stir the sleeping embers" (307, 316). Throughout this long novel, not a single opportunity for political or social elaboration on then (and still current) issues is developed. A secondary character, Fares, feels resentment because he is an outsider to the southern village; he is a Maronite from Mount Lebanon and questions the legitimacy of the larger nation. But his resentment and political musings are only fleetingly mentioned and come to nothing. The motivation to emigrate, supposedly every villager's dream, is left unconvincing, since everyone seems to be a rather satisfied landowner, yet feudalism, political oppression, and poverty were more the rule than the exception in these villages. Muslim/Christian coexistence and tension in the South (as across all of Lebanon) are never a reality in this novel. The Lebanese Christian migration to the Americas would soon be followed by Muslim Shi'a emigration to West Africa, but the wealth accumulated by a minority Shi'a and the social transformation resulting from the returning multiconfessional immigrants are left unbroached.

The novel is also void of a potentially liberating feminist agenda. In 1962, Nasrallah had written *Tuyur Aylul* [September birds], a novel that inaugurated her concerns for a female consciousness. Most of her works since then have focused on women, and she has earned a reputation as an Arab feminist author. Certainly the opportunity for a political agenda to emerge through gender issues exists, but it does not occur. The novel *Sleeping Embers* is dedicated to the "spirit of Lea," a character who is humiliated in the village when supposedly she is discovered not to be a virgin on her wedding night. We later find out that her husband was impotent and that she suffered a great injustice, but her character is neither central nor is her gendered plight elaborated on. The main character, Nuzha (the impotent man's second wife), promises at first to be a feminist heroine. She returns to the village as the successful immigrant searching for a groom (a reversal of the usual gendered formula), but she remains hopelessly in love with a confirmed bachelor and coward who is unmoved by her flirtatious attempts. The book's cover, in fact, is graced by an image of that same bachelor, presented always as a man of conscience, wisdom, and great restraint. He seems to represent the novel's moral core, and whatever feminist concerns exist are left trailing in the book's wake.

In her other recent stories, feminist issues are totally dissociated from their sociopolitical contexts. Repeatedly, Nasrallah undermines the realities of the watan [nation] to focus on the private lives of her female protagonists. In "Sahwa" [Awakening], for example, a middle-aged woman, unhappily married to a sick man she no longer loves, fancies herself in love with another. She reflects upon her marriage and notes that, like her nation after sixteen years of war, it too has declined. A brief paragraph then describes the ravages of war and postwar; this is the "reality that surrounds her . . . the reality of her nation," she muses (105). In a flash, however, all that reality is erased as she recalls the face of her lover (105). She later feels guilty at being so immersed in her own feelings, but this is not a story that develops that potentially interesting conflict between private lives and public space. The real point of crisis that leads to her "awakening" is when her supposed lover comes to visit her at the end of the story and surprisingly introduces her to his young fiancée! The plight of the nation not only does not consume the protagonist; it is hardly a factor in her very being. This is not to say that thwarted love is not a legitimate crisis, but it is worth noting that the personal is so disconnected from the social that it is especially challenging to detect a political (including gender) discourse.

Other stories in the same collection, *Mahattat al-rahil*, introduce female characters like Hanan in "Sik bara'a" [Document of innocence] or Selma in "Wa yabki al-zahr" [And the flowers weep] who have emerged from sixteen years of war totally unaltered. The author deliberately, in fact, states that all outside forces left no impression on them, but this is not elaborated on as a philosophical point. Social and political forces are not especially formative in Nasrallah's discourse; they exist to temporarily impinge upon supposedly insular human lives. They may or may not disrupt one's routine, initiate new thoughts or feelings, but they do not take center stage as constructing a base that might determine all subsequent human action. Consequently, Nasrallah the humanist who has chosen a feminist/womanist mission constantly prioritizes the internal voices of women as legitimate and worthy metanarratives. It is a syndrome reminiscent of earlier twentieth-century Western feminist discourse when the incentive was to demarginalize female voices. The prioritization of this mission often led to depoliticization, a condition then countered by certain first and third world women feminists who reclaimed a feminist agenda from within a broader nationalist cause.[16]

Despite these shortcomings, Nasrallah's fiction cannot be so easily dismissed. She has, for one, consistently provided a much needed discursive space for women's consciousness, even though that consciousness is generally severed from its sociopolitical source. When one considers the dismal record of women's rights in countries like Lebanon, any foregrounding of women is obviously important work. The fact that Nasrallah's texts are popular also ensures that they have entered the public domain and reach a wide audience.

The real impact of her post-1990 texts, however, lies in her concerted effort to re-create a mythology of national consciousness, a collective memory of an idealized Lebanon. One cannot but be jolted in "Thahiba ila Beirut" [She is going to Beirut] when the author carefully describes, as Da'if had done, the Burj with its cinemas, hotels, and lively souks. In "Sanduq al-firji" [The wonder box], Nasrallah recalls the chants of the gypsy-like travelers of her childhood; they came to the village with the box of wonders and called for the kids to take a peep inside and relive the glories of the great epics.

The nostalgic quality to these stories is captured as well in her novel *Sleeping Embers*. Like the short stories, this novel's inspiration comes from Nasrallah's remarkable ability to evoke some of the nuances of her childhood culture in the South. Almost ethnographic, the novel records customs and values, describes homes and the church, and perhaps most importantly foregrounds the dialogue between the villagers, giving the reader a good chance to "hear" the numerous proverbs, expressions of greeting and hospitality, and overall cadences of the colloquial rural southern Lebanese Arabic language. These were the supposed good days, and there is almost a desperate sense to record them before they disappear forever from the nation's collective memory. Neither Da'if nor Daoud seems motivated in precisely this direction. Nasrallah's nostalgia reinforces the sense that the past was better, simpler, and purer than our present. In interviews, she has stated that she has wanted to educate a new generation, to give them solid values and a secure sense of the past to offset the anarchy of the war years (Cooke, "Globalization," 184). It is a well-meaning incentive certainly, but not one shared by the authors previously discussed in this section.

This same incentive, I believe, continues to drive the Lebanese baccalaureate curriculum and helps shape much of the cultural reproduction of the nation. Gramsci talks at length about the role of education in fostering a thinking citizen within the evolving nation (*Selections from Prison* 37–40). Elementary Arabic textbooks of the 1990s reveal an interesting selection of texts. While there are many excerpts from Lebanese authors of the twentieth century in the current books, they are mostly defanged of political, economic, or social issues. The great majority are descriptive pieces, often on the village and almost always set in a previous generation. Quasi-nationalistic poems praise an idealized Lebanon no one has ever experienced, but there is no conscious irony, dialectic, or humor. Khalil Gibran's glorification of the Lebanese peasant and mountainside are represented, as are Maroun Abboud's relatively unproblematized pro-independence stories, and Emily Nasrallah's quaint portrayal of the south Lebanese village. This is a curriculum that still, in some schools, uses a geography textbook with pictures of downtown Beirut taken in 1970 (the downtown no longer exists—not a single building was left intact). Most history books make no mention of Lebanon's recent wars (and the revised book will only make nominal references to the sixteen-year war, focusing on leaders' names and dates of treaties only). These ludicrous omissions are deeply entrenched as well in the rhetoric of political leaders who deliver speeches that every Lebanese recognizes as lies, but that tension between what is said and what is known is also part of the culture. The gap between the mythology, if you will, and the reality (whatever that may be) allows for irony, humor, and a playful dialectic that we witness in many cultural productions. So even while the texts may be inherently devoid of irony, in their reception another irony is often revealed.

Ernest Renan wrote that "forgetting" and "historical error" are essential qualities to any nation formation (11). Benedict Anderson would later develop the theory that nations exist partially as the result of the narratives that "imagine" them.[17] Hence myths, stories, folklore—exaggerated and only marginally historically relevant—cannot be dismissed as mere sentimental wishful thinking. They too serve a purpose in creating a popular discourse. Gramsci advocates taking folklore seriously as it could bring about the birth of a new culture (*Selections from Cultural* 191). Although national myths and symbols can (and certainly have been) harmful, they can also reinforce positive feelings of national solidarity. It is possible that Nasrallah's work may function at this level, providing something like national memory—even though the memory is of no real time or place.

Nasrallah's narratives serve to demonstrate that even when one admits to constructionist theories of nation, the power and impact of national myths are real. As with all nations, there seem to be entire cultural industries in Lebanon intent on preserving a distorted national memory. It is the Lebanon of Gibran, the dabke dance, and the glorious singer Fayruz; the Lebanon of snow-capped mountains, red-roofed village homes, the "holy" cedars, and Phoenician coast. One of Lebanon's 1996 big "hits" was the Caracalla dance troupe's production of *Elissa*, story of the ninth-century B.C. Phoenician princess of Tyre who kills herself after founding Carthage rather than be wedded to a man she does not love. The drama then shifts to "present Lebanon" and the upcoming wedding of a village couple. The bride-to-be, initially refusing her groom, is quickly seduced (unlike the virtuous Elissa) by his wealth. Instead of being a damning critique of Lebanon, which has seemingly lost its pristine Phoenician values, the production concludes with the festive marriage and a riveting traditional dabke dance. Clearly described as "present Lebanon" in the program, this last scene is actually set in an undefined static past—neither Ottoman-dominated nor during the French mandate nor under Lebanon's post-independence government. It is the Lebanon of many popular songs, stories, and myths. A quick look at the contributors to the production reveals the broad range of talent across Lebanon's creative spheres. Besides the choreography and directorship by members of the Caracalla family, the poems and script are by none other than Sa'id 'Aql, perhaps Lebanon's key spokesman for the Phoenician and mythic dimensions of the country. Yet the lyrics are by the noted poet Talal Haidar, and the music composed by a variety of figures, including the populist leftist Marcel Khalife (to many considered the conscience of the Palestinian resistance and the artistic spokesman of al-Junub, the South).

The power of myth to invoke national sentiment needs to be acknowledged in any theory that attempts to study culture in conjunction with politics. Nasrallah's contribution to the discourse on national consciousness exists at the level of folklore. Especially while the nation is in crisis, the folkloric or the mythic can take on special poignancy and significance. The devastation brought upon the social fabric of Lebanon has resulted in a special need for healing. Narratives that assert an uplifting value-laden mythic Lebanon can certainly assist in that healing process.

At the far end of the literary spectrum from Nasrallah is Elias Khoury, whose recent novels also conjure up the folkloric, specifically on Palestinian culture. But for Khoury the folkloric is what is true, what is so true that it need not be authored. The oral narratives that have survived in the public consciousness are here recorded in this "era of registration," giving them a new life and an aesthetic form. Moreover, the Palestinian revival in Khoury's fiction becomes a charge for the Lebanese nation as it searches for its new identity in this postwar period. Lebanon can and should be the cultural and intellectual center for the Arab Middle East. This means primarily freedom of speech and expression, and encouraging a forum for the underrepresented and the politically downtrodden. The intertwined fates of Lebanese and Palestinians suggest a program of rejuvenation that prescribes the nation in new ways. For Nasrallah, the folkloric is derived from the idealism of childhood and is hence flavored with the hope to educate. The question of truth becomes less relevant than the issue of ethics. Her concerns are with acknowledging a positive Lebanese past that would then warrant attention to current Lebanon. It is an unabashedly patriotic stance, intentionally selecting its memories to construct a specific national consciousness.

This chapter has looked at literary examples that are primarily set outside of Lebanon's war years, but only Nasrallah seems intent on reviving the image of a nation that must presuppose a modicum of amnesia. Revivals of 1960s TV comedies like *Abu Milhem* and *Abu Selim*, plus frequent reruns on Lebanese TV of old Egyptian movies filmed in prewar Lebanon, serve a similar function of recalling a happier era that, somehow, might help justify sticking with the weary nation. Popular theatrical productions like the annual Caracalla shows or the 1998 musical by Mansour Rahbani, *The Last Days of Socrates*, also utilize a historical setting, but often do so to highlight differences between a better "then" and a disappointing "present." The Rahbani play, for example, promotes the figure of the outspoken Socrates (performed by the prominent Rafiq Ali Ahmed) against an oppressive state as a clear parallel to Lebanon's current predicament.

The great majority of the fiction examined here, all written in the 1990s, broadens and complicates constructions of Lebanon. Choosing to imagine fictions in prewar Lebanon or outside of Lebanon proper, these authors compel the reader to take a harder look. The novels assist in understanding Lebanese culture, institutions, and identity. They also provide a collective memory, especially for a younger generation that only experienced a limited, and warped, Lebanon. They record stories before they disappear, offering a lived and vivid testimony of a past that feeds into a future. With so many narratives composed about the war, these texts take us elsewhere, but most either lead up specifically to the war or keep the reader aware of the war by its juxtaposed absence. There is an argument that to write about the immediate present is too close—a perspective has not yet been formulated, the stories have not had the chance to coalesce. Others would say that Lebanon's current political climate is such that honest disclosure is too dangerous. For all the reasons listed above and more, the justification for these novels of resurrected pasts is warranted. In fact, the conscious relocation of the imagined text might be one of the most helpful strategies for reconstructing Lebanon today.

7

The Elusive Present

An ugly war creates an uglier peace.

Yahya Jaber, *Ibtasim anta Lubnani* [Smile, you're Lebanese]

This chapter continues the work of the previous one by looking at a cultural output of the postwar period that is explicitly set during the war or in the difficult-to-conceptualize present. Many of the texts (primarily novels) in this category feature a narrator, often tormented, who is searching within a fragmented reality. They bespeak volumes, literally, of a confused nation and citizenry. Despite occasional shafts of optimism, these collective texts reinforce the notion that the damage of war is far from over.

The first novels examined here are all set during the war, although they were published after it ended. This fact alone suggests that while the fighting may generally be over, the effects and implications of the war are very much alive. Moreover, the reasons for the war still need to be understood. Authors differ radically on how to approach these issues. Da'if's 1991 novel, for example, chooses to tell a story that is not set in Beirut and is not ostensibly about the war. In *Ghaflat al-turab* [Negligence of the dirt],[1] the central tragedy focuses on the inadvertent death of two men in a freak quicksand accident. This event takes place in the northern town of Ihden while the Aoun wars of 1989–90 are raging in Beirut. The war, as in Da'if's earlier *Techniques,* is only occasionally mentioned, but the opportunity is afforded here to narrate and consequently better understand the people and the nation at war.

First of all, Da'if intentionally shifts the locale of his fiction from Beirut (the site of much of the war and the site of previous novels) to his own village and Zogharta's summer resort, Ihden. In the process of carefully describing the town's squares, coffee shops, and characters, he tells anecdotes about the villagers. Gradually, we begin to understand something wonderful and terrifying about these rural folk that might shed some light on the Lebanese as a whole.

On the one hand, many of these stories reveal something positive about Lebanon. The photographer Sayed, for example, who escaped the war in the 1980s to live in New York, realizes that he loves Lebanon too much to leave. Muhsin, who raised a family in Caracas, finally returns to Lebanon (though still at war) because he cannot face the prospect of isolation and loneliness abroad. Indeed, the power of the extended family, the clan, the community, the village, is what provides for meaning and identity as the novel unfolds, but this same collective spirit constantly threatens danger for the villagers. For example, a lovely evening and dinner on the square is almost spoiled when one group favors the intrusion of a festive drummer and another group opposes it (32). They almost come to blows over this disagreement.

Opportunities for group cohesion and loyalty can invariably turn sour. With everyone armed to the teeth and tension always running high, Da'if captures the sense of the miraculous when disaster is, in fact, averted. In the tribal mentality that governs this northern region, honor and revenge are blessed qualities. So when Muhsin's son Charbel good-heartedly leaps into the trench to try to save Butros, the bulldozer driver who is sinking beneath the dirt, the drama is set. Both young men die, leaving the villagers ready to assign blame. Certainly foolishness played a part in this accident, and so did goodwill, but the law of the land dictates that any relative of the deceased can now "hunt down" anyone from his murderer's family (72). Translated, this means that Butros is responsible for Charbel's death, so all hell can now break loose.

As Da'if meticulously describes the incident itself, as well as the reactions to the tragedy by family and friends, and finally the huge double funeral, the undercurrent of danger is always present. At any moment this already sad event could burst into a truly uncontrollable disaster. After all, it has already been told that the five ruling families in traditional conflict with each other are currently contained only because of the larger war taking place in the nation (69). It would not take much to ignite an already vulnerable and volatile situation.

Da'if's mastery is in his ability to depict village customs and authentic mourning while also communicating something of their absurdity. Boutros's mother cannot let go of her son's pants, now wrapped around her neck, as she chants and dances before his body, cooing for him to stay, to take care. As she supervises the shaving of his face, she and the other women break into festive lines for the "bridegroom," screaming at the barber to be careful, reprimanding him for not using hot enough water. It is a touching scene, magnified as the funeral procession begins with the villagers taking up their age-old functions of walking, carrying, wailing, throwing perfume, dancing, chanting. This unmistakable collective outpouring of grief, however, is also energized by incessant shooting into the air. Hundreds of men, representing all factions of the village, are positioned around and within the funeral. Their function is to empty as many rounds of ammunition as possible. One of them fires from within the crowd, circling upon himself in a frenzy and gradually turning his vertical shooting into a horizontal aim that could prove disastrous (139). It is a miracle that no one is killed.

For days, according to the villagers, there have been miracles, strange occurrences, inexplicable sightings that must be premonitions. When the statue of Yusuf Bek Karam is seen printed on the ground in blue, the folklore explains: "When Lebanon and the Maronites are in danger, the iron of the Bek's statue becomes too tight" (25). This ridiculous interpretation is never condemned. After all, the villagers also believe the church and the mountain later turn blue. There are odd lurking clouds, and the statue of the Bek is reported missing; only his proud horse remains.[2] Clearly, a miracle has taken place. As militiamen race about with their walkie-talkies attempting to solve these mysteries, the church bells ring in alarm, creating havoc before the funeral. With Maronite superstitions riding high, anything is now possible.

The specific focus on the funeral of two young men accidentally killed in Ihden is juxtaposed (chronologically) against the violent Aoun years, when, among other events, Maronites fought other Maronites. Lebanon and the Maronites certainly are in danger, but this danger is not only exhibited when Aounist loyalists and Lebanese Forces militiamen fight each other; it is also visible in the daily manifestations of Maronite existence as here exemplified by these stories from Ihden. Nor are these stories purely tragic. In fact, Sayed condemns this Ihden mentality. Like the mentality of all Maronites, Christians, and Arabs, they can "only find sorrow—for their poetry, songs, and customs" (99). In their telling, Da'if's

stories are often funny, familiar, charming, even when sad or their subjects stupid.

One anecdote by the very old Ghassub describes how he heroically saved
the day back in 1932 when the statue was to be inaugurated in the square
and the concealing curtain got stuck just as the statue was to be unveiled.
The then young Ghassub leapt on the pedestal, unhooked the stuck string,
and released the curtain to reveal the magnificent statue of the Bek on his
horse. He then inexplicably leapt on the back of the stone horse and defiantly came face to face with the Bek's visage. The crowd was breathless at
his possible insurrection. In a surprising final move, however, Ghassub
suddenly embraced the adored Bek to the cheers of the relieved crowd and
descended a hero in their midst (22). Ghassub lives and breathes this perhaps apocryphal story. Although seemingly trite, the situation could have
been disastrous had he decided not to embrace but to defy the leadership
while on the horse. This is yet another example of what a fine line there is
between survival and death. Much in Daʿif's novel illustrates this precari-
ousness of existence in Lebanon.

By offering narratives from the past, from the village, and about events
unrelated to the current war, Daʿif's novel is reminiscent of the group of
novels discussed in the previous chapter. Like them, much of the energy
here is geared away from the contemporary urban war scene, but Daʿif's
text specifically takes place during the last years of the war, so one is forced
to juxtapose the narration against the contemporary political climate. In
this unusual way, Daʿif succeeds in commenting indirectly about that war
and about a mentality or a culture that participates in it. Daʿif also succeeds in constructing a palpable and endearing, if contradictory, image of
a people engaged both in positive values of loyalty and in negative ones of
violence.

Hanan al-Shaykh provides a different kind of discourse from Daʿif's. Her
novel is much more ostensibly about the war. Whereas Daʿif forces the
reexamination of a basic Lebanese mentality, Shaykh explores how that
mentality has changed because of war. Also in contrast to Nasrallah's presentation of a relatively static and positive Lebanon entity (discussed in
chapter 6), Shaykh intentionally demystifies Lebanon, constantly undercutting and dislodging her subject so that it is virtually impossible to formulate a fixed, let alone a positive, sense of the nation. Her 1992 *Barid*

Beirut (translated in 1995 as *Beirut Blues*) is an important example of another post-1990 extended narrative that offers new ways of imagining the nation.[3]

Unlike Nasrallah's or Daoud's works, Shaykh's fiction is overtly political. Similar to Daʿif's *Ghaflat*, which occurs against a backdrop of inter-Maronite strife, Shaykh's novel is set in 1985 as rival Shiʿa militias are battling for dominance in Beirut. When Hizballah gains ground in the Dahia, the Syrians intervene on the side of Amal. The PLO, evacuated after the 1982 Israeli invasion, is replaced by other groups. The Christian factions, Lebanese government, Iranian fighters, and Israeli army are all players in the arena as well. This military and political reality, however, is not merely a backdrop for Shaykh's fiction; it is an intrusive and transformative reality. Like earlier novels by Khoury and Daʿif, Shaykh's *Beirut Blues* is a war novel after the war has ended. No one in her fiction has been left unaltered by the events of the war. Everyone and everything has changed. Beirut is a divided city, and its people no longer know how to relate to each other. Cityscapes and landscapes have been forever distorted by bombs, by ugly rebuilding, by cannabis and opium poppies. Unlike Nasrallah's characters, the very lives, values, and thoughts of Shaykh's Lebanese have been altered. In a 1994 interview, Shaykh responds to a question on whether the war wounds have started to heal: "I believe that the Lebanese people don't want to look back and discuss the war or even think about it. They don't want to understand it; they don't want to analyze it so that they can live peacefully with it. They are putting it in a dark closet and saying, 'We don't want to deal with it'" (qtd. in Sunderman 306). One of the objectives, or certainly the consequences, of reading Shaykh's fiction is that it forces the Lebanese reader to reconfront the war. As mentioned previously, there is an active Lebanese cultural and educational industry that blatantly denies the complicated and messy internal Lebanese reality. Shaykh's cultural output, like that of many other writers, is an example of an opposite industry that attempts to keep the difficult issues alive and in the public domain.

Unfortunately, Shaykh's fiction is not especially popular within Lebanon. Despite excerpts and positive reviews of her work in leading newspapers and journals, her output remains rather isolated within intellectual circles.[4] She does not fulfill a folkloric criterion deemed suitable for the government educational curriculum, nor has she been able to claim a voice from within the larger public. Constantly aware of her position as a writer living in London away from the community she writes about in *Beirut Blues*, she tackles this question of positionality in her fiction. Asmahan, the narrator and writer of the letters that constitute the novel, is very careful to distinguish herself from another observer and writer/photographer, her lover Jawad. Especially toward the end of the novel, as Asma gradually realizes that she will not leave Lebanon, she criticizes Jawad for recording, as if for some scientific experiment or a folkloric project, everything he observes in Lebanon. Fresh from Paris and thrown into the tumults of war, Jawad is fascinated by the experience. Asma notes, "We are specimens under your microscope" (207). "You regard us with a foreigner's eye. . . . You see us as folklore" (225).

The folkloric is hence that which supposedly identifies Lebanon for the outsider; it can be defined, labeled, studied, appropriated, passed on. As we saw with Nasrallah, it also resides in a past and has static qualities that need to be remembered and commemorated narratively and mythically. With Asma as her mouthpiece, Shaykh seems scornful of any attempts to crystallize the past or reduce Lebanon to a folkloric mythology.

Asma is especially bitter when she realizes that Jawad is using Lebanon as material for his novel: "I'm irritated at the way he continues to look at everything as if he is turning it into a work of literature" (276). Almost like a vulture, his art thrives on the death of his subject. He admits: "I pick the bitter fruits of war and write in a Western language about the emotions which lie between my language and my conscience. The more successful I am, the more my conscience troubles me, because I always used to long for this country to be destroyed" (359).

Jawad's remarks capture a generally unspoken and insidious consequence of Lebanon's wars: the capitalization of the tragedy by entrepreneurs. The numerous journalists' accounts, artistic renditions, academic studies, and documentaries on Lebanon's war are also salable products inspired by Lebanon's demise. Shaykh fears that her own work might be regarded in this way: "I was terrified when [*Beirut Blues*] was published in Arabic in 1993 as to whether or not the Lebanese were going to judge my novel as being from the point of view of a *voyeur* writing about 'their' war" (qtd. in Sunderman 303). Although her positive reviews in Lebanon dispelled those fears, they are still warranted.

In one of the most revealing admissions on this subject at the end of the novel, Asma declares:

[Jawad] only sees what is in his camera lens and recorded in his note-book. I don't want to become like him, collecting situations and faces and objects, recording what people around me say, to give my life some meaning away from here. I don't want to keep my country imprisoned in my memory. For memories, however clear, are just memories ob-scured and watered down by passing time. There are many empty cor-ners between remembering and forgetting. I want things to be as they are, exposed to the sun and air, not hidden in the twists and turns of my mind. (360)

Asma decides to remain in Lebanon and live out the days rather than attempt to capture/reduce the experience while living abroad. Jawad's art, like her own memory, will end up limiting and simplifying the real-ity of Lebanon, and this she will refuse to do. Not coincidentally, in her own art, Shaykh does all she can to counter the impulse to reduce Leba-non in any way. By providing many voices, differing perspectives, intri-cate details, conflicting scenarios, unresolved emotions, etc., Shaykh pre-sents a vibrant and lived reality. It is not static and not comforting. On the contrary, Shaykh's Lebanon is disturbing and fluid. Asma notes: "The country was as hard to grasp as beads of mercury" (89). People and places were not what they seemed; even the language had changed. The nation could not be held in the palm of one's hand, could not be recalled by memories of an idyllic past, could not be identified by its traditional folk-loric practices.

One of Shaykh's most effective means of accentuating the very fluidity of the nation is in her depiction of the various political parties within Leba-non. Not only is every group undermined and demystified but the com-munities (and hence the individuals) linked to those groups are also impli-cated and, by association, undercut. The overall effect is an unsentimental portrayal of citizens, institutions, societies, and the larger nation.

Many of Shaykh's political barbs are bold and confrontational in that they go against public political discourse in Lebanon. The Palestinians, depicted mainly through flashbacks linked to Asma's fida'i boyfriend Naser, are only reservedly praised. Though their "cause" against Israel may be just, and their expulsion after the 1982 invasion tragic, they are also pre-sented as damaging to Lebanon. Asma suggests that perhaps the Palestin-ians should leave Beirut so that Israeli retaliations would not destroy the city she loves (74). Asma's grandfather, like many Shi'a from the South, detests the Palestinians who have occupied and abused his land (108, 134); their "cause," in other words, has not always been clean. In fact, Asma confronts Naser on exactly this point: "You confused the words for wealth [tharwa] and revolution [thawra], which sound similar in Arabic, and I said it was not a slip of the tongue, but a slip of the soul" (79).

Shaykh's depiction of Hizballah is equally disconcerting. While she describes the Dahia in all its vibrancy with its many shops, narrow streets, and inhabitants, and she presents characters, like Fadila, who praise the social services provided by Hizballah (303), Shaykh does not hesitate to voice criticism of their "cult" of kidnapping and desire for martyrdom. A veiled Shi'a woman in Asma's village in the South lashes out at the young men so eager to become famous martyrs, their portraits painted before their suicide missions: "Well, Asmahan, did you see those madmen's pictures? See how stupid they are. They're the death of their families. Their mothers put up with all the pain of giving birth to them, sweep up cowshit for their sakes, and raise them. The fathers die a thousand deaths to keep their mouths stuffed with food, and go out begging to make sure they have an education. As soon as they're old enough, they say, 'Bye. We're off now'" (156).

Whatever ideologies the various militias might have espoused, they are almost overshadowed in this novel by a desire for a quick buck. Drugs, ransom, theft are the order of the day. The fields in the South are overrun by cannabis and poppy plants, militiamen (counseled by foreign drug experts) manage the drug trade, and the villagers partake actively in the daily work of cultivation, manufacture, and packaging. It is a thriving business that involves all Lebanese denominations and factions: "Here each party, each sect, needed the other. Who would distribute these sacks of hashish apart from the Christians with their connections with the outside world? Who would plant the cannabis, irrigate it, and harvest it, other than the Shiites? Who would handle the cocaine if the Druzes didn't?" (250). In the English translation of this novel (which the author oversaw), Shaykh also implicates the Syrians in the drug trade. One of the American-educated sons of a drug family designed a small plane to use for "short runs into Syria" (113). The Syrians are feared and need to be placated. They enter the Dahia to assist the Amal movement against Hizballah and bring terror to the inhabitants. An interrogator, however, who kidnaps and then releases Jawad lectures him on the many benefits the Syrians have brought to Lebanon: They succeeded in releasing the hostages, stopped fighting between internal Lebanese factions, and were intent on restoring Lebanese sovereignty (340).

Although the political players may be the most obvious target of moral degeneration in the novel, few of the ordinary citizens come off as much better. People are primarily motivated by self-interest. Shaykh's presentation, though, is not overly judgmental and steers clear from any sense of moral superiority. The overall effect of reading Shaykh's fiction is of a refreshing honesty in the depiction of human nature. Characters' thoughts and feelings are often trivial, funny, and contradictory, and they constantly undermine sentimental and abstract grand notions of self or other.

Asma herself is perhaps the most vividly drawn. Her self-portrait is highly ironic, humorous, and self-involved. When her friend living abroad questions Asma about the import of the war and assumes that she is immersed in large sociopolitical issues, she has no way of knowing that, in fact, Asma (as she herself admits) is "absorbed with the trivia of love and sex, and at the moment with the rat" (3). Later as she is being evacuated from Beirut in a tank, she worries not about the gravity of the precarious situation at hand but about her failure to attract men. The militiaman has ignored her: "I must have stopped being attractive. He hadn't responded to my smile," Asma panics (64). Even when she makes one of her most insightful comments in the novel criticizing Jawad's regarding "us with a foreign eye" (225), she pauses to reflect on her own motives for attacking him. "Is the heart of the problem that you [Jawad] are not attracted to me? Am I jealous of Juhayna and her youth?" (225–26).

The extent to which Shaykh undermines political discourse is matched by her willingness to undercut all forms of traditional Lebanese discourse. Nothing, not even the land, not even memory, is sacred. All is subject to review and exposure. Shaykh intends to stir the waters, not to leave them safely unperturbed. In contrast to the already mentioned impulse of the educational curriculum to avoid harsh Lebanese realities in recent textbooks, here, on the contrary, we meet a schoolteacher who balks at teaching the expected history and geography classes: "He could no longer stand the hypocrisy of explaining with apparent objectivity how the administrative districts of Lebanon had been reorganized, found himself unable to ramble on about its snowcapped mountains and ski resorts when there were armed men at the top of the runs keeping the skiers in line" (228). Shaykh is not interested in preserving a distorted national memory or identity. Her direct approach has the effect of discomforting readers even while they recognize the truth of what they read. It is an honesty occasionally seen in TV talk shows like *al-Shatir yihki* that do not hesitate to expose some of the most taboo subjects in Lebanese society; it is a directness matched in recent drama by Ziad al-Rahbani or Rafiq Ali Ahmed; it is an unsettling discourse witnessed in the writings of Elias Khoury, Rashid al-Daʿif, and ʿAbdo Wazen. It is part of a cultural opposition [muʿarada] that has not yet met its match in a sociopolitical transformative movement, but its power resides in its potential to invoke change.

At the 1994 Middle East Studies Association convention in Arizona, Shaykh spoke about how she attempted to capture the Beirut she remembered before the war altered it forever. In *Beirut Blues*, one of the letters was addressed to Beirut and, before revisions, was over 300 pages long. Cut down to about sixty-five pages in the actual Arabic publication (and English translation), the letter to Beirut was only marginally reminiscent. In an interesting contrast to the segments by Daʿif or Nasrallah (discussed in the previous chapter), the flashbacks to "sahat al-Burj," for example, are not simple and sad contrasts to Beirut in ruins. The city now has soul, Asma notes:

> Even the alley cats have become real cats, catching flies, missing an eye or a leg. . . . My city . . . had begun to pulsate with life like cities with long histories, Cairo for example. Characters emerged who seemed eternal and had some kinship with the half-collapsed wall; apartments which previously dreamed only of the smell of food and the rustle of soft dresses became houses for convictions, ideas, where people could breathe freely and make love. . . . I was like a bee, discovering the honeycomb city with you [Naser]. I sat facing the sea, the hookahs bubbling around me, and found I was not distracted by the images of devastation and dead bodies the way I used to be. (81–82)

There is no time or place in Shaykh for nostalgia, for fixating on a past that never was (nor could have been) ideal. Hers is a narrative that proceeds with an irony not encountered in Nasrallah. It offers not solutions per se but potential discourses of transformation that, perhaps alongside the national myths, can also serve a function in Lebanon's search for meaning. By refusing to store memories and events in a "dark closet," by insisting on wanting things to be "exposed to the sun and air," Shaykh forces the Lebanese to confront who they are and what their nation has become.

With the horrors of war as recent national memories, Shaykh's fiction seems to steer a course away from sentimentality and an ideology of victimization. The South that she presents is complex, containing within it some of the seeds of its own destruction. The Lebanese have a knack for placing the blame elsewhere, but Shaykh is not willing to let them off the hook so easily. Her narrative deconstructs the nation with all its trappings and poses a great challenge to the reader/citizen who must then endure the glare of painful recognition.

Another innovative female novelist writing after the war but about the war is Hoda Barakat. Her second novel, *Ahl al-hawa* [People of the breeze], centers, like her previous *Stone of Laughter,* on a man. Now Barakat places the burden of narration fully on that man, whose perspective allows for gender tensions in the text. The two main characters, a He and a She, remain unnamed. He begins the novel with his admission of her murder, how he then drank her spirit and became whole. Suddenly we realize he is in a psychiatric ward because, as his sister Asma' keeps telling him, he was traumatized by a long kidnapping. He then narrates how he ran down the mountain with blood on him and was captured by militiamen and taken hostage. These events occur just when, according to him, things had seemingly achieved absolute perfection.

Part II presents his version of the problematic relationship between him and her: Do they love or hate each other? Are they obsessed or bored with each other? As the war intensifies, she is trapped on his side of the city (away from her husband), and they spend days together in a shelter. He reveals himself to be a delusional, tortured, and impassioned narrator infatuated with this woman whose portrayal is afforded us only through his diseased mind.

The third section describes her attempt to escape from him and how he pursues and finds her at the crossover checkpoint negotiating her passage. She frantically tells the soldier that he has kidnapped her. But he takes the soldier aside and talks to him "man to man": The woman is his wife, hoping to run off to her lover on the other side of town. Why would he want to kidnap a woman? He is a teacher at a good school, not an armed man, and he provides names of relatives. Besides, he sidles up to the soldier, you know how women get stricken sometimes (141). The soldier is easily convinced by his story and asks him to take his "wife" and go home with God's protection. The entire episode is rather wondrous to behold, primarily because the female author has chosen a male narrative voice, allowing it to go to the very edge of the gender dividing line (perhaps paralleled by the geographical crossover point). Barakat's convincing impersonation of man talk is bold and new, as she turns the tables on one's gender expectations. From this fresh perspective, the man's false story to the soldier and his believing it are disturbing examples of male dominance. His entire narration must then be reconfigured in order to locate the woman, the female voice, which is cleverly concealed as the author's.

After he brings her back "home," she grows increasingly quiet, passive, and distant. He beats and rapes her in his desperate attempt to possess her, but she seems to be slipping through his fingers. It is only a matter of time before his insane desire will lead him to kill her and "drink her spirit." From the first page, the text has prepared us for this conclusion.

The conclusion, however, is ambiguous. The man now admits his mental illness and feels he could not have killed anyone: "I doubt very much that I grabbed her head and knocked it against the rocks until it cracked and she died" (188). Besides, he muses, she wasn't there when the militiamen found and kidnapped him. Maybe she returned to her husband. Indeed, at no point in the narrative is there reference to the supposed victim. His entire stint in the psychiatric ward reinforces the notion that his mental condition is a result of his kidnapping. A murder is never mentioned by his sister or hospital assistants. Besides, his state is such that she might never have existed, certainly not in the intimate relationship that he imagines or projects. What is noteworthy is that his depiction of his being a tortured hostage is amazingly similar both to his depiction of himself as an abused mental patient and to *her* battered imprisonment within his home. The blending here of situations and characters is reinforced by the gender crossover theme that runs through the novel.

He, for example, finds himself attracted to masculine women. He remembers falling in love with her when he was still an embryo having only the female XX chromosomes before the Y entered the picture and transformed him into a man. Even then he swam in the female womb resisting total maleness (112). His yearning for her can be explained as his desire to retrieve that feminine self within him. He is constantly frustrated by the inflexible binaries that divide. At one point he is standing inside gazing at her outside. He wonders where to put this woman inside him when she is standing there rigidly outside the window: "Where do I put her inside me. What space do I reserve for her. In joy or sorrow. In memory or forgetfulness. In desire or boredom" (44).

Barakat's exploration of gender issues was cleverly depicted in her first novel, *Stone of Laughter*, through the homosexual character of Khalil, attempting to negotiate his existence by means of his sexuality during war (see chapter 5). Like Shaykh, Barakat chooses to place this fiction within war. The shooting may have stopped, but the war is still playing itself out within the individual psyche. The nation witnessed the physical damage produced by the war; now it is time to assess the more difficult psychological damage. Barakat's *Ahl* offers a narrative of how complex and vulnerable the human animal is and how entwined sex, violence, and identity are. She pushes the boundaries of perception, internalizing the war, while complicating notions of sexuality and subjectivity.

The novels of Ilham Mansur, the 1991 *Ila Hiba: Sira ula* and the 1994 *Hiba fi rihlat al-jasad*, are also interesting in terms of thematic and stylistic innovations. In a semi-autobiographical format, Hiba narrates her life before and during the war. In her article "Ilham Mansur's 'Ila Hiba,'" Michelle Hartman notes that Mansur's work can be didactic but that there is much to admire in her "interlinguistic technique" of incorporating both French and colloquial Arabic in her texts. She hence "seeks to reclaim a language lost in writing—how people in the Arab world, specifically in Lebanon, express themselves on a daily basis" (153). In addition, Mansur extends the discourse by delving openly into taboo subjects, especially regarding sexuality. Hartman concludes that the author "embraces the vibrancy of Arabic as a living and changing language, by integrating the different languages that people in Lebanon use in speech."

Another set of books written during this period explicitly focuses on Lebanese emigrants, generally struggling to locate themselves abroad or in Lebanon to where they have returned. Shaykh's most recent novel consciously relocates her Lebanese subject.[5] Having lived in London for many years, Shaykh is now interested in capturing the lives of Lebanese and Arabs abroad. Although most of her earlier novels do contain an expatriate and emigration component, her more recent narratives are set outside of Lebanon proper. The war was primarily responsible for massive waves of emigration, and these now coming-of-age displaced Lebanese have their own stories to tell.

Ghada Samman's 1994 collection of short stories, *Al-Qamar al-murabba'*, translated by Issa Boullata in 1999 as *The Square Moon*, is set primarily in Paris, introducing narratives of Lebanese in conflict between two cultures.

As a Syrian who lived and published in Lebanon for many years but is now residing in Paris, Samman is an example of the increasingly cosmopolitan reality of Lebanon. The gripping first story, "Qata'a ra'is al-qatt" [Beheading the cat], highlights the tension between traditionalism and modernity, as a young Lebanese man, Abdul, is trapped between the Arab ideal of the submissive wife or the liberated Lebanese woman Nadine who left Beirut when she was ten to grow up in Paris. The latter is a resourceful and confident woman who loves to bungee jump. She realizes, however, that Abdul is the "Lebanese Hamlet," undecided and unable to act (on whether to bungee jump, for example). He is also both loved and tormented by the Shakespearean ghost, here his traditional aunt with her powerful incitements on male superiority and female subjugation. She is, of course, part of who he is—his past, his Lebanese male identity. By postponing his proposal to Nadine, Abdul is left dangling like a yo-yo, caught between his two realities.

In another story, "Thalathuna 'aman fi al-nahl" [Thirty years of bees], a woman is married to a writer living in France. On their way to an honorary function, he ignores her while talking to a male friend in the car. Suddenly this frustrated woman emits a swarm of poisonous bees. They sting the men, leaving her alone. In this and other stories of the collection, Samman is experimenting with a form of magical realism to further explore central concerns like women's rights. Together the ten stories trace realities of Lebanese and Arab culture, set in relief against a European landscape. Both in technique and in perspective, these narratives push the limits of Lebanese borders, allowing for the nation to be imagined outside the homeland proper.

Another text that proceeds from the premise of emigration is Muhammad Abi Samra's 1995 novel, *Al-Rajul al-sabiq* [The previous man]. Here the narrator returns to Lebanon after spending seventeen years in France, where he has married and started a family. He describes his life in France in bleak and convoluted terms: His wife has scabies, his children are distant, his house smells like rot. Oddly enough, everything about France reminds him of the poor Beirut neighborhood he grew up in. Whereas at first he felt that in France everything was cut off from its past, after he marries and has kids there he feels as if "we had all just picked up our belongings and ourselves from the neighborhood of Selim Masaad to live in this country" (70). Now time and place are so blended that he cannot tell where he is.

As he continues to explore his state of mind, he confronts increasingly disturbing images of his mother. Whenever she called him, he would feel his body turn into a "worm swimming in the fluids of a huge stomach, exactly as I would imagine it in her body, before she gave birth to me through her ass while she barked like a dog" (88). After this disgusting birth, she threw him and his siblings into the filth of the neighborhood, and yet, the narrator screams out, she actually expected him to become the "doctor of the future" (88).

Now, seventeen years later, he returns for a visit and walks up the many steps, in the dark, to the apartment his relatives have rented for his reception. They are all inside to greet him, his mother and others smothering him with kisses and fawning over him, "the doctor." But his mother's greetings quickly begin to grate: It's bad enough that you married a French woman, but why didn't you bring your children so I could see them before I die? Your cousins have built beautiful villas in the village where their mothers live like queens! The narrator regards his mother with hatred and remains quiet and pensive during the reunion (100).

The next day, they all go down to the village to see the rest of the relatives, but they are in mourning over militia killings. Although they seem happy to see him and ask many questions, they do not care to hear his responses. He feels distant from them and almost breaks into laughter in the midst of their public display of sorrow. He peruses the villagers, the women indistinguishable from each other in their headscarves and long dresses. When his younger brother eagerly asks his opinion of his fiancée, the narrator has no idea which covered one she is (102).

He visits the old neighborhood and his old girlfriend, but realizes that Beirut is finally behind him. When he left seventeen years earlier, he did not really leave. Beirut was always with him. He had to return to discover that it had gone. This realization, in the last lines of the novel, does not sadden him, but what did was that "I leave behind what has passed of my life, as I await what is yet to come, but many years late for both" (106). For years he has lived "on hold" in France, always comparing and juxtaposing his life to a powerful and often sordid image of home. In this way, he has missed out both on a past and a present. The novel leaves us wondering about the future.

The text provides an interesting perspective on exile, on the psychological effects of relocation. Lebanese, emigrating for over a century, have a tradition of writing from the "Mahjar" (abroad). Abi Samra's novel brings that tradition up-to-date by offering a frank introspective set in contemporary postwar Lebanon. The changes both he and the country have undergone lead finally to alienation. It is a solemn outlook that disturbingly confirms something about his mother, whom he realizes he never recalls laughing.

Other texts like Etel Adnan's 1993 *Of Cities and Women (Letters to Fawwaz)* and Mai Ghoussoub's 1998 *Leaving Beirut: Women and the Wars Within* are written in English and extend the dialogue outside Lebanon in different ways. Here the narrators are either leaving or returning to Beirut, and they offer insights (not in fictional form) gathered from their experiences abroad.[6]

Interestingly, only a few novels written during the 1990s are actually set in present-day Lebanon. Perhaps it is a Lebanon that is too current, too close, and too fluctuating to provide a solid backdrop. This might explain one of the main features of Rabih Jaber's 1996 *Al-Bayt al-akhir* [The last house].[7] The novel is blatantly derivative, taking place in a world constructed by another novelist. The story (set mainly in 1993) foregrounds its connectedness to the novels of Yusuf Habshi al-Ashqar (discussed in chapter 5), by analyzing and continuing the story of Ashqar's main characters. Jaber's own characters are not only themselves echoes of Ashqar's but are referential in other ways. One of the protagonists is a writer and an avid reader known as K. In Kafkaesque fashion, this K lives alone, has no real family or community connections, and reads constantly, deriving his life's value only through novels.

He is particularly taken by Ashqar's *The Shadow and the Echo* and provides extensive commentary on the novel to his friend, the filmmaker Maroun Baghdadi, promising to write him a screenplay that would be a sequel to Ashqar's novel. K's obsession with Ashqar has resulted in his introducing himself as Unsi Iskander al-Hamani from the village of Kfarmallat. (In Ashqar's novel, Iskander was the loner from Kfarmallat who opposed the war and lived in a mansion in Beirut. As far as we know, he had no children and was probably killed by militiamen when he visited the cemetery where his mother was soon to be buried.) According to K, however, Iskander was not killed, and he had a son, Unsi, named after his good friend from a previous Ashqar novel, *La Tanbut juthur fi al-sama'* [Roots don't grow in the sky, 1971]. K identifies not only with a fictional son of Iskander but with Iskander himself.

The references continue, for K's friend and fellow protagonist is Maroun Baghdadi, the name of an actual Lebanese filmmaker. He is also compared to the complex Yusuf, the son of Khalil (Iskander's best friend). (In Ashqar's novel, Yusuf comes to both hate and love Iskander.) Baghdadi, who lives in France, discusses K's screenplay with him over the phone, and they decide to go ahead with production, but it soon becomes apparent that they have very different stories to tell. K believes that the film should focus on Yusuf's search for Iskander and hence for himself. Baghdadi, on the other hand, sees a story of revenge and focuses the plot on Yusuf's search for his own father's killers. The plot thickens after K disappears, and Baghdadi flies back to Beirut to search for him. In an interesting development, Baghdadi inhabits K's empty apartment, reading his journals, wearing his clothes, eating his food, and sleeping in his bed. Gradually he understands that K had wanted to make a film about the game of their friendship (174). Maroun's search for K, which had paralleled Yusuf's search for Iskander, is now over.

K reappears, although it is not clear that he ever really disappeared. Because he does not exist except as a fictional or referential character, his disappearance is only a matter of perception (namely Baghdadi's). While sitting at the barber's one day, K reads that his friend, the prominent filmmaker Maroun Baghdadi, has just died by falling down a stairwell (a reference to the true death of Baghdadi in 1993). The barber refers to K as Rabih, suggesting of course the author's name. The novel ends with an exchange: "And now it's my turn, right?" The role-playing is hence foregrounded as a final condition of being.

Other real-life characters, like the novelists Hasan Daoud and Elias Khoury, also have minor roles in this drama. Indeed, the world of novels (as created by Ashqar, Khoury, Daoud, or Jaber) is itself the subject of K's existence. Many other references to the Western authors that K reads also dot this text, making it a collage of references and cross-references. Here, fictional and real characters step in and out of each other's lives, interchanging places or acting as foils to one another. As a result, the text relies for its very existence on worlds constructed in other fictions. They, and especially Ashqar's masterpiece, are validated. They become edifices upon which other structures are built. Jaber's novel can then be read both as a tribute to and an extension of the novel genre itself. Like the works of previous writers, it can also be read as questioning the very issue of verity.

There is much in Jaber's novel that is derivative in other ways. Not only does he openly rely on Ashqar, but his themes, style, and structure are reminiscent, in varying degrees, of both Khoury and Da'if. When Baghdadi's body is found in the stairwell, the police and doctor's reports are provided (much as they were in Khoury's *White Faces* with the death of—is this another coincidence?—Ahmed Jaber). Sections describing K's meticulous and lonely existence are reminiscent of Da'if's portrait of Hashem in *Techniques of Misery*. The fiction/reality dynamic is a technique explored in many novels of the war years as are the shifts in narrative voices and perspectives. Despite Jaber's innovative composition, however, much of the dialogue is stilted, and entire sections (like the extended analysis and summaries of Ashqar's novels on 24–34) seem forced.

Jaber's insistence on basing his novel on a world generated in another novel is significant, as it places the burden of expression on a fiction that becomes a reality. According to K, for example, our entire lives are merely imitations of novels (185); they are the true measure of verity. Jaber toys with this notion as his text relies on worlds constructed in Lebanese fictions—worlds that have become public enough to be borrowed, perceived, and acted upon by others. Jaber's intertextuality, different than Maalouf's, also suggests that the world of fiction is more real, certainly more knowable and narratable, than current Lebanon.

In Da'if's 1997 *Nahiyat al-bara'a* [This side of innocence], the question of how to narrate current Lebanon lurks behind the text. The narrator has been accused of tearing the picture of a leader and supposedly has been taken hostage and interrogated. The novel focuses on a microscopic description of his thoughts and observations as he waits endlessly in an office. This meticulous narration also reveals another vague truth, a gruesome reality that is exposed only in snippets within parentheses. About halfway through the novel, the protagonist suddenly shifts his narration to the previously untold story of what happened in his house, with his wife and son present. Here, the three (or four) men who are interrogating him (or taking him hostage) have descended upon his private family space. The two distant worlds of armed men and family have suddenly collided, and the narrator seems unable to coherently depict the consequences. As he continues to narrate against the truth, it gradually occurs to the reader that, like the narrator of Barakat's *Ahl*, he cannot confront the horrors of his situation. His innocence is on the line as he increasingly, and perhaps unconsciously, implicates himself as guilty. By the end of the novel, he obviously can hold in the truth no longer, and he becomes incoherent, even delusional.

This difficult and intentionally ambiguous tale posits central questions on state oppression, on systematic torture, and on the psychological strain of a man perhaps both a victim and a perpetrator of unspeakable violence. It is as if to suggest that after what the Lebanese have witnessed and committed, there are certain things that just cannot be spoken. The novel is couched in obscurity, as it gradually leads the captive reader toward an elusive conclusion.

More than anything, the novel effectively captures a mentality that might have been produced during the war but that is significantly present now. It is a mentality of the hostage, as Da'if confirmed to me during a phone interview on June 15, 1998. The Lebanese are either the victims or the perpetrators of the kidnappings, not just literally but in a broader sense as well. The war is still raging within even if its most obvious external manifestations have ended. Reviewer Hashem Qasem noted that the novel, which begins with the ripping of a poster, is really about the ripping apart of an individual. Poet Yusuf Bazzi pointed out in *Al-Kuwaytiyya* the narrator has lost everything: his innocence, dignity, humanity, individuality, house (after the occupation by his interrogators/kidnappers), wife, and son. "The narrator is only his narrative." This psychological and philosophical novel tests the limits of what the novel has traditionally done, and it suggests the ominous conditions under which the Lebanese now live. In dealing with the question of how to narrate Lebanon now, Da'if's text disturbingly suggests that certain things cannot be narrated.

While the focus in this chapter until now has been on novels, some examples from other narratives will now be considered. 'Abdo Wazen's banned 1993 *Hadiqat al-hawass* is worth examining here, not only for the controversy it generated—suggesting a defiance on the part of the author—but for the new uses to which Wazen put the language. This text describes the encounter between an anonymous man and woman. She steps into his life, into his room, where they have sex, bathe, are together. They decide to commit suicide as if to preserve the intensity of their encounter, but she departs silently, leaving the door open. The light wakes him up, and now he is alone in the void, before the white pages on his desk. He tries to write about the encounter in order to preserve her and to construct meaning in his life:

I write to give to writing the taste of her body that I no longer remember. I write to kill my loneliness, the most extreme case of loneliness
when I open my eyes and don't find her.

I didn't have a need for words then. Her body was then between my
hands able to say what needs to be said. (54)

This is a man suspended in time and space. Except for her (and subsequently his commitment to record her), he has no points of reference. He
lives in total darkness, silence, and isolation—until she steps in to activate
him. It is no wonder that she becomes his narrative, his text.

Entire pages, for example, are devoted to a detailed description of her
body. Amyuni notes that Wazen draws from an esteemed erotic tradition
and consulted Lisan al-'Arab, "the classical Arabic lexical encyclopedia, in
search of precise words to describe women's genitalia and the sexual act"
(148). The result is a highly learned, exact, and classical style that manages
also to be sensual and poetic. This style is set against the absurdist condition of the narrator, in a text that defies easy categorization, creating a unique
opportunity for new ways of expression. Wazen hence extends the possibilities of Lebanese narratives by scripting, mainly, a state of mind in ostensibly concrete terms. Moreover, the state of mind subtly reproduces the
effects of war. Although the war is never overtly mentioned, its incompre-
hensibility and violence are forever present, exhibited not only in the state
of mind of the characters but engraved on their bodies.

The woman's white body, we soon learn, is covered with wounds and
scars that she tries to hide. He is mesmerized by them and soon realizes
that they are too red to be old. In fact, they are recent and bloody, but
their source is never revealed. She becomes the woman of wounds, the
nameless woman of secrets. Sitting before his empty papers after she has
left, the man recognizes the need to inscribe her—literally and figuratively. The text becomes the literal body. It needs to be written if it is to
be fully realized. As he records the wounds or markings upon the body,
he is not only creating the text but writing the body politic. In an oblique
way, Amyuni writes, Wazen records Lebanon's war: "By allusion only,
the contained violence of the inner monologue betrays the bloody historical context in which 'Abdo Wazen wrote his text" (150). The violence is hence internalized, reimagined, and reembodied. Wazen has
not only opened up sexual boundaries by his approach; he is semiotically
innovative. The worst thing is to be unmarked or unwritten. The crisis of

the white page reveals how important it is to be inscribed, for the writing is ultimately enabling: "Her body drips like ink on the white page before me, on the white in my eyes. . . . The words revive her body. . . . I write her to construct her, so the writing will construct her. . . . I write her nakedness now to polish the language with it, in its clarity, in its purity. I write the body now to preserve writing itself, to protect language from the ruin that descends upon us like the night, the pitch-black night" (133). The language in the original Arabic is beautifully rhythmic, replete with parallelisms and internal rhymes. It harks back to the poetic classical tradition of the Arabic "qasida," and yet its subject is contemporary and its vision is surprisingly reflective of Lebanon's condition at this juncture of its development.

The Wazen text invokes Sabah al-Khrat Zwein's 1995 *Al-Bayt al ma'il, wa al-waqt wa al-judran* [The leaning house, and time and walls]. Although written in prose, this is not a novel but a series of seventy-five plates or vignettes, which she describes as a "dramatic poem." Each consists of a single long sentence (typically over a page) that depicts the tortured condition of the female narrator.

Like the protagonists of many Lebanese novels of the last two decades, she is unnamed and featureless. She is hovering on the doorstep of a house that she finally enters only to be surrounded by four white walls. She recollects a tumultuous relationship with an unspecified He. She, like the narrator of Wazen's *Hadiqat*, must write in order to give meaning to her self, but it is an alienated and disturbed self. With no mention of the war, here is another cultural product that can be read only against the backdrop of the war. The violence and confusion suffuse every vignette, reinforcing the internalized psychological damage that the war-torn Lebanese must now recognize.[8]

The spirit of the prose poems of Zwein is matched by a wide variety of free verse and traditional poetry produced in the 1990s. Besides the continued publications of poets who became prominent in the 1980s like Shawqi Bzai' and Abbas Beydoun, others emerged as well. These include Yousuf Bazzi, Yahya Jaber, Bassam Hajjar, Iskander Habash, Bilal Khbeiz, and Hasan Zayd. Other poets like Henri Zoghaib, more in the traditional aesthetic tradition of Sa'id 'Aql, also remained active not only in writing but in promoting a literary movement.[9]

The work of Yahya Jaber, a poet turned critic and journalist, is an example of some of the innovations and thematics of this postwar era. In 1991 he published *Al-Zu'ran* [The scoundrels] privately, not through the existing presses, which he accused of charging high rates for their books. The book was then sold in cafes around Beirut for a mere LL 3,000 (around $2) and was heavily reviewed from 1992 to 1994. Jaber represents a generation of war poets who participated in and were disillusioned by the war. His writing is obsessed by the dynamics of life during the war as reflected in his stark and rough colloquialisms. As such he is a discerning critic of contemporary Lebanon. His 1994 collection, *Khuth al-kikab bi-quwwa* [Take the book by force], begins with an address to Beirut entitled "This Wall." Here Jaber creates a pastiche of graffiti and slogans that reconstruct a Lebanon quite different from the official government projection. Here are some selections: "Don't throw garbage, you asshole. Support the Resistance. Don't pee here. The government is ruling—they passed by here. Hizballah are the victors in 'Police Jeans.' Socialism is our path. Tetra Milk with Marcel Khalife. Bashir is not dead. Your Aoun is from God. On LBC. Good morning . . . on Beirut . . . that's a wall" (9–13). The poetry that follows uses daily expressions, current slang, and vivid imagery. It is noteworthy that the book was the biggest seller at the 1994 Beirut Exhibit that year.

Some of his critical articles published in *al-Naqid* magazine from 1992 to 1994 were collected in *Nujum al-zhuhr* [Stars at noon, 1995]. These generally bitter pieces reflect a bleak and pessimistic outlook on the new Lebanon emerging after the war. Below are some quotations from "Ayyuha al-Lubnaniyyun" [O Lebanese]:

> We're the country of 20,000 Sri Lankans and 20,000 Filipinos.
> We're in the country of summer resorts for prostitutes from Russia,
> Poland, and Romania.
> Smile, you're in Beirut.
> Where the soccer fans after a defeat destroy the bleachers and
> toilets and chase the Tunisian referee to the airport.
> Smile for this vivacious, resilient people who copy ideas and imitate
> and counterfeit—from the doctor's prescription to whiskey.
> Smile for this clever Lebanese, this merchant. . . .
> Those who loved Beirut, the queen of all capitals, is now Beirut,
> the disgrace of capitals.
> Love in my country is supervised by Coca-Cola.

We're going to die from something else; some call it degradation,
others peace.
The war is not over. . . .
I'm a person who hates his country, as a state and a people. . . .
Perhaps at another time I might love and respect them . . . and
thank you. (117–21)

One can detect Jaber's scorn when he describes the Lebanese as a generous people like a "meza" [culinary display of a wide assortment of appetiz-
ers], who allow all kinds of armies and militias in their midst (117). Now
all is nylon and plastic; there is no vision. He feels alone, betrayed, or-
phaned, and anguished by the current state of affairs.

In 1995 he wrote and put on a play, *Ibtasim anta Lubnani* [Smile, you're
Lebanese]. Here, Abdo and Rose search futilely for an appropriate apartment to rent in Beirut. In the process, Abdo provides a running commentary on contemporary life in Lebanon. He acknowledges, for example, that
it is good the war is now over, but at least then people were together and
looked out for each other. Also during the war, everyone, rich or poor, was
forced to resort to shelters. Now that the war has ended, he laments, each
has come out caring only about himself. Indeed, "an ugly war creates an
uglier peace" (87).

Abdo's frustration with people's materialism, selfishness, and narrow-
mindedness is matched by his genuine fear:

> Curses on war and its hours, but why is it still raging? You walk past
> these shop windows and the prices start to whizz by over my head. I
> walk in the supermarket and put my head down so no one hits me with
> a Howitzer! . . . I still tremble like during the war. I'm terrified the
> dollar will become 10,000 lira. . . . Before we used to die quickly, but
> now we're being buried in SLOW MOTION." (86)

Like the war, the dramatic rise in the cost of living has affected every Lebanese. It has led to devastations, physical and psychological. Rose and Abdo,
unable to make a home together, end up separating at the play's close.
When Abdo half-seriously makes as if to burn down the hotel that has been
their temporary place of dwelling, he stops short: "There's a cockroach in
the basement—the hotel's going to collapse on its own" (109). This ominous ending hearkens back to some of the prewar narratives that anticipated violence ahead for Lebanon. Certainly much of the literature exam-

ined in this section puts forth a grim picture of a Lebanese state of mind that seems to reflect on the nation itself. The official and highly publicized reconstruction efforts, however, are unapologetically positive.

A quick look through Solidère's beautiful 1996 coffee-table book, *Beirut Reborn: The Restoration and Development of the Central District,* will illustrate. Carefully crafted and documented with hundreds of maps, graphs, and photographs, the book is unabashedly celebratory. The current reconstruction of the downtown is depicted in only positive terms: "Almost 300 retained and heritage buildings will be restored." Over 20,000 jobs will be created; around 8,000 residents will be housed. Beirut's ancient heritage will be preserved, its holy sites (including the Wadi Abu Jamil synagogue) will be restored, public and private domains will be created. And all of this effort, the world's most "challenging urban regeneration project," will be coordinated by the government's Council for Development and Reconstruction (CDR) and taken on by Solidère, the private-sector company established in 1994.

The optimism of this vision is undermined by most of the narratives just discussed and, increasingly, by the growing number of plays, like Jaber's. Much of the theater in the 1990s was brazen in its condemnation of the reconstruction efforts of the regime. Authors sought to portray disillusionment as a main feature of Lebanese society.[10] With the end of the war, many theaters came to life again. The reopening of the Théâtre de Beyrouth and other theaters across Lebanon inaugurated a renaissance of sorts for drama in the 1990s. Even the novelist Elias Khoury wrote two plays that were performed in the nineties: *Muthakkarat Ayyub* [The memoirs of Job, 1993] and *Habs al-Raml* [Al-Raml Prison, 1994]. Although most of the stagings were rarely from original Lebanese scripts, many were powerful adaptations of previous works.[11] Not surprisingly, the work of Ziad Rahbani continued to be critical and cynical of the regime and current societal trends, as witnessed in his 1993 *Bi-Khusus al-karami wa al-shaʿb al-ʿanid* [With regard to honor and the stubborn people] and his 1994 *Lawla fushatul amali* [If not for the space of hope].

The title of the first play is a reference to a patriotic Fayruz song popular during the war, and the second comes from a proverb. An article in the April 1993 issue of *The Lebanon Report* points out how the average Lebanese in Rahbani's *Bi-Khusus* is not to be trusted; he is a liar and a thief and uses a deceptive and incoherent language. The new postwar world is also

one overpowered by the modern media, as the action of the play is constantly interrupted by a foreign TV crew attempting to do a documentary
on Lebanon. Also, above the stage is a large TV screen (also a feature in
Lawla) with regular broadcasts, loud advertisements, and the occasional
screening of what is transpiring onstage. As the play proceeds, the society
literally disintegrates, reverting to the dark ages of cavemen and beasts.
Not surprisingly, this disturbing play was not popular. Perhaps, as the article suggests, people don't enjoy seeing a negative image of themselves
reflected in a mirror.[12]

As Lebanon approached the fiftieth anniversary of its independence in
1993, many cultural events, like Roger Assaf's productions of Elias Khoury's
Muthakkarat Ayyub, question the direction in which the country is headed.[13]
In the same spirit of resistance, Lebanon's Writers' Federation issued a
communiqué to the Interior Ministry to reverse its decision on the banning of Wazen's *Hadiqat al-hawass*, and some 200 cultural figures meeting at the Beirut Theater noted that the decision "damaged the image of
Beirut which was, and remains, a city of freedoms, and a cultural labora-
tory for ideas and for original [cultural] experiments."[14]

Plays, like *Al-Jaras* [The bell] and *Al-Muftah* [The key] featuring the
prominent actor Rafiq Ali Ahmed, were staged to positive reviews, suggesting the revival of an intellectual and popular theater in Lebanon.
The consistently high-caliber productions of Roger Assaf continued to
push the boundaries of aesthetic and thematic interpretation, as in the
1998 revival of *Junaynat al-Sanayi'* [Sanayi' Public Garden]. Sponsored
by an antiviolence campaign, the series of interrelated minidramas confront some of Lebanon's most insidious crimes, including violence against
women and servants. A powerful sequence delves into the intricacies of
Lebanese atrocities against their Sri Lankan maids. The prejudice is so
deep that the actress who will play the part of the abused maid at first
refuses to belittle herself by taking on this subservient role. Once she acts
the part, however, she transforms her character totally into the servant's,
humanizing her tragic story of rape and abuse. The subject of racism is
one rarely dealt with in Lebanese society, but television talk shows have
done a good job in the last few years of airing this and other subjects
usually considered taboo.

The primary story of Assaf's play centers around the brutal killings
and dismemberment of women by a man who is later accused and hung

in Beirut's only public garden. As the play unfolds, it becomes clear that solving this crime is an easy example only for those eager to lay blame and restore order. There are innumerable and unspeakable crimes plaguing Lebanese society now, even though the violent war is behind us. Certainly the public hanging of a disturbed man will not provide a solution. This incident, based on an actual hanging in 1983 in the Sanayiʿ Public Garden of a man accused of mutilating women, proved to be a rallying point for a number of writers.

In April 1983, Elias Khoury wrote an article in the newspaper *Safir* (later collected in his *Zaman al-ihtilal*) on the hanging of Ibrahim Tarraf, killer of Mathilde and Marcelle Bahout. The government with media backup declared that this hanging proved that the war was now over and a new form of justice was at hand. The war, however, was not over, and the populace could hardly be reassured knowing that countless killers would never be brought to justice. Khoury maintains that the Lebanese do not know what to do with their guilty consciences. The man hung in Beirut's public garden was a scapegoat for a guilty nation (48). Ironically, the hanging occurred in a children's play area.

Yahya Jaber, in a poem dedicated to fellow poet Iskander Habash, also criticizes the hanging. In "Hadiqat min maʿdan" [Garden of steel], collected in his 1991 *Al-Zuʿran*, Jaber recalls the dismembered women in bags and the murderer hung in the garden. This is a garden in disrepair, where whores, beggars, and the senile roam as shells go off dangerously:

> The Sanayiʿ Garden
> To exhibit perfectly whole bodies
> A patrol for security forces.
> Two lovers embrace on green grass
> Where a woman is buried
> Unwound from the hip. (92)

Assaf's play, performed almost a decade after Yahya's poem and fifteen years after Khoury's article, elaborates on this powerfully symbolic episode primarily as a way to critique the current climate. It is significant that the episode has already presented itself textually and is now translated to a performance. As such, it is an example of how an idea can gradually make its way into the public sphere. Assaf's play, well attended and reviewed, dramatizes the episode so that it becomes the central motif in a multivaried series of skits on contemporary Lebanon.

The play's primary prop is a bulky cranelike object that accommodates itself to the rapidly changing scenes onstage until it transforms into the final gallows. The overriding message is that all kinds of abuses have persisted, and even intensified, since the war ended. Sectarian differences still divide, as exemplified by open scorn for a woman in a headdress. Women are mistreated, raped, and even killed by their husbands. Men feel like dogs. The stage is crammed with actors beneath the foreboding crane. There is an oppressive heaviness that suggests lack of urban public space. The Sanayi' Garden, originally designed for gentle pastimes, ironically becomes the stage for the play's final act of violence. (Coincidentally, a few months after the performance of this play, the first public hangings in decades took place, amid much controversy, in May 1998.)[15]

At the end of each performance, Assaf appears onstage to discuss the play and answer questions from the audience. One staging in March 1998 was reserved especially for a group from the Dahia, an audience (as newspapers reported) usually seen at Hizballah functions. The main criticism from this group related to the play's openly sexual themes and scenes, a perhaps expected knee-jerk reaction by so-called fundamentalists. That issues of sexual propriety override all others may only be a function of strategy rather than substance. The public outcry against sexual promiscuity is a captivating and mobilizing position that tends to mask other more intricate and more difficult-to-grasp Islamicist views. The sex banner has an especial appeal to those less versed in the nuances of fundamentalist theory. The novelist Hasan Daoud also recounts that one of the characters in his *Sanat al-automatik* was based on an old friend who, after joining the Hizballah fighters, was dismayed and angered at Daoud's earlier presentation of him as one who lusted after women.[16] Assaf's play and Daoud's novel do much more than discuss sex, of course, but how they are read and subsequently interpreted suggest the many disparate cultures understandably coexisting in Lebanon.

The spirit of much of the theater is oppositional, or critical of Lebanon's postwar society and trajectory. Though audiences remained relatively small for these productions, this does not mean that the message is not without impact, especially when the message is reinforced in other media. In fact, much of the oppositional culture was evident on television, a medium that was relatively dormant during the war. Television truly proliferated with the official end of hostilities in the 1990s. Dependent on an intermittent and unreliable source of electricity during the war, Lebanese TV was erratic at best. Numerous militias took over or created their own stations, broadcasting syndicated or pirated shows. With few original programs and highly subjective news reports, TV offered little that was especially revealing or reflective. After the war, and despite the somewhat restrictive and limiting audiovisual legislation, the possibilities for TV were greatly enhanced. This is evident in the late 1990s, as large numbers of Lebanese tuned in every evening, especially to the talk shows and political interviews.

Despite the expected light TV fare, a surprising number of talk shows (like *Al-Shatir yihki* with Ziad Njeim)[17] and other political formats with call-in participation sprouted. Some interviewers (as in *Maggie Farah, Hiwar al-ʿumr, Kalam al-nas, ʿAla Madar al-Saʿa, al-Layli layltak*) engaged candidates in frank discussions. The opportunity for real debate (sometimes enhanced by callers) often led to programs running well over three hours. By the next morning, one noticed that large segments of the population carried on the discussion in the workplace and at home. The Lebanese Broadcasting Corporation and Murr Television (MTV) tended to present the most controversial of these programs. MTV broadcast a highly controversial interview in January 1998 from France, for example, with the exiled Michel Aoun, one of the leading oppositional figures to the government.

More examples of populist critiques appeared on the Lebanese cultural scene. The songs of the popular Marcel Khalife, Julia Butros, and Majida al-Roumi, for example, confronted many of Lebanon's woes, drawing attention to political oppression, unacceptable poverty, and general disillusionment.[18] Newspaper editorials were often openly oppositional, though carefully worded to avoid appearing too anti-Syrian. Many political cartoons, local jokes, and popular discourse remained cynically antigovernment and anti-Syrian. One could almost discern a unified national culture of resistance, except that its very admission would probably ensure its immediate collapse.

Of course, not all of the cultural output of the 1990s is oppositional. A large segment of what was available on TV, for example, was either mindless entertainment or pure nostalgia. Much was also openly derivative of American shows. Lebanon featured its own talk shows, game shows, exercise programs, music clips, and morning quasi-news hours. In addition, much was not homegrown but imported directly from Egypt, from Mexico, and from the United States. In fact, Lebanon remained the country with one of the highest percentages of imported programming in the world.[19]

Again, with the return to peace, a sudden infiltration of Western-style programming filled the airwaves, so that programs like *Seinfeld* and *ER* became regular features. The phenomenon of Mexican soap operas dominated much of the 1990s. These Spanish-language programs are dubbed
into a classical Arabic, making them known as "al-baramij al-mudablaja,"
meaning the dubbed—after the French *doublage*—programs). A big percentage of air time was also filled with old Egyptian films and other syndicated shows (some local). A few recent original programs like *As'al shi*
[The most obnoxious] was especially popular with the young. With the
onset of satellite and cable, many Lebanese were now exposed to a broader
range of programming, including the ubiquitous CNN and other Western
news channels as well as the hard-hitting Al-Jazira Arabic news channel
from Qatar. Other sites like The Movie Channel or Discovery Channel
along with Eurosport and Euronews speak for themselves.

With the entertainment industry gaining its share of the cultural market, it is no revelation that provocative and intellectual narratives are not
especially sought after these days, even though now is the time when they
are most needed. Instead, national symbols and myths continue to be resurrected or constructed. The 1996 play on the poet Gibran (discussed at
the end of chapter 1) highlighted the character of the aloof genius from
the rugged mountains of Lebanon whose magical language transformed a
people. He is the visionary Gibran, whose birth is an almost messianic
event. Despite hammy performances and a sentimental script, some of
Gibran's lines certainly sounded prophetic the night of the performance.
Similarly, a revival of another national symbol, Fayruz, continues. The
Baalbek festival, for example, in the summer of 1998 once again featured
Fayruz after a prolonged absence. Her presence onstage beneath the grand
Roman columns of Baalbek tapped directly into the national consciousness, recalling the collective memory of better times. Fayruz's success was
further apparent in her well-publicized (and reviewed) performance in Las
Vegas (May 1999). Lebanese flocked to see her from as far away as Lebanon, while American reviewers puzzled over the audience hysteria she generated.

Set against the national symbols are narratives of nation that perplex
and disturb. Most of the texts examined in this chapter suggest confused
and damaged identities; indeed, some wonder how the self and the nation can be narrated at all. There is a preponderance of loss, of despair,

of alienation. As if the end of the war presented a new beginning, a tabula rasa, the authors inscribe their narratives on the white paper, the white body, but the words are pained and the body is scarred. The physical devastation of the war has now been internalized. The most difficult reparations lay ahead.

Afterword

At the beginning of the new millennium, one can only wonder how much Damascus will be "calling the shots" for Lebanon and how much the deteriorating Israeli/Palestinian relationship will affect internal Lebanese politics. Will the Lebanese state be able to deal responsively with political and economic challenges in the context of ongoing regional changes? Will the next parliamentary elections succeed in bringing necessary change to the class of political leaders? Will confessionalism still largely determine political representation and social identity? Will the economy continue its downward spiral? Will class differences widen, threatening the social order? Will emigration, poverty, and rapid commercialization further disintegrate the family? Will the effects of the war continue to ravage the physical and psychological landscapes of the Lebanese?

Examining a century of literary narratives helps one to ask and respond to some of these questions. I have attempted to present texts that speak to Lebanon's evolution, that offer multiple perspectives on the cultures within Lebanon, and that extend the possibilities for imagining the nation. Some of the more salient findings of this examination are summarized below.

Gibran's multiple narratives are significant because they occurred while Lebanon was emerging as a nation-state, helped define a Lebanese identity, and remain influential still. His self-narrative was an important precedent to the increasingly relevant stories of Lebanese emigrants pining for the homeland. His self-glorification raised him to the stature of a prophet, providing the new nation with a much-needed symbol of its own greatness. His fictional narratives set in the mountains of Lebanon helped consecrate that terrain in the Lebanese imagination. The Phoenician and religious dimensions to that land rooted it historically and spiritually, offering a mythology of nationhood that proved enduring, especially to

Lebanese Christians. Gibran was an advocate of freedom and a spokesman for the downtrodden, as his writings against prejudice and injustice
attest. This oppositional impulse is one that some of today's artists, intellectuals, and leaders aspire to, recognizing that Lebanon offers a relatively free climate but is also threatened by oppression. Gibran's narratives were also formative, as they acknowledged the problematics of state
designations (Syria or Lebanon) and admitted to the difficulties of defining a nation.

The contents of Gibran's works would not, in themselves, warrant his
huge influence were it not for the style in which he expressed himself.
Although he was not the only writer of that period to manipulate the Arabic language in order for it to more honestly articulate ideas, Gibran's language would be reproduced textually over the decades, inscribed in the
national educational curriculum, memorized by generations of Lebanese,
and reconfigured in popular songs. Lebanon discovered, in part, its national language through Gibran.

The narratives to follow Gibran's suggest a multiplicity of perspectives
coinciding with the many ideologies affecting Lebanon, especially following independence. The Phoenician, Christian, and Mediterranean image
of Lebanon was reinforced through the works of Sa'id 'Aql, who went so
far as to Latinize Arabic to transform it into a distinct Lebanese language.
Though not ostensibly anti-Arab or anti-Muslim, other Christian authors
like Ilyas Abu Shabaka, Maroun Abboud, and Anis Freiha narrated Lebanon nostalgically and, almost solely, through its village mountain culture.
The locus of national attention was still centered in Mount Lebanon and
especially reinforced by a program of folklorization that took effect in the
early 1960s. The successful Fayruz/Rahbani team dominated popular culture by resurrecting narratives of a romantic, idealized, rural Lebanon. That
perspective would gradually change as Palestine was lost and refugees spilled
into Lebanon, as Arab nationalism and other Ba'thist and revolutionary
ideologies spread across the region, and as continued sectarian divisions
threatened national unity.

Cultural narratives increasingly shifted to Beirut, where writers convened
to discuss pressing intellectual and political issues. The poets of *Shi'r* magazine espoused a Western modernist aesthetic situated firmly in this cosmopolitan city, which sheltered the Arab ideologies of the time. Yusuf al-Khal,
Adonis, and Khalil Hawi experimented with a scholarly diction and syntax

that reflected the complex identity issues in the Arab world. Suheil Idriss and others would narrate fictions that assumed Lebanon to be a natural part of a larger Arab nation, not a separate essentialized entity. The image of Lebanon was hence changing rapidly to incorporate urban and regional elements.

When Tewfiq Awwad published *Tawahin Beirut* in 1972, the cultural and political climate was hardly recognizable as the narrated Lebanon of the earlier romantics. Student riots, Palestinian frustrations, and Lebanese nationalist insecurities had created an atmosphere of national tension. Awwad's narrative anticipates the civil war and helps one understand its sources. Ziad Rahbani would also begin his sudden rise to stardom with his 1974 *Nazl al-surur*, a play that would systematically debunk the myths of the serene and sacred rural Lebanon. Ironically, while chipping away at the state apparatus, Rahbani bolstered the Lebanese language itself by total reliance on popular idiom and familiar dialect.

This study of earlier narratives established that they can be indicative, descriptive, and even prophetic in better gauging the nation. The narratives of the war and postwar years are offered not merely to help understand Lebanon but to suggest where Lebanon should go. The broad historical framework of this project illustrates the changing nature of Lebanon and the changing demands on its cultural output. At this juncture of its national history, Lebanon has survived a sixteen-year war and is in the midst of reconstruction. The more recent narratives are useful in Lebanon's attempts to reimagine itself.

Juxtaposed against a backdrop of warring factions, rhetorical posturing, and propagandistic cultural display, most of the narratives selected for examination in part II are in stark contrast to those discussed in part I. The novels of Elias Khoury narrate the war so that its verity is captured in the very style and structure of the text. The blatant honesty of this approach allows the reader to fully trust the written word. The writings of Rachid al-Daʿif also manipulate the language to say hitherto inexpressible things about the minutiae that characterize the deadly routine of daily life during war. Khoury and Daʿif construct Lebanon in new ways by telling stories in a style that is both utterly familiar yet surprisingly fresh. The novels of Hanan al-Shaykh, Hassan Daoud, Yusuf Habshi al-Ashqar, and Hoda Barakat further internalize the war, suggesting that its roots are far more imbedded in the psyche, in the family, in sexuality, in the deep recesses of the culture, than in external forces. These authors seem to suggest that the Lebanese have sought to blame others far too long. It is time to take account of themselves. As such, these narratives extend the boundaries of the nation by exploring new regions of its influence. The nation is not merely an exterior place, a shared society or culture, but a state of mind, a psychological entity. Internalizing the nation validates it to some extent by recognizing its broad and deep dimensions.

While Beirut remains the main focus of much of the cultural output, a new locus appears in the South (al-Junub), especially after the 1982 Israeli invasion. Paralleling Gibran's earlier veneration of the Christian mountain village, many writers (especially the Poets of the South) steered their energies to the plight of the Shi'a southern village. Lebanon, therefore, was increasingly imagined from multiple sites, including both the victimized rural community and the urban national capital. These narratives repeatedly challenge a romantic nationalism that sought to imagine Lebanon within a strictly beautiful, physical landscape. Many contemporary texts are situated in ugly spaces—congested, war-ravaged, and polluted.

As seen in part III, many works published after the war continue to confront its aftereffects. Bitterness and alienation color the narratives of Muhammad Abi Samra, 'Abdo Wazen, Rabih Jaber, Sabah al-Khrat Zwein, Ziad Rahbani, Roger Assaf, and Yahya Jaber. Jaber insists that an "ugly war creates an uglier peace," whereby people strive aimlessly for material and sexual gratification, where media and glossy entertainment products clutter the cultural scene, and where amnesia and escapism define the average citizen. It is a bleak assessment countered, in part, by a slew of other narratives that are consciously set in an earlier historic period or that focus, as in the case of Khoury's later novels, on a primarily non-Lebanese story—that of the Palestinians.

Each of the texts offered in this category also helps in assessing Lebanon. Some, like those of Amin Maalouf, Daoud, and Da'if, clarify sociopolitical climates and cultural norms. Khoury's insistence on Palestine forces Lebanon to reconsider its political and cultural connectedness and responsibility in the region. The work of Emily Nasrallah reminds us that cultural narratives sometimes have a national, even patriotic, duty in constructing the myths that the public consciousness requires.

Throughout this examination of a century of narratives there have been examples where, in the face of complicated political realities, reductionist notions of the nation have persisted. Gibran defined Lebanon as possessing essence, despite confusions over geographic, political, and cultural boundaries. The romantic writers who followed reduced Lebanon to idealist principles even while the young nation was working out a complicated compromise document known as the National Pact. As regional ideologies raged across Lebanon in the 1960s, a simple rural vision of Lebanon emerged in the folkloric popular musicals. Even during and after the disruptive war years, some sought to narrate Lebanon nostalgically in the hopes of reviving a tangible positive image of the nation. It is an interesting phenomenon that as Lebanon becomes increasingly difficult to define, the essentialist imaginations of it continue to materialize. The process of mythologizing seems necessary for nation formation, as the power of these narratives to mobilize popular reaction and to generate emotional response is undeniable.

Most of the texts examined from the war and afterward are clearly not in the "mythic" camp. They are hard-hitting, primarily realistic fictions that proved innovative on many fronts. Women writers joined the ranks as notable recorders and narrators of the nation, building upon the earlier work of Layla Baalbaki, Ghada Samman, Nadia Tueni, and Emily Nasrallah, among others. The novels of Shaykh and Barakat extend the boundaries of perceptions on the nation by insisting on the complex interrelationships between gender, sexuality, violence, and identity. Their fictions not only internalize the war so that its battles are fought as much psychologically as they are physically, they also offer a vital gendered perspective of Lebanon.

Another noteworthy feature of the recent narratives is an undeniable confidence in the language. Experimentation with syntax, with diction, with modes and subjects of expression, yielded a more vibrant literary style, more representative of the cadences of Lebanese dialect and experiences. In many texts the fusha [written classical Arabic] gives way to ʿammiyya [spoken Arabic], so that a Lebanese dialect emerges. In an evolution that began with Gibran, by the 1990s the language seems to have become (as Gramsci would put it) a "national fact." The printing and dissemination of the stories told in that language further enhance its viability. Although some writers continued to compose in French (and occasionally in English), and although some of the narratives are especially derivative of Western models, one increasingly senses a distinctively Lebanese texture to the war and postwar narratives. Gramsci's concerns over excessive cosmopolitanism and external influences on the formation of the nation seem, surprisingly, less warranted in the Lebanon of the 1990s. While Lebanon remains exceedingly regionalist and internationalist in most aspects of its social and cultural expression, its language is frequently Lebanese—not Syrian, not Palestinian, and not Arab nationalist. So the Lebanese, ironically, narrated themselves most effectively in the period when the nation was, politically and physically at least, disintegrating. More specifically in Lebanon's case, the novel, which Anderson saw as the receptor of cultural and national union, would validate certain criteria of the nation (like language) when the nation was hardly discernible.

The diversity of the texts themselves suggests that cultural output is much more broadly based than it was earlier in the century. Then, Christian writers, intellectuals, and entertainers dominated Lebanon, reinforcing the obvious notion that the privileged class has better access to modes of production and publication. Many of the newer narratives, for example, are from Shi'a writers. Religion hardly seems a relevant factor in how authors currently narrate Lebanon. The texts also differ widely irrespective of confessional identity. Discourses of transformation, national commemoration, cynical exegesis, psychological probing, and a critique of confessionalism suggest a healthy pluralism within Lebanon. This cultural pluralism stands in the face of the confessional pluralism that has plagued Lebanon's political history in the past century.

When Pablo Picasso was told that his portrait of Gertrude Stein did not look like her, he is said to have responded, "No matter; it will" (Edelman 12). This confident declaration speaks to the power of art to convert reality: Stein would change to become what Picasso had captured in his portrait. In different terms, Antonio Gramsci would argue that culture was a life force that played an effective role in transforming social and political life. Gramsci, like Georg Lukács, Benedict Anderson, and Richard Rorty, concentrated the work of culture in textual artifacts like the novel. Rorty, for example, believed that George Orwell's fiction was exactly right for the times: "His description of a particular historical contingency was, it turned out, just what was required to make a difference to the future of liberal politics" (169–70).[1] It is difficult, if not impossible, to make such a claim today about Lebanese fiction when one does not have the advantage of hindsight. Although there are some impressive narratives discussed here, it is too soon to tell which will endure and which have redefined (as Picasso claimed) the object they seek to create (or narrate). Focusing on a single author, Gibran, at the outset of this project was justifiable in part because he has withstood the test of time. In examining Lebanon's more contemporary period, it has been necessary to consider a much wider selection of authors and narratives, as one can only speculate upon what might be most relevant and influential.

Today, the novel as well as other textual artifacts must be considered alongside an increasingly wide array of cultural products. Whereas the novel emerges as the strongest repository of cultural expression in nineteenth-century Europe, the novel came late into Lebanon and has had to compete with many more popular forms of culture, especially in the audiovisual media. As such, the novels and most of the other textual narratives here presented are not especially well known. According to many writers, booksellers, and publishers, Lebanon has a relatively small market for literature. There is a general anti-intellectualism in the country now, most people have little interest in reading serious works, and books are expensive. But this is not to say that these materials exist in a vacuum. They do interact with each other and with narratives from a broader cultural base. Issues evident in literary narratives have seeped into the public consciousness through popular drama or television shows.

Certainly one objective of this study has been to draw attention to these textual narratives that have been read by too few and seriously considered by fewer still. Their perspectives are often critical, even negative; as such, they keep the difficult issues alive and in the public domain. There is no doubt that the texts examined here raise unsettling questions about Lebanon and the Lebanese, and they come at a time when most Lebanese feel in need of a rest—or at least good escapism. After a long war, it is understandable why intellectual confrontation might be evaded, but now is the time when it is most needed. The candor and depth of many of these narratives suggest new ways of understanding and constructing Lebanese identity. They refuse to accede to the rhetoric of politicians, to the amnesia of the populace, or to the soothing antidotes of consumerism. The war may be over, and much of the physical damage has been attended to, but the causes of the war and the psychological effects of it have yet to be seriously addressed. Any attempt to construct Lebanon now must take into account issues raised in the narratives discussed.

The oppositional nature of these cultural narratives should ideally find their match in the political field. Unfortunately, this is a slow and difficult process. Political culture has remained sterile, despite the cataclysmic changes of the last two decades. There are also, however, some signs of positive change: More elected officials, especially in the municipalities, have a civic and pro-environmental outlook. Cynicism against the traditional political rhetoricians and money-flaunting leaders is at an all-time high, as are complaints against ineffective bureaucracy and corruption. Many seem to want political change, but Lebanon has been unable to put forth a truly oppositional political party, leaving many of the cultural demands on hold.

The difficulties of conjoining cultural and political agendas might also be a feature of late-twentieth-century and early-twenty-first-century nationalism. The global and internationalist influences along with strong regional and local pulls both contaminate and enrich the national entity. The cultural pluralisms mirror, only superficially, the sectarian differences within Lebanon. Other larger considerations complicate easy transference between the cultural and the political, and yet, as we have seen, important insights and therefore possible strategies for action have emerged. Lebanon is offered here as a case study of a nation that within a compressed century underwent a series of changes. A study of its narratives can be used as a model for how other "national" literatures can inform political constructions.[2]

In Lebanon's case, there is currently a wide disparity between the literary narratives and the political reality. However, instead of building on that disparity to promote change, the Lebanese have an uncanny ability to live with, even thrive on, disparity. Maybe recognition-without-action has become part of the Lebanese character. The Lebanese who gets by often does so through *shatara* (cleverness), through negotiation and compromise, and through blame and avoidance. It is an expected norm to complain, but there is no concerted tradition of successful Lebanese struggle. Nor for that matter are there nationally recognized political narratives that have convincingly constructed that struggle, for perhaps they could not be sustained in Lebanon's climate of open cynicism and division.

"Al-haq 'al Tilyan" [it's the fault of the Italians] was a popular phrase used before Lebanon's independence that still resonates today. Because of Lebanon's delicate confessional balance, it was difficult to lay blame on the president of the republic or the prime minister, for example. Instead, the phrase above was adopted, and responsibility was deflected. This is the material of political humor. Often in Lebanon's history blame has been placed on "al shakhs al-talit" [the third person]. This mentality helps explain why the Israelis are a useful psychological entity for the Lebanese. This constant transference of responsibility, however, has more than comic effects. There may be serious ramifications when a nation seems to promote a culture that lacks guilt. Politicians, militia leaders, combatants, and even community members are all left feeling guiltless after sixteen years of atrocities. While narratives of blame and accusation abound, there is little self-analysis. The project for the nation seems to say, "Sweep away the debris and move on."

National narratives are often symbolized in powerful landmarks, but in Lebanon many of those landmarks have been altered or damaged. The popular downtown Burj featured still on postcards was decimated; the majestic Baalbek temples were taken over by Hizballah; the symbolic cedars confiscated by the Christian Marada group are now threatened by disease and pollution; Lebanon's once pristine coastline is an environmental nightmare. Beiteddine Palace and the successful festivals it hosts each summer are both a testimony to Druze domination of the Chouf and a showcase for the sophisticated wealthy who can afford the price of admission.[3] What new landmarks can the nation offer besides the Solidère vision of a rebuilt downtown and a commemorative site at Qana? For one, it could construct a complicated landmark that forces the Lebanese to take a hard look at themselves. Qana (site of the Israeli bombardment of the United Nations compound in 1996) hardly psychologizes or internalizes the war. The aggressor is clearly external, Israel, and the victims are clearly Lebanese. Lebanon has too easily resorted to these kinds of simplistic national symbols. It is time to probe deeper, to create national symbols that specifically force the Lebanese to confront themselves, not others. As such, preserving buildings or sites devastated by the civil war as clear reminders of recent national history would be a constructive act. At the very least, a museum, school textbooks, programs in the popular media, should recall the significance and the impact of the war that pitted

Lebanese against Lebanese. National memory, specifically national grief, is a good criterion for nation-building, yet it has not been effectively capitalized on.

There are those who would like to believe that the war created something of a national culture. By virtue of having experienced a terrible war, the Lebanese have become more unified. Perhaps, but a counterargument is that the Lebanese actually experienced different wars. Though consistent in its indiscriminate violence, the war significantly altered the economic foundations of the country. Simply put, new groups found wealth while a large majority sank into an unexpected poverty—especially evident not during the war per se but in the 1990s and beyond. Unfortunately, these new economic conditions seem to have produced thicker callousness to poverty and misfortune, as if to say, "Don't brandish your misery. We have all suffered." Indeed, a vulgar display of riches accompanies a shocking abuse of the working classes and domestic labor in the country. The Sri Lankan maid, for example, is blamed for her ignorance, but few attempts are made to learn her language, understand her plight, or assist her in her employment. It is not a healthy culture where prosperous children are often encouraged to lash out at their dark-skinned servants, while their mothers line up for yet another plastic surgery miracle. In a desperate search for gratification, many Lebanese have resorted to a lifestyle of materialistic pursuits, putting things on credit when they cannot afford them, contributing little toward addressing their own real frustrations and the current ills of the nation. In the meantime, more and more Lebanese can no longer pay their bills, new levels of poverty are evident just off the modern highways cutting through reconstructed Beirut, and crime is on the rise.

The civil war was no accident, and the current peace might be no more than a lull brought on by exhaustion of the factions as well as by Syrian pressure. The state has not seriously addressed the causes of the war nor made sufficient amends, but the state is not alone to blame. Many Lebanese still refuse to implicate themselves or their families or their communities, and as economic conditions worsen, prospects for an "examined life" seem hardly forthcoming. That is why attention to contemporary cultural production is especially needed if we want to construct Lebanon for tomorrow. The narratives presented here do the groundbreaking work by locating, exposing, and foregrounding the difficult issues facing the self and the nation. They constitute a still untapped body of rich material that is especially needed in these unimaginative times. The provocative narratives suggest a new language, vocabulary, style, approach, and thematics that expand the possibilities for Lebanon. They are, after all, the nation's stories and, though fictions, the most telling.

Notes

Nature and Culture

1. Some scholars say we are moving into a postnational era, "dominated by the globalizing forces of an international division of labor, transnational companies, great power blocs, ideology of mass consumerism, and the growth of vast networks of communications." See Hutchinson and Smith, *Nationalism*, 11.

2. Some of the leading theorists on nation include Ernest Renan, Max Weber, Anthony Smith, Ernest Gellner, Benedict Anderson, Eric Hobsbawm, and Partha Chatterjee. For studies on Arab nationalism, consider William Cleveland, C. Ernest Dawn, James Jankowski and Israel Gershoni, Bassam Tibi, Philip Khoury, and Rashid Khalidi. Refer to the bibliography for complete citations.

3. Chapters on Arab historiography and narrativity are collected in Jankowski and Gershoni, eds., *Rethinking Nationalism in the Arab Middle East*. Drawing from the important theories of Hayden White on modern historiography, Israel Gershoni studies the narrative components of Arab nationalism, and Gabriel Piterberg explores the construction of narratives of identity in Egypt. In his article, William Cleveland discusses the narrative impulse of George Antonius, and Rashid Khalidi writes on the intricate formation of Palestinian identity.

4. Natalie Zemon Davis's 1987 *Fiction in the Archives: Pardon Tales and Their Tellers in Sixteenth-Century France* studies the fictional aspects of historical documents and how they are crafted as narratives. Indeed, the "artifice of fiction [does] not necessarily lend falsity to an account; it might well bring verisimilitude or a moral truth" (4). Shahid Amin's 1995 *Event, Metaphor, Memory: Chauri Chaura, 1922–1992* focuses explicitly on a violent historical event from the "nonviolent" era of the Gandhian nationalist movement. He traces how this event is at first ignored in the narrative of the nation but then appropriated; in the process one witnesses the formation of nationalist history itself. Afsaneh Najmabadi, in her 1998 *Story of the Daughters of Quchan*, also examines how a historical occurrence (from 1906 Iran) is told, retold, and forgotten. The amnesia is hence linked to a political culture, revealing much about modernist historiography.

5. I obviously do not intend to offer a survey of the extensive work on the nation, but I make reference to those theorists who have spurred my own thinking.

6. See Stuart Hall, "The Toad in the Garden: Thatcherism among the Theorists": "Gramsci represented a kind of test of historical concreteness for me against the over-theoretical claims of structuralism. . . . [He hoped to] always reproduce the concrete in thought—not to generate another good theory, but to give a better theorized account of concrete historical reality. This is not an antitheoretical stance. I need theory in order to do this" (69).

7. For an interesting discussion of Gramsci's applicability to the Middle East, consult the work of Peter Gran, *The Islamic Roots of Capitalism* and *Beyond Eurocentrism*.

8. For some of the most salient theorizing on the culture concept, see Raymond Williams's *Culture and Society*, Clifford Geertz's *Interpretation of Cultures*, James Clifford's *Predicament of Culture*, Renato Rosaldo's *Culture and Truth*, Virginia Dominguez's "Invoking Culture: The Messy Side of 'Cultural Politics,'" and Akhil Gupta and James Ferguson's "Beyond 'Culture': Space, Identity, and the Politics of Difference." The range of the above writings suggests that culture is not a conceptual given but a complex and highly flexible human construction.

9. Michael Gilsenan's *Lords of the Lebanese Marches: Violence and Narrative in an Arab Society* examines the role of narratives in constituting social honor, collective biography, and shared memory/forgetting in "Akkar, a northern province in Lebanon.

10. According to Benedict Anderson, novels and newspapers are both versions of "books," the "first modern-style mass-produced industrial commodities" (34). They reproduce experiences that are consumed (read) by thousands. In this way "fiction seeps quietly and continuously into reality, creating that remarkable confidence of community in anonymity which is the hallmark of modern nations" (*Imagined Communities*, 36).

11. Because of time and logistical constraints, I did not consider texts published after 1998.

Chapter 1. Nation Formation

Note to readers: Unless otherwise indicated, all references to Gibran's texts come from *Al-Majmu'a al-kamila li mu'allafat Jubran Khalil Jubran* [Gibran's complete Arabic works], 4 vols. (Beirut: Dar al-Jil, 1994). The volumes are unnumbered, but I will number them here to facilitate referencing. The titles of the volumes are vol. 1, *The Arabic*, ed. Jamil Jabr; vol. 2, *Translated from the English*, ed. Jamil Jabr; vol. 3, *The Letters*, ed. Antoine al-Quwwal; vol. 4, *Texts Outside the Collection*, ed. Antoine al-Quwwal. Translations are mine.

1. Martyrs' Square once stood at the center of downtown Beirut, but it was destroyed early in Lebanon's civil war. The area has now been bulldozed to make way for the new Beirut reconstruction. The famous statue of the martyrs ("al-Shuhada'") was severely scarred during the war, and discussion was under way on whether to repair it totally or to leave remnants of the war as a reminder of Lebanon's history.

2. The text in French reads, "Confiants en la France, mère patrie de la liberté . . . qui fit la plus grande des révolutions pour les droits de l'homme. . . . Nous sommes sûrs qu'il ne nous sera jamais refuse le droit de disposer librement de nos propres destinées et que nous ne serons jamais annexes à n'importe quelle partie dans un plebiscite légal comprenant exclusivement les habitants des parties qu'on voudrait annexer."

3. Although the five nation-states (Lebanon, Syria, Palestine, Transjordan, and Iraq) that emerged after the defeat of the Ottomans were all artificially carved out of Arab territory and consequently did not possess inherent or natural national coherence, each strove to claim narratives of legitimization, but each today still suffers from the very arbitrariness of its existence. Interestingly enough, it is Lebanon, Salibi argues, which has been perceived as most artificial. The reason is precisely because of the fervor of a Lebanese nationalism (distinct from an Arab nationalism) that inspired the Christians and motivated them to seek a separate political entity. For the other four states, a local nationalism was always concurrent with an Arab and, at times, an Islamic nationalism. The Lebanese example was different, and the country would pay a heavy price for it (32).

4. Some of Rihani's Arabic works were published by the influential al-Hoda Press in New York with Naʿum Makarzal. The elaborate "Ameen Rihani Home Page" claims that he was the "founding father of Arab-American literature" and the first Lebanese Arab to "introduce free verse to modern Arabic poetry." He helped establish a modern Arabic literary movement that would culminate in al-Rabita al-Qalamiyya (the Pen Society), organized in New York by Rihani and presided over by Gibran in 1920.

5. Gibran's *Broken Wings*, in fact, has been compared to Rihani's 1911 *Book of Khalid*. Both have lovers meeting in deserted ancient ruins; both depict the tyranny of the church and the misery it brings upon the lovers; both are pagan in tone and adulatory in terms of Lebanon's mountainous nature.

6. Among Mikhail Naimy's works as a critic are the 1913 *Al-Ghirbal*. His most famous play is his 1917 *Al-Abaʾ wa al-bunun* [Fathers and sons], collection of stories *Kan ma kan*, and poetry *Hams al-jufun*. Probably his most famous work is *The Book of Mirdad*, originally written in English and published in Beirut in 1948.

7. Gibran was not the only writer to use Lebanon's Phoenician past as a source of national glory. In the late nineteenth century and early twentieth, poets like Khalil al-Khoury, ʿIssa al-Maʿlouf, and Khalil Mutran did the same. See William al-Khazen's monumental study, *Al-Shiʿr wa al-wataniyya fi Lubnan*.

8. Consider Yumna al-Eid's study on the early literary romantic movement in Lebanon, *Al-Dalala al-ijtimaʿiyya li-harakat al-adab: al-romantiqiyya fi Lubnan*. She discusses Gibran as a key example of this literary phenomenon.

9. In one of his most famous works, *The Book of Mirdad*, Mikhail Naimy writes an allegorical tale set in Mount Sannine (in Mount Lebanon). Like earlier examples by Rihani and Gibran, this text also reinforces the divinity of the Lebanese landscape. So we see a burgeoning literary movement, that of the Mahjar or immigrant Lebanese

authors based in New York, which constructed a powerful and memorable image of the homeland they left behind. The Lebanon that coalesced in these narratives would continue to be reinforced in other literary texts produced throughout the century. Despite the examples of Rihani and Naimy, it is Gibran's writings that would become most popular and, through the generations, assimilated into a national consciousness.

10. One of the most critical studies of Gibran is the 1963 book by Khalil Hawi. One of Hawi's arguments is that Gibran advocated not only for the collapse of a feudal order but for the transformation of Maronites into Protestants. As evidence, Hawi cites Gibran's many references to the Gospels and the spirit of the New Testament.

11. Hawi writes that Gibran was very disturbed by the suffering in Lebanon during World War I and was one of the few Lebanese in America who "attempted to relieve their homeland by forming the Syrian–Mount Lebanon Relief Committee, in which he served as a secretary" (106).

12. Other writers like Amin Takyiddine, Nicola Nakkash, Shibli Mallat, Chahine 'Atiyyeh, and Khalil Mutran also expressed what can be called a Lebanese nationalism in their poetry decades before the nation-state ever existed (Khazen 420).

13. The traumatic effect of World War I on Mount Lebanon resulted in a host of poems pleading Lebanon's case. For example, in 1914, al-Akhtal al-Saghir published his long poem "Nahnu fi Lubnan" [We in Lebanon]; and in 1917 Khalil Mutran wrote his "Maja'a Lubnan" [Lebanon's famine]. Again note the designation of Lebanon as an actual sociopolitical locale.

14. Hawi takes issue with another critic, Jamil Jabir, who wrote a study of Gibran in 1958. According to Hawi, Jabir's belief in "Lebanese nationalism" encouraged him to suppress "facts concerning Gibran's interest in Syrian nationalism and Arab culture" (80). This accusation is interesting because Hawi, at that time, was a supporter of the Syrian Social Nationalist Party (SSNP).

15. For a provocative discussion of the long-term reception of *The Prophet* in the West, see Irfan Shahid's "Gibran and the American Literary Canon." Here, Shahid exposes the hypocrisy of American academics who have snubbed this most popular of books.

16. There is a long tradition of discussing Arabic literature in relation to the Nahda. Pioneering works include George Antonius's *The Arab Awakening* and Hisham Sharabi's *Arab Intellectuals and the West*. More recently Stephen Sheehi has been examining the formation of modern Arab subjectivity during the nineteenth-century Arab renaissance. His articles on Jurji Zaydan and Butros al-Bustani are cited in the bibliography.

17. Khalil Hawi maintains that Gibran, though original, was heavily indebted to earlier innovators like Faris al-Shidyaq, Francis Marrash, and Adib Ishaq, who helped construct Gibran's "national heritage" (44).

18. Gramsci, as mentioned in the introduction, developed a strong argument linking Italy's weakness as a nation to the overabundance of external and cosmopolitan

forces (*Prison Notebooks*, 17, 117) without the establishment of a strong vernacular language. Italian was not a "national fact" (*Cultural Writings*, 268).

19. There are multiple translations, of course, including "Two Voices" in Mounah Khoury and Hamid Algar's *Anthology*, 22–25. This English version does not replicate the meter of the original, although its content is quite accurate and beautifully rendered.

20. The Kheirallah translation, which does replicate the original meter, appears on 45–47 of Suheil Bushrui's edited *Introduction to Khalil Gibran* (Beirut: Dar al-Mashreq, 1970).

21. Alasdair MacIntyre discusses how a language contains a worldview, a cosmology, that cannot be fully represented in another language; a certain alteration is necessary in order for the meaning to be intelligible in another language. He writes: "Concepts are first acquired and understood in terms of poetic images, and the movement of thought from the concreteness and particularity of the imaged to the abstractness of the conceptual never completely leaves that concreteness and particularity behind" (188).

22. Khazen notes that the phenomenon of emigration resulted in a poetry from abroad that featured "tenderness towards the nation" (398, 442–48).

23. Hawi persists that Gibran clearly fashioned himself by creating an "aura of sanctity." He maintained that Gibran came from a rich and wonderful family in Lebanon, that he had received many honors, and he promoted the notion of the hermit or the "oriental sage" (67–69).

24. Khazen records that many Lebanese poets (not surprisingly most were non-Sunni) criticized Turkish rule during the late Ottoman period. Shibli Mallat, Iliyya Abu Madi, and al-Sha'ir al-Qurawi are some examples.

25. See Fawzi 'Atweh's *Jubran Khalil Jubran: 'Abqari min Lubnan* [Gibran: Genius in Lebanon]. 'Atweh expresses a strong sense of gratitude and adulation for the poet who placed Lebanon on the global map. See also Suleiman Kattani, *Jubran Khalil Jubran fi masrah hayatihi* [Gibran in his life's play], written as a thirteen-part television documentary. The text glorifies the young Gibran from Bsherri, who grew up to stun the world with his genius, etc.

26. This fifty-minute video documentary was directed and produced by Eliza Haddad for Beryl Productions in Canada. See my review of it under Manganaro, *MESA Bulletin*.

27. I will be discussing Hawi's own literary contribution in following chapters. Mikhail Naimy's study of Gibran in 1934 (the English version was called *Khalil Gibran: His Life and His Works*) is also important, but too much speculation abounds on the nature of Naimy's relationship to Gibran and the possible resentment and jealousy of the latter's success. Another useful text is Khalil Ahmed Khalil's *Al-Ma'rifa al-ijtima'iyya fi adab Jubran* [Social concerns in the literature of Gibran]. This study approaches Gibran within a larger social and cultural context, admitting to his role in Lebanese and Arab national culture.

28. Liesl Schillinger's review of Waterfield's *Prophet* in the *New York Times Book Review* (December 13, 1998) states that Waterfield writes a "pathography." Here is an "unforgiving portrait" of a "narcissistic pretender who did not care about his family and who may have cruelly manipulated his chief patroness, literary collaborator and one-time fiancée, Mary Haskell Minis, for financial ends."

29. Nabil Karami, himself an author, wrote a sentimental book on Gibran, promoting the notion of the grander-than-life poet and prophet. The book begins with a glorification of Gibran who, from the moment he raised his voice in the cause of freedom, began to "chip away at the edifice of colonialism, feudalism, and backwardness." See *Jubran Khalil Jubran wa al-qawmiyya al-'Arabiyya* [Gibran and Arab nationalism].

30. See Antoine Khuweiri's *Jubran Khalil Jubran* for specifics on the burial and museum. This is yet another example of an adulatory text on Gibran.

31. Today the Gibran museum is a quiet, tastefully renovated series of rooms in the old monastery with soft lighting and background flute music. Each room holds a collection of Gibran's drawings and occasional samples of his handwritten notes. The "cave" has been furnished to look like the poet's austere bedroom and study. It is also where he is buried—a tomb and a shrine, according to another adulatory text, Wahib Kayrouz's *Gibran in His Museum*.

32. See Suheil Bushrui's *An Introduction to Khalil Gibran*, xiv. The book was published on the occasion, in fact, of the May 23–30, 1970, Gibran Festival.

33. Another series of celebrations took place in Detroit in 1995 (100 years after Gibran's emigration from Lebanon to America).

34. This collection of 1983 essays by Lebanese university professors was also in collaboration with al-Hay'a al-'Ulya li-Sanat Jubran al-'Alamiyya. The introductory lectures are very exclamatory, rhetorical, and nationalistic.

35. The play, *Gibran Wa Al-qa'ida*, was written by Ya'qub al Shidrawi.

36. Khazen's 500–page study of Lebanese poetry before World War II isolates four influences on nationalism: (1) the Ottoman current; (2) the Eastern current: despite some criticism of eastern primitiveness and occasional praise for Western technology and French culture, most poems tended to fault the West for its domination and praise the East (to which Lebanon belonged) for its Arab and, at times, Islamic cultures; (3) the Arab current; (4) the Lebanese current that tended to sentimentalize and glorify Lebanon's beauty and past, but also pleaded its suffering at the hands of Turkish oppressors.

Chapter 2. Contest of Ideologies

1. This legal practice was still in existence in the late 1990s.

2. President Chamoun also attempted to extend his term in 1958. President Shihab, though offered an extended mandate in 1964, refused, as did President Sarkis in 1982. President Gemayel appointed General Aoun in 1988 to head a military cabinet. Aoun assumed the presidency and refused to be ousted for two years. President Hrawi's man-

date was extended in 1995 for three more years. In October 1998 the constitution was amended to allow for a grade-one civil servant (like an army commander) to become president. This paved the way for the election of General Emile Lahoud as Lebanon's eleventh president later that month.

3. Michel Chiha's legacy has been revived, in fact, with an exhibit entitled "Historical Pages of Lebanon: Archives of Michel Chiha" at the Sursock Museum in Beirut in the summer of 2001. In addition, two publications by Michelle Hartman on Chiha are forthcoming (see bibliography).

4. The 1940s also saw the emergence of rabitat al-zajal [popular poetry groups] that identified with the newly independent Lebanon. Some of the leading poets of this movement included Ali al-Hajj, Tanius al-Hamalawi, Anis Ruhana, and Emile Rizkallah (see Khazen 11).

5. Freiha's book was first published in 1956. Its stories are regularly taught in elementary school curricula.

6. During the presidency of Camille Chamoun, the Baalbek Festival was launched in 1956. The initial committee focused on Western productions, however, and did not include any examples of Lebanese culture until 1959 (as represented by the Rahbani/Fayruz team). This Lebanese folklorization would climax in the 1960s (see chapter 3).

7. 'Asi and Mansur Rahbani had entered Lebanon's musical scene in the 1950s. In 1954, 'Asi married Nuhad Haddad, virtually creating the sensation of Fayruz.

8. Georges Corm, an economic consultant who has been living in Paris, was critical of the Hariri regime in the 1990s. He was chosen to be in the new cabinet under Selim Hoss in late 1998.

9. For a good summary and discussion of Baalbaki's novel, see Bouthaina Shaaban's useful examination of a century of Arab women novels: *100 'am min al-riwaya al-nisa'iyya al-'arabiyya*, 98–102.

10. In his insightful book, *The Precarious Republic: Political Modernization in Lebanon*, Michael Hudson admits to some of Lebanon's successes, but primarily exposes the weaknesses upon which the state was built.

11. Arab nationalism, as Israel Gershoni has argued, is itself a narrative. Gabriel Piterberg and William Cleveland have also demonstrated the narrative components of historical texts on Arab nationalism. For a partial list of writers on Arab nationalism, refer to endnote 2 of the Introduction and consult Jankowski and Gershoni's edited *Rethinking Nationalism in the Arab Middle East*, 1997.

12. Chamoun also attempted to extend his presidential term in 1958, but under U.S. pressure he stepped down in favor of the army commander, Fouad Shihab.

13. For a full discussion of Hawi's role in advocating and then becoming disillusioned with Arab ideologies, see chapter 2 of Fouad Ajami's *The Dream Palace of the Arabs*.

14. Fredric Jameson believes that cultural texts contain a political unconscious, buried narratives, and social experiences that are not easily perceptible.

Chapter 3. Development and Dissent

1. Omar al-Zaʿinni (1895–1961) had established a distinct Lebanese musical formula with famous songs like "Lubnan mahla fayyatak" and "Law kint hisan." Other Lebanese artists who rebelled against the dominant Egyptian flavor were Nicola al-Manni, Yahya al-Lababidi, and Sami al-Saidawi. For more information on the early phase of Lebanese music, see Nabil Abu Murad's *Al-Akhwan Rahbani.*

2. The six plays are *Mawsim al-ʿizz* [Season of glory, 1960]; *Al-Baalbakiyya* [The woman from Baalbek, 1961]; *Jisr al-qamar* [Bridge of the moon, 1962]; *Al-Layl wa al-qandil* [The night and the lantern, 1963]; *Biyyaʿ al-khawatem* [Seller of rings, 1965]; and *Dawalib al hawa* [Wheels of the wind, 1965].

3. I am indebted here to Abu Murad's insightful examination of the Rahbani musicals in *Al-Akhwan Rahbani.*

4. In *The Precarious Republic*, Michael Hudson praises Shihab's efforts and maintains that none of the presidents to follow were up to the task of governing complicated Lebanon (xiv).

5. See Awad's "Economics of Coincidence and Disaster in Lebanon," 83–86.

6. Hudson maintains that Lebanon's seeming prosperity was primarily a result of the inflow of funds from the Arab oil-producing states and remittances from emigrants to their families. This source of revenue, though, masked three important problems: unemployment, the uneven distribution of prosperity, and Lebanon's too heavy dependence on outside investment (63–66).

7. Hudson asserts that Lebanon's heavy reliance on outside investment meant that changes in the international and Arab financial and political situation could have serious repercussions in Lebanon. That was painfully evident with the 1966 Intra Bank crisis (64).

8. For this presentation of Zurayq, I have relied on Laroui's translated 1976 *Crisis of the Arab Intellectual: Traditionalism or Historicism?*

9. See Rosemary Sayigh's *Palestinians: From Peasants to Revolutionaries,* 164–65. Here she quotes a refugee returning to his camp after the 1969 "revolution": "The first moment I got down from the car I saw the Palestinian flag instead of the Lebanese flag, and a group of Palestinians in *fedayeen* clothes instead of the Lebanese police. As I moved through the camp I saw the happiness on people's faces, and in the schools there wasn't the frustration of before. . . . Before there had been a political and ideological siege around us, but now the camp radio played revolutionary songs and speeches."

10. For a lucid discussion of Arab intellectual history, see Issa Boullata, *Trends and Issues in Contemporary Arab Thought.*

11. A newly translated version of *China Tree* appears in Jayyusi and Allen, eds., *Modern Arabic Drama.* In the introduction, M. M. Badawi sums up the play as a "cross between a surrealist, nightmarish variation on the Oedipal situation and a strikingly Kafkaesque brand of 'absurdist' drama. . . . It is more the work of an elitist Arab intellec-

tual thoroughly at home in the latest Western vogue than a truly Arab play that can appeal to the average Arab reader or audience" (17).

12. Abu Murad discusses these later musicals in his book on the Rahbani brothers. The plays include *Hala wa al-malek* [Hala and the king, 1967], *Al-Shakhs* [The person, 1968], *Sah al-nawm* [Good morning, 1970], *Ya'ish ya'ish* [Long live, long live, 1971], *Al-Mahatta* [The station, 1973], *Lulu* (1974), and *Mays al-rim*, 1975.

13. In the 1950s and 1960s, the Lebanese University (the only national institution of higher learning) and the Arab University founded by the Muslim Philanthropic and Benevolent Society of Beirut in cooperation with the University of Alexandria in Egypt enrolled the largest number of students. By 1969, only 13,637 of the total 32,376 students in higher education were Lebanese. This lopsided ratio of non-Lebanese to Lebanese students has significant cultural and political implications (Elie Salem 36–38).

14. In the next decade, Hanan al-Shaykh would create another victimized Shi'a woman in her powerful *Story of Zahra*. Like Tamima, Zahra is scarred by politics and violence and abused by her hypocritical brother.

15. I disagree with Fredric Jameson, who tends to fault "the cultural monuments and masterworks that have survived" because they "tend necessarily to perpetuate only a single voice in this class dialogue." Jameson, *The Political Unconscious*, 85. Awwad's text is an example that defies this tendency.

16. For a spirited testimony of Arab women writers from the seventh century to the present, see Bouthaina Shaaban's "Arab Women Writers: 'Are There Any?'" Shaaban refutes the claim that the Egyptian Hussayn Haykal wrote the first modern Arabic novel, *Zainab*, in 1914. A Lebanese woman, Afifa Karam, published *Badi'a wa Fouad* in 1906 in the *Al-Huda* newspaper in New York.

17. Note the many awards Nasrallah has won, including the Book Friends Society Award in 1962 and the Sa'id 'Aql Prize for *Tuyur aylul* (Zeidan, *Arab Women Novelists*, 300).

18. A prolific writer, Samman has her own press and has published many collections of poems, stories, and essays. Some of her titles not discussed here include the 1976 *A'lantu 'alayka al-hubb*, the 1986 *Ghurbah tahta al-sifr*, and the 1987 *Al-'am al-muhtallah*.

19. Indeed, the reality of Syrians in Lebanon today remains a complicated and paradoxical relationship. While Syria has great political and military influence over weaker Lebanon, many Syrian laborers in Lebanon are themselves subject to their more powerful Lebanese employers and live in fear of their own government.

20. See my "Imagining Lebanon through Rahbani Musicals" for a discussion of two generations of Rahbanis who helped construct changing ideas of Lebanon.

Chapter 4. Disintegration

1. Ziad Rahbani and Jean Chamoun broadcast a very popular radio show for a few months in 1976 called *We're Still OK*. Janet Stevens provides excerpts and a brief analy-

sis of their colloquialisms and acerbic wit in her article, "'We're Still O.K.': The Lebanese Tapes."

2. Fuad Awad argues that significant economic changes affected Lebanon irrespective of its war: Arab banking transferred to London and New York because Beirut could no longer handle the large volume; the entry of American and other Western companies directly into the Gulf and other Arab states reduced Lebanon's role as liaison; the technical and educational advances in Arab countries lessened Lebanon's seeming advantage in doing business with the West; and the reopening of the Suez Canal after the Egyptian/Israeli 1978 peace treaty meant a decline in the need for an overland transit route to the Arab interior. All of this meant a severe drop in Lebanon's economic activity, rising inflation and depreciation of the national currency, rising public and foreign debt, and emigration. See Awad, "The Economics of Coincidence and Disaster in Lebanon."

3. Unless otherwise indicated, all Khoury quotations and references come from the original Arabic texts; translations are mine.

4. See Zeidan, *Arab Women Novelists*, 204.

5. See Cooke, *War's Other Voices*, 50–60; Accad, *Sexuality and War*, 43–63; Zeidan, *Arab Women Novelists*, 205–17; and Shaaban, *100 'am min al-riwaya al-nisa'iyya al-'Arabiyya*, 168–83.

6. All references here are to the English translation.

7. In his section on Shaykh's *Story of Zahra* in his *Arab Women Novelists*, 205–17, Zeidan discusses the paradox of Zahra's madness in conjunction with the mad society at war. He refers to Barbara Hill Rigney's *Madness and Sexual Politics in the Feminist Novel* as a key text in explaining women's madness as a "reasonable response to living in a patriarchal culture" (Zeidan 211).

8. For a more extended discussion of these issues, see my "Negotiating Feminist Ideologies within Lebanese Women's Writings."

9. In *I Speak for Lebanon*, Kamal Joumblatt admits to the failings of his movement, including the looting and irrational behavior of the young: "It still amazes me how disappointingly immature and callow the young people turned out to be in this respect, for all their heroism, their commitment and their honesty. The young people treated the battle as a game" (111).

10. During an interview with Khoury in June 1998, he told me that it is in this novel that he felt he had perfected his writing: He was able to write as he talked. This was an exciting and rare discovery. An English translation has yet to appear.

11. The chapter on Khoury is entitled "Al-Harb wa al-nass: Al-Wujuh al-bayda' li Elias Khoury" (The War and the Text: The White Faces of Elias Khoury), 193–253. Other chapters focus on the work of Naguib Mahfouz, Ghassan Kanafani, Tayeb Salih, Yasin Riaiyya, and Jabra Ibrahim Jabra.

12. According to Stefan Meyer, "The Contemporary Arabic Novel in the Levant," 250, this novel is strikingly similar to Gibran's "The Madman."

13. In a warning to the reader at the beginning of *Nothing Is Beyond Description*,

Da'if refuses to classify the genre of this text; in fact, he says, he wouldn't even know how to do so.

14. I am indebted to Michelle Hartman for pointing out that Arabs have been known as ahl al dhad [the people of the heavy *d* sound].

15. For translations of all of these poetic works, see my 1994 edited volume of the *Literary Review* titled "Bearing Witness."

16. There is a good published translation of this poem by Sharif Elmusa and Jeremy Reed in Qabbani, *On Entering the Sea*, 143.

Chapter 5. Living with War

1. Besides his poetry (including the famous "Tal al-Za'tar"), Darwish published *Thakira li al-nisyan* [Memory for forgetfulness] about the 1982 invasion and siege of Beirut. This combination of reflections, analyses, and laments occasionally takes on the poetic quality reminiscent of Qabbani's poem to Beirut. Beirut remains an enigma, once the site of culture and publishing, but now? "Is it a shelter or an anthem? It no sooner ends than it begins, and the opposite is also true" (115). In 1995, the University of California published an English translation.

For further information on the central role of Beirut in the literature of the 1970s and 1980s, consult Mona Takieddine Amyuni's "The Image of the City: Wounded Beirut." Amyuni considers novels like Awwad's *Death in Beirut* and Khoury's *Gates of the City*, along with the poetry of Nadia Tueini, Claire Gebeyli, and Adonis.

2. Translated by Samuel Hazo as part of "The Desert: Diary of Beirut under Siege, 1983" and appearing in my volume "Bearing Witness: Recent Literature from Lebanon," 456–57.

3. I will be using Paula Haydar's translation of Khoury's novel.

4. For a discussion on the reasons behind Hawi's suicide, see Fouad Ajami's chapter on Hawi in *The Dream Palace of the Arabs*.

5. For an ironic example of how Palestinian losses finesse all others, consider Barbara Harlow's "Palestine or Andalusia: The Literary Response to the Israeli Invasion of Lebanon."

6. This essay appears in Shehadi and Mills, *Lebanon: A History of Conflict and Consensus*, 305–14.

7. This poem is from Bzai''s collection, *Ughniyat hubb 'ala nahr al-Litani* [Love songs by the Litani River]. Eid's discussion is from her *Al-Kitaba*, 125–26.

8. Translated by Sharif S. Elmusa in my volume "Bearing Witness," 475–76.

9. This poem is translated by Sabah al-Ghandour in "Bearing Witness," 481.

10. Muhammad 'Ali Shams al-Din, "A Hand Not Ready for Birds," 1987, trans. Mansour Ajami, in "Bearing Witness," 525.

11. In May 1987, the Lebanese Parliament abrogated the 1969 Cairo Agreement. Ironically, the Palestinians continued to fight (though now each other) in Lebanon.

12. Hanf (639) lists some of these groups that from 1985 to 1987 marched in demon-

strations for peace and national unity. These groups include Women Against War who marched on Parliament and the presidential palace; war cripples who protested on crutches and wheelchairs from Tripoli to Beirut; the Lebanese Association of Lawyers and the Medical Association; and various trade unions.

13. Amyuni notes that women continued to be excluded from studies involving intellectuals and professionals in Lebanon. In 1987, however, a public conference of professional women was held in Paris under the title of "Lebanese Woman, Witness of the War." See her article, "And Life Went On . . . in War-Torn Lebanon."

14. For a more comprehensive study on French-language authors in Lebanon, see Michelle Hartman's forthcoming *Ecrire l'arabe en français*.

15. First published in Beirut by Dar al-Tanwir in 1983, this novel had a second printing in Cairo in 1998 by Afaq al-Kitaba. There is a 1999 English translation by Paul Theroux, *The House of Mathilde*.

16. The subtitle for this book is *Kitab al-balighin* [The book of eloquent ones or rhetoricians]—an irony since Da"if intends to blast the balagha [eloquence/rhetoric] that has so informed traditional Arabic writing. This book was translated into French by Edgard Weber.

17. The 1992 translation is *Passage au Crépuscule*. An excerpt in English (translated by Mona T. Amyuni) is in "Bearing Witness," 395–401. Other portions are translated in Stefan Meyer's dissertation, 275–82. The Arabic edition is out of print and out of stock.

18. This novel was translated by Edgard Weber in 1997 with the title *Insolence du Serpent ou les Creatures l'ombre*.

19. Among Ashqar's publications are the award-winning *Layl al-shita'* [Winter night, 1954] and *Al-Ard al-qadima* [The old earth, 1963], plus the more recent *Arba'at afras humr* [Four red horses] and *La tanbut juthur fi al-sama'* [Roots don't grow in the sky]. His 1989 novel, *Al-Zhull wa al-sada*, is being translated by Adnan and Paula Haydar as *The Shadow and the Echo*. The first chapter was excerpted in *Aljadid* 20 (summer 1997): 16–18.

20. Two positive reviews of this novel include Sabri Hafez's in *Al-Arab* and Isa Makhlouf's in *Hayat*.

21. Hanf explains the gradual economic collapse of Lebanon that intensified after the 1982 expulsion of the PLO; huge resources of funding stopped, coinciding with a recession in the Gulf states. The government of Amin Gemayel also borrowed heavily from banks, leading to a recession by 1984. Unable to raise enough credit, the state resorted to printing more money. "The result was inevitable: inflation soared and the currency collapsed" (354). By 1986, "the buying power of the minimum wage has fallen by 40%, that of the average income of salaried employees by 60%." By the late 1980s, the threat of hunger loomed across Lebanon (353–57).

22. See Samir Khalaf's *Lebanon's Predicament* on this issue: In order to guarantee water, electricity, telephone, and fuel, the Lebanese "spends much of his time and resources doing endless and futile chores simply to cope with the sheer exigencies of sur-

vival." This trivialization of daily life, whereby a disproportionate amount of energy is wasted, leads to a "pervasive feeling of entropy and lifelessness" (243–44).

23. The debate over Taef continues. Many in the Christian camp viewed the new document as being a total sellout. Phares writes that the Taef Agreement "shifted the power from Christians to Muslims, consecrated an Arab identity in Lebanon, and ensured Syria of much more influence in the country" (162).

24. Hanf quotes Professor Labaki for this information in an unpublished survey, 597.

25. It won the 1990 prestigious al-Naqid prize. The English version is translated by Sophie Bennett and is part of the Emerging Voices series of New International Fiction published by Interlink Books in New York. All references are to this translation.

26. One of Fayruz's most popular pro-Lebanese songs during the war was "Bhibbak ya Lubnan" [I love you, O Lebanon].

Chapter 6. Reworking the Past

1. Opening paragraph of the Treaty of Brotherhood, Cooperation, and Coordination concluded between Lebanon and Syria on May 22, 1991. For the full translated text, see *Beirut Review* 2 (fall 1991): 115–19.

2. *Lebanon Report* 5, no. 7 (July 1994): 6.

3. See *Lebanon Report* 5, no. 1 (January 1994): 3.

4. *Beirut Review* 5 (spring 1993): 136.

5. See Nabil Beyhum's "Beirut's Three Reconstruction Plans."

6. George Shehadeh, Nadia Tueni, Etel Adnan, and Amin Maalouf are all cases in point. There is a broad range of authorial experiences, and hence there are various reasons why francophone literature is a reality in Lebanon.

7. An English translation with the title *Gate of the Sun* is under way by Paula Haydar.

8. The tales of Juha are folkloric Arab anecdotes that revolve around the antics of a dim-witted country bumpkin.

9. The novel received the second annual Palestine Award for the Arts and Humanities in 1998. It was also adapted into a play by Najeeb Ghlal and George Ibrahim, directed by Najeeb Ghlal and performed in July 2000 in Jerusalem (Palestinian National Theater) and Ramallah (Al-Kasaba Theater).

10. To the right of the title page, Barakat acknowledges the contribution of Al-Nasser Khmeir. Originally conceived as a screenplay in Morocco, the text was later transformed into a novel.

11. In an interview on April 29, 1998, Da"if told me that Kawabata has, like himself, lived his thoughts and feelings. He also both thinks his emotions and feels his thoughts.

12. As discussed in chapter 3, Tewfiq Awwad's novel *Death in Beirut* revolved around this era in Lebanon's history.

13. Much of this novel is autobiographical. Daoud (whose real last name is Zebib) grew up near his father's bakery on Bliss Street, across from the Main Gate of the

American University of Beirut. Whereas countless accounts of the university and its clientele have been written, this novel offers a totally fresh vantage point of that neighborhood.

14. By the late 1990s, much of the pluralistic spirit of Ras Beirut had returned.

15. Other works include his *Leo the African, Samarkand,* and *The First Century after Beatrice.*

16. Gayatri Spivak, Chandra Mohanty, Nawal al-Saadawi, and Benita Parry are just a few examples of feminists who have sought to theorize on third world literature in broad political terms.

17. In his *Imagined Communities,* Benedict Anderson argues that narratives (popularized and disseminated through the advent of print capitalism) help construct the cultural communities that become the modern nations (24–26).

Chapter 7. The Elusive Present

1. The title is difficult to translate: *ghaflat* means negligence or foolishness, as well as unexpected or sudden death; *turab* means dirt, which could give us *Murder by Dirt.*

2. After the Arab defeat of 1967, many in Lebanon swore that a huge statue (known locally as Harissa, protectress) of the Virgin Mary overlooking the Bay of Jounieh turned toward Jerusalem in her sorrow over its loss. I recall heated debates with our Maronite neighbors who were convinced that Harissa used to face west and was now pointed south—an indisputable miracle.

3. All references are to the English translation by Catherine Cobham.

4. Shaykh herself admits that she is more popular abroad than in her own country. Most of her fiction has been translated into English, and she has achieved a reputation as a leading Arab woman writer, a title, by the way, that she dislikes because it is too reductionist.

5. Shaykh's novel *Innaha London ya ʿazizi* [It's London, my dear] was published in Beirut by Dal al-Adab Press in 2001. It concerns Lebanese and Arabs living in London. *Zawj min waraq* [Paper husband] was staged in London at the Hampstead Theatre in 1998. This "black comedy" centers on a Moroccan woman in London.

6. I have not explored in this book the full role of Lebanese narratives not written in Arabic. I have chosen generally to refer only briefly to French or English texts. The already broad scope of this study precluded me from expanding on this potentially interesting and relevant component of Lebanese literature. Suffice it to say that I do not intend to exclude English-speaking Lebanese, for example, from their contributions to the nation. With the legacy of immigrant Gibran and the growing Lebanese-American cultural output and my own scholarly book written in English, I clearly admit to the relevance of non-Arabic production. But I had to make some choices and generally opted to view Arabic texts as a more focused way to talk about national construction in Lebanon.

7. Rabih Jaber is one of the most recent contributors to the Lebanese novel. Another

is Ahmed Ali al-Zein, whose *Ma'bar al-nadm* [Threshold of regret] was published in 1998.

8. The reaction of a group of undergraduates to this text (as well as to Wazen's and Barakat's) was in evidence on May 27, 1998, at a talk delivered by Dr. Mona Amyuni at the American University of Beirut. When a senior professor objected to the premise that the war generated a specific literature and asked whether these texts spoke for a generation, many raised their hands to confirm that alienation, confusion, and despair accurately described their current condition. They then eloquently explained how the war specifically was responsible for their malaise.

9. Zoghaib established the Odyssee publishing house in 1978 and the poetry magazine bearing the same name in 1982 (this monthly was issued for three years). In 1994 he established the Odyssee Committee, which has been actively commemorating, in monthly celebrations, the work of a broad range of writers. Besides celebrating living writers like the Lebanese poet Shawqi Bzai', the literary group has also honored historians, calligraphers, and fiction writers from around the Arab world. In addition, special events marking the anniversaries of writers' deaths have become popular. Some of those gatherings have honored the poet Amin Nakhli (an event attended by the president of the Republic), the composer/poet 'Asi Rahbani, and Elias Abu Chabaki.

10. The plays of Fadi Abu Khalil are a case in point. His *Popcorn*, for example, explores the problematic postwar atmosphere.

11. The director Siham Nasser is a good example of a consciously postmodern artist whose plays are intricate and intellectually stimulating collages. Her plays include *Aljidar* and *Crime and Punishment*.

12. "Foul and Fair: Ziad al-Rahbani and the Nightmare of Postwar Culture," *Lebanon Report* 4 (April 1993): 6–7.

13. See Mazen Khalid's "Awakenings: Theater Symbolizes Beirut's Cultural Regeneration," which discusses the reopening of the Beirut Theater and its growing importance in reestablishing Beirut's cultural centrality.

14. This quote is taken from Michael Young's "Inconvenient Reminders," 114.

15. The hangings of two criminals took place in the public square in Tabarja, a town north of Beirut. Attended by a large crowd, the event was also graphically captured by the media. A week later, a young girl almost died in a copycat hanging. The entire event sparked a heated debate on capital punishment in Lebanon.

16. As reported to me during an interview in his *Hayat* office on May 27, 1998.

17. This program consistently raised the largest number of difficult social issues facing contemporary Lebanon. Some of the topics discussed included racism, civil marriage, religious tolerance, adoption, citizenship, superstition, imported TV soap operas, and issues related to health and sex.

18. In a song composed by Henri Zoghaib and Habib Yunus, "Sayyidi al-ra'is" [Mr. President], al-Roumi attacks the current leadership. She performed the song abroad in 1998, and some Arab countries then banned it. Zoghaib also composed "Ya Ayyuha al-kibar" [O ye mighty ones] for Julia Butros, a song about Lebanon's starving people. The

work of Khalife is well known for its defense for the victimized and oppressed sectors of society.

19. In a 1992 study on prime-time television in various countries, most showed nationally produced programs overshadowing American and regional imports. In Lebanon, however, the national, regional, and American programming were each about 30 percent. In the other countries, national programming was usually around 90 percent. See Straubhaar's *Communications Media*, 128.

Afterword

1. See Rorty's *Contingency, Irony, and Solidarity*, esp. chaps. 7 and 8 on the novelists Nabokov and Orwell. Their fictions enable the reader to see the "effects of our private idiosyncrasies on others" (142). More specifically, they both illustrate how cruelty is the worst thing we do.

2. This book has presented a broad selection of primarily Lebanese authors, writing and publishing from within Lebanon in Arabic. They constitute a body of material on Lebanon, but I am not claiming that this is simply a "national literature," for that would imply a state-sponsored agenda.

3. The popular summer festivals, though bringing in artists from the region and around the world, still are linked to specific cultural regions and communities. The Baalbek Festival (housed in Shi'a territory but controlled by a committee of aging grandes dames of the prewar aristocracy) must coordinate its evening programs with the mosque's call to prayer. The well-organized and high-caliber Beiteddine Festival has been a showcase for the Druze leadership. Other summer festivals include those in Sour (Tyre), Beirut, Jbeil (Byblos), Douma, and Deir al-Kamar.

Bibliography

'Abbud, Marun. *Al-Shiʿr al ʿami: Amthal al-qarya al-Lubnaniyya wa aghaniha wa sahratha wa al-lugha al-ʿamiyya fiha* [Colloquial poetry: Examples from the Lebanese village along with its songs and musical evenings]. Beirut: Dar Maroun Abboud Dar al-Thaqafa, 1968.

———. *Ahadith al-qariya: Aqasis wa thikrayat* [Village tales: Stories and remembrances]. Beirut: Dar Maroun Abboud, 1984.

Abi Samara, Muhammad. *Al-Rajul al-sabiq* [The previous man]. Beirut: Dar al-Jedid, 1995.

Abu-Deeb, Kamal. "The Perplexity of All-Knowing: A Study of Adonis." *Journal of International Literature and the Arts* 10.1 (1977): 163–81.

Abu Jawdeh, Naoum. *Al-Mujtamʿ al-mithali fi fikr Jubran wa Naimy* [The ideal society in Gibran and Naimy]. Beirut: Dar al-Fikr al-Lubnani, 1981.

Abu Murad, Nabil. *Al-Akhwan Rahbani: Hayat wa masrah—Khasaʾis al-kitaba al-dramiyya* [The Rahbani brothers: Life and stage—qualities of dramatic writing]. Beirut: Dar Amjad li al-Nashr wa al-Tawziʿ, 1990.

Accad, Evelyne. "Contemporary Arab Women Writers." In *Contemporary Arab Women Writers and Poets*, by Accad and Rose Ghurayyib, 10–81. Monograph Series. Beirut University College, 1985.

———. *Sexuality and War: Literary Masks of the Middle East.* New York: New York University Press, 1990.

Accad, Evelyne, and Françoise Collier, eds. *Les cahiers du grif: Liban.* Paris: Editions Tierce, 1990.

Achebe, Chinua. *Hopes and Impediments: Selected Essays.* New York: Doubleday, 1989.

Al-Adab: Majalla shahriyya taʿni bi shuʾun al-fikr (Revue mensuelle culterelle). Ed. Souheil Idriss, 1953–. Beirut: Dar al-Adab.

Adnan, Etel. *Sitt Marie Rose.* Trans. Georgina Kleege. Sausalito, Calif.: Post-Apollo Press, 1982.

———. *Of Cities and Women (Letters to Fawwaz).* Sausalito, Calif.: Post-Apollo Press, 1993.

Adonis. *The Blood of Adonis*. Trans. Samuel Hazo. Pittsburgh: University of Pittsburgh Press, 1971.

———. *Al-Thabit wa al-mutahawwil: Bahth fi al-ittiba ʿwa al-ibdaʿ al-ʿArabi* [Continuity and change: A study of conformity and creativity among the Arabs]. Beirut: Dar al-ʿwda, 1977.

———. *Kitab al-hisar: Huzeyran '82, Huzeyran '85* [Book of siege: June '82 to June '85]. Beirut: Dar al-Adab, 1985.

———. *Al-Nizham wa al-kalam* [Order and the word]. Beirut: Dar al-Adab, 1993.

———. Lecture, University of Balamand, January 1998.

Aflaq, Michel. *Fi sabil al-Baʿth* [For the renaissance]. Beirut: Dar al-Taliʿa, 1959.

Ahmad, Aijaz. "Jameson's Rhetoric of Otherness and the National Allegory." *Social Text* 17 (fall 1987): 3–25.

———. *In Theory: Classes, Nations, Literatures*. London: Verso, 1992.

Ajami, Fouad. *The Dream Palace of the Arabs: A Generation's Odyssey*. New York: Pantheon Books, 1998.

Al-Ali, Mosbah. "Bsharri Honors Gibran." *Daily Star*, August 2, 1999.

Amin, Shahid. *Event, Metaphor, Memory: Chauri Chaura, 1922–1992*. Berkeley: University of California Press, 1995.

Amyuni, Mona Takieddine. "The Image of the City: Wounded Beirut." *Alif: Journal of Comparative Poetics* 7 (spring 1987): 27–51.

———. "And Life Went On . . . in War-Torn Lebanon." *Arab Studies Quarterly* 15.2 (spring 1993): 1–13.

———. Review of "Hadiqat al-hawass" by Abdo Wazen. *Beirut Review* 7 (spring 1994): 145–52.

———. "Style as Politics in the Poems and Novels of Rashid al-Daʿif." *International Journal of Middle East Studies* 28 (1996): 177–92.

Anderson, Benedict. *Imagined Communities*. London: Verso, 1983.

Antonius, George. *The Arab Awakening: The Story of the Arab National Movement*. Beirut: Librairie du Liban, 1938.

ʿAql, Saʿid. *Lubnan in haka* [Should Lebanon speak]. Beirut: Muʾassasat Nawfal, 1960.

al-Ashqar, Yusuf Habshi. *Al-Zhull wa al-sada* [The shadow and the echo]. Beirut: Dar al-Nahar li al-nashr, 1989.

ʿAtweh, Fawzi. *Jubran Khalil Jubran: ʿAbqari min Lubnan* [Gibran: Genius in Lebanon]. Beirut: al-Shurka al-Lubnaniyya li al-kitab, 1971.

Awad, Fuad. "The Economics of Coincidence and Disaster in Lebanon." *Beirut Review* 2 (fall 1991): 82–95.

Awwad, Tewfiq. *Tawahin Beirut* [Mills of Beirut]. Beirut, 1972.

———. *Death in Beirut*. Trans. Leslie McLoughlin. London: Heinemann, 1976.

Ayalon, Ami. *Language and Change in the Arab Middle East: The Evolution of Modern Political Discourse*. New York: Oxford University Press, 1987.

Ayubi, Nazih. *Over-stating the Arab State: Politics and Society in the Middle East*. London: I. B. Tauris, 1995.

Baalbaki, Layla. *Ana ahya* [I live]. Beirut: Al-Maktab al-tijari, 1958.

———. *Al-Aliha al-mamsukha* [The deformed goddess]. Beirut: Al-Maktab al-tijari, 1960.

Barakat, Halim. *The Arab World: Society, Culture, and State*. Berkeley: University of California Press, 1993.

Barakat, Hoda. *Hajar al-duhk*. London: Riad El-Rayyes Books, 1990.

———. *Ahl al-hawa* [People of the breeze]. Beirut: Dar al-Nahar, 1993.

———. *The Stone of Laughter*. Trans. Sophie Bennett. New York: Interlink Books, 1995.

Barakat, Najwa. *Bas al-awadim* [Bus of decent folk]. Beirut: Dar al-Adab, 1996.

Baron, Beth. "Nationalist Iconography: Egypt as Woman." In *Rethinking Nationalism in the Arab Middle East*, ed. Jankowski and Gershoni, 105–24.

Bazzi, Youssef. *That al-matraqa* [Under the hammer]. London: Riad el-Rayyess, 1997.

———. Review of Da'if's *Nahiat al-bara'a*. *Al-Kuwaytiyya*, July 7, 1997.

Beirut Review. Journal published by the Lebanese Center for Policy Studies, Beirut. Vols. 1–8, 1991–94.

Beydoun, Ahmad. "Restoring Lebanese Culture." In *State and Society in Lebanon*, ed. Leila Fawaz, 63–74. London: Centre for Lebanese Studies and Tufts University, 1991.

Beyhum, Nabil. "Beirut's Three Reconstruction Plans." *Beirut Review* 4 (fall 1992): 43–62.

———, ed. *Reconstruire Beyrouth: Les Paris sur le possible*. Lyon: Etudes sur le Monde Arabe, #5, 1991.

Bhabha, Homi K., ed. *Nation and Narration*. New York: Routledge, 1990.

Boullata, Issa J. *Trends and Issues in Contemporary Arab Thought*. Albany: State University of New York Press, 1990.

———. "Mikhail Naimy: Poet of Meditative Verse." *Journal of Arabic Literature* 24.2 (1993).

Brennan, Timothy. "The National Longing for Form." In *Nation and Narration*, ed. Bhabha, 44–70.

Brooks, Peter. *Reading for the Plot: Design and Invention in Narrative*. New York: Knopf, 1984.

Brown, John Pairman. *The Lebanon and Phoenicia: Ancient Texts Illustrating Their Physical Geography and Native Industries*. Beirut: American University of Beirut Press, 1969.

Bushrui, Suheil B., ed. *An Introduction to Khalil Gibran*. Beirut: Dar al-Mashreq, 1970.

Bzai', Shawqi. *Ughniyat hubb 'ala nahr al-Litani* [Love songs by the Litani River]. Beirut: Dar al-Adab, 1985.

Chatterjee, Partha. *The Nation and Its Fragments: Colonial and Postcolonial Histories*. Princeton: Princeton University Press, 1993.

Chedid, Andrée. *The Return to Beirut*. Trans. Ros Schwartz. London: Serpent's Tail, 1989.

Chiha, Michel. *Visage et présence du Liban*. Beirut, 1964.

————. *Politique intérieure.* Beirut: Editions du Trident, 1966.

————. *Liban d'aujourd'hui.* Beirut, 1949.

Cleveland, William. "The Arab Nationalism of George Antonius Reconsidered." In *Rethinking Nationalism in the Arab Middle East,* ed. Jankowski and Gershoni, 65–86.

Clifford, James. *The Predicament of Culture: Twentieth-Century Ethnography, Literature, and Art.* Cambridge: Harvard University Press, 1988.

Connor, Walker. "A Nation Is a Nation, Is a State, Is an Ethnic Group, Is an . . ." In *Nationalism,* ed. Hutchinson and Smith, 36–46.

Cooke, Miriam. *War's Other Voices: Women Writers on the Lebanese Civil War.* Cambridge: Cambridge University Press, 1988.

————. "The Globalization of Arab Women Writers." *Bahithat* 2 (1995): 175–98.

————. "Reimagining Lebanon." *South Atlantic Quarterly* 94 (fall 1995): 1075–1102.

Corm, Charles. *La Montagne Inspirée.* Beirut: La Revue Phénicienne, 1964.

————. *La Revue phénicienne.* Beirut: Dar al-Nahar, 1996.

Corm, Georges. *Géopolitique du conflit Libanais.* Paris, 1986.

————. *Liban: Les guerres de l'Europe et de l'Orient, 1840–1992.* Paris: Gallimard, 1992.

————. *Madkhal ila Lubnan wa al-Lubnaniyyin talih iqtirahat fi al-islah* [Introduction to Lebanon and the Lebanese: Reform proposals]. Beirut: Dar al-Jedid, 1996.

al-Da'if, Rachid. *Hin halla al-sayf 'ala al-sayf* [When the sword cut short the summer]. Beirut: Dar al-Farabi, 1979.

————. *La Shay' yafuq al-wasf* [Nothing is beyond description]. Beirut: Manshurat Lubnan al-Jedid, 1980.

————. *Ansi yalhu ma'Rita* [Ansi plays with Rita]. Beirut: Mukhtarat, 1983.

————. *Al-Mustabidd* [The tyrant]. Beirut: Dar Aba'ad, 1983.

————. *Fusha mustahdafa bayna al-na'usi wa al-nawm* [Trapped between drowsiness and sleep]. Beirut: Mukhtarat, 1986.

————. *Ahl al-zhull* [People of the shadow]. Beirut: Mukhtarat, 1987.

————. *Tiqniyyat al-Bu's* [Techniques of misery]. Beirut: Mukhtarat, 1989.

————. *Ghaflat al-turab* [Negligence of the dirt]. Beirut: Mukhtarat, 1991.

————. *Ay thalj yahbut bi-salam* [What snow falls lightly]. Beirut: Mukhtarat, 1993.

————. *'Azizi al-Sayyed Kawabata* [My dear Mr. Kawabata]. Beirut: Sharikat al-Taba' wa al-nashr al-Lubnaniyya, 1995.

————. *Nahiat al-bara'a* [This side of innocence]. Beirut: al-Masar, 1997.

————. Interviews, January, May, June 1998.

————. *Dear Mr. Kawabata.* Trans. Paul Starkey. Foreword by Margaret Drabble. London: Quartet Books, 1999.

Daoud, Hasan. *Binayat Matilde.* Beirut: Dar al-Tanwir, 1983.

————. *Ayyam za'ida* [Extra days]. Beirut: Dar al-Jedid, 1990.

————. *Nuzhat al-Malak* [Promenade of the angel]. Beirut: Dar al-Jedid, 1992.

———. *Sanat al-automatic* [Year of the automatic]. Beirut: Dar al-Nahar li al-nashr, 1996.

———. Interview, May 1998.

———. *The House of Mathilde.* Trans. Peter Theroux. London: Granta, 1999.

Darwish, Mahmoud. *Thakira li al-nisyan; al-Zaman, Beirut. Al-Makan, yawm min al-ayyam ʿam 1982* [Memory for forgetfulness: The time, Beirut; the place, one of the days of August 1982]. Beirut: Al-Muʾassasa al-ʿArabiyya li al-dirasat wa al-nashr, 1987.

———. *Memory for Forgetfulness: August, Beirut, 1982.* Trans. Ibrahim Muhawi. Berkeley: University of California Press, 1995.

Davis, Natalie Zemon. *Fiction in the Archives: Pardon Tales and Their Tellers in Sixteenth-Century France.* Stanford: Stanford University Press, 1987.

Dawn, C. Ernest. "The Origins of Arab Nationalism." In *The Origins of Arab Nationalism,* ed. Khalidi et al., 3–30.

Death of the Prophet. 1995 Documentary on Khalil Gibran. Dir/Prod: Eliza Haddad for Beryl Productions, Canada.

Dominguez, Virginia. "Invoking Culture: The Messy Side of 'Cultural Politics.'" *South Atlantic Quarterly* 91 (winter 1992): 19–42.

During, Simon. "Literature—Nationalism's Other? The Case for Revision." In *Nation and Narration,* ed. Bhabha, 138–53.

Edelman, Murray. *From Art to Politics: How Artistic Creations Shape Political Conceptions.* Chicago: University of Chicago Press, 1995.

al-Eid, Yumna. *Al-Dalala al-ijtimaʿiyya li-harakat al-adab: al-Romantiqiyya fi Lubnan* [Social conditions for literary movement: Romanticism in Lebanon]. 2d ed. Beirut: Dar al-Farabi, 1988.

———. *Al-Kitaba: Tahawwul fi al-tahawwul: Muqaraba li al-kitaba al-adabiyya fi zaman al-harb al-Lubnaniyya.* [Writing: Transformation of the transformation: A study of comparative literature during the Lebanese war years]. Beirut: Dar al-Adab, 1993.

Fadil, Jihad. *Al-Adab al-hadith fi Lubnan: Nathra mughayyira* [Modern literature in Lebanon: A different perspective]. London: Riad El-Rayyes Books, 1996.

Fawaz, Leila Tarazi. *An Occasion for War: Civil Conflict in Lebanon and Damascus in 1860.* Berkeley: University of California Press, 1994.

Fernea, Elizabeth. "An Account of Her [Layla Baalbaki] Trial on Charges of Obscenity and Endangering Public Morality." In *Middle Eastern Muslim Women Speak,* ed. Fernea and Basima Bezirgan, 280–90. Austin: University of Texas Press, 1977.

———. "Case of Sitt Marie Rose: Ethnographic Novel." *Literature and Anthropology,* 1989.

Ferris, Anthony, ed. and trans. *Kahlil Gibran: A Self-Portrait.* New York: Citadel Press, 1969.

Fisk, Robert. *Pity the Nation: Lebanon at War.* London: Andre Deutsch, 1990.

"Foul and Fair: Ziad al-Rahbani and the Nightmare of Postwar Culture." *The Lebanon Report* 4 (April 1993): 6–7.

Freiha, Anis. *Isma'ya Rida* [Listen, O Rida]. Jounieh: Al-Karim, 1956; Beirut: Dar al-Matbu'at al-musawwara, 1968.

Gavin, Angus, and Ramez Maluf. *Beirut Reborn: The Restoration and Development of the Central District*. Beirut: Solidere, 1996.

Geertz, Clifford. *The Interpretation of Cultures*. New York: Basic Books, 1973.

Gellner, Ernest. *Nations and Nationalism*. Ithaca: Cornell University Press, 1983.

———. *Encounters with Nationalism*. Oxford: Blackwell, 1994.

Gershoni, Israel. "Rethinking the Formation of Arab Nationalism in the Middle East, 1920–1945: Old and New Narratives." In *Rethinking Nationalism in the Arab Middle East*, ed. Jankowski and Gershoni, 3–25.

Ghandour, Sabah. Foreword to *Gates of the City* by Elias Khoury. Minneapolis: University of Minnesota Press, 1993.

———. Foreword to *The Journey of Little Gandhi* by Elias Khoury. Minneapolis: University of Minnesota Press, 1994.

Ghoussoub, Mai. *Leaving Beirut: Women and the Wars Within*. London: Saqi Books, 1998.

Gibran, Jean, and Kahlil Gibran. *Kahlil Gibran: His Life and World*. New York: Interlink Books, 1991.

Gibran, Khalil. *Al-Arwah al-mutamarrida* [Rebellious spirits]. Beirut, 1908.

———. *The Garden and the Prophet*. London: Heinemann, 1934.

———. *The Broken Wings*. Trans. Anthony Ferris. New York: Citadel Press, 1957.

———. *Mirrors of the Soul*. Trans. Joseph Sheban. New York: Philosophical Library, 1965.

———. *The Wanderer: His Parables and His Sayings*. 1932; rpt., New York: Knopf, 1966.

———. *Al-Majmu'a al-kamila li mu'allafat Jubran Khalil Jubran al-'Arabiyya* [Gibran's complete Arabic works]. Beirut: al-Jil, 1994.

Gilsenan, Michael. *Lords of the Lebanese Marches: Violence and Narrative in an Arab Society*. Berkeley: University of California Press, 1996.

Gordon, David. *The Republic of Lebanon: Nation in Jeopardy*. Boulder, Colo.: Westview Press, 1983.

Gramsci, Antonio. *Selections from the Prison Notebooks*. Trans. and ed. Quintin Hoare and Geoffrey Nowell Smith. New York: International, 1971.

———. *Selections from Cultural Writings*. Ed. David Forgacs and Geoffrey Nowell-Smith. Cambridge: Harvard University Press, 1985.

Gran, Peter. *The Islamic Roots of Capitalism: Egypt, 1760–1840*. Austin: University of Texas Press, 1979.

———. *Beyond Eurocentrism: A New View of Modern World History*. Syracuse: Syracuse University Press, 1996.

Groden, Michael, and Martin Kreiswirth, eds. *The Johns Hopkins Guide to Critical Theory and Criticism*. Baltimore: Johns Hopkins University Press, 1994.

Gupta, Akhil, and James Ferguson. "Beyond 'Culture': Space, Identity, and the Politics of Difference." *Cultural Anthropology* 7 (February 1992).

Hafez, Sabri. Review of al-Da'if's "Tiqniyyat al-Bu's." *Al-'Arab*, November 22, 1994.

Hall, Stuart. "The Toad in the Garden: Thatcherism among the Theorists." In *Marxism and the Interpretation of Culture*, ed. Cary Nelson and Lawrence Grossberg. Urbana: University of Illinois Press, 1988.

———. "Gramsci's Relevance for the Study of Race and Ethnicity." *Journal of Communications Inquiry* (winter 1993): 5–27.

Hanf, Theodor. *Coexistence in Wartime Lebanon: Decline of a State and Rise of a Nation*. Trans. John Richardson. London: Centre for Lebanese Studies, 1993.

Harik, Iliya. *Politics and Change in a Traditional Society: Lebanon, 1711–1845*. Princeton: Princeton University Press, 1968.

Harlow, Barbara. "Palestine or Andalusia: The Literary Response to the Israeli Invasion of Lebanon." *Race and Class* 26.2 (1984): 33–43.

Harris, William. *Faces of Lebanon: Sects, Wars, and Global Extensions*. Princeton: Markus Wiener, 1997.

Hartman, Michelle. "Ilham Mansur's 'Ila Hiba: Sira ula' and 'Hiba fi rihlat al-jasad: Sira thaniya.'" *Arabic and Middle Eastern Literatures* 2.2 (1999): 141–58.

———. *The Complete Translation of Michel Chiha's Works in English*. Beirut: Dar al-Nahar, 2003.

———. *An Anthology of Selected Writing of Michel Chiha*. London: I. B. Tauris, forthcoming.

———. *Ecrire l'arabe en français: Language and Identity in Literature from Lebanon*. London: I. B. Tauris, forthcoming.

Hawi, Khalil. *Kahlil Gibran: His Background, Character, and Works*. Beirut: American University of Beirut Press, 1963.

al-Hayek, René. *Bortret li al-nisyan* [Portrait of forgetfulness]. Beirut: Al-Markaz al-thaqafi al-'Arabi, 1994.

Hitti, Philip. *Lebanon in History: From the Earliest Times to the Present*. London: Macmillan, 1957.

Hobsbawm, E. J. *Nations and Nationalism since 1780: Programme, Myth, Reality*. New York: Cambridge University Press, 1990.

Hourani, Albert. "Ideologies of the Mountain and the City." In Roger Owen, ed., *Essays on the Crisis in Lebanon*, 33–41. London: Ithaca Press, 1976.

———. *A History of the Arab People*. Cambridge: Harvard University Press, 1991.

Hourani, Albert, and Nadim Shehadi, eds. *The Lebanese in the World: A Century of Emigration*. London: Centre for Lebanese Studies and I. B. Tauris, 1992.

Hudson, Michael. *The Precarious Republic: Political Modernization in Lebanon*. 1968; rpt., Boulder, Colo.: Westview Press, 1985.

Hutchinson, John, and Anthony D. Smith, eds. *Nationalism*. New York: Oxford University Press, 1994.

Idriss, Suheil. "Al-Tal wa al-nawrass" [The hill and the seagull]. *Al-Adab*, nos. 7–9 (July–September 1976): 90–96.

———. *Al-Khandaq al-ghamiq*. 5th ed. Beirut: Dar al-Adab, 1986.

———, ed. *Al-Adab: Majalla shahriyya ta'ni bi-shu'un al-fikr* [Revue mensuelle culterelle]. Beirut: Dar al-Adab, 1953–.

Ignatieff, Michael. *Blood and Belonging: Journeys into the New Nationalisms*. New York: Farrar, Straus and Giroux, 1993.

Issa, Samira. Review of Khoury's *Bab al-shams*. Supplement of newspaper *Al-Nahar*, May 9, 1998, 18.

Issawi, Charles. "The Historical Background of Lebanese Emigration, 1800–1914." In *The Lebanese in the World*, ed. Hourani and Shehadi, 13–31.

Jabbur, Mona. *Fatat tafiha* [A worthless girl]. Beirut: Maktabat Dar al-Hayat, 1962.

Jaber, Rabih. *Al-Bayt al-akhir* [The last house]. Beirut: Dar al-Adab, 1996.

Jaber, Yahya. *Al-Zu'ran* [The scoundrels]. Private printing, 1991.

———. *Khuth al-kitab bi quwwa* [Take the book by force]. London: Riad el-Rayyess Books, 1994.

———. *Nujum al-zhuhr* [Stars at noon]. London: Riad el-Rayyess Books, 1995.

———. *Ibtasim anta Lubnani* [Smile, you're Lebanese]. London: Riad el-Rayyess Books, 1997.

Jabir, Jamil. *Jubran*. Beirut, 1958.

al-Jabiri, Muhammad. *Ishkaliyat al-fikr al-'Arabi al-mu'asir* [The problematics of Arab contemporary thought]. Beirut: Markaz al-dirasat al-wihda al-'Arabiyya, 1989.

Jackson, Peter, and Jan Penrose, eds. *Constructions of Race, Place and Nation*. Minneapolis: University of Minnesota Press, 1993.

Jameson, Fredric. *The Political Unconscious: Narrative as a Socially Symbolic Act*. Ithaca: Cornell University Press, 1981.

———. "Third World Literature in the Era of Multinational Capitalism." *Social Text* 15 (fall 1986): 65–88.

———. *Postmodernism, or the Cultural Logic of Late Capitalism*. Durham, N.C.: Duke University Press, 1991.

Jankowski, James, and Israel Gershoni, eds. *Rethinking Nationalism in the Arab Middle East*. New York: Columbia University Press, 1997.

Jayyusi, Salma Khadra. Foreword to Jean and Kahlil Gibran's *Kahlil Gibran*. New York: Avenal Books, 1991.

———, ed. *Modern Arabic Poetry: An Anthology*. New York: Columbia University Press, 1987.

Jayyusi, Salma Khadra, and Roger Allen, eds. *Modern Arabic Drama: An Anthology*. Bloomington: Indiana University Press, 1995.

Joumblatt, Kamal. *I Speak for Lebanon*. Trans. Michael Pallis. London: Zed Press, 1982.

Jubran. Beirut: Al-Nadi al-thaqafi al-ʿArabi, 1984.

Karami, Nabil. *Jubran Khalil Jubran wa al-qawmiyya al-ʿArabiyya* [Gibran and Arab nationalism]. Beirut: Manshurat dar al-rabita al-thaqafiyya li al-tabaʿ wa al-nashr wa al-tawziʿ, 1961.

al-Kasem, Jean. *Al-Rahbaniyyun wa Fayruz: Alf ʿamal fanni, khamsun ʿamal min al-ʿata'* [The Rahbanis and Fayruz: One thousand works of art, fifty years of giving]. Damascus: Dar Tlas li al-dirasat wa al-tarjama wa al-nashr, 1987.

Kattani, Suleiman. *Jubran Khalil Jubran fi masrah hayatihi* [Gibran in his life's play]. 1983 TV series.

Kayrouz, Wahib. *Gibran in His Museum.* Bacharia, 1995.

al-Khal, Yusuf. *Shiʿr* 1.4 (fall 1957): 109–10.

Khalaf, Samir. *Lebanon's Predicament.* New York: Columbia University Press, 1987.

———. *Beirut Reclaimed.* Beirut: Dar al-Nahar, 1993.

Khalaf, Samir, and Philip Khoury, eds. *Recovering Beirut: Urban Design and Postwar Reconstruction.* Leiden: E. J. Brill, 1993.

Khalid, Mazen. "Awakenings: Theater Symbolizes Beirut's Cultural Regeneration." *Lebanon Report* 4 (November 1993): 10.

Khalidi, Rashid. "The Formation of Palestinian Identity: The Critical Years, 1917–1923." In *Rethinking Nationalism in the Arab Middle East,* ed. Jankowski and Gershoni, 171–90.

Khalidi, Rashid, Lisa Anderson, Muhammad Muslih, and Reeva Simon, eds. *The Origins of Arab Nationalism.* New York: Columbia University Press, 1991.

Khalidi, Walid. *Conflict and Violence in Lebanon: Confrontation in the Middle East.* Cambridge: Harvard Center for International Affairs, 1979.

Khalil, Khalil Ahmed. *Al-Maʿrifa al-ijtimaʿiyya fi adab Jubran* [Social concerns in the literature of Gibran]. Beirut: Dar Ibn Khaldun, 1981.

Khatibi, Abdelkebir. *Love in Two Languages.* Trans. Richard Howard. Minneapolis: University of Minnesota Press, 1990.

al-Khazen, William. *Al-Shiʿr wa al-wataniyya fi Lubnan wa al-bilad al-ʿArabiyya: Min matlaʿ al-nahda ila ʿam 1939* [Poetry and nationalism in Lebanon and the Arab world: From the beginning of the Renaissance to 1939]. Beirut: Dar al-Mashreq, 1979.

Khoury, Elias. *Al-Jabal al-saghir.* Beirut: Muʾassasat al-abhath al-ʿArabiyya, 1977.

———. "Al-Naqd wa al-nass al-naqdi" [Criticism and the critical text]. *Al-Mawaqif* (fall 1981): 11–23.

———. *Al-Wujuh al-bayda'* [The white faces]. Beirut: Muʾassasat al-abhath al-ʿArabiyya, 1981.

———. *Abwab al-medina.* Beirut: Dar al-Adab, 1981.

———. *Zaman al-ihtilal* [Time of occupation]. Beirut: Muʾassasat al-abhath al-ʿArabiyya, 1985.

———. *The Little Mountain.* Trans. Maia Tabet. Minneapolis: University of Minnesota Press, 1989.

———. *Rihlat Ghandi al-saghir.* Beirut: Dar al-Adab, 1989.

———. *Gates of the City.* Trans. Paula Haydar. Minneapolis: University of Minnesota Press, 1993.

———. *Kingdom of Strangers.* 1993.

———. *Mamlakat al-ghuraba'.* Beirut: Dar al-Adab, 1993.

———. *The Journey of Little Gandhi.* Trans. Paula Haydar. Minneapolis: University of Minnesota Press, 1994.

———. *Majma' al-asrar* [Collection of secrets]. Beirut: Dar al-Adab, 1994.

———. *Bab al-shams* [Gate of the sun]. Beirut: Dar al-Adab, 1998.

———. Interviews, July 1995, March, May, June 1998.

Khoury, Mounah. "A Critique of Adonis's Perspectives on Arabic Literature and Culture." *Studies in Contemporary Arabic Poetry and Criticism.* Middle Eastern Series #16. Piedmont, Calif.: Jahon Books, 1987: 13–41.

Khoury, Mounah, and Hamid Algar, eds. and trans. *An Anthology of Modern Arabic Poetry.* Berkeley: University of California Press, 1974.

Khoury, Philip. *Syria and the French Mandate: The Politics of Arab Nationalism, 1920–1945.* Princeton: Princeton University Press, 1987.

Khuweiri, Antoine. *Jubran Khalil Jubran: Al-Nabigha al-Lubnani* [Gibran: The Lebanese genius]. Beirut: Markaz al-i'lam wa al-tawthiq, 1981.

Kiwan, Fadia, ed. *Le Liban aujourd'hui.* Paris: CNRS Editions, 1994.

Knowlton, Clark S. "The Social and Spatial Mobility of the Syrian and Lebanese Communities in São Paulo, Brazil." In *The Lebanese in the World,* ed. Hourani and Shehadi, 285–311.

Kristeva, Julia. *Nations without Nationalism.* Trans. Leon S. Rowdiez. New York: Columbia University Press, 1993.

Kundera, Milan. *The Art of the Novel.* New York: Grove Press, 1986.

Labaki, Boutros. "Development Policy in Lebanon between Past and Future." *The Beirut Review* 6 (fall 1993): 97–111.

Laroui, Abdallah. *The Crisis of the Arab Intellectual: Traditionalism or Historicism?* Trans. Diamid Cammell. Berkeley: University of California Press, 1976.

Lebanon Report. Monthly and then quarterly publication by the Lebanese Center for Policy Studies, Beirut, 1990–98.

Lloyd, David. *Nationalism and Minor Literature: James Clarence Mangan and the Emergence of Irish Cultural Nationalism.* Berkeley: University of California Press, 1987.

Luciani, Giacomo, ed. *The Arab State.* Berkeley: University of California Press, 1990.

Lukács, Georg. *The Historical Novel.* Trans. Hannal and Stanley Mitchell. Lincoln: University of Nebraska Press, 1983.

Maalouf, Amin. *The Rock of Tanios.* Trans. Dorothy Blair. London: Abacus, 1994.

MacIntyre, Alasdair. "Relativism, Power, and Philosophy." In *Relativism: Interpretation and Confrontation,* ed. Michael Kravs. Notre Dame: Notre Dame Press, 1989.

Makhlouf, Issa. Review of al-Da'if's 'Tiqniyyat al-Bu's.' *Hayat. Mawaqif: li al-hurriyya wa al-ibda' wa al-ta'bir* [Positions: For freedom, creativity, and expression]. Magazine edited by Adonis: 1968–75, 1980–81, 1983–93 (not including 1985–87 or 1990), 1994.

Manganaro, Elise Salem. *See* Salem Manganaro, Elise.

Meyer, Stefan G. "The Contemporary Arabic Novel in the Levant: A Case Study in the Development of Literary Modernism." Ph.D. diss., Rutgers University, 1996.

———. *The Experimental Arabic Novel: Postcolonial Literary Modernism in the Levant.* Albany: SUNY Press, 2001.

Mina, Hana. *Adab al-harb* [The literature of war]. Damascus: Manshurat wizarat al-thaqafa wa al-irshad al-qawmi, 1976.

Modern Poetry of the Arab World. Trans. Abdullah al-Udhari. New York: Penguin Books, 1986.

Moses, Michael Valdez. *The Novel and the Globalization of Culture.* New York: Oxford University Press, 1995.

Al-Muqawama fi al-ta'bir al-adabi [Resistance in literary expression]. Beirut: Al-Majlis al-thaqafi li Lubnan al-junubi, 1985.

Naff, Alixa. "Lebanese Immigration into the United States: 1880 to the Present." In Hourani and Shehadi's *The Lebanese in the World,* 141–65.

Naimy, Mikhail. *Khalil Gibran: His Life and His Works.* Beirut: Khayats, 1964 (orig. in Arabic, 1934).

Naimy, Nadeem. *The Lebanese Prophets of New York.* Beirut: American University of Beirut Press, 1985.

———. Interview, April 1996.

Najmabadi, Afsaneh. *The Story of the Daughters of Quchan: Gender and National Memory in Iranian History.* Syracuse: Syracuse University Press, 1998.

Naked in Exile: Khalil Hawi's The Threshing Floors of Hunger. Trans. Adnan Haydar and Michael Beard. Washington, D.C.: Three Continents Press, 1984.

Nasrallah, Emily. *Tuyur aylul* [September birds]. Beirut: Mu'assasat Nawfal, 1962.

———. *Shajrat al-difla* [Oleander tree]. Beirut: Mu'assasat Nawfal, 1968.

———. *Tilka al-thikrayat* [Those memories]. Beirut: Nawfal, 1978.

———. *Flight against Time.* Trans. Issa J. Boullata. Charlottetown, PEI: Ragweed Press, 1987.

———. *A House Not Her Own: Stories from Beirut.* Trans. Thuraya Khalil-Khouri. Charlottetown, PEI: Gynergy Books, 1992.

———. *Al-Jamr al-ghafi* [Sleeping embers]. Beirut: Nawfal, 1995.

Osseiran, Layla. "*Asafir al-fajr* [Birds of dawn]. Beirut: Sharikat al-matbu'at li al-tawzi' wa al-nashr, 1991.

Otto, Annie Salem. *The Parables of Kahlil Gibran: An Interpretation of His Writings and His Art.* New York: Citadel Press, 1963.

Owen, Roger, ed. *Essays on the Crisis in Lebanon.* London: Ithaca Press, 1976.

Parker, Andrew, Mary Russo, Doris Sommer, and Patricia Yaeger, eds. *Nationalisms and Sexualities.* New York: Routledge, 1992.

Penrose, Jan. "Reification in the Name of Change: The Impact of Nationalism on Social Constructions of Nation, People, and Place in Scotland and the United Kingdom." In *Constructions of Race, Place and Nation*, ed. Jackson and Penrose, 27–49.

Phares, Walid. *Lebanese Christian Nationalism: The Rise and Fall of an Ethnic Resistance*. Boulder, Colo.: Lynne Rienner, 1995.

Piterberg, Gabriel. "The Tropes of Stagnation and Awakening in Nationalist Historical Consciousness: The Egyptian Case." In *Rethinking Nationalism in the Arab Middle East*, ed. Jankowski and Gershoni, 42–61.

Qabbani, Nizar. *On Entering the Sea: The Erotic and Other Poetry of Nizar Qabbani*. Trans. Sharif Elmusa, Lena Jayyusi, and Jeremy Reed. New York: Interlink Books, 1996.

Qasem, Hashem. Review of al-Da'if's *Nahiat al-bara'a*. *Al-Nahar*, July 20, 1997.

al-Rahbani, Ziad. *Nazl al-surur*. Play presented in 1974.

———. *Bilnisbi la bukra shu?* Play presented in 1978.

———. *Film Amirki tawil*. Play presented in 1980.

———. *Shi fashil*. Play presented in 1983.

Randal, Jonathan C. *Going All the Way: Christian Warlords, Israeli Adventurers, and the War in Lebanon*. New York: Viking Press, 1983.

Renan, Ernest. "What Is a Nation?" Trans. Martin Thom. In Bhabha's *Nation and Narration*, 8–22.

Rigney, Barbara Hill. *Madness and Sexual Politics in the Feminist Novel*. Madison: University of Wisconsin Press, 1980.

Rorty, Richard. *Contingency, Irony, and Solidarity*. Berkeley: University of California Press, 1989.

Rosaldo, Renato. *Culture and Truth: The Remaking of Social Analysis*. Boston: Beacon Press, 1989.

Rowe, Peter, and Hashim Sarkis, eds. *Projecting Beirut: Episodes in the Construction and Reconstruction of a Modern City*. Munich: Prestel, 1998.

Said, Edward. *Orientalism*. New York: Vintage, 1978.

———. Foreword to *Little Mountain* by Elias Khoury. Minneapolis: University of Minnesota Press, 1989.

———. *Culture and Imperialism*. New York: Vintage, 1993.

———. *The Politics of Dispossession: The Struggle for Palestinian Self-Determination, 1969–1994*. New York: Pantheon Books, 1994.

Salem, Elie A. *Modernization without Revolution*. Bloomington: Indiana University Press, 1973.

———. *Violence and Diplomacy in Lebanon: The Troubled Years, 1982–1988*. London: I. B. Tauris, 1995.

Salem Manganaro, Elise. "Bearing Witness: Recent Literature from Lebanon." *Literary Review* 37.3 (spring 1994).

———. Review of "Death of the Prophet." *MESA Bulletin* 30 (July 1996): 133–34.

———. "Negotiating Feminist Ideologies within Lebanese Women's Writings." *Bahithat: Women and Writing* 2 (1995–96): 163–73.

———. "Imagining Lebanon through Rahbani Musicals." *Aljadid* (fall 1999): 4–6.

Salem, Paul. *Bitter Legacy: Ideology and Politics in the Arab World*. Syracuse: Syracuse University Press, 1994.

Salibi, Kamal. *A House of Many Mansions: The History of Lebanon Reconsidered*. Berkeley: University of California Press, 1988.

Samman, Ghada. *Beirut '75*. Beirut: Dar al-Adab, 1975.

———. *Kawabis Beirut* [Beirut nightmares]. Beirut: Manshurat Ghada Samman, 1976.

———. *Al-Qamar al-murabba*ʿ [The square moon]. Beirut: Ghada Samman, 1994.

———. *Beirut '75*. Trans. Nancy N. Roberts. Fayetteville: University of Arkansas Press, 1995.

———. *Beirut Nightmares*. Trans. Nancy N. Roberts. London: Quartet Books, 1997.

———. *The Square Moon: Supernatural Tales*. Trans. Issa J. Boullata. Fayetteville: University of Arkansas Press, 1999.

Sayigh, Rosemary. *Palestinians: From Peasants to Revolutionaries*. London: Zed Books, 1979.

Shaaban, Bouthaina. "Arab Women Writers: 'Are There Any?'" *Washington Report on Middle East Affairs*, February 1993, 36 ff.

———. *100 ʿam min al-riwaya al-nisaʾiyya al-ʿArabiyya* [One hundred years of the Arab female novel, 1899–1999]. Beirut: Dar al-Adab, 1999.

Shahid, Irfan. "Gibran and the American Literary Canon: The Problem of *The Prophet*." In *Tradition, Modernity, and Postmodernity in Arabic Literature: Essays in Honor of Professor Issa J. Boullata*, ed. Kamal Abdel-Malek and Wael Hallaq, 321–34. Leiden: Brill, 2000.

Shammas, Anton. *Arabesques*. Trans. Vivian Eden. New York: Harper and Row, 1988.

Sharabi, Hisham. *Nationalism and Revolution in the Arab World: The Middle East and North Africa*. Princeton: D. Van Nostrand, 1966.

———. *Arab Intellectuals and the West: The Formative Years, 1875–1914*. Baltimore: Johns Hopkins University Press, 1970.

———, ed. *The Next Arab Decade: Alternative Futures*. Boulder, Colo.: Westview Press, 1988.

———, ed. *Theory, Politics, and the Arab World*. New York: Routledge, 1990.

al-Shaykh, Hanan. *Hikayat Zahra*. Beirut: Dar al-Adab, 1980.

———. *The Story of Zahra*. Trans. Peter Ford. London: Quartet Books, 1986.

———. *Misk al-ghazal*. Beirut: Dar al-Adab, 1988.

———. *Women of Sand and Myrrh*. Trans. Catherine Cobham. New York: Doubleday, 1989.

———. *Barid Beirut*. Beirut: Dar al-hilal, 1992.

———. *Ukannis al-Shams ʿan al-sutuh* [I sweep the sun from the roofs]. Beirut: Dar al-Adab, 1994.

————. *Beirut Blues.* Trans. Catherine Cobham. London: Vintage, 1996.

————. Interview with the author, London, February 4, 1999.

Sheehi, Stephen. "Doubleness and Duality: Allegories of Becoming in Jurji Zaydan's 'al-Mamluk al-sharid.'" *Journal of Arabic Literature* 30.1 (spring 1999).

————. "Inscribing the Arab Self: Butrus al-Bustani's 'Nafir Suriyah' and the Discourse of National Subjectivity." *British Journal of the Middle East* (spring 2000).

Shehadi, Nadim, and Dana Haffar Mills, eds. *Lebanon: A History of Conflict and Consensus.* London: Centre for Lebanese Studies and I. B. Tauris, 1988.

Shi'r [Poetry] Magazine. Ed. Khal et al. Beirut: Dar Majallat Shi'r, 1957–.

Stevens, Janet. "'We're Still OK': The Lebanese Tapes." *Arab Studies Quarterly* 3.3 (autumn 1981): 275–84.

Straubhaar, Joseph, and Robert LaRose. *Communications Media in the Information Society.* Belmont, Calif.: Wadsworth, 1996.

Suleiman, Michael. *Political Parties in Lebanon: The Challenge of a Fragmented Political Culture.* Ithaca: Cornell University Press, 1967.

Sunderman, Paula. "Between Two Worlds: An Interview with Hanan al-Shaykh." *Literary Review* 40.2 (winter 1997): 297–308.

Sweidan, Sami. *Abhath fi al-nass al-riwa'i al-'Arabi* [Studies in Arabic literary texts]. Beirut: Mu'assasat al-abhath al-'Arabiyya, 1986.

Tibi, Bassam. *Arab Nationalism: A Critical Inquiry.* Trans. and ed. Marion Farouk-Sluglett and Peter Sluglett. New York: St. Martin's Press, 1990.

Tinaoui, Simone Ghazi. "An Analysis of the Syrian-Lebanese Economic Cooperation Agreements." *Beirut Review* 8 (fall 1994): 97–112.

Van Leeuwen, Richard. "Fakhr al-Din in Lebanese National History." *Beirut Review* 4 (fall 1992): 97–103.

Venuti, Lawrence, ed. *Rethinking Translation: Discourse, Subjectivity, Ideology.* New York: Routledge, 1992.

Waterfield, Robin. *Prophet: The Life and Times of Khalil Gibran.* New York: St. Martin's Press, 1998.

Wazen, 'Abdo. *Hadiqat al-hawass* [Garden of the senses]. Beirut: Dar al-Jadid, 1993.

Weber, Edgard. Interview regarding his translation of Rachid al-Da'if. *Nahar al-Kutub,* February 18, 1998.

Weber, Max. *Essays in Sociology.* Trans. and ed. H. H. Gerth and C. Wright Mills. New York: Routledge and Kegan Paul, 1948.

Wicker, Brian. *The Story-Shaped World: Fiction and Metaphysics, Some Variations on a Theme.* Notre Dame: University of Notre Dame Press, 1975.

Williams, Raymond. *Culture and Society, 1780–1950.* 1958; rpt., New York: Columbia University Press, 1993.

Yared, Nazek Saba. "Un autre visage du Liban." In *Les cahiers du grif: Liban,* ed. Accad and Collier, 99–106.

Young, Barbara. *This Man from Lebanon: A Study of Kahlil Gibran.* New York: Knopf, 1945.

Young, Michael Bacos. "Politics and Culture in Lebanon: Interview with Elias Khoury." *Beirut Review* 5 (spring 1993): 131–42.

———. "Inconvenient Reminders: Reading a Selection of CLS Papers." *Beirut Review* 6 (fall 1993): 113–23.

Zamir, Meir. *The Formation of Modern Lebanon.* London: Croom Helm, 1995.

———. *Lebanon's Quest: The Road to Statehood, 1926–1939.* London: I. B. Tauris, 1997.

Zeidan, Joseph T. *Arab Women Novelists: The Formative Years and Beyond.* Albany: State University of New York Press, 1995.

Zwein, Sabah al-Khrat. *Al-Bayt al-ma'il, wa al-waqt wa al-judran* [The leaning house, and time and walls]. Beirut: Amwaj li al-nashr wa al-tawzi', 1995.

Index

· · ·

Elise Salem is a professor of literature and assistant dean for academic planning at Fairleigh Dickinson University in Madison, New Jersey. She was born and raised in Beirut. In 1994, she edited a special issue of the *Literary Review* on contemporary Lebanese literature, and she has published numerous articles on Lebanese literature and culture.

CONCURRENT SENTENCES

CONCURRENT

A True Story of Murder, Love and Redemption

SENTENCES

BY

DENISE BECK-CLARK

New Horizon Press
Far Hills, New Jersey

New Horizon Press
P.O. Box 669
Far Hills, NJ 07931

Denise Beck-Clark
    Concurrent Sentences: A True Story of Murder, Love and Redemption

Interior Design: Susan M. Sanderson

Library of Congress Catalog Card Number: 99-70155

ISBN: 0-88282-188-1
New Horizon Press

Manufactured in the U.S.A.

2004   2003   2002   2001   2000   /   5   4   3   2   1

For Victor and Raphael
with love and gratitude
and
For people everywhere
yearning to be free

The Indestructible is one; it is every individual
man, and at the same time it is common to all,
and this is the reason for the unparalleled,
inseparable union of mankind.

Franz Kafka
Meditations

TABLE OF CONTENTS

Author's Note

This book is based on the experiences of Denise Beck-Clark and Victor Clark and reflects our perceptions of the past, present, and future. The personalities, events, actions, and conversations portrayed within the story have been taken from our memories, extensive interviews, research, court documents, letters, personal papers, press accounts, and the memories of participants.

In an effort to safeguard the privacy of certain people, we have changed their names and the names of certain places and in some cases, altered otherwise identifying characteristics. Events involving the characters happened as described. Only minor details have been changed.

PROLOGUE

The storefront of 1088 Clarkson Avenue with its black door and dark walls through which no light penetrated was known throughout the neighborhood as a social club. By eleven-thirty on the evening of Thursday, March 30, the party which had begun at nine with only about thirty teenagers was an evident success. Now fifty to seventy-five young people were dancing or socializing. Gail Roberts, one of the women who had helped the kids organize the party to raise funds for the graduating class of Sullivan High, was standing by the front door to make sure that no problems erupted. Unfortunately, the place was so dimly lit that she could not even see to the back wall. The center of the club was designated as the dance floor. It now teemed with the bulk of the guests bopping, jiving, and grooving to rock 'n' roll blaring from the record player behind the bar.

As small and cramped as the club was, the dancing went on, surprisingly, without commotion. Sheila Eaton was one of the people on the dance floor, chatting and dancing with her three girlfriends. Those who were not dancing sat at tables which were set flush against the two side walls to make more room for the dance floor. Here, boys and girls were engrossed in gossip about other party patrons or obsessing over different ways to ask that special someone to dance. A small group of teens located themselves behind the five-foot-long bar in the back of the store. One of the student organizers of the party, Kate Rogers, was there talking with her friend Carrie Conrad and others, including those hanging out by the deep freezer to the immediate left of the bar. On the freezer sat Todd Richter, his legs wrapped around the waist of his girlfriend, Beth Gossard.

The guests, so involved with each other and themselves, did not pay attention to much else. After all, this was a party, and all they wanted to do was relax, drink sodas, have fun with their friends, and leave their problems and people from their urban world right where they belonged—outside. In fact, that was the mood which prevailed.

And so, when three young men walked in a couple minutes before midnight, no one paid attention.

One of the men approached Sheila Eaton and said to her, "Get out if you don't want to get shot." Then he walked away. Sheila thought she recognized the man despite the dim lights in the place. But she wasn't concerned about who he was at the time; rather, she was frightened about what he had said. No one had ever said anything like that to her before, and hearing him mouth his warning terrified her. Feeling threatened, Sheila immediately interrupted her friends Jill, Marsha, and Davida and whispered that they should all quietly leave. The four young girls told no one else where and why they were going in such a hurry as they exited the front door, darted across the street, huddled one block away on a street corner facing the storefront, and stood there, curious as to what was going to happen. The streetlights in front of the store enabled them to dimly see the club entrance, the sidewalk in front, and parked cars on the street.

At about the same time, inside the club one of the men approached Gail Roberts still standing near the front door. The man took his gun out and pointed it at the stupefied woman who immediately reached into the pocket of her dungarees, and dug out the twenty dollars she had borrowed from her brother earlier in the evening. Gail was in shock and didn't make a sound or even a slight movement. She didn't recognize the man, and she didn't think anyone else could see what was happening to her in the obscure shadows. The closest light she could see anything by was a haloed red one in the ceiling. Regardless, Gail didn't want to look at the man. But she couldn't help seeing his gun. After he snatched the twenty dollars from her hand, the man ran away from Gail and melted into the crowd. She prayed that he was gone.

Shortly before midnight, the three men took their places. One stood on the dance floor near the left wall about twenty feet away from the bar. The second stood near the right wall, and the third quickly moved towards the bar. The men conspired that with this particular configuration they'd be able to control the crowd. In his haste, however, the third man may have tripped on the electrical cords of the lights located behind the bar, or could have intentionally turned off the lights to let the others know to prepare for the signal. Whatever the cause, the lights towards the front of the bar flickered and then went out. With the darkness to hide them, they were confident that their identities were shielded and their crime all the more perfect.

At midnight, the three men drew their guns and the one on the dance floor fired his revolver.

"Everybody freeze! This is a stickup! Don't move!" screamed the man on the dance floor who fired the signal shot.

Carrie Conrad was behind the bar when the man yelled, and she saw one of the men wielding guns come toward the bar where she stood. Carrie panicked. She wondered if her classmates, most of whom were still dancing, could even distinguish that the loud bang was a gunshot and not drums from the music. She began to think the whole thing might be all in her head, but then she noticed that some friends near her were looking towards where the gun was fired. Confused and scared, Carrie did not know what to do, so she did the only thing which in her confused mind made any sense: she took the record off the phonograph, hoping to clue everyone that something was wrong. Someone from the crowd screamed to turn the music back on. Believing it to be one of the men with guns giving her an order, Carrie did as she was told. All of a sudden, one of the gunmen approached her, pressing his weapon to her head. He did not say a thing, and she did not move. Carrie had never felt terror like this before, and it was even more ominous that some of the party guests still did not realize what was happening. Of course, Carrie herself did not really know what was going on: the man stood there watching her terror then slithered away so quickly in the darkness that he was a blur to her. In short order, he found another target at whom to point his gun. Meanwhile, most of the kids continued unaware, and, amid their dancing, Carrie felt immobile and helpless.

The man behind the bar slunk towards Kate Rogers. In the same fashion, he held his gun to her head, but this time he spoke. "Where is the money?" he called out. A frightened Kate tried to tell the man she had no money and pleaded with him not to shoot her. He seemed to pause for thought. Then he demanded she start pulling down coats from behind the bar. Kate obeyed, although she did not know why—all she could think about was the gun and her fear of being shot. At that point the man could have asked Kate to do almost anything, and she would have obliged. He surprised her when he began helping her pull down the coats. The two of them were knocking records and cans of soda off the bar while they were throwing around the coats. Kate was not sure if he was looking for a particular jacket or for wallets or money in the pockets, but her immense fear told her not to question his motives and to just keep doing what he asked. The last thing she needed was to agitate this man.

Suddenly, as if frustrated, the man moved away from Kate and the coats and stepped towards the deep freezer where Beth Gossard stood with Todd Richter's legs wrapped around her waist. Todd saw the agitated man approaching, unwrapped his legs from Beth's waist, and told her to move away. The girl stood absolutely still, paralyzed with fear. Presumably, to get her to move, Todd pushed Beth. She fell backwards against the wall and stayed there. The man held his gun up and ordered Todd to step down from the freezer. The man seemed upset because he had not found any money. Without a word, Todd obeyed, trying not to make the gunman any angrier. However, as Todd slowly slid down from the top of the deep freezer, at least one shot rang out.

Beth saw the flash from the gun. She did not scream and she did not run. The girl was in shock as Todd, his head bleeding, fell to the floor dead. The man with the gun fled onto the dance floor, and he and his cohorts became lost in the crowd. Why had the gunman shot Todd? Beth had no idea. She was still in a daze, her mind lost amidst the confusion, commotion, and questions about the senseless tragedy. She still was in this state when a friend grabbed her arm, pulled her into another room, and brought her back to reality.

Having finally caught on that there was trouble, most of the teenagers on the dance floor suddenly started screaming and running out of the club. Some kids did not realize a robbery was going on or that someone had been hurt, but happy and giggling, followed the rest of their friends outside as if dancing in a conga line. They wondered why everyone was in such a rush to leave. Outside, Sheila saw the people spill out of the club. She also noticed some men jumping into a light blue car which sped away.

Behind the bar, Kate had fainted. She did not revive until after everyone left. The affair which she had helped to organize, the party which was supposed to celebrate the graduating seniors before they went out into "the real world," was over. At 12:15 A.M. Friday morning, NYPD Officer John Kelly, the first policeman to reach the scene of the crime, had to explain to the young people that there had been a murder and the horrors of "the real world" had just entered their lives.

INTRODUCTION

On a steamy July Tuesday in 1988, I left the stink of Manhattan streets in a borrowed rust-colored coupe with dirty velour seats and no air-conditioning. Once outside the city, I rolled down the windows and breathed the clean air deeply. What a luxury to be driving to the country on a weekday morning instead of going to work in the congested city. I drank in the sight of the thick leafy maple trees that flourish just a few miles beyond New York City. I drove on through several small idyllic towns. I couldn't relax, however, because of the intense butterflies churning in my stomach; I tried to sidestep my jitters by interposing memories of bygone summer days traveling on a bus with other rambunctious teenagers, on the way to the Delaware River Water Gap. The radio station I tuned in seemed in sync with me, playing songs from that era such as "Help" and "Groovin'."

But today my excitement was different. For, unlike those earlier years, I was not on my way to some idyllic summer setting; now I was on my way to a state penitentiary. I was going to meet the inmate with whom I'd formed a strong bond after corresponding through the mail and talking on the telephone. Victor was serving a twenty-year-to-life sentence for a homicide committed during a robbery.

I have always had a strange fascination with women who form attachments to men in prison. You see them from time to time in reports on television: the man in drab prison garb looking hungry and eager as the woman walks through the iron gates and into the confines of the prison walls just to be with him. Perhaps my fascination is, in part, because I am a social worker and seek to understand the workings of the mind, or maybe I have whatever it is that motivates those women inside me. When I've wondered what would motivate a woman to do that, I'd usually come to the same conclusions: she has poor self-esteem, or feels sorry for him, or confuses love with compassion, or is masochistic and attracted to brutes, or has a problem with intimacy and wants a dream lover but not a normal relationship in which she must wake up and go to sleep with a man, risking that all-too-common occurrence of contempt born from familiarity.

Today as I drove along Route 17 en route to where Victor was imprisoned, the irony was inescapable. For, though I have always considered myself attractive and well-grounded in reality, I was now one of "those women."

And there was no avoiding it. I was nervous: nervous about myself, nervous about meeting Victor, nervous about going inside a prison.

Finally, the sign I was watching for announcing the town of Napanoch appeared. My heartbeat accelerated, for I knew the Eastern New York Correctional Facility would be a short distance beyond. And then, there it was: it looked like a phony medieval castle erected for a movie set, complete with turrets and towers with the addition of gun towers. I drove through the gate and headed for one of the parking lots for visitors. Surprised to find it full, I went to the next one, finally parking on the edge of a field of waving four-foot-high grass. The white sleeveless blouse and stone-washed denim skirt I wore were not the coolest clothing I could have chosen, but I hadn't wanted to go into a men's prison with too much skin showing.

The entrance had battleship-gray double doors which I had to lean my whole body against to open. Inside, a few men wearing light blue uniforms turned their heads as I entered and stopped talking. One with a bulbous nose and graying hair asked if I was there to visit an inmate. When I said yes, he informed me, "You're in the wrong place. Go out and walk to the left." Anxious but relieved to have more time to compose myself, I walked slowly. Questions ricocheted through my mind. *What if Victor is not the warm and loving man I have come to know through letters and phone calls? What if he is just another inmate conning a sucker? What if he looks different from his pictures? What if he is a predator?*

At the visitors' entrance another heavy iron door, this one painted black, was propped open. I walked through a small vestibule lined with lockers and into a waiting room with a formica counter at either end of the room, wooden benches, beat-up red plastic chairs, and male and female restrooms. At the far end guards were processing visitors. Two women, one young, one old, placed the contents of their pockets and wallets onto the counter. An officer did a cursory inspection of their things and signaled them on; the women walked one by one through a metal detector.

It was my turn next, and I, who usually questioned and pondered the world around me as well as figures of authority, humbly did exactly as I was told. I was allowed to keep my wallet, but I had to go back to the lockers to leave my handbag, along with a book of stamps and gum. "The stamps are contraband," the burly officer told me. Walking back, I thought it strange that they didn't allow stamps to be brought in, but I later learned it was because stamps are considered tender, and inmates are not allowed to handle money. At the same time, I was allowed to bring in my wallet which contained money. It didn't make any sense. But I was too nervous then to be concerned with their absurd rules. I longed for the moment when the fluttering butterflies in my stomach would be calmed.

As I got back in line and once more waited, the guard asked me abruptly, "What's the inmate's name and number?" Though I knew the number by heart, I read it with a shaky voice off a piece of paper. The corrections officers were businesslike and humorless. As I usually do when nervous, I wanted to crack jokes, but I didn't dare.

After gathering my remaining possessions, I walked through the metal detector practically on tiptoe and when it didn't go off, the first door was buzzed open for me. Through a window in that door and the one beyond, I could see the visitors' room. Men wearing white, red, green, or pink shirts with baggy forest green prison pants walked with their visitors or sat with them in parallel rows of plastic chairs and at tables. As I stood between the two doors, my heart began to pound, and my knees felt rubbery. How long did they plan to keep me in that airless cubicle! What if there were some problem? Victor had told me I could get something to drink while I waited for him, but I knew I would be too nervous to do anything but sit and wait.

As I clasped and unclasped my hands, the second door finally buzzed. A female officer motioned that I should go through. In the room another officer seated at a desk beckoned to me to give her the paper I had been given outside. After doing so, I scanned the room, then zeroed in on where to sit: somewhere to the right of the door where the inmates entered the room. I wanted to be noticed and inconspicuous at the same time. Victor knew that my hair was a noticeable mixture of chestnut, auburn, and dark brown, and, because he had seen my picture, I figured he'd recognize me. I hoped from the photos he'd sent to me I'd recognize him as well.

I looked around at what would have been a typically bland institutional room with its dirty, pale blue walls and gray linoleum floor, except just below the high ceiling was a mural painted in vivid colors of daisies and tulips, robins and blue jays, and an entanglement of green leaves. Next to the door through which the inmates came was a long one-way mirror in which I was startled to see my reflection. Sounds bounced from one wall to the other, as the high ceiling created bad acoustics.

Every couple of minutes the door opened, and each time my heart leapt to my throat as I thought, *This is him* and turned out to be wrong. After ten minutes I was sweating. After fifteen I frantically looked around to see if anyone noticed me sitting there alone, but of course no one did. Inmates and their wives, lovers, friends, and children were completely immersed in each other. As more time passed, the wait seemed endless. *Should I ask the guard what was taking so long? No. I don't want to do that and single myself out.* Finally, a small, muscular man with a sparkling smile and a mane of black hair touched by gray, wearing a white mesh and cotton shirt over the green pants, appeared at the door and scoured the room.

When our eyes met, I was sure it was him. I felt immediately attracted to him as he headed straight toward me with a bounce in his step and took my hand gently in his. "How are you?" Victor asked in a rich, resonant voice as if he really cared.

"I'm fine now," I somehow murmured.

"Thank you for coming," he said, still holding my hand.

My heart started to beat fiercely. At that moment I knew that I was embarking on a long journey that had only just begun.

PART
ONE

Somebody must have been telling lies about
Joseph K., for without having done anything
wrong he was arrested one fine morning.

Franz Kafka
The Trial

CHAPTER ONE

VICTOR'S WORLD

He stood hidden by the brush and watched the helicopter in the sky as it was struck by Vietnamese gun fire and erupted into flames. Victor Clark was on a mission with Recon Bravo company which had sent him out to the Khe Sahn where the North Vietnamese army was supposed to be on the move. He kept his eyes on the burning copter as it fell from the sky. With a mud-encrusted hand, he wiped his sweating brow and followed the descent of the helicopter until it hit the ground not far from him. He could see the pilot was trapped. There was no time to waste.

Under heavy enemy fire Victor ran to the copter. Flames yapped at his face and body, but he was not going to be stopped. Somehow he wedged open the door and got inside the cockpit. The pilot was still alive. He was moaning and not fully conscious.

"It's going to be all right," Victor comforted the man, realizing the pilot could be of no help in his own rescue. Using his knife, Victor cut the pilot out of his seat belt. He slung the man over his shoulder in a fireman's carry. Meanwhile, bullets flew about them. Victor continued on. Half-walking, half-crawling, he got the two of them to safety in the brush and cradled the pilot as they waited for the medivac unit.

It was a long wait. As he sat there holding the pilot, Victor's mind spun back to the beginning of his life, to what had brought him to this day, this hour, which was to earn him the Bronze Star.

Six days before Ruthie, his mother, would turn seventeen, Victor Jerome Clark was born in Bellevue Hospital in Manhattan. His mother and father brought him home to a one-family house in Hollis, Queens, then an up-and-coming working class neighborhood for the black bourgeoisie. An unskilled laborer, his father, Walter, had been in the signal corps of the army during the Korean Conflict and was able to buy the house financed by the GI loan program. The house had two stories and a finished basement. The bedrooms were on the second floor, Victor's in the front, his parents' in the rear. His room contained dark mahogany furniture, a bed with rounded posts, and a bureau. In the basement he had a scooter, a wagon, and a tricycle. The epitome of an only child, his parents bought him everything.

This included Trixie, a big-boned German shepherd who was trained by Walter to be Victor's baby-sitter and slept in his room. When they were out in the yard, Trixie wouldn't let Victor out or anyone else in. Trixie enabled Walter and Ruthie to leave Victor alone, even at a young age. They would brag to relatives that Victor was so intelligent he was able to answer or dial a telephone at age three if he needed help.

When Walter and Ruthie went off to Florida for a vacation, they left Victor with his godmother, Anne. He developed a fever, and Anne took him to Bellevue and left him there, in a room with pea green walls with brown trim. Because she wasn't a blood relative, Anne was not allowed back in either to visit Victor or take him home when he was well enough, so he had to remain there for a week until his mother came up from Florida to get him. One of many early abandonments, while he was in the hospital Victor kicked his heels until they turned bloody red, and he wouldn't stop screaming. No one held him; he was only a small child but completely alone.

Two years later, his father burned down their house in a jealous rage. Victor heard Walter yelling at Ruthie, then there was fire roaring all around them. All that could be heard was screaming and yelling, an anarchy of voices, until Victor felt the breath being snatched out of him. This was his Aunt Nell grabbing him, pushing him out of the way of a table lamp which came sailing through the air, crashing into her head instead of his. Outside, someone wrapped Nell's head entirely in white gauze except on the top, where Victor could see a bit of her black hair peeking through. For a long time they stood in the dark and starry night; fire engines were all over, and there was the thunderous noise of sirens and fire truck horns blasting.

Life changed a lot for Victor after the fire: no more dad, no more Trixie, no more house. He was brought to Florida to live with his grandmother who was full of religious fire and righteousness, but he spent as much time as he could next door with his great grandmother. Soft and warm to the touch, Maisie had gnarled, chubby hands and was always humming "Amazing Grace." She held Victor on her lap as she stomped her feet to a regular beat, rocking back and forth in the rocking chair. Her kitchen was always warm and fragrant with the scent of freshly baked biscuits which sat in an aluminum pot with a glass cover. Victor ate them as if they were cookies. Like his great grandmother, they were soft, soothing and succulent, and full of love.

One Thursday, Victor was sitting on Maisie's lap when he said, "Momma, I just want to die."

"Why would you say something like that, Child?" she responded with surprise.

"Because nobody loves me. Nobody wants me."

"You shouldn't talk such foolishness. I love you."

If Maisie was like a mother to Victor, William, her husband, was Daddy. Dark and leathery with a blue ring around his black pupils, which Victor inherited, he would take Victor by the hand and together they would walk to the railroad station about a mile away. As they walked, he would tell Victor about life, why grasshoppers and trees and fruits and vegetables exist, and when they got to the station, they'd watch the trains come in, diesel fumes piercing their nostrils. Back at the house, they'd sit in the backyard while Victor caught yellow grasshoppers which he'd keep as pets. Like men chewing tobacco, the grasshoppers chewed brown stuff and spat it out.

Not all of Victor's experiences in the South were happy. Sometimes older cousins took him to the movies. They'd bring their brown paper bags containing baloney sandwiches, and after going through the main entrance to buy tickets at the same price as everyone in the theater, they'd be directed outside and up the outdoor stairs to the balcony. They couldn't buy popcorn because "coloreds" weren't allowed inside on the main floor of the theater.

On one trip south, Victor and his mother were somewhere below the Mason-Dixon line. They stopped at a Howard Johnson's restaurant and headed straight for the back where Victor saw several black adults dressed in white cooks' uniforms. One of them handed Ruthie a brown paper bag. Other blacks were sitting outdoors and eating at picnic tables. Upon returning to their car, Victor looked in the restaurant window and saw it full of white people. He didn't understand until he was older that he and his mother had taken their hamburgers out in a bag because they had to. His parents had never talked to him about discrimination nor had they told him not to talk to anyone white.

One weekend morning, Victor was working in his aunt's vegetable patch when the owner of the fields where his family worked pulled up in his truck. Victor ran in to tell his aunt, who proceeded to beat him because he didn't call the boss "Mister." This was hard for Victor to understand because the boss called his aunt and uncle by their first names even though they were older than him. A few years later when he was twelve, Victor and his cousin were in town in Blackville, South Carolina, sitting on a bench, eating salted peanuts. Two white boys around their same age came along, stepped on his cousin's foot, and kept walking. Victor turned to his cousin and said, "You're gonna let him get away with that?" In New York that would have been unheard of. So they followed them. One white kid turned around and said, "What do you niggers want?"

"You stepped on my cousin's foot," Victor said. "Ain't you gonna tell him you're sorry?"

"Sorry? We don't apologize to no niggers," the boy said in a heavy drawl. Victor beat up the first one then the other, even though he was smaller than both of them, while his frightened cousin stood there watching. Victor's anger was so fierce that the two white boys were scared and unable to fight, thinking that Victor was crazy. His cousin, too, had terror on his face as he took Victor by the arm and led him away saying, "You can get hung for that kind of thing down here." Together they ran like crazy. Within a couple of days, his aunt took him to another county and put him on the train. He never went back to his cousins'.

A few months later, Victor came upon his grandmother sitting in the front yard wailing away as if someone had died. In an effort to soothe her, he told her everything would be okay, not knowing that the cause of her tears was his mother showing up to take him back up north. After living in Florida for about two years, Victor's mother decided he was ready to return to school and life in New York City.

Victor attended second grade, his grandmother worked in a dry cleaners, and his mother took care of white folks' kids. He only saw her once a week because she had a sleep-in job which was fine with Victor, because often when his mother was home she was either too tired to show him affection or else was dishing out corporal punishment for that week's transgressions. Whether he had been bad in school or did something to displease her, he got a beating. This went on for years.

Victor's mother Ruthie had a boyfriend named Sam who found out something she had been keeping from him. Even though Victor was a child and had nothing to do with her business, she believed he was the one who had told Sam her secret, so she beat him with an iron cord, a fan belt, and an extension cord. She often beat him so badly that in order to make her stop, Victor would punch himself in the nose until it bled, then smear the blood over his face. He'd keep hitting himself and running, eventually stopping to turn around to face her. Thinking she had hit him in the face, Ruthie was scared by the sight of all that blood.

She'd yell and curse at him, then tell him to go wash up. When he walked past her she'd get her last lick in.

Victor was terrified all the time and hated the weekends, because it meant his mother was coming home. When she came home she'd talk to his grandmother about how smart cousin Loretha was or about the white kids she looked after, how smart Joey was, how pretty Kathy was. To her, Victor could do no right. His grandmother, who gave him milk and ginger snaps after school and never beat him, was his only comfort. When he would try to do multiplication tables, his mother would smack him in the face until he got it right. To this day, Victor can't do multiplication tables.

When his mother was gone, Victor and his grandmother danced in the living room to the Contours singing, "Do You Love Me?". One day that song was playing, and there were a bunch of people in the house. As the only child, Victor couldn't go out to play, so to entertain himself he was playing under his grandmother's bed; in the darkness he couldn't see and pretended he was in a cave. Searching around blindly, his hand found a match box. He struck one match and then another. There was a loud whoosh as the whole underside of the bed went up in flames. Victor ran to the kitchen, grabbed water in a cup, ran back and threw it under the bed. He repeated this about seven times until the smoke reached the other room and the guests came running in. The men threw the bed over and put the fire out. While his mother screamed at him, his grandmother shielded him, saying, "The fire probably started from a wire because that wall socket is no good and sparks must have flew. Ain't that it?"

"Yes, Ma," Victor said, grateful for his grandmother's protection.

In the second grade Mrs. Halpern was Victor's teacher; he liked the way she talked with him and allowed him to be creative in her class. Then she became a guidance counselor and protected Victor in the third grade by helping to settle any problems that arose. In fourth grade Mr. Le Roi, a dark West Indian, used corporal punishment on the boys though not on the girls. They would hold out their hands and he'd hit their palms with a thick yardstick. He did this for any small thing. Victor vowed that when he got bigger he would come back and kick Mr. Le Roi's ass.

In fifth grade his teacher was Ms. Blackshear, the prettiest black woman Victor had ever seen. She was brown-skinned with little freckles and a little turned up nose, cute, not matronly like most of the white female teachers. She was also smart, and Victor's class, 5-2 (grade five, level two), was the second smartest group of kids (Victor remained in this level of class through the eighth grade). All the boys liked Ms. Blackshear because she was so pretty. One day the next year she came into Victor's sixth grade class where the teacher was once again Mr. Le Roi. She was crying, and all the boys felt protective towards her, wondering what was wrong. Mr. Le Roi held Ms. Blackshear, making Victor and his friends want to kick his ass even more, but by then Victor had learned how to play the ruler game on Mr. Le Roi: if you looked him in the face and didn't try to withdraw your hand, he'd hit you once and that would be it. These practices made them hate authority more and want to rebel. After school that day, Victor learned why Ms. Blackshear had cried: President Kennedy had been shot. There was much grieving in his community where every black household had a picture of John F. Kennedy.

After graduating from Public School 262, Victor started that fall at Junior High School 35, which turned out to be uneventful. Still trying to please his mother, Victor continued his elementary school record and never missed a day of school. He matriculated into the neighborhood high school, Franklin K. Lane, without taking any placement tests, but once in school he passed two entrance tests for better, more prestigious schools. He began to attend one of them in tenth grade, but then started to play hooky. Even though he had passed the tests, Ruthie never praised him. Victor figured, if he couldn't get any reward for being good, why bother.

Around this same time, Ruthie got married again. Victor was surprised when this took place because he didn't even know that her relationship with her boyfriend Norman was serious.

One day she told him they were moving; it was the first time he would be away from his grandmother in years. Suddenly, it was just Victor, his mother, and her husband. It was 1967, and Victor stopped going to school and started hanging out with friends, something he had never done before. He started coming home later and later.

One night soon after, his stepfather tried to stop him from going out. When Victor ignored him, they began fighting. During the fight Norman pushed Victor toward the window. In Victor's mind, Norman was trying to push him out the window. Victor beat Norman back and down, got dressed, and left the house. He came back early in the morning and went to sleep. Next thing he knew, his mother was pulling the covers off him and beating him with an extension cord. While she was beating him, he told her that Norman had tried to push him out the window. She said, "I don't care." Upon hearing this, something in Victor snapped, and he pushed her hard. She flew about ten feet into the door which she then slid down. Looking at Victor with fear in her eyes, she got up and fled from the room. For the first time, Victor did not play the victim to Ruthie's tirades. Victor barricaded himself in, pushing a dresser and chairs against the door. When he wouldn't come out, Ruthie called the cops; they talked to Victor through the door, trying unsuccessfully to get him out. Victor's relationship with Ruthie was forever changed.

Several months later, Victor, now sixteen, was fixing his bicycle in the hall of the building. When the superintendent came by and told him he couldn't work on his bike there, Victor became defiant. The super disappeared and returned with a .22 rifle and pointed it at Victor. When Victor cursed at him and didn't back down, the super called the cops and said that Victor had pulled a knife on him. Victor was brought to the Brooklyn Criminal Courthouse, where the judge was going to dismiss the case. Then Ruthie showed up and said she didn't want Victor home anyway. The judge agreed, and Victor remained locked up in the Brooklyn House of Detention until the next court appearance three weeks later. A small and young-looking sixteen, he had to endure a lot of threats and taunting from other inmates and was terrified the whole time. No one in his family came to visit him; he endured the whole stay with no support or sympathy.

Many of Victor's friends were into first, alcohol, and later, drugs. While Victor abstained, having seen the bad effects of alcohol on some of his relatives, his friends drank Cold Duck, Boone's Farm, pre-mixed screwdrivers, Twister, Thunderbird, Ballantine ale, Mad Dog 20/20, Nighttrain Express, and Swiss Up. They'd get ripped on the stuff, sit in the park, and sing old songs, trying to sound like the Delphonics and the Dells. They all thought they were the Temptations. Together they sang sad love songs. They were almost all children of the street from single parent families, and the parent they lived with either couldn't or wouldn't care for them, and found them a burden. The one thing the street kids had was each other. They often lived and died for that reason alone.

Victor's school district was entirely white, and the people who lived there didn't like the idea of black kids coming to their neighborhood. Victor would come out of school to see the white kids armed with baseball bats and knives. The cops wouldn't do anything to them, yet in the classroom the black kids were the ones the cops were abusing and locking up.

In the hot weather it was especially bad. The mostly Italian kids saw them as an enemy even though crimes in their community were being committed by whites because blacks weren't even allowed to walk in that area. Especially after sundown, any black person seen walking the street would be picked up by the cops. The white kids would block the black kids from leaving the community even though this is what they wanted, and the black kids would have to fight to get down the block to the subway. For Victor, it was a hassle having to fight three and four times a week, then go home and get beaten by his mother for having ripped his clothes and have her tell him the fight was his fault. In her mind, that type of racism only existed in the South.

Eventually, Victor's friends from Bedford-Stuyvesant and Crown Heights went from alcohol to heroin, bypassing marijuana for the two-dollar bag. Some of them overdosed and died. Victor wasn't into the drug scene and one day surprised Ruthie with the news that he wanted to join the Marines. To her this was a blessing, since she felt caring for the teenager kept her from independence. On his seventeenth birthday, she took him to the recruiting station in the Williamsburg bus depot, adjacent to the Williamsburg Bridge. Both Victor and Ruthie signed all the papers, and six days later, on her birthday, Victor reported to Fort Hamilton in Brooklyn. There he swore his allegiance to the United States and took a battery of tests. He was then taken to Penn Station where he caught a train to Beaufort, South Carolina.

On the train there was a mixture of boys, aged seventeen to twenty, from all over the country, all nationalities and races. In Beaufort they were met by a Greyhound bus and a drill instructor who wore olive drab pants, a khaki shirt, and a Smokey the Bear hat. He wore a smile that was contagious and seemed very nice and helpful, going out of his way to help the new recruits put their luggage on the bus. On the bus he didn't speak much. As they rode along, guys smoked cigarettes and talked about their pasts. A lot of them came from gangs or had been rescued from the criminal justice system when the judge offered the military as an alternative to jail sentence.

Like Victor, his fellow recruits were poor, came from troubled families, and were searching for some kind of meaning in a difficult life. What better place to find it than the place they'd heard was the epitome of a war machine: the Marine Corps. These kids had all thought of themselves as "bad asses," and bad asses didn't go to the navy or army. They were seduced by the Marine Corps mystique, the truth of which was later revealed.

Suddenly, Victor looked out the window and saw that they had pulled up to the guard house, a red brick hut where a Marine stood looking very sharp, wearing navy blue pants with a red stripe down the side, a khaki shirt with creases like razor blades, and a dress cap shining black like a mirror with the white on the cap cover so bright it was blinding in the sun. Holding a clipboard, he checked the recruits in. At this point the smiling drill instructor's attitude changed. There was no more smile, and his body language was no longer relaxed; it was as if he had gone through a transformation, the significance of which was as yet unknown.

A few miles into the base they pulled up before Quonset huts and wooden barracks, and on the ground in front were hundreds of yellow footprints. Out of his peripheral vision, Victor saw green school buses and hundreds of guys that looked like the drill instructor pour out of the buses with their Smokey the Bear hats and rocklike jaws. They surrounded his bus. As the drill instructor on the bus stood up, he seemed to keep growing. He looked much bigger than when they had first met him. The first words the instructor spoke were, "Okay, you fucking maggots, get off my bus. This is my bus and the last motherfucker off here's ass belongs to me."

Grabbing them by the belt or the nape of the neck, he threw the recruits off. Here were guys who were warlords in their neighborhoods, and now they weren't fighting back. As they got off the bus, the drill instructors on the ground were screaming at them to stand on the yellow footprints. The instructors surrounded the recruits, yelling constantly; the recruits had no time to think. Then, as they stood on the footprints, the drill instructor picked out one young kid and yelled, "What are you looking at?"

"Nothing, sir."

"Nothing? You're calling me nothing?"

"No, sir!"

"Then what are you looking at?"

"You, sir!"

"Do I look like a female sheep to you?"

"No, sir!"

"Then why are you calling me a ewe?"

Most of the guys didn't even know what a ewe was. But the drill instructor continued shouting orders in their faces. There was mass confusion and chaos. The instructors knew they were dealing with street kids, and they had to let the thugs know who was really the toughest and who was in charge. The recruits were told to put their noses on the back of the next guy's head. "Asshole to belly button," they had to run like that for half a mile. Recruits were falling while the drill instructors called them maggots and sissies.

That was the beginning of twelve weeks of torture, what the Marines called training. In reality Victor felt it was brainwashing, a mind game of pulling apart the recruits' identity and stripping them of their dignity, making them feel inadequate, then building them up through the identity of the Marine Corps brotherhood. They came to believe that there was only one color, green, for that's what Marines wore. Any transgression of the rules was met by humiliation. If a recruit referred to a rifle as a gun, he was forced to grab his rifle with the left hand while grabbing his crotch with the right, clad only in underwear. Then he was ordered to run around the platoon in front of eighty people standing at attention, shouting, "This is my rifle, this is my gun, this is for shooting, this is for fun," while continuing to hold his crotch. He had to do this until he was about to fall. If anyone laughed he would get punched in the solar plexus by the drill instructor, knocking the victim to his knees. The exercise was used to foster teamsmanship and empathy for their fellow Marines.

In school, if a child were to misbehave, he would be reprimanded and the class would laugh. In boot camp, "the class" would be punished for one person's wrongdoing with no explanation. For example, if someone couldn't do a simple exercise, the drill instructor would bring out a lounge chair and an umbrella and have the guy sit there and sip on lemonade while the rest of the platoon did the exercise because, "She doesn't know how." The drill instructor would say, "Okay, ladies, do it!" He knew that that night the platoon would throw a blanket party on the guy: four men would throw a blanket lightly over him while he was sleeping, then tie the four corners down tightly. The rest of the platoon would then beat him with socks stuffed with bars of soap.

After two weeks, Victor began to hate the drill instructor. When he received a letter from a girlfriend that had loving words on the envelope, he had to eat the envelope because it was United States property that had been defaced and he was now a United

States employee. Any pictures of wives or girlfriends were put on the "hogboard," so everyone could ogle the women. Everything was shared by everyone. In the evening at mail call, known as "school circle," everyone in the barracks had to run simultaneously up to the drill instructor at the front of the room. At reveille they were conditioned to swing out of bed and have every foot hit the floor at the same time so that when the drill instructor came in and turned on the lights, all the recruits were out of bed and standing at attention simultaneously.

All cigarettes were confiscated by the drill instructor and given out at specified times when the smoking lamp was lit, indicating permission to smoke. The recruits stood by a long wash basin and faucet in a concrete table outdoors where clothes were washed. Everyone, whether they smoked or not, lined up around the table. The platoon leader would jump on the table and light as many cigarettes as he could from one match. If he missed you, you were out of luck, and if he got you, you had to smoke at attention as recruits were always at attention. Obese recruits had the words "obese" or "midriff" written on their foreheads and arms and were fed only lettuce. When eating, all recruits ate in unison.

The Marine Corps is unique in that you can't be a Marine without completing Marine Corps boot camp, whereas you can go into other branches of the military, after completing your first enlistment contract, without going through their boot camps. The same is true for Marine officers. The Corps is a brotherhood, and being in this elite club made the hell of boot camp worthwhile. The day Victor graduated was the first day the drill instructor smiled at him and called him a Marine. Victor was proud and so was Ruthie, who happened to be in the South and showed up for graduation. After a couple of hours of freedom, Victor reported back and packed his bags.

The next morning the bus came and took Victor to Camp Lejeune, North Carolina. From there he went to second battalion, reconnaissance on a Mediterranean cruise in which he learned beach maneuvers, or how to make beach assaults. When he wasn't involved in doing the maneuvers, he had liberty in those European countries, including Spain, France, Greece, and Italy. A lot of maneuvers were done on the Greek and Italian islands. When this was finished, Victor received his orders for Vietnam. When he told his mother, she said, "That's okay. I'll just buy you an insurance policy, and don't worry, only the good die young anyway."

At the age of eighteen, Victor went from Camp Lejeune to the staging area at Camp Pendleton, California, and from there to Anchorage, Alaska, next to Hawaii, and then Okinawa. In Okinawa, his American dollars were replaced with military payment certificates; he was supplied with camouflage uniforms and jungle boots, and was given inoculations. From there his unit went to Vietnam. In Vietnam the company to which he was assigned arrived in a jeep to pick up Victor and those with him. It was extremely hot. One of the first things he learned from the "old salts" was that the Army of the Republic of Vietnam, called ARVN's, wouldn't fight, so you always had to watch your back when you were out in the bush. Very few Marine units ever worked side by side with an ARVN unit.

Another thing he learned upon arrival was how to do dap, the black man's handshake which involved hitting each other's fists in a specific pattern. There was a brotherhood among black servicemen. They would give each other the black power salute or dap. Whites were alienated from this process, and there was no white brotherhood. It was part of a ritual that blacks wouldn't show to whites; it was a connection which said *I'm with you, and I've got your back.* They knew that back in the States, blacks were being disproportionately sent to the front lines and that they couldn't burn their draft cards even if they had wanted to. Going to Vietnam was a way to advance, and in Vietnam guns made everyone equal. You couldn't be called a nigger because you had a gun.

The roar of the arriving medivac helicopter interrupted his memories. Victor helped the medical corpsmen lift the still moaning pilot onto a stretcher. Along with the Bronze Star Victor received for his rescue of the downed pilot with disregard to his personal safety under heavy fire, Victor and his unit received a Presidential citation. Victor also received three star clusters.

Victor wound up doing two tours in Vietnam, the first of which lasted nine months. The second ended after seven months because he had "gone native." He put water buffalo dung on his body before going out in the bush and then stayed out there for months at a time, gathering intelligence. Many of the operations he went on were classified, which made a very stressful situation even more pressured.

One guy, Jake, wore ears around his neck, which he had cut off the people he killed. Ears were the least obtrusive thing you could wear, and Jake wore them for good luck, even though they stunk like hell. As the operations became more perilous and desperate, Victor and Jake used speed to go out on patrols and lay out in ambush. For days they lay in mud without moving during the monsoon season. They were in a state of heightened vigilance and would shoot at anything that moved, including tree branches, leeches, worms, and bugs. The "shorter" a soldier got, meaning the fewer days left until he was going home, was the time when many soldiers died because they got careless. Victor got reckless, taking chances, going head-on into the bush, not caring whether he'd come back.

Once, after he had been in the bush for two weeks, Victor returned and had to report to a sergeant who was new from the States and unfamiliar with the ways in Vietnam. He told Victor to do something which Victor felt he shouldn't have to do since he had just come in from the bush. When Victor refused, the sergeant spat out, "I won't be spoken to like that by a nigger." This triggered an exchange of insults, and that night the sergeant attacked Victor in his bed. Victor pulled a knife down from the wall, and the sergeant received a cut that wasn't serious. The sergeant told the gunnery sergeant, who told him to forget about it. "Victor's a hell of a soldier in this kind of warfare. Right now he's high strung, because he just came out of the bush. Just let it go."

Thinking the issue had been resolved, Victor went back into the bush. About four months later, he was remanded and told that the sergeant would not let the issue drop, that he had gone over the head of the gunnery sergeant, an unusual move in a group which believed individual issues were not as important as the cohesiveness of the whole and loyalty to peers. The sergeant went to the commanding officer and reported that Victor had pulled a knife on him and that the gunnery sergeant hadn't done anything about it. He didn't say that he had called Victor a nigger nor that he had attacked Victor. Victor was given three months in the third MAF brig in Danang where he became known as "Brother Blackenize."

In the brig, all the prisoners were black while all the keepers were white. Once a week Victor was taken out to the company commander who wore an army uniform and whom Victor cursed out. He was then removed from Vietnam in handcuffs and sent to Camp Pendleton to finish his sentence. Doing time there was hard, with minimum rations of bread and water three times a day. Victor was in such a rebellious state that he refused to follow prison requirements, including showering and eating.

After thirty days Victor was sent to Hawaii. He was still reeling from his experiences in Vietnam. He kept getting into fights with whites, always over something racial, such as when a white guy said, "All you guys..." or called him a nigger. If the whites lost the fight, they'd report Victor to the white sergeant, and it was Victor's word against theirs. During this time, Victor had a psychological evaluation, and, unbeknownst to him, was found to have post-traumatic stress syndrome. Based on this, he should have received an honorable medical discharge which would have entitled him to disability payments, rather than the administrative discharge which he received. He returned to Brooklyn burned out and seething with anger over having served his country, risking his life and sanity while Richard Nixon pardoned all the draft-age men who went to Canada, and those same men, who'd stayed home, spat on and vilified those who'd done their duty.

In Brooklyn, he found himself back with his mother, now divorced from her second husband. He took a job in a factory making rope on the midnight shift so he could go to college during the day, although he hadn't yet been accepted to a school. The work involved lifting hundred-pound spools with archaic and dangerous machinery, and was dirty and degrading. He felt humiliated being there, knowing he ought to be doing better than earning crumbs as an unskilled laborer. As in Vietnam and all situations throughout his life until then, the foremen were white males. No one of color ran anything. The idea was always the same: he did the dirty work; they got the credit.

When he slept, which was very little, Victor had nightmares and cold sweats. During his breaks at work he'd walk the streets alone, finding comfort in the late-night darkness. Sometimes he'd just stand on the sidewalk to see if he could hear things the way he did in the bush. At home, he and his mother, Ruthie, stayed out of each other's way. She treated him the way many people did, as if he were crazy. Like other veterans of Vietnam, he didn't feel like sitting around pontificating about bullshit, and he didn't want to socialize the way others wanted him to.

The world to which Victor returned hated Vietnam veterans. He quickly learned not to tell people where he had been because being a vet they would have thought him crazy, and being a Marine, totally insane. The vets who were lucky enough to be able to work often wound up with menial jobs like the one Victor had in the rope factory. Many of the others joined the ranks of the unemployed, some of them homeless.

One night, about ten months after his return from the jungles of Southeast Asia, Victor was taking a break at work, lying with his eyes closed in the middle of fifteen-foot-high stacks of cartons containing rope. Above the deafening noise of the machines, he heard someone shout, "Are you Victor Clark?" He opened his eyes to see six white plainclothes cops pointing shotguns and revolvers at him, repeatedly asking if he was Victor Clark. He was stunned as one of them with an angry red face grabbed him, spun him around, handcuffed him, and said, "Oh, you think you're a fucking tough guy, huh?" The cop hit Victor in the head with a leather-covered chunk of lead called a blackjack, a weapon often carried by cops but not a part of their issued arsenal.

Knocked unconscious and dragged, he came to outside the building where he worked, with one cop holding each of his arms. When they opened the back door of the squad car to push him in, Victor saw his mother sitting in the back seat. "Why did you bring her here?" Victor cried.

"Just tell him to cooperate," the cop with the angry expression told Ruthie.

"Fuck you! You just beat me up, and I haven't done anything."

To Ruthie the cop said, "We didn't touch him, and you need to tell him to cooperate."

They drove to the precinct. There Victor was read his rights and told he was under arrest for the murder of Todd Richter and the robbery of a social club. He was then locked up in the Brooklyn House of Detention for Men. Not only was he furious, he felt he was being railroaded. A friend of his and another guy he didn't know were also arrested for the crime. The bail was set at one million dollars, even though Victor had roots in the community and no money with which to flee. While locked up in the county jail system for the next two years, he felt as if the bail were a ransom. Between April 1973 and February 1975, Victor fought his case in the Brooklyn Supreme Court, being treated as guilty the whole time, with no rights for contact visits, mail, or money.

The district attorney gave Victor the opportunity to cop a guilty plea and receive the minimum life sentence of fifteen years to life, but Victor would not admit to a murder he said he didn't do and trusted that the judicial process would prove his innocence. On the contrary, the trial proved to be a farce from beginning to end. The prosecutor's, Dick Conways, main evidence was identification through a mug shot, yet Victor had never been convicted of a crime so there were no mug shots of him. When Victor's lawyer, Harry Borso, demonstrated that mug shots of Victor didn't exist, the judge allowed the prosecutor leeway with cross examination, providing flexibility with the rules of identification, implying that the mug shots did, in fact, exist. What followed was like the principle of the fruit of the poisonous tree: the identification of Victor was tainted, and therefore everything that happened afterward was also tainted. At one point during the trial, Harry Borso asked one of the witnesses, "When was the last time you saw Victor?" Mistaken, or not telling the truth, she said, "A year ago." At that point, Ruthie, who was sitting in the back of the courtroom, jumped up and screamed, "She's lying. My son has been in jail over two years."

The judge ordered Ruthie removed from the courtroom. After a long pause, Borso asked the witness, "Where did you see him a year ago?"

"Around where we live." The lawyer asked for details which were provided, even though Victor was in jail at the time. Nevertheless, he was found guilty, while the two men arrested with him were acquitted. Victor was given twenty years to life in prison which was many years more than if he had copped a plea.

Two years later, locked up in state prison and in possession of all his records and the trial transcript, Victor continued to seek justice. By this time he had run out of money, so all of his motions were *pro se*; meaning he did the legal work himself or else paid jailhouse lawyers with cigarettes. He learned that when he was first arrested one of the witnesses had identified a guy who lived in Victor's building as the man who had fired a shot and said, "This is a stick-up." Two months later, the witness changed her story and said the assailant was Victor, leaving him to speculate as to why the man she had originally identified was not arrested in April when she had first identified him. Victor filed several appeals on identification which were denied. He was told that the police officer who reportedly had the mug shots in his possession had died in a car accident, and the mug shot book could not be located. Nor could the arresting officer's notes of the case ever be found.

CHAPTER
TWO

DENISE'S WORLD

Slim, leggy, and bleached blond, my mother, Sylvia, had ambitions for us all. My grandfather had been a Russian immigrant who, some years after coming to the United States, went to college and became a civil engineer. Throughout my childhood my mother boasted of the fact that while other families suffered economic ruin during the Great Depression living lives of poverty and deprivation, the Schulmans kept their comfortable lifestyle. Sylvia wanted to make sure that she not only kept that style but surpassed it. Why, then, would she choose for a mate my father, Lenny Beck, whom she later referred to as a "poolroom bum?"

The answer was love, or at least, lust. For years those two were as infatuated with each other as they were with themselves. Lenny, with his slim build, blue eyes, and glib tongue, could charm any woman. Raised by his mother and sisters after his father died, he seemed to instinctively know what women wanted, and the stronger-willed the better. Sylvia found in him a charming boy-man eager to please and to be led. She also found someone witty and exciting, just as he found someone both gullible and snobbish. They gave each other that challenge of differences which alchemized into romance and, after Lenny returned from the war, marriage.

When I came along they had already enjoyed each other's company alone for five years. Making the transition into familyhood wasn't necessarily a smooth one, as it tied Sylvia down into a domestic stay-at-home role which didn't agree with her glamour-girl image. Now, when Lenny went out to the race-track, she had to stay home unless she got her parents who lived nearby to baby-sit. Was the bitterness I later perceived a result of her feeling trapped in a role she didn't really want? Perhaps.

But she was also orchestrating an escape from ordinariness. After my first two-and-a-half years in the Bronx apartment building in which they had been living since their wedding, we packed up and headed for greener pastures in Little Neck, Queens (West Egg in *The Great Gatsby*). It wasn't exactly Beverly Hills, but it was bucolic compared to the cement pavements and high rises of the Grand Concourse. Part of a large complex, our apartment was the upper unit of a two-story garden apartment with lawns and shrubs in front and back. It was here that I spent my formative years. Like the neighborhood we left in the Bronx, this was a Jewish enclave where anyone not Jewish was considered weird and an outsider. Anyone nonwhite was a maid.

The apartment had five small rooms. The kitchen faced east, and one morning ritual I relished was sitting on the kitchen table by the window listening to the crows and watching the sky change colors as the sun rose. Another favorite ritual was watching my dad shave. I'd sit on the toilet lid while he stood before the mirror in his white T-shirt and boxer shorts. I'd watch, fascinated as he sprinkled water on the soap in the dish, whisked it up with his brush, then solemnly painted his face with the lather. Then he would purse his lips, push them to either side of his face, suck in his cheeks, and point his chin to the ceiling, in order to get every last hair. Of particular interest to me was the evenness of the scraping sound the razor made against his face. At the end he'd be red-faced and gleaming, smelling sweetly of Aqua Velva aftershave.

For almost five years I was treated like a princess with abundant attention from both my parents, my grandparents, and my mother's unmarried sister. Each night before I went to sleep, my mother and I would lie on my bed and read books, initiating my lifelong love of literature. I had my own room, my favorite dolls and toys, and a record player. And then, one snowy December day, my brother arrived. They put this baby boy in my room, and life was never the same. Not only was the attention no longer all mine, but I also had to help take care of Barry for many years to come.

My mother continued pursuing her dream of fame and fortune through me. When I appeared on television on *The Merry Mailman* at age four, I screamed and cried. It was at this age, too, that Sylvia and I had the first argument I remember, about me wearing a pair of shorts that I liked and she didn't. Our arguments seriously escalated when, at age seven, I began piano and ballet lessons. She took these very seriously and when I did not want to practice on a daily basis, we fought. We also fought each time there was a recital and I had to get up on stage. My parents pushed me into this situation, yet they were so nervous the night before a recital you would think they were the ones who had to perform.

During these years the fights they were having with each other were also increasing. Lenny liked to take some of his hard-earned money and gamble at the racetrack. Sylvia didn't mind if he went once in a while, as long as she was with him. So arguments would erupt if he went one too many times or left her at home. Even when they did go out together they would argue because he thought she wasn't dressed sexy enough or because he felt she was nagging him. She also told him who his friends should and shouldn't be, and she was fond of calling his friends "lowlifes" and "animals." When I would ask her, "Do you and Daddy love each other?" she would explain that they did, but that people who love each other sometimes argue. I found this hard to grasp, especially as I was being bombarded with rock 'n roll which idealized love as a perfect state.

Sylvia's next attempt at stardom, through substitution, came when I was nine and she decided I should become a model.

At the request of modeling agencies we had composites made which were sheets of pictures of me in different poses and costumes. These we gave out at every potential gig, of which I wound up having a few. Sylvia really enjoyed running around on Madison Avenue and hobnobbing with the beautiful, rich, and famous. At an agency Christmas party we went to she was in her glory. For me the whole thing was strange; for one thing, I wasn't particularly good at modeling. I couldn't smile convincingly on demand, and my voice didn't have that high pitched lilt that children in television commercials have. It was never particularly fun, even when I went on *The Price Is Right* and walked on stage wearing a matching mother-daughter dress with a former Miss Rheingold. The dress, a gorgeous emerald green chiffon with matching fur collar, I wasn't even allowed to keep!

School became the main place that I loved. I excelled scholastically, was popular with my peers, and was often the teacher's pet. Once again, as in my early years, I had the attention afforded to someone special.

Notwithstanding my love for school, the happiest times were summers. Early on we would go to Rockaway. Dad would stay in the city and come out on weekends. Each day my mother, Barry, and I would go to the beach, walk the boardwalk, and play skeeball. I became comfortable playing in the ocean at a young age and became a proficient swimmer. Every Fourth of July, fireworks were set off from a barge offshore, and they were nothing short of spectacular to me.

After Rockaway, we retreated to the heart of the suburbs, the Roslyn Country Club, a few miles and a socioeconomic class away from where we lived in Queens. The club had sprawling green lawns which glistened like diamonds beneath undulating sprinklers. I lost myself in the sights and sounds of the lavish rose bushes and exotic birds and sparkling turquoise water of the pools where I perfected my swimming strokes and learned to dive. For three years we lived a two-month life of luxury and leisure.

One summer I recognized a pattern in my behavior. I always seemed to want to take care of the underdog. At day camp it was Larry, a boy in my age group with cerebral palsy. His head hung to one side, and he wore a towel on his shoulder to catch the drool. At first I was repulsed by him but then became his fast friend and protector. The summer before at the country club, I hung out with Kerry, a girl with deformed hands who was undergoing skin grafts. On the block where I lived I was always defending Marilyn, a girl frequently ridiculed because her mother was in and out of Creedmoor, the nearby state mental hospital. It was a trait and a role I took on and grew to be proud of, but at the same time I had to fight the tendency to lose my patience with those people who couldn't keep up. It was this summer that I began to think about career helping people, in addition to becoming a writer.

At about the same time, my father bought a dress business. When he and my mother thought it was doing well enough, they decided to buy a house. It seemed as if they looked at houses for years before making a decision, and though I was only ten, I knew intuitively that their long indecision came out of their ambivalence about each other. Married for fifteen years, they appeared bored with each other, and without the sexual passion of their earlier years, there didn't seem to be much else. A house was at least some interest they could share. They kept looking and finally opted for a house in a development that was not yet built.

Not long after we moved into the new house, Sylvia barged into my room and started to yell at me, "You've been spoiled for too long. You're no longer going to get what you ask for, and you'd better get used to it."

This was out of the blue; what had I done? Her overall mood went from bad to worse. I told myself it wasn't me, but when someone who's supposed to love you is always angry, it's hard to believe. Once it started, the yelling went on and on from morning until night. She yelled at all of us, and we all yelled back. My father began to come home later and drunker. Sylvia began having her late afternoon cocktail earlier. Alcohol seemed to be the only thing they enjoyed together. Barry and I spent a lot of time in bars waiting for them. The black and red waiting room at Gam Wah, a Chinese restaurant we went to often, became as familiar to me as my bedroom. From the phone booths there I'd pass the time by calling friends as Barry played on the leather couches. By the time we got to the table, Sylvia and Lenny would be plastered and would mortify me and Barry either by yelling at each other or by making obnoxious comments to the waiters. While home life was crazy and depressing, school was exciting. I both hungered for and dreaded the newness of the intense peer pressure, the competition, and the socializing. As if the normal trials and tribulations of puberty weren't enough, the air fairly sizzled with the electricity of political and media events, particularly the assassination of JFK and the arrival of the Beatles on their first trip to the United States from England. Amid the routines of daily life we all knew that we were living in history-making times. With so much to think about, including life, boys, music, my friends, my clothes, and how to deal with my parents, I left behind the A student I had been throughout elementary school. To her list of things about me that made her unhappy, my mother added my B grades. She counseled me continuously on how I had to make something of myself, to have a career to "fall back on" in case my marriage wouldn't work out. She also counseled me on the kind of man I should look for: looks were not important, but being rich and generous were.

In the mid-nineteen sixties, Greenwich Village became the place for young people to be. It had been hip for years and held a great mystique for having been the setting for so much of the Beatnik movement. Now, those of us in a state of rebellion and high dudgeon looked toward its dark smoky cafes, narrow winding streets, galleries, and offbeat stores as a natural home. We went there as often as possible, sometimes legitimately with our parents' permission on weekends and sometimes illicitly, cutting school and lying. Sometimes this involved changing clothes from something schoolgirlish into something black and existentially dire, including putting on frosty lipstick, shades, and dangling silver earrings. We'd walk the streets, stopping at the tiny stores that sold jewelry, music, and incense. A couple of years later they were called head shops, offering rolling paper, hash pipes and other drug paraphernalia, and they proliferated, sometimes with several on a single block.

Many of my friends came from wealthy, permissive families. They lived in very large houses and even if their parents were home it was still easy to raid the liquor cabinet or disappear into a part of the house and not even see them. This was in direct contrast to the paranoid environment that existed in my house where the rooms were small and close to each other, and I was not allowed a lock on my door.

With greater frequency I began to turn to writing as an outlet. An early poem I wrote was titled "The Block of Ice," a metaphor for how I felt. When I showed it to Sylvia, she said, "You don't feel like that." I felt down all the time and thought continuously about leaving home. But I never had an answer to the question of where I would go, and I knew that not finishing high school would cause me a lot of problems in the future; so I comforted myself by focusing on age eighteen when I would go away to college. Whenever I mentioned how I felt to either Lenny or Sylvia, they got angry and said things like, "If you don't stop talking like that I'll make you feel really bad."

Their relationship worsened to the point that they were throwing punches at each other, and one or both often had black and blue marks and swollen lips. One night, after hours of screaming and cursing, my mother came into my room. I said, "Why don't you leave him?"

She said, "Because I will not be alone."

"You mean it's better to live like this than to be alone?"

"Yes."

She went to a psychiatrist who put her on all kinds of sleeping pills and tranquilizers, despite the fact that she was heavily into alcohol. One day she and Barry went out shopping; I became alarmed when Barry, who was about twelve, came home by himself.

"Where is she?" I asked.

"She was acting crazy so I left her and walked home," he said.

A few minutes later I heard the car screech to a halt in the driveway.

"Are you okay?" I asked as she walked through the door.

With slurred words my mother responded incoherently. Then she began saying things that got me scared because they had little or no basis in reality. I got on the phone and called my grandparents who lived about twenty miles away. They said they would come if I would pick them up. I jumped into the Cadillac and did about eighty miles an hour the whole way, because I was scared to leave my mother alone with Barry. When we finally got back, I was relieved to have someone else there to take care of things and to witness what was going on. Later that night, we learned that she had overdosed on her pills and had also gotten stopped on the road by police who noticed her erratic driving. This was the first in a series of driving while intoxicated incidents that my mother had. My father had his share of these, too.

Not only did I live for the weekends but also for the summers when I would go away to camp. Nestled in the rolling hills of Pennsylvania, Camp Laconda provided for me a haven away from my parents; in addition, I loved the outdoors and participating in sports in which I excelled. I also enjoyed living in a cabin with other girls my age and having a campus full of boys a few yards away. Each summer I had a boyfriend and became an expert on all the good make out spots around the camp.

In the spring of 1968, my own sense of despair intensified as the aura of societal anarchy deepened with the murders of Robert Kennedy and Martin Luther King. There was a pervasive feeling among my friends of why serve your country or other people when those who are brave and humanitarian get assassinated? It felt like everything and everyone was going to hell around me. This strengthened my need to help people one by one. What a relief it was that summer to escape to camp.

One balmy night, way out on the fragrant grass of the golf course beneath a sky full of stars, my boyfriend Joshua poured out from a film canister a chunk of yellow-brown hashish. He put a piece the size of a grape in a small metal pipe and demonstrated how to hold the lighter over the hash while inhaling. After coughing for five minutes, I felt a warmth envelop my head and my eyelids grow heavy as a smile settled on my lips. I achieved that state twice more that summer, and at the end of August, after camp was over, I entrusted myself once again to Joshua by losing my virginity. As the Chicago convention blasted away on the television, my virginity was lost on my friend Sally's parents' bed.

I entered senior year with optimism as the silver lining in my depressive cloud, for I would soon be submitting applications for college. The end was in sight, and this made the craziness at home more bearable. I began hanging out with Andy and his friends, a somewhat hippie-ish group, and soon Andy became my new boyfriend. Kind, smart, and down-to-earth, Andy often rescued me from my house, bringing me to his beautiful home where his parents were smart, sane, and protective toward me.

At our high school graduation in June 1969, we all wore black armbands on our gowns in protest of the Vietnam war. My friend Patti and I had smoked a joint before going to the school which made everything seem a bit more surreal than it probably would have anyway. I had some nervousness about being with my family while high, but by the time I joined them I had come down. After the graduation ceremony, I had to part from my friends and go with my parents, brother, and grandparents to a restaurant which overlooked Long Island Sound. I was grateful for my grandparents' presence, because my parents didn't totally let loose with their rage when they were around. Even so, the meal was tense and unpleasant, and I couldn't wait for that evening when I could join Andy.

The summer of '69 I didn't go to Woodstock, mainly because I knew my parents would make life a living hell for me if I did. Patti and a couple of other friends did go, however, and when they returned with tales of tripping on acid in the rain and mud, I was vaguely glad I hadn't gone. At the same time, I regretted having missed a historical event. Most of the summer I spent with Andy at his parents' beach house in Bridgehampton, Long Island. We were preparing for our separation at the end of August when I would head for Boston University and he for a dorm at the New York University campus in the Bronx. I was torn by my conflicting feelings: sadness to be leaving Andy and euphoria over finally being released from the prison I was in at home, a jail which over the past year had grown increasingly unbearable.

One night Lenny had gone after Sylvia with an ax, practically chopping down the bathroom door. On another occasion, Sylvia shared some mind-boggling news with me and Barry. We were at dinner when, with her lips pursed as she ate grapefruit, my mother, in a hollow voice, said, "I have something to tell you" and started to cry. Barry, thirteen at the time, slammed down his spoon. "Oh, come on," he cried, used to meals that wound up in chaos. "Can't we eat in peace for once?"

"Your father's been indicted," she sobbed.

"Indicted? For what?" I asked, the vein in my head pulsing. "When was he arrested?"

It was one of those moments that confirmed my suspicions that these people called my parents had sordid things going on in their lives about which I had absolutely no idea. Like the affairs my mother was having, which I knew about only because I had eavesdropped on her telephone calls. The idea that my father could be arrested for something and I didn't know about it was preposterous.

"Income tax evasion."

"Income tax evasion?" What the hell was that?

"Yes, do you remember when we first moved to this house and we had that drawer where we put all our receipts? Well...." She then described how my father and his business partner had kept two sets of books as advised by their lowlife accountant and how the accountant was so incompetent he couldn't even cheat successfully. At that moment it became clear to me, at least in part, why she had suddenly turned and made life a living hell for me for all those years. I had a fleeting moment of sympathy for both her and my father; that was soon replaced with anger.

When I left Long Island that hot August day in the car filled with my clothes and other possessions, the only thing that was wrong was that my parents were in the car too. They had insisted on accompanying me to Boston. That night we stayed in a motel on Commonwealth Avenue near the Boston University campus; they typically got drunk and argued all night. The next morning at breakfast, the knots in my stomach made the scrambled eggs seem sickening. None of us were able to say anything in normal or civil tones. After breakfast they brought me to Shelton Hall dormitory on Bay State Road. The goodbyes were awkward, and I knew that when my eyes filled with tears, they were caused by the realization of how sad all our lives had become and because I was dismayed to feel so happy to finally be away from all their madness. When I sat down on my bed and looked around at the thick walls and worn carpeting, I was scared but thrilled with the potential of the great unknown that lay before me.

Some three years later, I returned to New York, and my life as a single woman on her own in the big city began. But I was to learn that what begins as exciting and fulfilling doesn't always turn out that way.

CHAPTER THREE

FROM DOOR TO DOOR

City life was lonely and unfulfilling. Without a degree, the jobs available to me were limited. The positions I took were boring and menial. I gravitated from job to job until I was hired for a secretarial post at Columbia University School of Law. This position would enable me to get free tuition at Columbia's School of General Studies. I found an apartment in Morningside Heights, with space, sunlight, and views, overlooking the Cathedral of St. John the Divine.

On my first day at work, the assistant dean to whom I reported said, "Welcome to Paradise." Compared to the cubicles of the business world, the wood paneled, academic environment which I encountered was a great improvement. I was also happy to be around students and intellectual types, and I quickly ferreted out the looker and radical on the law faculty, and proceeded to have a mad crush on him from a distance. At that point, my romantic life was not as important as my classes, which I loved, and so this fantasy relationship was fun, albeit frustrating. I was also serious about writing, studying Zen, and astrology; the latter I had been learning for years and had become proficient enough at developing charts to supplement my income. For a year, as I meditated on my future, I drank no alcohol, took no drugs, ate no meat or sugar, and stopped smoking. After two years of working and attending school part-time, Columbia awarded me a scholarship, and I finished my bachelor's degree full-time. At graduation in 1980 I received a prize for excellence in the field of psychology, my major.

My friend Yvonne, who also wanted to write and supported herself as a secretary, told me she had met a guy in a bar who, when asked what he did, said he was a poet. When she asked, "How do you make a living?" he answered, "Vydec." Yvonne and I agreed that Vydec, one of the early word-processing systems, was the way to go. My writing had taken a back seat long enough, and I needed now to organize my life around it. Word processing would allow for flexible hours with high hourly pay. After a brief training course, I took a job with a major Wall Street law firm in its word-processing pool; I chose the five-to-midnight shift so I could use my energy in the early part of the day for writing.

For a while my routine was gratifying: I'd awaken at a reasonable hour, have coffee and read *The New York Times*, then I'd write for two to three hours. Or at least, I'd sit in a chair and think about writing for two to three hours. Often nothing productive came from these sessions, and I'd be plagued with doubts: what if I spend my whole life trying to write and I'm never successful? Then I will have given up family, money, traveling, etc. for nothing. I will have spent my time in a way that didn't help humanity in any way and it will all have been a waste. These feelings were especially prevalent when I received rejection letters for the stories, poems, and articles I had sent out.

After two years of working at Vydec, Daconics, and Wang, and having none of my writing published, I decided my life seemed too meaningless; I needed to do something that would be of importance, that would benefit the world in some way. It was then I remembered my childhood preoccupation with taking care of those to whom life had dealt mean blows with which they could not cope. I decided to become a psychotherapist. I considered a doctorate in psychology but figuring that would take too long, opted for a master's degree in social work. Once again, I became a student at Columbia University. Talking to my first client, a learning disabled college student, seemed so natural I knew I had made the right decision. I was good at counseling, and eventually I'd make enough money per hour that I could cut my working time in half and devote that much more time to writing. That was the plan.

That same year, my father, who had been divorced and banished by my mother a few years before, was diagnosed with throat cancer. He had been told that a benign throat polyp would become malignant if he continued to smoke and drink; he had already survived a serious bout of cirrhosis of the liver but having sold his business and moved alone to Florida, his will to live wasn't that strong. I missed my first semester finals in social work school when I went to Florida to make arrangements for my father to be buried in New York, his home.

The following year, when my grandmother died, I was in my mid-thirties and for the first time heard the ticking of my biological clock. I saw an image of my grandmother, my mother, and me on a treadmill: as my mother and I moved up in position after my grandmother dropped off the end, I saw no one behind me. I had moved back to my apartment, and my boyfriend, who had told me early on he was not father material, and I still spent weekends together. I told him, "I need to see if having children is in the cards for me." I gave a lot of thought to the idea of being a mother and read all the books and articles that were proliferating about "older mothers." One thing I knew I didn't want was a child outside of a relationship; I realized that what I wanted wasn't so much a child as a family. I wanted a man with whom I could visualize that kind of family future.

Being single was no picnic. The statistics seemed so true: it was easier to get hit by lightning than to be a woman over thirty-five in New York City and get married. As common knowledge had it, all the "good" men were either taken or gay. My friend Clara had recently had some success with personal ads, so I started to study them and responded to several. I met a few men this way though nothing lasted.

I was beginning to feel anxious and frustrated. Then, as if serendipity struck, I acquired a job in which I hoped I could make a difference: I became a social worker at a state mental hospital.

I began my job with high hopes, fervently believing that this was my chance to really help others, but it soon became apparent that getting anything accomplished in the state mental health system was a struggle. Walking through the doors of the state hospital, I tried convincing myself that I was fortunate to be earning my living doing what I had always wanted, something spiritually virtuous and vital, serving the poor and the sick, but as soon as I got to the ward my anger at the system rose. The smell of unwashed bodies of patients lying on the floor screaming my name, not to mention the weird and crazy goings-on of the staff made it hard to remember the good I was committed to doing.

I kept thinking I could do more if I could get into private practice where I could earn enough and then contribute pro bono hours as an advocate for poor people.

But to do so I'd have to attend a psychotherapy institute, and I had all kinds of reasons why I did not want to do that. I had attended some of their free seminars, open houses, and lectures, and to me they all seemed exclusionary to the point of being cultish. While I knew that not everyone in an institute ascribed to only that institute's point of view, I also knew that as a student, conformity was required. I maintained a basic cynicism about psychotherapy because, despite all this expertise, many deep personal problems remained unsolved.

In a way, as a social worker in the state hospital system, I was part of the problem, not the solution which I so earnestly wanted to find. Yet the state hospital philosophy of incarceration was achieving some good ends, I had to admit. On the ward we saw it all the time: kids came in wild, driven by fear, rage, and psychosis, acting like snarling animals, chomping at the bit, waiting to spring at the first opportunity. As time went on, they became calmer and more resigned. Their hallucinations and delusions subsided or at least got quieter. Some of this was due, in addition to medication, to becoming institutionalized, some was the mellowing process. I, too, was growing calmer with age, having acquired in my mid-thirties a sense of my mortality.

Paradoxically, I also felt as if the bars of imprisonment were being locked tighter by diminishing opportunity and potential. I had become increasingly aware of what I was not accomplishing. I began to have a growing dread knowing that much of what there was to do in the world I most likely would not see and experience. Increasingly, I felt imprisoned by the confines of my own set of characteristics, abilities, shortcomings, and personal qualities that in themselves were neither good nor bad, but often I experienced as holding me in custody. I had been born female, white, and Jewish in mid twentieth-century New York City. What did it all mean?

Each day as I went to my job I was acutely aware that I was alone, unhappy, or, perhaps more accurately, dissatisfied, awash in my unmet desires. "I Can't Get No Satisfaction" was my theme song.

I soon left the state hospital job for what I hoped would be a more rewarding position at a mental health clinic. Though the clinic paid less than the state hospital and I had to travel over an hour by subway and bus to get to the new job in Brooklyn, once there and working with the patients I was happy. I swore to myself I would never again work for the state bureaucracy. Professionally things were finally going well but in the personal arena there was emptiness.

After years of struggling with the dilemma of being a single woman wanting to meet Mr. Right in New York City, I went ahead and did what I had several years before decried as completely unsuitable: I ran a personal ad in the *Village Voice*. I asked for someone "beautiful, brilliant, thoughtful and socially conscious." Answers began to trickle in within days of the ad's appearance. Although I laughed over some of the responses, there was one which strangely enough stood out from the rest.

On one of those muggy June days when you can feel the city's heat through the soles of your sandals, I walked up Broadway, all the time conscious of the envelope stamped with the logo "Eastern New York Correctional Facility, Napanoch, New York" in my Channel 13 tote bag. I had never heard of the Eastern New York Correctional Facility or Napanoch, New York, though I knew they were on the same road as the Nevele Hotel, where at least a small portion of my teenage angst had found an outlet. When it came to New York State penitentiaries, I was aware of Sing Sing and Attica. I had also heard of Auburn, Woodburne, Dannemora, and Bedford Hills, all of which I pictured as mysterious places behind high walls in which horrendous things happened among despicable people. But Eastern New York Correctional Facility called up no images.

When I saw that logo on the envelope of Victor's first letter to me, I approached it with a mixture of interest, humor, and cynicism. I was intrigued at the writing on the letter which was an elegant script font, neat and professional. As I began to read, I also became intrigued by what it said and how: literate, unassuming, and friendly, it was unlike many of the other letters I received. I didn't know what to do about Victor's letter. Wouldn't answering an inmate's letter be asking for trouble? But he sounded so normal and even appealing. I postponed a decision by placing his letter in Pile Two, the "I don't knows," as distinguished from the definite noes and yeses. In the meantime, there was at least one definite yes whose sun sign was Aries like mine and who shared other things in common with me. I called him and we had a conversation which became more exciting with each belief and value we shared in common. In the enthusiasm of newness, we met for a drink, and what was exciting on the phone fizzled in person. Perhaps we were too alike, or maybe the physical chemistry just wasn't there. Whatever the reason, we had no further contact, and I became even more tempted to answer Victor's letter.

When I did so several days later, he answered immediately with a letter that was longer and more charming than the first. This time he sent a photograph which showed him with intense dark eyes, a long Afro, and a body that had been tightened by at least a moderate amount of working out. On the back of the snapshot he wrote his date of birth and "Gemini" which made me gasp. Just a few months before, an astrologer had read my chart and told me I would soon be meeting the "love of my life" who would probably be a Gemini. *Now here he is,* I thought. And wasn't it typical of my life that he should make himself known in this way. My life rarely followed the usual patterns. Of course, my choices had something to do with this. In this case, I could have decided not to respond to Victor's first letter, but given a choice between the practical and the intriguing, I went for the latter. So I responded, and Victor Clark again wrote back immediately. And so, our correspondence began.

Then, one June morning, the streets of Morningside Heights were empty, most of the Columbia students having fled for their homes around the country, and the local residents who were fortunate enough were at country homes and beaches, avoiding the hot pavement. I felt left behind, as I always did in summer, memories of my childhood by the sea, pools, and lakes as fresh as if they were yesterday. Walking past the newly converted West End Cafe, then down 116th Street, the ghosts of some well-known past Columbia students — Jack Kerouac, Allen Ginsburg — rose in the air with the heat waves. The West End's conversion from a dark smokey hangout, where inebriated poets and intellectuals pontificated and debated all night, into a bright, plant-filled restaurant was testimony to the absence of the likes of Kerouac et. al., not to mention the activists of the late 1960s. These days the streets were quiet, the old political movements were gone, and individuals just lived out their mundane dramas, not the least of which was mine.

The trees of Riverside Park created a dark and leafy bower over the cobblestone path. After settling on a bench that was half-sunny, half-shaded, I took out Victor's latest letter and reread it for the eighth time. This one was more detailed than the others. Victor wrote that he was an ex-Marine who had served in Vietnam for sixteen months, winning the Bronze Star, a presidential citation, and other medals; that ten months after his return to the States he was arrested for a homicide and robbery he did not commit. Though his early years in prison had been angry and bitter, in spite of his uncertain future he was trying to make a difference in prison. Now he was trying to improve conditions by helping inmates with physical and mental limitations.

Reading his words, I felt inspired. Though he might never again be part of the outside world, he was committed to making his world a better place. How many of us incarcerated in our own prisons could say the same? His photo showed him to be a man of beauty, strength, and seriousness. Was he brilliant? Maybe not breaking IQ test records, but obviously highly intelligent. And the rest? The only one that had yet to reveal itself was "thoughtful." I was intrigued. What could be more fascinating and inspiring than a man who had been victimized by the system yet was committed to helping others? This was Zen at work; I was starting to believe that Fate had sent Victor to me to teach me some lessons.

Lifting my gaze from the page, I became aware that the air was awash with the scent of honeysuckle. A small woman was being pulled by a Weimaraner. I smiled as I thought of how I had been wishing that something wonderful would happen to me. I was tired of coming home from work, feeling I had nothing to look forward to except junk mail and bills in the mailbox. In the subway on the way home from work I would frequently entertain myself by imagining something unexpected in the mail, such as an announcement that I had won a million dollars, or else a declaration of love from a secret admirer. Anything that would rescue me from the mundaneness of my existence.

And now, here it was: large envelopes bearing the *Village Voice* logo, inside of which were Victor's letters in their envelopes bearing the Eastern New York C.F. logo with its red star. For several weeks we shared our hopes, fears, and experiences in these letters. We exchanged opinions about many subjects and were gratified to learn we had much in common, including interests in politics, literature, and the arts. Because of the way we had met, I felt entitled to be completely myself and to have my correspondent be exactly whom I wanted. Victor claimed he was being completely himself in his letters, and I hoped he was not just telling me what he thought I wanted to hear.

Sitting on the bench opposite the ornate architecture of the early twentieth century buildings on Riverside Drive, reveling in the balmy scented air, I thought about what my next step should be as the *Voice* box number would shortly expire. I could either get another post office box, or else give Victor my address. I also thought about giving him my phone number, for despite all the words we were exchanging they were always cased in silence; I wanted to hear his voice. I wanted to confirm that he sounded normal and not like some homicidal maniac, as if a brief phone conversation could prove it one way or the other. I had mentioned this to my friend Clara on the phone the night before.

"He's an inmate, a convicted felon," she said.

"He claims he didn't do it."

"They all say that."

"Well, whether it's true or not, even if he killed someone twenty years ago, that's not who he is today."

"But, Denise, he's in prison. What kind of relationship can you have?"

"I guess I'll find out. When is there ever a guarantee?"

Clara sighed, probably thinking of her own troubled relationship with an artist who was passionate, vibrant, and an alcoholic. "I know I'll be seeing you off on the bus next week."

Writing was never as easy for me as when I wrote to Victor; the words rushed from my pen in a torrent of feeling. My hand cramped as I tried to write fast enough. As I wrote my phone number, I was infused with that thrilling sense of potential and possibility. The following Tuesday at 7:30 the phone rang.

"This is the AT&T operator with a collect call from Victor at a correctional facility. Will you accept the charges?" I was a bit taken aback as I hadn't been expecting the call to be collect.

"Yes," I said breathlessly.

"How're you doing?" Victor said in a voice that matched what I had imagined: friendly, warm, bright. "I'm only allowed ten minutes and I'm sure we can't possibly say everything we want to, but, how are you?"

"I'm good. I can't believe I'm finally talking to you."

"It's great to hear you too. You sound great."

For the next several minutes we talked somewhat nervously. From the way he spoke as well as what he said, I made an on-the-spot determination that he wasn't violent, sex-crazed, or desperate so I gave him my address. I told him the *Voice* box was expiring and he'd have to write me at home.

When we had been on the phone for nine minutes, Victor said, "There's a guard signaling me to hang up. I really don't want to, but I'm gonna have to."

"I wish you didn't have to go."

"Me, too, Denise, but if it's okay with you I'd like to call again on Thursday. My assigned days for phone calls are Tuesday, Thursday, and Sunday."

"Well," I said, "I know Fate is with us now because Tuesday and Thursday are the days I don't work in the clinic, and I'm home in the evenings."

"I'll be counting the hours until Thursday. Is seven-thirty okay?"

"Yes."

"Hey, I can feel you grinning, like a teenager."

"So in addition to all your other talents you can hear people smiling on the phone?"

"Not people. You."

From then on, my Tuesdays, Thursdays, and Sundays were focused around that ten minutes in the evening when he called me. For three weeks our conversations were peppered with allusions to me eventually visiting him, and then one day in July, after we had been corresponding for two months, I asked, "How do I get to Napanoch?"

CHAPTER
FOUR

SOMETHING MORE IMPORTANT THAN FEAR

Waiting to go upstate for further processing, Victor watched the guard stopping in front of his cell in Sing Sing. "Clark." The guard smiled slyly. "You're going to Great Meadow."

Victor smiled back, thinking he had done well on the skills test and as a result would be sent to a better place where, because of the name, Great Meadow, he imagined there would be trees, grass, and rolling hills. "Perhaps I'll work on a farm while going to school." Red, a fellow inmate in the cell next to him, said, "Fool, don't you know what Great Meadow is? It's Comstock—gladiator school." Victor's heart sank, as he replayed in his mind all the horror stories he had heard about Comstock: rapes, beatings, murders, robberies, all by both convicts and guards, everything characteristic of a brutal and sadistic society. Comstock was like Spartacus, where you learn how to fight if you didn't fight before, and where you learn the meaning of the words, "Blood on my knife or shit on my dick."

Despite the fact that 99 percent of the inmates at Comstock were minorities, it had only one black officer. This was after the Attica riots when part of the settlement stated that there would be more minority corrections officers in the prison system. What Attica didn't take into account, as no legislated desegregation policy can, is that the rank and file guards weren't going to accept "colored people" into their ranks when the only people of color to whom they were accustomed were convicts. The worst part was the arbitrariness of the rules as administered by the guards which made it impossible to figure out how they should be obeyed. Victor watched as the tiny number of white inmates were favored and protected.

When Victor received his first ticket, for talking after nine o'clock, he had no recreation and no commissary for two weeks. In accordance with a rule that said everybody had to go to a shop, Victor chose welding. Without a shop job, an inmate stayed in his cell for twenty-three hours a day. Wanting to get an education, Victor also enrolled in a college program but couldn't keep up with the work and dropped out. Every day he tried to live through the rapes and violence occurring around him.

One day he was working as a clerk in the reception center and a white inmate who called himself Chief was sitting at the desk using Victor's typewriter. Though the typewriter wasn't actually his, in prison everyone became very property-oriented and claimed things for their own. When Victor said, "Look, you're using my typewriter, and I need it," the guy responded, "Too bad. I guess we both can see whose need is greater."

Victor replied, "We can go up to the top floor and settle this," which was where inmate fights usually took place. When he turned to go upstairs, Chief took a steel bar and slammed Victor twice in his head, then left him there for dead.

The next thing Victor knew, someone was smacking his face and asking, "What's your name?" As he became more conscious, Victor realized the person was a nurse and he was in a hospital, but he didn't know where and couldn't remember his name. After a couple of hours, the incident started to come back to him. He learned he had received eighteen stitches in his head and remained in the hospital for ten days. During this time, an officer from the adjustment committee came and gave Victor his second ticket, for being assaulted. They gave him time served for the ten days he had been in the hospital.

When Victor left the hospital, he learned that Chief, the

inmate who had assaulted him as well as a lot of others, was
locked up in protective custody. But even there Chief wasn't safe
as inmates were known to burn other inmates alive by tossing
jars filled with lighter fluid into their cells. Victor, who still had
his Marine Corps and gang honor codes, told Chief, "Don't
worry, no one in here will bother you. You did what you had to
do," not realizing that the jailhouse code said he should have
killed the guy. According to Victor's code, Victor had gotten
what was coming to him because he had been stupid enough to
threaten Chief, then turn his back. Victor's peers, on the other
hand, told him he should have killed the guy or else told them
and they would have taken care of him.

Victor's next encounter was with Red, an inmate who had
a head four times the size of a normal head, weighed two hundred
and fifty pounds, and looked like an ape. It was a Saturday morning, and the cells were open for cleanup time. Victor was in his cell
making a cup of coffee by boiling water in a jar with a "stinger,"
a metal coil that heats up when it's plugged in. Suddenly he felt
someone's eyes on him. He turned to see this guy leaning on the
bars of his cell, looking at him. Victor, clad only in boxer shorts,
said, "What are you looking at?"

"I'm looking at you," Red said in a seductive voice. At
that moment, everything Victor had ever heard about Comstock
became a reality. Through his mind flashed something an old
timer had told him which was, the first time someone becomes a
threat to you, attack them immediately. You don't talk, you
don't stare them down, you don't try to reason, you don't try to
be logical: the only thing an animal respects is fear and pain. So
Victor grabbed the jar of boiling water, burning his own hand,
spun around, and threw it at Red's face. The jar crashed against
the bars and shattered, cutting and burning Red at the same
time. Victor then lunged at him and ran down the gallery,
yelling, "You wanna fuck somebody, huh, I'll give you something to fuck all right." The officer let Red through a gate before
Victor could get to him. For this Victor received his third ticket.
Both he and Red got locked up.

After Victor had been at Comstock two years, some of

the inmates staged a riot and a work stoppage because no one was getting transferred, and because black inmates were being killed in solitary or the box. At twelve on the night the riot ended, officers came and searched the cells, then inmates were shipped out to other prisons in order to break them up, whether they had been part of the riot or not. Those who had been actively involved were sent farther upstate to places like Attica or Clinton, which was near the Canadian border and had a reputation for being particularly brutal to black inmates. Victor was sent to Green Haven which was considered a reward as it was closer to New York City.

The loneliness, callous guards, and brutal regime made the reward seem a meager one. At night, Victor often lay awake on the thin mattress that passed for a bed and thought, *Jessie Jackson didn't coin the phrase "keep hope alive;" it was invented in the bowels of prisons eons ago.* Including two years in a county jail waiting for his trial, Victor had by this time been in prison for seven years. After being found guilty, he spent the last five years continuing to fight his case, but now finally defeated, he gave up. He realized no one was listening, there was no one who cared about his claim that he was innocent. Everyone here made similar claims, whether or not they were true. There was no way he could eventually be paroled without admitting guilt, and he couldn't admit guilt and still fight; plus, no one in the system wanted to hear about anyone being innocent. Everywhere he turned, he ran up against a brick wall. It was on these long, desperate nights that Victor came to grips with his fate and his anger at it, and all that preceded that destiny.

His education thus far had been in the Marines where he had learned how to hunt people down and kill them. One night he had an epiphany in which it became clear that he needed to find out about himself as an individual and also as a member of his people. The next day he started on his quest for knowledge by entering the pre-GED program to prepare eventually for college. At the same time that he was learning the traditional subjects in school, on his own he began reading literature about those discriminated against, including George Jackson's *Blood in My Eye*, Franz Fanon's *Wretched of the Earth*, Viktor Frankl, Che Guevara, Mao Tse Tung, and Machiavelli.

Living in a world of hurt and pain, Victor began to come to the difficult realization that the only way he could survive was to embrace his fate. The guys he saw who fought it either killed themselves, got killed, killed someone else, or went insane. He knew he couldn't find himself until he had a focus, understanding and control of his feelings. Studying began to bring this about but it also made him angrier. In prison, knowledge was dangerous; the guards preferred that inmates stay ignorant and do ignorant things to justify their existence. Victor became convinced that the true means to transcending this kind of oppression, both in prison and back in the world, was education.

Victor found out that, miraculously, the jail had a college program. He entered Marist College on a Higher Education Opportunity Program (HEOP) scholarship. Going to college in prison required that he relinquish recreation because the college program ran at night, and he had to have a full-time institutional job during the day. From 8:30 to 4:00 he worked, and from 6:00 to 9:00 he attended classes given by teachers from Marist who came into the prison. His own evolution brought a further realization that college was a real vehicle for inmates to effect change. Victor set out to convince the teachers that the prison needed a tutorial program because of the high dropout rate. When he succeeded, they sent him Neal Ritter, a young guy with a ponytail who didn't know the first thing about prisons or prisoners.

Victor was not about to give up. Together, he and Neal designed a tutorial program, the goal being to help students effectively cope with the academic rigors of college along with the harsh reality of prison life. Research had shown Victor that if a person could survive the demands of prison while managing to get an academic foundation, the chances of him returning to prison after release were slim. However, though he now had a program, Victor found there were two major things against the program succeeding: other convicts and the guards.

They didn't like the uppity inmate who, though he had given up his own fight for justice, was trying to change the system from within. Out of jealousy, the convicts resented the fact that he was trying to pull himself up; Out of pure hatred, the guards resented that he was getting a free education which they couldn't. Despite these drawbacks, Victor was determined to emerge from this seemingly impossible situation with a stronger driving determination to bring about change, not only in himself, but in a system that he had assumed was unbeatable because it had put him there.

At least part of Victor's resolve came from conversations he had with some of the "old timers" who sat around and talked about what was wrong with the prison system. Many of these inmates, like "Big Black," whom Victor had met in the Brooklyn House of Detention, knew they would never get out or see the light of day.

Victor began to feel strongly that individuals and their attitudes had to be changed, especially about prison. He observed some guys who, upon returning to prison and being placed in reception with their movement restricted, could be heard saying through the gate to their friends, "Put me on the callout for the basketball game" so they could be included in activities. What struck Victor was that they didn't appear distraught or even upset that they were there. Prison became an acceptable part of their lives. They believed they had no means of going anywhere better.

In his junior year of the college program, Victor decided to matriculate as a psychology major because of the atrocities he saw around him. He knew there was something insane about the abusive treatment. How could the attitudes and cruelty result in positive ends? It was understandable that the prisoners were warped—that's why they were there—but no one seemed to question the sanity of the guards who brutalized them or the system that justified the brutality. It was commonplace that guards would destroy personal possessions; often Victor came back to his cell to find it had been turned upside down and that pictures and letters were ripped, soiled, or missing. Victor, as were the others, was left feeling violated and impotent while the guards spoke to the inmates as if they were the judge, jury, and executioner, whose sole purpose was to punish the inmates. This was the constant message. Inmates learned that if you had power you could do anything you wanted. It was a horrible message to send to the incarcerated because it was this kind of thinking — that if they had power through a gun or intimidation, they were cool — that had gotten them there in the first place.

Thus, when Victor became a clerk in the Academic Vocational Program, the AVP, and met the assigned guard, Norm Thompson, Victor was suspicious. About five-feet-six-inches tall, though Norm always said five-seven, Thompson was a Neanderthal throwback. In his fifties, Norm's hard life as an unskilled laborer made him look weather-beaten and ten years older than he was. He had worked delivering ice and coal, and as a construction worker. His hands, which were hard and cal-loused like stone, were so gnarled from arthritis, weather, and age that they could barely hold anything. Yet Norm was able to use them despite what must have been constant pain. At first Victor didn't like or trust Norm who looked to him like an old redneck and came into the AVP unit criticizing everything.

The AVP was an offshoot of the psychiatric satellite unit where the severely psychiatrically ill inmates were sent. AVP was for guys with psychiatric problems and diagnoses who didn't require acute hospitalization. About forty-four of them in all, these inmates psychologically just couldn't do the time. Some tried to kill themselves and often acted out in bizarre ways, such as talking to themselves and yelling and screaming at imaginary enemies. In the middle of a screaming tirade they would stop and calmly say, "Excuse me. Do you have a cigarette?" then return to ranting and raving. Victor's duties as the clerk were organizing the patients' days and the inmate staff's payroll. Officially, inmates could not be in charge of other inmates, but in reality Victor was in charge; the officers depended on him to run the program. The clerks had their pulses on everything, seeing to all the mundane administrative details, while the officers were the figureheads.

One day Victor complained that the inmates looked disheveled. When the next day Norm brought in an ironing board, Victor began to see Norm less as a stereotype and more as a person amenable to the changes Victor was looking for. However, the AVP inmate population were looked on as loonies by the rest of the population, who were afraid of them. As a result they were unable to barter or trade for any of the things they wanted. At commissary they got robbed all the time. One inmate, Brownie, white, retarded, and in his fifties, went to commissary one time and came back with nothing. "Why?" Victor asked.

Brownie stuttered, "Some guys asked for my stuff so I gave it to them." Brownie was incarcerated for arson, having admitted setting a fire because someone had told him to.

When Norm found out what happened, he marched them all down to the commissary which was in the basement. Norm banged on the door, saying, "Open the goddamn door." The guard opened the door, and Norm said, "Brownie, which one of these fuckers took your stuff?" Brownie pointed to some big, black guys. Norm told them, "All those bags, give them all to him," indicating Brownie.

The guys said, "What are you talking about?"

Norm replied, "If you don't I'll kick your asses." Victor stared at the white guard sticking up for them. Then the commissary guard faded into the background. The forty big guys standing behind Norm, with their unkempt hair, drooling, talking to themselves, muttering, "Let's kill 'em" made the toughs give Brownie back his things. Victor was developing respect for Norm's ideas and methods.

Unlike the rest of the unit, the AVP unit had a racial and ethnic mix, and there was a feeling of closeness between the inmate staff and the inmate patients with whom they would socialize in the evenings in the yard. Though other inmates looked at Victor and the others like they were weird, the guys with the psychiatric labels for the most part were lovable, conscientious, and caring.

When Victor's cell was set on fire because a snitch's cell was next to his, he was put on lockdown while an investigation went on. The next morning he saw some of the AVP guys outside of his cell who explained that Norm had told them what happened, and they wanted to make sure Victor was safe. When lockdown was over, they followed Victor around, which was their way of repaying him for him taking good care of them.

In fair weather, the AVP inmates would go out to Fay Field and play softball against other prison groups, such as the metal shop or furniture shop. They'd wager cases of soda. Because they were considered "handicapped," Victor's team was allowed to have as many people in the field as they wanted. Norm was the only corrections officer out there, and he acted as the umpire. The guys really couldn't play, but they never struck out with Norm as the umpire. After they got one run, Norm would end the game so they always won. The guys would run around and brag, not knowing that the wins were planned.

Because he did his studying at night after classes, Victor usually didn't get to sleep before two or three in the morning, and he was up by seven-thirty. He'd leave his housing unit and go to the A block where the AVP unit was housed and wake them up. There he always encountered Norm opening the cells. Victor helped the guys get up and get washed and dressed. From there they'd go to the hospital to get medication, then to breakfast, then spend the day in the J block school area. As Norm gave them directions, he was fair and firm. He acted like a father to them, letting it be known that he would rip into any inmate or guard who made fun of them.

Norm was also like a father to Victor, who had warmed up to the older man and good-naturedly teased Norm, saying, "You must have been hell when you were a young officer. I guess this is your way of repenting." Norm never responded to such comments one way or the other. Though Norm referred to blacks as "colored people," Victor was not offended because he knew

Norm was of that generation. Norm encouraged Victor's academic pursuits, introducing him to another sympathetic supporter, Frank De Luca, a psychologist in the psychiatric satellite unit. One day when Victor told De Luca that when he became a senior he wanted to take an internship which corrections wouldn't allow, Dr. De Luca said he would intervene.

During the time that Victor and Norm were in the AVP unit there were no fights or assaults. After he had been working there a while, Victor went to Norm. "I really think these guys need something more than medication. I envision them in general population programs such as GED classes and workshops."

"Let's both work on it," Norm replied. Slowly, the administration started to let this happen; at first, they'd go out for two hours. One inmate got into the college program.

Not long afterward, staff from the Central New York Psychiatric Center (commonly referred to as "Marcy") came to observe the AVP unit. As people from the outside often did, they talked around the inmates as if they didn't exist. They talked to Norm with their backs to Victor, and upon hearing inmates laughing down the hall, they asked, "Do you allow that down here?"

Norm said, "They're playing cards and having a good time."

The visitors said, "We shut them up and put them in solitary when they make noise."

Unable to remain quiet, Victor turned around and said, "That's why we catch so much hell here because when they go to you, you brutalize them or ignore them like Ralph Ellison's Invisible Man, so when we get them they act out violently."

A short balding guy shot Victor a look then turned to Norm and said, "We don't allow inmates to work in our offices."

Norm said, "You'd better leave then; this is not the place for you."

In Victor's senior year, Frank De Luca kept his promise. For the first and only time in the history of corrections, an inmate was allowed to do an internship in a psychiatric satellite unit of a prison. Under Frank's supervision, Victor counseled the patients. Victor graduated magna cum laude, with a Bachelor of Arts degree in psychology. He was the class valedictorian. At the graduation, Norm was heard to say, "That's my boy."

After graduation, Victor continued to work in the tutorial program with Neal Ritter, whose two sons were in special education classes. Neal introduced him to special education teachers from the State University of New York at New Paltz who offered Victor a graduate program but said he would have to pay the tuition as there were no grants. This was another first. Having managed to save six thousand dollars from his earnings, Victor started graduate school that September. Because he had letters from the academic dean and chairman of the psychology department at Marist, he was allowed to take nineteen credits per semester, seven more than the standard amount. By the following August, he had completed the course work, graduated with a 4.0 cumulative average, and was awarded a master's degree in special education. As part of his master's thesis he designed the tutorial program and education mainstreaming program for the psychiatric satellite unit. Everything he had learned in school, he applied to the prison system, to improve the lives of inmates, to give them more choices.

While he was working in the AVP unit, Victor became friendly with Carole, a female guard who worked there as Norm's relief. Over time Carole and Victor began talking, and she wound up telling Victor about the abuse she was suffering at the hands of her ex-husband. At a loss for what to do, Carole was afraid to go through the system. Victor got information for her about organizations that helped abused women, including an employee assistance program representative whom Carole didn't want to see because she didn't want her problems to become the subject of gossip around the facility. Victor had written all the information down and when another guard found this piece of paper in Victor's cell, it was assumed that he had more involvement with Carole than just friendship. Victor was investigated and locked up in solitary. Carole was chastised and told what to say. Rather than say things about Victor that were untrue, Carole quit. Though eventually the investigation showed that the woman had been abused, Victor's counselor said that Corrections would never apologize or even admit they were wrong. However, instead of punishing him by sending him to Comstock, they would send him to a better prison, but far away from the AVP Unit, Norm, Neal, and Carole.

Two weeks later Victor found out he was being sent to the Eastern New York Correctional Facility, a less secure prison, in Napanoch, New York. Saying goodbye to Norm made the move bittersweet, especially since true to form, Norm had never asked Victor whether the accusations about Victor's relationship with Carole were true because to him it didn't matter.

Upon his arrival at Eastern, Victor found there was no program for him, but wanting to work at something, anything, he was allowed to take a job as a porter in the vocational school area. While there, after working hours and because of his prior experience with the deaf and blind, he was able to design a disabled unit after working hours. An area in a basement under a housing unit had been carved out. At the end of the day, after Victor finished his porter duties, he read through catalogues, making lists of all the equipment he would need such as Telecommunication Devices for the Deaf, visual aids, and Braille machines. Once again, Victor's determination cut through custom. Soon the equipment started to materialize, though it happened under cover, because inmates normally didn't do this kind of thing.

It was necessary to have someone other than an inmate as the official head of the program and to control the keys, so they hired Taylor Bradley, a young guy who had never done prison social work before. It was a marriage of oil and water, as Taylor knew that Victor had more experience than he did, that Victor was fluent in sign language, and that he had designed a program that Taylor envied. At the same time that he hated Victor, Taylor needed him in order for the program to succeed. He took credit for Victor's teaching, coordinating, and designing when all Taylor really did was sign his name. When the blind inmates decided that they didn't want to play softball, Taylor blamed Victor and used it as an excuse to fire him. While Victor was there, one blind inmate got a GED; after Victor left, there were no more graduates. In fact, after Victor left, the program started to fail, and Victor was blamed for this too. Because the inmates were Victor's peers and they were returning to the same kind of communities from which he'd come, Victor had a vested interest in having them succeed. Taylor didn't have the same kind of investment, nor did he subscribe to what Norm had been fond of saying: "Corrections is everybody's business."

In 1986, Victor enrolled in another SUNY New Paltz graduate program, this one in sociology. Around the same time, he was contacted by a publisher to write a vignette about the issues in teaching the handicapped, to be included in a book on special education in the criminal justice system. This was published in 1987 when Victor was also awarded his second master's degree, graduating with a 3.8 cumulative average. He now had made as good an adjustment to his fate as he could. Though he was despairing about his own future, at least he was contributing to the positive futures of others.

One night, Victor was sitting in his cell reading the *Village Voice.* With nothing to do when he finished reading the news, he idly perused the personal ads. Like his future, Victor had given up on relationships. What kind of relationship could anyone from outside have with someone condemned to life in prison? Despite his cynicism, one ad from a "psychotherapist, writer, astrologer" who was looking for someone "socially conscious" among other things, caught his eye. Though he didn't know why and had no hope of a reply, he wrote a response. He was shocked to receive a letter from her. As she kept writing, so did he, and then one day she sent a phone number. He was amazed that someone trusted him enough to give him a number and allow him to hear her voice. The letters and phone calls continued until that day in July when Denise came to Napanoch.

PART
TWO

"If only," Frieda said, slowly, quietly almost relaxedly, as if she knew she could have only a very short spell of peace resting on K.'s shoulder, but wanted to enjoy it to the full, "if only we had emigrated somewhere that first night, we would be in safety somewhere, always together, your hand always close enough to take hold of; how I need you near me, how desolate I have been, ever since I have known you, when you are not near; believe me, having you near me is the only dream I ever dream, no other."

Franz Kafka
The Castle

CHAPTER
FIVE

At First Glance

"Let's sit over there," Victor said, indicating seats that were out of the path of inmates entering the visiting room. He sat opposite me with his arms curved around the backs of adjacent chairs. Shyly I told him about my experience of going through the wrong door and finally coming into the right place and being processed. Then, even though in letters and on the phone we had already been more intimate, we talked about things that are typical of first dates — weather, hating and loving New York City, the difficulties of life in the late twentieth century. He gave me the names and numbers of other inmates' wives, "Just in case you have any questions you don't want to ask me," he said shyly. As I told him about renewing my lease and my building turning condominium, part of me thought, *what could this possibly mean to him, being locked up for so many years?* But Victor had kept abreast of everything going on in the world, and actually he knew more about condo conversions than I did.

After a while we got up and walked hand in hand to the food machines. His hand was gentle, strong, and protective.

"That's the child care room I wrote to you about," he said, indicating a small room off the main room. "We have to rotate jobs; It's my new one. I really enjoy working in there with the kids, though handling them and their parents can be quite challenging."

"What made you request working in there?"

"Well, wherever they put me, I want to feel like I'm really helping people. And I like to work with kids."

I couldn't stop myself from thinking, *Good father material* and felt my face color.

So that he wouldn't notice, I turned my attention to the odd red, white, and green shapes in the windows of the machines. Finding healthy food in the machines was a challenge. The drinks available were only lukewarm soda, milk, and coffee. As the temperature was at least eighty-five degrees, orange soda seemed the least offensive. The selection of food was not much better, and I passed on that. Who was hungry, anyway? Back at our seats, the hours passed in the blink of an eye, and I regretted that I had gotten there late. I hadn't wanted to push it. After all, what if I hadn't liked him or we didn't get along? I had also come prepared with an excuse if I needed to leave early, just as I might do on a blind date with someone on the outside. So we really only had a few hours together until 3:30 P.M. when visiting time would end.

When the announcement came that the visiting time was almost up, I felt sad and at the same time, exhilarated and inspired. Though I told myself to tread lightly and use caution, I wondered if I could be falling in love. Slowly, along with all the other visitors and inmates crowded in the room, I got up and made my way toward the door. There, many of the couples were passionately embracing and kissing each other. Women had tears in their eyes. Children tugged at their daddies' legs. Victor and I looked into each other's eyes. "Thank you for coming," he said gently.

"I'll be back very soon," I said and reached out to hug him. He was startled and stiff hugging me back, as if touching a woman was part of an experience too painful to remember. Both of us were wooden, as if stunned by the intensity of our meeting, intimidated by the intimacy of having entered each other's destiny. When the door was opened by the officer on the other side, I, along with the other visitors, shuffled into the vestibule between the doors while the inmates hung back and watched. Then the second door buzzed open, we went through it, and when I looked back, the visiting room was empty.

With trembling fingers, I took the locker key from my wallet and retrieved my things. Walking out, I felt ablaze like the four o'clock sun above me and dazed, as if I had been baking under its heat for hours. I floated across the parking lot to the car, which, when I opened the door, was like a furnace. Sweat began pouring from all parts of my body. After removing my contact lenses from red and gritty eyes, I started the engine and pulled out of the parking spot. As I made my way toward the exit, I became acutely aware of not wanting to leave, and the irony of it struck me: I didn't want to leave a prison. I saw the men in the gun towers. I saw the bars on the windows. I also saw, not with my eyes but with my heart, the man I'd just met but seemed to have known forever, from whom I was now driving away. But I told myself, *I'll be back; I will be back.* For though it was only our first meeting, I felt we were meant to be together.

I made my way along Route 209, past bungalow colonies, hotels, quaint banks, and discount beverage stores, and finally back to Route 17. I was loathe to leave the mountains and the sweet smelling air. As if the car were driving me, I found us exiting the highway at a thickly wooded area and onto a small country road. Every few hundred feet there was a house nestled in woods which were pierced by iridescent rays of sunlight, straight out of sixteenth century oil paintings. I wished one of those houses were mine, that I could pull into the driveway and be home, and that a pool in the backyard waited to welcome me with its softly lapping waters. And, of course, to make the fantasy complete, Victor would be home from work in an hour or two, and we would spend a happy and gratifying evening together, sharing the day's experiences and life in general. Ah, fantasy, so sweet and unattainable. The question was, could I actually live in the moment, in reality?

Suddenly through the trees I noticed the glinting of light off water. I turned onto a dirt road and followed the light. Further down the road, a few cars were parked, and people fished on the edge of a vast shimmering lake. Not wanting to be near anyone, I pulled off to the side, got out of the car taking my camera, and walked into the woods. The emerald mossy pine smell was invigorating. I was starved for Nature; during the past several years of my adult life, I had gotten stuck in the inner city, and getting out was not easy.

Like I've been in prison, I mused as I sat on a tree stump, enchanted by flitting yellow and orange butterflies and scurrying chipmunks; Victor's and my life did have parallels. We both had had less than gratifying relationships with parents and wound up angry and rebellious. Now here we were, adults waiting to be freed, him by external forces and me by internal ones.

The breeze had an almost ethereal softness, like down. Suddenly I was overcome with the desire to have Victor there with me, to experience with him the pastoral scene. How would I be able to stand being without him for years? Suddenly, amid the saplings and foliage a deer appeared, then stood stock still. How majestic and without fear it looked, so at home in its natural environment. Slowly and deliberately I picked up my camera, captured the deer in the viewfinder, and snapped a picture. I continued to watch the deer as it ambled away.

When the pictures came out, there was the deer staring at me head on. I had it blown up into an eleven-by-fourteen enlargement which I framed and hung in my office to feast on as I provided psychotherapy to my clients. I imagined that the deer had Victor's spirit.

The next night, Friday, I was surprised when the phone rang and it was Victor.

"I promised a guy some cigarettes for his phone time. I just had to call you and thank you for yesterday," Victor said.

"It was my pleasure."

"I can't begin to tell you how much the visit meant to me, and then, when you hugged me...."

"I hope that was okay. I mean, it was kind of awkward."

"Denise, what you're calling awkward was my terror. No one has hugged me like that in years; it's like I've been in an isolation tank, and suddenly here you were reaching out like that and enveloping me. It's hard for me to describe how cared for you made me feel."

"I'm so glad; I felt the same way."

"I can't wait to see you again."

"Same here."

Over the next few weeks we had two more visits, in which we talked of not only the momentous but also small things which made us unique. I love flowers, especially roses. One day I confided, "I will live in the country and have my own rose garden."

"I'd like that," he said, participating in my daydream.

One night on the phone I informed Victor of a decision I had made. "I'm going to spend my vacation with you," I announced.

Victor laughed. "How're you gonna do that?"

"Well I figured I'd stay in the Terrace Motel...."

"I think it's safe, if not terribly attractive. At least that's where Marian, the woman whose number I gave you, stays."

I nodded. "I pass it on the way to see you and it looks like a decent enough place; so I figured I'd stay there and come to see you every day." I paused for a moment. "If you want me to that is."

"Nah, I would hate to see you every day," he joked.

I laughed. "I know, I'm so tired of seeing you for a few hours a week as it is."

"Seriously, Denise, I would be honored if you'd spend your vacation near me. I would love it."

"I'm so happy to hear you say that. You know, we'll be right down the road from each other."

"I know."

"Maybe I can camp out under your window."

"Sure, and if anyone sees you, tell them you thought it was a campground."

"Yeah, right. A campground with a fortress."

We chatted for a few minutes more until Victor was given the signal that his time was almost up.

"I'll speak to you Thursday. Take care of yourself, and don't worry about me."

"Don't Worry, Be Happy." The song was always playing in the visitors' waiting room, which struck me as both ironic and appropriate. All those inmates' wives and relatives who were both worrying and very unhappy indeed needed some good advice and uplifting words. Marian, whose number Victor had given me, was the girlfriend of an inmate Victor was friendly with. I had called her and listened to what she undoubtedly thought was the voice of experience, telling me that Victor was "one of the good ones" and how, generally speaking, it was not a good idea to get involved with an inmate, even though she had. When I saw Marian, who was overweight with long stringy hair, I thought she fit the stereotype imagined by many of women involved with inmates. Though I always try not to pigeonhole people, I could not help seeing her as the lonely, bitter type who can't find a mate and who have to meet men in this way. But I also wondered, what did that say about me? I was pretty confident in my ability to meet men, and Lord knew I'd had enough relationships. Nevertheless, I had not run from this situation for I also knew that it was already too late for well-meaning advice. My heart was telling me to stay.

As I told Victor, I had driven past the unprepossessing Terrace Motel on Route 209 in Ellenville many times over the past several weeks, so when I walked into the combination lobby, reception counter, and office for the first time it seemed perfectly natural that the space was decorated like an oriental gift shop, with plaster bonsai trees in porcelain pots, a peacock with a glittering tail made of waving fiberglass wands, and shimmering pictures on the walls of waterfalls and lakes. Tiny china ashtrays and plaster figurines littered the low coffee tables which crowded pale mauve and blue sofas and chairs. A bridge table held a Mr. Coffee machine and Cremora, and an easel stuffed with brochures of local tourist attractions stood in the corner. The proprietors, a petite middle-aged Korean couple, he small and silver haired and she with a jet black bun held by a small plastic ivory look-alike

comb, greeted me from behind the counter and were accommo-
dating when I asked for the quietest room, farthest from the road.
"Number nineteen," the husband told me, and handed me the key
in exchange for my MasterCard.

Room nineteen, the last room on the second floor, had a
chalet-style wall over the bed, dark wood beams on the ceiling,
and opposite the door leading to the catwalk, a sliding glass door
leading to a small terrace. The decor was an eclectic mixture of
green and blue polyester, cotton, and plastic. The air smelled of
pine disinfectant poorly masking stale cigarette smoke. Below the
window was one of those units that's both a heater and air conditioner, the latter of which I put on full blast. In a tiny alcove sat a
two-foot-long cylindrical bar with three wire hangers, a small coffee pot with packets of instant coffee and creamer, and two small
teacups with caffeine and lipstick stains. The bathroom had no
window and was dimly lit by one bare bulb over the sink. There
was no hygienic paper strip around the toilet though there were
two paper-wrapped glasses and a tiny bar of soap.

It wasn't the Plaza, but I was thrilled to be there. I had
promised I was going to spend my vacation with Victor and the
Terrace was the next best thing to camping out under his window.
I lifted my suitcase onto one of the two double beds and hung up
my shirts, slacks, and jacket. Reveling in all the free, unencum-
bered time that stretched before me, I walked out onto the terrace
and looked toward where I knew Victor to be, a few miles down
the road. I knew his schedule. His time was well regimented; how
he spent it didn't vary much from day to day. Like those of us not
incarcerated, he had holidays and breaks from work and school,
but they weren't particularly welcomed in the drab prison world
because of the void they created. *Exactly the opposite of me*, I
thought, straining to see the prison through the trees. I coveted
free time and dreamed about the traveling I would do if I had
enough of it. For now, however, I was content to be spending several days out of the city, near Victor.

It was midday and since visiting hours went on until 3:30
P.M., I decided to take a ride down the road and surprise him. I got

into the rented silver blue car and rolled down the windows. Here in the country I loved having the sizzling wind blowing in my face, whereas in the city, open car windows were stifling.

It was strange, I couldn't help thinking, how the implausible can so quickly become the norm. Visiting a prison was hardly a reality I had ever contemplated when I'd watched those stranger, unknown women—wives and girlfriends of inmates—whom I'd seen on television, yet now I was busy figuring out how and when such interludes could best be scheduled, and I was already taking it as a matter of course.

Midday during the week, I had already found out, was the best time to visit prisons since there was no one else waiting to get in and be processed. The normally crowded, noisy waiting room was empty, and I walked right up to the counter. A male corrections officer with a partially bald head stood at the end reading a newspaper. He must have heard me, but he didn't look up.

"Excuse me," I said, "I'm here to visit Victor Clark."

Into his newspaper, he said, "What's his number?"

"75-A-0518." I recited his number from memory. This was one of a series of ID numbers Victor had. The "75" indicated the year that Victor entered the state system. He had been locked up since '73 but the first two years were in the city. The "A" indicated the facility (Sing Sing) where he was processed into the system. Slowly, I was getting accustomed to the man I loved having a number follow his name.

The guard pulled a dog-eared manilla folder out of a file cabinet. "Victor Clark?" he read the label. "Sign here." In the folder they kept a running log of visitors. When he pushed it toward me he covered the lines above the line I was signing with an index card. They now did that in case the inmate had a visitor he didn't want his wife to know about; it had been commonplace for women signing in to start shrieking and cursing at the guard, and supposedly more than one woman had tried to tear up the log when she saw a name that didn't belong there. Personally, I was glad they did that because if anything like that was happening, I didn't want to find out about it that way.

I signed my name and put down my car license number (I assumed they took that so that in the event of an escape they could track the inmate down in his visitor's car), showed my driver's license, then walked through the metal detector, leaving my sandals on. I had heard that in other facilities they made you walk through barefoot, though for the life of me I couldn't imagine how you could hide anything in a sandal. At this point, the officer reached for a phone on the desk and punched in four digits. "You got Victor Clark there?" My heart pounded in anticipation, for fear there would be a no. When the guard hesitated, looking down for a few seconds, I began to get anxious. Then he said, "He's not there? Okay, thanks." Looking at me he pressed down the receiver button. Why wouldn't he tell me what was going on? He dialed another number. "Hey, you got Victor Clark there?" He was calling all over the prison. *How come no one knew where Victor was?* "Yeah, he's got a visit." I let out my breath, having been unaware that I had been holding it. I was relieved that Victor was okay; in this place you could never take anything for granted.

The officer buzzed open the door to the vestibule, and I walked through after gathering the personal items I was bringing in with me. I could see through the window that the visiting room was fairly empty; maybe a third of the seats were taken. After a minute or so, the next door buzzed open, and I entered the visiting room, heading straight to the officer's desk on the side of the room near the entrance. A heavy, dark-skinned woman stood on the other side of the room talking to a guard. I just stood near the desk hoping she'd look at me so I could leave the identifying paper. She was very involved in her conversation and was not looking around the room. Finally she turned around and saw me, said something to the guard she was talking with, and scowling, came over. *Uh oh, what did I do now?* I thought. Because the overriding theme of the place was rules and punishment, even as a visitor I was often intimidated into feeling that if I broke a rule they had a cell waiting for me.

I took the seat I usually did while waiting for Victor to emerge from the bowels of the fortress. As the minutes ticked away, I got more anxious; I considered walking to the vending machine area, but did not want to miss Victor's entrance. With a very loud click the door kept opening, and inmates wearing either a complete set of prison greens or just the pants with a red or white shirt walked through. Each time I was disappointed by someone else appearing, I sat back thinking that the next one would be him. When it finally was, he smiled broadly and sauntered over to me saying, "This is a surprise. I didn't expect you till tomorrow. I was at work." Then we embraced, being careful to cut it off after a few seconds, as it was against the rules to embrace for more than a brief instant. "Are you thirsty, hungry? Do you want to sit here or shall we move?" he asked.

Unfortunately, the yard wasn't open during the week even though it was at least ninety degrees in the room. "How about by the wall?" It was the one corner of the room which afforded couples any privacy and there were a few people there already. We sat in an empty row in two seats facing each other next to the pale blue cinder block wall. "How are you?" Victor took my hands and leaned forward to kiss me passionately. As we broke apart, I said, "I'm great. All checked in at the Terrace and looking forward to spending the week with you."

"Thank you for spending your vacation with me, Denise. There aren't many people who would voluntarily choose to spend their vacation in prison." He leaned towards me and said gently, "You know, a relationship with me is going to be very difficult. I'd completely understand if you felt after reflecting that it would be too much for you to undertake."

"I want nothing as much as to be here." I smiled, feeling myself blushing deeply.

"The things we do for love," Victor said, gazing intently at me.

"It's amazing," I replied. As I gazed back, I couldn't help but notice over his shoulder the curved back of a woman whose head was lap level, bobbing up and down. "Victor," I whispered.

"What?"

"Behind you," I said, leaning in to Victor. "I think that woman is giving the guy oral sex."

Victor blushed and gestured for me to look away. "Come on, let's go get something to drink."

As if what I had just seen were an ordinary occurrence, we got up, hand in hand, and headed toward the vending machines. Victor put his arm around my shoulder, fingers cool and dry on my neck. As we stood behind two people on line at the soda machine, I could feel Victor's body touching mine and the smoothness of his arms. For a moment it was as if we were far from this place and finally alone to touch and explore each other. Then the murmurs of conversation and the clink of the machine brought us both back to a reality we could never dismiss. We began to discuss the various options we had for food and drink. As the vending machine fare didn't much interest me, I opted for a giant Pepperidge Farm cookie and ginger ale, the least toxic items I could find. He got the same. As we walked slowly back to our seats, I tried not to look at the other couples: one of the many unspoken rules that I was learning. On the other hand, I didn't want to stare at Victor for fear my real hunger might return. I inadvertently noticed that the couple who had engaged in oral sex was a twenty-something black guy, with bulging muscles and fade hair cut, and a fortyish white woman with hair pulled back in a ponytail and wearing a navy and gold Chanel suit and navy pumps. Quickly I looked away.

"They don't mind if you're not at your job?" I asked as we settled into our seats.

"Well, they'd prefer it if I'm there, but a visit always takes precedence. I'm on the deaf and blind unit again. It's tough but rewarding," Victor said with pride in his voice. I felt proud just to hear him talk about it. After all, Victor had not only helped establish this unit but now it served as a model for similar programs in prisons across the country.

"Last time I was working on this unit, one of the staff, Taylor Bradley, felt so threatened by me because I was an inmate, yet I got more done in a day than he did in a week. A lot of my ideas he claimed as his own."

"That must have been so frustrating for you," I said.

"It was, but just recently these people from Albany came to

observe the program, and one of them, a woman, kept addressing her comments and questions to me, not realizing I was an inmate. When someone finally told her, she was visibly shaken and embarrassed. She stopped talking to me and wouldn't even look at me."

"As if she had done something she wasn't supposed to," I said, shaking my head. "Or, like she might get contaminated or something, just by talking to you."

"She was really blown away because I must have shattered her stereotype of what an inmate is like."

"You are quite unusual, you know."

Victor kissed me. "You're just prejudiced."

"Who me?" I said, grinning, feeling heady.

The next three hours passed in a flash, proving that hideous paradox of life: the rate at which time seems to pass is directly proportionate to how you're feeling—the happier you are, the faster the time passes, and conversely, the more miserable, the more time drags, prolonging the agony. Before we knew it the voice came over the speaker saying, "Five more minutes left to visiting hours." At that moment everyone in the visiting room tried to intensify the time left with their loved ones. Many people embraced tightly, despite the rule against it. Victor and I stared into each other's eyes. "I can't believe I'll be back tomorrow," I whispered.

"I know. Don't worry if it takes a while before I show up. It just means I'm at work. And don't feel like you have to get here first thing. Don't forget, you're on vacation, so you should sleep late." I was gratified that Victor was proving he fit that other word in my personal ad's description: thoughtful.

"Okay, people, visiting hours are now over. I repeat, visiting hours are now over."

We stood up and put our arms around each other. "Thank you for coming, sweetheart. I can't wait until tomorrow." We walked toward the door where all the inmates and their guests were gathering. I noticed again that some of the women and children were crying. I might have been teary too had I not known I'd be back the next day as well as several days following.

"Inmates report to the back," the announcement blared.

With those words everyone got in a final hug and kiss, then the inmates all headed toward the door where they came in, many walking backwards and turning around waving at their guests. Then our door buzzed open and as many guests as could fit in the vestibule shuffled in. I made sure to be in that first group because I didn't want to linger, especially after Victor was gone from the room.

Outside the weather was perfect, mellow, and sun-kissed, and I felt both ecstatic and heartsick at once. The essence of life, Yin/Yang. "The measure of a person's sanity is the degree to which he is able to hold two opposing concepts in his intellect at once," wrote F. Scott Fitzgerald, who, judging by his copious consumption of alcohol, had difficulty meeting this challenge. But it was true for me: here I was, madly in love, and the object and cause of this state was locked away from me. As I walked toward the car, I was overwhelmed by the sweetness of the hot breeze, the hazy aquamarine sky, the grasses waving lazily in the field off the parking lot, and by the thought of the man sitting in an airless cell, writing to me.

That night, I took a ride over the mountain to the town of Woodstock. After walking around and window shopping, I chose a street café with outdoor tables and ordered a glass of Chablis. A not bad looking guy with longish dirty blond hair and designer jeans asked if he could sit with me.

"Nice night, eh? I'm Brad," he said.

I was both flattered and annoyed.

"Yeah, it's beautiful." There was a crescent moon; the ink blue sky was lit with a few stars, and the air was balmy.

He asked the usual what-are-you-doing-here type questions, and I told him, "I'm visiting my boyfriend in prison."

"Really? What's he in prison for?"

"Well, I don't really want to discuss that with you."

"Oh, sorry for asking. You knew him before he went to prison?"

"Well, if you must know, no. I met him there."

"Yeah? Well you must be a good person to do that."

I smiled, the wine beginning to mellow my mood.

"Hey, I hope you have a nice stay up here and enjoy visiting your man," Brad said as he got up and left. I was relieved, wanting to be alone with the flowery night air and my thoughts. I ordered chicken Marsala, which was delicious, and began to fantasize about coming here with Victor. The ride back to Ellenville was like a ride through paradise. The road over the mountain was virtually empty, the sky dense with stars. Driving slower than usual, I barely felt the road and floated the whole way back, Victor's image never leaving my consciousness for more than a few seconds. The incessant song of the cicadas played an accompanying symphony.

The next morning I awoke with the sun and walked out on the terrace. It was going to be another hot day and would be scorching in the visiting room. I would have to dress to be cool. I dressed modestly, in walking shorts and a plaid top. Even though I had seen women go in with skin-tight pants, tops, and miniskirts, the prison didn't allow tank tops, the rationale being that they were too provocative. After washing one of the stained cups, I fixed myself some instant coffee which was vile. Pouring it down the sink, I splashed water on my face and left to grab a newspaper and something to eat. Outside the car glistened with dew. Driving down the road I stopped and bought a large Styrofoam cup of coffee (not great but better than the instant), a jelly doughnut, and *The New York Times*. Back at the motel I wiped down a lawn chair and eased into the day, listening to the birds and communing with the trees and mountains in the distance. Thoughts of Victor streamed through my mind. What must it be like for him waking up in prison each day? Had he gotten used to it, or, even after all these years, did his imprisonment strike him anew each time he arose in the morning?

I got to the prison earlier than the day before, and it was more crowded. Women piled shopping bags and cartons full of food, clothing, and other assorted items on the counter where packages for inmates were received. Finally I was at the front of the line and couldn't believe my ears. The officer said, "Sorry, tank tops are not allowed."

"This isn't a tank top." I was wearing a sleeveless, loose fitting green plaid button-down.

He smiled. "Yes it is." Angry and helpless, I was beginning to get a firsthand sense of what Victor had been telling me, that one of the most difficult aspects of prison was the arbitrariness of the rules. You never knew what to do, or how to act from one day to the next, as the rules depended on who was enforcing them. Even the same person enforcing the same rule could vary in his interpretation from day to day depending on his mood. So even though I had seen several women go in who were really wearing tank tops, today this guard decided that what I was wearing was a tank top, and I couldn't wear it. Tomorrow if I wore the same thing he might not feel the same way. Each judgment was a roll of the dice.

"So what am I supposed to do?" I was growing more frustrated with each passing minute. What was I going to have to do, drive all the way back to the motel to change my shirt while Victor agonized about what had happened to me?

"I don't know. You have something in your car you could put over it?"

"No, it's ninety degrees out. Why would I?"

"Well, I'm sorry, Miss, you'll have to get something. Please step aside."

I moved to the side and let the next person sign in, thinking the quickest thing would be to go to a nearby mall and buy something, when a woman on line said, "I have a sweater in my car if you'd like to borrow it." Despite how hot it would be, I was so grateful that I thanked her profusely and said I would. Five minutes later she was back from her car handing me a geranium red acrylic sweater. Thanking her again, I told her I'd return it at the end of the visiting hours. "Okay?" I said to the guard wanting to curse him for being so petty.

"Okay," he said and finally processed me.

As I sat and watched the door, my rancor subsided. It took Victor a while to arrive, and when he finally burst through the door we hugged joyously. "What's with this sweater? It's so hot."

I told him about the guard calling my shirt a tank top. "I'm sorry that happened to you, but now you've seen what most people never get to see and don't understand about Corrections, how arbitrary and bizarre it is. How can such actions teach those who already are devoid of respect for rules why and how rules are important? Like if the guard says 'There's a peacock sitting on your head,' you'd better hope it doesn't shit, or else risk a beating or lockup. They treat everyone like that, even visitors and civilian staff."

"It must be so damn hard to have to tolerate such unfair treatment. I'm furious, and this is one petty incident."

"You can't take it personally or seriously. You just have to yes them to death and forget about it. Otherwise you make yourself sick. You try to obey the rules the best you can, but expect that these guys are going to make it really difficult for you."

"Victor, it's almost as if they want to reduce you and anyone connected with you to a subhuman level. What's that supposed to correct?" I shook my head.

He smiled and kissed me on the nose. "Come on, let's get something cool to drink. You're gonna need it."

We got sodas and took seats near the wall. I couldn't help but notice that many of the inmates and their guests stared at each other lustfully. Victor leaned forward, took my hands, and I felt myself start to sweat. Would we eventually be surreptitiously groping at each other as appeared to be the practice? "What do people do about making love?" I asked softly.

He paused and answered, "Where there's a will there's a way." And then he added, "What are you doing Columbus Day weekend?"

"I don't know. Why?"

"Can I entice you to spend it here at Chez Victor?"

"You know I'll be here at least two out of the three days."

"I mean overnight.'

"Overnight? What do you mean?"

"I'll tell you more as soon as I can."

"Victor, you don't know how much I want to spend a night with you." We stared into each other's eyes; my head started to swim, and my fingertips felt electrified.

"I'm working on it," he said quietly.

"Well, that certainly is mysterious."

"For now, let's just be happy we're together."

Victor stood up. "Denise, I'll be right back. I need to use the bathroom. By the way, did you know I'm considered a third gender? Look at how the bathroom doors are labeled."

I looked at the doors. "Men and Women. So?"

"You forgot one." He pointed to a door at the other end of the room which said *Inmates*. "We're not considered men in the eyes of Corrections."

"Why do they do that?"

"Oh, supposedly they don't want us going into the bathroom with visitors. They feel we can exchange clothes or contraband more easily which, of course, is ridiculous. If you brought me contraband or drugs you could give it to me right now, and I could walk right into the inmates' bathroom and stick it up my butt. In fact, this way it's easier because if they saw an inmate and a visitor walk together into the bathroom you can be sure a guard would be following close behind. This way there's no suspicion."

I slowly shook my head. "It's right out of a Kafka story."

"It's worse. You know, two guys did escape once. Their visitors brought them women's clothing which they changed into and walked right out with the visitors."

"How did that happen?"

"The officer that was on, although new, had already adopted the 'don't-fraternize-with-inmates' attitude and was typically hostile toward inmates. He looked at their forged passes without looking at the men. Deciding the passes were okay, he let them through. The guard who used to be on visiting room duty treated us like people, like individuals. He would sit and talk with inmates and their wives. These guys could never have gotten past him because he would have looked at their faces, not just at their passes."

"What a crazy system."

"You're telling me." He kissed me on the top of the head and walked away.

Despite the usual sadness I experienced upon leaving Victor, on this day I was also vastly relieved to get that cloying, red sweater off my sweating body. Back at the Terrace I got into my purple and black bathing suit, gratified that someone had had the sense to make a two-piece that covers the stomach but is high enough on the legs to flatter narrow hips. Upon diving into the Terrace pool and shaking the water out of my eyes and ears when I surfaced, I understood the meaning of the cliche, high on life. In contrast to the burning sun and humid air, the coolness of the water in the turquoise pool was spectacular. I felt so alive as I treaded water and stared at the woods in the distance. There was nowhere I would rather have been, knowing Victor was down the road, and I had nothing to do but swim and daydream about the man with whom I was falling in love.

After reading the local paper and taking a nap, I got in the car and headed to Petit Chateau, an old stone inn in Stone Ridge. It was weird passing the prison on the way there and thinking about Victor being inside. I fantasized about the possibility of helping Victor over the wall. Arriving at the restaurant, I was given a small table and ordered a glass of wine. I looked around at my surroundings. The inn was charming and atmospheric with a flagstone floor, stone walls, and a wood-burning fireplace that would be cozy when lit. I imagined what it would be like if Victor were there with me. Would he like sitting in an inn like this? Would we really have as much in common as we were now saying we did? I was willing to gamble that we did. But here I was in love and alone. Was it a fear of commitment because of my parents' volatile marriage that made loving someone at a distance more comfortable? I couldn't be sure of the cause, but I was sure that I was becoming more and more in love with Victor. If, in fact, I was afraid of a committed relationship, I would certainly have plenty of time to ease my way into this one. But no matter how long it took, I now suspected that this was the man with whom I wanted to spend the rest of my life.

The rest of my vacation flew by. Each day I awoke around 7:30 A.M., drove up the street for coffee, pastry, and the newspaper, which I would enjoy as I sat on a bench on the grounds of the Terrace. Except for a couple of brief late afternoon thunderstorms, the weather was brilliant, matching my mood. Each day I went and sat with Victor in that room where we talked, held hands, and savored every moment, drinking in the knowledge we were gaining about each other. Intoxicated on the newness of love, we parted each day with a bittersweet mixture of feelings until the last day when we knew it would be at least a week until I was back.

"Your mailbox should be overflowing," Victor said in an effort to make me feel better. "I've continued to write you every day even though you've been here."

"What could you possibly have to say in a letter after we've talked all day?"

"I'll always have things to say to you."

I felt a lump in my throat. "It's really hard to leave you."

"Denise, I feel the same way but I can't stand to see you so sad. It reminds me of once when my cousin Marc was six years old and he came to visit. When it was time to leave he started crying and screaming, 'I won't leave you here. I won't go without you.' His parents told me he had nightmares for days after."

I looked at Victor. He had tears in his eyes, and I knew my own mirrored his.

"Oh, Victor how sad."

"Sweetheart, I told you this wasn't going to be easy. Remember, I said prison relationships can be very difficult and painful. I want you to think about that."

I smiled. "What is there to think about? I'm already committed."

Victor put his hand on my hair, stroking it gently. "I hear you, Denise, but you still have a choice, and with each day that goes by, the choice will get harder and harder. As we grow closer, this whole thing," he gestured to indicate the prison, "will become more offensive and oppressive to you, and seeing how they treat me will really hurt you at times."

I nodded, not trusting myself to speak. He went on. "The irrationality of the rules, the randomness of clemency, work release, and parole means there are no guarantees," he said. "Even when my time is up it doesn't mean I'll get out. Loving me means you'll be infuriated as you see the travesty that passes for justice around here. Not to mention the simple fact of our separation, not being able to see or speak to me when you want, not being able to do and share things with me.... Think about it long and hard."

"But I love you. What am I supposed to do, just put that aside and pretend we never met?"

"I love you, too," he whispered.

The loudspeaker crackled, and a voice announced, "Five minutes left to visiting hours. I repeat, five more minutes."

We spent those last minutes comforting each other and embracing. "One day we'll be taking vacations together," I said.

"I hope so," Victor held me tighter. "Anyway, these days have meant so much to me."

"And me," I whispered back.

"I feel so protective of you. If anything happened to you my life would be over."

"Shh, let's not talk like that."

"I'll speak to you later, sweetheart. Get home safe."

And then I was back in the car, tears in my eyes spilling down my cheeks, driving south on Route 209, knowing I would not see Victor again until the following week.

CHAPTER

SIX

IN NAPANOCH

During the week, on the days I wasn't working as a psychotherapist at the clinic in Brooklyn or in my new and fledgling private practice, I had to be creative to make ends meet. I got some free-lance word-processing work, and I arranged my patients' appointments so I could have at least one whole weekday free to go upstate. During the week, there were always fewer visitors to the prison than on weekends which made my time with Victor a little more private. Even though I tried to return to the city by five-thirty or six o'clock, I was usually so drained by the long trip and all the pent-up feelings being with Victor unleashed that all I was motivated to do was bask in my feelings, daydream, and await Victor's call. However, this week had been an especially heavy one workwise so my next visit to Napanoch was the following Saturday, the first time I was there on a weekend.

What a difference between weekday and weekend. Even though I had gotten up at 5:30 A.M. and was on the road by 6:30 A.M., there was already a crowd of women and children waiting at the prison door when I got there. They all seemed to know each other and had staked out their places in line like homesteaders; I had the sense that these women would defend their spots with as much, if not more, rigor than the settlers of the old West. I claimed my territory at the end of the line, then became aware that there were women waiting in cars though their places on line were known by all the regulars. I looked around. Most of the women had more than one child or baby to whom they barked, "Shut up" and "What did I tell you?" Many of them smoked ferociously, taking long powerful drags on lipstick-stained cigarettes, and some of them looked as though they might have done time themselves with their spandex clothes, tattoos, and dyed, teased hair. It didn't take me long to realize that when you have many people in front of you and limited time, you become feral.

After a nervous half hour, the guards finally opened the heavy black iron door, and we all filed in and signed the list of visitors. I was number seventeen. Then everyone waited some more as the guards called people's names from the list. Once they called my name I went up to the counter, showed my driver's license, signed the log, and handed over the stuff I was bringing in with me, including lipstick, a pen, my wallet, glasses, tissues, and keys. What they didn't get to see was the three-inch-square marble coffee cake I had in my pocket. No food of any type, including gum and cough drops, could be given directly to an inmate. But this certainly didn't stop people. Victor told me there were women who smuggled in Big Macs between their breasts, and home-cooked chickens and ribs under large flowing skirts and blouses. It was absurd that the guards looked through my wallet when I could have hidden any number of things on my body.

The processing finished, I was once again buzzed through the double doors and into the visiting room which already was more crowded than I was used to. I was beginning to feel less conspicuous and self-conscious and more like I belonged there, as bizarre as that was. With disappointment, I noticed that the seats next to the wall were almost all taken, and I sat where I knew I would be the first person Victor saw when he walked through the door. When he finally did, we beamed at each other and embraced.

"Hey, sweetheart, you look beautiful. But then you always look beautiful." He leaned back and looked me over again. From the beginning, I was eager to believe Victor when he said loving or complimentary things to me, though how could I not help but wonder whether he was sincere or had not been close to a woman for a long time. Nonetheless, he always made me feel beautiful, so it was easy to believe him when he said things that validated me.

"Let's go out to the yard. Are you thirsty, hungry? Maybe we should get something now before it gets too crowded by the machines."

With arms around each other's shoulders we walked to the machines. I gave Victor the square of cake I'd smuggled in and we fed it to each other on the line. Being close to Victor like that was always electric. Maybe because we could not be physically intimate in any real way, the intimation of it was striking. Feeling his skin, his muscles, even his clothing, and breathing in the scent of his skin and hair was incredibly erotic. By the time we got to the vending machines all the desire I felt for him was overwhelming. As we usually did, we waited on line in an embrace and made small talk. I told him about the trip up—uneventful—and getting into the prison—absurd. Together we marveled over the Kafkaesque nature of the prison experience.

"Have you become used to it?" I asked him.

"Denise, I will never be used to this. I tolerate it; I know what to expect, but used to it, no. On any given day I can be reminded of what a bizarre and cruel place prison is. It's not anything you ever get used to."

"How have you been able to stand it?"

"I've had no choice. It's like what happened when I was being sentenced. The judge said, 'I hereby sentence you to life imprisonment for the murder of so and so. Do you have anything to say?' I replied, 'Your honor, I can't do that kind of time when I didn't do it.' And in this seemingly fatherly way, he said, 'That's all right, son, I understand. Just do the best you can. However much you can do, that'll be just fine.'"

"He really said that?" I was appalled. "What did he mean? That if you couldn't do it you could kill yourself?"

"I suppose so. Either that or go crazy."

"God, how could a judge who is supposed to be just say something like that? It's so abusive, making you believe he's being kind and understanding while in reality he's telling you to kill yourself."

"That's the system for you. Once you're branded an inmate that's it. You're the lowest form of scum on the earth. All that Christian dogma of forgiveness everyone always preaches goes right out the window."

We got our ginger ale and cookies and headed toward the door of the yard where the August morning sun was intense. The din of the visiting room had doubled over the last ten minutes, and stepping out into the yard was a relief. It was a grassy expanse about one-quarter the size of a football field with several picnic tables, a few of which had faded umbrellas.

"Let's grab that table," Victor said, leading me by the hand to the one vacant table which had an umbrella. "It gets real hot out here under the sun."

And then, more shock as we sat side by side on the bench. We had never been able to sit this close, with our thighs touching. It felt at once so natural and, at the same time, almost too intoxicating to tolerate. No wonder couples around us resorted to groping each other or worse in public. Victor tilted the umbrella to provide us with a circle of shade. "This also gives us a modicum of privacy." He nodded toward the several windows on the wall in front of us. "You can't see them easily because of the glare, but there are guys in a lot of those windows. They have nothing better to do than sit there and watch the visitors in the visiting yard."

"I guess they don't see too many women."

"Oh, we see women all the time. Plenty of women work in the prison, but watching couples go at it is like porno movies for some of them."

"Do inmates hit on the female staff?"

Victor leaned back to look at me. "Is the Pope Catholic? Some of these guys are so sex-starved they'll hit on the seventy-year-old nurse who looks like their grandmother. The thing is, all a female has to do is be polite to them and they think she's coming on to them. Some of them are really desperate, but I think they'd probably be just as desperate if they were in the street."

I looked up at the windows. Beyond the umbrella, barely

visible in the glaring sun, were faces in the lower corners of the windows. I felt like I was on display.

"Just ignore them," Victor said.

"What else can we do?"

"Nothing."

He changed the subject. "This building behind us is the O.M., the officers' mess hall."

I turned to see a single-story extension of the building, with windows covered by shades.

"That one down there is a housing unit, and behind it there is the auditorium where we see movies."

"You see movies?"

"Sure."

"Recent ones?"

"Well, as soon as they're out on tape. Before videos we'd see a movie as soon as the local movie theater was done with it. The prison leased it from them so the theater made some money off the prison. The prisons make life a lot more lucrative and pleasant for all these little upstate towns. Despite that—and in many cases, I don't blame them—they hate inmates' guts, but a lot of people wouldn't have jobs if it weren't for these prisons. Especially since Cuomo came in and built a lot of new facilities. Prisons are the state's leading industry, and meanwhile the number of inmates, especially repeats, grows and crime is never ending." He looked off in the distance. "Something must be done to change the mind-set of criminals. The question is, what?" He paused and then said as if he didn't want to burden me, "Come on, sweetheart, let's walk."

We left my pen and a pack of tissues on the table and bench to mark it as our spot and, hand in hand, began to walk the perimeter of the yard. A feeling of peace and contentment descended upon me as the sun warmed our bodies and a gentle breeze ruffled our hair. I knew I never wanted to let go of his hand.

"I'll wait for you forever if I have to." I looked at Victor and smiled. We stopped right there and embraced. Victor looked into my eyes.

"Thank you," he whispered. "Hopefully it'll be less than

forever." We continued our stroll. Little kids ran in and out of our path. Instead of being annoyed I patted their heads and joked with them. I had been noticing that I was becoming less angry and more patient with others. Was it being in love, or was it the example set by Victor? He amazed me. I thought someone innocent being locked up all those years would be a raving madman. It boggled my mind that not only was he not, but he was kind, accepting, and good. I often wondered if he were just bottling it all up inside and was saving his rage for some future date when he would explode. Or was he cultivating a serious disease? He seemed too good to be true.

"A penny for your thoughts," he said.

"Oh, my thoughts, they're about you, of course. About how much I admire you for not being angry or bitter."

"Denise, I've been all those things and more. I'm not a saint, so don't idolize me. I have had to learn to live with my fate and to use it to become the best person I can. Do you know the poetry of Richard Lovelace?"

"I don't think I do."

"He was an English poet who was sentenced to prison unfairly by Charles I, and he wrote a love poem to Althea, the woman he left behind:

> "Stone walls do not a prison make,
> Nor iron bars a cage:
> Minds innocent and quiet take
> That for an hermitage.
> If I have freedom in my love,
> And in my soul am free,
> Angels alone, that soar above,
> Enjoy such liberty."

"Lovelace was very Zen," I said, smiling.

We had gone full circle and were back at our table. We decided to sit and walk more later. We were talking quietly when someone came out and yelled, "Click-Click!"

"What's Click-Click?" I asked.

I learned it was picture-taking in the prisons, sponsored by a charitable organization, the Jaycees. Supervised by prison staff and run by inmates, it enabled inmates and their guests to have Polaroid snapshots taken of themselves.

"Would you like to have pictures taken?" Victor asked.

"I'd love to."

"Come on." We walked over to the bottom of the stairs where two inmates sat at a table with a metal box and a receipt book. We paid for two pictures and waited with two other couples for our turn. An inmate, his wife (all the women were called wives whether they were or not), and a little girl with pink ribbons in her hair were now posing by the side of the stairs. On the wall was a realistic mural of a waterfall descending into a pool in shimmering blues, silver, and white. An inmate had painted the mural and pictures were always taken in front of it. Another scene was of a forest.

"This guy must have been really talented," I mused.

"A lot of guys who wind up here discover talents they never knew they had. That's what happens when you've got nothing but time. People on the outside get upset that someone who committed a crime has the opportunity to do something like paint. I understand that prison isn't and shouldn't be a country club, but what they don't realize is that if inmates had had the opportunity to do these things on the outside, a lot of them wouldn't have wound up here in the first place."

"Somehow the ideal of corrections has gone astray. A lot of people don't think criminals can be rehabilitated."

"Never mind *re*habilitated, how about habilitated? In order to re-habilitate there has to be something there to put back. Most of the guys in here come out of such impoverished backgrounds they're not starting with anything. They were never educated, never walked the right path. They've been bad their whole lives, because they were never taught anything else and never felt they had the opportunity for anything else.

"The driving force behind corrections is not trying to change these men so that they will give to rather than destroy society, but to inflict revenge and punishment on them. You went wrong? Well the hell with you, you deserve to die. Or at least spend your life rotting away in a jail cell." He shook his head. "I know better than most that that is the only solution for some who are just too far gone, but I think there has to be a better solution for the others. There has to be a way to reclaim them because the alternative is they'll be back on the streets angrier and meaner than ever. And that's what's happening now."

"Right, and people wonder why there's so much recidivism."

"Clark!" the inmate with the Polaroid camera shouted.

Victor and I walked over and stood in front of the waterfall, putting an arm around each other's backs for our first picture. For the next shot we faced each other, and Victor took my hands. We took the developing prints and returned to our picnic table. The pictures came out really well, especially the profile with us staring amorously into each other's eyes. Victor said he would take them back with him and have copies made through a mail order company.

"I thought you weren't allowed to bring pictures back with you." On a recent visit I had brought Victor a photograph of me which he told me I'd have to mail him because he couldn't take it inside with him.

"We're allowed to bring photographs that are taken by Click-Click. Any others have to go through the package room because they're considered contraband, the same as if you brought me, say, a gun."

"They can't differentiate between a photograph and a gun?"

Victor laughed. "There you go being logical again." He kissed me on the nose. "The rules don't make sense. You know, we're allowed to bring out a closed pack of cigarettes on a visit. It can't be open. And then we can't take it back."

"I can understand not being able to take cigarettes back, but what's the rationale behind not being able to bring out an open pack?"

"Beats me. I guess if the pack were open they'd feel they had to go through it."

"Why? You might smuggle something out to your visitor

in a cigarette? I would think they'd worry about the other way around, that someone on the outside might try to smuggle something back to you."

"I know. It makes no sense. Like them pat-frisking us before we come out on a visit and making us take off our shoes."

"Why is that? In case you're smuggling out a weapon to kill your visitor?"

"Yeah, but they're certainly not gonna find anything with a pat frisk or looking in a shoe. When we come back from a visit we're strip searched."

"Is that as awful as it seems?"

"It's humiliating and degrading, especially when they tell you to bend over and spread 'em."

"What do they think they're going to find in there?"

"Well, to put it bluntly, guys shove drugs up their asses all the time."

"Why don't the guards catch them?"

"Because they don't look that closely."

"I guess if they really looked someone might think they were weird."

Victor laughed again as he stroked my fingers on the table. "That reminds me of something crude but hilarious that once happened." He stopped for a moment before telling me, "Sometimes I'm not sure how much I should tell you, whether the truth may be too offensive for you, and yet I want you to know everything."

"I want to know everything," I said quickly. "And remember, I have worked with the criminally insane. Nobody knows better than I that gallows humor sometimes keeps you sane."

Victor smiled and continued his story. "This old timer named Rosey Stewart was coming back from a visit and was being strip searched. After you've been in the system as long as he had you know the drill, you know what to do, and you do it by rote. So he took off his clothes, ran his fingers through his hair, ran his fingers around his teeth and gums, lifted his tongue, pulled his ears back, lifted his arms to show his armpits...."

"You have to do all that?"

"You never know when someone's gonna hide something behind his ears. So anyway, then Rosey turned around, showed the soles of his feet, wiggled his toes, then he grabbed each cheek of his butt and spread them apart. After that he turned back around and lifted his genitals so Tim Clavin, the guard, could look under his balls. After Rosey did all this, Clavin told him, 'I didn't see nothing, do it again.' So Rosey ran through the whole routine again, and Clavin said, 'No Rosey I didn't see, you got to do it again.' So then Rosey started to smile and he said, 'Wait a minute, I know what you want' and he began to fondle himself until he got hard, and walked around the table toward the guard, saying, 'I know what you want baby' and then the cop started to run. Rosey started to chase him saying, 'Just give me a minute, I know what you want! I know what you want!' Finally, the officer, his face flaming red from embarrassment, yelled across the room to Rosey, "Get dressed and get the hell out of here." The other officers were standing there with their mouths hanging open. They were in such shock that they couldn't even react to stop Rosey from chasing the officer. And you know, the guard never even wrote him up. I guess he was too embarrassed."

I shook my head. "You have to deal with people like that every day? How do you do it?"

He nodded. "Let me tell you, it's difficult. Especially with guards like Clavin who make careers out of messing with people's heads. They get a great charge out of it. Clavin does things like stop you in the hall and ask for your pass. He looks at it, asks you your name and number which are right there on the card. If you say something like 'It's on the card,' he threatens to write you up for disobeying a direct order."

"So you're better off not saying anything."

"The system teaches you to suppress all your thoughts and feelings. You're not supposed to be a human being. And the guards are rewarded for fucking with you if you do express anything. Like Clavin, that guard Rosey chased around, is now a sergeant."

I looked at Victor, shaking my head. "It's really an 'us versus them' mentality."

"That's what makes it so crazy. The criminal justice system would be a lot different if it weren't like that." He paused and looked lovingly at me, realizing I was upset. "Hey, enough about this. Let's talk about you."

We walked to a small patch of grass and sat there. As we touched, our desire mounted. We were dying to lie down in each others' arms; instead we had to make sure to sit upright and not touch each other in any way that might be considered untoward. We had no words to say what we were feeling, and words might have kindled the fire inside us. Instead, our fingers linked, we sat side by side and each time we drew a breath our bodies grew fiery.

At three o'clock an officer announced, "The visiting yard is closed. Everyone has to go inside." The visiting room was so crowded we practically had to yell to make ourselves heard. We sat at one of the tables near the door to the yard and contented ourselves with holding hands and staring into each other's eyes until the warning came that visiting hours were almost over.

"Remember, we're going to be together for a night soon," Victor said as we stood and prepared to leave.

"What night?"

"Ah hah, what night, the lady wants to know." He put his arms around me. "Thank you for coming today, Denise."

"Changing the subject, are we?"

"What subject?"

We were interrupted by the blaring public address system: "Visiting hours are now over. All inmates report to the back." A kiss and a hug later, I was walking through the double doors, as always, alone.

On my way back to New York City, I reflected on Victor's ability to handle his fate. To be imprisoned unfairly for most of his adult life—how could anyone stand it? What would I do in those circumstances—kill myself, I supposed, or go crazy or strike out at everyone around me. From where did Victor get his strength of character, his sense of humor, his calmness in the face of such horror? I thought of the poem he'd recited, of the college degrees he was amassing, of our growing love for each other. Thoughts swirled in my consciousness as I drove through the darkening night.

At home I found two envelopes in the mailbox, both of which had colorful cartoon creatures drawn on them with dialogue bubbles containing words of love. I didn't open them immediately, preferring first to go through my ritual of changing my clothes, pouring a glass of white wine, then lying down to read his letters. I opened the thinner envelope first, and read: "You are cordially invited to a slumber party at Chez Victor October 10-12, 1988. Dress informal. RSVP." Beautifully drawn hearts and flowers adorned the paper. I drank some of the wine and looked at the long, graceful philodendron vines that hung in the window like a curtain. What could this mean? Victor had alluded to some sort of overnight visit, and now he actually had a date? I knew they had such things as conjugal visits for wives and even family visits where an inmate's children or parents could visit, but certainly I didn't fall into any of these categories. I wondered what he had in mind as I opened the other envelope. Perhaps the explanation would be in there. It wasn't, and I knew I'd have to remain in suspense until the next day. When he called Sunday night he was equally cryptic and said he would discuss it with me in person.

"You mean I have to wait a week or more to find out what this overnight visit is all about?"

"Yes, my dear, but trust me, it will be just fine. You'll find the accommodations suitable and the company, I hope, scintillating."

"You have more than piqued my curiosity, Victor. You are driving me crazy." I smiled.

"Good. I can hear you smiling. I like that. I hope this will keep you smiling through the week."

"As long as you are in my life, I'll always be smiling."

"Me, too, sweetheart. Me, too."

CHAPTER
SEVEN

Roses for Remembrance

The week crawled by. One night, I was home in my typical position: prone on the living room couch, reading some case histories. The 5,000-BTU air conditioner was doing a poor job of cooling the room from the hundred-degree heat wave bearing down on Manhattan. But it sure beat an open window and a fan, not only because of the heat but because of the noise coming from the next block, which sounded as if it came from next door, of Spanish rhythms blasting. Closing the window and putting on the air conditioner barely kept out the beat. In fact, no matter what I did to shut out the sound, the incessant beat of Latin percussion, guitar, and vocals pounded in my brain. Occasionally I was in the mood to hear it, but the vast majority of time it generated in me fantasies of violent revenge on that stereo.

I tried to focus my attention on the clients about whom I was reading, but every few minutes I realized that I was staring at the ceiling dreaming of Victor. Suddenly the phone rang. Normally I would let the answering machine get it, but because it might be Victor calling, I jumped up and said, "Hello."

"Is this Ms. Denise Beck?"

"Yes."

"This is Grace Florist. Will you be home in an hour or so?"

"Yes."

"Good. Do you live at...." The woman proceeded to recite my address which I confirmed. "See you in an hour."

I walked over to the window. Elongated raindrops streaked the glass like accent marks. Above the pulsing Latin music I could hear faint thunder. I was annoyed that I couldn't open the window and hear the melodic rhythm of the rain on the window, or feel the warm gusts. That florist, I thought as I watched the storm clouds, would be coming here in a major downpour. She hadn't said where from, and an even more interesting question was, who was sending me flowers? My first thought was Victor, but I dropped that quickly. How could Victor send flowers from prison? Who else was there? I knew it couldn't be my ex-boyfriend Greg; even when our relationship was at its best, sending flowers was not the kind of thing he would have done, especially on a day that wasn't a special occasion. Maybe I had a secret admirer.

Resuming my position on the couch, I began to review the case I was working on again, but after reading a sentence four times without knowing what it said, I conceded my mind was elsewhere. How would I pass the time until the flowers arrived? Well, I could try to sleep, but that was probably impossible. I could watch television, but I knew I couldn't concentrate on the usual pap. I could write to my beloved. I could meditate, I could do exercise. There were many things; there were people I could call. Then how come I didn't feel like doing anything more than lolling on a stupid couch? Was I lazy not in the common sense but because my fantasies were so consuming? How much of my life had I lived thinking, imagining, and visualizing? Way too much. And in a way, that's what I was doing with Victor. Perhaps that's why the relationship was not as aversive to me as it would be to many people. I had a great capacity for living in the mind, if not an aversion to actually doing things.

Tired of psychoanalyzing myself, I flipped on Channel 13. A concert from Lincoln Center came into view and blotted out the Latin rhythms from the street. The glamour and glory of artists who played music which satisfied the soul created a wonderful world, I thought. Did Victor like classical music? Did he ever get the opportunity to listen to it? I imagined him and me walking hand in hand by the fountain at Lincoln Center and staring up at the Marc Chagalls and chandeliers in the Metropolitan Opera House. Victor, of course, would turn out to be mad about Beethoven, as I was, and we would breeze along in that rarified world together. Somehow I knew, or was it another fantasy, that despite his having grown up in the ghetto and spending his young adult life in the swamps and jungles of Vietnam and the dank dungeons of New York State penitentiaries, he would have this exquisite sensitivity to art of all kinds, as well as impeccable taste which, of course, I'd be the one to determine.

The phone rang again. It was the same woman.

"I'm at Ninety-Sixth and Broadway, just got off the West Side Highway. You're near here, right?"

"Yes." Since when did women start making flower deliveries? And did they usually call en route? My curiosity was piqued, to say the least.

Fifteen minutes later the doorman rang up. "Grace Flowers."

Then the apartment doorbell rang, and when I opened the door, a heavy-set, caramel-skinned woman dressed fashionably in a black suit peered out from behind an enormous bouquet of roses. She certainly did not look like the typical delivery boy.

"Hi, are you Denise Beck?"

I nodded, and, holding out the three-foot-high bouquet, she said, "Here, enjoy." I took it, closing my eyes as I breathed in the fragrance. When I opened them, the woman was gone. I looked down the hall and saw her standing at the elevator, smiling. Somehow I sensed that I was not supposed to ask her any questions or even give her a tip. I watched, speechless, as she called back, "Take care" and disappeared into the elevator.

"Thank you," I finally called out though she was gone.

I brought the vase of magnificent pink, yellow, and peach roses in and set it on the coffee table. Pulling out the little card attached to the cellophane wrapping, I read, "To my darling

Denise. All my love, Victor." I couldn't believe it. How could he have done this? Even more fabulous than the logistics was that he thought of it at all; he must have remembered the time I happened to mention that I adore roses and that a fantasy of mine was to have a rose garden. No man I had ever been with was that thoughtful, attentive, or kind. I was stunned and humbled at the same time. I had never been one of those women who expected nor wanted men to shower me with gifts. Now, here I was accepting an extravagant bouquet of flowers from a man, and he was in prison.

That I could not call him to thank him, no less be with him, was torture. I had a sense of deep longing, even so it was not nearly as painful as the longing that had existed before Victor came into my life. For the current ache was overshadowed by love and joy. I took off the cellophane and touched the rose petals as if they were Victor's flesh; breathing in the rose essence, I reveled in the heady fragrance. Then I remembered the "flower deliverer" and wondered just who she was. Luckily I only had a day to wait to speak to Victor. Having specific calling days not only gave structure to our relationship but also to my feelings; at least with Victor that awful anxiety that came with wondering when your man was going to call was alleviated.

The next evening, I came home, turned on the air conditioner, and sat back with my glass of wine and a letter from Victor. Before opening the letter, I stared at the front of the envelope on which he had written "Photo enclosed—please hand cancel." Hand cancel? I had never seen that particular message before. I wondered if there was such a thing as hand canceling, and, if there was, would the postal workers actually honor such a request? Or was this something that they used to do when Victor first went away, but now many years later it was as obsolete as phonographs? I pressed the edges of the envelope with my fingers; it felt stiff like two Polaroids. Since meeting Victor I was amazed at the number of photographs he was able to have taken of himself. I imagined the Click-Click people perpetually floating around the prison with Polaroid cameras. Perhaps it was Victor's influence and popularity which enabled him to take advantage of such opportunities. Whatever the explanation, I was pleased to find this added surprise in the mail.

When I opened the envelope, the loving words on the inside made me gasp. As the blood rose up through my chest into my neck, I unfolded the several-paged letter and saw the two pictures. Victor was sitting on the grass, squinting into the sun. Words of passion were written on the white border of the picture. Oh, if only I could dive into the picture and be next to him on that grass. But did I really want to be in a prison yard? No, as long as I was fantasizing, I might as well make the setting somewhere out in the country, or perhaps a tropical beach. I wondered if Victor had ever been to the Caribbean. Not that I'd spent so much time there, but I loved the area. Before I knew it, I was deep in fantasy, imagining us together in Aruba, or perhaps Martinique, or Jamaica. When would that be possible? God, what would I do until then?

The letter was full of news of his daily doings as well as his love for me and his hopes and dreams for the future, our future. In the beginning Victor had only written of the present. It was as if he could not bear to plan what might never be, but he said I had changed all that. I could only hope the change was more than our fantasy. As I looked around the living room, I imagined how it would look to Victor. I assumed he would like the books and plants and my choice of artwork as much as I did. But then again, even if I lived in a stark white room with folding chairs and a cot it would beat what he was accustomed to! Now he was living in an eight-by-eight cell that had a door with a small window in it. There was just enough room in there for the bed, a two-foot-high locker, and the metal toilet/sink unit. Many guys put up shelves, though it was against the rules. They stayed until a guard with an attitude came in with a hammer and smashed them up. If the guard were calm enough to say, "You know you're not supposed to have those," the inmate would say, "Hey these were here when I got here" and hope that the officer would let it go.

I looked at my watch: 7:20 P.M. He was due to call at 7:30, though as he reminded me almost every time we spoke, there was never a guarantee that he would call at a specific time. "Don't get nervous if you don't hear from me exactly at seven-thirty or any other time I say I'm going to call," he had warned me. But I believed Victor could do anything, and if he said he'd call at 7:30 P.M., well, it was highly unlikely that anything would prevent him from doing so. The procedure was that he had to go out to the yard and get on line. He could never be sure that this would happen when it was supposed to. So far, however, he had been pretty consistent in calling when he said he would.

At 7:29 P.M. the phone rang. "This is a collect call from Victor Clark at a correctional facility. Will you accept the charges?"

"You bet I will!" I was already thinking that if I had to work extra hours to pay for my inflated phone bill I would do so and happily: a small price to pay for love.

"How is my love?" he said softly. It was so good to hear his voice.

"I'm happy now. How are you?"

"Much better now."

"Why, is anything wrong?"

"Other than being locked up in a maximum security prison? No," he joked.

"Hey, I received a beautiful gift last night from you."

"From me? How could you receive a beautiful gift from me?"

"That's what I'd like to know."

"And what was the gift?" he said playfully.

"Oh, listen to you acting like you don't know."

"Hmm."

"The roses," I said. "Two dozen gorgeous pastel roses. Oh, Victor, I love them."

"I'm so glad. I'd do anything to make you happy."

"Likewise. Thank you so much."

"My pleasure, sweetheart."

"But how could you manage to do that from where you are?"

"Ah," he said quietly, "where there's a will there's a way to do anything. Remember I told you that."

"Do you know the woman who delivered them?"

"What did she look like?"

I described the deliverer of the roses. Victor laughed. "It's my first cousin, Loretha. She's more like a sister to me. She drove all the way up there in the rain to deliver them."

"She's so good." I felt gratified to know that there were people looking out for Victor.

"Yeah, she's stuck by me through thick and thin. You two will have to meet for real one of these days."

A few weeks later Loretha and I did get to meet, in a way that was not unlike someone's parent checking out a prospective suitor for their son or daughter. Over a bottle of Chablis in a dimly lit, incense-fragrant Indian restaurant in downtown Brooklyn, we exchanged information about each other. "You know, Victor was with me at my apartment the night they say he shot that man," she said. We both had tears in our eyes, thinking how much time had been lost, how much pain inflicted and still to be felt because others had lied. Though we recognized the differences in our lifestyles and backgrounds, she a wife and mother living in Brooklyn, me a single Manhattanite, we came away from the dinner having formed an indelible bond. Considering her close relationship with Victor, I was glad to have her approval.

CHAPTER
EIGHT

BREAK-IN

The mountain rose outside the window of McDonald's as if it had been built there like the town nestled at its base. There was a safe feeling generated by this stalwart monolith, knowing nothing would budge it. On this morning, however, nothing could anchor me or calm my nervousness. I had barely slept the night before, in anticipation of this morning when I was going to break into the maximum security state penitentiary. There, accompanied by Victor's aunt Hattie, I would try to pass myself off as Victor's nineteen-year-old sister in order to have a trailer visit with him.

This was what Victor had been planning for months. Apparently, inmates and their loved ones did it all the time. Each inmate had a list of relatives who were approved to come on a family overnight visit. However, if you checked the identities of people in those trailers, you'd find many individuals related by neither blood nor marriage. I was particularly uptight, because the guard would have to be either completely color blind or else dazed to mistake me for Victor's sister who was both a different race and twenty years younger than I was.

"They don't care. As long as you have the proper identification, that's all they care about," Victor said.

"So you mean when they look at Charlene's birth certificate and see the year of her birth as nineteen years ago and they look at me, they won't question it? I mean," I said slowly, "I know I look young for my age, but this is stretching it."

"Sweetheart, believe me, they won't even read the birth certificate. Only the name. And her work ID card. Just make sure you can sign her name the way it is on the card. Believe me, I wouldn't have you do this if I wasn't sure it would work."

We had had this conversation several times in the weeks after I received the Chez Victor invitation. I also asked once again what would happen if we got caught.

"Nothing serious," he said. "They'll send you home and deny me trailer visits for a while."

I had visions of them dragging me inside the prison and throwing me into a cell.

"Don't worry," Victor said, teasing me. "They'll take you to Bedford Hills, the women's prison."

"That makes me feel much better."

Talking about the Columbus Day weekend had been a favorite activity of ours in letters, on the phone, and in person. We even decided upon our menu: Chinese food one night and on the next a special dish that Victor was eager to make for me, the ingredients of which he wouldn't reveal in advance. Sitting in McDonald's with Victor's cousin Loretha and his aunt Hattie that Saturday morning, I wondered what we would do with all this Chinese food if they didn't let me in.

"Don't be so nervous, Denise," Loretha said. "If Victor said it will be all right, it will. I'm sure he knows what he's talking about. You think he'd drag us all the way up here if he didn't think there was a good chance you'd get in?"

"Yeah." Hattie shook her head and patted my hand. "And me come all the way from Rochester?" His aunt Hattie was the one who was making this all possible because even passing myself off as Victor's sister wouldn't have done the trick, as anyone under twenty-one had to be accompanied by an adult. Victor had talked a lot about Hattie and convinced me that because of Hattie's loving personality I wouldn't feel awkward with her presence at our first really intimate time with each other. Hattie truly was the jolly, plump, good-natured aunt who, without children of her own, lavished generosity and good spirits on those she loved. I knew this as soon as she had hugged me at the United Airlines gate the day before.

Wearing a daffodil yellow suit with a matching headband in her shiny black bouffant hair, she was immediately likeable. After several more hugs, she and Loretha had caught up on news of mutual acquaintances while we drove back to Manhattan in Loretha's Toyota. They were both to spend the night in my apartment in preparation for leaving at the crack of dawn the next morning. The night with them reminded me of a teenage slumber party, complete with mattresses on the floor and punchy laughter. However, their laughter was truly from the gut; mine was a nervous tee-hee, part of my concerted effort to be in the here and now and not worry about the next day. The problem was, I was so scared Victor's and my visit wasn't going to happen. After all this planning and anticipation, not to mention highly charged sexual tension, the thought of something going wrong was uppermost in my mind. But I tried to join in the merriment, not wanting to seem neurotic to these women whose opinions mattered to Victor.

"Anybody want anything else? I'm getting another cup of coffee." Loretha lifted herself out of the blue and red formica seat/table unit.

"No thanks," Hattie and I both said and looked at our watches. We were scheduled to be at the prison at ten. We had killed an hour but it still wasn't quite nine. After Loretha had her coffee and a piece of apple pie and Hattie told her, joking, "You need that as badly as I do," we decided to head over to the facility and hang out in the parking lot if they wouldn't let us wait inside.

The trailer area was located off to the left of the main buildings. On more than one occasion when visiting Victor, I had seen cars go off in that direction, opposite the way I went, and wondered where they were going. Now I would see for myself, though there wasn't much to see. Beside a small parking lot there was a grassy area littered with rusty farm equipment and a low, one-story whitewashed building. The mountains loomed in the distance; above them the sky looked like dust balls.

"How do I look?" I asked Loretha and Hattie. "Not a day over nineteen, right?" I tried to joke.

I had fixed my hair in braids as if that more youthful style would get me in if the guards had any doubts!

"Victor's robbing the cradle," Hattie said, smiling. "I'm really gonna have to supervise you two."

"Assuming we get in," I said nervously.

We went into the white building and sat on a long, narrow bench. I resisted the temptation to believe that the guard standing behind the counter knew I was an imposter. *I am Victor's light-skinned sister*, I told myself, and Hattie's niece, despite the lack of resemblance. There was one other family there, a woman of about twenty with a blond little girl about five years old. After a while, more visitors came in, and soon it was crowded. I was growing more shaky by the minute; my stomach growled as if it had taken on the burden of anxiety for the rest of my body. After what seemed like hours, the guard called out, "Line up in the order in which you got here and have your ID's ready." The moment of truth at last.

Loretha kissed us both. "Now you have a great time with your brother," she said to me with a wink. "I'll see you Sunday."

With Charlene's birth certificate and employee ID card becoming soggy in my sweaty hand, I stood behind Hattie, deriving comfort from her being older and larger than me, as if I really were a child in her care. I surreptitiously looked once again at the signature on the ID card and hoped I'd reproduce it as well as I had at home after dozens of practice attempts. Finally we were in front of the guard, who, unlike most of his blue-clad counterparts, was wearing a mild grayish-beige uniform which made him seem less threatening. Pushing a log book in front of us, he told us, "Sign your names, addresses, and who you are visiting, and then hand me your ID's." Careful not to look at him, I signed the faked signature; happily, it came out like the one on the ID card. Contrary to what I had feared, I did not blank out on Charlene's Rochester address. So far so good. Assuming the guard did not want to engage in further conversation or look too closely at me, I was in.

We were directed to take our bags to the other side of the room where we waited for the other families to be processed. For what seemed like the first time in days, I let out a deep breath and grinned at Hattie. Suddenly the smell of the Chinese food she was carrying was appetizing instead of sickening.

"How you feeling, Charlene?" Hattie smiled.

"I can't wait to see my brother."

"I'll bet." Her eyes twinkled.

Suddenly a state van appeared out of nowhere. An officer jumped out, swung open the door, and told us, "Load your stuff." We and the other families put in our things, and with all of us packed in, we proceeded along a road which ran next to the wall, then went around a turn and stopped in front of an iron gate set into the wall. Right over the gate a guard sat poised in a gun tower. In fact, there was a guard in a gun tower above every gate in the wall. Though the sight made me tremble, I told myself it made sense since an inmate could theoretically make a run for it through one of those gates.

We sat in eager anticipation as a corrections officer searched under the van. Victor later informed me that this was standard procedure for vehicles entering or leaving the compound, making sure that no person or thing was being smuggled in or out. As I often did when visiting there, I had the uneasy feeling that I had broken the law or done something wrong. Actually, in this case I had! But I did not care. I was joyous at the prospect of spending almost two whole days and nights with the man I loved.

The gate slid open, and the van slowly proceeded into a small enclosed area where five men in green prison garb were standing in front of a semicircle of trailers. My heart surged as I saw Victor grinning in front of trailer Two. Hattie and I gathered our bags and made our way out of the van. Victor was allowed to help us.

"Hey, Sis, give me a hug," he said loudly, and then in my ear he whispered, "Sweetheart, you made it. God, I'm so glad you're here."

After he and Hattie hugged, we all carried the food and our bags to trailer Two.

"Home sweet home," Victor said. "This is it for two days."

The trailer had a small faux wood-paneled living room with an early American style pull-out sofa, a table, television set, and easy chair. The kitchenette was off to the side as was the bathroom. A small bedroom was on the other side, with the same phoney wood paneling. Victor brought my bags in there and left Hattie's on the couch where she would be sleeping. Standing next to the bed we embraced and began kissing, then stopped as Hattie called out something which was unintelligible to us.

"We'll come back," Victor whispered in response to my look of interrupted passion.

Hattie looked at us when we emerged and, smiling, said, "Hey, you didn't have to come out of there. I just wanted to know where the coffeepot was."

"Over here," Victor said, seeming to derive pleasure from his role as host and opening a cabinet. "Who wants coffee or tea?"

Both Hattie and I said we'd like coffee, and I went to the kitchen area and started putting away groceries. Transferring the milk, eggs, vegetables, and other items from shopping bags to the refrigerator and cabinets, I became aware of feeling elated, that sense that I was doing just what I should be doing, that there was nowhere else I'd rather be. I chuckled out loud. Victor looked lovingly at me.

"I feel so relieved, so happy that they actually let me in."

"I feel the same way," he said. "But they kind of intentionally look the other way. I mean, they know you're not really my sister. But I guess they figure, if we keep 'em happy they'll give us less trouble."

"That seems pretty enlightened."

"Yeah, that's real nice," Hattie said.

"They're not this lenient in all facilities," Victor said. "In some of them they actually take pictures of your eligible family members when you first get to the facility and then match the visitor to the picture when they come for a trailer visit."

"I'm sure glad they don't do that here. I wouldn't be here if they did." I truly was grateful, as Victor and I wouldn't be able to be alone together for years, unless of course we found a way to get married. But a prison wedding? Was that really something I was prepared for? Although in the back of my mind I felt I knew the answer, I quickly pushed the thought out of my head to concentrate on the here and now.

"Why don't you sit down and rest. I'll finish unpacking," Victor told me. "Being in a place like this that's like a home with a kitchen and a living room and no guards breathing down my neck every minute, with people I love, this is like heaven to me. Just to be able to serve you coffee, bring you what you want, it's really special for me."

Victor was true to his word: he waited on Hattie and me all weekend, and if this were a treat for him, it was also quite a treat for me. I had never been with a man who wanted to take care of me. They had all had the attitude that I could take care of myself. Now here was someone very different who wanted to care for others even in an atmosphere of repression and rigidity. The concept was fascinating, not to mention seductive; it felt great having someone consider my needs and say, "You just sit and let me bring it to you," or "Don't worry, I'll take care of that. You just enjoy yourself."

Sinking back in the couch next to Hattie, I watched Victor and undressed him with my eyes. I couldn't wait to be with him; it was amazing and impressive to me, the will power that he had. All around, Victor presented himself as a disciplined man, a species I was not familiar with, beginning with my father, who had been charming, childlike, and alcoholic. Victor brought over two cups of coffee.

"Say, why don't you two drink yours in the other room? I need a little peace and quiet out here so I can take a nap," Hattie winked at us. Victor and I looked at each other. "Okay," Victor said. "Come on." With cups in hand, we retreated once again to the other room, placed the cups on the dresser and threw our arms around each other. Our mouths merged. Tongues and lips greeted each other like long lost lovers reuniting after years. Victor felt so right, so familiar; there in that prison trailer I felt like I was truly home. After not too long we were rolling around on the bed which creaked loudly.

"Think of all those three-hundred-pound women who have bounced around on this," I whispered. "It's a wonder the springs aren't totally shot." We giggled, picturing some of the enormous women we regularly saw in the visiting room.

"Yeah, you know these trailers really rock during some of these visits," Victor said.

Our bodies entwined, our hands and mouths groped over each other's flesh, as we engaged in some of the sweetest love-making I have ever experienced, different from past encounters in the presence of both love and lust. Afterward, we lay there in each other's arms and talked quietly, hearing only the television in the next room and birds outside. Suddenly a phone rang, and I jumped. "There's a phone here?"

"Damn, it's the count. I forgot all about it." Victor kissed me and jumped up, pulling on his prison greens. "Don't go away, I'll be right back."

Grabbing his shirt, he ran into the other room and picked up the phone which, unlike normal phones, had no breaks in the ring, making it sound urgent. "Yeah, okay, right." The front door of the trailer closed as Victor stepped outside. I had no desire to move; I lay there under the sheet, tired and happy from lovemaking and lack of sleep, and finally being able to relax after all those hours of tension. I stared at the woody walls and yellow-curtained window which provided no light. *How would I be able to leave this man?* I commanded myself not to think about that. We had about forty hours of bliss remaining, and I didn't want to tarnish it in any way, least of all by thinking of its end. As all the Zen books I read taught, what's meaningful is the experience, not possessing it or how long it lasts. It was a comforting theory intellectually, but really accepting it in my gut I found to be another story.

The front door opened and closed again. I heard Victor tell Hattie, "They have to count us when they count the rest of the population, as if I might have gone somewhere."

I didn't hear Hattie's response, but they laughed. Then Victor was back in our room, ripping off his clothes and diving onto the bed. I screamed with joy and we laughed. "Hey, keep it down in there, you two," Hattie called jocularly. "Shhhh."

We squirmed and giggled softly like two mice.

Two hours later, we emerged into the living room where the only light in the late afternoon dusk was from the television. Inside, the trailers were darker than it was in the yard because the high prison wall prevented much daylight from getting in. Hattie, snoozing on the couch, opened her eyes. "Hey, you two. I thought you might stay in there all night and leave me out here to starve. So what's for dinner?"

"Well, if it's all right with you ladies, I would like to save my special dish for tomorrow and indulge in that great-smelling Chinese food that you lugged all the way up here," Victor said.

"Sounds good to me," Hattie said.

"Hey, at Chez Victor we aim to please."

"I'm very pleased," I said, walking over to the refrigerator.

"You look it," said Hattie.

"Now I'm embarrassed," Victor said, not looking very embarrassed.

"Do you think these are clean?" I asked, pointing to the plastic dishes, glasses, and silverware stacked on the kitchen table, thinking about all the inmates and their families who used the utensils daily.

"They're supposed to be. I've got a copy of the rules. Wait till you see what we have to go through before we leave here Monday morning. Everything is supposed to be spotless. The C.O. will come through here with white gloves on. But I cleaned everything anyway because I don't trust them. So, yeah, those dishes are clean because I washed everything while I was waiting for you."

We laid out the Chinese food on the coffee table, and with a Clint Eastwood movie on television, dug in.

"God, this is fantastic," Victor said. "Thank you, sweetheart." He leaned over and kissed me.

"When was the last time you had Chinese food?"

"Well, occasionally an officer or a teacher in the program will treat us to Chinese food or pizza, but it isn't anything like this."

This was a melange of hot and spicy Szechuan and Hunan chicken, shrimp, and vegetables from one of the myriad of Chinese restaurants on upper Broadway.

"I think the Chinese restaurant in Ellenville has one hot and spicy dish on its menu. But believe me, I could have it over and over. Whatever dish they bring in, it's fine with me; it beats having that institutional food day in and day out."

"I guess the food you get in here must be really horrendous," I said.

Hattie frowned. "I know someone whose son did some time and he lost about twenty pounds in three months because the food was so bad."

"It is. It's tasteless, nutritionless food, but I don't eat it much anyway. I do my own cooking."

"How do you do that?" Hattie asked.

"Well, from packages that people are kind enough to bring me," Victor winked at me, "and from the commissary. You learn how to be creative with basic ingredients. For me, it's a challenge that I enjoy because I love to cook."

"What do you cook?" I asked.

"Well, you'll get a sample tomorrow. It's a kind of Chinese pasta dish. I make different things with rice, vegetables, meat, whatever's around. It's what I do with it that makes it special."

"Do you have access to a stove?"

"Now I do, but in the old days we'd have to use a coil or cook over a lightbulb. You wouldn't believe what you can do using a little ingenuity."

"It seems amazing that you can actually cook in prison."

"It's true," Victor said, piling more Szechuan mushrooms on his plate. "When you deprive people of the means to provide for themselves, they become very resourceful. Unless you manage to kill their spirit—which happens all the time—their will and desires are as strong as ever. Maybe even stronger because of the deprivation."

"Prison doesn't sound as bad as I always thought it was," I said, putting down my chopsticks.

"Believe me, it's worse. Just because we may have television sometimes or access to a stove, prison is still hell. You're in a constant state of tension, of readiness to be abused, to be treated like scum by people who despise you. And that's the guards. Then there's your fellow inmates. Imagine living side by side with people you don't want to be near, most of whom are uneducated, demoralized, and uninterested in becoming anyone other than the seamy person who got arrested and thrown in jail. Some of these guys are real animals."

"Victor, do you see a lot of attacks?" Hattie asked.

"They happen every day. The guards are always acting like they have a lot to worry about from the inmates, but that's rare. Most of the violence that happens in prison happens between inmates. Half the time if a guard sees a fight, he doesn't even try to break it up. Or else they jump in and make it worse."

"Have you ever been attacked?" I asked, suddenly concerned.

"Hey, let's not talk about that stuff now. I'm trying to forget all that out here. I want to concentrate on you."

Besides not wanting to think about rotten prison facts of life while taking a temporary refuge from them, Victor was also embarrassed in front of Hattie. In a way, I was relieved, for even though a part of me was curious, another part dreaded hearing more about what Victor experienced in prison, knowing I could obsess my way into a constant state of worry.

"I can't believe it's dark out," I said, looking toward the black square of a window.

Victor looked at me gratefully. "We have a saying about these trailers, that once the first night is over, the end is already looming."

I could feel his sadness, even though he smoothed it over by smiling and stroking my hand. Fighting my own dread over having to leave him in thirty-six hours, I tried hard to emulate Victor's ability to enjoy whatever was good in the moment and not dwell on its ending. After fifteen years in jail, he'd had plenty of practice.

After kibitzing with Hattie for a few more minutes, we retired to the bedroom. Victor draped one of his T-shirts over the lamp on the dresser, creating a dim, diffuse light, then joined me on the bed.

"You know, I didn't want to talk about it in front of Hattie but I want to tell you everything," he said softly. "I was almost raped, three times." He stretched out on his side, head in hand, leaning on an elbow.

"Tell me what happened," I said, feeling my psychotherapist training kick in. Painful though it was to hear about the man I loved being abused, I knew he needed to get it out, and I needed to listen.

"Well, one of the times was at Green Haven. They had a boxing team, and a majority of the trainers on the team were bandits, a term for people who stalk and rape other men."

"You mean 'booty bandits?'" I had heard the term in a movie.

He nodded. "The bandits are into boxing in the first place, because a lot of the young guys coming in from Elmira and Coxsackie can be convinced to get into boxing under the pretext that they're learning how to protect themselves. Meantime, the guys teaching them are the ones they need protection from. One day after working out, I was showering in the gym workers' shower area. I worked in the gym at that time because I had two jobs in order to pay school tuition. This guy Sam came into the shower room fully clothed. I was the only one in there. He had a shank in his hand, and he said, 'Yo, Blood, you think you better than everyone else because you're going to school. You know what this is?' I didn't respond. I just looked at him as the water ran on me. He came closer to me, oblivious of the water splashing on him, and holding the shank in his left hand, he punched me in my chest with his right.

"One of the things that flashed through my mind," Victor continued, "was in anti-guerrilla warfare school we learned that when you're confronted with an enemy who has an advantage over you, you have to turn it into your advantage. You have to think it out. So knowing that Sam came in there to rape me, I had to disarm him and let him think he was completely superior to me. I purposely avoided eye contact, lowered my eyes to the floor, and became humble and meek, dropping my hands so I wasn't threatening. He hit me again in the chest, then I moved two feet to my left which put me directly in the corner of the rear of the shower which was eleven feet by eight feet. Before you even got to the shower room there were the officers' office and the supply room, so no one could hear you scream."

"What happened next?" I asked, trying to quiet my pounding heart.

"Well, he was assuming he had the advantage, because he had pummeled me in my chest and I looked terrified of him. In reality, I was pulling him into me to make him drop his guard because he still had a weapon. He then said, 'I don't need no shank for you; you're a punk,' and he put the shank in his back pocket. Then I hit him hard in the jaw. Even though he was a boxer he was stunned: he had gotten sucker punched because he wasn't expecting it. My nakedness was to my advantage in that I wasn't sliding, but he slid because he was wearing boots, and this scared him. I was standing over him, and I kicked him; he was clamoring to get out, but off balance, he kept slipping. I refused to let him go. I took the shank out of his pocket and threw it to the side, cutting my hand. He finally got up and ran out."

"What a nightmare."

Victor nodded. His voice was steady, but his face was contorted with the painful memory. "I was drying off, and his partner, another bandit, came in. He didn't say anything, coming in under the pretense of getting a towel, but I could see him scoping me for my next move. See, they had had a plan which was that the partner, after standing outside playing chickie, would then come in and get some for himself. They had it all figured out. They were known bandits and that's how they operated. They purposely worked in the gym, because during eleven to one when everyone else is locked down, there are some kids in the gym with just one officer. The bandits get the kid at this time because the officer is sitting in his office with his feet on his desk."

"Well, what was the attitude of these guys after this?"

"After I left and was in the big gym, Sam approached me and said, 'I don't give a fuck if you go and get your boys.' He meant the guys I worked out with. I was then faced with a choice. I was getting ready to graduate college. Despite being in prison, I was turning my life around. In my heart, my survival instincts wanted to kill him, but I knew what I was becoming and what I was trying to leave behind.

"When my weight-lifting group heard about it, they said, 'Let's go kill that motherfucker,' meaning I should kill him and they would watch. I told them that I had already handled it. In their eyes I was a coward because I didn't kill him. My settling it wasn't good enough. In order for me to maintain a standard of manliness, I should have killed him. After that, I was no longer part of the weight-lifting crew. But the bandits never messed with me again, because they knew that I was not to be fucked with. You have to establish that, because if you don't, they get you and you wind up doing your whole sentence either in protective custody or on someone's arm, being passed like a whore from person to person."

"It must be a terrible way to live, to be constantly worried that some predator will come after you."

"For me it was especially hard." He hugged me close. "Prison's a horrible place, Denise. That's why I always keep this with me." He got up and went to his toiletry bag, from which he pulled out a small leather wallet.

"I've been carrying this with me for years." Off a laminated card he read in his own writing: "'Everything can be taken from a man but one thing: the last of the human freedoms — to choose one's attitude in any given set of circumstances, to choose one's own way.'

"That's Viktor E. Frankl," Victor said. "Another man who found himself in a dire set of circumstances not of his own making. His was much worse in Auschwitz. He wrote about it in his book *Man's Search for Meaning*: 'To be alive,' Frankl said, 'is to suffer, but to find meaning in one's suffering is to survive.' His words have had great meaning for me over the years."

"I can understand why," I said softly, wondering how I would react if I had experienced the suffering of a wrongful imprisonment.

"Hey, come here," Victor said, putting the card on the dresser. "Enough of this morbid talk."

With our arms around each other we lay quietly, momentarily absorbed in our own thoughts. I wondered about other traumatic things that had happened to Victor, but didn't ask, knowing there would be other times in the future for him to tell me about them. Now I wanted to enjoy the reality of all I had been anticipating for so long.

Though we stayed up most of the night, it passed by as if in a dream, the euphoric kind that you don't want to end. The sun was barely up when the phone screamed its incessant ring, and Victor had to step outside to be counted, as if he could have escaped in the middle of the night beyond the wall and the gun towers.

Sunday, our one full day, we spent like the previous one: reveling in each other's company, making love, eating, laughing, watching television, and goofing with Hattie. Though we were confined to a small space with just a brief break, when we went out in the yard the minutes flew by, and it was as if the hours never existed.

Around 11:00 A.M., the three of us went outside after a guard knocked on the door and announced "Click-Click" just like they had in the visiting room. On the grass stood an inmate with a Polaroid camera, accompanied by a guard, ready to take pictures. Being together in the crisp, autumn air took on a special poignancy, but we had to keep in mind that I was supposed to be Victor's kid sister. We toned down what otherwise would have been more passionate poses: me on his lap on the jungle gym and on the swings. Instead, we took one of him holding me up next to the basketball hoop, about to slam dunk a basket. We each posed with Hattie and then took one of the three of us together. As the pictures developed within minutes, we saw that despite the circles under our eyes, we all wore joyful smiles.

In the evening, as the sun was going down, despite our fervent wishing that it wouldn't, Victor prepared his special meal, adamantly insisting that Hattie and I not come into the kitchen while the chef was at work. Our curiosity piqued, he finally put before us two heaping plates of noodles.

He waited as we tasted the dish. "So, how do you like it?"

We ate till we were stuffed, assuring Victor the food was delicious, which it was. "The mystery ingredient is pulpo," he said. He paused as we looked mystified and, smiling, said, "Octopus."

"If I had known that, I wouldn't have eaten it." Hattie, who'd already had two helpings, squirmed in her chair.

"That's why I didn't tell you!" Victor said. "When I make this stuff for the guys, they rave over it."

I envied "the guys" being fed by Victor.

"And now for the coup de grace." He emerged from the kitchen with a cheesecake. "Coffee anyone?"

"You made this?" I asked. "It's fabulous."

I envisioned a future with this man cooking and feeding me. "Will you still love me when I weigh three hundred pounds?"

"Baby, I'll love you if you weigh a thousand pounds!"

"Now I don't know about that," Hattie joined in.

Could Victor really be as wonderful as he seemed? I wondered as we savored the creamy cake and watched a movie. I knew I was bringing so much to him. Did he really love me for myself or for how I was enhancing his life? It was a question I could have tortured myself with, but by the time the sky was lightening on doomsday morning, I had made up my mind.

"Victor," I said as we lay in each other's arms, sweaty and tired, "if we have to get married in order to do this again, I am prepared to do so." Were those words really coming from my mouth, I, who had always been so wary of relationships? It was as if I were surrendering, but I was so smitten, so desirous of being near this man as much as possible, I was ready to do anything.

"Denise, my future is so uncertain. How could I ask you to share it?"

I interrupted him, "Darling, you're going to get out. We're going to fight to get you out."

Then he added, "And on top of the uncertainty, I can't get married," he said.

"What!" I sat up and looked at him.

"Lifers cannot get married in prison, but some guy has a class action suit claiming it's discriminatory. His argument is that there are married guys who come in to serve life sentences, so it doesn't make sense to prohibit those of us who aren't married from doing so."

"Why didn't you tell me this before?" I asked, my voice rising, despite telling myself to stay calm, as if that would have made a difference.

"I thought I did. I thought you knew."

"No, I've been dreaming of marrying you." I felt my face growing hot. I was devastated, wondering what our future would be.

"Denise, I can't even promise you when we can be together like this again." Victor's voice was tinged with sadness, but he tried to smile. Tears ran down my cheeks.

"Don't worry, sweetheart. Come here," he pulled me down into his arms. "Where there's a will, there's a way," he said, as if reading my mind. "People say there's a good chance the suit will come out in our favor, and I even have some names of people you can contact if you want to try to do something to help us be together."

Suddenly I saw the years stretching out before me: coming up each week to visit him, dying to make love, wanting our child. And him locked up for what seemed like forever. I could feel myself locked up too, thwarted as I was in my desires and my ability to pursue my goals. But Victor had already warned me that being involved with an inmate is like doing time yourself. Now I knew he was right.

My heart was breaking as we packed, mopped, dusted, and shined. Victor immersed himself in the cleanup of the trailer, not only because of his natural meticulousness, but because it was the only way to avert the pain of leaving. I tried to do the same, but I was unable to laugh and joke the way he did. At eight o'clock we hugged and kissed briefly, then Hattie and I with our belongings, along with the other tired and sad inmates' loved ones, were loaded into the van. The sight of Victor standing there in his dark greens, waving and blowing kisses, was a new heartbreak for me to bear this time.

It was a lot easier to get out of the prison than in. It seemed to take only seconds for the van to bump along the dirt road that led to the parking lot where Loretha was waiting. She was still her usual ebullient self despite having gotten up at 5:00 A.M. to make the drive to get us. As she and Hattie chatted on the drive to the city, I sat back in a daze of conflicting feelings. Victor's imprisonment would now be mine as well. Was I up to coping with a prison sentence? Could I really fight for his freedom? Did I really have a choice at this point? I knew the answer to the latter was no, and to the first question, well, I thought of what the judge had told Victor when Victor asked the judge how he could serve life in prison for a crime he didn't do. "Do as much as you can, son. Just do the best you can."

CHAPTER NINE

SYNCHRONICITY

It was a blustery and sunny March day, and the ride up to Ellenville was made more enjoyable by the tape of Beethoven overtures, in particular, the *Egmont*, which I played repeatedly. Especially in my amorous state, the trumpets made me feel that I was at the gates of heaven. These drives on long stretches of empty highway always felt liberating, perhaps all the more so in contrast to my destination. I was glad it was a Thursday, because when I arrived, the crowd waiting to get in was not large. I had that familiar mixture of excitement and anxiety as I waited. My adrenaline really surged when the guard behind the counter said, "Have a seat," instead of ushering me to the metal detector.

"Why? Is something wrong?" I felt my stomach contract.

"No," he said looking at some invisible speck on the wall behind me. The guards often spoke without looking at me, and often didn't provide any directions. Was it that I was unworthy of information, or was it something I shouldn't know, or was it that the guards were just mean? Whatever the reason, it was infuriating to be treated that way.

"Is something wrong?" I asked again.

"I don't know," he said, picking up the telephone.

My imagination spun. I looked around and suddenly everything took on a surreal quality: the women draped with infants, toddlers, and children; the fiberglass chairs, the soiled, pale blue walls, the grimy windows that were too high to see out of. It was as if a glass partition had come between me and them, and I was alone in a bubble of fear. Had he been hurt in a fight? Did something happen and he was in the box? Victor had told me that the cops rarely threw you into solitary confinement without beating you. While rationally I knew that he was not involved in anything that would land him there and that no one had any serious grievances against him, in this environment you never knew. People could set you up, plant things on you. You never knew when a guy you were all right with might think you looked at him funny and come after you with a knife. I felt my fingertips get icy as the blood drained from my extremities.

Somewhere from the crevices of my brain came the echo of a voice strangely like my mother's: *Well, what do you expect, being in a place like this? What are you doing here anyway? This place is for animals: the inmates are psychopaths and lowlifes, and their women are no better. Is this what you think of yourself?*

"Uh, excuse me." I ran over to the guard.

"Can you tell me where Victor Clark is?" I asked desperately.

"Clark is being transferred today, so you won't be able to see him."

"What? Where is he going? You mean I came all the way up here and I can't even see him?"

"I don't know where he's going. Wait a minute." He walked to the back and spoke to another uniformed individual.

The idea that Victor was being transferred was at once exciting and frightening. It was exciting because it might mean that he was progressing to a less restrictive environment. It was frightening because it meant change. In the ten months we had known each other, things had remained remarkably consistent, in part because the prison environment provided for a limited number of factors, just about none of which were alterable in any way. The inmate had very little choice; each day he woke up and knew where he would be and whom he would see.

The guard came back. "We're trying to see if we can get him down here for a few minutes."

"Oh, thank you," I said sincerely. Because Victor had been around a long time, was polite, and didn't get into trouble, some of the guards had better attitudes toward him and were more likely to stick their necks out for him than for other inmates.

"Okay, come on." He beckoned me toward the metal detector. I walked through and was relieved when the alarm didn't go off, even though I knew I had nothing metal on me.

"You'll only be able to stay for a short time," the guard said as I waited to be buzzed into the vestibule where I would wait for the next buzz. A moment later I entered the waiting room.

Victor came in, breathless and smiling. "I'm going to Walkill," he whispered, clutching my hands. "But I'm not supposed to know it."

"Why not?"

"Inmates usually don't know where they're going, and if they do, they never know until an hour before they're told to pack up because they're afraid the inmate would get someone to hijack the bus."

"So how do you know you're going to Walkill?"

"Simmons told me." Simmons was a guard with whom Victor had worked in the child care room.

"So if I follow you will they think I'm trying to hijack you?"

"Yes, they will. You'd better not." We kissed passionately.

"Oh, I'm so excited for you, sweetheart."

Actually, Victor was getting what we had hoped for. A few weeks before, anticipating his becoming eligible for a medium security facility, he had put in a request to be transferred to Walkill. Walkill would be a better atmosphere for our relationship, because it was one of the few medium security prisons with trailers and was relatively close to the city. Normally, inmates didn't request specific transfers, because it was rare that an inmate's preference was considered. But it didn't hurt to try, especially when you had the good reputation Victor did.

I looked around the room, feeling an unexpected fondness for it. Love changed one. Being in love made everything seem so much softer, so much more benign. I even felt love for the prison and had been inspired to photograph and draw it. From the balcony of my room at the Terrace Motel where I had stayed for a second time on Thanksgiving, I had done several sketches of Eastern. I had been thrilled to find that, unlike when I stayed there during my vacation in August, in November the nakedness of the trees enabled me to see the gray stones and turrets of the prison.

"So what are you saying, I should just go home?"

"Denise, remember there are no guarantees about anything here. The best thing after you've done all you can is to relax. Go home. Read a good book, sweetheart."

"But when will I see you?"

"Well, how about Saturday? You're working tomorrow, so come Saturday."

Fifteen minutes later, the guard came over and told Victor I had to leave. As I exited Eastern's parking lot, I wondered if Victor felt sad or nostalgic since he had been there for about five years. Could someone be nostalgic for a prison? Victor had spent a good deal of his adult life in them and, though sometimes bitter, he also spoke with sincere fondness about the football teams he had played on, as well as his friendships with many inmates and even some staff.

I spent the afternoon feeling free and at the same time, vaguely guilty that I wasn't working more. In my profession, being published is helpful. I had tried in the recent past to do some writing on psychological subjects, but found myself blocked and unable to write or think about anything but Victor. And letters to him were hardly the professional papers I needed to write for career advancement. But I didn't care, for now

Victor's freedom was my concern. So I spent my free time that day writing to congressmen and others, trying to acquaint them with Victor's case.

Victor often wrote two or three letters a day, and regularly sent me photographs, cards, and computer-generated banners declaring our love. Every day I could hardly wait for the mail carrier to arrive. On the day when Victor was transferred and our visit aborted, the mail finally arrived at four. By then I was on pins and needles. Two letters from him soothed my mind.

On Saturday I arose eagerly at 5:00 A.M. in order to get an early start. As I lathered up my hair in the shower, I thought about how getting out of bed so early on weekends would have been impossible except that I was motivated by love for Victor. As a therapist, I was aware that motivation, or lack of it, was the driving force behind most problems, and if therapists could figure out how to inject motivation into their patients, they'd go out of business because so many of their patients would be immediately cured.

As I walked to my car, 110th Street was surrealistically still and deserted. In the monochromatic gray light it was difficult to predict whether the day would be sunny or cloudy. Ever vigilant, I looked around as I got into the silver gray five-year-old Toyota I had bought the month before, my first automotive purchase. At thirty-seven, I was still living hand-to-mouth, and the used car was about all I could afford. I comforted myself by thinking that I would not want a nice car now anyway, not after years of seeing all those smashed car windows littering the streets of Manhattan like confetti and all those nights I was kept awake by screaming car alarms.

The previous day I had called Walkill Correctional Facility and gotten directions; I was thrilled that it was nearer to the city than Eastern, but it was still an hour-and-a-half drive. I drove purposefully. Only once en route did I lose my way.

"Where's Walkill?" I asked a female toll booth attendant.

"You mean the hamlet of Walkill?"

The hamlet? What was this, medieval Europe? "No, I mean the prison."

"Oh." She looked at me strangely and stumbling, gave directions as if no one had ever asked before. The prison was outside the hamlet. In fact, the prison was out in the middle of rolling fields, looking from the distance like a large farm complex. Again I felt the irony: visiting this man in prison upstate took me out of the city and into the country where I longed to be. Yet freedom in this case equaled imprisonment. It seemed to me this was both a metaphoric and factual irony. As I explored the thought further, I began to see that I had been in my own prison created by the bars of my own limitations, my own negativity, and my own belief that the glass was half empty.

Like Victor, being in love had caused my attitude to change: now my optimism was strong, if cautious. As I neared the prison, I envisioned staying there overnight with Victor. After a night of continuous lovemaking, we would walk into a lush, green field and breathe deeply, filling our lungs with the fragrance of freshly cut hay.

I was glad to find that the waiting area was smaller and less congested than the one at Eastern, and the processing went much faster. Walking into a spacious room that had large windows providing copious light and panoramic views of the fields, I found a table next to a window. When Victor entered the room, we beamed at each other and embraced.

"Are you doing all right?" he asked, gently as always.

"Just fine. And you? How is it here? It seems lower key than Eastern."

"It is, it is," he said excitedly. "From what I hear, the personnel here have a pretty good attitude, and most important, because it's small, they give us trailer visits about every two months. I don't know yet how strict they are about who they let in for trailer visits, but you know I'm hopeful."

"Victor, I've been thinking of the law about our not getting married. Maybe we should work to get it changed."

He smiled. "Any ideas?"

"I have several." I smiled back. "You know, if we are able to get married we can have our trailer visitors legitimately." We were passionately holding hands. Since our illicit trailer visit at Eastern, we had begun to surreptitiously grope at each other, but in this new place we knew we had to be cautious until Victor learned the unwritten codes of behavior and the rules that were okay to break, or at least bend.

"Let's talk about it later." He seemed to want to change the subject. I had already begun to work with Frankie Mendoza, an inmate Victor had once mentioned, to alter the rule about life-sentence prisoners being able to marry. Mendoza was out on work release at the Long Island law firm where he was a paralegal. At his suggestion, I had also written to congressmen and anyone else I felt could help Victor and myself, and told them why we felt the law was discriminatory. Meanwhile, Mendoza's class action suit was pending.

"Shall we check out the machines?" Victor placed his red bandanna on the table and led me the short distance to the ubiquitous vending machines. Walking with him I had that same feeling I had always had at Eastern: a mixture of pride and the intensity that comes from being entirely in the moment. The uniqueness of this way of being was the absence of the feeling, sometimes vague, sometimes glaring, but almost always with me, that life at that moment was wrong and should be otherwise. When I was with Victor, everything seemed crystal clear, simple and comfortable. I suspected that this was what the word "happy" meant.

What also fascinated me was how time always redefined itself when we were together. The few hours, eight-thirty to three, that we were allowed to spend together passed in a flash without so much as a look at the clock because we wanted time to stand still. One of those things I once again wondered about vis-à-vis the "human condition" was why time spent in unpleasant moments could drag on interminably while time to be savored zipped by. The cruelty of this paradox presented itself to me daily and was one of several features of life on earth as a human being that I just couldn't fathom but knew was a fact. Thus, I was soon kissing Victor goodbye, and he was telling me the usual consoling and uplifting things he always said at the end of our visits. Now, however, we were both buoyed by a new sense of enthusiasm and hope, for Victor was more free than he had been since being incarcerated sixteen years before.

As I walked to my car, I reflected on the fact that a lot happens and doesn't in sixteen years, and a few minutes later as I tried to stop the car from being blown into the next lane by the wind, I realized how much had—or hadn't—happened to me. I had gone from girlhood to womanhood, a major transition, and while I didn't want to believe that I hadn't accomplished much, in my heart, I knew that was true. Victor, despite the uncertainty of his future, was amassing graduate degrees and skills, starting programs that served others, while I was trying hard to write and not be depressed. On that April day in 1973 when Victor had been arrested for robbery and homicide, I was living with my parents who were abusing each other. I was attending Hofstra University where I couldn't figure out what to do with my life, swallowing uppers to stay up and downers to get down.

Like many young people in the late sixties and early seventies, recreational drugs were the background music for my life. Those years were also manic depressive for Victor, but the details were different. Winding up in prison solved the dilemma which many Vietnam veterans found themselves facing—being unable to fit into so-called normal life after having experienced the extreme highs and lows of daily life-on-the-edge intensity and misery of the steamy jungles of Vietnam. Prison provided a suitable enough facsimile with its daily unpredictable life and death encounters with other men.

Early in his sentence, Victor forged a friendship with an older inmate who became like a mentor to him. One day as they were walking in the yard, Larry said to Victor, "You don't belong here. You're not like the rest of these guys." To Victor, that was the reawakening of how he thought about himself as he fought for survival in his family and the ghetto. He had always been smart, studious, and able to master whatever challenge confronted him. Though nothing would change his status of confinement, he began working toward his inner liberation.

On Sunday I spent several hours perfecting a letter I intended to send to as many people as I thought might be interested in championing Victor's application for clemency. I knew this approach was working to get the support of Governor Cuomo for Gary McGivern, a white cop killer and prison escapee who not only wasn't innocent but who hadn't accomplished half of what Victor had; McGivern had people like William Buckley championing his cause. How could people fail to lend their support to Victor, who, even if they didn't know he was innocent, had dedicated his prison life to helping others and deserved to be recognized?

After spending the morning working on more letters for Victor's and my future, I spent the next part of the day in a small brick building on Flatbush Avenue in Brooklyn, administering psychotherapy mostly to adult women, with a sprinkling of men and children. Between sessions I chatted with colleagues, keeping the news of my relationship to myself except for Janine, a woman whom I decided might not judge but understand the story of how Victor and I had met and where he was. To tell or not to tell was always an issue for me and one that Victor had difficulty understanding. "Why do you have to tell anyone anything?" he asked.

"Because that's my style. You are the most important thing in my life. How can I be really honest with people and not talk about you?"

But the reality was I didn't tell most people. Sometimes I found myself in an awkward situation if others were talking about their mates or lovers or families. "Oh, I'm seeing someone," I'd say and change the subject before they could ask detailed questions. Janine, however, seemed politically progressive and nonjudgmental enough to handle my telling her about my relationship in a sympathetic and inoffensive way, and at the beginning, she was.

"I once had a boyfriend who was in jail," she said excitedly as I looked with admiration at the many floral pictures and knickknacks that decorated her office. "He was a political activist and drug dealer who got busted. I used to visit him upstate all the time."

We laughed as we commiserated about visiting someone in prison, and I felt great comradery with her for confirming that my seeing Victor was not quite so bizarre after all. A few days later, however, Janine said to me, "Are you sure you know what you're doing? After all he could be a psychopath," and gave me a little lecture. As we walked back from lunch through a neighborhood playground in the cold March afternoon, I answered, "Janine, I've thought a lot about this and am fully aware of all possibilities. Especially as a therapist, you should know it's not helpful to tell someone who's in love anything even remotely negative about their lover. It only alienates them."

Janine apologized. "I'm only expressing my concern." She half-frowned, half-smiled, and added, "You sure seem to know what you're doing." Happily enough, Janine never raised any doubts again and was always enthusiastic and supportive. She was the only person at work that I could talk to, at least until I felt comfortable enough to tell others. That night when Victor called, I was just about to tell him that I had made a supportive friend when he confided some bizarre news.

"I'm being transferred."

"What? Again?" Once again, fear hit me in the gut. Had something happened?

"The superintendent thinks I've been locked up too long to be in such an open environment."

"Why, what does he think you're gonna do?"

"Run. After all, when you're outside here, it's pretty easy to keep going over the fields and over the fence."

"But legally you're entitled to be there.'

"Yeah, that's why I'm here."

"So, can he do that? I mean, what he says can supercede corrections law?"

"He can and is."

"What a system. So where are they going to send you this time?"

"I'm not sure but it'll probably be either Mid-Orange or Otisville. They're both medium security facilities but not as open as this one."

"Oh, sweetheart, I'm sorry. I know you were so happy to be there."

"I'm okay. It's you I'm concerned about, Denise. I know how much making these drives takes out of you, and I was so glad this place was closer. The worst thing, though, is there are no trailers at either of those other facilities."

"Oh no, you're kidding."

"No." He sounded truly down. Victor had told me about how before I came into his life the guards chided him for never smiling and how he just tolerated most of each day. "Hey, Clark, how come you always look so down and you never smile?" they would ask him.

"I'm locked up in prison for something I didn't do," he always replied.

Since we'd met, he always smiled and was upbeat. I understood that at least some of this was for my benefit; he knew how difficult our relationship and his imprisonment could be for me, and he didn't want me to get discouraged, but some element of the change in both his attitude and outlook was occasioned because we both now had a future for which to plan and hope.

"Don't worry, honey. We'll manage. We've been managing so far, and we'll continue," I said, feeling sad for him; how frustrating it must be for a man to know he was innocent and to have no recourse. And then to get a further kick in the teeth for having been so active in helping others and not being rewarded. How could he not be seething with anger?

"Listen, nothing is promised in this system, and you have to expect the worst. Let's look at the bright side: I'll still be closer to you than I was at Eastern, and I'll be in a medium security facility which will help when it comes time to apply for work release."

"When will that be?"

"In two years."

I sighed heavily despite telling myself not to betray my disappointment. *Even if that occurred, it would still be another two years of driving upstate and dealing with that system. Two more years of making love with our eyes in a room full of people.* I paused and, taking a deep breath, tried to get better hold of my emotions. Whatever it took, I was committed. I was in this with him. I was writing officials in the hope that my efforts to get him clemency would be rewarded. Maybe the remotest possibility of all would happen: Governor Cuomo would read through Victor's voluminous file and recognize that here was a man who deserved to be set free. After all, wasn't that what clemency was all about? If not justice, forgiveness? Mercy?

"Hey, before we hang up, let me tell you something good. What do they call it when something happens and it seems like a coincidence, but has such meaning you know it can't be?" Victor said.

"Synchronicity."

"Right. Well, listen to this. I was in the yard this morning; I had just found out they were going to transfer me and I was feeling really depressed when I happened on a big rock, more like a boulder. As I walked past it, I noticed writing carved into it. You want to hear what it said?"

"Of course," I said softly.

"'Whatsoever is brought upon thee, take cheerfully and be patient when thou art changed to a low estate. For gold is tried in the fire and acceptable men in the furnace of adversity.'"

"That's amazing, as if it were there just for you to read at that moment."

"Denise, there may be rhyme or reason to all this madness. Perhaps we just have to be receptive to it."

"And as Jesse Jackson says, 'Keep hope alive.'"

"Amen."

CHAPTER
TEN

ANOTHER DAY, ANOTHER PRISON

Otisville Correctional Facility is located on Sanatorium Road in the hills of Orange County, right next to the Federal Correctional Facility which you pass first when coming from the east. They occupy their space on this back country road like twin guard dogs. The ride up had been pleasant enough: across Route 17, through Middletown, past mall after mall, then the Mid-Hudson Psychiatric Center, about which I would hear a lot more in the coming months and years. Finally, the road wound around hills, past farms and sheep grazing in meadows, and then past a couple of auto body shops and a cinder block cafe with two large Honda hogs out front. This was the country; idyllic with the faint greenness of new buds shimmering in the air. Then came the two prisons.

The first thing I noticed about the Otisville facility was that it was smaller than the other prisons I'd seen and that it was encircled by a fence crowned with razor wire. Soon I came to a small shack where I had to stop and tell a corrections officer the name and number of the inmate I was visiting while a second officer copied down my license plate number. When they were satisfied I was who I said I was, they opened a sliding gate. I drove through, and the gate locked behind me. I drove up the road to a small parking lot in front of what could have been a ski lodge complete with stone chimney. Walking in, I noticed the waiting room was rustic and less institutional than either Walkill or Eastern. While being processed, I had to go through the same procedures as the other prisons, but I had less of a feeling that the guards were trying to nab me for something.

The guard in charge of this visiting room was a tall, broad-chested, white man with a leonine head of white hair. There was no mistaking his position of authority as he sat elevated at the front of the room like a judge presiding over a courtroom. The only other people in there when I entered were a female guard standing near him, and one visitor pulling out a chair at a table by the window. I observed that a table by the window as far from the front as possible would be the most private, so I walked quickly to stake my claim. Looking out the window, the view was of the same rolling hills I had driven through and a valley in which were nestled gingerbread houses. Later I would come to learn that a table more toward the middle was better, because this far back, we were too close to the guard sitting by the door through which the inmates came and went. With great expectancy and hardly breathing, I watched this door; within minutes Victor appeared. Once again I experienced that same thrill seeing him. We embraced and he pulled his chair close to mine.

"How are you, sweetheart?" he whispered.

"Fine now," I said, breathing in his scent.

We sat with our knees touching, fingers entwined, drinking in each other's faces. His eyes were wide and joyful. Part of what made being in love with Victor so intoxicating was watching him take such pleasure in my existence. At other times I was just me, an ordinary person with both flaws and assets, whereas in our love, the flaws receded into the background.

The day passed with a happy peace as we sat and talked quietly, at intervals getting up to stroll arm and arm to the wall of vending machines. All seemed right with the world, except, of course, when the reality of the end of visiting hours came upon us. We shared the sadness of our final embrace, and I left by myself, feeling that I was abandoning Victor, leaving him alone with his fate. When I expressed this to him, he jokingly said, "Okay, wait outside the gate. I'll meet you there." Especially in the medium security facilities, all an inmate would need in order to escape was a blanket to cover the razor wire and some good climbing and running shoes. I had asked Victor if he ever seriously considered escaping and his response was that sure, everyone at least thinks about it, but he knew it wasn't the way to go. Even if he were able to beat the odds and not get caught, he didn't want to live as a fugitive. But since I had come into his life, he said, he thought about it more. Also, as your time got "short," as you got closer to the end, it became harder to do. That made sense to me as I lived my life that way: when I believed that there was no way out of a situation I would resign myself and settle down with it. As soon as I believed there was a way out, I would be unable to whole-heartedly get into it, as I was too conscious of its end.

Very un-Zenlike. For years I had been immersing myself in Zen literature and philosophy, meditating sporadically, yet I still found it difficult to accept "what is." I always got caught up in the "what ifs" and "shouldn't bes," believing that there was always room to make a change or to abandon a situation entirely. It was the part of the Serenity Prayer that refers to the wisdom to know the difference between what you can and can't change that was the challenge for me: I could easily accept not being able to change something if only I knew for sure that I couldn't, but much of the time, there was no certainty and that was the hard part. On the other hand, there were times when I was glad I was a tena-cious person who would not give up on something I believed in. Perhaps the wisdom lies in knowing when to stop being stubborn and surrender.

The days grew longer, the air in the hills became greener, and Victor settled into Otisville. There was no school program, nor much of any program there, but Victor wanted to work at something so he passed his days as a porter, mopping floors and cleaning toilets, earning seventy-five cents a day. Though he did his best to accept his tasks with equanimity, he felt bored and frustrated, as well as concerned that working as a porter would not look good on his resume when it came time to apply for work release. But I encouraged him to look toward our future. In each free minute, I continued to write letters on Victor's behalf and also on behalf of overturning the law against our marrying. At the same time, I was bringing up to date my own resume since I had decided to make a job change.

After three years of riding the Number 2 train to the end of the line and then getting on a bus to the only job I've ever liked, I decided to break two vows I had made to myself: that I would never again work at an unfulfilling job and I would never again work for the state bureaucracy. If we were going to start saving for our future, I needed to have a more substantial income. I needed to put my individual needs aside and buckle down. I wanted to take responsibility for my life, our life.

My present goals, although I felt them difficult to attain, were a far cry from my past illusory dreams. I took heart from Victor's grounding in reality. After all, he was a model of such good sense and responsibility, and I had such great admiration for him, how could I not emulate him? I decided in order to earn more, I would go back to working at the state hospital, back to a state civil service position. The state job made sense also because unlike the job at the clinic, where my clients suffered and I felt guilty if I missed a day, in the state hospital there were always others to assume your duties.

Two days before I started my new job on the male admissions ward of the Bronx Psychiatric Center, Victor and I had a momentous visit. We had settled in at our usual table by the window, which by now I knew to make a run for as soon as I got there. At the next table I saw Junior and Chita, a husband and wife Victor knew. They both had silvery hair, flashing dark eyes, and large, toothy smiles. Before the men came out, Chita had said to me conspiratorially, "I think your husband will have a surprise for you today." Oh? Normally I would have been somewhat defensive, like, why is this stranger telling me about my husband? But love often caused me to respond out of character, for the better.

"That would be nice. What is it?" I turned my head from watching the door for Victor to look at her.

"I'm sorry, I can't tell you. He wants to tell you."

Victor and Junior came in one after the other. Junior, a Latin-lover type, flashed me a perfect white-toothed smile on his way to his wife. Usually, after the men came in, there was no socializing for a while, but on this day, after about two minutes, Junior passed us a folded piece of paper.

"Hmmm, what could this be?" Victor took it from him with a wink.

My heart began to beat faster. If it weren't for all of their joviality, I would have been scared. Then, Victor looked at me meaningfully, said, "I love you," and unfolded the paper. It was a copy of a newspaper article with the heading: JUDGE OVER-TURNS LAW PROHIBITING LIFERS FROM MARRYING.

"Oh my God!" I threw my arms around him and over his shoulder saw Junior and Chita beaming their approval. "Congratulations," Chita said.

"I don't believe it," I whispered.

"I know, sweetheart. It's as if Fate is really looking out for us. This law has been in existence for so long and now they change it."

"Yes, thanks to Frankie Mendoza," I said.

"And you." Victor looked at me lovingly. "You just don't give up."

"I never will," I said. "And now we'll be united. It will be our fight for our future."

"Denise, before you say yes, I want you to give this serious thought; we shouldn't just rush into this."

I looked at him, alarmed. "What are you saying? Do you have doubts that we should get married?"

"I want to marry you more than anything in the world. I'm just saying I want you to think about it. Being married to an inmate is not easy. Like I've told you so many times, nothing is guaranteed. I may not get work release, and parole could be a long way off."

"So what are you saying? How will us being married make things any different than they are? Do you think I'm less committed now than if we were married?"

"No, it's just that you're expecting that in a couple of years we'll start to live in a way that approaches normal. I'm just warning you that that might not happen, might never happen."

"Victor, when you talk like this you scare me."

"Oh, sweetheart, I don't mean to. I just want to make sure you're completely aware of what you're getting yourself into. I don't want you to be disappointed."

I stared out at the hills that were now verdant with only chimneys and corners of houses visible, covered as they were by greenery. I knew he was right about letting myself in for hardship.

"Of course I'll think about it. And you should too. Is marriage to me something you really want after all these years of being locked up?"

"Why, are you saying you're gonna lock me up?" His face was practically touching mine.

"Yeah," I breathed. "I'm gonna handcuff you to the bed and have my way with you."

"Mmm, sounds pretty good to me." We devoured each other's tongues and lips, our appetites for each other ignited.

"Seriously," I whispered.

"What?" He looked at me. "I know for sure that I want to spend the rest of my life with you, Denise, but you're right. I'll follow my advice to you and think about it."

"Yes, marriage is something we shouldn't rush into."

Normally an indecisive person, I didn't have to give much thought to whether or not to marry Victor. I had devoted much time to thinking and meditating about our relationship and whether I was crazy to be pursuing it. That Saturday night when I arrived home, the balmy May air served to heighten my feeling that I was being taken care of by Providence; this was unfamiliar territory as I had spent so much time feeling the opposite. The apartment smelled of dust and cat food; despite the blasting salsa music outside, I threw open the windows to air the place out. I imagined Victor there. What would he do? What would we do? It was Saturday night; would we go out somewhere or would we enjoy each other's company at home, perhaps renting a video? Would we be happy? Would we have a family?

I poured myself a glass of white zinfandel and sat on my bed thinking. I always kept in mind the words of Bo Lozoff, spiritual director of the Prison Ashram Project: the most important consideration was not what would happen years down the road or whenever Victor would come home, but rather the quality of the relationship in the present. And that's how I was living it: the relationship with Victor was deeply rewarding for me in the present, and saying yes to marriage was part of the present.

My new job, on the other hand, was far from rewarding. Going to the dismal state hospital each day was nightmarish; from the first day I entered the ward with its dark yellow and feces-brown hallways, I felt depressed. Psychotic men thronged around me when I came through the door, all whining, "Ms. Beck" at the same time, and followed me to my office, the door of which, unlike other staff members, I kept open. Many of the ward staff were openly hostile to the patients, leaving me wondering how they could be in a position to care for others. Each weekday I awoke with the dread of going there, but I pushed myself because of my commitment to my and Victor's future and my dedication to the patients. I resolved to do all I could for the poor souls in my charge who were so much like Victor once had been, hopeless and alone.

Meanwhile, Victor's situation with officials at the prison was once again repetitive of those we had found in the past. Victor's counselor, Bill, tall, blond, and rugged looking, clearly had disdain for the inmates and for his job. He didn't know Victor, nor did he care to, and basically thought of him as any other scumbag inmate, despite Victor's weighty file full of praise. I was resigned to these types but unfortunately, it was he on the facility level who had to give Victor permission to get married, which legally, he had no reason not to. As part of the process, I was required to meet with him. So one humid day in late June, when there were late visiting hours, I left the mental hospital at noon and took the familiar drive across Route 17 to Middletown. About an hour into my visit with Victor, Bill came in and led me to a table on the other side of the room. He had Victor's file open on the table and flipped through it as we spoke.

"Do you know why Victor is here?" he asked.

"Of course," I said.

"Did you know that he had a previous arrest?"

"What?" Uh-oh, my worst fears come true: Victor had been lying to me all along. There were hideous details in his past that he had hidden from me.

"He was arrested as a juvenile for getting into a fight with the superintendent in his building."

That was all? Victor had told me about this. "That's not supposed to be part of his adult record," I said.

He shot me a glance which I took to mean, *Shut up, you wiseass,* and said in a condescending tone, "It's my job to make sure you know who you're getting involved with."

"Are you aware he got his two master's degrees while in prison, not outside? Yes, Victor has told me all about himself."

He looked at me patronizingly. "Yes, I'm sure Victor wasted no time in telling you all the good things about himself. They're all like that here, even though most of them don't have much good to relate." Though I knew that most of the staff here was hardened I couldn't help but wonder why this so-called counselor was so begrudging about acknowledging all the positive things Victor had done. How could he act as an advocate for the prisoners he counseled if he thought of them as scum with no chance for redemption? Didn't this negate any chance for change that they had?

Still looking at the file as if he had never seen it before he said, "He took LSD as a teenager." Suddenly I felt almost jocular. *Well, that's it, the marriage is off,* I thought sarcastically. But to the counselor I just solemnly nodded my head.

"Okay," he sighed with resignation. "I'll let Victor know what he needs to do next. Good luck to you."

"Thank you for that," I said seriously.

Upon rejoining Victor I told him about the interview. "Bill acted as though people never change—once bad, always bad. I know in many cases, he's right; but what's hard to swallow is the tendency of most prison personnel to lump all inmates into one group and not see individuals." Especially for Victor, this was frustrating as he was uniquely different, yet to the officials, all inmates were the same. Your basic garden variety prejudice. As a black person in America, Victor was too familiar with prejudice, and he had learned once again how to cope with it as an inmate. For me as a social worker working with the disadvantaged, being so close to such blatant discrimination was also not new, and yet my rage flared whenever I encountered it.

Nevertheless, I would let no one, not even Bill, destroy Victor's and my first taste of victory. The next step in preparing for our marriage was Victor contacting Reverend Jones, the prison chaplain. Together, they arranged for having our birth certificates sent to the Office of the Clerk in Otisville, which would issue our marriage license. Victor and the reverend chose August 10, a Thursday, since that was the day the paperwork would be completed.

Like any bride-to-be, I anticipated the wedding with a combination of joy and fear. There was also a bit of amusement and irony thrown in because for many years I didn't think I would get married at all. Now that it was going to happen, it felt right. What made me chuckle was *how* I was getting married. I had always been attracted to that which was different. The ordinary usually held no interest for me though I didn't consciously seek out the extraordinary.

As we were only allowed four guests, we asked my brother Barry and Victor's cousin Loretha, both of whom were pleased to accept. Loretha asked if she could bring her daughter Tiffany, and there was no one besides Barry whom I felt comfortable having there. Though I was pleased that the wedding would be small, I told Victor, "We'll have a big wedding when you are home, on our fifth or tenth anniversary."

"Or whenever," Victor said wistfully.

Sitting at our table in the Otisville visitors' room overlooking the voluptuous hills, we discussed what we would wear. Victor's decision-making was limited by the narrow dress code imposed on inmates, so he opted for a white silk shirt to go with his green pants, along with a light green knit tie he already had. The shirt I would bring to him in a package. For myself, I planned to look for a dress at Loehmann's, where I could find something affordable and suitable for the occasion. I enjoyed shopping at Loehmann's for this reason: I always found one-of-a-kind items there at bargain prices. Like playing the lottery, looking through their racks was a matter of luck, and I won big with the wedding dress. It was perfect. The fabric was white linen with embroidered scalloping along the neckline and hem, and it would not have been out of place among Renoir paintings of ladies of another era.

The other shopping I had to do was for our rings. Victor felt badly that I had to do this myself, and he made sure to impress upon me that he would pay for them. "How can you afford to pay for rings?" I asked.

"I've told you, my love, I'm great at saving. Every dime I make here I put away, and you know what? After a while, even seventy-five cents a day adds up. So go ahead, sweetheart, get something you really like."

It was amazing to me that earning so little money, he made it go so far. On Saturday, I went to the diamond district, for-getting that because of the Jewish Sabbath most of the stores would be closed. It was one of those scorching days at the end of July when everyone has fled Manhattan for cooler scenes. The sidewalks were virtually deserted and steaming. It was in one of the few stores that was opened that I bought our rings. They were beautiful and unique with yellow and white gold that glittered in the light like precious stones. At Victor's suggestion, I had each inscribed with the loving phrases we often used with each other. On the phone I excitedly told him about the rings. "If you picked them out, I'm sure they are beautiful, and I will love them," he said.

Being without him during this time was harder than usual, for I longed to share the details of planning the wedding, small as they were, with him. I was lonely doing them by myself. Even though his love was always with me, I was sad that he could not partake in the wedding preparations more directly, for I knew how much he would have enjoyed them.

CHAPTER ELEVEN

Strange Wedding Day

On August 10 the sun rose around 5:30 A.M. with a weather pre-
diction of a sultry summer day, a good omen, I thought, remembering the old saying, "Happy is the bride upon whom the sun
shines." Victor's cousin Loretha and her daughter, bright and colorful in summery pastel silk dresses, got on the subway with the
early shift riders and arrived at my house in time for us to leave
by 7:30. On our way up Broadway, we stopped at the corner of
122nd Street where my brother, Barry, was living with his girlfriend. Since he worked at night, arising before noon was rough
for him, but he had gone to bed early the night before in order not
to be too bleary-eyed for the wedding. While Loretha had visited
Victor in the past, Barry had never been inside a prison.

"So, Barry, how do you feel about going into a prison?"
I looked at his face which seemed strangely pale through the
rearview mirror.

"Uh, yeah, I'm thrilled," he said grumpily, his eyes half-
closed.

"No, really, I remember you once telling me you were
curious about prisons and what it's like being locked up."

His eyes opened a bit wider. "Yeah, a few years ago I was."

"But now you're not?"

"Yeah, I guess I still am."

I was starting to feel a familiar frustration that sisters often feel when conversing with their brothers.

"Oh, you'll find it interesting all right," Loretha chimed in.

"Make sure you don't have anything incriminating in your pockets."

"I wish you had told me that before, I would have left my Uzi at home."

Loretha and I both turned around.

"I'm only kidding," he said, grinning, and closed his eyes again, leaning back against the seat.

"What a sense of humor," I said, turning back to scan the road. Focusing on the tiger lilies and daisies growing wild along the parkway, I was grateful that my brother and the others were half-dozing so I could daydream. There was more than a small sense of unreality that I was on my way to my wedding and my bridegroom was locked behind bars.

It felt strange entering the flagstone prison building in my wedding attire with Barry, Loretha, and Tiffany at my side. Along with the white linen dress, I wore a crystal necklace, gold brooch, and gold and silver sandals. Even the guards smiled at me approvingly and were unusually friendly as they processed us through. I led Barry, Loretha, and Tiffany into the visiting room as if it were my living room. Settling into a table for four, Barry brought over an additional chair, which, happily, none of the guards hassled us about. The morning sun beamed in on us as we awaited Victor.

"This doesn't look so bad," Barry said, looking around.

"Well, this isn't what a cell looks like," I said.

"Yeah," Loretha said. "This is just what's presented to the public."

Spotting Victor coming in across the room, I said, "Here comes the groom."

We embraced lovingly, beaming at each other. After he hugged Loretha and Tiffany, I introduced Barry. "This is your future brother-in-law." They embraced.

"I've heard so much about you. I'm so happy to meet you," Victor said.

"Me too," Barry said self-consciously.

"You want anything to eat or drink? Anyone want anything? It's not exactly gourmet cuisine, but it's all we have," Victor said, indicating the machines.

They went to the machines in shifts while Victor and I clutched at each other.

"You look beautiful," Victor said. "People are admiring you."

"Thank you. Do I look like a bride?"

"Yes! You look like *my* bride."

"What time is the good reverend supposed to arrive?" I asked, vaguely uncomfortable with the idea of being married by a reverend. My father, though not a religious Jew, would have turned over in his grave if he knew I was being married by a Christian clergyman, though my marrying someone black and a gentile would not have bothered him as much.

"I don't know. Could be any time."

It turned out to be eleven o'clock. Reverend Jones, someone whom I didn't know but who was about to play an important part in my life, was large, with a navy windbreaker barely concealing his portly gut. His round, bespectacled face was serious but kindly. Victor walked over to him, and they exchanged a few words. Then Victor came back and got the rest of us. We followed him to the back of the visiting room where no one else was sitting. After introductions, the reverend, in a slow tired voice told us the procedure, where we would stand, and when the ring would be given.

"Any questions?" he asked, inclining his head like a teacher.

We took our places in front of yet another example of inmate talent: a trompe l'oeil wall of cherry wood bookcases, filled with colorful leather tomes bearing golden titles, in the center of which was a door, ajar, with a sparkling gold light shining from a room beyond; an artistic creation so realistic that people seeing the photographs afterward never questioned its veracity.

The reverend opened his book and began to read the standard wedding ceremony.

If the door behind us seemed real, the moment itself did not. It was another one of those times in which the observing self steps back and provides a running commentary; in this case it was saying, *Well you're finally getting married. You thought it would never happen, but here it is with those same words you've read and heard in movies a million times.* That's why when the reverend asked, "Denise, will you take Victor " instead of "Denise, *do* you take Victor" I was a bit thrown and responded "I do" anyway. Who ever says "I will"? Then, after the words "in sickness and in health, till death do you part" I choked up and answered with a cracking voice and tears. At the same moment, some of the inmates and visitors in the other part of the room came into my line of vision; they were watching, and it was weird to have this group of strangers, prisoners at that, partaking in such an intimate moment with me.

After Victor dutifully exclaimed his "I will," we embraced, and Barry came forward with the rings, which we gingerly placed on each other's fingers.

"You may kiss the bride," the reverend said, and we kissed and embraced. Loretha, a choir singer, broke into a rendition of "Giving You the Best That I've Got," and Victor and I stood there, holding hands, beaming, while the omnipresent "Click-Click" person loaded the camera. He took several shots of just Victor and me and then of all of us; the pictures were all beautiful, full of smiles, with the gleam of the burnished wood paneling and books behind us so rich that we could have been in an exclusive men's club library. Victor made me promise that I would bring the wedding dress to our first trailer visit so he could carry me over the threshold.

The reverend lingered and chatted with us for a few minutes before departing; then we returned to our table. A couple of people nearby congratulated us, and I sat there, trying to discern whether I felt different. On some level I did, demonstrating to me the power of rites to which I usually pay short shrift. Now, magically, the unit formed by Victor and me was official; we legally belonged to each other. It felt good, really good, but in this case, I knew, was no potential guarantee against loneliness. What felt strange, as always, was leaving him there, though this time a representation of him—the beautiful, shining band on my finger—came with me.

After dropping Loretha and Tiffany off at the A train and Barry at his apartment, I drove home. Walking through the door of my apartment, I patted my cat, Yin, saying, "Hey, I'm married now, baby." After turning on the air conditioner, I sat down on the couch, took off my shoes, and stared out the window at the familiar skyline of rooftops and water towers. Everything looked the same as always, and here I was home, alone as always, yet something was different, if only in its potential for the future. In the present my wedding day was a bittersweet reality, a happiness with an emptiness, a marriage with no wedding night. But at least now Victor and I knew that we were each other's next of kin. That's why though physically alone, I felt very much connected to him, and that made all the difference.

CHAPTER
TWELVE

FAMILY AFFAIRS

Going to work Monday morning a newly married woman was odd, because there was only one person there who knew about my marriage, a fellow social worker with whom I had become friendly. When I had expressed to Victor my concern about how I would explain the sudden appearance on my hand of a wedding band, his response was, "Don't worry about it. Probably no one will notice." This did not turn out to be the case.

You could be away from the hospital for weeks and upon your return the patients always acted as though you had never left, as if your life were only an extension of theirs. When I came in Monday, several tired, disheveled men of all colors, ages, and sizes, some of whom were violent criminals, hovered near the door.

Every morning the staff had rounds in the nurses' station, a rectangular room with a long Plexiglas wall and a door on each end. They would sit down and begin discussing patients and bitching and moaning about working in such a horrible place, while I worried about the effect on the patients who hovered outside the windows, staring at us, calling to us, or mumbling to themselves. Often they knocked and shouted in an effort to get the staff's attention. As usual on Monday mornings, the staff straggled in looking tired and depressed. Howie, one of the nurses, read the communication book, a large log in which staff members wrote of any incidents that might have taken place and messages to each other. Then specific patient care issues, most of which were painfully repetitive, were discussed. It was while we were talking about whether a very regressed elderly patient had been sexually abused by one of the young criminals there that my supervisor, Roberta, looked at my left hand and then at me with a quizzical smile. I smiled back at her and mouthed, "I'll talk to you later."

Rounds dragged on for about an hour, during which the nurses' station became filled with the usual hot air and tension. Leaving the nurses' station was like stepping from the safety of a car in a theme park into the wild where the animals roam free. As we walked down the hall to my office, Roberta and I stepped around patients who were sprawled out on the floor. Before she could ask any questions, I handed her one of the letters I had sent to Governor Cuomo in support of Victor's application for clemency. Anticipating people's questions, I had figured the letter would supply answers as it spelled out in glowing terms Victor's phoenixlike rise out of the ashes of Bedford-Stuyvesant and Vietnam, and how even though convicted of a crime for which he maintained his innocence, he had gotten two master's degrees, while growing in sensitivity and compassion, and was an inspiration to us all. Roberta read the three single-spaced pages and looked up.

"And the ring?"

"We got married Thursday."

She shook her head, looked at me thoughtfully with what I hoped was understanding, for I respected and admired Roberta, and her opinion was important to me.

"This must be very hard for you. How long have you known him?"

"A year. It is hard, but it's meaningful. He's a wonderful person. What's hard is coming here and seeing murderers like Barry Roberts and Ted Hutchinson coming and going as they please, yet they would not let Victor, who insists he's innocent, stay at a medium security prison because they thought it was too open."

"That must be very frustrating."

"It is. The system is awful. Corrections makes the Office of Mental Health look like a humane and charitable organization. They feel justified in treating people with cruelty. Victor always says he doesn't know why they call it 'Corrections,' especially these days."

"You have a lot of courage, Denise."

"I have to believe in him and our future, or else I'm just a foolhardy risk taker."

"Well, how can it be wrong to follow your heart? When I was a young girl in high school, I was very much in love with a boy. We planned to get married, but my family did not like his family. They told me that I should not marry him, so eventually I broke up with him to please my parents."

"Why didn't they like him?"

"Oh, he'd been in some trouble when he was younger, and he was poor and just starting out, and they felt he could not provide well enough for me."

"That's too bad." I nodded sympathetically.

"Denise," Roberta said, meeting my eyes, "I never got over it. Even after I married Don, I always wondered what my life would have been like if I had stayed with that boy. That's why I believe one should summon the courage to follow one's heart."

I sighed heavily. "Yes, that's what I'm doing, following my heart. I can only hope it will lead to the future about which Victor and I dream, but at this point there are no guarantees. At least that's what Victor keeps reminding me. Nevertheless, I have to take that chance."

At that moment we heard shouting in the hall. We stared at each other. "Who was that?" Roberta asked.

"It's the new patient we got yesterday. He doesn't want to be here."

As Roberta got up to leave, I was grateful for her support. I stared out the window at the red maples blowing in the hot August wind. What would the future bring? How could I know? I had to have faith that Victor would get out of prison eventually, and even more important, I needed to feel good in the present. I had encouraged Victor to apply once more for clemency. He said there was not much chance of him getting it, but I knew he deserved it, and sometimes the Universe or God or the powers that be actually gave us what we deserved. Sometimes I wondered whether Victor didn't have some horrendous karma that caused him to be locked up in prison when he was innocent. Often I wondered about my karma, too, and about karma in general. Many people liked to say things like, "What goes around comes around," but I always found that hard to believe because many people who are evil get rewards and never get punished for their wicked deeds. And others who are good like Martin Luther King, Indira Gandhi or Nelson Mandela are punished or cut down. Perhaps it's all random, and we're like flowers and trees: is there any reason why this tree instead of that is blown down in a hurricane or a volcano eruption destroys one town and not another?

I looked around the cell that I called my office and wondered if it was a divine plan which had me coming daily to a place like this. In fact, it did seem like a plan, because state mental hospitals had been in my life before. As a child in Little Neck, New York, Creedmoor State Hospital loomed over our neighborhood, a constant threat of what inhumanity to the afflicted could permit. One of the kids on the block was shunned because her mother was in and out of Creedmoor. On the other hand, I imagined myself a Jeanne d'Arc, restoring mercy to Creedmoor, that complex of mammoth, tan brick buildings, tiered like a wedding cake with its hundreds of screened and barred windows. When I was thirteen, a popular book among the pre-teen set was about young girls volunteering as Candy Stripers, and I wanted nothing more than to volunteer at Creedmoor so that I could so something about the conditions. When my mother took me there to inquire about my helping out, they looked at us as if *we* were crazy. In junior high school I participated in a trip to the infamous Pilgrim State Hospital, and a tour through dark, foul-smelling hallways that housed lobotomized patients confirmed my suspicions about the inhumane way we treated those who are mentally ill.

Perhaps my dreams came as the result of a collective unconscious memory passed on by my father who had returned from World War II with the emotional disturbance they called *shell shock.* They sent him to Pilgrim State. Though he never actually spoke to me about his two-month stay there, when I heard about it as an adult, it was as if I already knew. Even my astrology chart showing Pluto in Scorpio transiting my twelfth house foretold an intimate involvement with hospitals and prisons and people being confined in one way or another. Well, I was really in it, sunk in the basement of my twelfth house. Sometimes it seemed, despite all my plans for helping those imprisoned, here I too was helpless, locked away in my own prison's deepest, most remote corners. Nevertheless, I labored on.

When I went to see Victor the Saturday after our wedding, the rings on our fingers were not the only difference: my parents and brother were no longer my primary family; this muscular, bronze-skinned man who looked at me adoringly was. Now I was thinking of the future not as an individual but as part of a family unit. What was as natural as the birds and the bees suddenly dawned on me: this is why people procreate. This is what happens when two people who are in love want to have a family. Although just before I had begun my relationship with Victor, I had been struck by the fact that my biological clock was ticking. I had never really understood it before, the desire to have your own little unit of people which you actually create with someone you love. It was amazing to me that something so simple could seem so profound. "Raising a family." It's one of those phrases that's with us from the time we're children and one that we take for granted, yet because my family background was so troubled, I grew up thinking of family as toxic and an oppressor, and never realized how good being in a family could feel.

So here I was in my mid-thirties experiencing these homey domestic feelings, despite the fact that Victor wasn't even home. I became more nostalgic about my own parents. I started to watch more baseball on television, which reminded me of my father. I suddenly became a Mets fan (though my Bronx father was born and died rooting for the Yankees). Then I found myself watching cooking and home repair shows. To feel productive while doing all this sitting and watching, I resumed my old hobby of knitting. I had a habit of starting and abandoning knitting projects like a child with new toys; sweaters without arms and vests without sides cluttered my closet, but in this case I felt on a mission. In a month, I completed a brick red cowl-necked sweater for Victor, perhaps a little large, but fashioned with love. If only I could bottle the energy created by our union.

We started to talk about getting pregnant. At first Victor said all the correct things like, "This isn't the time" and "We don't know when I'll get out. How can we create a child who we may not be able to parent the right way?"

But I objected. "We are going to be together. I know it, and you must too. We have to fight for your freedom together, just as we fought to get married, and have confidence that this is meant to be."

We agreed to start trying. Now that we were married we were able to have regular trailer visits, and we discussed the possibility of trying to schedule them when I'd be ovulating. But we knew that if we had to wait for trailer visits it could take months or even years to get pregnant. So we discussed our options and came up with a plan.

The following Saturday when I was processed for entry to the visiting room, I had two items on me that the guards did not see: one was a brown, plastic drug store vial with a cap. The other was a vaginal inserter, the kind that comes with cream for yeast infections. Both were nestled snugly in my underwear.

After Victor and I secured our table by the window, I transferred them to one of the large pockets on the front of the long black cotton sundress I wore for the occasion. *If Corrections were really on top of things, they would ban long dresses and skirts from the visiting room since it is so easy for women to hide things under them and use them as camouflaging shields,* I could not help thinking.

Dark clouds filled the sky outside the window, and the pungent scents of earth and humidity mixed with the sweet scents of each other. This was the eleventh day into my menstrual cycle and we were psyched with a profound sense of potential. We were so drawn to each other; at no time was our skin not touching even if it was only a small patch on the back of our hands. We craved connection, merging. We took note that the regular staff was in place, the leonine male officer who reigned supreme from his perch up front and one of the regulars at the back of the room. We were as hidden as possible by families at nearby tables. We passed the hours as usual: romantic sojourns to the vending machines; standing embraces; knees touching; whispering; talking delightedly about the children we would have, until we realized it was getting late and if we were to accomplish our mission, we couldn't postpone it any longer. Both of the guards were occupied, and as we spoke erotic words to each other Victor's hand disappeared under my skirt and mine into his open fly. As Victor's eyes met mine, I handed him the vial under the table which he then strategically placed so as to retrieve the fluid which would help create our family. Then, carefully placing the cap on it, he handed it to me, and with a parting kiss, I palmed the warm vial in my pocket and headed for the ladies room. There, locked in the stall, I poured the fluid into the vaginal inserter and put it inside me as deeply as possible, followed by a tampon to prevent leakage. I left the dark, littered bathroom feeling less alone, as though I now walked with a companion, and for the first time had an inkling as to how a wanted pregnancy must feel. Throughout the next day I walked around feeling smug: I was not alone; my husband was with me at all times.

We decided that I would take a long weekend away from work and go back to the prison that Monday so we could repeat our efforts. So once again with vial and applicator in the black sundress and Beethoven's Ninth filling the car with majesty, I set out for the hills of Orange County, joyful to be going to my love. Monday morning at the prison was uncrowded and quiet, people seeming too tired and hung over to be energetic about anything. Relieved, I got through the processing with no trouble and walked into the spacious and warm visiting room glistening with the early morning sun. I was glad to see that the guard at the front of the room was not the usual one but a female guard who in the past had shown herself to be quite laid back, even disinterested, preferring to sit at the desk and nap or file her nails.

When Victor came in, he whispered, "We could forego the vial method and do it the 'real' way."

"I was thinking the same thing." I smiled at him.

The thought fed our erotic fires like a match on gas-soaked charcoals. For the next two hours our love talk was detailed and graphic, until we determined that the time was right: there were no guards nearby, and the one at the front was dozing. People sitting at tables near us were providing a functional block. I left Victor to go to the bathroom and remove my panties which I carried back to the table in the large pocket of my sundress. I now understood why not wearing underwear could be such a turn-on; as the air hit my inner thighs and pubis, I felt so exposed, yet no one knew! Back at the table, Victor pulled my chair toward him in such a way that we were at right angles to each other. Though I tried to get close enough to him that our bodies could make contact, we were unable to do so. I turned my chair to face him, and Victor held the jacket he had brought up as a shield. After looking around to make sure no one was watching, I put my legs over his, covered by the dress. He pressed against me and then with some difficulty, began to push his way into me.

In high school, when my friend and I would sneak a joint

in her room while her mother was down the hall cooking dinner, I'd be too uptight to do it. Whenever I tried to do something sneaky or illicit, the nervousness I experienced almost rendered the act not worthwhile. This is what happened that day at Otisville. I was so anxious that my muscles were tight, and he could barely enter me. Once he did, I couldn't relax and enjoy it; I just wanted him to come and get it over with. The act became purely utilitarian, a means to an end. After he pulled out, my original level of excitement returned, and I felt its "afterglow." Surreptitiously, I looked at our neighbors to see if they were all gaping at us, but no one seemed conscious of our existence. The guard at the front was barely awake. While normally people's unconsciousness got me angry, this time it was a blessing.

"Here, why don't you sit on this and put your legs up so they are elevated." Victor folded his jacket and put it under me. The idea was to give the sperm every advantage on their journey into my uterus. I tried to relax knowing that gave us the best chance to conceive.

Our remaining time together vanished seemingly in seconds, and then I was on my way home once again, feeling part of Victor was with me. When I got to my block, I was fortunate that a car pulled out and gave me a parking spot right near my building.

Lying on my bed with my Sunday *New York Times* crossword and my beloved Yin, nothing felt bad, except that Victor was not by my side, and even that was tolerable because the existence of our love superseded everything. But two weeks later when I went to the bathroom one morning and felt that familiar pressure in my pelvis, then saw the watery, brown blood on the toilet paper, my disappointment for the first time at not being pregnant struck me, and I wept. When I told Victor that night on the phone, he was typically upbeat, "Don't worry, my love. We'll just keep on trying. It will happen."

I could not help but be struck by the irony. When I was younger, I was always in a state of high anxiety if my period were even a day late. This was a serious problem for a single woman, and birth control was a major challenge. At the age of nineteen, my college friends and I had joined the women of the ghetto in Roxbury, Massachusetts to become among the first in the country to receive the Dalkon Shield into our wombs. For three years I tolerated massive periods with profuse bleeding. Three years later I had it removed at St. Luke's Hospital in New York City after several days of incessant bleeding. Around this time, horror stories of hysterectomies and infertility resulting from the Dalkon Shield were beginning to make media headlines.

Optimistic and hopeful, I had accepted another intra-uterine device. The Safe-T Coil was less offensive than the Dalkon Shield, at least until it fell out. At this point you might think I'd have learned my lesson, but what was the choice? Pills? A diaphragm?

I succumbed to the diaphragm, plus periods of withdrawal and abstinence. In my thirties, I was fed up with the battle against what Nature meant to have happen, but I had no choice.

With Victor in my life, magically procreation became the beautiful act that everyone claimed. How sadly ironic it was then, that for me, finally at this juncture in which I was ready and eager for pregnancy, having sex with the man I loved, my husband, was the major challenge instead of birth control.

A few weeks later on a Saturday, Victor and I had an opportunity to discuss this and other profundities in a somewhat different setting than we were used to. The Muslim prisoners' group was hosting a family day picnic, and though we weren't Muslim, Victor had a good rapport with some guys in the group who encouraged us to attend their picnic anyway as a kind of honeymoon. The ten dollar fee entitled us to a barbecue, live music, and five hours in each other's company out in the fresh air, surrounded by the rolling hills and farmlands, with the guards at enough distance that they weren't breathing down our necks. One of the pleasures of visiting Victor at Otisville was catching sight of him on my way in through the gate where he waited up the hill. He couldn't wave, though, since technically he wasn't supposed to be there waiting. On the morning of the picnic he was there as usual, and when I saw him, all seemed right with the world.

After parking, I proceeded to a different area than I normally did for processing. This in itself was fun, as was any break in the routine. We lined up in a small, low-ceilinged corridor and were processed by officers at a heavy wooden desk. There they did the usual inspection of our possessions and ran a handheld metal detector over our persons. Then we were ushered out a back door and into a bus the color of mushroom soup which shuttled us down to the field. On the way, we passed a group of inmates walking on the road, and all the women in the bus craned their necks to see if their man was in the group. Mine was there at the front, grinning as widely as any of them. Now it was okay for him to wave, and I waved back.

On the field, a four-member band was warming up, and chicken, franks, and burgers were cooking on several grills; as the inmates and their guests found each other there were shrieks and squeals. Like children on summer vacation, Victor and I almost skipped out into the field holding hands. For a while, we sat on weather-worn bleachers, then walked back to the tables where most of the people were congregating. After Victor introduced me to some acquaintances and we saw that the food wasn't ready, we went back to the grass to lie down. A few minutes later a guard walked toward us.

"You two have to sit up. From where I was standing it looked like you were doing something you shouldn't be," the lanky guard said from behind his shades.

We looked at each other and sat up. "Sorry, Officer," Victor said.

"No problem," the guard said and walked away.

"Even when you're not doing something, they think you are," Victor said.

"It's their job to be suspicious," I said.

"Come on, my love, let's go eat."

We savored the barbecued chicken, corn on the cob, and salad as the hot sun baked our heads. As we were finishing up, the band started to play.

"They're pretty good," Victor said, turning to face the four men who, in their prison clothes, were playing guitars, drums, and a saxophone. After one rendition of a popular song, we got up and strolled toward them. The singer was saying something about "Congratulations to the newlyweds," and Victor said, "This is for us." I was vaguely embarrassed as we stood and swayed with the music, but pleased at the sentiment.

The only thing that was wrong with an otherwise perfect visit was it ended too soon, earlier than regular visiting hours. It seemed the sun had barely passed the point of high noon when the guards were ushering us back into the bus. As I drove through the prison front gate, I saw Victor off to the side, standing on the road, waving. Out the window I held up my hand with thumb, forefinger, and pinkie raised in the American Sign Language word for "I love you." In the mirror I saw him do the same.

The days that we spent apart inched by. My thoughts focused on the time Victor and I could be together. Now that we were married, we were eligible for the family reunion program, more commonly known to the public as conjugal visits and to inmates and their loved ones as trailer visits. There was only one small problem: there were no trailers at Otisville. Program opportunities were also minimal, and Victor, with his two master's degrees, was cleaning toilets. Victor usually kept a stiff upper lip and rarely complained, but one day he said, depressed, "I've always felt I was in here for a reason, and when they let me get an education and start those programs for disabled inmates I thought perhaps that was it, but I can't conceive what the rationale for this is."

"What about my writing some more letters, this time to try to get you transferred?" I offered.

"It probably won't help."

"But it may," I insisted.

"Maybe Fishkill," he mused, quickly regaining his usual positive outlook. "At least we could have trailer visits there."

I smiled. "A taste of heaven."

At that moment, neither of us spoke of how or when he would get out permanently. Victor had tried all the legal avenues he could to get a new trial with no success, and we didn't want to speak of my hitherto unsuccessful campaign, so we focused on the present. Unlike when a person is staying someplace voluntarily, such as a school or hospital, an inmate is moved around like a pawn on a chessboard. It didn't hurt to tell the right people what you wanted, however, as had happened a few months before when Victor was transferred to Walkill. Even though it wasn't admitted openly, someone might say or do something behind the scenes which would bring about what you wanted.

A few days later, Victor was mopping in the school area when he ran into Yvette Williams, whom he had known as a teacher at Eastern. They greeted each other heartily; he had always liked Yvette, a tall, handsome, white woman who had been married to one of the nicer corrections officers who was black and had a drinking problem.

"Hey, Victor, how're you doing? I can't believe I'm seeing you of all people mopping the floor."

"Well, funny you should say that. My wife and I were just talking about it."

"You got married? Congratulations."

"Thanks. What are you doing here? Are you teaching?"

"Well, no. Actually, I'm the education director." She smiled.

"Oh, that's great. Any chance there might be a job for me here?"

"No, I'm sorry, Victor. I wish there was. There really isn't much going on here in that way."

"My wife and I were wishing that I could get a transfer to Fishkill. I know they have a tutoring program where I could be of some help to the other guys."

"That's a good idea. Let me know if I can help in any way. I've got to get going. Good luck."

He watched Yvette walk off, thinking that maybe Fate was with him. Victor was known and respected in the education departments of all the facilities he had been in, and most of the teachers like Yvette had positive attitudes toward inmates, especially the ones who went to school and showed the desire and ambition to get an education. While I began another letter writing campaign, a few days later, Victor met with Bill, his counselor.

"Well, I can't just transfer you. You know it doesn't work like that," the counselor said with his usual dour face.

"What do I need to do?" Victor asked. "I would like to get involved in the program there to help the other inmates. Also, they have the Juvenile Justice certificate which I'm just a few credits shy of completing."

"Look, if you can get a letter from someone at Fishkill saying they have a need for you to work there, then I'd have reason to put through the transfer. Otherwise, there's nothing I can do," Bill told him.

Back in his cell, Victor wracked his brain. Who did he know at Fishkill? Then he remembered that Neal Ritter, the teacher with whom he had tutored at Green Haven, was now at Fishkill. The next time we talked, Victor asked me to call or visit Neal and ask if he'd consider writing the necessary letter.

I felt nervous speaking to someone I didn't know, but I was ready to do anything I could to advance Victor's cause. The next open day I had, I went to see Neal.

"Of course," Neal said, "I'd be happy to." Everyone was eager to help Victor. Everyone, of course, but people in a position to give him a new trial or help shorten or commute his sentence. Another person who had become a devoted fan of Victor's was Beatrice, an elderly woman who had come with the Jaycees, a charitable group, to visit the prison one day. Amongst other things, they went into prisons to cheer up the inmates by keeping them company and giving them small gifts. Beatrice had gotten to talking with Victor on one of these visits and had been exchanging letters with him for years. A devoted New York City Upper West Sider, Beatrice actually lived near me, and I was eager to meet her. Perhaps she would have new ideas for me to try to free Victor. On the phone, she had the type of voice that made me picture Tallulah Bankhead or Marlene Dietrich. We arranged to meet at a local pastry shop.

We had a strange conversation, Beatrice sitting across

from me in her worn, tan designer trench coat and trademark floppy hat. She had a Sunset Boulevard fading glamour, including an unreal English accent. But she was reaching out to Victor and was not afraid to go into a prison to help someone, so she commanded my respect. Their worlds were so divergent, I couldn't help but wonder, if Victor had met her under other circumstances, what, if any, relationship he would have had with her.

Neal sent the letter within days. Victor brought it to his counselor who said, "I'll see what I can do but I wouldn't count on anything. They're probably going to know you really want to move because you just got married and want trailer visits."

"But I have this letter requesting my presence in the tutoring program at Fishkill."

"Well, like I said, I'll send it and we'll see what happens."

Once Victor had met with his counselor, I sought out Yvette Williams and told her about what had transpired, including Victor's depressing conversation with Bill.

She frowned. "I wonder how they think we can stop these guys from coming back if we don't help them find another way of life. I'll make some calls in my capacity as Education Director." She was as good as her word. And whether it was Neal's letter or my efforts or Yvette's intercession or a combination thereof, not long afterward the word came down that Victor would be transferred.

CHAPTER
THIRTEEN

FISHKILL CORRECTIONAL FACILITY

At the foot of the Catskills, Beacon, New York is a working class town at the end of Route 52, off Interstate 84. Overlooking the Hudson River, it should be a lot prettier than it is. One of Beacon's main sources of revenue and employment is the Fishkill Correctional Facility on the outskirts of town. On I-84 a sign warns passing drivers "CORRECTIONAL FACILITY AREA," presumably in the event a green-clad inmate is seen escaping across the highway. In its proximity to the town, Fishkill Correctional Facility is different than many New York State penitentiaries.

The prison, a sprawling series of one-story, dark red brick buildings, many with turrets, along with some taller, light tan buildings, is enclosed and protected by miles of chain-link fence topped with razor wire. Unlike Otisville, there are also gun towers. Overall, as it comes into view, the impression is one of a place where there should be tunnels and torture chambers, hidden rooms where unspeakable things happen. This is not far from reality; Fishkill used to be the Mattawan State Hospital for the criminally insane, and tales abound about the torturous things that were done to its helpless inmates.

Victor was transferred to Fishkill on one of those brilliantly sunny September days when it seems impossible to believe that snow and 4:40 P.M. darkness are just around the corner. We were ecstatic, anticipating trailer visits and dreaming of Victor getting work release when he would be eligible.

I was eager to see Victor in his new setting and take advantage of the evening visiting hours. After a long, arduous ride up the narrow, winding Taconic Parkway, I made my way west on Route 52 and finally saw the sign "Fishkill Correctional Facility." I turned off and drove along a bumpy road on which there were houses with children playing in front yards; at the end were signs warning against arms and other contraband and stating that unauthorized people would be prosecuted. Straight ahead was the parking lot, adjacent to one of the many brick buildings which housed some of the fourteen hundred inmates. As I got out of the car, I noticed a few men standing in the windows seemingly staring at me. I felt vaguely uncomfortable, assuming them to be horny and deprived.

The waiting area was a trailer which contained the standard decor of lockers and benches. On this Thursday afternoon there was no one there but a guard sitting at a desk which I approached.

"Sign the book." He indicated a large log open on the desk. This established your presence and the order of arrival when crowds were present. After I signed, he scrutinized my signature so long I thought he was going to ask for further identification. The officer went to a phone nearby and informed someone that I was there.

"Okay."

"Could you tell me where I go?" I asked. Why did I always have to pry information from them?

"Out there," he said, shrugging. He indicated a door behind his desk which led outside to a wire cage. I stood and waited until the first gate buzzed open. When I walked into the cage, it shut behind me as my heart beat faster. Then the other gate opened and I walked up some stairs and into a building where I waited while three officers in the adjoining room paid no attention to me, chatting and laughing as if I were invisible. Finally, one of them called, "Hey you, you can go in." I had to show a picture ID and sign Victor's visitor's sheet. Here again, they took great pains to make sure all the signatures above mine were covered.

Next was the metal detector, which, like everything else, was a greater production here than in other facilities. I had the usual anxiety, hoping I wouldn't set it off by some overlooked metal I might be carrying. I was not totally unprepared when told to remove my shoes as Victor had warned me about, but it was still unsettling to have to remove clothing with all the implications of strip searches. Happily, everything went well, and with relief I walked to the end of the corridor into yet another room which led into the first of the two visiting rooms.

None of this in itself was terrible; what made it somewhat trying was the attitude of the guards. More than in any of the other facilities, they conveyed the feeling that they thought you were scum, and it was your fault that they were in such a horrible place doing such reprehensible work. This was conveyed by the way they talked down to you and looked at you without making eye contact. It was clear to me that they had absolutely no respect for anyone who was personally connected with an inmate. They didn't know, nor care, that I was their peer, a fellow state worker and civil servant; to them I was garbage, even though I probably made more money than most of them and certainly had more education, as did Victor.

After what seemed like a long journey through a maze, I was in the visiting room where I was dismayed to see long rows of tables. The privacy afforded in other facilities at which Victor had been imprisoned did not exist here. One wall was lined with about a dozen vending machines, and opposite this was the "No Smoking" area which basically meant you could not smoke at that table and but could at the one next to it. I took a seat at the end, farthest from the front desk where the corrections officer was perched. Victor came in after about ten minutes from the other side of the room, and as always when we embraced, the foulness of the scene around us diminished as we created our own little universe. I told him about my drive up the Taconic, making sure to give as much detail about cars, the road, the forests, and hills along the road. I always tried to convey to him as much of the outside world as possible. He smiled and then asked, "Was it all right getting in?"

I frowned.

"Yeah, this place is rough," Victor said. "It's a medium security facility, yet they have more rules than anywhere. Did you know that I'm forbidden from going to the vending machines?"

"Why, what do they think you're going to do there?"

"It's another way of controlling and demeaning us," Victor said.

"I hate you being here."

"I know," he said quietly, "and no more than I hate it and hate putting you through all this." He paused. "We're not supposed to embrace either."

"That's pretty awful," I said, feeling disappointed that we would not have the opportunity to hold each other. Walking together to the vending machines had been one opportunity to be close during hours spent sitting at a table. My heart went out to Victor, as I witnessed him being humiliated and infantilized by the system. "So how are you supposed to decide what you want from the machines?"

"I guess you go up and see what's there, come back, and report to me. Then I tell you, and you go back and get it."

Our joy at Victor being transferred gradually diminished, like air slowly seeping from a tire, as we began to have a sense of what this facility was like.

"Oh, God, sweetheart, we've got to get you out of here."

"I just got here." He leaned in and kissed me. "But don't worry about me, honey. It's you I worry about. Are you gonna be okay?"

I was feeling little wings of doubt fluttering somewhere in my gut, but I said, "Of course. As long as you're okay, I'll be fine. Anyway, I'm so glad that you're that much closer to home, both in space and time."

"Is this much closer to the city?"

"Oh yeah, it's closer than any of the places I've visited you in so far."

"Good, I'm glad you don't have to drive so far."

"Listen, I'd follow you to the ends of the earth if I had to. Anyway, I love to drive — at least when I get out of the city."

"I look forward to driving with you."

"Oh, I can't wait."

"Shall we venture a walk outside, my love?"

"Outside" was a twenty-five-foot-square courtyard in the center of the building. There was a cement path around its perimeter and grass in the center with four weatherbeaten picnic tables and an oak tree already shedding dry yellowing leaves. Along each wall were benches, erratically placed. We stepped out past the guard and started to walk.

"Well, it ain't Central Park, but at least it's air," Victor said.

"Look at all those windows." We were surrounded by them; three of the walls were in the visiting room, and the other we would later find out was the school area where Victor would be working.

"Yeah, you never know who's gonna be observing you when you're out here."

There were only a handful of inmates and their visitors in the yard, so we were able to sit on a bench and not be on top of other people. We talked quietly, enjoying the warm air, grateful for the presence of the one tree with its leaves rustling. Soon the guard announced that the yard would close in five minutes, so we headed back inside.

As the day wore on and the daylight waned, it got darker in the visiting room and the overhead fluorescent lights cast a harsh glare. "I think I'll leave when it's still light out so my ride will be easier." Victor was able to walk me as far as the desk. Our goodbye was brief and minimally physical as there were eight guards standing there.

"Why are there so many of them?" I whispered in his ear.

He laughed. "Shhh, they're protecting you. Get home safely. I'll call you tomorrow, sweetheart. I love you madly."

When I got home, exhausted but happy, there was a letter and a card from Victor, both with elaborate colorful designs on the envelopes, and a letter from one of the legislators to whom I had written about Victor. The letter was brief, stating that the bill he had written regarding time off for good behavior for lifers was on the back burner now as there were several pressing issues facing the legislature, and this was not a very popular bill anyway. Letters like this reminded me that while I might be in love with a prison inmate, most people looked on the incarcerated with contempt. There was much more sympathy for the mental patients I worked with each day, for even though many of them had committed heinous crimes, their mental illness relieved them of responsibility. The mood in the country had changed, and many people in the general public seemed to be in favor of punishing inmates and exacting revenge. The death penalty was coming back in favor, though recently an editorial in the newspapers had told of a series of innocent people, especially minorities, who served long prison sentences or even were executed. I shuddered thinking Victor could have been one of the latter. Moreover, I knew, though many in the outside world appeared to have forgotten, that most inmates would eventually return to the streets, and it behooved the system to prepare them. At times like these I felt I was climbing uphill, making little progress. It was difficult to accept that Victor was not only innocent but had worked every year of his confinement for the betterment of himself and others and yet had to remain in that environment. Each day when I went to work, I watched truly dangerous people going out to the streets, and I was overwhelmed with the absurdity and unfairness of it all.

One day, three weeks after Victor got to Fishkill, I had just finished seeing one of my private patients. For close to an hour, I had listened to this anxious, depressed woman talk about how her life was dictated by her inability to drive over bridges through tunnels, or ride in elevators. I quickly changed into shorts, a T-shirt, and running shoes, and went downstairs. The doorman, a portly Dominican man, said, "Denise, you know someone named Charlie?"

"Yes," I told him. I hadn't seen my old boyfriend in years.

"Well, he was here. He didn't look very good," he said and lowered his voice. "He smelled like liquor. So I told him you were not home."

For a second, I stood there looking at him with my mouth hanging open, thinking, *how dare you manipulate the truth like that*; then I concluded it wasn't worth getting into a confrontation with the doorman, especially since he had known I had my patient upstairs, so I thanked him instead.

"He left you this note."

Sure enough, there was Charlie's meticulous but erratic handwriting in a brief, friendly message which ended with his phone number and address, the Terminal Hotel on Twenty-third Street. I felt suddenly depressed. It was a hotel populated by drunks and junkies. As I jogged along the outside of Riverside Park, I thought about calling him. Perhaps I could help him. No, I probably wouldn't be much help, and anyway, I didn't want to discuss Victor with him.

He also might take my calling him as an invitation to call regularly, and I didn't want him to do that.

On Saturday morning my alarm went off at 4:30. As I did each pre-dawn Saturday, I thought, only love could make me do this, especially after getting up at 6:00 all week to go to work. My drive began easily, however, on virtually empty roads as the sun slowly rose. At the point on the Taconic Parkway where construction forced all cars into one lane, it became stressful as I wound up behind someone going thirty miles an hour. It was hard to have patience behind the wheel when I wanted to be one of the first visitors to arrive at Fishkill.

On the weekends at Fishkill the trailer quickly filled up with visitors well before the time they started letting us in. I pulled into the parking lot, and another woman entering the trailer let me know that she was ahead of me. We stood around making small talk, mostly about our husbands (every inmate was called a husband, married or not). We talked about how hard it was being a prison wife and how much longer we had to serve what had become a joint sentence. After half an hour that seemed like half a day, the phone rang; it was an officer inside instructing the guard in the trailer to start sending us in.

"Okay," he called. "Numbers one through ten, line up."

We lined up by the door, everyone slightly pushing, and waited for the guard to open it. Once outside, we waited again, this time for the first gate of the cage to open, then we shuffled into the cage and had to wait until everyone was inside before the other gate would close. Inevitably, one person lagged behind, and the rest of us got more annoyed as the minutes ticked away, robbing us of time with our men.

By nine o'clock when I was finally united with Victor, I was tired and ready to relax. To my chagrin, the visit began with an encounter with Sergeant Regis, a tall corrections officer with slicked-back hair and a bulging gut above his belt, who stopped me as I entered the smaller visiting room through which others walked in order to get to the main room.

"This room is closed."

"I'm just going to the machines."

"Sorry, it's closed."

The room was actually open, but for some reason we weren't allowed to sit there; I didn't know why. As Victor often said, "There you go being logical again."

"The machines in there have a kind of muffin that the machines in this room don't have," I told Regis.

"Well, okay, I'll allow it this time but that's it."

"Thank you," I said humbly.

After completing my mission, I returned to Victor and told him what had happened.

"That's what prison is all about: nonsensical rules that don't even get enforced all the time. Whether a rule gets enforced has to do with the enforcer and what mood they're in: did he have a fight with his wife this morning, did he get laid last night, did his supervisor reprimand him?"

"I know. It really puts you in a no-win situation. I guess the only way you can deal with it is by always following the rules and never questioning them."

"That's what I try to do. Sometimes it's hard because so many of the rules are so stupid, but I keep trying." He put his head down as if meditating.

I became silent too, watching him wistfully.

A little later, people were sitting in the small visiting room which was not supposed to be open.

Victor looked up. "That's what I mean. There's no rhyme or reason."

We chitchatted for several minutes. Then I said, "An old boyfriend stopped by to see me."

"Who?" Victor asked.

"Charlie. He seems to have fallen on hard times. He's living at the Terminal Hotel where a lot of drunks and junkies live," I said softly.

"He's a drunk?"

"And a junkie. He always liked to escape one way or another."

"You didn't let him in, I hope."

"No, I didn't, but what if I had?"

He looked at me as if I had said something in Martian. "Denise, I can't believe I'm hearing you say that. The guy's a drug addict. You don't know what he might have wanted."

"But he's not just some stranger off the street. He's someone I know. You really think I would have let him in if I thought he would do something abusive or harmful?" I felt a vague panic in my stomach; this was mine and Victor's first real disagreement. Did he have an irrational, jealous side to him that I hadn't met before? What if the mild-mannered, sweet, thoughtful man I thought I knew was only one small part of him, and along with that resided a monster?

Perhaps he was wondering, too, if he had married a flake with poor judgment. "Look, this is a guy," he went on, "who you haven't seen in several years. You don't know where he's at. For all you know he's down and out looking for money for a fix and was planning to rob you."

"No, I know that's not the case."

"How do you know?"

"I know him." Both of us looked out of the corners of our eyes behind us where the guard that had been strolling decided to stop. Under his breath Victor said, "I don't believe he's going to stop right next to us."

"Ignore him," I said. "Anyway, look, honey, I understand you're concerned about my welfare, but you have to trust me."

"How can I trust you when you tell me you almost let a junkie into your apartment to be alone with you?" His voice was getting louder.

Victor put his head in his hands. The guard strolled down a few feet and positioned himself at a diagonal from us, crossed his arms across his chest, and watched us. Victor looked up at him.

"Is there a problem, officer?" Victor called.

The guard walked toward us. "What?"

"I was wondering why you're staring at my wife." Then in a completely uncharacteristic reaction, Victor lost his usual even temper. "Can't we talk with each other without having you watch us?" I cringed, knowing Victor was transferring his exasperation with me to the guard, and hoped he wouldn't really lose it.

"Come with me." The guard motioned to Victor as he started to walk. Victor said, "Wait here," and followed him to a table nearby.

I watched them as Victor's eyes grew dark with frustration and the guard's hand jabbed the air. I nervously hoped Victor would maintain control. At the least, the guard could terminate our visit, and at worst, lock Victor in solitary. Normally Victor was so calm, polite, and rational with everyone, but now he was defending not only himself but me as well, and I feared that macho pride might rear its obstreperous head and get the better of him. Suddenly I felt scared and alone, as if I had entered a foreign land in which I didn't belong, full of snarling men. When Victor came back, I was relieved. "He's going to write me up, but he said we could continue the visit as long as I remain calm."

"God, what did he think, you were going to start throwing punches?"

"It's okay, Denise. I can handle it." He stared straight ahead with his jaw clenched. I ached for him as another man in a position of authority threatened his autonomy as a man and a husband. I put my arm around him. "I'm sorry, sweetheart. Don't worry, I won't let anyone in until you are home."

"Look, I'm not saying that. I just worry about you, that's all. I don't know if you can imagine my feeling of helplessness here. I don't know what I would do if anything happened to you. It's so frustrating not being there to help you."

"But you do. You don't know what a tremendous effect you have on my life without even being present."

"I know, but if there's any physical threat to you..."

"Hey, I love you, Victor, and I will not do anything to put myself at any kind of risk, but I need you to promise me the same, which includes not getting into anything with these fools here."

"Oh, I didn't really get into anything with this guy. You know I get along with them really well. Nothing bad will happen to me. I don't want you to worry, okay? I love you."

We kissed passionately but broke it off quickly as we knew we were being closely watched. "They go on alert when they see people arguing in here because there have been incidents of people losing it and hitting each other."

"Yeah? People actually have the nerve to hit each other here? What do the guards do then?"

"I've seen a few times where the guy's wife hauled off and hit him. The guards just terminated the visit and gave the inmate a ticket."

"So you'll be okay?"

"Yeah. Listen, please bear with me if I get jealous. As I said, it's very frustrating being locked up in here, knowing you are out there with a guy who might come on to you or worse. Not that I don't trust you," Victor looked me in the eyes, "but I know how difficult this can be for you, how you might get lonely or whatever."

"Sweetheart, you can be sure I will not let anyone in my home, nor would I be with anyone else anywhere. I'm married to you and no matter how lonely I might feel, I will always be loyal to you."

"Thank you," he whispered. "I love you so much."

"We'll both feel a lot better once we have a trailer visit and are able to be alone even for a short while."

"That's for sure," Victor said.

"The visiting yard is now open!" One of the guards at the front announced.

"Come on," Victor said, "I need some air."

"Me too."

The rest of the day we were cautious under the scrutiny of the guards, and I left feeling more sad than usual. While driving home, I relived our first fight and told myself it had been inevitable, that no one could get along as well as we had been, that arguing was part of every relationship. On the one hand, it scared me as I had watched my parents' relationship degenerate in proportion to the amount they argued. On the other hand, I was almost relieved that the perfectness of Victor's and my relationship had been broken, since it had seemed too good to be true. Arguing for us, I told myself, was a sign of normalcy, proving that our relationship was like those in the outside world. I admitted to myself that Victor was not entirely wrong in his concern about my letting Charlie in; once, Charlie had pushed his way into my apartment and forcibly took the stereo. I hadn't tried too hard to stop him, having assumed that he was on something and capable of violence. He then sold the stereo for drugs. The last time he was in my home was years before when I had invited him over just to visit. After I had rebuked his advances to make love, he left without protest. But I understood that this was not so much about Charlie as it was about Victor feeling protective and helpless, one of the things that being in jail did in locking you away from your loved ones.

On Sunday morning I awoke to warm sun and cool breezes coming in through the window. Rather than lie there and have my brain rehash the same thoughts over and over, I jumped out of bed, fed Yin, and made coffee. Then, as I had done every morning for many years, I sat in my chartreuse velour chair and wrote in my journal. Doing this was a way of clarifying and organizing my thoughts, though sometimes when I was younger I wondered if this writing didn't contribute to obsessing and fantasizing, thinking about life instead of living it. But it felt good so I continued. How would I do it once Victor was there? Would his presence inhibit my self-expression? But Victor continuously claimed that part of loving me was helping me become all I could. He planned to dedicate himself to this pursuit. How seductive this was: having the man I loved promise to facilitate my goals. It seemed too good to be true!

After I had written in the journal, I turned to writing an initial draft for my letter to Governor Cuomo in support of Victor gaining his freedom. I had been composing it in my head for weeks, and it was now ready to emerge. Though it was doubtful that Cuomo would actually read the letter, I wrote it as if he were going to, thinking about him as I wrote. In an effort to understand him, I had recently finished reading his biography. In the book and to the public, he presented himself as a thoughtful, intellectual, religious, and highly moral man who was governor because he truly wanted to serve people, especially the people of New York State. Because he had forged that reputation of a sincere public servant driven by a Christian ethic, I had high hopes of appealing to him directly, person to person, if not as a Democratic constituent who had voted for him or as one of his state employees. I fantasized that if the governor read about Victor and his life, he would be duly impressed and morally driven to grant him clemency.

My letter described in detail how Victor, after receiving his many medals in Vietnam, had left the service embittered and gotten in with the wrong crowd but was a good man. I described his attempts to educate himself and to benefit others in prison. I did not talk about his innocence. I intended the letter to appeal to the governor's understanding of the concept of "mercy," which in my and Victor's belief, was what granting clemency should be about, though we knew that most of the minuscule number of clemencies given in recent years had little or nothing to do with mercy.

The letter came out in a heated rush of words and feelings; I put it aside to let it cool before I edited it. Surrounded on my bed by manilla folders and newspaper and magazine clippings, I thought about who else might support Victor's clemency application. I made up my mind to contact everyone who might be even a remote possibility and began to make a list. Suddenly my eyes grew very heavy, and when I awoke some time later, the windows were dark between the slats of the blinds. I smiled. Victor would be calling soon. I pretended he would be telling me he would be there soon for cocktails and dinner. Life at that moment would have been perfect if it weren't for the nagging thought that in reality we wouldn't see each other for fifteen hours and then it would be across a table in a prison.

I called to order Chinese food delivered. Eating it, I read a voluminous report from the New York State Office of Research and Development, on recidivism statistics of New York State parolees. The results in every study showed that though their crimes were the most violent, men serving hard time had the lowest recidivism rates upon release. This was due at least in part to age and to a greater motivation to stay out. As I read, my resolve to help Victor get clemency, or at least work release, was fueled. Some modicum of mercy, if not justice, would prevail if I had anything to do with it.

CHAPTER
FOURTEEN

REUNION

Our marriage was three months old, and we were waiting anxiously for a trailer visit. It was over a year since we had spent the night together in the trailer at Eastern, and our visiting room dalliances notwithstanding, we were proof that nothing whets the sexual appetite more than forced abstinence. For someone who has chosen a celibate life, say for religious reasons, the convictions and sense of morality might be enough to annihilate carnal desires, but not so for us ordinary mortals caught in the hectic pursuits of everyday, where relationships have little time to flourish. For us, sexual love can sometimes be the only expression of how deeply we feel, and its expression heals us.

We had met with Ginnie, the plump, blond, and piquant-faced Family Reunion Coordinator, after cornering her as she passed through the visiting room. We beseeched her to expedite our so-called family reunion. Later that day she returned with a Polaroid camera and took us off to one of the small, empty rooms that preceded the visiting room. Sitting next to Victor on a couch was itself a novelty and fanned the flames of desire. Ginnie asked us each a series of questions and wrote down our answers. We each signed an agreement to follow the Family Reunion Program rules, and then she took my picture.

"You'll be hearing from Minister O'Brien, who will come to your home, and after that, you'll officially be on the list," Ginnie told me.

"Ginnie, how long do you think it will be once the minister visits Denise?" Victor anxiously asked.

"Well, usually it's sixty to ninety days, but I'll tell you what, if there are any cancellations I'll call you first. Could you come up at a last minute's notice?" she asked me.

"Definitely."

"Okay, I'll keep that in mind, but don't get your hopes up because usually if someone calls at all to cancel it's right before the visit. Most of the time they just don't show, which is terrible, because they're depriving someone else of that time slot. But we'll see. Maybe you two will be lucky. You look so happy together."

We thanked her and later agreed that she seemed like a nice person who really cared, a unique commodity in that place.

Minister O'Brien called me the following week, and we arranged a time for him to make a home visit. When he arrived, a slim, fast-talking black guy wearing dark gray polyester slacks and a burgundy sports jacket, he explained that the home visit was more for my sake than theirs.

"Oh?"

"Well, the Family Reunion program wants to make sure that the family is coping all right with their loved one being away."

I realized that the minister was not used to a situation like mine in which the family member did not leave the family to become an inmate, but rather became the family member while he was already an inmate. Rather than go into this with him, I said, "Well, I'm coping as well as can be expected, but an overnight visit with my husband would really mean a lot to both of us."

"I hear you." He was no more interested in discussion than I was, and the visit was short and sweet.

"Well, Mrs. Clark, you take care. If you need anything, don't hesitate to call. Here's where I can be reached." He handed me a paper with an address and phone number and closed the door behind him. Remembering Victor's upset over my ex-boyfriend's visit, I wondered whether Victor would be upset about this man being alone in the apartment with me. If he would, I felt certain that his happiness over expediting the trailer visit would supersede any anxiety he might have about a member of the male gender being in my home with me.

I went into the bedroom, which was on a corner of the building and had windows facing east and south. I never tired of either view, and today's clear aquamarine sky in the east was exceptional. I could see airplanes taking off and landing at LaGuardia Airport. In the distance were both the Whitestone and Triboro Bridges, glistening silver structures which, at night, were great arcs of diamonds against the sky. Just outside and to the left, the Cathedral of St. John the Divine was surrounded by a park full of trees. From the southern view I could see buildings all the way to midtown Manhattan, which, while not pic-turesque, offered air and space, and at night, golden light from thousands of windows. On nights when there were fireworks displays over Central Park, I could see their colors burst upon the darkness and even hear park concerts when the wind was right.

Awaiting my private client who was due shortly, I noticed that the trees by the cathedral and in Central Park were turning mostly deep golden browns with a sprinkling of rust and crimson. This whet my appetite to see real foliage; my usual dread of autumn had been transformed by Victor's presence and our love into a joyous appreciation of this stage of the seasonal cycle. As I anticipated our upcoming trailer visit, I savored the crisp air and November winds whose arrival normally made me want to flee to tropical climates.

My client arrived seven minutes late. Joan Todesta was a stylish woman in her late twenties whose abundant intelli-gence and creativity were hampered by her crippling anxiety, depression, and virtually nonexistent self-esteem. Because of my work, I didn't know whether I had developed a biased view of humanity, at least in New York City, or whether my impression that many people were dysfunctional was accurate. Certainly, I and many of my friends had at times shared this affliction in which the life force was distorted, if not destroyed, by negative influences. Sometimes it seemed miraculous to me that people could wind up healthy, that they could love and work without being led down paths of self-destruction.

I was learning cognitive therapy, and of the many therapies I had studied and experienced, I thought it made a lot of sense. I had always been fascinated by language; one of my many unrealized dreams had been to study psycholinguistics, for I believed that the relationship between our psyches and the language we speak has a strong bearing on our daily experience of life. Cognitive therapy addresses our thinking and our use of language and the effects of these on our emotions. To tell someone, "Just change your thinking!" seemed to me like a much more effective and clinically sound way of helping that person. Unfortunately, people cannot "just" do anything, especially if they're in the clutches of neurotic personality structures and lifelong demons.

Although Joan cried throughout our session, I felt we made progress in that she seemed to understand why she was crying and that there were alternative ways of viewing things. She left tearful, but hopeful. I always had difficulty when patients left in the grips of their pain and had to assure myself that they would be okay without me until their next session. That was one of the traditional tenets of psychotherapy which struck me as misconceived in some way: you help people to get in touch with their pain, then tell them their time is up and they must leave.

After seeing two more clients, I had the rest of the evening free. I walked out to the Chinese restaurant on the corner and bought hot and sour soup and an egg roll. It was dark and cold out, unmistakably November. Clouds raced by in the sky, intermittently lit by a three-quarter moon. I began to think about seeing Victor soon. This Thanksgiving I was again going to stay in a motel near Victor and spend the holiday with him. I had sent away for "I Love New York" brochures for Dutchess, Ulster, and Orange counties and had studied them in an effort to find the right place in which to stay.

I loved perusing travel brochures. I had traveled vicariously to Switzerland, Greece, Tahiti, Mexico, and Australia, not to mention Vermont, New Mexico, and Arizona, by reading travel books and publications made available by libraries and bookstores, travel agencies, and chambers of commerce. I liked to read all the descriptions and look at the pictures of lodgings, then pick my top three choices. Lately as I read, I saw myself with Victor on a terrace overlooking a Swiss lake, or us drinking coffee in a French cafe filled with exotic plants, strangers, and art, or spending a day floating in the perfectly turquoise waters of the South Seas.

I still vividly remembered traveling to Puerto Rico at age nineteen and how entranced I was by the riot of colored foliage, the exotic food, and the rhythm of the music. Since then I've been fascinated with the idea of going to a place steeped in a foreign culture, but I hadn't done so, caught up as I had been in other pursuits such as earning a living and finding love.

Slowly, the weeks passed.

Finally, I was on my way to the Hopewell Junction Motel the day before Thanksgiving, feeling very free of hassles. It was exhilarating to drive through the snow-covered countryside to my love. The weather people were all atwitter because there hadn't been snow before Thanksgiving in thirty years or so. The pristine white fields were beautiful. Then again, the way I was feeling, I could have been riding through the pre-cleanup Love Canal and felt inspired.

Upon arriving at the motel, I saw people in the lobby wearing slippers and bathrobes, talking to each other like neighbors. When I had chosen the place, I hadn't realized it was a motel where people lived. Victor, always concerned for my safety, had asked, "Are you sure you'll be okay there?"

"Of course, these places are very safe," I said with more conviction than I felt. "You just have to make sure you put the chain on the door." I didn't tell him about the recent *Sixty*

Minutes report which showed an increasing number of people getting robbed and attacked in roadside motels.

"Make sure you put a chair under the doorknob," he had said.

Walking toward the front desk, I remembered Victor's words about putting the chair under the doorknob, though generally it was not the people living in motels that robbed others, but people off the street. Yet, I felt odd and paranoid checking in, as if I were the only one there that was just staying for two nights rather than living there. Whenever I felt that I stood out I became acutely self-conscious, as if I were the only thing on everyone's mind. I knew that self-consciousness and paranoia are forms of grandiosity, the implication being that I was so important to other people, when in reality they were much less aware of my existence than I was of theirs. Once I had gone to a relatively unknown movie on a weekday afternoon, luxuriating in the emptiness of the theater, there being only two other people besides me. I was appalled and astonished when a woman came in and sat in the seat right next to me.

"Excuse me," I said. "There's a whole empty theater and you sit right next to me?"

She turned and in a contemptuous voice said, "I didn't even notice you."

I often wonder what it must be like to be so blissfully unaware of others.

Having checked in, I walked up the hallway to my room. Inside, it had flattened, worn red carpeting, and the air intimated old cigarettes and loud music though it was quiet. I wondered who was on the other side of the wall and whether they were wondering about me. When I unzipped my bag and laid my book down on the night table, I imagined they heard. I thought of turning on the television just for the sound but dismissed the idea. Anyway, I was going to leave soon for the prison.

Seeing Victor, my heart soared. At first, we sat with our fingers entwined, while in my thoughts visions whirled of lying naked with him, our bodies entangled. To cool our desires we decided to go outside and began to talk of more cerebral concerns. "Tell me about life here," I said.

"Life in prison is merely a microcosm of life in the outer world. I know I've said that before but it's true, and it's not unique to minorities or the poor but spans the range of ethnic and economic groups. Especially in the late twentieth century, prison is a very American experience," Victor said.

"But the poor are more familiar with it, more able to handle it," I said. "It's almost a given that if you have a street life, prison could be a part of it at sometime, whereas middle and upper class people find it more disturbing and foreign to their lives."

"Prison is horrible for all classes, Denise, believe me," Victor said.

"Of course. All I'm saying is if a person already has an unstable life and lives in a hovel, being uprooted and put in this place would be less disturbing than if an individual lives in a big house in the suburbs and is used to all kinds of material comforts."

"That's true, and though there are a lot of miserable people, there are even guys who are happy to be here. I've heard guys say they didn't want to leave here because all their friends are here."

"That's a really sad commentary on the kind of lives some people live."

"I know," Victor said, "but few people are connected. Most, as Thoreau said, live lives of quiet desperation."

We strolled through the yard listening to the mustard-colored leaves crunch beneath our feet. A small patch of gray sky loomed above us.

"It smells like snow," Victor said.

"Well, I just hope it holds off till I get home so I don't have to drive through a blizzard," I said, holding tightly to his hand.

On the road back to the motel I saw a Taco Bell and pulled into the drive-thru. There was a newspaper stand, so I bought the local paper, and with warm food smells filling the car,

I arrived back at the Hopewell Junction Motel. The desk clerk, a bespectacled, balding black man, nodded slightly as I entered, and I made a beeline for my room. Closing the door behind me, I heard music blaring from both sides. Taking the chair from the desk, I put the back under the doorknob, with the legs sticking out. For the life of me, though Victor thought it would, I couldn't understand how this barrier would prevent someone from entering if they wanted to and pushed hard enough.

I spread my food out on the bed along with my newspaper, books, and magazines. Despite the shabbiness, I was glad to be there, for I loved motels, perhaps dating back to trips I took as a child with my family. These were always happy occasions filled with the excitement of being somewhere new. The anonymity of a motel contained such promise and freedom. I turned the television on and ate my burritos. Hearing voices right outside my door gave me some anxiety, but basically I believed I was safe.

Bright and early Thanksgiving morning I awoke and much to my chagrin found the motel coffee shop closed. I quickly realized that here was my opportunity to give up coffee which I had been wanting to do. Now I was forced to by circumstance. Though I didn't drink a lot of coffee, I resented being dependent on that one morning cup. Attempts to give it up in the past had been met with such excruciating headaches that I always continued. This was a good time to try again. I figured that if a headache overtook me, I could always drink the swill from the visiting room vending machine.

Because of the holiday there were fewer guards on duty at Fishkill, and the ones that were working were clearly not thrilled about it. They were more surly and depersonalizing than usual.

"Put your bags over there." Snarl.

"Take off your shoes." Growl.

"Sign here." Hiss.

One of the things I particularly hated was when the guards had me stand at the gate for an interminable time and wait while they chatted and gossiped with each other, as if I were invisible. Eventually I got in, and Victor entered the room minutes later. Each time I saw him it was as if it were the first. We went through our usual hugs, kisses, and little rituals of obtaining food from the machines. With great relief I noticed that I hadn't developed a headache. Having surmounted more than one addiction in the past, I was happy to add caffeine to the list. I didn't want to have to depend on anything, except, perhaps, my husband.

We celebrated Thanksgiving by giving thanks to each other and eating turkey sandwiches from the machine. Parting was not too sorrowful as we knew I'd spend the night down the road and be back the next morning. That night at the motel I saw a Meals on Wheels truck which delivered turkey dinners to the residents. I opted for pizza delivery. After a few slices, I slept somewhat fitfully, notwithstanding the chair under the doorknob. In the morning it felt strange when I realized I would not have coffee. Having grapefruit juice instead made me feel I was doing something very healthy. With both relief to be leaving that place and sorrow since I would soon be leaving the vicinity of where Victor was, I packed my bag, checked out, and drove over to Fishkill. The sun was bright, and the roads dripped with melting snow. As I drove, I remembered how at the age of nine, my best friend and I had wanted to be hoboes riding the rails. But one day we realized girls couldn't do that and felt a great loss, the beginning, perhaps, of my imprisonment.

The guards were still less than pleased to be at work, which regretfully is the nature of such jobs, but is particularly unfortunate when your job impacts directly on other people. Unless people have careers they love, most spend their days angry and bitter except for days off and vacations. About three hours into the visit, we spotted someone across the room who did seem to like her job.

"Wow, I'm surprised Ginnie's here today," Victor said. "I know she has a family."

"Well, unlike the majority of the guards, she actually enjoys helping people and is not prejudiced against inmates and their families. She probably catches hell from most of the staff here."

"Oh yeah," Victor said. "You *know* they don't like anyone who treats inmates with any degree of humanity."

Looking around, Ginnie spotted us and sauntered over with a big smile on her face. "Hi, guys. I have some good news. A family canceled for this weekend. Would you be able to take it?"

"Would we?" we both said at once, our faces beaming.

"It would start Saturday morning and end Monday morning."

"I can leave soon, go home, and get everything together," I said excitedly.

"You sure you can do that, sweetheart? I mean, by the time you get home...."

"Are you kidding? I'd fly to be with you. If I leave in a few minutes, I'll be home by one. Then I can shop and pack."

"Great," Ginnie said. "As soon as this guy's wife called me, I thought of you. I was going to call but figured I'd check in here first. Oh, I'm so glad you can make it."

"So are we," we both said.

"We're so grateful to you," Victor said with feeling. "Thanks a lot."

"Hey, I know you've been waiting a long time."

"Yeah, you're wonderful," I told her, tears rising to my eyes.

As she walked off, I said to Victor, "I wish I were ovulating this weekend."

"It's not even close?"

"No, but who cares? At least now we know we'll have opportunities."

We spent a few minutes deciding what food I should bring and then Victor took my hand. "I'm going to devour you," he said. "You don't know how much I want you."

"And I you," I replied. Then, feeling somewhat limp with desire, I said, "Let me get going." He walked me to the door where we embraced, our bodies clinging to each other like electrically charged magnets.

"I'll try to call you tonight," Victor said, "but if you don't hear from me, don't worry, I'll see you in the morning."

"I can't wait," I said.

"And don't forget the wedding dress," Victor called after me. "Remember, I'm going to carry you over the threshold."

Less than twenty-four hours later, I was on the road at 4:00 A.M. and back in the parking lot at dawn beneath the gaze of the knowing inmates watching from the windows. Today it was even more awkward than on a regular visit, because where I had to wait, they knew I was there for a forty-five-hour tryst. The first one there for the trailers, I stood in a small fenced-in area adjacent to the housing unit. Though it was cold out, I chose to wait there with all my bags rather than wait in the car and have another wife come along and say she was there first. The order was significant as the first one was the first to be with their loved one. As it got closer to 10:30, other families arrived, all carrying stuffed overnight bags and shopping bags of food. I had with me a Famous Famiglia everything pizza, which I had raved to Victor about and couldn't wait to share with him. I tried to read a *Times Herald Record* but couldn't concentrate. This would be the first time Victor and I were really alone together since our first trailer visit, and that had been with Hattie. I half listened to the corrections officers grousing to each other and watched state vans come and go. As it was Saturday morning, the visitors' parking lot filled up fast. Every other minute I looked at my watch until finally one of the officers in the small building beckoned me forward, asked for my picture ID, and told me to sign my name and address in the book. Then I lugged all my stuff over to the waiting van where the guard, to my pleasant surprise, helped me in. When we were all boarded, the guard got in the driver's seat, and we took off slowly as dark-green-clad inmates walked next to us along the road. It was like being in a theme park like Six Flags

Great Adventure, only we were the attraction. All of the inmates stared; some made cat calls.

The trailers were located down a hill; behind them stretched a field and I-84. Our hosts were eagerly waiting in the trailer area, all smiling and waving as we arrived. Upon debarking from the van, we were ushered into the guards' trailer where they proceeded to look through our bags and keep anything that wasn't allowed in, such as glass containers, or anything that might contain alcohol, including shampoos and perfumes. Of course, if someone was intent upon bringing in alcohol, all she had to do was put it in a container with a label that did not list alcohol. As usual, we had to empty our pockets and be scanned with the metal detector. I was pleased and relieved that the overall process felt less accusatory and hostile than it was on a regular visit. Suddenly there was Victor at the door smiling, asking if he could help me with my bags, and they said it was okay. We didn't embrace until we were inside, and then the floodgates opened, the torrents of our contained passion released.

"Would you like something to drink?" Victor whispered.

"All I want right now is you," I said.

"Don't you think we should put the food away?" he asked, nibbling at my ear.

"Yes," I breathed.

"Okay, let's." We fell onto the couch.

"Seriously, come on." We broke apart, panting.

"Don't forget where we left off, but I have to carry you over the threshold for our wedding night. Did you bring the dress?" Victor said.

"Yes. Shall I put it on?"

He smiled. "Why don't you put it on while I start putting the food away?"

Emerging from the bedroom in the slightly wrinkled white linen dress, I stood and watched Victor place the last of the food in the refrigerator.

"I can't wait to try this pizza I've heard so much about," he called, not realizing I was right there.

When he looked up, I grinned. "But I'd rather try you." He held out his arms, and I went right into them.

"Come on," he whispered.

We stepped outside the door of the trailer, and I tried to ignore the inmates walking by on the road.

"Are you ready, my blushing bride?"

"Yes," and with that he scooped me up, stepped back into the trailer, heading for the bedroom. As we fell together onto the creaking bed, Victor said, "Why don't we take this beautiful dress off. I wouldn't want anything to happen to it."

After helping me off with the dress, Victor began to massage my back, and it wasn't long before we were devouring each other. Not only was our desire at a peak, but for me it was a very different experience, not thinking about birth control, and on the contrary, being eager to have that torrent of precious fluid explode into my womb. Even though I wasn't ovulating, I hoped that this would be one of those freak times they always warned you about, when you'd get pregnant even though you thought it was a safe time.

About two hours later we returned to the living room. "Are you hungry, my love?" Victor asked, turning on the television.

In addition to the pizza, our other meal would be barbecued chicken, which we planned to cook indoors though there were grills outside. As he had done during our previous visit, Victor had washed all the dishes and silverware and stacked them on the table. Looking out the back window, I discovered the view of the field which had the golden straw colors of a Breughel painting. Victor came up behind me and together we looked out at the field, separated from the prison by two razor wired fences.

"All you need is a blanket to throw over the razor wire," Victor said softly.

"Yeah, and then go running over the fence to I-84 and hitch a ride home."

"Right," Victor said. "Seriously, why don't we sit down?"

The rest of the visit was perfect. I was locked up with my lover with guards outside forbidding me to leave. Other than periodic phone calls from the guard beckoning Victor for the inmate count, we had no contact with the outside world. Late at night and just before dawn, our desires momentarily satiated, we lay in bed, eyes level with the window, and watched deer emerge dreamlike out of the mist. At times, a guard on a horse trotted across the field. We watched television, ate a lot of food, played Scrabble, and made love. As on our first trailer visit and on every subsequent one, we tried not to think about the dreaded morning when the idyll would come to an end. It inevitably did, demonstrating once again that sadistic quality of time: when you wanted it, it vanished, and when you wanted to get rid of it, it refused to flee.

When I awoke before dawn, Victor was staring at me as if he was memorizing everything about me. "Hi, sweetheart," he said softly.

"Did you sleep at all?" I asked.

"A little. Sleeping when you're out here seems like such a waste of time. Especially on the second night it's hard to sleep, knowing the morning's on its way and then we'll have to part."

We held each other while looking out at the smoky gray light. "Look, there's a deer," Victor said, pointing.

I could barely make it out, but then sure enough, there was a graceful fawn, and then another, and another. "There's a lot of them out there."

"One day soon we'll be walking in a field like this together."

"I can't wait," I said. Trying not to think about the fact that we did not know when that time would be, we kissed hungrily and caressed each other's tired bodies. Then we melted into each other again. Afterwards, we lay in each other's arms. "I love you," I said.

"I love you," he replied.

Reluctantly, we got up and began to put the trailer back together so it was not only in the condition in which we found it but better. Victor threw himself with a vengeance into cleaning the dishes, mopping the floor, and dusting the furniture, thereby avoiding acknowledgment of our impending separation.

As always, our goodbye was bittersweet, containing both the joy of the visit and the sadness of the parting. Victor walked me to the processing trailer, and, after one last embrace, I was back to being alone.

The van ride back to the front gate was as strange as the one out, except this time I imagined the inmates who leered into the van were thinking, *well they got some this weekend*. I resented them as they ambled along near the van, for they got to be with Victor all the time while I only got him for brief interludes.

In the parking lot the car was covered with frost but seemed none the worse for its two days there. I watched two of the women who had also been in the trailers heading for the visiting room in order to spend more time with their men. Victor and I had agreed that we didn't want to do this, for after being alone together so intimately and physically close without anyone watching our every move, sitting in the visiting room would be oppressive. I headed out. I stopped at the deli down the road and bought the *Times Herald Record*, thought about coffee, and bought orange juice and a Danish instead. I had considered going straight to work from upstate but I felt that would tarnish the beauty of the weekend, so I called in sick. After driving home, I used the day off to rest and regroup. I needed to slowly ease back into the details of daily living. It was strange being back to the "real" world after being sequestered away with the man I loved for almost two days. *What will it be like*, I asked myself, *for Victor when he comes back to the "real" world after so many years imprisoned?*

Upon awakening from a nap later that day, I pored over the newspaper as I had gotten into the habit of doing, looking for clues and ideas on how to approach Victor's impending applications for clemency and work release. The papers often had articles on prisons and inmates; it was important to keep abreast of the prevailing political views so that I could take the most promising approach. I had file folders full of newspaper clippings and research from the library, which provided me not only with information, but with quotes for the letters that I was writing and the meetings I had begun having. On this Monday, the newspaper contained nothing prison-related. So I went on having a day of solitude, mentally preparing myself for the return to the world of the insane the next day.

CHAPTER FIFTEEN

PSYCHIC CONNECTION

Each day as I went to my job I was acutely aware that I had spent much of my adult life frustrated and lacking contentment, consumed as I was with desires that went unsatisfied. Now, at last, I had found love and gotten married, albeit under strange circumstances, yet my future was still uncertain. Was it possible to "have everything" as the catch phrase of our times put it? My union with Victor implied that I believed one could. But what was the reality? Buddhism, which I'd long studied, said it was my desire that was the problem. So I meditated. Upon returning to my apartment in the evenings, I got into a half-lotus position on a pillow on the floor, breathed slowly and evenly, listened to the city sounds, and watched my thoughts and emotions come and go. Though I well understood the concept of temporality, the understanding didn't translate into how I felt.

One day on a whim I decided to see a psychic. Having gone to a few in the past, I took what they said with a grain of salt. Some people I knew, including my friend Isabella, didn't make any major moves in their lives without getting a reading. Isabella couldn't say enough about the psychic she was seeing whose ability, according to Isabella, was uncanny. So I made an appointment to see Elizabeth in her home office in the basement apartment of a brownstone in the West Eighties. According to Isabella, Elizabeth was more involved with the spirit world than most psychics. We sat on large pillows in a brick-walled room that smelled faintly of incense. She explained that she would start by contacting people in "the other world."

"Your father sends his love and says that he's fine."

"Really?" It was now six years since my father had died, and I still missed him, despite our relationship having been a mixed blessing equally concocted of pain and affection.

"Your father loved you very much, but he was weak in some ways."

I thought it was amazing that the woman could know this, though skeptics might say it was a statement that could apply to anyone.

"He is concerned about you and wants you to find a good man." She had her eyes closed and rocked slightly back and forth, side to side.

"Well, what do you see in that area?" I asked.

"Wait, we'll get to that. I'm still sensing those on the other side."

I stared at this stocky, blond woman whose fine facial features were suggestive of an English doll and wondered how she came to inhabit this world of spirits, and what it was like for her.

"Is there anyone else you would like to know about?"

"My grandmother died three years ago."

"She's fine and sends her love.... Now to the here and now." There was a subtle shift in Elizabeth's posture and facial expression. "I see a short, dark man who is inhibited in some way—he is unable to go where he wants or express himself the way he would like to."

"Do you see that changing, I mean, will he be less restricted in the future?"

She paused, her eyes closed, and then said, "Yes, I think so." Another pause. "I see children. Do you have any?"

When I said no, she said, "You do, or you will."

She went on. "Is there a young boy?"

I couldn't think of anyone.

Her head nodded back and forth. "Perhaps you will have a son."

I told her about where Victor was; she began talking about what a good person he was, and how he was innocent of the charges against him. "He will be freed," she went on, "and have a life together with you."

"When?" I asked anxiously, despite my usual reserve with such people.

"It won't be too far off." I had noticed that many psychics do not have a time frame, but she continued. "I see you having at least one child in the near future, a son, born naturally, without technological means." Her blue china-doll eyes opened wide. "I see you persisting in your quest to free him and eventually succeeding."

Thanking her profusely, I paid her, and though I told myself not to count too much on her words, there was something so real about her that I felt energized as I went out into the cold December night. All the resolve and determination that I carried with me like an engine strapped to my back were charged and fired up, and I thought about Victor with fresh optimism. It was without my usual envy that I stared at the couples dining in the restaurant adjacent to the bus stop, for I imagined that soon Victor and I would be eating out together, on nights that we didn't feel like staying home with the kids. Neither the system that conspired to keep him locked up nor the fact of our separation would stop us from achieving our goals.

Later that night, as if serendipitously, I watched a television news magazine show that featured a story of an inmate to whom the governor was granting clemency. He was forty years old from the South Bronx and had been given fifteen years to life for selling four ounces of cocaine under the tough Rockefeller drug laws. In prison, his artistic talents had had a chance to blossom, and his paintings had been discovered by an art gallery, which was instrumental in garnering the political support which influenced the governor. Now he was coming home. When the inmate was asked how he would support himself and his family, he said, "I'll try to get a good job so I don't have to return to my old bag of tricks."

On the phone, when I told him about the man, Victor was incensed. "The guy still thinks like a criminal if he even considers returning to what he used to do as a possibility." Victor went on, "If he really wants to have a different life, he's got to be willing to say 'I'm going to work at McDonald's if I can't get anything else.' That's why so many of these guys don't make it on the outside and why you can predict who will and who won't. The ones who refuse to have a job while they're locked up because they won't accept making a dollar thirty-five a day won't make it on the outside either, because their egos won't let them. You know how many guys I've heard say, 'Hey I'm great with kids, I'm gonna go into childcare.' Or, 'Yeah, man, I'm good at math, I'm gonna have me my own business.' But they don't even have a GED and refuse to go to school!"

It wasn't that we were against this particular inmate or any other one getting clemency. It was just that we asked ourselves, if this inmate could receive clemency, why couldn't Victor? Then again, as he pointed out, "How many of the people who've gotten clemency in recent years have been black? Do you think that even with Norman Mailer pushing for it they would have let out that murderer Jack Henry Abbott if he had been black? Or even this guy from the South Bronx? If he had been dark skinned or Hispanic instead of white, they wouldn't have given it to him. Race always plays a major role, though no one would ever admit to it."

"The statistics prove it," I agreed. "I'm sure there are people out there who are eager to prove they're on the right side of the struggle for racial justice and would be happy to embrace your cause."

"I wouldn't be so sure of it," Victor said. "I don't mean to be cynical, and believe me, sweetheart, I'm grateful for all your efforts, but there's just not that many people who are willing to put themselves or their reputations on the line for some inmate, especially a black one."

I felt my jaw set. "Well, if they're out there, I'll find them. Why should a guy like this who doesn't have half your accomplishments get out early, and you, who are innocent and have so much to offer society, have to rot away in prison."

Despite Victor's words about the prejudice involved in gaining clemency and our discouragement about his ever getting justice, I was strategizing and working to get commitments of help from people who might be in a position to influence the governor. My resolve to get my husband freed was continuously being strengthened. In addition to my affirming reports from the psychic and the fueling anger that came from learning about other people getting clemency, there was the ongoing freeing of the violent, mentally ill at my job. I knew that the plea of insanity was oftentimes a legal strategy for the guilty to avoid punishment. A week later, I went to the hospital to learn that shortly after a former patient of mine had been discharged, he beat his elderly mother to death with a lamp. I, along with many other staff, was interrogated in an effort by the bureaucrats to place blame on someone. I knew it wouldn't be me, for I had documented that the patient should never live with his mother. But the staff who treated him after me gave in to the patient's pathological attachment to his mother, the result of which, ironically, was that he now would be living without her forever.

It infuriated me that so many of the murderers, rapists, and truly dangerous people I walked among every day were set free, and Victor was not. The hospital was increasingly accepting parolees from prisons as patients, which was Corrections' way of abdicating responsibility to the mental health system. So here I was, working with all these paroled convicts, many of whom were not only psychiatrically ill but also illiterate, borderline retarded, and heavy drug users. Many of them had little, if any, sense of right and wrong. It was obvious that if they weren't already, they would become repeat offenders. Yet Victor remained locked up.

Convinced that the media not only reported the news but created it, I took it upon myself to try and get Victor's story publicized. I wrote and rewrote a synopsis of Victor's story and sent it to *60 Minutes, 20/20, Primetime Live, Dateline,* and others. I also sent it to talk show hosts including *Oprah, Donahue,* and *Maury Povich.* But my experience was similar to sending query letters and manuscripts to magazines and receiving one rejection letter after another, except in this case what was being rejected was the opportunity to strongly influence a good and innocent person's life. It was exasperating to come home from a day spent with violent criminals at the hospital who were gaining their freedom to find a letter in the mailbox saying, "We receive hundreds of proposals like yours, and we regret that we cannot use it. . . ," as if "it" were only a storyline.

But I wasn't about to quit. Nothing would ever make me give up on Victor's and my future. I decided I needed to read Victor's trial minutes so in the event that someone did respond positively, I'd be able to talk with authority about his wrongful conviction and imprisonment. I really didn't want to read the minutes, assuming it would be painful to see the travesty of justice that had happened to him, but I knew I needed to. One copy was in the possession of Sasha and Blaine, a couple who had become Victor's friends and advocates. Blaine had been a teacher of Victor's, and her husband, Sasha, was a writer and house husband who often visited Victor. I called Sasha and he agreed to send the minutes. A week later they arrived in a carton, a stack of papers six inches high.

Sitting in my favorite chartreuse chair, I began to read the trial transcript, becoming more and more incensed. Slowly, I read the testimony of one of the witnesses the prosecutor called, Kate Rogers, who stated that the lights went out around midnight before the shooting. This definitely would have been a major hindrance for her, I thought, to recognize who put a gun to her head. It could therefore only be speculative how she identified Victor, whom she said she had only met once at the home of her good friend Jennie, whose last name escaped her. How could Rogers' memory of the facts be reliable when she could not even remember her good friend's last name?

And more doubts were confirmed for me from the testimony of Gail Roberts who was very vague about what happened that night. "As far as I remember, someone came up to me and held a gun on me and took money out of my pocket." She could not identify who robbed her because, she said, "The place was so dimly lit." I did not see how Gail Roberts could have been regarded as a reliable witness to a robbery if she was not aware of her surroundings, could hardly see anything, and couldn't identify the gunman. No one else testified to this robbery and there was absolutely no proof that Victor had anything to do with it.

Up to this point in the trial there should have been a presumption of innocence on the part of an unbiased jury about Victor and certainly room for reasonable doubt.

Next, I read the words of Beth Gossard whose testimony, as I became more and more immersed in it, in and of itself raised even more questions. She testified the lights went dimmer at the time of the crime, so how could she have identified anyone correctly? Moreover, right after the crime she testified to the district attorney that someone else, a boy named Brad Morgan, had been the gunman. Her story for the next two weeks kept changing and she'd already admitted to being confused only one night after the incident. Why had Beth's testimony kept changing, I asked myself—her own doubts, prosecutorial pressure? The only thing sustainable from her testimony that I could discern, after carefully going over it, was her confusion!

I became even more dubious about Victor being at the scene when I read how Sheila Eaton, one of the girls who'd been at the party, identified Victor fleeing the scene. She was one block away from the storefront, and she saw "some people" leave the store and get into a blue car and did not recognize any of the people who got in. She did not even know Victor's last name until someone at the police station told her the next day.

And then there was the angry testimony of Marilee Singer who had, at first, confirmed Victor's alibi and later recanted her words. After breaking up with Victor's cousin — Loretha's brother — and trying to have their mother arrested, she had struck out at Victor. How could she be a reliable and unbiased witness?

The testimony of Dr. Joseph Bajor further confirmed my suspicions about the trial verdict's veracity. He testified that the path of the bullet which struck Todd Richter was on an angle from the left eye toward the right rear side of Todd Richter's head. According to Beth's testimony, she was in front of Todd whose back was turned into the room. The boy she first identified as Brad Morgan and later as Victor Clark was to her left and Todd's right, and the gun was in his right hand. The forensic evidence spoke for itself. So how was it possible that Victor, if he had actually been there and positioned where Beth said, could have shot Todd Richter at such a range, with such a bullet path, with a gun in his right hand? It simply wasn't impossible.

In addition to all these refuting facts, Victor had testified that he never had a mug shot or picture taken by an official agency, yet pictures were given to Beth Gossard and Kate Rogers to identify Victor before he was brought in, arrested, fingerprinted, and had mug shots taken. So what pictures did they look at? The mug shots were missing at the trial. And where was Carrie Thomas, who had been behind the bar and might have seen something concrete? Most important of all, what happened to Brad Morgan, whom Beth Gossard first identified as the killer and who Victor testified he saw under arrest at the police station when Victor was brought in? The question as to the whereabouts of Brad Morgan, who never appeared, was one of the big mysteries of the trial.

The final evidence for me was Victor's young and inexperienced but fervent lawyer's summation in which the lawyer, Harry Borso, tried to point out all the ambiguities and inconsistencies in the prosecution's case, to no avail:

MR. BORSO: May it please the Court, counsel, members of the jury. At this time it is customary for the attorneys to address the jury and to present to the jury their viewpoints of the evidence. It so happens in this particular trial, it is my turn to address you first. Then counsel for the other two defendants and finally the district attorney. I will not have an opportunity to rebut anything that the district attorney says to you, so I hope that after this chain of summaries that you hear, you will give as much consideration to the arguments that I make as you will to the arguments that Mr. Conways makes.

The district attorney comes into this Court with an indictment that charges, so far as Victor Clark is concerned, that on the early morning of March thirty-first, nineteen seventy-three, he committed various crimes, murder, robbery, grand larceny and possession of a weapon. He has presented on behalf or pursuant to that indictment certain witnesses and certain evidence to you. I am going to ask you to let me have your indulgence for a few minutes while I recite to you a chain of circumstances based solely upon the evidence presented in this case and then leave the conclusion to you.

I am going to start with a situation where a boy and a girl go together, keep company, for an indefinite period of time and there comes a time when this relationship breaks up and the girl takes up with another boy and then, in the course of events, there comes the fateful night of March thirtieth, nineteen seventy-three, and the girl either goes with or meets a certain boy at this party that we are concerned with on Clarkson Avenue. Under her testimony, at that particular time that this incident took place, the boy, in the girl's words, has his legs wrapped around her and had his hands on her pants. Now, according to the same girl's testimony, we have it that the first boy was there, he had a gun and he fired the gun off, and the second boy dropped dead. We all know that the second boy is Todd Richter and the first boy is not Victor Clark. The first boy is Brad Morgan. The testimony is that he had the gun. The testimony is that he shot the gun off and the testimony is that he had the motive.

Now, you say there is something omitted from this? The girl said that it was Victor Clark who shot Todd Richter. But was it? What motive did Victor Clark have to shoot Todd Richter? Did he know him? No. Was there a robbery in this place?

Gail Roberts said that she was there but she didn't know anybody in the place. She said that sometime during the course of the night, twenty dollars was taken from her while she was in the front of the store. Was this at the time the shooting occurred? I don't know. I don't remember what her testimony was in that respect, but at any rate, nobody shot her to take the money from her and there is no proof in this case as to who it was who took the money from her. What possible motive did Victor Clark have to shoot Todd Richter? Was it Todd Richter who was robbed here? No. It was Brad Morgan who had the motive, who had the opportunity, who had the gun and the gun shot off, and furthermore it was Brad Morgan who was in custody four or five days later when he was showed into Mrs. Clark's apartment by the detective who said that he is mixed up in a homicide and we want to talk to Victor. Who was mixed up in the homicide? Brad Morgan and Morgan was seen at the police station in confinement. Where is Brad Morgan today?

You heard the testimony. You know there are three mysteries in the twentieth century. What happened to Judge Crater, who promoted Perez, and where is Brad Morgan? I must go a little bit further and see if you have any reasonable doubt as to whether or not it was Victor Clark who shot and killed Todd Richter.

There is testimony here on page ninety in which, if I may have your indulgence for a moment, this is Beth Gossard's testimony cross-examination by me:

"Question. And you said that just around midnight, when this shot went off and you heard somebody say this is a stickup, you say the lights got dimmer then?

"Answer. The lights were dimmer just before that happened.

"Question. Right before that happened they got dimmer?

"Answer. Yes.

"Question. And they were dim to begin with, weren't they?

"Answer. They were dim, yes."

Now, at page thirty-seven, the testimony of Kate Rogers:

"Question. Now, you say that there—while you were at the party, sometime around midnight, the lights went out, is that what you said?

"Answer. I said they went dim because there was a light behind the bar.

"Question. Well, could you make the light dimmer and brighter, or —

"Answer. No.

"Question. Well, do you know whether they went out?

"Answer. I saw the lights go dim. I—well, I guess they went out, if I saw them go dim.

"Question. You saw them go out?

"Answer. Yes."

We have various testimony here with respect to how dim the lights were. One girl said that you couldn't even read a newspaper by the light, but there isn't any dispute but they were dim and one girl said they went out. Now, here we have a party in a little storefront with at least seventy-five people packed into this area. I am going to ask you to look for a moment at the defendant, Victor Clark, and take a look at his complexion and tell me whether or not anybody at that party could possibly identify Victor Clark in a place where the lights had gone out, according to the prosecution's witness?

Now, furthermore, we have Kate Rogers who said she knew Victor Clark and she said somebody at this party came up to her with a gun and pointed a gun at her head and this person was face-to-face with her and she said that she did not know who that person was. She said on the next day she was taken to the police station and she was shown some photographs, and then for the first time after looking at the photographs she said it was Victor Clark who held the gun to her head when she was face-to-face with him and didn't recognize him.

And in the case of Beth Gossard — if she couldn't see him in the dark when he was face-to-face with her, then how could Beth Gossard identify him or anybody else for that matter? Do you have a reasonable doubt that it was Victor Clark who shot and killed Todd Richter?

Furthermore, the photographs Kate Rogers said she couldn't identify Victor Clark face-to-face, Beth Gossard says that she recognized Victor Clark, but the very next day at a time when she was shown photographs along with Kate Rogers, she could not pick out Victor Clark's photograph. *Where are the photographs? This is the second mystery in this case.*

You heard the testimony of Victor Clark that he had never been photographed by the police or by any law enforcement agency. In other words, he had never had a mug shot taken. He had never been convicted of a crime. If there was any official police photograph or FBI photograph of Victor Clark, you can be sure it would be in Court today. How can a man be identified from a mug shot which doesn't exist?

THE PROSECUTOR: I object, and I ask Your Honor to instruct the jury regarding this matter.

THE JUDGE: No, the jury heard the evidence. They can use their own good sense and judgment.

MR. BORSO: You are all reasonable men. You know the answer to the question.

There was some question here in the colloquy with His Honor, if I may divert here for just a minute, page one hundred seventy-three of the minutes, Beth Gossard's cross-examination by Mr. Borso:

"Question. Was there a time you were in the police station with Kate Rogers?

"Answer. Yes.

"Question. At that time, were you shown some photographs by the police officer?

"Answer. Yes.

"Question. All right. Now, at that time were you able to pick out Victor Clark's picture from the photographs that were shown to you.

"Answer. No."

Now, going back just a minute to the testimony of Sheila Eaton, she was at the party and someone came up to her and told her to get out if she didn't want to get shot or something like that. So she left. She went to a corner a block away and she stood there. Now, if somebody had threatened her or told her to leave some place or leave some party because she might get shot, do you think it was natural for her to stand on the corner a block away and not call the police? She might not call the police, but she would run away as fast as she could. She would not stand there waiting for something to happen if she were anticipating something to happen — she would call the police. But, she said she stood on the corner a block away, in the dark, and then she heard a shot. She said a shot.

Kate Rogers testified to only one shot, as far as I recall, and if you take the testimony of Beth Gossard, one place she said it was two shots and another place she said it was three shots. But Sheila Eaton said right after the first shot, or the only shot, she heard three people came out of that store and got into a car which she said was Victor Clark's. Victor Clark's. Why was it Victor Clark's? Because it was light blue and it was a small car. How many light blue, small cars are there in the City of New York? Was there anything else about that car that identified it to her as Victor Clark's car? Nothing.

If you stand in front of the Court House for a half hour, you could count twenty small, light blue cars that pass by. Do you have a reasonable doubt that it was Victor Clark who shot Todd Richter?

Let's come to the physical facts. We have the testimony of Beth Gossard who testified to almost anything that she was asked. She contradicted herself I don't know how many times on the witness stand. At any rate, that is the testimony that the district attorney relies upon for a conviction in this case. She said that just before the shot that killed Todd Richter was fired, she was facing the front of the store and facing Todd Richter; that Todd Richter had his legs around her and as she, as he fell, he had his hand on her pants. Now that is how close they were together. At this time, in response to my questions on cross-examination, she testified *that Victor Clark, if it was Victor Clark, was to the right*, to the *right* of Todd Richter and to her left. Dr. Bajor, the medical examiner, testified that when the bullet was removed from Todd Richter's head, they found *the bullet had entered Todd Richter's left eye at an angle and it was found in the right rear side of his head.*

I'm going to ask you for just a moment, if I stand here and I am Todd Richter and Victor Clark is to my right and he has a gun in his right hand, how is he going to fire that gun through the eye of Todd Richter at this kind of angle so that it comes out over here and is taken out of the right rear side — it's just impossible.

Now, suppose you take some other testimony in this case. There is some testimony, I think, that states Victor Clark was behind the bar, but according to it if he was there he was, according to that testimony, to the left of Beth Gossard. There is no question about that. If he was to the left of Beth Gossard and Beth Gossard is here [indicating], and Todd Richter is directly in front of her facing her, how in the world was Victor Clark going to fire his gun from over this way to get the bullet to go that way? Can you rely on such testimony to convict Victor Clark? Do you have reasonable doubt? This is the testimony of the prosecution's witnesses.

You have a long way to go in this case and I don't want to take up too much of your time. But I must also bring up the testimony of Marilee Singer. Please don't convict Victor Clark on the testimony of Marilee Singer. Here is a girl, a woman, who meets me with Loretha Carter, her ex-boyfriend Franklin Carter, at Loretha Carter's apartment. She said to me and she admits on the witness stand that I told her that I wanted nothing but the truth and she told me at that time that Victor Clark was at Loretha's apartment, and she was there all that night. Then she comes in here, takes the witness stand, and says she doesn't know Victor Clark and she was not there. Now, is this the kind of witness you are going to believe? She is called in rebuttal, get this, she is called in rebuttal to the testimony of Loretha Carter, an upstanding business owner and community activist, who states unequivocally that Victor was at her place all night. The district attorney had asked out of the clear blue sky, he asked Loretha Carter whether or not Todd Richter had given her a gun and whether she disposed of it, and her answer was no. Then he called in Marilee to contradict that testimony and Marilee takes the witness stand and she testifies that on some occasion last summer, about a year and a half after the crime took place, she was approached by Loretha Carter who asked her to testify about a party that Victor Clark was at back on October thirtieth or rather March thirtieth, nineteen seventy-three, and she further testified that Loretha Carter told her that Victor Clark had given her a gun and some bullets and she had disposed of them.

Now, this is the testimony that the district attorney asks you to believe, but my question to you is if the district attorney himself believes that witness, why didn't he arrest Loretha Carter for aiding and abetting a crime?

THE PROSECUTOR: I object to that.

THE COURT: That is objectionable and the jury will disregard that statement.

MR. BORSO: Why would Loretha Carter confide this kind of situation to Marilee Singer who was responsible for filing a complaint and putting Loretha Carter's mother in jail? Why would Ms. Carter confide in Marilee when her brother Franklin had broken an engagement to her, and wasn't this the reason she first

tried to get Ms. Carter's mother and now Victor Clark
into jail?

THE PROSECUTOR: Objection.

MR. BORSO: She said she broke it up.

THE COURT: No, I consider Mr. Borso's words to be
fair comment on the evidence. It is up to the jury to
determine which part of it is credible or not.

MR. BORSO: Page three hundred forty-nine, cross-
examination of Marilee Singer by Mr. Borso:

"Question. Did you know before you went
there to Loretha Carter's apartment the night I met her
what we were going to talk about?

"Answer. Yes.

"Question. Did I tell you at that time that all I
wanted was the truth?

"Answer. Yes.

"Question. And you understood that, didn't
you?

"Answer. Yes.

"Question. Did I ask you if you were present
in Loretha Carter's house on March thirty, nineteen
hundred seventy-three?

"Answer. Yes.

"Question. Was a party going on then?

"Answer. Yes.

"Question. And I asked you if Victor Clark
was there?

"Answer. Yes.

"Question. I asked you the times that you
were there?

"Answer. Yes.

"Question. I mean you arrived there about six-
thirty or so with Franklin and you left about seven
o'clock and you came back at eight-thirty?

"Answer. Yes.

"Question. And these are all the things that
you told me?

"Answer. Yes.

"Question. I didn't put any of these words in your mouth, did I?

"Answer. No.

"Question. And I told you I wanted the truth, didn't I?

"Answer. Yes.

"Question. And you told me that from eight-thirty until some time after midnight, that Victor Clark never left the apartment, didn't you?

"Answer. Yes.

"Question. *And what you told me on October seventeen, when I told you to tell me the truth, was not the truth; is that what you are saying?*

"Answer. *Right.*"

Now, is that the kind of witness you are going to believe on this trial? Do you have a reasonable doubt? If she wasn't at the party at Loretha Carter's house, how does she know if Victor Clark was there or not?

Now, when you go into that jury room after listening to the other lawyers and have the judge charge you on the law of this case, you are going to have in your hands the fate of my client, Victor Clark. You will be the final and the only judges of the facts in this case; the law you will get from the judge. I ask you to be as fair as you can, and to come in here with a verdict of acquittal for Victor Clark.

As I spoke to Sasha that night, my heart ached for Victor.

"It was infuriating; everything Victor had said was apparent in the minutes. Despite the alibi that his cousin Loretha had provided, the jury believed the shaky testimony given and then recanted by two girls, one of whom had first identified someone else and the other of whom said she identified him from a mug shot, though he had never been convicted before, that Victor was the trigger man in a shooting of a high school kid in a neighborhood social club. The missing mug shot of Victor—which could not have been taken before this crime since he'd never been convicted of any crime—was a major point in the case."

What blew my mind the most, however, was when Victor told me at our next meeting that he always knew who had actually fired the fatal shot.

"Why didn't you tell them?" I fervently asked.

Victor explained in more detail what he had only alluded to earlier. "You just don't do that," he said. "When you're on the street it's part of the code: you don't tell on anyone to the cops."

"Even if it means going away for life?" I asked incredulously.

"Denise, I didn't think I'd go away for life. I believed that the system would work: because I was innocent I would get off. That's why I didn't take the prosecution's offer of a plea for fifteen-to-life. What I didn't know then is that the system only works for you if you have the money to hire the right lawyers. If you're poor and a minority you don't stand much of a chance of having justice prevail."

"So knowing this you chose to be loyal to your buddies rather than feed them to the system, even though you had to have known on some level that the system might not work for you."

"Freedom," he said quizzically. "If I had turned someone else in, my freedom would have been short-lived. Not only for the ethical aspect of it, but the brother of the guy would have come after me."

"So it was like blackmail."

"Well, yes, in a way."

"God, that sucks."

"Yes, it does. The whole situation sucked. Any way I looked at it, my choices were really lousy. I chose the one which let me live. But, you see, no one in Corrections or Parole wants to hear this. In fact, Sasha and I finally figured out that the main reason my first clemency application was denied was because I was still proclaiming my innocence. They don't want to hear that. They want remorse. They want me to say I'll never do it again, and I'm sorry I killed the guy."

"Even though you didn't?"

"Yes! Because according to the court I'm guilty. So if I want them to give me any kind of a break I need to go along with what they want. When I apply for clemency the next time I'm going to do exactly what they want. I'm going to say I've had this breakthrough, and I'm full of remorse. I mean, it's not like I haven't done bad things in my life. But I haven't murdered anyone, other than in Vietnam which is what I was sent there to do." He paused, and then said in a quiet, emotion-filled voice, "I guess all this is happening to me for the things that I did do."

"What did you do?" We were sitting close to each other in the visiting room, and I really didn't want to know what Victor had done, but I needed to know.

He held my hand and stroked it. "Let's put it like this: I've snatched a couple of purses. I've hit people. Then there was the time at Shea Stadium I stole the hat vendor's money. I was an angry kid, always acting on my belief that life gave me a raw deal so it owed me."

I nodded, experiencing a mixture of emotions. It was weird hearing that this gentle, loving person had performed these hostile acts. But then again, I thought of the acts that I had performed in my youth, the difference being that mine were directed against me and his were against others. *More healthy*, I thought. I always suspected that if I had been more willing to go against others rather than myself I would have been better off. Instead I was the archetypical female, always ready to defer to the other, to be the martyr, to accept the burnt piece of toast or the messed-up egg. Then again, Victor really did the same thing on a grand scale, by going to prison rather than give up those other guys.

"Do you believe in karma?" Victor asked.

"Well, sort of. I believe we've been here before in some

form and our present incarnation has some relationship to other lives. What about you?"

"Hey, I must have done something in a past life to deserve all of this."

"Including me?"

Kissing me on the lips, he said, "You are the changing of my karma. Maybe God is ready to forgive me for all my sins."

"You believe in God?"

"I was raised by a church-going, God-fearing family."

Suddenly I noticed the couple at the table directly in front of us. The stout bleached blond was straddling the lap of her dread locked boyfriend who was as tall and lanky as she was the opposite. Their loud breathing was noticeable.

"Not to change the subject," I whispered, "but I think they're having sex."

"Shhh, don't look."

"They're right in front of us."

"So turn this way. Look at me." Victor turned me more toward him. We had gotten into the routine of sitting in the smaller visiting room, all the way in the back because there was less scrutiny by the guards. There was also a steady stream of people walking through to get to the larger visiting room. Given that we were both small and surrounded as we were by so many people, we were as obscure as we could be.

"Like I said," Victor went on, "God has brought me you so I must be doing something right."

"You're doing a lot right. You're doing more right than most people."

"I really need to hear that from you, sweetheart. And I want you to know that I believe the same about you. Not just because of what you've done for me but also because of your work; it's not everyone who goes into the state mental hospital and works with hardcore down-and-out mental patients. Most people could never do that kind of work. Your patients are very fortunate to have you. I wish I could be with you for eight hours every day."

"You will," I breathed as I felt the warmth of Victor's fingers on my thigh. "What are you doing?"

"I love the softness of your skin."

"Here comes Henry," I whispered, referring to the thin, red-faced guard who was strolling between the tables.

The rule was all hands visible on the table. Victor put his in mine.

"Any plans for tomorrow?" Victor asked.

"Well, there's laundry, the Sunday *Times*, and thee."

"Oh?"

"Yes, you know I work on something Victor-related every Sunday."

"You shouldn't, sweetheart; you need to go out more. Spend time on yourself."

"Spending time on you is spending time on myself."

That Sunday for diversion I read the *Times Magazine*. It was interesting but not crucial to my daily existence. These days, relevant reading was anything that related to prisons or the New York State government. I read an article about a woman who survived breast cancer, and I felt inspired by her fortitude in fighting the odds. Then I got out my Victor folders.

Getting material from everyone I could who was interested in Victor's case, I started polishing the hundred-page-thick package of letters and other documents in support of Victor's early release. In addition to the dozens of heartfelt letters from friends, family, and teachers, I had got in several from corrections officers and other prison personnel. It also contained copies of all his diplomas and degrees, his school transcripts showing his consistently high grade point averages and school honors, including dean's list and valedictorian. This clemency package was the story of a man's life, in this case the man I loved, and I prayed that it was impressive enough to get Victor further along in the clemency process.

Initially, the clemency materials are screened by the Department of Parole which handles clemency applications, and they disallow most of the applications. If the application somehow survives, the inmate is interviewed by a panel of parole officers, and the prospective home where the inmate would live is visited and inspected by parole officers. I began drafting letters to various prisoners' rights groups and advocates, including the Sentencing Project and the New York State Coalition Prisoners' Association. Though it was beautiful weather outside, I had my work cut out for me inside. I kept working until well after midnight.

PART
THREE

A heavy downpour. Stand out in the rain, let
the iron bars go right through you, glide along
in the water that is trying to sweep you away,
but stay erect and wait till the sun comes
streaming suddenly, endlessly in.

Franz Kafka
Diary

CHAPTER
SIXTEEN

SMALL MISSIONS

We were having trailer visits about every three-and-a-half to four months. As soon as one ended we began planning the next so that the loneliness in between would be assuaged. Each visit developed its own character. For instance, there was one in the middle of March during which there was a freak heat spell. What a delight to have the warm humidity of June when normally the radiators would be hissing. Though we spent the whole time inside the trailer, we kept the back windows wide open, and mellow air flowed in. Especially in bed, having the sweet, balmy breezes caress our bodies was an unexpected pleasure. And, as the day went on and temperatures rose, turning on the air conditioner for Victor was a luxury.

Another visit began on the same day as the Persian Gulf War. As children of the sixties and seventies, Victor and I still identified with the Vietnam War. The Gulf War, in our eyes, seemed dwarfed in comparison. But during our two days of conjugal bliss we learned its every nuance as that was the only thing we could get on television. For Victor, one notable element was the lack of casualties, which clashed with his memories of the horrors of comrades dying around him in Vietnam, about which he still had nightmares. We were frustrated that we had to watch it because we had looked forward to the escapism of watching movies together. Instead, all there was was war.

One bizarre thing that happened that weekend was when a guard, Ms. Hardcastle, decided to pay us a call. We were lying in bed when there was a knock at the door. We looked at each other in shock; having a guard come to your trailer during a visit was such a rare occurrence that we got paranoid. Victor said, "Stay here," and putting on his shirt, went out to see her. I listened as they chatted and heard them walk to the bathroom; after more talking the trailer door closed. I let out my breath, unaware that I had been holding it. A few minutes later, appearing in the doorway of the bedroom, Victor said, "She wanted to look at the shower because they're going to fix it after we leave Monday. But guess what?"

"What?"

"You're not going to believe this. We left your pills out, and she saw them."

I knew having drugs of any kind was a cause for having our visit terminated. "Oh shit," I breathed, feeling a sense of panic. "What did she say?"

He came in and sat down. "She saw the dish on the table and said, 'What's this?' and me thinking quickly on my feet, replied, 'They were there when we got here.'"

"She believed you?"

"I don't know, but she took them with her."

"Oh, wow. Do you think anything's going to happen?"

"I don't know, maybe not. They'll probably contact the guy that was in here before us and ask him if he left some pills. He'll say no, and it'll be my word against his."

"Well, it's not like they're illicit drugs, you know. It's just vitamins, Tylenol, and my fertility medication."

He gave me a worried look. "Will it matter if you miss a couple of those pills?"

"No, I don't think so."

In an effort to increase the possibility that the artificial inseminations I'd been having would work, I began taking fertility pills. While packing for the trailer visit, I had put two days' worth of the pills, my vitamin regimen for two, and some Tylenol in a tissue which I carefully folded into a two-by-two square, sealed with scotch tape, and placed in my bra. I had done this before with no problem, and upon entering the trailer I removed the packet and emptied the pills into a small saucer which we kept on the kitchen table as we had no expectation of anyone being there besides us. So startled were we by the intrusion of Ms. Hardcastle that we totally forgot about the pills on the table. The pills were quickly analyzed and found not to be street drugs, so the issue was dropped.

In the visiting room on our next visit, Victor and I noticed how many of the inmates' wives showed up pregnant.

"This can't all be happening here in this room," I said.

"No, most of it happens in the trailers."

"But it's not happening to us."

"No, it isn't, at least not yet. But it will, I know it will."

"I think we should try to make it happen sooner, otherwise we're relying on this visit every three to four months when I may or may not be ovulating."

We had started trying in Otisville and were still utilizing the crude method of collecting Victor's semen in the vial and using the inserter for insemination. One day while riding through the congenial town of Fishkill, New York, I noticed a sign announcing Gynecology and Obstetrics Associates, and I came up with my latest brilliant idea. Immediately upon seeing Victor I conveyed it to him. "Maybe the prison administration will let us legally obtain semen from you which I can then bring to these nearby doctors, and they will inseminate me."

He smiled at me. "You can try," he said gently, "but it's a long shot."

A few days later I made an appointment with Dr. Nyquist, my New York gynecologist. Handsome and famous, he was eager to be helpful and was happy to write a letter to the prison officials. We went through Ginnie, the Family Reunion program liaison, figuring she, too, would want to help, but all she could do was pass the request on. After two weeks, the response came from Albany where the chain of command originated. The answer was no. We were disappointed, but not surprised.

Dr. Nyquist assured me that if I could get Victor's sperm to New York fast enough and store it in a bank, it would be possible for him to artificially inseminate me with it. He also suggested that we increase the fertility medication, progressing from pills to injections. Giving yourself injections is one of those experiences you don't think you can do until you actually have to. This was not about one-inch insulin needles quickly jabbed into the thigh, but rather Pergonal, which is administered via a three-inch needle into the upper part of the butt. I practiced in the office with Nancy, the nurse, who instructed me with a shot of Vitamin B_{12}. Standing in front of a mirror, I located a spot a few inches in from my hip, swabbed it with alcohol, then plunged in the needle with the medication. I was left vaguely queasy, but determined. At home I marveled at the way the medication came neatly packaged in rows of small, thin glass vials, along with pristine vials of sterile water in which to dissolve the caps of powder. The medical insurance at my job covered the forty-four-dollar-a-vial, ten-vial-a-month medication.

The next and more challenging step was to get Victor's precious seminal fluid from Beacon, New York, to Madison Avenue in under two hours, which, according to Dr. Goldstein of Fertilab, was the absolute longest that unrefrigerated air-exposed sperm could remain alive. I was relieved Dr. Goldstein hadn't asked questions when I said I wanted to bring in my husband's sperm rather than have him produce it on the spot. Ironically, this sperm bank had just emerged from a cloud of media attention in which one of their white female clients gave birth to a brown-skinned baby and sued Fertilab for giving her the wrong sperm.

On the chosen day I arrived at the prison early with the vial safely ensconced in my underwear, camouflaged by a billowing sundress. Because it was a weekday, much of the visiting room was closed off, and those of us who were there were sitting close together. I sat in what appeared to be the most discreet spot, but the location was far from ideal. I began to feel anxious about how Victor and I would be able to accomplish our mission with all of us—guards, inmates, and visitors—in such close proximity.

Normally Victor arrived about ten minutes after I did so when fifteen minutes went by and he still hadn't arrived, I started to get even more nervous. Soon the whirring of huge fans and the hum of the vending machines were really setting my nerves on edge; I was going to approach the guard's desk when the phone rang. The officer answered it, said a few words, and looked at me. My solar plexus contracted as if I had been punched. What could have happened? He came down from the elevated desk and approached me. It seemed amazing to me that this stonefaced stranger in a blue uniform could have a large impact on my life.

"Mrs. Clark?"

"Yes?"

"Your husband, Victor, will be a little late as he's meeting with the parole officer."

"The parole officer?" I was stunned. Victor had no parole officer, and he was years away from parole. What could this mean? Certainly nothing bad, I hoped.

"Thanks," I said, forcing a meek smile.

I looked around, making sure not to let my gaze linger on any one person for too long. Couples huddled together; fathers joked with their children; the guards talked with each other while their eyes scanned the room. I didn't know what to do with myself. After buying a can of Blue Bird orange juice from a vending machine, I stopped at the guard's desk and asked for a pencil. I was given one that was about an inch-and-a-half long with no eraser. I sat and doodled on a paper towel, drawing the leaves on the yard tree, whose branches bisected one of the windows. I grew more and more nervous that Victor wouldn't get there in time for us to do what we had to do. It was crucial that I leave before rush hour in order to get to the city in time to park uptown, get on the subway, and make it to Fertilab before the two-hour deadline.

Finally, after an hour, Victor walked in. He had an intense look on his face, and the wideness of his eyes suggested that he was as hyped up as I was. Instead of sidling up as he sometimes did so we could savor the distant view of each other, he walked briskly and directly towards me. I stood, and, as we embraced, he said, "You're not going to believe this . . . I had to see this parole officer for a clemency hearing."

"What?"

He must have read on my face joy at the thought that this somehow meant he would be coming home soon. He took my hand as we sat. "It was just a formality, sweetheart. I met with this guy who asked me a few questions in preparation for an actual hearing which I'll have in a couple of weeks in front of a three-member panel, just like when you actually go before the board for the purpose of parole."

"But this is fantastic, that you're actually getting this far in the clemency process again!"

Victor agreed. "But don't get too excited; they're most likely not going to give it to me."

"Still, who knows, maybe Cuomo will have a burst of compassion and good will the day they put it on his desk."

Victor smiled. "Let's not count on it. So how are you, my love?" He kissed me passionately, but we broke after a few seconds as guards prowled nearby.

"I'm great, just a little anxious about our mission."

"What time do you have to leave?"

"Oh, by two." It was now a little after twelve. The sun beamed in the window. The room was steamy, and we were both slightly sickened by the discount store perfume which hung in the air.

"Would you like to take a walk outside?" Victor asked.

"Do you think we'll be able to accomplish our goal out there?" I said secretively.

"Well, I don't know, but if not, at least we can walk for a

few minutes. Let's leave stuff here so we can come back to these seats if we need to."

Marking our spot with my sweater and a half-empty tissue pack, we went out into the sunlit yard. Holding hands, we began to walk.

"If only it were really possible that they'd grant you clemency....."

"You know, I think there's a chance that the parole board would, but I don't think Cuomo ever would, because it wouldn't be politically expedient for him. Except for a guy who is white and has the right political connections."

"What a system."

"Really! Hey, enough about me, how are you, my love? It's so good to see you, a wonderful treat in the middle of the week."

"I know. For me too. Of course, any reason that I'm not at the pit makes me happy, but this is really great. I'm just a little worried about getting to the city on time."

"Don't worry; everything will go fine."

We walked the perimeter of the yard about eight times then sat on one of the few benches that fell in the shadow of the building. The bench was warm.

"Definitely can't do it out here," Victor said. "Too many windows."

"So let's go in."

"Okay. Let's sit out here for about five minutes and then go in."

"I wish we could sit out here all day and night. Then again, as long as we're wishing...."

Back inside, both the temperature and the noise level had risen. In a way, this was good since it would help conceal our activities. It didn't exactly make for an erotic setting, however. Not that it usually was, but when we weren't involved in doing something specific the way we were that day, we could get into each other at our leisure, and being next to each other for hours was erotic in itself. On this day, besides being distracted by our tension, the other people, and the time limit, we also knew that the culmination of love play would be the end of the visit.

But, loving each other as we did and with our joint desire for a family, we did what we had to do. We were able to touch and caress each other's arms and other areas of skin not covered by clothing, and then our hands found their respective way into pants and under dress. Quietly oohing and ahhing, looking into each other's glazed eyes, I said, "Tell me when," and Victor said, "Okay," and I slowly brought the open vial from my pocket to Victor's hand under the table which he strategically placed. With each pulsation, I thought of the vial filling up, and when he was done, he capped the vial, we kissed, and I placed the vial in my pocket. "I feel so badly that I have to leave you," I said.

"Love 'em and leave 'em," Victor joked.

"Ha ha. I'm not even sure I can walk at this point," I said, my face shining like a beacon.

"I know you're in a hurry, but please drive safely," he whispered as we embraced by the exit.

"I will," I said, thinking I would be speeding the whole way down the Taconic Parkway.

As I drove, I tried not to watch the clock. With the air conditioning on, the power of the engine was diminished, and the car fought me the whole way, especially on inclines. Nevertheless, somehow I made it to the Bronx in an hour; there the traffic slowed to a crawl, and I felt as if my blood pressure were skyrocketing. As I sat cursing New York City, suddenly there appeared in my line of vision that shimmering bolt of light that signaled to me the onset of a migraine headache. Of all things, I was chagrined to have a migraine come on at a time when I needed to perform optimally. Getting a migraine while driving was something I always feared, since I knew my vision would become marred by my malfunctioning brain. I thought about pulling over by the Third Avenue Bridge and finding the nearest subway, but I knew I had to make it at least into

Manhattan. Staying to the right and driving with extra caution, I
made it to Ninety-sixth Street and Lexington Avenue and found
a parking spot with not too much trouble. My heart raced.
Another fifteen minutes and it would be two hours, the end of
the time limit the doctor had set for the sperm to be viable. As I
stood waiting for the Number 6 train, a light show blazed before
my eyes, and the pounding headache began. The train came
with a roar that threatened to blow my head right off my shoulders. I rode to Fifty-ninth Street where I jumped out and ran,
head throbbing. Through the crowds I made my way, weaving
in and out like a running back, and got to Fertilab with three
minutes to spare.

Inside, I was glad to see the lighting was cool and sub-
dued; there were firm but comfortable gray couches, and a clipboard and pen with which I filled out the necessary papers,
squinting through my head pain. Trembling, I handed over the
vial, and the white-coated technician told me to wait as they
tested its contents. I sat back on the charcoal couch and tried to
take deep, slow breaths. After a few minutes the red-haired technician beckoned me to a small sterile room where she gave me
the good news: "Much of the sperm is still alive, and it is a good
count." *Good old Victor, what a man*, I thought, chuckling. She
handed me a printed sheet of instructions for retrieving sperm
from the bank. Despite my still throbbing temples, I walked out
into the sunlight smiling.

With Victor's sperm nearby and intact, I went into the
fertility process full force. Each morning when I woke up, I took
my temperature with the OvulIndex thermometer, specially
designed to get as exact a reading as possible. Then I entered the
temperature readings on a graph, which was supposed to show
two things: the rising of the temperature mid-cycle which indicated that ovulation had taken place, and if it remained elevated
at the end of the cycle, this indicated pregnancy. This procedure
gave new meaning to my mornings; there was a suspense in the
process that was powerfully motivating.

The doctor instructed me to have my hormone levels

tested on the tenth day of the cycle. Sitting in the crowded waiting room, I looked with envy at the women who had men with
them. I wondered how many women were there because they
were ill, how many were pregnant, how many were happy. I
wanted to assume that all the pregnant ones were happy, but of
course I knew realistically that many pregnant women are anything but happy. So much of life is a matter of timing; you may
crave something desperately today that tomorrow you will do
anything to avoid.

On the tenth night I would begin the shots. I couldn't
help but think of all the junkies I treated and what a valuable
commodity syringes were. Who would have thought that ordinary people got prescriptions for syringes and had them filled at
the neighborhood pharmacy?

Preparing myself for an elaborate ritual, I laid out all the
materials on a surface near the full length mirror. Careful not to
mishandle the fragile glass vials, I mixed the medication, a powder made from the urine of postmenopausal nuns in Italy, with
the sterile water. Did those nuns know that their urine was being
used to help women become pregnant? I wondered. I took a
five-inch-long hypodermic and plunged in a formula made of
their urine. The sickening aspect of this was superseded by my
desire to do anything to have a child with Victor. I walked
around for days with black and blue marks symmetrically
placed on the upper outer corners of each buttock.

It was uncomfortable to sit down during this time. More
than ever, I identified with being female and enduring pain. I
could not help thinking, *no wonder we're so good at it. With our
bodies as vehicles, how can we be sensitive to a little pain?* People are
always poking and prodding inside us; our bodies are not our
own, unlike men whose bodies, for the most part, remain intact
and off limits to others. As women, we get to know this experience from the first time someone tells us, "Open your legs."

Dr. Nyquist suggested that we continue to try and get
pregnant by whatever ingenious ways we could come up with,
and he would also inseminate me with Victor's sperm on the

optimal day of the cycle, perhaps twice. Thus began a series of visits to Dr. Nyquist's office at odd times, even on weekends and holidays when his office was closed and he had to make a special trip in because I was ovulating. I admired Dr. Nyquist for his dedication; his whole life seemed to revolve around the thousands of women who were his patients and the thousands of lives he had helped to bring into the world.

On the appropriate day, Dr. Nyquist's office phoned, and Fertilab shipped Victor's sperm in a two-foot-high silver tank to the office. It was kept inside long, thin straw-like containers which were also used in the insemination process. I was apprehensive at first that the process would hurt, but all of the times except one it didn't. That cold night Dr. Nyquist was either overzealous or else just plain careless and inserted the sperm too quickly; suddenly I felt uterine contractions so severe that I wound up writhing on the floor in agony. I told myself that this was practice for when I would be in labor; small consolation.

The following week our visit had a sadder tone as I had gotten my period one morning. The amazing thing about the temperature method was that you knew ahead of time that you'd get your period because that morning your temperature dropped. It was with great chagrin that I saw the 98.3 reading, down from 99 the day before. Denial of the truth worked only until the faint redness appeared on the toilet paper, and then reality set in: we'll have to go through the whole thing again in the new cycle—the temperature charts, the bloodwork, the shots, the insemination. It seemed like a losing battle. For the rest of the day I walked around feeling lost, alone, and deprived. Practically every woman I passed on the street seemed to be pregnant, and the ones who weren't had babies and little children in tow.

"Maybe it's for the best," Victor said, always the optimist. "I mean, just think of how difficult it could be for you having a baby to care for on your own. After all, I'm not there, and we don't know when I will be there."

"That's true," I said as we walked the yard, holding hands, watching our breath in the cold. "But I like to think I would manage. After all, I have your family now as a support system, and I'm sure they would help me."

"They would, but they're in Brooklyn and you're in Manhattan, and at two or six o'clock in the morning they won't be there. Working and bringing up a child is not easy for anyone, but without a partner it's even tougher."

"Maybe you're right," I said wistfully. "But I believe in us and in our future, and I know we'll make wonderful parents or else I wouldn't be going through all this. Believe me, it's no picnic going through all these shots and visits to the doctor."

"You're doing that because you want to. If you're uncomfortable with it you should stop."

"Hey, I'm just complaining. Don't mind me. I won't stop the discomfort. I want to have your child. But the doctor told me that I can't take these medications indefinitely, so at some point I'll at least take a break."

"Honey, do whatever feels right for you. It's your body, and even though I'm as anxious for you to get pregnant as you are, I want you to feel good and not stressed out. So whatever you decide, I will be supportive."

We stopped in the middle of the yard and hugged.

"Clark!" A guard standing a few feet away was motioning with his hand for us to move on.

Victor and an inmate standing nearby looked at each other with exasperation.

"Come on." I took his hand, and we continued to walk as the sky overhead got grayer.

That night I drank Harvey's Bristol Cream in one of the engraved Depression Era wine glasses I inherited from my grandmother and rented *Roman Holiday* with Audrey Hepburn and Gregory Peck. I watched the dark burgundy liquid cling to the rose-colored glass. Everything in life seemed delicate and tentative; as Victor was always saying, "There are no guarantees." *Roman Holiday* was captivating, set as it was in a time and place and with people so different from my daily existence. With its *carpe diem* message about love and duty, I was lulled into a warm, pleasant escape and then sleep.

Back to reality the next night, I got scared when I heard Victor's voice on the phone sounding husky and almost tearful. I had never heard him like this.

"Hi there," he said. "How are you?"

"Never mind me, how are you? You sound so sad."

"I am." He stopped, and I could hear him crying. Had someone died?

"Victor, what is it?"

"I've been crying since this afternoon when I went for the clemency hearing."

"What happened?"

"This officer 'of mercy' told me, 'I don't get the sense that you've suffered. You've done so well for yourself; prison seems to have been a positive experience for you.' When he said that, that I haven't suffered, I was stunned. It's precisely because I used all my pain over the years that I was able to accomplish what I did, and when I heard him say that, the floodgates opened."

"Oh, I'm so sorry for you, sweetheart," I said, feeling tearful myself.

Victor rushed on, his voice broken. "It's as if now that the feeling has come out it doesn't want to stop. Also, I knew right then and there that my chances for clemency were over."

"It's as if you're being penalized for having done so well."

"You're right, and in truth, the only reason we were even sitting there was because I've done well."

"You're damned if you do, damned if you don't."

"And this is not a place where you can show what you're feeling. After I left the room where the hearing was held, I walked down this long corridor. I knew I was going to cry, so I ducked into the stairwell. Luckily, no one came along."

"What would a guard do if he saw you crying?"

"Probably send me for a psychological evaluation."

"That's unbelievable. How do guys cope with sadness there?"

"Most of them get violent, that's how, and that's considered okay. 'Cause when you're violent or verbally abusive, you get sent to the box—you know, solitary confinement—for thirty days, and that's that. If you cry, everyone gets real uncomfortable and doesn't know what to do, so they send you to the shrink."

"What if you refuse?"

"You can't. Or else you're thrown in the box for defying a direct order."

"What a place."

Silence. Then Victor said in a muffled tone, "Denise, someone's signaling me. I have to go."

"Are you going to be okay, sweetheart?"

"Yes, I didn't mean to worry you. I'll be fine so long as I don't show them how I feel."

"No, no, it's good for you to feel. Please don't ever think you can't express your feelings to me."

"I won't. I'm just kind of fucked up right now." I could hear in his voice the tears starting again. "See you Saturday?"

"Absolutely."

On Saturday, Victor's pain was still flowing. As a therapist, I wondered if this parole officer hadn't done Victor a favor; as a wife, I hated the man's guts. I tried to comfort Victor the best I could, but ultimately I knew that the ache of the last eighteen years was so great, he had to bear it on his own.

CHAPTER
SEVENTEEN

A LONG JOURNEY

Going upstate to visit Victor every week started to wear on me in the third year. Here I was, longing for a family life, yet I had entered a situation which didn't allow for anything even resembling what was normal, at least not now. Then again, I told myself this was the year Victor would become eligible for work or school release. *With his prison record and performance, how can he not get one of them as soon as he is eligible?* I kept telling myself. On the other hand, Victor kept telling me that nothing was guaranteed, especially in the prison system, and warned me that I should expect the worst and hope for the best. Despite his advice, I dreamed constantly of his being home working or studying by the latest, September.

On March 18, a memo we'd drawn up was submitted by Victor to the chairman of the Fishkill Correctional Facility Temporary Release Committee, with a copy to his counselor, Ms. Keenan, stating he would like to be scheduled for an interview in order to determine his point score and to submit an application for temporary release. Ms. Keenan, a short, heavyset white woman, saw to it that the committee got the memo and scheduled an interview for Victor. The point score determination, which looked at the nature of the crime for which the inmate was serving time, his past convictions, participation in programs, and institutional behavior, established an inmate's basic eligibility for temporary release; without scoring above a designated minimum he couldn't even proceed with the application. As we had anticipated, Victor's point score was high, so Ms. Keenan proceeded with the next step, which was to submit the application. Victor and I had drawn up lists of people from whom to request support of his application for work or school release.

Thinking of people to write to and meet with had become an obsession for me. I needed to work for Victor's release or I would have gone mad, for by this time my longing to have him with me was so consuming.

On Sundays and days off there were the meetings I had arranged and the actual writing of the letters. Victor did his share too. Between the two of us, we generated hundreds of pages, all of which described his life in detail, how he deserved work or school release, and how greatly the support of the reader was needed. Some of the people we wrote to or I met with were people in Corrections, including one first deputy commissioner who played a direct role in the signing of work release approvals; another first deputy commissioner who had known Victor personally at Green Haven where he had been the educational director; a first deputy superintendent who had also known Victor at Green Haven; a parole commissioner who had been the head of the clemency board and several times had reviewed Victor's voluminous clemency package; Charles Hynes, the Brooklyn District Attorney; Henry Louis Gates, the eminent African-American scholar and educator; Charles Rangel, New York Congressman; and Assemblymen Franz Leichter and Ed Sullivan. I also continued writing to the producers of television shows like *Oprah*, *Maury Povich*, *60 Minutes*, *20/20*, and *Primetime Live*.

Had this been twelve or fifteen years before, I might have had a whole team of people eager to have their names affiliated with the cause of Victor's release. Now, we were grateful to get the meager responses we did. They ranged from enthusiasm from the two assemblymen I met with and Professor Gates, to well-wishing from the prison personnel, to an either neutral or negative response from the rest. Several of my friends generously offered to write letters of support, but I told them that the Department of Corrections was not so much interested in what a few individuals had to say as in the larger public voice, which, as a whole, was becoming increasingly punitive and vengeful. If anyone could possibly influence Corrections, it would be politicians who theoretically could be held accountable if Victor were released and then committed a crime. Hardly anyone was willing to take that chance, especially as the 1988 presidential campaign and Willie Horton still remained in the public memory.

September, the date I'd set in my mind as the one when Victor would gain work release, came and went. It was particularly frustrating and heartbreaking to us when, that Christmas, clemency was bestowed by the governor upon Gary McGivern, the white inmate who had been convicted for a cop killing and escaping from prison, to name just two of his crimes. It was a purely political move, which made us ache from the injustice, that a man like this who had an extensive criminal history and a much weaker record of rehabilitative activities than Victor would be set free while Victor remained imprisoned. It was hard for me to not blame myself as it was McGivern's wife who had been the driving force behind the campaign to get her husband out of jail, and she had done something right, which I, with all my zeal, had not been able to do. Helping her, however, was the fact that when she began the campaign, public attitudes toward inmates were less vindictive, and of course, the fact that her husband was white. Victor and I rationalized all this when we saw McGivern's face in the news and drew small comfort from the huge outcry of so many in the law enforcement community.

Meanwhile, our other mission continued. Continuing to give myself shots of fertility medication, I grew fat as I approached my fortieth birthday. I anticipated that birthday with dread, as with each dawn I became increasingly aware of my life growing shorter and the family life I had come to desire still lacking. Here I was, middle aged and not yet a parent. I was a wife with no husband by my side. I had a mildly successful career as a psychotherapist and a few writing credits. I had no money; no property. *What do I have to show for twenty years as an adult?* I asked myself.

More questions, more uncertainty. In this period of self-doubt, I sat across from my psychotherapy clients feeling like a fraud. Who was I to give people guidance? Over and over, I had to remind myself that I wasn't so much guiding them as helping them with techniques to guide themselves. The techniques I was employing at the time were both rational emotive and cognitive therapy. These belief systems put forth that we are what we think, and if we examine and refute our thoughts, we will feel better. Feeling more comfortable with this system than with previous ones, I went weekly for therapy with one of the directors of the Institute for Rational Emotive Therapy and became personally more centered and less uncomfortable with life. Rational emotive therapy bases its philosophy on that of Marcus Aurelius and the Stoics, who believed that we can live successfully through anything depending on how we view it. For instance, if a patient says, "I can't stand to be alone," the therapist would respond, "You may not like being alone, but you can certainly stand it." A more extreme example of this would be if the patient says, "I don't want to fly on an airplane because I'm afraid it will crash and I'll die," and the therapist responds, "What would happen if you die? It might be difficult for you and your loved ones, but they and the world will go on." At least some degree of ego strength is needed to work with this system, not to mention intelligence. Although some patients benefitted from the more reparative nature of a relationship with a therapist, I suspected that the compromise of a combination of the two techniques would be optimal.

One person I contacted to ask for support for Victor was a former therapist of mine, Paul Monasch, who was now running a program for ex-offenders, drug addicts, and people with HIV and AIDS. Paul had played a major role in my life in the early 1980s when I had gotten his name from a friend's therapist whom I wanted to see but couldn't because he was too expensive. The first time I saw Paul I was stunned. "He's incredible looking," I told my friend Yvonne.

"Which actor does he look like?" she asked.

"He's in the arena of Gregory Peck and Richard Gere," I responded.

"How are you gonna get into the therapy? You'll probably just sit there and lust after him the whole time," Yvonne said.

"I don't know, but I'll love sitting there looking at him for an hour."

A follower of Bhagwan Sree Rajneesh, the guru with twenty-three Rolls-Royces, Paul dressed in red all the time, often wearing clashing shades of maroon, crimson, and tomato. Around his neck he wore a mala, a necklace of beads with a picture of Rajneesh, and he had a few affectations resulting from the group's teachings. One of these was that at the end of a session, he would hug me while taking deep breaths which caused his stomach to expand and contract. I always found this more comical than erotic, though it was meant to be neither, because his stomach was like a balloon pressing against my chest. I did go through a period of transference with him in which I was frustrated by my desire for him. When I told him about my physical attraction to him, he asked, "Would you rather have me as a lover or a therapist?" I gave the sought-after answer which, of course, was "a therapist," the implication being that handsome, sensitive lovers are a dime a dozen, but a good therapist is hard to come by. Compared to the therapists I had seen before him, Paul was rare in his frankness, compassion, and Eastern orientation. To help the growth process, I joined a therapy group that Paul ran, and for over two years I cried, hugged, confessed, and raged with a variety of different personalities. I eventually left when I got tired of hearing them say, "We don't want to hear what you think. What do you feel?" They were so into feelings that they always gave short shrift to my intellect. Because my brain was something I had a reasonable degree of confidence in and my feelings were not, I felt they were being too dogmatic and doing me an injustice.

While I was sitting in these rooms examining my soul, Victor was also in rooms, albeit ones with bars on them. The Alternatives to Violence Program was, and continues to be, a strong presence in prisons across the country. Run by the Quakers, the program trains inmates as leaders, or facilitators, of the groups. Early on, Victor became a facilitator and remained involved over the years. Instead of a weekly meeting, like most ordinary therapy groups, the AVP group met for two to three days twice a year. During these intensive sessions, the inmates opened up with each other, sharing their experiences and feelings. Particularly in the repressive atmosphere of prison, these encounters were cathartic and productive, for there was also training and education which provided the participants with new ways of acting and thinking, the goal being just what the name implied: they'd find ways other than violence to express themselves and get what they wanted. For Victor, it was an opportunity to have a deeper level of friendship and intimacy than he ordinarily could, to examine his own feelings and behaviors, and to teach, which he loved to do.

Now, as our mission for his freedom went through periods of optimism and despair, the lessons I learned under Paul's counsel as well as Victor's experiences in the Quaker program provided us both with the ability to better manage our pent-up feelings.

On January 23, Victor's counselor, Ms. Keenan, submitted Victor's work release application to the Temporary Release Committee in the facility. For inmates convicted of violent felonies, applying for work release was a three-tier process; first, approval was needed on the facility level, then by the Office of Temporary Release in Albany, and then, for a lifer, the approval had to be signed off by the Commissioner of Corrections. I was more excited about the process than Victor, perhaps because I hadn't been frustrated in my appeals for justice for eighteen years. His experience with the system made him shelter his feelings.

"Hope for the best and expect the worst," Victor told me again. We were sitting in our usual spot at the back of the smaller visiting room. It was a cold gray day, and the visiting room was warm with the smell of old perfume on heavy wool and fake furs. Victor carried his heavy green state jacket. I had left my coat in the car and wore a dark gray wool cardigan. After I procured our vending machine breakfast of hot chocolate and bran muffins, we sat with our arms entwined.

"What about when the statistics are in your favor?" I said.

"Denise," Victor's voice stiffened, "I want you to understand that in this case they are not. Too many people have to approve this who probably won't."

"How can they not? If they don't give someone like you work release, who are they going to give it to? I mean you're innocent, and you've far surpassed their requirements."

"Unfortunately, the first definitely and the latter may not matter. I mean, don't get me wrong, I have more chance than if I had just been hanging around pumping iron all the time, but not a whole lot."

I leaned forward to hear him. The room hummed with conversation. Though Victor often told me not to, I watched the couple that usually sat in front of us. He was at least a head taller than her, and though he was brown-skinned with dreads and she was blond with dark roots, their hair had the similar look of spider plants. They squirmed about, their hands and mouths groping each other, making me wonder if they were going to have sex as I had seen them do in the past.

I sighed, thinking of my new frustration, and tried to keep my mind on our conversation.

"So you're saying they're more likely to give work release to non-violent offenders even though they keep going in and out of the system?"

"Yeah, they consider drug offenders to be non-violent, but how do you think most of the cops get killed in the city? Drug-related crimes."

He changed the subject. "Hey, sweetheart, want to go outside? It might be a little chilly, but I can offer you some watery vending machine hot chocolate and the warmth of my hands and heart."

"Mmmm, sounds good to me."

There were only a handful of people in the yard, and the quiet out there after the din inside was palpable. Small patches of snow were scattered about like discarded papers and crunched as we stepped upon them. The gunmetal square of sky above us had an ominous, smokey look. Had it been before Christmas, I would have had a sense of dread that we were being closed in upon by the darkness, but now that the winter solstice had come and gone, I knew that the days were getting longer, and light hovered in the near future. I could look with optimism on the melting snow, knowing its days were numbered, rather than in August when I always looked sadly at the trees, knowing the leaves were dry and old, waiting to fall.

"How long do you think it will take before you get a response?" I asked as we slowly strolled around the yard breathing in the cold crisp air.

"Who knows, it could take a week or it could take a month. We just have to forget about it and be surprised, hopefully pleasantly, when it comes."

That night Victor had an unpleasant reminder that he was still very much in prison. After speaking to me on the phone, he went back to his cell and found a pot on the floor just inside the door. Then he noticed that the lock on his locker had been busted. Fortunately, he had returned before they could take anything.

"It was some lowlifes," he told me when I visited the next night. "They knew that I would be out of my cell at that time so they had someone stand guard and watch for me while another one was into my stuff."

"Your cell stays open?" I asked.

"Sure, while I'm not in it. The guards have the key, not me."

"Honey, I'm so sorry."

"That's how it is here," Victor said quietly. "At least I got back before they could take anything."

"You're surrounded by criminals."

Victor laughed. "You've got that right. Hey, remember it was only a few months ago that some jerk took my jacket."

I had felt badly for him. His beloved jacket, saved from the Marines twenty years before, had disappeared while in the laundry. He had felt a real loss because the jacket had survived Vietnam with him; I knew how I would have felt, especially living in a situation in which physical possessions were so threatened and temporary. It was hazardous to your sanity to get attached to anything. As Victor had learned to do, he didn't hold on, and when his aunt sent him a new military jacket, he quickly broke it in.

"This work release better come through or I might break you out of here myself," I said.

"Don't worry about me, Denise. I've been dealing with this kind of thing for so long I'm used to disappointment. It's you I'm concerned about."

"Listen, sweetheart, I've told you so many times: as long as you're okay, I'm okay. Just like that story of the woman who cut off her hair to buy her husband a watch chain when the man bought her the comb by selling his watch." We identified with O. Henry's *The Gift of the Magi*, each feeling that we would sacrifice everything for the other, and though we might be left with nothing, what mattered was that we would have our love and each other.

In addition to applying for work release, Victor also applied for school release. This was a lesser known part of the temporary release program, not as commonly utilized as work release, as education was not high on the Department of Corrections' list of priorities (since then, most of the education programs have been eliminated). Several months before submitting the initial application, we had put together a list of doctoral programs which interested Victor and for which he might qualify. He wrote letters explaining his situation to the special education department heads at Columbia University's Teacher's College, City University of New York, State University of New York at Albany and New Paltz, and St.

John's University. The responses were overwhelmingly favorable.

"You see," I told him, "people are impressed by your accomplishments, not to mention that black male professionals are in demand out there."

Our hopes were soon dashed. He showed me Form 4134, "Temporary Release Program Notification to Inmate." Along with his point score of forty-one, which was high as ever, the box that was checked was "The Temporary Release Committee has disapproved your application." In the space provided for comments, it said, "Your good facility adjustment and programming is recognized; however, the seriousness of the present offense... indicates that you would be a poor risk for Temporary Release. Reapply January 1992 with NO MISBEHAVIOR REPORTS."

"What's so difficult to take," I said as we once again walked the perimeter of the visiting room yard, "is that the idea of redemption never enters their mind. Even if you had really committed the crime, all that you've done since that event eighteen years ago has to mean something."

"I wish it did. I wish they knew the truth, but neither appears probable."

Tears rose to my eyes. "I guess they can deny it forever because the 'offense' will never change."

"That's right, and believe me, you'll see, this is not the only time they'll use it with me."

That afternoon we wrote a letter of appeal of the decision. We chose to be brief and understated, for they had already heard how much Victor had done within the confines of the prison to better himself and many others. It was clear that there was nothing they didn't know about Victor that could convince them.

"Don't count on this appeal doing anything, sweetheart. Think about it: the appeal is handled by the same people who made the original decision."

The following Saturday when I left Victor, I stopped at the mom and pop candy store down the road, bought a Lotto ticket, and picked up a *Times Herald Record*. I liked patronizing the stores in that area since they were small and uncrowded, with friendly proprietors, completely unlike shopping in the city. Over time, I began to do more and more of my shopping up there. On page three of the *Record* was an article with the headline: "PRISONS ORDERED TO RELEASE INMATES TO WORK PROGRAMS." I felt renewed hope as I read about how the work release program was expanding, and Corrections was encouraging inmates to apply. When I told Victor though, he gently explained, "It sounds good, darling, but it doesn't really refer to me since I've had a violent felony conviction."

All this should have made me resigned, but one thing I learned working for the state and being married to a ward of the state is to never underestimate the unpredictable nature of bureaucracy. One might suspect the opposite would be true, that bureaucracies would be deadly in their predictability, but in actuality, the arbitrariness of the rules predominates. Thus, on May 23, when Victor received the memo re: Approval for Temporary Release, our moods were immediately uplifted. For about three or four weeks we were buoyant. Even going to work was less difficult, for I wasn't consumed with a feeling of injustice seeing truly violent people go free while Victor remained behind bars for an offense from eighteen years before, a crime I believed he hadn't really committed.

Our happiness was short-lived. Within the next two weeks we received two separate memos of denial of the work release, one on the facility level and one from Albany, bringing to mind the cliche, "One hand doesn't know what the other is doing." The first memo, dated June 6, was the denial of the appeal and stated, "The seriousness of the instant offense in which a life was taken raises community safety concerns. Your excellent institutional record is noted; however, the instant offense warrants a denial at this time. Reevaluation is set for January 1992." As if the seriousness of the offense would change over the next six months! The form also had checked off that Victor should continue in a vocation [sic] program and an acad-

emic program, as if the years of education and innovative programming he had engaged in didn't exist.

The next one, dated July 18, was from the Director of
Temporary Release Programs in Albany. It contained a description of the crime and then conceded that Victor "has an exceptional institutional record.... His help in many special programs
for inmates is noted." However, "The seriousness of the instant
offense of murder raises community safety concerns at this time.
Reevaluation is set for January 1992 with continued good
record." Once again we submitted an appeal, this time attacking
the concept of the "seriousness of the instant offense;" why it
wouldn't be any different in six months, how they were just
warehousing Victor at this point, and how he couldn't possibly
prove any further how qualified and deserving he was to be
released to work or school release.

Once again, I was alone with the company of my
thoughts, which, as usual, focused on Victor. When would he
finally come home? I couldn't, shouldn't daydream of this, I told
myself. Now I just had to focus my thoughts and efforts on con-
quering the bureaucratic juggernaut which controlled his life,
and by extension, mine. Yes, a nice, modest task I'd set for
myself this time. What made me think I could do it? Was I delusional? Sometimes I wondered.

CHAPTER
EIGHTEEN

A "FESTABLE" OF SONGS

On the third Saturday in June, Marist College held the graduation ceremony for its students who were also inmates. Victor had given me my invitation about two weeks before, as if there were a chance that I wouldn't attend! I was so glad I'd be able to celebrate his latest academic achievement, earning a Certificate in Juvenile Justice, with him. We both looked forward to the chance to have a Saturday together in a setting other than the visiting room.

For the occasion I wore a tan and gray checked rayon skirt, a black top, and sandals that were silvery with thin straps. One of the first to arrive at 7:30 that morning, I went into the visitors' trailer, where a sign next to the sign-in book read FOR FESTABLE GO TO BUILDING A. "Festable"? I followed the signs to Building A; the weather couldn't have been better: a cloudless sky, balmy temperatures. A breeze blew my hair across my face; I couldn't wait to sit with my husband in the sensual air.

In a different location, we went through the usual processing: waiting in line, signing papers, emptying pockets, going through the metal detector. Then we boarded a dingy, dark green school bus which proceeded to transport us along the same road on which the conjugal trailers were located. In the distance were rolling fields and hills and I-84. Just passing the trailer site caused a sudden warmth in my loins as I remembered with fondness our last visit and realized with glee that we had only three weeks until our next one.

The bus let us off just past the trailers in front of a large, old stone building which housed the gymnasium. I hoped and expected Victor to be out there waiting for me, and sure enough, there he was, waiting to receive me as I stepped off the bus. Most of the other visitors ambled around on their own looking lost, but Victor always made sure that he was right there in the forefront, especially when I was involved. Taking each other's hands, we walked through the gymnasium which was in a state of semi-preparedness, and where inmates and staff intermingled with visitors. Compared to a regular visiting day, there was an overall greater sense of intimacy, freedom, and normalcy. While there were corrections officers everywhere, the suspicious and accusatory air they usually had was camouflaged beneath smiles and friendly faces. Many of them congratulated Victor, who introduced them to me. I also met many inmates, as well as educational staff Victor worked with, including Neal Ritter, the Harrison Ford look-alike with dark hair, wire-framed glasses, and a friendly manner.

For the graduation ceremony we sat on benches, the inmates a ten-row deep sea of dark green at the front. Ms. Smith, the Fishkill educational director, along with Neal, stood on a platform and after a short speech, called up each graduate. The men, some young, some middle aged, each rose, and with the intense pride that comes from surmounting a difficult struggle, walked to the front. My eyes teared as I understood the kind of pasts that they had overcome and the great effort and commitment it had taken for them to be receiving their diplomas. Even more than in the outside community, receiving degrees on the inside carried the hopeful aspiration of a new and positive lifestyle. The men and their families grinned, clapped, and cheered in affirmation of this.

At one point during the ceremony Victor got up and went to the men's room. Unfortunately it was during this time that they called his name. From the stage, Neal looked over in my direction after he proudly extolled Victor, his accomplishments, and his invaluable contribution to the Marist program. The audience turned and looked at me. I was self-conscious as I motioned that Victor had left the room. There was a momentary awkward silence; they were about to move on to the next person when Victor appeared. Flashbulbs exploded as he shook hands with everyone on stage, then returned to sit next to me.

After the ceremony the side doors of the gymnasium were opened, and we filed outside to the grassy area where picnic tables had been set up. Music boomed from a loudspeaker, and the mood was festive despite the tall double razor-wire fence that contained us. Victor and I sat on a bench looking out over the rolling green expanse into the distance, as if seeking our future. After a while, someone announced that food was being served, so we got on line. The strong breeze caused the corners of the paper tablecloths to flap, and lightweight items like cups and napkins flew to the ground. With our plates piled with chicken, corn, and salad, we returned to our table where we were joined by Neal and a couple of Victor's friends and their families. When it was time for the dessert, Neal, in his laconic way, said, "Are you guys ready for a surprise?" Victor looked at me quizzically. "Ready?" Neal asked. Suddenly over the loudspeaker we heard, "You can make it by railway," the opening strains of "Get Here," a song we had come to think of as our song.

"I don't believe Neal," Victor said, hugging me.

Goose bumps rippled over my skin, and a lump hardened in my throat. Neal came over, beaming.

"Thanks, man," Victor slapped him fondly on the back, then stared at me, mouthing the words of the song: "I don't care how you get here, just get here if you can."

My eyes were still moist as we sat back down at the table. Usually, tender emotion like this made me uncomfortable, but with Victor I felt I could handle anything. It had always been easier for me to say "I hate you" or "I'm angry at you" than "I love you." Victor expressed his love a lot, and not only to me. He expressed positive sentiments to his family and friends, and while someone else might have seemed effusive, I knew Victor was sincere; having been surrounded by ugliness, hatred, and anger for so long, he knew the importance of perpetuating love and warmth. Even I had become softer since being with Victor, but the skeptic in me sometimes wondered where all his anger had gone and if it would resurface someday when he was freer to be himself.

As it inevitably did, our time together quickly drew to a close. By 2:30 they were announcing that visitors had to report to the bus to be brought back to the main building. It was always more difficult to leave Victor from visits like this one, after several hours of the semblance of being in the "real" world together, as opposed to the prison visiting room.

"Just think, in only three weeks we'll be together for a whole weekend," Victor said during our parting embrace.

"I can't wait."

In order to prolong the time spent near him, rather than go directly home, I stopped at the nearby Dutchess Mall and went into a card store. It was hard to find a romantic card to send Victor because over the past three years, I had exhausted the supply from all the stores I frequented. But I continued to look with the expectation that card companies were always turning out new ones. Victor was at a distinct disadvantage with cards since, obviously, he couldn't shop, yet I continued to receive a steady stream of romantic mail from him, much of which he made himself. Having access to the computer in the school, he created different designs and wrote the verses himself. He made huge posters, some for holidays, some declaring his undying love for me.

The summer passed. We were immersed in our efforts to get Victor work release. I spent a couple of long weekends at a

Holiday Inn near the prison, cooling off in the pool, watching movies on HBO, ordering room service, and fantasizing that Victor was there in bed with me. I couldn't see Victor each day as I had done in the past because the Department of Corrections had eliminated weekday visiting hours in the medium security facilities. One very long day I realized how burnt out I was: weary, spent, in need of some rest and esthetic stimulation. With Victor's encouragement, I decided to take a vacation somewhere not too far away. After perusing some travel books, I decided Maine would be a good choice. I had mixed feelings about traveling alone: on the one hand, there was the experience of total freedom, of not having to answer to anyone or anything, and on the other, as a woman I always felt limitations on where I could and could not go and feel comfortable. When I had gone to Puerto Rico alone a few years before, I had visited places where I felt too conspicuous to stay. Even driving around in my rented car, men on the streets yelled comments at me, making me feel self-conscious and mildly threatened.

Though I wouldn't be going too far away, it would be strange not to be able to speak with Victor on a regular basis. I would miss hearing his voice. Nonetheless, I chose a motel in Ogunquit and made a reservation for the week after Labor Day when it would be less crowded. I spent the Sunday before Labor Day with Victor and retreated to the Holiday Inn in Fishkill with a vial of Victor's sperm, retrieved in our usual under-the-table method. My temperature-taking had indicated that I was ovulating so I didn't want to miss the opportunity. I was pleased with the timing, thinking that I'd be taking a part of him with me to Maine, and perhaps conception would be facilitated by the relaxation I would have there.

The motel turned out to be a two-story condominium with units overlapping in a zigzag formation. I liked the room, an efficiency with a terrace overlooking a placid inlet off the ocean where tall grasses blew in the salty ocean breeze. Private, yet right in the heart of bustling Ogunquit, it afforded me peaceful solitude amid people and activity. I quickly fell into a routine which began with waking up around 7:30 or 8:00, walking the three blocks to the delicatessen which had the basic essentials of an ideal start to a day — juice, pastry, and newspapers. I returned with these to my room's terrace where my attention would alternate between the water and sky, the newspaper, and my writing paper. Each day I added to a letter to Victor and mailed it the day I was leaving. I also attempted to write other things such as poetry but didn't produce much more than an expression of feelings. Because this was vacation, which was all about *not* having to do anything, I didn't feel too guilty.

I divided the late morning and afternoon hours between swimming in the motel's pool and sunbathing on the beach a block away. At times, I preferred the pool. The beach held memories of my early childhood, reminiscent of the young families reclining on blankets, picnicking, or chasing each other into the water. As much as I tried not to, I felt old and odd. These young men and women with their babies and toddlers seemed so *normal*. What was I doing, forty years old, alone on a beach in a resort town? Even though I was married, I had no husband here, though having the knowledge of Victor somewhat ameliorated the strangeness for me. Nevertheless, I alternated between feeling like an oddity and an old maid, either way unfit to be around these families in the full bloom of their youthful and fresh togetherness.

In the late afternoon I returned to the room, flush with the day's sunburn, showered, and indulged in that greatest of luxuries, the nap. During the first few seconds after awakening, I felt disoriented, then made my way out to the terrace where I was vaguely melancholy as the reflection of the setting sun burned on the surface of the inlet. Usually I sat and perused all the books, brochures, and local newspapers I had accumulated and decided which restaurant I'd feel the most comfortable in alone. The main criterion was proximity to the ocean, the closer the better. Then, either I'd take a leisurely stroll, desiring everything I saw in every quaint and charming store window, or I'd ride on the old fashioned Ogunquit trolley. It didn't take long before a vacation phenomenon set in of wanting to live there. It appeared to have everything Manhattan didn't: the streets were clean, uncrowded, and quiet, and the buildings were one or two stories, painted light colors, containing all the aesthetically pleasing food, clothing, books, and services that one could want. And of course, there was the ocean, the blue of the water so dramatic and the cloud formations in the summer dusk sky so majestic. How would it have been different if Victor were there? It would have been that much more beautiful. It would have defined the concept of perfection. A fiery sunset, a lobster dinner, and my love. That would be paradise enough.

One night I went to the Ogunquit movie house and saw *The Doctor* starring William Hurt and Christine Lahti. The movie, showing the evolving character of a doctor whose serious illness makes him more human, reminded me of Victor's metamorphosis. But almost more enjoyable was the theater itself, which, with its one modest-sized screen and soft seats enclosed by wooden railings, was a pre-computer era throwback. Spending time in a place like this, I could begin to understand people who were reactionary, who didn't want anything to change, who wanted to live wholesome, if not restricted lives. I wondered how Victor would feel in a place like Ogunquit in which people of color were few and far between and probably welcome only if the numbers stayed sparse. I wouldn't want to live in a place, no matter how quaint, that was racist or right wing, but I liked visiting towns that were fairy-tale pretty and mostly apolitical. Victor always claimed he wanted to travel to such places, as did I, and I wanted to share all my experiences with him.

When I left Maine it was with ambivalence. I told myself it was better than the awful feeling of dread and despair when one's vacation is over and it has been an escape from a terrible life. I had had those feelings in the past, but this time I felt like the week had served its purpose: I felt relaxed and rested and ready to get back to my *real* life, the one in which my husband needed my help to get out of prison.

Awaiting me at home, along with my cat, Yin, was a stuffy, cluttered apartment, including a stack of mail. After planting several kisses on Yin's little gray and white head, I went through the stack which contained mostly cards and thick letters from Victor. There were also responses from *Oprah, 60 Minutes*, and a lawyer specializing in prisoners' issues to whom I had written after reading an article about him in *The New York Times*. The first two letters were the standard rejections I had become used to; the latter was an original addressed to me, saying there was nothing he could do but why didn't I contact prisoners' rights groups, which I had, in fact, already done. Two of these organizations had also said there was nothing they could do for Victor and that getting work release was a privilege, not a right, so Corrections could do what they wanted. They were astute enough to understand that even though Victor was a model prisoner and presumably would be the ideal kind of person the program was created for—had served hard time, helped others, and would benefit by a transition to the community rather than a direct release to the street after so many years—Corrections was more concerned with politics and image than with what was fair.

Victor and I had had so many discussions about this, how absurd it was that prison officials gave work release to mostly the young repeat offenders who had one-to-three-year sentences, usually for drug related offenses, and invariably returned, rather than to the inmates for whom the program was intended, those like Victor who needed to reenter community life gradually with an opportunity to work, save money, and reunite with family, all while under Corrections' supervision. Instead, Corrections chose to see those men, who statistically had the lowest recidivism rate, as undeserving of work release because they were convicted of violent crimes, and then Corrections paroled them with no transition. Victor had known for many years, and I more recently, that logic was not one of the state bureaucracy's strong points. I saw examples of this all the time at work and more so in the prison system. I developed more respect for Franz Kafka. I had by this time read all his works and remembered his writing about the phenomenon that today is alive and well in its sickness.

Shortly after returning from Maine, I began to be bombarded daily with catalogues ablaze with the oranges, reds, and greens of the coming season's holidays. The four last months of the year always seemed to me a chaotic whirlwind of academic flurry, intense consumerism, and nose-to-the-grindstone ambition in business, the arts, and politics. In direct contrast to the laid back attitude of the summer, it made me anxious; during the summer you could be a relaxed version of yourself, whereas once September arrived, there was no more fooling around.

Though the New York State Department of Corrections seemed to want to keep Victor forever, at the hospital we were being pressured to discharge, discharge, discharge, a continuation of the "deinstitutionalization" trend which began with humanitarian intentions in the 1960s. The idea was that people with mental problems did not necessarily need to remain in the hospital for thirty years, and the advent of psychotropic medications made it possible for them to exist on the outside. Unfortunately, this was taken to an absurd extreme, leaving the streets of New York City littered with filthy, wide-eyed people, babbling and screaming to themselves, and the cardboard boxes in which they slept. In particular, the streets of Manhattan's Upper West Side came to be known as the world's largest psychiatric outpatient clinic.

As we were constantly being told to discharge patients, at the same time we were being threatened with job layoffs because the state was downsizing the mental health system. I became more and more concerned, not because I thought I would be without a job, but because I was trying to have a child. In case I should succeed, I figured no one would hire me pregnant. Despite the putrid environment, violent patients, bizarre staff, and irrational system, I had chosen to remain. Nevertheless, all the staff including me felt we were being victimized. Many came in late, left early, called in sick continuously, and fell behind in their work. Treated badly, they felt, as many do, justified in treating others badly. Even in the prison system, this axiom applied. After being abused by the guards, the inmates came to see themselves as victims, forgetting that they were the ones who had victimized someone, and that that was why they were in prison. It came back to the idea of karma: if someone treated them well, they returned it. If someone treated them terribly, they returned that too.

It was a role Victor did not espouse. Victor did not act out in prison. No matter how inhumanely the guards spoke to him, he never lost his temper, never cursed, always spoke to them respectfully. Through this he maintained his dignity and often nonplused the guards, as they were used to the surly, snarling inmate who would be a hair's breadth away from striking them and in some cases did so. One day, Victor told me, when he had just gotten to Fishkill, he was headed for the library and stopped a guard to ask directions.

"Excuse me," Victor said. "Can you please tell me which way is the library?"

"What?" the guard responded.

"How do I get to the library?"

Again the guard didn't understand, and when Victor repeated the question once again in a louder voice, he finally got an answer.

"He was not used to being spoken to in a polite way. He was used to some jitterbug coming up in his face with hands splayed, saying, 'Yo, man, where the library at?' They're threatened when an inmate speaks to them in a tone that's not angry and hostile, because then what justification do they have to speak to the inmate like an animal?"

Two bureaucracies, related like fraternal twins, and my life had become inextricably entwined in both of them. At times it felt like "the State," meaning Governor Cuomo and the other bureaucratic bigwigs, were our parents, and if we could only show them what good children we were, they would give us what we wanted, which was Victor's work release. If only everyone were like Cliff Austin, an idealistic young lawyer who was the assistant to State Senator David Patterson. Earlier in the year, I had sent the senator a copy of Victor's clemency package in an effort to enlist his support of Victor's applications for clemency and work release. Cliff Austin had responded with a phone call expressing how impressed he was and invited me to come and talk with him.

One sleety winter day I left the Bronx early and went to the State Office Building on 125th Street in Harlem. I had not been there for the five years since I had had a makeshift office on the eighth floor which housed Manhattan Psychiatric Center's outpatient clinic. When I stopped in to say hello to whomever might still be there that I knew, the dark, dreary walls and depressed staff reminded me of how I had hated going there each day. At least in the Bronx there are landscaped grounds with trees. A couple of flights up was Senator Patterson's office which had an entirely different feel about it. Senator Patterson's strong features shown from posters in every direction I turned. There was a lot of paper and people and phones ringing. Everyone seemed seriously engaged, and the air buzzed with importance. In the midst of all this, clad in a tan corduroy suit, Cliff Austin with his quiet, polite demeanor and modest preppy style welcomed me. Bringing me into a small office with a window that looked out on the brownstones of a Harlem side street, he shook my hand.

"Thank you for coming," he said. "I was so impressed when I read this." He held the clemency package.

"Thank *you*. It means so much to have someone respond so positively, to believe in the redemption of another human being as I do."

He perched on the corner of the gray metal desk. "I haven't quite read the whole thing, but I saw the degrees and the article about the deaf/blind unit; he certainly is an example of someone who's changed."

"Yes," I fairly shouted. Remembering Victor's words that no one wanted to hear of his innocence, I simply agreed. "This is why everyone who knows him thought he would be ideal for clemency and certainly work release."

"Well, I'm sure I don't need to tell you about Governor Cuomo's attitude toward clemency."

"No, you don't. That's why we're focusing on something that seems possible, like work release."

I went on to tell him what we were doing and how we felt a letter or phone call of support from David Patterson could be helpful.

"Well, I'll definitely show this to the senator and tell him about our meeting."

"Great. We appreciate your interest."

Smiling, he said, "Do you think it would be possible for me to meet Victor? I mean not just for the purpose of helping him but for selfish reasons. I'm so fascinated by what he's been able to accomplish, and I have a lot of questions to ask him."

Was this man an angel sent by God? "I'm sure Victor would love to talk with you, but of course, I'll have to ask him and let you know. If it's all right with him, you could come up with me one Saturday."

"I'd love that." He walked me through the bustle of the outer office to the door. We shook hands and agreed to speak within the week. Descending in the rattling metal elevators, I felt more hopeful and optimistic than I had in a long time. What a charge it was to have a complete stranger validate what you knew to be true but were unable to get others to accept. As I stepped out into the building's plaza, the colors of the neon lights in store windows on 125th Street seemed more vibrant, and the cold drizzle sparkled here and there like fireflies. I couldn't wait to get home and write to my husband.

I found out that despite those who are quick to mouth platitudes and slow to act, some people (or angels) are as good as their word.

Two weeks later, Cliff accompanied me to Fishkill. It was another gray day, though not raining, and only moderately cold. We were able to spend a good part of the day out in the yard.

Cliff had never been inside a prison before, and on the ride up I told him about some of the procedures and what it was like there. An easygoing guy, he seemed to take it all in stride, and we passed through the various gates smoothly. I could tell that Victor thought some of Cliff's questions were naive, and that even though Cliff was black, he was coming from a sheltered middle class background and knew little about the street or prison. Nevertheless, Cliff's compassion and Victor's warmth were a bridge, and they hit it off well. When we left, I felt a little cheated in that Victor and I had missed our weekly private time with each other but knew it was for a good cause. On the car ride home, Cliff said, "You know, my initial impression of Victor on paper has been confirmed by meeting him in person." Then he added the words that made my heart soar. "I would have no hesitation in helping in whatever way I can."

Within days he had gotten Senator Patterson to write a letter of support. For a while, we heard nothing, but one day that summer Cliff called.

"Well, I might have some good news," he told me as I stared out my office window at the leafy, dark green maples. "I'm going to be leaving here and going to work in the governor's office."

"You're kidding," I said, my mind instantly becoming awash with fantasies of Cliff as Governor Cuomo's right hand man and him carrying his impression of Victor's worthiness to the governor.

"I'll be the Coordinator of African-American Affairs in the governor's office, and I'll be having a lot of input into things like Victor's case."

"That's fantastic. Please let me know your address and phone when you move."

"I will," he promised. And again Cliff was as good as his word.

It was a Saturday in mid-November when Victor greeted me in the visiting room waving a paper, saying, "Sit down. Look at this." He handed the sheet to me. Because he wasn't smiling I got a little scared. I knew if it weren't something of major importance he would have waited while I got us juice and muffins, and then he would have related it to me. My fingers trembling, I unfolded the paper. I recognized it to be one of Corrections' notices pertaining to work release, similar to the ones Victor had received during the past year. I scanned it and then looked again, my heart thumping. This one had an X in the box next to the words "Your appeal has been approved," and under that another X next to "But statutory requirements necessitate further approval."

I looked at him in amazement. "What does this mean?"

"Look at the bottom."

It said, "Comments: Approval is conditional upon your continuing good behavior and final approval from the commissioner."

He grabbed my hands. "What this means is that if the commissioner says it's okay, we have to start sending out my resume."

"I don't believe it." Without thinking we jumped up and hugged until we noticed Sergeant Regis a few feet away watching us with a scowl on his face.

"Soon we won't have to worry about jerks like Regis," Victor whispered.

"I don't know," I said, trying to lighten his mood. "Maybe you should bring a few of them with you to make you feel more at home."

"You're all I need to feel at home."

"Well," I said, a smile filling my face, "I'd better start cleaning the closets and making some room."

For the rest of the day, the visiting room didn't look as bad as it usually did, and we felt more kindly toward the guards, even the nastier ones.

"Honey, listen," Victor said as I was leaving. "I know I keep saying this, but I don't want you to be disappointed. There's no guarantee that the commissioner will sign off on this, and then I'll have to reapply."

"Let me speak to Ed Sullivan," I said quietly.

The following week I went to see Ed, our assemblyman, who happened to personally know the commissioner, and his office assistant was as gracious and helpful as always. Each time I went or called there I wished that everyone with whom I had the occasion to do business was as solicitous and conscientious as she was. Ed told me to give him a copy of the notice, and he would take it from there. I also called Cliff Austin in his new capacity in the governor's office to put him on the alert, just in case Ed's intervention would be unsuccessful. In late December, Ed called to let me know that he had spoken at length with the commissioner. He indicated that the commissioner was reluctant, for if anything should go wrong, i.e., should Victor get into trouble, the commissioner's butt would be on the line. But because Ed had presented Victor in such a favorable light, the commissioner had said he would probably do it. "He trusts me," Ed went on. Thanking Ed profusely, I said, "All elected officials should be like you, truly there to help people and take a risk when it is called for."

Ed expressed his pleasure in helping, saying, "Most of politics is removed from the people, and cases like yours in which I am personally involved and can see the fruits of my labor are rare and fulfilling." I promised him that we wouldn't let him down.

As I had done for the last four years, I spent Christmas Day in prison with Victor. Though Jewish, as a child I had been enchanted at this season by the multicolored lights sparkling on people's houses and over their lawns, and I had envied them their festivities. My nonreligious parents gave in to my childhood desire to be part of the major culture, so along with our perfunctory Chanukah menorah, we put up stockings on Christmas Eve and got our presents Christmas morning. This ritual held for me the same magic and excitement it did for many Christian children; the same anticipation wouldn't let me fall asleep until midnight and caused me to awaken at 5:00 A.M. to peer out my bedroom door, trying to catch a glimpse of the presents by the ersatz fireplace in the living room. Victor must have taken his own childhood memories of Christmas and stashed them in some unreachable and invulnerable place in his consciousness, for he confirmed that holidays can be seriously depressing for those in institutions. The first year I said I was going to come up, he had said I didn't have to, that the day meant nothing to him anyway. Unconvinced, I had insisted, and his happiness at seeing me was gift enough.

This year Victor and I felt especially festive with the prospect of the impending work release. But the holidays didn't fulfill their promise. Two tension-filled months went by as we waited for word on the work release application. Finally, at the end of February, with Victor now entering his nineteenth year of incarceration, he received a memo from the head of temporary release at Fishkill, saying that his application for work release had been approved by the Temporary Release Committee and the superintendent, and it had been forwarded to Central Office in Albany for final review. This was actually what had been said in the memo in November, but we recognized that this was closer to the final step than it had been, and having been signed by the assistant deputy superintendent, was official. We now knew for sure it was in the commissioner's hands.

The communique we were waiting for, Form 4141, STATE OF NEW YORK—DEPARTMENT OF CORRECTIONAL SERVICES NOTICE OF APPROVAL FOR TEMPORARY RELEASE, dated March 10, came to Victor the following week, though at the bottom of the form it indicated the approval was done on February 18. Mired in the bureaucratic world, one became cognizant of all the minute details on a piece of paper. The day he brought this paper to the visiting room was mild in temperature, and we walked through the yard. We stopped to look at the tree, its limbs lush with buds ready to open. New shoots of grass enlivened the scruffy patch of old grass. A couple of yellow jonquil buds almost defiantly exclaimed their presence. Even the air smelled fresh.

"It truly is a new beginning," I said to Victor, beaming.

"Yes, I can hardly believe it's real."

"I've cleared space in the closets for you."

"Thank you, sweetheart."

"I can't imagine how you must be feeling right now, coming home after all this time."

"Well," he stopped and looked at me. "It is strange and scary, but wondrous. Actually, each minute that I'm here feels even stranger now."

"Come on," I joked, " you know you'll miss it."

"Yeah, right," he smiled back, clasping my hand tighter.

We spent most of that day discussing the logistics of getting Victor a job and suitable work clothes. In true Corrections fashion, he didn't know the exact date he would be home. He told me he would find out the next week, on the day before he was scheduled to have his first real taste of freedom in nineteen years.

PART
FOUR

The babble of voices in these rooms had something extremely joyful about it. At one moment it sounded like the rejoicing of children getting ready for an excursion, at another like the first stirrings in a hen-coop, like the joy of being in complete accord with the awakening day.

Franz Kafka
The Castle

CHAPTER
NINETEEN

ANOTHER WORLD

Though I had passed by the nondescript, rust-colored brick building hundreds of times over the past fifteen years, I never knew it was a prison. But of course, what else could it be but a mental hospital or prison, with its windows rendered invisible by thick iron grills and screens. It had gone through several metamorphoses as various institutions of confinement, most recently a drug treatment facility, and now it was the minimum security work release prison, Lincoln Correctional Facility. Synchronicity certainly was at work here: Victor couldn't have planned it better if he had tried, meeting and marrying a woman who lived on the same block as a work release facility. Though he was originally from Brooklyn and had spent little time in upper Manhattan, that's where his new home was, and that's where he was headed on April 3, 1992, having been granted work release.

It was a Friday, and Victor was not allowed out of the facility for the weekend, nor was he allowed to have visitors; I was permitted, however, to drop off clothing for his job search. I looked out my bedroom window over the urban landscape of Harlem and Central Park, toward the Whitestone and Triboro

Bridges, and the planes rising up out of LaGuardia Airport, hoping I could see Lincoln, and without realizing it then, the black iron cage on Lincoln's rooftop was in my path of vision. It seemed incredible that he was right down the street; I couldn't begin to imagine what being there must have been like for him. After nineteen years, here he was, back in the world, in a different venue than he had started out, with a wife and a new home.

For the previous two weeks we had been busy lining up job prospects since having a job was required to be on work release. We put together a resume for him as well as something called a biographical profile in anticipation of the questions that prospective employers would ask once they found out he was on work release. The profile described in detail his arrest, conviction, and subsequent years in prison. I put both of these documents on the computer, then sent them to agencies that advertised for help in the Sunday *New York Times*. It seemed like a long shot that anyone would be eager to hire a convicted felon fresh out of prison after so long, but I was hopeful that Victor's impressive accomplishments would win someone over, and they did.

The same Friday that Victor came to the city I got a call from Rabbi Bergman at the New York Society for the Deaf. He had received Victor's resume and wanted to set up an appointment for an interview. As always, it was gratifying when another person was willing to take a risk and give Victor the chance that he deserved. We scheduled a time for the following Tuesday when Victor would be allowed out to go on job interviews.

On Saturday, a chilly, gray spring morning, I set out down Broadway and hit the few men's stores in the neighborhood to get Victor some basics so he would have something to wear besides his prison greens and sweatshirts. In the afternoon I took the bus east across 110th Street to the Lincoln Correctional Facility, carrying a bag containing, in addition to jeans and T-shirts, a gray-blue tweed sports jacket, slacks, light blue shirt, striped tie, and a pair of black wingtips. As I walked up the front steps with Central Park faintly green behind me, I was tense with the kind of anxiousness that is hard to distinguish from excitement. Since I wasn't actually visiting him but was just there to deliver things, I didn't have to go through a search or any of the processing that I had been used to upstate.

The officer in the front booth called upstairs on the phone to tell them to send Victor down, then indicated a dirty plastic chair where I was to have a seat. I stood instead and paced in a small circle. The officer held the bag of clothing. Suddenly, a stairway door opened and out came Victor wearing his greens which seemed so strange here in the city, looking like a cross between a garage attendant's uniform and pajamas. We hugged ferociously, the mutual excitement flowing between us.

"Okay, come on," the guard called to us.

We walked over to where the guard had placed the bag on a table and watched while he proceeded to take out each item and write a list. As the bag was emptied, Victor whispered, "Nice choices, sweetheart. I knew I could count on you."

"I hope everything fits."

"I'm sure it will."

When the bag was empty, the guard said, "Okay, say goodbye."

"Wow, they're not kidding about no visiting."

"I'll see you Tuesday," Victor said, clutching my hand. "At home."

"Yes, at home," I responded and my heart surged.

Having requested Tuesday off, I watched for him that morning from my window. Through the branches of the newly blossoming trees I stared intently, knowing he would look different as a fellow inmate had cut off the dandelion of hair that had framed Victor's head. As one of the few things he had been able to control, his hair had symbolized a lot to him; he joked about Samson losing his strength along with his hair. I knew Victor would continue to be strong; but I also knew I'd miss his hair which felt so soft.

My heart swelled as I saw Victor emerge from the shadow of the Con Edison plant. I had alerted the doorman, who had received and held for me many of Victor's packages, that Victor would be arriving. For a second, I wondered what the doorman thought as he had seen Victor's return address with the number after his name and the correctional facility logo. More, I mused on what it must be like for Victor, his first day out, on a street where he had never been, alongside the majestic presence of the Cathedral of St. John the Divine, walking amid so many people on foot, bikes, rollerblades, and in cars, and then turning into the building of his wife's apartment, his new home.

Across the window in the living room, visible when you first walked in, I had strung one of those signs made of brightly colored metallic letters that spelled WELCOME HOME. In the bedroom "Get Here" was playing. When Victor walked in and heard "You can get here by railway," he broke into sobs. I put my arms around him and feeling my eyes fill up, didn't say anything; I could only guess at how he must have been feeling at that moment, to finally be free after nineteen years, his long nightmare nearing its end. We looked out the window. "I can't believe I'm here," he said, still tearful.

"I'm so happy."

"I know. I love you," he whispered, and we fell onto the bed, ripping at each other's clothes.

"Mustn't be late for the job interview," I whispered.

"The heck with the job interview," he said impetuously.

When I looked at him askance, he said, taking a deep breath, "Only kidding. We have a little time."

And so we did. As we made love on my bed where I had so many times fantasized about doing just that, I had a surreal feeling, as if it were still a fantasy. Suddenly, something that had been a vivid thought for so long crossed a dimensional line and existed in the physical world; the difference was striking yet subtle at the same time. When we lay in each other's arms afterward, I again said, "Welcome home, sweetheart."

"I'll never go away again," he said.

"You'd better not."

"I won't. Promise."

We showered and dressed, and as we were leaving the

apartment, Victor said, "Let me lock the door." I showed him which key was which, and as he held them, he sighed. "It's been so long since I've held keys."

"When was the last time you were in an elevator?" I asked as we stepped in.

"As long as since I last held keys."

On the way out of the building I introduced Victor as my husband to Ruben, the doorman, realizing that several people in the building would probably wonder where this husband popped up from, since they hadn't seen me with him before. While we headed toward the subway as I had done hundreds, if not thousands, of times, I was acutely aware that everything with which I was so familiar Victor was seeing for the first time. I started noticing the building with the gargoyles, the ginkgo trees, the doormen in front of apartment buildings, the pizza place on the corner, everything, also as if for the first time.

"Does all this look really strange to you?" I asked.

"Yes. It feels amazing just to be able to walk down the street and not have to account to someone and not have to think about who's behind me. Thanks to television, how things look isn't a total shock, but the cars really are a lot smaller."

On the subway, Victor looked around in wonder like a five-year-old. "When I left, the trains were old and beat up, covered with graffiti. These look beautiful," he said about the relatively new IRT trains.

"Did they still have those woven straw seats when you left?"

"Yeah, there were a few of them around. None of the trains had air conditioning."

"A lot of technology has happened. Wait till we go to the cash machine," I shouted over the roar of the train.

The sun greeted us when we emerged from the train at Eighteenth Street and Seventh Avenue.

"The sun's a lot warmer than it was twenty years ago, because more of the ozone layer is gone," I said.

He smiled, looked around, and took a deep breath. "It's beautiful."

"Of course," I said, smiling back.

We headed for his first appointment at the Fortune Society. We were incredibly early, so we strolled around aimlessly to use up the time.

"There's a lot of hookers around here," Victor said, referring to the many women he saw standing in front of buildings smoking cigarettes.

"They're not hookers," I laughed. "People can't smoke indoors anymore in most places. Smokers these days are treated like pariahs. That's what ultimately made me give it up. Can you imagine having to come outside in the middle of the winter just to smoke? What good is it if you can't light up where you are?"

"Yeah, that's a real change." He looked embarrassed. "I thought all those women out here were soliciting."

I shrugged. "Well, it's some kind of progress, I guess."

"Were the streets always this crowded?" Victor asked as we made our way through a throng of people along a typical weekday Manhattan sidewalk.

"Yeah, Manhattan's always been pretty crowded."

At the Fortune Society, an organization run by and for ex-convicts, Victor met briefly with a well-built young man who, despite having read Victor's resume and biographical profile, told him he would have to take a class on job hunting, which would cover resume writing and interviewing.

"What a waste of time that would be," Victor said, clutching my hand nervously as we walked east on Fourteenth Street. "I already have a resume, I know how to interview. What I need is a job."

"I guess most of the people they deal with don't have your credentials."

"Wow, that smells great," Victor said as we passed a food wagon hissing with shish kabobs and sausages.

"Are you hungry?" I asked.

"Nah. I'm too nervous to eat right now. Maybe after the interview."

Passing a doorway with a raggedy figure drinking from a brown paper bag, we came to sit on a bench in Union Square

Park, which, along with the homeless, had manicured lawns and benches full of well-dressed people. "It's schizoid," I murmured, staring. Across from us, a man sat next to a shopping cart that was packed and overflowing with bags, clothing, and newspapers, among other things.

"There weren't all these homeless people before I left," Victor said. "At that time we called them 'bag ladies.'"

"That seems almost quaint now."

"Yeah, this is pretty awful. Did you see that guy in the doorway we just passed?" Victor looked at his watch.

"Yeah, it's been like this for years. A lot of people actually live in doorways, parks, and cardboard boxes."

"How can this happen in such a wealthy country?"

"The rich get richer and the poor get poorer in this society."

"That's for sure. But I'll tell you one thing, homeless people or not, just being free to walk around sure beats the bench in the Fishkill visiting yard, wouldn't you say?"

I nodded. We kissed, and Victor looked at his watch for the fifth time in five minutes. "Almost time."

As we walked toward Broadway, making our way to the building which housed the New York Society for the Deaf, I asked Victor if he wanted me to go in with him and wait there.

"Yeah. I feel a little like a child on the first day of kindergarten: I need my mommy."

While Victor was being interviewed, I sat on a chrome and vinyl chair in NYSD's waiting area, watching all the people signing at each other. The place had a hushed, peaceful feeling, not like my workplace where everyone walked around yelling commands at themselves and each other. I told myself it was not infantilizing for me to be sitting there. Since this was Victor's first day out, he needed moral support as well as concrete guidance on getting around. When he came out smiling, but looking wary, and shook hands with the suited black woman who had interviewed him, I concluded that it must have gone well. After introducing me to her, we left, and he confirmed my feeling.

"My signing came back. I was a little rusty, but overall I

think she was impressed. Hey, let's go eat," he said as we got into the elevator.

"When was the last time you were in a restaurant?"

"You know, I don't remember, but it was over nineteen years ago."

"God, that's amazing."

We chose a nearby coffee shop where we could get a quick bite so Victor could be back by four. It was sad to think about parting so soon as it was just beginning to feel like a normal day out with my husband. That felt more like punishment than when he was totally locked up upstate.

"Believe me," Victor said, "even an hour of freedom is worth it. Just getting a taste of the outside world is so unbelievable. To be able to sit in a restaurant and order whatever I want to eat. You can't imagine how great that is until someone locks you in a cage and says, 'Here, eat this,' and it's pure shit. And when you're finished you just sit there and you stare at your cell and maybe at some creep you might share the cell with. I tell you, sweetheart, prison is one of those experiences you can't begin to imagine unless you've been there."

I nodded and reached for his hand.

The coffee shop was typical, with a charcoaled hamburger smell and the din of people conversing over the clattering of dishes. But Victor looked around taking in the atmosphere with obvious pleasure as if it were a four-star restaurant.

"I like this place," he said.

"It's unpretentious, but then coffee shops are usually pretty unpretentious."

"If I work at the New York Society for the Deaf I'll definitely come back."

"When did they say they'd let you know?"

"By the end of the week."

Victor called the next night, and I had a message for him. "Rabbi Bergman called," I told him, "and said you have an excellent chance. You're being considered along with another candidate. If possible, Victor, he wants you to call him." Victor was able to call from a pay phone, and, after they negotiated salary, the amount having mysteriously dropped since their first contact, Victor was offered the job. Though we assumed the salary dropped because they knew Victor was not in a position to negotiate, what was a thousand dollars or two when his freedom was at stake? Victor had a job, would start Monday, and then would be able to spend most of his nights at home, rather than in the facility.

That weekend Victor had to remain at the prison locked in, and I attended my cousin's wedding. Usually, I avoided those kinds of events, but it had been a while since I'd seen my aunt and cousins of whom I was fond, so I decided to go. It took place at a country club in Pelham, New York, and now and then I enjoyed entertaining myself with a glimpse into the world of luxury and opulence. Because they didn't know about Victor, I removed my wedding band and presented myself as an unmarried woman. I also began to drop hints that I was involved with someone, and that the reason I hadn't been more forthcoming was because he was not white.

"Oh, Denise, you could have brought him," my aunt said, planting an orangy-pink kiss on my cheek. "You know I don't care about that."

"I know, but...." What could I say? It's not really because he's black but because he's a convict that he's not here? What bothered me most was that anyone who knew me would know that I would not have hidden a relationship just because it was interracial. Then again, how could they guess the truth if I didn't tell them? Anyway, my aunt and cousins attempted to make me feel comfortable by introducing me to a black social worker who was the bride's cousin by marriage, and by emphasizing the interreligious nature of the wedding which was performed by both a rabbi and a priest. For my family this was liberal, and it felt vaguely related to my everyday reality. What I enjoyed most were the delicious brunch buffet, the thick carpeting and lavish bouquets, the elegant artwork, and the chamber music ensemble. After prisons and a mental hospital, this was a rarefied atmosphere, if only for a couple of hours!

The next Saturday was the day before my birthday, and

Victor came home in the morning carrying a small duffel bag. It was gray and rainy out, the way mid-April and my birthday often are, with the promise of spring right around the corner. During the week we had spent a day with his aunt and uncle who had come from Brooklyn to take Victor shopping for clothes on the Lower East Side. Aunt Nell and Uncle Max were immediately likeable with their matching silver gray hair and joking manner, throwing one-liners out as if stars of a sitcom. They were generous in buying him slacks, shirts, ties, and a trench coat so Victor had more than the one outfit I had bought him. I had looked forward to meeting Nell and Max, for Victor often spoke of them as the only happily married couple he knew growing up, and because Max was his role model. I sometimes wondered how Victor's and my marriage would fare, considering neither of us grew up in a household where there was a healthy marriage. The fact that Victor had Nell and Max nearby was more than I could claim for exposure to good marriages. With Victor coming home, I was to realize just how little I knew about marriage and what to expect from it.

From the minute he came into the house that Saturday, I understood that our relationship would be quite different than it had been for the previous four years. Whereas in prison we were always congratulating each other on how much we had in common, now we began to discover how divergent our views could be, beginning with the innocuous but meaningful detail of the front closet. To someone else my piles of paper and other things might not look organized, but there was nothing in my apartment I couldn't lay my hands on almost immediately, and after fifteen years I had accumulated a lot. When, some months before, it had seemed likely that Victor would be coming home on work release, I began to throw out and rearrange things so that he would have room for his possessions. This was no easy task, and when he came home, Victor let me know that I hadn't done an adequate job, for he proceeded to rearrange the whole front closet, which was relatively large with three walls of shelving stretching to the ceiling.

My stomach contracted into knots as I watched Victor carefully remove boxes of photos, old forty-five records, paint cans, books, hats, and other assorted items.

"I thought you said you had made room for me," he said when I commented.

"I did."

"No, you didn't," he insisted.

I went to the closet and looked in. He was right; I had emptied only a small part. Having assumed he wouldn't have that much stuff, I thought the space I had allotted would be adequate.

"That's okay, sweetheart, take as much space as you need," I said, feeling mounting panic. Maybe my worst fear would come true: the sweet, loving, judicious person I had married would now turn into an aggressive, macho male. As the day progressed, we bickered on and off, as we had never done before. We were both on edge: Victor was anxious about starting his new job and being in the world after nineteen years; I was anxious about having the man I loved, whom I thought I knew but with whom I hadn't shared all that much time, move into my sanctuary.

After the first two weeks, we settled into a routine in which Victor was home every night except Wednesdays and Thursdays when he went back and slept at the facility. Work release had what they called "day reporting" in which the inmate didn't have to spend any nights there, but Victor was ineligible for it as he had a violent felony conviction. He was supposed to go directly to the facility from work and directly to work from the facility, but because Lincoln was so close to where we lived, he was able to come home both before and after he was there. His having to go there was a disruption in our lives, but compared to the alternative of him being upstate, it was nothing.

Leaving for the facility was always heart-wrenching, especially for him. Here he was, working as a professional during the day, earning respect from colleagues, having increasingly greater responsibility for the lives of the agency's clients and their families; then he'd go to prison and be told to wash a sink or sweep a floor that wasn't even dirty. Perhaps most difficult was that many of the other inmates came back drunk or high on drugs; they stayed up smoking, watching television, and generally carrying on until the wee hours of the morning. Even when Victor was not in the dorm and had his own room, it was without a door and adjacent to where everyone else was. The lights stayed on all night, and the guards talked in loud tones, not thinking about Victor's or anyone else's need to sleep. He would come home in the morning, his hair and clothes reeking of cigarette smoke. With growing intensity, we set our hopes on January when Victor would go before the parole board. Thinking logically, it seemed likely that he would be granted parole: he was already out in the community, living in a stable home, and maintaining a good job, and he presented no problems of any kind at the facility. Yet we knew the bureaucracy was not about logic; each month our fear grew as the parole board came to the facility and denied parole to long-timers like Victor and granted it instead to young thugs who filtered in and out of prison.

One morning about a month after Victor gained work release, I awoke, took my temperature, and realized with great joy that it had remained up instead of dropping as it would when I was about to menstruate. After a second day with a high temperature and no period, I bought a home pregnancy test. When I took the test and saw its ambiguous blue dot, I didn't know what to believe. The next day after work, Victor accompanied me to a nearby women's center where I took an early pregnancy test. When the nurse came out after twenty minutes and handed me a slip with the word "positive," I started to cry.

"I can't believe it," I said to both her and Victor, and for her benefit, "I've been trying to get pregnant for a long time."

To say we were overjoyed is an understatement; after all those months and years of fertility shots and artificial inseminations, all it took was Victor being home for a few weeks, and I was pregnant. To have this presence in my body and to welcome it and feel blessed by it, rather than feel that I had been cursed with a hideous fate as I would have when single was true bliss. Unfortunately, "the Universe" had its own ideas about my fate. At six weeks, I went for a routine sonogram to confirm the viability of the pregnancy. After happily answering all the medical history questions of both Victor's and my family, I lay back on the table for the sonogram. On the screen was the staticky black and gray triangle, inside of which was supposed to be a small black spot; instead, there was nothing.

"I don't understand this," the young male doctor said, rolling the cool metal square over my pelvis. "We'll try a different machine."

A technician ushered me into another room and introduced me to another machine. It produced the same result.

"I'm so sorry, Denise, but it looks like you have an ectopic pregnancy. We're going to have to take blood and test your estrogen level to verify that you are, in fact, pregnant," the doctor said. I held back tears and fought back the thought, *I knew it was too good to be true* as he got on the phone with the fertility specialist who was also the surgeon. His response was that I'd immediately have to be admitted to the hospital, for ectopic pregnancies could have dire consequences if not removed as soon as possible. I called Victor and broke the news to him. He was able to leave work early and accompanied me to the hospital. Meeting us at the hospital, the doctor explained that he would do a laparoscopy early the next morning to determine the nature of the ectopic pregnancy, and hopefully major surgery would not be necessary. That turned out not to be the case.

Known as a cornual pregnancy, the embryo had embedded itself right at the juncture of the fallopian tube and the uterus where the uterine wall is particularly thick. The doctor couldn't extract it via the laparoscope; I had to be cut open, and I was under anesthesia for over three hours. When I awoke in the recovery room, Victor was right there. When I heard what had happened, I cried. "He or she almost made it. It was implanted just a little too soon."

"Well, my love," Victor said, "it wasn't meant to be this time, but we can take comfort in the fact that you got pregnant so easily and presumably can again."

Staying home over the July Fourth holiday was difficult. Long before, I had vowed to myself never to spend July Fourth at home because the neighborhood turned into a war zone with a nonstop barrage of explosions, but that year we had no choice. We buttoned up the windows, turned on the air conditioning full blast, and rented a lot of videos. Having Victor there giving me food, love, and tender loving care helped to heal me. We agreed that we'd go away for a weekend as soon as I was able.

Technically Victor was not supposed to leave New York City, but that was one of those rules that no one would be the wiser about when it was broken. Sometimes when we ventured to New Jersey or upstate, we'd joke about running into Mr. Riley, his parole officer, but fortunately that never happened.

The other major stipulation of work release was that Victor had to turn over his paycheck to the Department of Corrections, which kept ninety dollars; Victor was issued an allowance every two weeks to pay for living expenses, and the rest was placed in an account for him. Victor was good with money, so he was able to contribute to the household, have spending money, and put some away, but it was not easy. As always, we reminded ourselves of the alternative. Though Victor was still an inmate, the life we were now leading was vastly closer to a "normal" life than it had been. At least he had a much greater semblance of being free than if he were locked in upstate, and we were together, albeit five nights a week, with the opportunity to do most of the things that free people do.

In November, anticipating the upcoming parole board hearing in January, we once again began to think about garnering support for the hearing. There was a lot less to do this time, however, as we agreed that inundating the parole commissioners with papers praising Victor would probably serve to bore rather than impress them, and that understatement would be more effective. Again we appealed to our assemblyman, Ed

Sullivan, who by now had met Victor and had seen for himself that the man he had been supporting was worthy of his vote of trust. As he had done several times before, Ed wrote a wonderful letter, expressing his faith in Victor's rehabilitation, Victor's commitment to remaining nonviolent and free of crime, and his dedication to his work, family, and the community. A similar letter was written by the executive director of the New York Society for the Deaf, who had now been working with Victor for eight months and recognized his sincerity, integrity, and intelligence. The third expression of support was from Mr. Riley, the facility parole officer. We had grown quite fond of Riley, who would pay us periodic visits at home. A muscular, prematurely balding white man who always wore the orange and brown jacket of his beloved Cleveland Browns, he'd squeeze himself into our director's chair and chat with us about the inequities in Corrections, among other things. He seemed to truly appreciate having Victor on his caseload, for Victor was a success story. When an inmate got into trouble, the parole officer had his or her hands full. "Someone like Victor makes my job gratifying," he said. I thought it somewhat similar to my job in which everyone wanted the so-called "good" patients, the ones who made progress and responded to therapeutic interventions.

On January 14, 1993, almost twenty years after he had starting doing time, and nine months after he had come out on work release, Victor went before the three-member parole board. Although he had sat before them in the past for clemency hearings, we were both nervous. We kept reminding ourselves that the worst that could happen if they denied him parole was that he would continue as he had been on work release. "At least you're home." I clasped his hand.

But we really could not believe that they would deny him. On what grounds could they do that? That morning, after discussing what he should wear—look respectable and neat but not arrogant—we also discussed the tone he should take, firm and confident, but not pompous. I kissed him for luck, and he went off.

The day was significant for us for another reason; an article we had written together appeared in *New York Newsday*, a daily newspaper. The article discussed the issues of racial divisiveness in Crown Heights, Brooklyn, and how the media tended to fan the flames of the conflict by using oversimplified terms to describe the people involved, specifically "Blacks and Jews" rather than "Caribbeans and Hassidim." The article was well received by everyone, and we felt proud and accomplished.

At work all day I was on pins and needles as I waited for word from Victor. When I had heard nothing by three o'clock, I placed a call to Victor's counselor. "The parole has been denied," she said quietly. I was stunned, infuriated, and sickened. Once again the system seemed like a farce; politics ruled over substance. They granted parole to the young repeat offenders, but someone like Victor, who for all intents and purposes was already out, they denied. "The reason," she said, "was the nature of the crime." I wanted to shout, *But he was innocent*! But what good had that done Victor in the past? None. What good would it do us now? None. The scariest part was that theoretically they could use this reason forever, for the nature of the crime he had been convicted of would never change. I asked myself why would the nature of the crime be too serious to let him go now but not in two years? I told myself we had to turn our attention to the appeal. But I felt momentously shattered. The next day, however, Victor came home, and that's what mattered.

CHAPTER
TWENTY

END OF SENTENCE

The effect of the board's ruling, or "the hit" as inmates called it, was two years; two years before Victor could go to the parole board again. The worst part of this was the potential for Corrections to tell Victor, "Okay, you're no longer going to be on work release, you're going back upstate." Because work release is a privilege, not a right, Victor was at their mercy. Once, Victor asked Parole Officer Riley about the interest he was supposed to be earning on the thousands of dollars Corrections was saving for him. Riley's response was, "I wouldn't make waves about it if I were you; it would be very easy for them to find dirty urine on you." Even though Victor hadn't touched a drug since Vietnam, he was given frequent drug screens. The tests were a mild inconvenience, but the list he was given of drugs that could show up positive was ridiculous. It included over-the-counter medications like ibuprofen and dextromethorphan. It meant he had to think twice about taking Advil or Robitussin. He also had to beware of poppy seeds, as they reportedly could show up as positive for heroin.

"It's really something when the parole officer tells you not to ask questions for fear of negative reprisals," Victor said one night a couple of weeks after the parole denial as he sat before the television set, dicing zucchini and mushrooms.

"Well, look at it this way. At least you have someone like him around who's honest enough to let you know. What if he had told you to go ahead and ask about the interest?"

"What a system." Victor shook his head. "These are the people who are supposed to decide who would profit most from freedom. Who has the moral character to change. And you can't be honest with them." He slowly shook his head. "Anyway, honey, how was work?"

It had been a typical day and was now a typical evening. After working at the hospital, I had seen one patient in our living room which served as my office. At first, Victor was a little put off when I wouldn't allow him to display personal effects like sports trophies as it compromised the neutral atmosphere of the psychotherapy office, but he came to understand and accept my rationale. During my psychotherapy sessions, Victor absented himself and sat in neighborhood cafes such as the Hungarian Pastry Shop and listened to college students wax intellectual. Now home, he was going to cook while I did sit-ups, trying to eradicate the effects of his excellent cooking. Even though the cooking facilities were quite limited in our apartment, with half-size oven and refrigerator and no counter space, to him it was almost luxurious compared to what he had been used to. He cooked often, and since he had come home we had both gained weight, the result of Victor's culinary skills and also, for me, of having resumed fertility medication.

The fertility specialist, Dr. Timothy Daniels, was a dead ringer for the actor Michael J. Pollard, the murderous sidekick in the movie *Bonnie and Clyde*. When I first went to him I had doubts about putting myself in his short, stubby hands, but I persuaded myself that the physical packaging wasn't important. His knowledge and wisdom, in turn, convinced me that even though I had gotten pregnant naturally with no technological or pharmacological assistance, because of my age (forty-one), I should take an aggressive approach to trying to get pregnant again, and if I didn't get pregnant on my own within a few months, I should consider in vitro fertilization. So back on medication I went, but this time Victor was there. No longer did I have to twist and contort to jab myself with the long hypodermic in my back and upper buttocks. Victor approached the task like a trooper. "Look," he bragged when we talked about giving me a shot, "I've taken care of AIDS patients, and I nursed my aunt after she had her breasts removed because of cancer, so this will be a cinch." When it came time to actually doing it, however, he recoiled. "I don't want to stick you with this needle. I hate needles." But then he distracted himself by trying to make me feel more relaxed. Getting a nightly shot was not pleasant, but as before, the motivation for pregnancy made me almost look forward to it.

I loathed the idea of being in an operating room not even a year after I had had major surgery, but a couple of months later we agreed to try in vitro fertilization. At least this did not entail any overnight hospital stays. Basically it involved turning my body over to people who poked and prodded and became more familiar with my body than Victor and I were. For us, though deeply in love, making love became making a baby; the irony of the situation was inescapable, that here we were working so hard to achieve what for so many years I had worked so hard to avoid. I questioned why there weren't more frequent harmonious times of working in tandem with Life, getting what we want when we want it, and wanting what we get when we get it. Then Life would be easy, but as those people who believe Life is a school might say, what lessons would we learn? Frankly, by that time I was quite sick of learning lessons and ready for things to happen a bit more smoothly.

But then, who was asking me? So the emotional tests kept on coming. First, the ordeal of in vitro fertilization: having a long catheter inserted between my legs to remove ova from my ovary. Next, having to wait while the ova and Victor's sperm found each other in a petri dish. Then, once the doctor declared the meeting a success, I was back in the hospital, paper gown open to the back, with matching shoes and hat, unconscious for the few minutes it took them to insert the four embryos into my uterus, hopefully this time to implant themselves in the right spot. The wait was one of the more rigorous tests, though my superior ability to fantasize and visualize the best outcomes tided me through that. If nothing else, I enjoyed walking around with the knowledge that I was possibly carrying Victor's child inside me.

Each month, the taking of the morning temperature had increasing significance as I neared the time of menstruation. After doing the in vitro, the wait was imbued with the knowledge of money and time invested, not to mention the physical discomforts of injections, the side effects of hormones, and the invasions of blood drawing and vaginal sonograms. Thus, when one morning the thermometer indicated a significant drop, my heart dropped as well. We had gone through all of that for nothing. After watching me mope around for a couple of days, Victor said, "Sweetheart, there's no use dwelling on what's already happened. It's water under the bridge. Let's focus on trying again and being optimistic." While I agreed, I felt I had the right to mourn our loss and couldn't shake off my depression though I tried for both our sakes.

Though our love stayed strong, we were discovering to our chagrin that we had differences in style and the way we processed things; this gave rise to enough strife between us that we decided to go for couples therapy. Having both grown up with critical, dispassionate mothers, we were both extremely sensitive to perceived slights, real or otherwise, which often left each of us feeling hurt by the other, and angry. While each of us stubbornly clung to our points of view, we both were completely committed to our relationship. James, the therapist, helped us make inroads into the way we communicated and how we reacted to each other. Going weekly was painful, but ultimately helped us to deal better with our conflicts by being more conscious of what we said and how we said it, and by letting go of hurt and anger as soon as possible and moving on.

After the failed in vitro fertilization, we decided to

reevaluate. "Darling," Victor pleaded, "let's believe in each other and our future as a family and just make love naturally."

I clung to him. "That's what I want, too," I said.

In the past I had gone for acupuncture and I now resumed it; in addition, I increased my intake of fertility-enhancing herbs and began to eat a lot of yams. Victor began taking ginseng and other potency enhancers, including those mysterious liquids in small bottles sold next to the cash registers in delis and health food stores, whose labels boasted such ingredients as extract of bull testicles. For Valentine's Day, along with a box of Godiva chocolates and a bouquet of roses, Victor gave me a fertility idol, carved out of rich, dark mahogany. We gave this hermaphroditic creature, with its flat round head, pointy breasts, and erect penis, a prominent place over our bed. As Victor and my natural passion returned, my optimism grew stronger. Spring was coming. Again, an elevated body temperature was the first clue that something was happening. This time I didn't bother with the home pregnancy test, but headed straight for the women's center after waiting ten days as they instructed. Once again, Victor was there to hold me as I cried tears of happiness upon hearing the result. "It's meant to be," we agreed.

It was another elated spring. We were delighted that I was pregnant. Going to work for me became less offensive as I changed venues within the hospital and worked with patients who were less psychotic, which bode well for my upcoming months of pregnancy. That spring was a particularly beautiful time as the multitude of cherry blossom trees burst into color, and birdsong created a constant musical background. This time, before sending me to the obstetrician, the fertility doctor did a sonogram and checked for the fetal heartbeat. There was that tiny, black mass in the center of the triangle, and, as hoped for, the heartbeat, a slight but definite rhythmic pulsating. The baby was due in late December.

At eight weeks, I visited the same obstetrician who had done that fateful sonogram less than a year before. Since he already had my medical history on file, we went right to the sonogram. As he smoothed the cold metal over my abdomen, he stared thoughtfully at the screen without speaking.

"Is something wrong?" *Oh no, here we go again.*

"I don't know," he said pausing. Then, "I don't see the heartbeat."

"But we just saw it last week."

"I know, but this early on in the pregnancy anything can happen. I want Tim to see you," referring to the fertility doctor. It was like last year all over again. "I'm sorry."

"I don't believe this." Though my rational mind knew he wasn't, I was trying not to believe that this doctor was somehow responsible for the failure of these pregnancies.

Later that afternoon, I saw Dr. Daniels who confirmed that there was no heartbeat, that the fetus had died. "It's what we call a failed abortion, that is, a fetus which isn't viable and dies without expelling itself from the womb." Feeling beaten, the next day I went to Mount Sinai Hospital's ambulatory surgery clinic for dilation and curettage. Victor accompanied me, both of us feeling heavy with the burden of our latest loss. In therapy the next week, I said, "Maybe it really wasn't meant to be. After all, I'm forty-two years old, which, for many women, is too late." The doctor had reassured me, however, that I was still ovulating, and my hormone levels were more than adequate. So we decided to remain optimistic and keep on trying. Again, the doctor suggested that after my system got back to normal, we should consider fertility medication.

That summer we discovered Coolidge State Park in Vermont. Though Victor was not supposed to leave New York City, we had been sneaking off to Vermont since the first year he was home as his cousin Loretha was involved with a religious group which owned a house that people used as a retreat. A typical Vermont-style farmhouse, we had been there on a few occasions; we loved the Vermont countryside as well as the state's serenity and laid-back vibes. We felt not only peaceful there but safe, actually able, after our paranoia wore off, to leave the car door unlocked, something completely unthinkable in New York.

Victor and I shared in common a love for the outdoors, and we had begun to invest in camping equipment, intending our first trip to be July Fourth. We found Coolidge one day while driving around looking for another campground, and the woman we asked for directions happened to mention it.

We drove the twenty-five miles there and were awestruck by nature's beauty as we wound up the mile-long road to the park at the mountain top. The pine scent flowing in the windows from the cool, dark woods intoxicated us. When we reached the top, suddenly there was crystal sunlight. Miriam, a born-again Christian park ranger, warmly told us to drive through and see the place. Log cabin lean-tos were spaced far enough from each other to afford privacy and looked out on the green valley and towering mountain across the way. It was like no state park that we had seen before, and we fell in love with it. We were able to cancel our reservation at Taghkanic Park in New York and get the one remaining lean-to site at Coolidge; even though it was a five hour drive from home, it was worth it. We camped out several times that summer, and though our main obsessions of Victor's parole and my getting pregnant were never absent from our minds, they receded to the background as we enjoyed nature and renewed our passion for each other under the stars. We even went camping at Coolidge Columbus Day weekend and endured amazing weather changes, from frost and snow flurries to balmy wind and summer temperatures.

As the weather turned colder and once again fall activities accelerated everyone's pace, I told Victor that we needed to focus again on pregnancy, if for no other reason than to rule it out and think more seriously about adoption. Adoption was something that we mentioned now and then as a possible alternative, but I wanted to have Victor's baby; I knew I wanted more than just the experience of raising a baby with him. So, once again, the shots and fertility-related activities resumed. At the same time, I was starting to accept the sad possibility that I might never be a mother, at least of my own children.

On January 2, 1994, we gave in again to scheduled love-making in both the morning and the evening, knowing that this was *the* day of ovulation. I felt especially hopeful as it was the tenth anniversary of my father's death, the implication being that a baby conceived then might somehow be related to the soul or spirit of my father. We were given the opportunity for this metaphysical possibility with yet another pregnancy. It seemed unbelievable, yet completely fated: here I was, forty-two years old, and I had gotten pregnant three times in less than two years. I started to think of myself not only as not infertile, but as a super fertile woman, and that it was a miracle that I had avoided pregnancy as well as I had during the years I didn't want it. Then again, it could just have been the magic duet between Victor and me. Whatever the cosmic meaning, here we were again, going to the women's center, getting the test result back positive. This time we were skeptical and allowed our happiness to proceed with caution.

When the time came, I went to a different obstetrician, Dr. Sherman. He said this time it looked like everything was going to be okay. Because of my age, he strongly recommended genetic counseling, for which Victor and I went. Afterward, Victor and I discussed at length whether to have the amniocentesis and ultimately decided against it, agreeing that we would accept the child we were given, in whatever condition he or she might be. The idea of an abortion was unacceptable for us at that point. Having gone through so much, we wanted our child, no matter what might be "wrong" with the fetus. We went through the pregnancy with great joy; though I was big as a house, I loved every minute. At six months, I got a stress fracture in my left foot and limped around for a month with a soft cast and surgical shoe. As rotund as I was, people stared and/or laughed when I passed. I didn't care. Then I developed gestational diabetes which forced me to test my blood for sugar each time I ate and adhere to a special diet.

Despite all the physical anomalies of my pregnancy, those eight months were some of the happiest of my life.

Pregnancy was wonderful in that it was a time of being treated as special and feeling perfectly justified in accepting that kind of pampering. Especially after all I had been through, I felt I deserved it.

Because of all my previous uterine surgery, the obstetrician felt strongly that I shouldn't risk subjecting my uterus to the contractions of labor, that it might be too weak to withstand that kind of stress and could rupture with great risk to both me and the baby. Because of this, I agreed to his plan of scheduling a C-section three weeks before the baby was due.

The baby, whom we knew would be a boy, we planned to name Raphael. He was scheduled to arrive on Thursday, September 8, which would be convenient, not only for the doctors, but also because Victor would go to the prison that night and then would come out the following morning and could be with me without interruption until the following Wednesday. Perhaps fortuitously, he had left the New York Society for the Deaf a couple of weeks before in a mutually agreed upon decision. At first, we were anxious about the fact that I would soon give birth and he needed to have a job in order to remain on work release, but then we realized that not working would give him the opportunity to help me after the baby was born.

On the night of Labor Day, which also happened to be Rosh Hashanah, the Jewish New Year, I was in bed when I began to have pains. I woke Victor. "I think I'm having contractions." Usually not at a loss for words, Victor didn't say much. I decided to have a glass of sherry, having read that if the contractions are false, alcohol will relax the uterus and stop them, whereas if it's the real thing, they'll continue. Continue they did, and after calling the doctor, we packed a bag and went out into the cool pre-dawn stillness. After two yellow cabs passed him by, Victor got a gypsy cab to stop and take us to Mount Sinai Hospital. I was settled into a birthing room, even though I would have a C-section, and proceeded to have painful contractions, at first every ten minutes, then more frequently, as we waited for the doctor to arrive. The nurses and anesthesiologists hovered around me, each administering their own particular expertise. Finally Dr. Sherman arrived in a T-shirt and jeans, exclaiming, "You got me out of shul! I changed my clothes and rushed right over here."

Once again, I found myself in an operating room, but this time I was blissful. And though I was scared, the nurses were all so chipper and confident that they put me at ease. One of the things I was anxious about was meeting my baby for the first time. Who was going to emerge from me? I was given an epidural injection of anesthesia to numb me from the chest down. Victor stood by my head, encouraging me and reassuring me of his love. Suddenly the doctors and nurses were cheering and holding up a crying baby, confirming that he was, in fact, a boy. It was surreal: here was this new person in the room, who hadn't been there before, but had been in my body. My heart felt overjoyed. After cleaning and fixing him up, Raphy was brought to me, all tiny and red and swathed in a blanket with a little cap on his head; Victor snapped pictures as I held the baby and kissed his little face. Then all hell broke loose.

"Look at this! Do you see what's going on here?" I heard Dr. Sherman shout. I heard the commotion of people moving and talking. A few seconds later Dr. Sherman was by my head, looking down at me. "You are severely hemorrhaging. I don't want to do a transfusion, but we might have to remove the uterus."

Somewhat groggy, I said, "Isn't there anything you can do to save the uterus?"

"I'll try," he said, "But this is life threatening."

He went back to the lower portion of my body. Victor said, "Let him do what he needs to do. I want you to be safe."

Seconds later the doctor was back. "I tried stitching it, but the uterine wall is very thin and unable to hold the stitches, and the bleeding won't stop. You've already lost a good deal of blood. If we don't remove it now you might die. I'll leave the cervix and ovaries."

"Do what you have to do," I said. Some voice in my

mind said, *You're going to have a hysterectomy but it's better than dying. And remember, you have a son.* When I felt intense pressure bordering on pain in my pelvic area, despite the epidural, I realized he was doing the surgery while I was awake. At that point, they told Victor he could wait upstairs in the nursery with the baby, and they gave me general anesthesia. For the next twenty-four hours, I slept on and off in the recovery room. In a dream state I was aware of other women coming and going, having delivered their babies. Victor came by several times to comfort me, as did the doctors. One doctor who stopped by was a pediatrician who had been enlisted by Dr. Sherman. Her announcement stunned me.

"Mrs. Clark, I'm Dr. Arroyo, and I've examined your baby." She paused and looked down at me. "We think he might have Down syndrome."

"What?" I was appalled. Who was this strange woman telling me my son had Down syndrome?

"Well, there are his eyes. Your husband said oriental-type eyes run in his family, but there's also the baby's pinky, which is curved, and the extra roll of skin on his neck. I'm sorry, I know you've just had surgery, and all this is a lot to take in. I'm sure you'll want to have him tested."

I lay there in a state of disbelief. First I had lost my uterus in order to save my life; now I was hearing that my new son had Down syndrome.

Over the next few days there were many visitors to my hospital bed, including genetic counselors, heart specialists, pediatricians, and social workers. The blood test confirmed that Raphy had Down syndrome, and the echocardiogram showed a major heart defect. In between all this, every few hours the nurses brought a beautiful, tiny infant to me whom I held, and, with some intimidation tried to nurse and wound up giving a bottle. Victor became a familiar fixture in the nursery, tenderly holding and feeding Raphy, when he wasn't going on job interviews. Outside my window across Fifth Avenue, Central Park was still green and lush, and some small part of me wished all of this had never happened and that I could just be free, running on those sprawling lawns among the flower beds.

For weeks after Raphy's birth and especially after Victor returned to work a month later, I was in a state of shock. Not only was I grieving the loss of my uterus and my fantasy of a genius child, I also realized I had had only minimal contact with babies in the intervening years since my brother was born when I was a child. I was stunned by the vulnerability of this fragile creature who was completely dependent on me for his well-being and survival. Victor, on the other hand, had had more contact with babies and children, most recently in the child care room at the Eastern Correctional Facility, and earlier, as an adolescent when he had helped to raise his cousin. As I recovered from surgery, Victor provided much of the care for our baby.

On Wednesday and Thursday nights when Victor returned to Lincoln, I bade him farewell with great reluctance, and then I tried to manage. Despite the fact I still felt weak, I got up every few hours to feed Raphy, hold him, walk him when he cried, and change him; I did all those things that have to be done for an infant and put my own needs and weakened physical condition second. With great clarity, I came to understand what is meant by "a mother's love." It is not "I'll love you when it is convenient," but rather "I'll love you even when it's totally inconvenient, and I have to put myself last." This selfless love was what Victor and I had both lacked and were eager to provide for our child.

We were pleased to discover that despite Down syndrome, Raphy was an alert, curious, and charming baby. With his tawny complexion and limpid brown eyes, his physical beauty made him even more precious; however, we did not truly begin to relax until after his heart surgery at the age of six months. Before that, he took two different kinds of heart medication, and I had to take him for frequent echocardiograms. Each time he cried or was ill I harbored a fear that something was going wrong with his heart and he would have heart failure. But thanks to modern medicine, and perhaps Fate, none of this happened, and he came through the surgery like a trooper. For as long as I live, I will have enduring gratitude, respect, and admiration for the surgeon who was able with his fingers to take Raphy's heart, which was the size of a small apricot, and create a valve where none had been. After the operation, Raphy immediately began to thrive. His appetite increased, and he began to grow strong and hardy, turning into the stocky, little bulldog he is today.

One Indian summer day, a few weeks after Raphy's birth, we packed up his diaper bag and went to Brooklyn to visit Ruthie, Victor's mother, and his grandmother whom everyone calls "Mama." Victor's relationship with Ruthie had long since healed, and I was also growing close to her. While I was in the hospital recovering after Raphy's birth, she often came to visit me as if making up for the time she had not been able to devote to Victor.

With four generations proudly posing, Victor snapped picture after picture of his family.

CHAPTER TWENTY-ONE

SORROW, JOY, AND POLITICS

Time passed, our family life solidified, and in November 1994, the people of New York State voted out their three-term governor, Mario Cuomo, and elected an unknown conservative Republican named George Pataki. The general public, or at least the small minority that took it upon themselves to vote, apparently were tired of Governor Cuomo and particularly his antipathy toward the death penalty. They found in George Pataki a compatriot. One of his first acts as governor was to sign legislation to enact the death penalty. He also set the tone of his administration with a get-tough, hard-line attitude toward criminals, including prohibiting inmates convicted of violent felonies from participating in the work release program. Rumors flew through the Corrections network that guys who had been on work release for years were being sent back upstate after being denied parole. As January and Victor's second parole hearing approached, he grew increasingly nervous, especially now that he had been on work release for almost three years, and we had a child. In reality, we had what all Corrections officials should agree is the goal for every inmate: a stable home and family life, work, money, and ties to the community. There was nothing deviant or illegal, no drugs, no crime. But in this new political climate, we were uncertain of the verdict.

The wintery day of Victor's second parole hearing, shortly before the end of my maternity leave, I was home with Raphy when the parole officer, Mr. Riley, called me. "I'm afraid the news isn't good. They hit him again. Two years."

I was crushed. "Why? Why should they do this? How do they justify it when he's been living successfully in the community for three years?"

I could hear the disappointment in his voice. "It's Pataki. They're coming down really hard on people convicted of violent felonies."

How I wanted to cry out, *But he didn't do it*. I knew my cry would be useless. Instead, I said softly, "Will he be able to remain on work release?"

"Yeah, I think so. The guys who are already in the program will be grandfathered in. But you know they can do anything they want at any time. I don't mean to scare you, but you should be prepared for anything."

Again, the official reason for the denial was that "release at this time would depreciate the gravity of the crime." Victor reported that one of the parole commissioners, the sole woman on the panel, had leafed through his file during the hearing, looked up at him, and said, "I see here it says you took LSD when you were a teenager. What are you doing about your drug use?" When Victor responded that he hadn't used drugs in thirty years, she was unimpressed. In the ensuing weeks, I met with both Ed Sullivan, the assemblyman, and the then-acting Commissioner of Corrections, who, when he had been a facility superintendent, had known Victor. Both agreed that the denial was purely political and that it would not make sense to try and make waves legally or through the media; it could backfire and create serious negative repercussions for Victor. Corrections could always say work release was a privilege, not a right, and as revenge for making trouble, Victor's privilege could be revoked. I left it up to Victor whether he wanted me to pursue any avenue of rebuttal against the Department of Parole.

"No," he said. "At least I'm home, I'm with you and Raphy, and working. Why take the chance that they'll get angry and want to send me back upstate?"

Ultimately, I agreed, angry and sorrowful as I was at an unjust system. Once again, we got on with our lives.

By January 1997, the Pataki administration was in full swing, and inmates on work release who had violent felony convictions were being sent back upstate. Victor had now been on work release for almost five years and had seen many generations of youthful offenders come and go from the program. Even his parole officer, Frank Riley, had moved on; he now had Mr. Charles McDuffy, a small, West Indian Republican whom we feared would not be sympathetic or helpful. About a week before his third parole board hearing, in his usual calm way, Victor made arrangements in the event that he would be imprisoned again. He arranged for his paycheck and vacation pay to be sent to me; and he gave me pep talks. I assured him that Raphy and I would be all right, that I would not be shy about calling on his family to help out.

On January 14, a cold, sunny morning, we got in my car as we did every day, to drive Raphy to day care. Victor carried a backpack of clothes, toiletries, and other things he would need if he were shipped upstate. I waited in the car as he took Raphy up the stairs to the center, imagining how Victor must have felt saying goodbye to his son. When he emerged from the building, I got out of the car, and we embraced, enveloped in our fear. We knew we were dealing with an irrational system: even though we had rehearsed that he should say he had many letters of support and five solid years with no problems, they could say no just because they wanted to.

I drove to work in a fog, not knowing when I'd see Victor again. On the job, I went through the motions, talking with patients and colleagues, filling in charts, watching the clock continuously. As the hours ticked by, I tried to remain calm. When the call finally came, it was after three, and Victor sounded as if he'd been crying. My heart stopped.

"January twenty-eighth," he said.

"What?"

"I made it. They approved my release."

That's when I started to cry, the relief and joy were so great.

"We were wrong about McDuffy. He was there, and he seemed so happy for me. He told me he wrote a really good parole report for me."

"Oh, Victor, I'm so happy for you. Congratulations."

"Thank, you, sweetheart. And it looks like they're gonna let me come home tonight instead of keeping me here until I see the counselor. All our phone calls, meetings, and letters of support must have had an influence because someone said, 'Let Clark go, orders from Albany.'"

As of January 28, 1997, two weeks after the hearing, Victor's twenty-four-year long sentence would be over. He would have four more nights to spend at Lincoln, and then he would be a parolee reporting to the parole officer as often as was designated. When he came home that night, we couldn't let go of each other as we laughed with joy.

"'Free at last! Free at last! Thank God Almighty we are free at last!'" Victor sang, holding a squealing Raphy between us in the air. Then, holding me a bit apart, he looked into my eyes and said, "Thank you, Denise, my darling, for sticking with me through all of this. I know it hasn't been easy."

I smiled. "I love you," I said, "and finally I understand that true Freedom begins when we embrace Life, knowing that it will never be easy." That night, though only one of us really qualified, we all slept like babies.

Epilogue

Three o'clock in the morning, I awaken. There's a Barney song going through my head: "Just imagine, just imagine, just imagine all the things that we could be...." Victor is next to me, snoring lightly. Raphy is asleep in his room. Thinking about this book I have written, and how in a few months my and Victor's lives will become public information, puts my stomach in knots. I think I must be crazy, for I have always been such a private person. At the same time, I have also been someone who faces challenges and takes risks, and I am gratified to tell the world our story.

Taking a few slow, deep breaths makes me feel calmer. I listen to the silence, to the absence of crashing bottles, screams on the streets, and salsa music. Since we have moved out of the city, I miss none of that and am grateful daily for the birds singing and the trees waving outside the window. Finally, I go back to sleep.

My eyes fly open. Hearing the patter of little feet, I awaken to see the sweet innocence of Raphy's smiling brown eyes and his button nose. He climbs onto the bed. "Hi!" he exclaims.

"Hi." I whisper, "Shhh," indicating his Daddy who is still sleeping. Raphy takes my hand and starts to drag me out of bed. These days, if I get six hours of sleep it's a lot as there's so much to do, which is far preferable to having more time than you know what to do with. Raphy and I go into his room, which at 6:00 A.M. is already warming with sunlight. Though Raphy is four-and-a-half, he still wears a diaper, but he'll soon progress to training pants. Neither Victor nor I mind having him as a baby beyond the usual amount of time. Soon Raphy is happily sipping orange juice and watching Barney. While I prepare coffee and Raphy's lunch, Victor gets up. Over the next hour, we shower and dress, then after a fast embrace, head out to our respective destinations.

Victor and I both work in the community with psychiatric outpatients. He drives into Manhattan, first dropping off Raphy at his pre-school, then heading crosstown to East Harlem to the residence for homeless adults of which he is the director. My community service takes place in the Bronx; the knowledge that I am improving the quality of life for some people continues to provide meaning for me. Writing also continues to be a goal and a challenge. Most afternoons after work, I go into Manhattan to pick up Raphy, and when he shrieks with delight upon seeing me, my day is made.

On August 10, 1999, Victor and I celebrated our tenth wedding anniversary. Like most marriages, ours has been a mixture of pleasure and pain, joy and sorrow. Despite, or because, it began in prison, our courtship had a dreamlike quality with little opportunity to learn that in reality we didn't have the perfect relationship we believed it to be. For even though we couldn't be together often, when we were, our senses were heightened, and we were totally focused on each other; our need and desire for each other was so keen, so ravenous that our love was a thing apart from the desperate, seamy world around us. In the years since then, thanks to our tenacious love, commitment, and loyalty, we have weathered the shock and disappointment of learning that our relationship is not perfect, and found the contentment of loving each other as we are.

It was synchronistic that we picked the name "Raphael" for our son, not knowing that it means "God has healed," and that in the Old Testament, Raphael was the angel of healing. Our Raphael, with his joy and innocence, heals both Victor and me each day. He symbolizes all that we have now for which we are so grateful.